Bottom Line's
BIG BOOK OF CONSUMER SECRETS

Bottom Line
Books
www.MyBottomLine.com

Bottom Line's Big Book of Consumer Secrets

Copyright © 2015 by Boardroom® Inc.

10   9   8   7   6   5   4   3   2   1

ISBN 0-88723-732-0

Bottom Line Books® publishes the advice of expert authorities in many fields. These opinions
may at times conflict as there are often different approaches to solving problems. The use
of a book is not a substitute for legal, accounting, investment, health or any other professional
services. Consult competent professionals for answers to your specific questions.

Offers, prices, rates, addresses, telephone numbers and Web sites
listed in this book are accurate at the time of publication,
but they are subject to frequent change.

Bottom Line Books® is a registered trademark of
Boardroom® Inc.
281 Tresser Boulevard, Stamford, CT 06901

www.MyBottomLine.com

Bottom Line Books® is an imprint of Boardroom® Inc., publisher of print periodicals,
e-letters and books. We are dedicated to bringing you the best information from the most
knowledgeable sources in the world. Our goal is to help you gain greater wealth,
better health, more wisdom, extra time and increased happiness.

Printed in the United States of America

Contents

PART TWO: YOUR MONEY

7 • MONEYWISE

PART THREE: YOUR FINANCIAL FUTURE

12 • RICHER RETIREMENT

PART FOUR: YOUR LEISURE

13 • HAPPY TRAVELS

Preface

We are happy to bring you *Bottom Line's Big Book of Consumer Secrets*. You will find numerous helpful and practical ideas for yourself and for everyone in your family.

At Bottom Line Books, it is our mission to provide all of our readers with the best information to help them gain better health, greater wealth, more wisdom, extra time and increased happiness.

The *Big Book of Consumer Secrets* represents the very best and the most useful *Bottom Line* articles from the past year. Whether you are looking for ways to get the most from your money or land a new job in this challenging economy...relieve pain naturally or assert your rights with your doctor...keep your marriage strong or stop worrying so much, you'll find it all here...and a whole lot more.

Over the past 30 years, we have built a network of thousands of expert sources.

When you consult the *Big Book of Consumer Secrets*, you are accessing a stellar group of authorities in fields that range from natural and conventional medicine...to shopping, investing, taxes and insurance...to cars, travel, security and self-improvement. Our advisers are affiliated with the premier universities, financial institutions, law firms and hospitals. These experts are truly among the most knowledgeable people in the country.

As a reader of a *Bottom Line* book, you can be assured that you are receiving reliable, well-researched and up-to-date information from a trusted source.

We are very confident that *Bottom Line's Big Book of Consumer Secrets* can help you and your family have a healthier, wealthier, wiser life. Enjoy!

The Editors, *Bottom Line/Personal*
Stamford, CT

1

Health Update

5 Very Simple Ways to Cut Your Disease Risk *by 80%!* Start Now...

If you were to boil down all of our medical wisdom to just a few words, you would already know them—exercise, eat well, do not smoke and maintain a healthy weight. But an astonishing number of people are not following through. Only 9% of adults meet all of the criteria for a healthy lifestyle—that's right, only 9%!

The research, which looked at more than 23,000 participants between the ages of 35 and 65, found that those who improved any one of the factors above were 50% less likely to develop a chronic disease. Those who did all four at the start of the study had a nearly *80% reduced risk* for any chronic disease.

So why aren't we doing what we should? Because it seems too hard! *Here are little ways to get started...*

• **Stand up.** A report in *BMJ Open* suggests that you could gain an extra two years of life just by standing up. Researchers found that people who reduced their daily sitting to less than three hours tended to live longer than those who spent more of their days in a chair.

My advice: Remind yourself to move. At least once an hour, stand up for a few minutes. A fast walk through the halls will get the blood moving.

Better: Do high knee raises, jumping jacks or other calisthenics.

When I'm on a long car trip, I do isometric exercises by flexing my arms against the steering wheel. At home, stand up and flex your calves while talking on the phone or watching TV.

David L. Katz, MD, MPH, internist and preventive medicine specialist. He is cofounder and director of the Yale-Griffen Prevention Research Center, Derby, Connecticut, and clinical instructor at the Yale School of Medicine, New Haven, Connecticut. He is coauthor, with Stacey Colino, of *Disease-Proof: The Remarkable Truth About What Makes Us Well* (Hudson Street).

•**Eat popcorn.** Even if your diet is mainly healthy, you still will gain weight if you don't keep an eye on portion sizes. This is particularly important for those who eat processed foods, which typically pack a lot of calories into surprisingly small servings.

My advice: Eat foods with a high satiety index. Even small servings of these foods will fill you up, so you consume fewer calories. Popcorn is a good example. It contains a lot of air, which takes up space in the stomach. (But stay away from chemical-laden packaged microwave popcorn.)

Other high-satiety foods include those with a lot of water (such as soup or fruits)…protein (beans, lean meats, nuts, etc.)…and low-glycemic foods (such as sweet potatoes or whole grains), which are absorbed slowly into the bloodstream.

•**Go caveman.** Our Stone Age ancestors probably got about half of their calories from meat. This was not a problem because the meats they ate were much leaner than today's steaks and hamburgers. You do not have to avoid meat to be healthy. You do have to limit saturated fat.

The mass-produced beef, pork and poultry that most of us eat come from confined animals. They're fattened with grains and manufactured foods, an unnatural diet that makes meat tender but also increases saturated fat.

My advice: Eat meats only from animals that were given a more or less natural diet. Game meats, such as venison and antelope, are leaner than traditional beef and pork—and rich in omega-3 fatty acids.

If you don't care for the "wild" taste of game, look for beef or pork that is grass-fed and buy free-range poultry.

•**Get the *right* fiber.** The Centers for Disease Control and Prevention has reported that the prevalence of diabetes has increased by 45% in the last 20 years, with the greatest increase occurring in people 65 years old and older.

Self-defense: Studies have shown that soluble fiber—the type found in beans, lentils, berries, vegetables and whole grains, particularly oats—slows the rate at which sugar enters the bloodstream. If you eat oatmeal for breakfast, you will have a lower blood sugar response to whatever you eat for lunch.

My advice: In addition to adding more fiber to your diet—the optimal amount is 35 grams (g) or more a day—include foods with a high percentage of soluble fiber. For example, add a whole grain, an apple or avocado, raw spinach or cooked broccoli, or a bean dish to every meal.

•**Think movement, not exercise.** Even people who exercise often approach it as a formal, and not particularly fun, activity. This mind-set might explain why lack of physical activity now accounts for nearly 10% of premature deaths in the world each year.

In my experience, most people want to exercise, but they haven't found a natural way to integrate it into their lives. You might not realize that the accumulation of 20 to 30 minutes of daily physical activity provides up to 85% of the cardiovascular benefits of hard exercise.

My advice: Think about what you already do—and do those things more often. Dancing is good exercise. So is a stroll through a park. An hour spent gardening counts. So does moving furniture…a bike ride…and a yoga class.

Do You Have a Heart Attack Gene? Finding Out Could Save Your Life!

Bradley F. Bale, MD, cofounder of the Heart Attack & Stroke Prevention Center, Nashville, and medical director of the Heart Health Program, Grace Clinic, Lubbock, Texas. He is coauthor, with Amy Doneen, ARNP, and Lisa Collier Cool, of *Beat the Heart Attack Gene: The Revolutionary Plan to Prevent Heart Disease, Stroke, and Diabetes* (Turner).

E ven if you do everything right—you do not smoke, you're not overweight and you manage your cholesterol and blood pressure—your odds of having a heart attack might be higher than you think.

An eye-opening case: One of our patients, a 44-year-old executive whom we nicknamed

"Superman," appeared to be very healthy. His Framingham Risk Score (a standard measure of heart disease risk) predicted that he had only a 1% risk of having a heart attack over the next 10 years. That should have been good news—except that other tests we did, which most doctors do not routinely give, showed that his real risk was about 40 times higher.

THE TESTS YOU NEED

Many of the tests that are used to detect heart disease are decades old. Some look for risk factors (such as arterial narrowing) that have less to do with the actual risk of having a heart attack than most people think. Many of the tests that can make a difference still aren't used by most doctors.

Most cardiologists routinely recommend angiography, an imaging test that looks for large blockages in the coronary arteries. If a blockage of 70% or more is found, a patient might be advised to receive a stent or undergo a bypass, surgical procedures that don't always help and can have a high rate of complications.

Severely blocked arteries can be a problem, but a more common, and typically overlooked, threat is from small deposits inside artery walls. A patient might have dozens or even hundreds of deposits that are too small to be detected with angiography.

The risk: When these "hidden" deposits are exposed to inflammation—triggered by insulin resistance, smoking, a poor diet or stress, for example—they can rupture, tear the blood vessel lining and trigger a clot, the cause of most heart attacks.

New approaches: Doctors can now predict the risk for a heart attack with far more accuracy than in the past—if you know which tests to ask for. *Tests I recommend…*

•**Carotid intima-media thickness (CIMT).** This is an effective way to measure atherosclerosis inside an artery wall (between the *intima* and *media* layers). The FDA-approved test uses an ultrasound wand to look for the thickening of the carotid arteries that occurs when plaque between the two layers accumulates and pushes outward.

An isolated area of thickness measuring 1.3 millimeters (mm) or greater indicates plaque—and an increased risk for a heart attack or stroke.

Most patients who have excessive arterial thickening will be advised by their doctors to exercise more, eat a healthier diet and take a daily baby aspirin to reduce the risk for clots. A cholesterol-lowering statin drug also may be prescribed.

•**Genetic tests.** More than half of all Americans have one or more gene variations that increase the risk for a heart attack and a stroke. According to research published in *Circulation*, up to 70% of patients who are given the genetic tests described below will be reclassified as having a higher heart attack risk than their doctors originally thought. The cost of testing has dropped to about $100 per gene. Your insurance may cover the cost. *Important gene tests…*

•9P21. If you inherit two copies of this "heart attack gene" (one from each parent), your risk of developing heart disease or having a heart attack at an early age (in men, under age 45…in women, under age 55) is 102% higher than that of someone without the gene. And increased risk continues if you are already past these ages.

You'll also have a 74% increased risk for an *abdominal aortic aneurysm*, a dangerous weakening in the heart's largest blood vessel. If you test positive, your doctor will advise earlier and more frequent abdominal aortic ultrasounds. If you smoke, stop now. Most aortic aneurysms occur in smokers.

You should also exercise for at least 22 minutes daily (the amount found in research to be protective) and maintain healthy cholesterol and blood pressure levels.

Important: Patients with the 9P21 gene often are advised to have an *ankle-brachial index test*, which involves measuring blood pressure in the arms and ankles. It's used to diagnose peripheral artery disease (PAD), plaque buildups in the legs that quadruple or even quintuple the risk for a heart attack or stroke.

•Apo E. This gene affects how your body metabolizes nutrients. There are different types of Apo E. The *3/3 genotype*—64% of Americans have it—increases cardiovascular disease, but not as much as the 3/4 or 4/4 types. Those with 3/4 or 4/4 need to eat a very low-fat diet (with no more than 20% of calories from fat). Those with the 3/3 genotype are advised to eat a Mediterranean-style diet—focusing mainly on plant foods…fish…and olive oil.

•KIF6. Patients with the so-called arginine gene variant have up to a 55% increased risk for cardiovascular disease. There are no particular lifestyle changes known to be especially helpful for these patients. It's also useful to know if you're a noncarrier of KIF6—as such, you won't receive significant risk reduction if you are prescribed either *atorvastatin* (Lipitor) or *pravastatin* (Pravachol), two of the most popular statin drugs. Instead, you will need a different statin, such as *lovastatin* (Mevacor).

ANOTHER CRUCIAL TEST

An *oral glucose tolerance test* can detect insulin resistance years or even decades before it progresses to diabetes. But many doctors still use the simpler *A1C test*. It's more convenient—it doesn't require fasting—but it often fails to detect insulin resistance, one of the primary causes of heart attacks and strokes. Insulin resistance leads to inflammation that can trigger plaques to rupture and form clots.

With an oral glucose tolerance test, your blood sugar is measured. Then you drink a sweet solution, and your blood sugar is measured again two hours later. A level of 100 milligrams per deciliter (mg/dL) to 139 mg/dL could indicate insulin resistance. Higher levels may indicate prediabetes—or, if they're high enough, full-blown diabetes.

Next steps: Regular exercise is critical if you have insulin resistance or diabetes.

Also helpful: Weight loss, if needed, reduced intake of sugary beverages and foods, and a diet rich in fruits, vegetables and grains.

What Does the Weather Do to Your Heart?

Barry A. Franklin, PhD, director of preventive cardiology and rehabilitation at William Beaumont Hospital in Royal Oak, Michigan. He has served as president of the American Association of Cardiovascular and Pulmonary Rehabilitation and the American College of Sports Medicine. Dr. Franklin is coauthor of *109 Things You Can Do to Prevent, Halt & Reverse Heart Disease* (Workman).

During a typical winter, there are up to 36% more circulatory-related deaths than during warmer months. And it's not just cold weather that puts you at risk. Researchers have identified other types of weather—throughout the year—that trigger spikes in hospitalizations and death.

For details on the effects that weather can have on your heart, we spoke with Barry A. Franklin, PhD, a leading authority in cardiac rehabilitation.

•**We hear a lot about cold weather being hard on the heart. At what temperature does this really become an issue?** When it's cold enough to wear a winter jacket, it is cold enough to think about the health of your heart. In fact, research that was recently presented at the European Society of Cardiology Congress 2013 shows that the risk of having a heart attack increases by 7% for every 18°F drop below 73°F.

•**Why exactly is cold weather so dangerous?** Cold temperatures cause blood vessels throughout the body to temporarily constrict, raising blood pressure. Since the arteries that supply the heart are only about the thickness of cooked spaghetti, even a slight narrowing can cause reduced blood flow.

Winter temperatures don't generally pose a problem if you are young and active. But risk rises as you hit middle age and beyond. The risk is highest for adults who are ages 65 and older, particularly those with underlying health problems, such as diabetes, obesity or preexisting heart disease. For people in these groups, spending even a few minutes in below-freezing temperatures can trigger a 20- to 50-point rise in blood pressure.

That's why I advise older adults, in particular, to stay indoors on the coldest days if possible. When you do go outdoors, don't depend on a light jacket—you should really bundle up by wearing a hat and gloves and dressing in multiple loose layers under your coat. Each layer traps air that's been heated by the body and serves as insulation.

•**And what about hot weather—does it harm the heart?** Actually, heat kills more individuals every year than any other type of weather.

High temperatures, generally above 80°F, but especially greater than 90°F, can cause dizziness...heat syncope (fainting)...heat edema (swelling in the feet/ankles)...and heat stroke, in which the body's core temperature can rise above 104°F. People with atrial fibrillation or dementia are at a 6% to 8% increased risk of dying on hot days. Dementia affects the brain's ability to regulate the body's heat response and can prevent an individual from recognizing that he/she should get to a cooler area.

•**Why is strenuous exertion so dangerous for many people during weather extremes?** Snow shoveling provides a good example. This activity creates a "perfect storm" of demands on the heart. With snow shoveling, the real danger—particularly for those who are older and/or sedentary—is the exertion itself.

Moving snow is hard work. Each shovelful weighs about 16 pounds (including the weight of the shovel). If you lift the shovel once every five seconds and continue for 10 minutes, you'll have moved nearly one ton of snow. This exertion can have adverse effects on the heart.

The reason why: Snow shoveling involves isometric exercise and unaccustomed muscle tension, which increases heart rate and blood pressure. Your legs may stay "planted" when you shovel, which allows blood to pool and reduces circulation to the heart.

Also, people tend to hold their breath (this is known as a *Valsalva maneuver*, and it often occurs when people are straining to lift heavy loads) when they are wielding a shovel, which causes a further rise in heart rate and blood pressure. That's why every year, we read or hear about people who dropped dead while shoveling snow.

•**Is there any way to reduce the risk associated with snow shoveling?** If you have or suspect you have heart disease, I suggest that you do not shovel your own snow. Hire someone to do it for you.

If you are in good shape and want to shovel your own snow, it may be safer in the afternoon. In general, most heart attacks occur between 6 am and 10 am, when heart rate and blood pressure tend to be higher. You're also more likely to form blood clots early in the day.

Then make sure to shovel slowly...work for only a few minutes at a time...and keep your legs moving to circulate blood. And remember, it's best to push snow rather than lift it. This helps keep your legs moving and takes less exertion than lifting. There are snow shovels designed for pushing snow.

•**What types of exertion are especially dangerous during hot temperatures?** Racket sports, water skiing, marathon running and certain highly competitive sports seem to be associated with a greater incidence of cardiac events in hot, humid weather. Why? Heart rates are disproportionately increased. Electrolytes, such as sodium and potassium, also are lost, which can lead to dangerous heart rhythms.

•**What steps should people take to protect themselves in hot weather?** Everyone knows to drink water when it's hot. But even people who are consciously trying to stay hydrated often do not drink enough. Drink plenty of cool liquids before, during and after heat exposure. If you're sweating a lot, you might want to drink an electrolyte-rich sports drink such as Gatorade or Powerade. And be sure to wear lightweight, loose-fitting clothing when you go outdoors.

In addition, think about any medications you may be taking. Many common medicines, including certain antihistamines and antidepressants, have *anticholinergic effects*—they inhibit your body's ability to cool off.

To help your body adapt to heat and humidity: As the weather grows hotter, gradually increase your daily exposure to the heat. The body's circulation and cooling efficiency increases, generally in eight to 14 days. Afterward, the body is better able to cope with extremes in heat and humidity.

Low Blood Pressure May Harm the Brain

It's long been known that high blood pressure in middle age may cause brain shrinkage, or atrophy, later in life. But when 663 middle-aged patients with coronary artery disease or other vascular conditions were followed for about four years, those with *low* diastolic (bottom number) blood pressure readings (under 60 mm/Hg) also showed signs of atrophy.

Theory: Low blood pressure may be inadequate for healthy blood flow to the brain, which can lead to brain tissue loss. More research is needed to determine if low pressure should be treated to minimize risk for brain atrophy.

Majon Muller, MD, PhD, geriatrician, VU University Medical Center Amsterdam, the Netherlands.

New Hypertension Guidelines

People over age 60 can have higher blood pressure than previously recommended. The recommendations, released by a National Institutes of Health panel, say that people over age 60 can have blood pressure of 150/90 before starting treatment for hypertension—previously, it was 140/90. The change is based on clinical trials that indicate a reduction in blood pressure to less than 150/90 does not decrease risk for cardiovascular disease in these patients. Also, many people needed to take several medications in order to reach 140/90, and the panel noted that these medications can have side effects.

Mark Houston, MD, director, Hypertension Institute of Nashville, and coauthor of *What Your Doctor May Not Tell You About Hypertension* (Grand Central Life & Style) and author of *Handbook of Hypertension* (Wiley-Blackwell). The panel's findings were published in *The Journal of the American Medical Association*.

OK to Stop the Meds?

Many people wonder if they can stop taking blood pressure medications if their pressure has returned to normal and they have gone on a diet, started a regular exercise program and lost weight.

Many can stop taking these drugs or reduce the dose once blood pressure is under control, but it should be done only under a doctor's supervision. Medication may have to be tapered over several weeks or months. If it's stopped suddenly, the patient may experience rebound increases in blood pressure or other cardiovascular complications.

The ability to stop medication depends on many factors, such as a family history of high blood pressure, pretreatment blood pressure levels, other drugs you may be taking and healthy lifestyle practices. A patient may also need to monitor his/her blood pressure on a regular basis at home using a 24-hour monitor.

Mark Houston, MD, director, Hypertension Institute of Nashville.

Antidepressants May Increase Risk for Abnormal Heartbeat

Certain *selective serotonin reuptake inhibitors* (SSRIs), such as *citalopram* (Celexa) and *escitalopram* (Lexapro), may extend electrical activity in the heart—an indicator of abnormal heart rhythms and cardiac risk. The effect is most likely in people taking higher doses of the medicines. Talk to your doctor about whether a reduced dose or a different medicine might be just as effective.

Analysis of data on 38,000 adults by researchers at Center for Experimental Drugs and Diagnostics, department of psychiatry, Massachusetts General Hospital, Boston, published online in *BMJ*.

Beware...iPads May Cause Heart Implants to Malfunction

When placed close to the chest, the magnets in an iPad may alter the settings of *implantable cardioverter defibrillators* and possibly even deactivate them.

Recent finding: The heart devices in 30% of study participants were affected by iPads placed close to their chests. The risk occurs when the person falls asleep with the tablet on his/her chest. iPads are safe to use by defibrillator patients if they are held at normal reading distance.

Study of the iPad 2 by researchers at Central Valley Arrhythmia, Stockton, California, presented at the Heart Rhythm Society's annual meeting in Denver.

Job Burnout Worse for the Heart Than Smoking

Job burnout is worse for the heart than smoking, high cholesterol and other risk factors.

New study: Patients who measured in the top 20% of a burnout scale were 79% more likely to develop coronary disease than patients with lower scores.

Psychosomatic Medicine, a journal of the American Psychosomatic Society.

Calcium Caution

In a recent finding, men who took more than 1,000 milligrams (mg) a day of calcium were 19% more likely to die from heart disease than men who took no calcium. Excess calcium in blood vessels may narrow and harden coronary arteries.

The research is not definitive—some studies link calcium consumption to health benefits. Talk to your doctor.

Qian Xiao, PhD, a cancer prevention fellow at the National Cancer Institute, Bethesda, Maryland, and leader of a study published in *JAMA Internal Medicine*.

Cut Heart Disease Risk *Without* Losing Weight

If overweight people control blood pressure, cholesterol and blood sugar through lifestyle changes and medication, the increased heart disease risk associated with being overweight can be reduced by 50%...and stroke risk can be lowered by 75%. But overweight and obese people still have higher risks for heart disease than people of normal weight.

Study of 1.8 million people by researchers at Harvard School of Public Health, Boston, Imperial College London and University of Sydney, Australia, published in *The Lancet*.

Heart Disease Compromises Reasoning Ability

In a recent finding, women who had coronary artery disease, congestive heart failure or other cardiac problems were three times as likely as other women to have non-amnestic mild cognitive impairment. The condition affects reasoning abilities but not memory. Men with cardiac disease also had a higher risk for cognitive impairment, but the difference was not statistically significant.

Self-defense: Control blood pressure, cholesterol and glucose levels. Exercise regularly. Eat right. Don't smoke.

Rosebud Roberts, MB, ChB, professor of epidemiology, Mayo Clinic, Rochester, Minnesota, and leader of a study published in *JAMA Neurology*.

Unclogging Heart Arteries via the Wrist Gains Favor

For years, physicians have been opening blocked heart arteries by threading a catheter through the femoral artery in the groin.

Update: US cardiologists are increasingly unclogging heart arteries using a procedure known as *radial-percutaneous coronary intervention* (r-PCI), in which a catheter enters through the radial artery in the wrist. Widely used in Europe, r-PCI is now being performed in nearly one of every six artery-opening procedures done in the US. With r-PCI, there's less risk for bleeding compared with the traditional route.

Dmitriy N. Feldman, MD, director of endovascular services, New York-Presbyterian Hospital, New York City.

Common Pain Reliever Raises Risk for Heart Disease

People who took more than 400 milligrams (mg)/day of *celecoxib* (Celebrex) had one-third higher risk for cardiovascular disease than people who took less, a recent study reports.

One alternative: Naproxen (Aleve). At doses as high as 1,000 mg/day, it does not raise heart risk and may even have protective effects.

Garret A. FitzGerald, MD, professor at the Institute for Translational Medicine and Therapeutics, Perelman School of Medicine, University of Pennsylvania, Philadelphia, and a participant in an analysis of studies published in *The Lancet*.

Better Time to Take Preventive Aspirin

Adults with a history of stroke or heart disease who took a 100-milligram (mg) aspirin tablet at bedtime had less of the blood stickiness that is associated with heart attack than when aspirin was taken in the morning. Because blood stickiness tends to peak in the morning, taking a nighttime aspirin allows for adequate time for absorption.

Tobias Bonten, MD, researcher, Leiden University Medical Center, the Netherlands.

Keep the Noise Down!

Ongoing and lengthy exposure to everyday noises, such as cell phone rings or traffic, increases heart rate and decreases heart rate variability—two risk factors for cardiac problems and stroke.

Self-defense: Take deep breaths to ease your body's response to noise. Block out loud noises with earplugs, sound-blocking headphones and/or white noise.

Seth Goldbarg, MD, electrophysiologist, New York Hospital, New York City, writing in *Prevention*.

Anxiety/Stroke Link

People with high levels of anxiety were 33% more likely to have strokes than those with low levels, according to a recent 22-year study of 6,000 adults.

Possible reasons: Higher levels of stress hormones, elevated heart rate and blood pressure, as well as anxiety-related behaviors such as smoking and physical inactivity, may be to blame.

Maya Lambiase, PhD, postdoctoral fellow, University of Pittsburgh.

When Neck Pain Means a Serious Problem

Seek medical attention if your neck pain precedes or accompanies a headache—it could indicate an impending stroke...when the pain radiates to your shoulders or arm or is accompanied by leg weakness or difficulty walking—this may be a sign of a herniated disk...if the pain worsens at night or is accompanied by fever or weight loss—this may indicate an infection or another serious condition, such as cancer. Neck pain can also be a symptom of a heart attack.

Mayo Clinic Health Letter. HealthLetter.MayoClinic. com

Sinus Infections May Raise Odds of Stroke

People diagnosed with a sinus infection were 39% more likely to have a stroke than those without infected sinuses.

Possible reason: Inflamed sinus tissue may put pressure on brain arteries.

Saline nasal sprays may help reduce inflammation. Ask your doctor for details.

Study by researchers at Taipei Medical University, Taiwan, published in *American Journal of Rhinology & Allergy*.

Little-Known Rheumatoid Arthritis Risk

In a recent finding, people with rheumatoid arthritis had a 30% greater risk of having a stroke and a 40% greater chance of having *atrial fibrillation*, a common heart arrhythmia.

If you have rheumatoid arthritis: Get screened regularly for atrial fibrillation, a major risk factor for stroke.

Study of 18,247 people by researchers at Copenhagen University Hospital Gentofte, Hellerup, Denmark, published in *BMJ*.

IBD and Stroke

Inflammatory bowel disease (IBD) increases risk for stroke and heart attack by 10% to 25%. The most common forms of IBD are Crohn's disease and ulcerative colitis, both of which are caused by inflammation. Inflammation is believed to be responsible for the increased cardiovascular risk.

Self-defense: IBD can be kept under control with medication, diet and moderate aerobic exercise.

Siddharth Singh, MBBS, an instructor of medicine in the division of gastroenterology and hepatology at the Mayo Clinic, Rochester, Minnesota. His analysis of nine studies was presented at the American College of Gastroenterology's Annual Scientific Meeting in San Diego.

Better Stroke Prevention

In a study of 451 patients at high risk for stroke, those who took medication to lower cholesterol, blood pressure and clotting were 9% less likely to have a stroke within three years than those who took the same drugs and had stent surgery in the brain to open narrowed arteries.

Possible reason: Complications from surgery in small brain arteries can lead to stroke.

Colin Derdeyn, MD, director, Center for Stroke and Cerebrovascular Disease, Washington University School of Medicine, St. Louis, Missouri.

FDA Approves New Stroke Prevention Drug

A new drug has been approved to prevent stroke in people with atrial fibrillation and at least one other stroke risk factor. *Apixaban* (Eliquis) is more effective for patients in this group than the traditional medicine *warfarin*. It is not approved for use in patients who have had a recent hemorrhage or who have faulty or artificial heart valves. Ask your doctor for details.

Rafael Alexander Ortiz, MD, director of Center for Stroke and Neuro-Endovascular Surgery, Lenox Hill Hospital, New York City.

Better Stroke Care

When adults who had mild or moderate strokes got the clot-busting drug *tissue plasminogen activator* (tPA) within 90 minutes of having symptoms (rather than within 3 hours, as specified by the package insert), they were much more likely to have little or no disability at a three-month follow-up than those who were given tPA later.

Takeaway: Call 911 if you have any sign of stroke—sudden numbness or weakness on one side of the body, facial drooping, speech difficulties, inability to walk or loss of vision—even if it lasts for only a few minutes.

Daniel Strbian, MD, PhD, associate professor of neurology, Helsinki University Central Hospital, Finland.

WHAT TO DO...

Signs of Stroke? Call an Ambulance!

Even though an ambulance is the fastest way for someone suffering symptoms of a stroke to get to a hospital—a crucial factor in stroke survival and recovery—the records of 204,591 stroke patients show that more than one in three were driven by someone else or they drove themselves. Among the ambulance patients, 67.3% received a clot-busting drug within three hours (an important cutoff period for this stroke treatment), compared with 44.1% of the others.

Bonus: Ambulance personnel can contact the hospital in advance so staff is ready when the stroke patient arrives.

Best: Have the ambulance take the stroke patient to a "Stroke Center" if at all possible.

To learn the signs of a stroke, go to *Stroke Association.org* and click on "Warning Signs."

Jeffrey L. Saver, MD, director, UCLA Comprehensive Stroke Center, Los Angeles

Seafood Caution

In a recent finding, young adults who consumed high levels of mercury increased their risk for type 2 diabetes later in life by 65%. (*Editor's note:* For a list of fish and their mercury levels, go to *NRDC.org* and search for "mercury in fish.")

Study of 3,875 people by researchers at Indiana University, Bloomington School of Public Health, reported online in *Diabetes Care.*

Some Statins Reduce Risk for Diabetes... Some Raise It

The cholesterol-lowering medication *pravastatin* (Pravachol) has been shown to decrease risk for diabetes by as much as 30%. According to a recent study, two other statins—*fluvastatin* (Lescol) and *lovastatin* (Mevacor)—also are associated with a lower risk when compared with *atorvastatin* (Lipitor), *rosuvastatin* (Crestor) and *simvastatin* (Zocor). The relative rise in diabetes risk for atorvastatin, rosuvastatin and simvastatin was 22%, 18% and 10%, respectively. If you take any of these statins, talk to your doctor.

Muhammad Mamdani, MPH, PharmD, associate professor of medicine and pharmacy, University of Toronto, Ontario, and director of the Applied Health Research Centre, St. Michael's Hospital, also in Toronto. He is senior author of a study published in *BMJ*.

Alert: New Diabetes Drugs *Double* Risk for Pancreatitis

The newest class of diabetes medications—*glucagon-like peptide-1-based therapies* (GLP-1)—are effective in lowering blood glucose. But the drugs *sitagliptin* (Januvia), taken orally, and *exenatide* (Byetta), an injection, foster the formation of lesions in the pancreas and cause inflammation. People taking these drugs should tell their doctors if they experience symptoms of pancreatitis, such as nausea, vomiting and abdominal pain.

Study of 1,269 type 2 diabetes patients who filled at least one GLP-1 prescription by researchers at Johns Hopkins University School of Medicine, Baltimore, published online in *JAMA Internal Medicine*.

New Help for Diabetes

Sometimes the constant delivery of insulin causes blood sugar to drop too low—a potentially fatal condition called *hypoglycemia*. Medtronic's MiniMed 530G has a sensor that alerts patients to this danger and, if the person is asleep or unconscious, shuts off automatically for two hours. The pump has been used in Europe for over two years and was approved in the US in September 2013.

Joel Zonszein, MD, FACE, FACP, director of the Clinical Diabetes Center, Montefiore Medical Center, the Bronx, New York.

Diabetes Medications That Lower Cancer Risk

In a recent finding, women with type 2 diabetes taking *insulin sensitizers*, including the diabetes medication *metformin* (Glucophage), or *thiazolidinediones*, such as *pioglitazone* (Actos), had a 21% lower risk for cancer than women taking *insulin secretagogues*. Insulin secretagogues include *sulfonylureas*, such as *glimepiride* (Amaryl), and *meglitinides*, such as *nateglinide* (Starlix).

Sangeeta Kashyap, MD, an endocrinologist and associate professor of medicine at the Cleveland Clinic's Endocrinology & Metabolism Institute. She is lead author of a study published in *Diabetes, Obesity and Metabolism*.

Statins May Reduce Risk for Esophageal Cancer by One-Third!

In a recent finding, people taking statins had one-third lower risk for esophageal cancer than people not taking the cholesterol-lowering drugs. People who took aspirin as well as statins had a 72% lower risk.

Possible reason: The drugs' anti-inflammatory effects may decrease cancer-related inflammation.

Editor's note: Research also suggests that statins may decrease the risk of dying from prostate, breast and kidney cancers.

Review of 13 studies of statins by researchers at Mayo Clinic, Rochester, Minnesota, presented at a meeting of the American College of Gastroenterology.

Aspirin May Reduce Cancer Risk

In recent research, aspirin and other *non-steroidal anti-inflammatory drugs* (NSAIDs) were found to help prevent the growth of cancer cells when taken at least once a week for six months.

Study led by researchers at University of California, San Francisco, published in *PLOS Genetics*.

New Blood Test for Early-Stage Cancer on the Way?

The new blood test checks for *serum-free fatty acids*, which are much higher in people with lung cancer and prostate cancer. The test accurately identified cancer patients 70% of the time in a small study. More research is needed.

Study of 95 cancer patients by researchers at Cleveland Clinic, Ohio, presented at the annual meeting of the American Society of Anesthesiologists in San Francisco.

All Skin Cancers Are Dangerous

Every year, nearly three million people in the US are diagnosed with *basal cell car-*

cinoma (BCC) and another 700,000 with *squamous cell carcinoma* (SCC). Neither of these is as serious as melanoma.

But: BCC and SCC can spread, damaging tissue and bone, and become infected or cause disfigurement if untreated. Surgical removal may be needed.

The Skin Cancer Foundation. *SkinCancer.org*

EASY-TO-DO...

Stop the Tanning!

Just one session in a tanning bed increases risk for melanoma by 20%. Frequent tanning sessions raise melanoma risk by 42%.

Meta-analysis of 27 studies of indoor-tanning devices by researchers at the International Prevention Research Institute, Lyon, France, published in *BMJ*.

Stress of Cancer Scare Lingers for Years

In a recent finding, women who received a false-positive on a mammogram could suffer psychological distress, including problems sleeping and eating, for up to three years. In the US and Europe, the rate of false-positives can be as high as 60%.

Study of 1,310 women by researchers at University of Copenhagen, Denmark, published in *Annals of Family Medicine*.

Benefits of Quitting Smoking Outweigh Risk of Weight Gain

Smokers who quit gain an average of six to 13 pounds over the first six months, but those extra pounds won't hurt your heart as much as continuing to smoke will. Despite the weight gain, former smokers have a 50% lower risk for cardiovascular disease than smokers.

An analysis of data from the Framingham Offspring Study by researchers at Harvard Medical School, Boston, published in *The Journal of the American Medical Association.*

Are E-Cigarettes Safe?

We do not really know. Electronic cigarettes, commonly known as e-cigarettes, look a lot like the conventional version but use a battery to heat a small cartridge containing liquid nicotine or a synthetic substitute, turning it into a vapor that is inhaled. Manufacturers claim that e-cigarettes are safe, but there's a wide variation in the chemicals in each brand. The FDA recently found detectable levels of toxic cancer-causing chemicals in two leading brands of e-cigarettes and in 18 cartridges that are used as refills.

Until more is known about the potential health risks, it is best not to use e-cigarettes. They have not been found by the FDA to be a safe or an effective method to help smokers quit. If your spouse needs help to stop smoking, he should talk to his doctor or take part in the American Lung Association's free-of-charge Freedom from Smoking group clinic or online program. Get more information at *FFSonline.org* or call 1-800-LUNGUSA.

Erika Sward, assistant vice president of national advocacy, American Lung Association, Washington, DC.

Better Screening for Lung Cancer

New risk-calculating software that was used when reading the CT scans of nearly 2,700 current or former smokers predicted with more than 90% accuracy which nodules were benign or malignant.

Implication: After an initial CT scan, doctors can now better determine what type of

follow-up is needed—a second CT scan, biopsy or surgery.

If you need a CT scan to screen for lung cancer: Your doctor can use the risk-calculating spreadsheet at *Brocku.ca/Lung-Cancer-Risk-Calculator.*

Stephen Lam, MD, professor of medicine, The University of British Columbia, Vancouver, Canada.

Lymphoma Breakthrough

In a recent study, cancer patients with *chemotherapy-resistant, large B-cell lymphoma* who were treated with *azacitidine* (Vidaza)—a *DNA methyltransferase* (DNMT) *inhibitor*—responded to chemo after taking the drug and then went into remission.

Possible reason: DNMT inhibitors genetically reprogram cancer cells, which seems to help chemo drugs work better. Larger studies are under way to see if DNMT is effective for other cancers.

Leandro Cerchietti, MD, assistant professor of medicine, Weill Cornell Medical College, New York City.

Very Overweight Patients May Not Get Enough Chemotherapy

Recent guidelines from the American Society of Clinical Oncology (ASCO) recommend basing chemotherapy dosage on body surface area, height and weight. This gives obese patients the best chance of recovering from cancer and does not increase their risk for side effects.

Gary H. Lyman, MD, MPH, professor of medicine, division of medical oncology, department of internal medicine, Duke University School of Medicine, Durham, North Carolina.

Steroid Shots May Raise Fracture Risk

A recent study found a 21% higher risk for vertebral fractures (cracks in the bones of the spine) in patients who were given steroid shots for low-back and leg pain. But the study did not prove that the injections caused the fractures, and your risk may depend on your bone health. Talk to your doctor about the risks and benefits of steroid injections.

Shlomo S. Mandel, MD, director of the Center for Spinal Disorders, Henry Ford Hospital, Detroit, and leader of a study of 6,000 patients, published in *The Journal of Bone & Joint Surgery.*

Common Household Chemical Linked to Arthritis

In a recent finding, women exposed to high levels of *PFC chemicals* had nearly double the risk for osteoarthritis compared with women exposed to lower levels. PFC chemicals are found in nonstick cookware, take-out food containers, stain- and water-resistant fabrics used in carpeting and upholstery, and some personal-care products, such as shampoo and dental floss. Previous studies have linked PFC chemicals to premature onset of menopause, higher LDL (bad) cholesterol and reduced effectiveness of vaccinations.

Study of more than 4,000 people by researchers at Yale School of Forestry & Environmental Studies, New Haven, Connecticut, published online in *Environmental Health Perspectives.*

5 Myths About Arthritis...Plus Ways to Ease the Aches

C. Thomas Vangsness, Jr., MD, professor of orthopaedic surgery and chief of sports medicine at Keck School of Medicine at University of Southern California, Los Angeles. He is also on the editorial boards of *Arthroscopy: The Journal of Arthroscopy and Related Surgery* and *The Journal of Knee Surgery,* and he is author, with Greg Ptacek, of *The New Science of Overcoming Arthritis: Prevent or Reverse Your Pain, Discomfort and Limitations* (Da Capo Lifelong).

About one in six Americans will have to cope with osteoarthritis* during his or her lifetime. But even though so many people have it, there's still a lot of misinformation about it. *What's true about osteoarthritis—and what's not...*

Myth: **Running causes arthritis.** It would seem likely that the pounding the body receives during running could damage cartilage and increase the risk for arthritis. Not true.

A study that followed nearly 75,000 people for seven years found that those who ran 1.2 miles a day were 15% less likely to develop osteoarthritis and 35% less likely to need a hip replacement than those who merely walked.

Even though runners strike the ground with a force that equals eight times their body weight, they take longer strides (and require fewer steps) than walkers. The cumulative jolts caused by running actually appear to be similar to the slower-speed impacts experienced by walkers.

That said, if you have, say, an arthritic knee, you should consult with a medical professional before beginning a running program. The joint stress from running could increase the progression in an already-damaged joint.

Myth: **Don't move when you are hurting.** The conventional arthritis advice is to give your joints total rest during flare-ups. Don't believe it.

You obviously don't want to overdo it when a joint is inflamed. But gentle movements keep joints mobile, flush out inflammatory

*The advice in this article may help with rheumatoid arthritis, too. Talk to your doctor.

chemicals and improve the flow of oxygen and nutrients to damaged tissues.

On the "good" days, you could swim, lift weights, jog, etc. Yoga is an excellent exercise because it strengthens muscles and joints in a controlled fashion. Tai chi is another excellent form of gentle exercise.

Important: If you have more pain than usual, talk to your doctor or physical therapist before starting—or continuing—exercise. You might need to adjust your workouts, including stopping/starting particular exercises.

Myth: **It's an age-related disease.** This is one of the most pervasive myths. Over the last few decades, people have begun to get osteoarthritis at younger and younger ages. Today, the average age at which symptoms start is 45—and the downward trend is likely to continue.

Experts aren't exactly sure how to explain the increase in younger adults. Americans are heavier than they used to be, and obesity is strongly associated with arthritis. Also, injuries to joints during sports can lead to joint pain down the road. Ongoing inflammation increases cartilage destruction in the joint.

Important: If you have had a joint injury—a torn meniscus in the knee, for example—at any age, there's a good chance that you eventually will develop arthritis in the same joint. Work with a physical therapist to strengthen the muscles and tendons that surround the joint before symptoms start.

Myth: **A little extra weight is OK.** Studies have shown that people who are obese have more inflammation, less joint mobility and more cartilage damage than those who are lean. But what if you're just a few pounds overweight?

It's still a problem. People tend to exercise less when they're overweight. Reduced movement leads to less joint mobility—and more pain. Also, even a small amount of extra weight increases pressure on the joints. Every 10 pounds that you add above the waist generates an extra 70 to 100 pounds of pressure on the knees when you walk.

Research has shown that women who lose about 11 pounds can reduce their risk of developing arthritis symptoms by more than 50%.

Myth: **You can't stop it.** Arthritis may be persistent, but it's rarely hard to treat. Most patients get good relief without high-tech treatments or expensive medications.

Though the American College of Rheumatology advises patients with knee and/or hip arthritis to start with *acetaminophen* (Tylenol), I tell my patients that acetaminophen is an effective painkiller, but it doesn't help with inflammation.

My advice: Take one of the NSAIDs (*nonsteroidal anti-inflammatory drugs*) such as aspirin, ibuprofen or naproxen. They reduce pain as well as inflammation. Follow the dosing directions on the label, or ask your doctor for advice.

Helpful: To reduce stomach irritation (a common side effect of all the NSAIDs), take an anti-ulcer medication, such as *cimetidine* (Tagamet). I also have been prescribing a newer medication, *misoprostol* (Cytotec), for stomach irritation. Ask your doctor whether either of these might help you.

Soft Drinks Worsen Knee Arthritis

Knee osteoarthritis progressed significantly faster in men who drank more than five nondiet sodas per week than in men who drank less sugar-sweetened soda. No such link was found in women.

Possible reasons: The phosphoric acid in soft drinks may interfere with calcium absorption and cause additional calcium loss...or the sugared soda may replace healthful foods and drinks, such as milk, dairy products and fruit, in the men's diets.

Study of more than 2,000 people by researchers at Brigham and Women's Hospital, Tufts Medical Center (both in Boston) and Brown University, Providence, presented at the annual meeting of the American College of Rheumatology in Washington, DC.

Better Hip-Replacement Surgery

Posterior hip-replacement surgery, in which the incision is made in the buttocks or the side of the hip, usually is a better choice because it is done with a smaller incision than *anterior surgery* (through the front of the hip)…has a lower risk for complications…and provides better cosmetic results. Anterior surgery has a slightly faster recovery—but a much higher rate of complications, including nerve damage and higher fracture risk. Discuss with your surgeon.

Geoffrey H. Westrich, MD, an orthopedic surgeon at Hospital for Special Surgery, New York City.

Has Your Hip or Knee Implant Been Recalled?

Hip and knee implants are sometimes recalled. If you are planning an implant surgery, you should inquire about the track record of the device the surgeon intends to use. If you already have an implant, you can contact your physician's office for information on the type of implant and then access the FDA website (*FDA.gov*) to see if it has been recalled. If it has, talk to your surgeon about next steps, which could include further surgery, monitoring or simply reassurance that the device is unlikely to be problematic.

Douglas E. Padgett, MD, chief of adult reconstruction and joint replacement, Hospital for Special Surgery, New York City.

Shoulder-Replacement Effective for Arthritis

In a recent finding, 93% of rheumatoid arthritis (RA) patients who had a total shoulder replacement…and 88% of those who had a partial replacement had pain relief and improved function. RA patients with severe shoulder pain and stiffness that are not relieved by medication or physical therapy may want to consider the surgery.

Note: Rehabilitation after shoulder surgery can take many months.

John Sperling, MD, an orthopedic surgeon at the Mayo Clinic, Rochester, Minnesota, and leader of a study published in *Journal of Shoulder and Elbow Surgery*.

These Common Antibiotics Can Cause Serious Nerve Damage

Fluoroquinolones, including *ciprofloxacin* (Cipro), *levofloxacin* (Levaquin), *moxifloxacin* (Avelox), *norfloxacin* (Noroxin) and others, often are used to treat respiratory, bladder and sinus infections. The nerve damage, *peripheral neuropathy*, is not common, but it can be severe when it does occur. If you take a fluoroquinolone and start having symptoms —such as nerve tingling, burning or weakness—immediately contact your doctor.

Jay S. Cohen, MD, adjunct associate professor of psychiatry and family and preventive medicine at University of California-San Diego and author of *Prostate Cancer Breakthroughs* (Oceansong).

5 Top Myths About Lyme Disease

Richard I. Horowitz, MD, an internist, integrative medicine practitioner and medical director of the Hudson Valley Healing Arts Center in Hyde Park, New York. He has treated more than 12,000 patients with Lyme and other tick-borne disorders. He is a past president of the International Lyme and Associated Diseases Educational Foundation and author of *Why Can't I Get Better? Solving the Mystery of Lyme & Chronic Disease* (St. Martin's). *CanGetBetter.com*

Your risk of getting Lyme disease is higher than you might think. Approximately 30,000 cases are reported to the

16

Centers for Disease Control and Prevention (CDC) each year. However, the CDC estimates the actual number of Lyme cases is roughly 10 times higher—about 300,000 per year.

If you assume that you are safe from Lyme, consider this: Although many people think that this disease occurs in isolated pockets around the country, it's actually now been reported in most parts of the US.

"The great imitator": Lyme, the most common disease that's spread by ticks, causes dozens of symptoms that can easily be mistaken for other conditions, such as chronic fatigue syndrome, fibromyalgia and autoimmune diseases including multiple sclerosis. Many patients with Lyme suffer unnecessarily because they never even know that they have the disease—and those who are diagnosed often are not given the best treatments.

Leading misconceptions about Lyme—and the facts…

Myth #1: **Lyme always causes a bull's-eye rash.** People who live in areas where Lyme disease is common are taught to look for a red, expanding rash known as *erythema migrans*. It resembles a bull's-eye and generally appears about seven days after a bite from an infected tick.

Fact: About half of Lyme patients develop a rash. But even when the rash is present, it resembles a bull's-eye in only about half of those cases. It's just as likely to appear as a "simple" rash that's easily mistaken for a spider bite or skin infection.

Myth #2: **Joint pain is the telltale symptom of Lyme.** Many Lyme patients will develop Lyme arthritis, severe joint pain and swelling that usually affects the knees or other large joints. But not every Lyme patient develops this symptom—so you can't assume that the absence of joint pain and swelling means that you don't have Lyme.

Fact: Most Lyme patients have at least a dozen different symptoms, but there is no one symptom that everyone with Lyme has. Among the most common symptoms are fatigue, migratory joint and muscle pain, tingling, numbness and burning sensations, a stiff neck, headache, memory and concentration problems and sleep disorders. These symptoms can range from mild to severe. The constellation of symptoms and ruling out other disorders point to Lyme.

Myth #3: **Lyme is fairly easy to diagnose with a blood test.** If you have Lyme symptoms, your doctor will probably recommend two-tiered blood testing (first the *ELISA test*, which measures the total amount of antibodies produced by the body in response to the Lyme bacterium (*Borrelia burgdorferi*)…and if that test is positive, the *Western blot*, which looks for specific protein patterns that are characteristic of Lyme).

Fact: The tests are not very accurate. One study, conducted by the New York State Department of Health, looked at more than 1,500 patients who had been diagnosed with Lyme disease. Two-tiered testing missed 81% of the cases. If tests are done early in the course of Lyme disease or if the patient has received an antibiotic, test results may indicate a false-negative.

Important: I recommend getting both the ELISA and Western blot tests. If your Western blot shows a 23, 31, 34, 39 and/or 83-93 band, this indicates Lyme. Other tests, such as a *DNA test* called *polymerase chain reaction* (PCR) and *antibody titers*, to check for other common tick-borne infections, such as *Babesia* (a malaria-like parasite) and *Bartonella* (which causes cat scratch fever), also can be helpful in diagnosing resistant symptoms.

Myth #4: **Doxycycline always cures Lyme quickly.** When Lyme is diagnosed and treated within two to four weeks of the tick bite that transmitted the disease, about 75% of patients will be cured with tetracycline antibiotics such as *doxycycline* or other types of antibiotics such as a *penicillin* or a *cephalosporin*.

But about one-quarter of these patients—and a higher percentage of those who don't get quick treatment—will develop a chronic infection that doesn't respond to simple antibiotic therapy. Although some doctors don't think Lyme bacteria survive after 30 days of antibiotic treatment, many studies have shown that they can.

Myth #5: **Medication is the only treatment.** Antibiotic therapy is the mainstay of Lyme treatment. But it's usually not enough.

Fact: Many Lyme symptoms—such as fatigue, muscle and joint pain, and memory loss—that persist despite antibiotics may be caused by more than one organism. Chinese herbs such as coptis, artemesia and cat's claw may help treat Lyme and these co-infections.

I often advise patients also to take low-dose *naltrexone*, a medication that helps reduce inflammation. A combination of naltrexone, *curcumin* (an anti-inflammatory compound found in the spice turmeric) and antioxidants like *glutathione* have helped relieve fatigue, pain and cognitive difficulty in many of my patients who have Lyme disease.

Also helpful: Diet is important. Some people feel better avoiding gluten, and for others, an alkaline diet with lots of fruits and vegetables counteracts the acidity and inflammation caused by infection.

BETTER TICK PROTECTION

People can prevent some cases of Lyme by carefully checking their skin and removing ticks with tweezers (within 24 hours) after spending time outdoors—but don't count on it.

Fact: The black-legged tick that causes Lyme is about the size of a sesame seed. Most people never see the ticks that bite them.

My advice: Whenever possible, wear long pants and high socks when you go outdoors during tick season. Spraying your clothing with a product that contains permethrin, a flower-based insect repellent, can help repel ticks. If it's just too hot and you prefer shorts or other summer clothes, you can apply the stronger insect repellent known as DEET to your skin, but wash it off as soon as you are out of the tick-infested area to reduce exposure to the chemical.

Helpful for tick removal: Tick Twister Pro, about $5.*

*Price subject to change.

Faster Treatment for Hepatitis C

The new drugs *sofosbuvir* and *simeprevir* are specifically designed to stop the hepatitis C virus from replicating. Studies show high cure rates for both drugs. In many patients, including some who previously had been unresponsive to treatment, the infection was gone within 12 to 24 weeks. Hepatitis C is an infectious disease that can scar the liver and lead to liver cirrhosis and/or liver cancer.

Downside: These new drugs are extremely expensive.

Robert Gish, MD, clinical professor of medicine at University of Nevada and senior medical director of Robert G. Gish Consultants, San Diego, a consulting firm that promotes liver health.

Common Vitamin Raises Risk for Kidney Stones

Men who took vitamin C supplements of 1,000 milligrams (mg) or more per day were twice as likely to develop kidney stones as those who did not take supplements. Multivitamins—which usually contain about 60 mg of vitamin C—were not associated with increased risk, nor were foods rich in vitamin C.

Agneta Åkesson, PhD, associate professor, Institute of Environmental Medicine (IMM), Karolinska Institute, Stockholm, and leader of a study published in *JAMA Internal Medicine*.

Probiotics Can Harm as Well as Heal

These dietary supplements contain bacteria that can help remove disease-causing microorganisms from the digestive system, relieving such problems as bloating, irregularity and gastroesophageal reflux disease (GERD). But probiotics can increase the risk for colitis, diverticulitis, irritable bowel syndrome (IBS) and other disorders—and they can cause allergic reactions. Probiotics vary in the types of bacteria...how they affect the body...and how they interact with medications. Talk to your doctor.

Andrew L. Rubman, ND, a naturopathic doctor and founder and director of Southbury Clinic for Traditional Medicines, Southbury, Connecticut. *Southbury Clinic.com*

Help for a Bad Nose Job

If you get a nose job that leaves you with a bump, microdroplets of liquid silicone can be injected into low areas to plump them up and disguise the bump. Most patients need to get three or four short treatments at six-week intervals.

Advantages over having another surgery: No anesthesia...no swelling or bruising...less recovery time...and it's significantly less expensive—a nose job can cost from $7,000 to $12,000.* The full round of silicone treatments typically costs about $2,000 to $4,000. Silicone filler is permanent, unlike such temporary fillers as Juvederm and Restylane.

Note: Silicone has gotten a bad reputation because of breast implant risks, but this product and technique are different—and safe.

Robert Kotler, MD, rhinoplastic surgeon in Beverly Hills, California, clinical instructor at the David Geffen School of Medicine, University of California–Los Angeles, and author of *The Essential Cosmetic Surgery Companion* and *Secrets of a Beverly Hills Cosmetic Surgeon* (both from Ernest Mitchell).

*Prices subject to change.

Statins May Increase Cataract Risk

Statins have been associated with a 9% higher risk for cataracts in a recent study.

Possible explanation: The cholesterol-lowering drugs may interfere with cell regeneration in the eye's lens, which requires cholesterol to maintain transparency.

But people with certain risk factors, such as a family history of heart disease, may need statins despite the risk.

Ishak Mansi, MD, staff internist at VA North Texas Health System and professor of medicine at University of Texas Southwestern, both in Dallas. He led a study published online in *JAMA Ophthalmology.*

Breakthrough: No-Stitch Cataract Surgery

The FDA recently approved the first gel sealant for the corneal incision that's required after cataract surgery. In clinical studies, ReSure was more effective than a single suture in preventing eye fluid from leaking through the incision. There were no significant differences between the gel sealant and suture in eye pain, corneal swelling or inflammation.

James J. Salz, MD, eye surgeon in private practice in Los Angeles.

DID YOU KNOW THAT...

Getting Cataracts Fixed Extends Life?

In a study of more than 350 people with cataracts, those who had cataract surgery were 40% less likely to die from any cause within a 15-year period than those whose cataracts went untreated.

Possible explanation: The better eyesight that results from cataract surgery can increase a person's optimism and motivation to pursue a healthy lifestyle.

Jie Jin Wang, PhD, senior research fellow, Westmead Millennium Institute, The University of Sydney, Australia.

Surprising: Depression May Weaken Shingles Vaccination

Researchers gave a shingles vaccination or a placebo to 92 patients, roughly half of whom had major depression.

Result: The shingles vaccine was less effective in patients with untreated depression than in those who were not depressed or undergoing treatment for depression.

Conclusion: Untreated depression weakens the body's immune response to the vaccine. The shingles vaccine is advised for adults age 60 and older.

Michael Irwin, MD, Cousins Professor of Psychiatry, University of California, Los Angeles.

Got a Rash? It Could Be from an Ailment You'd Never Expect to Affect Your Skin

Cindy Owen, MD, an assistant professor of dermatology and associate program director at the University of Louisville School of Medicine, where she practices medical and inpatient dermatology with a focus on the skin signs of internal disease and drug reactions. She has published many articles in medical journals such as the *Archives of Dermatology* and *Journal of Cutaneous Pathology*.

We all know that we should keep an eye on all moles and any other skin changes that might be a sign of skin cancer. *But there's another reason to look closely at your skin:* It can point to—or sometimes even predict—internal diseases that you might not be aware of.

Many internal diseases are accompanied by skin symptoms. The yellowish skin tint (jaundice) caused by hepatitis is a common one—but there are other serious health problems that most people do not associate with skin changes…

DIABETES

Skin symptoms: Rash or pimple-like eruptions (sometimes containing pus) under the breasts, between the buttocks or in other types of skinfolds.

Possible underlying cause: *Candidiasis*, a fungal infection that commonly affects people with diabetes. This infection also can lead to whitish spots on the tongue or inner cheeks.

Candidiasis of the skin or mucous membranes that is chronic or difficult to regulate could be a red flag for poor blood sugar control—and it can occur in patients who haven't yet been diagnosed with diabetes. People with poor blood sugar control often have impaired immunity, increasing their risk for infections such as Candidiasis.

Next step: Most Candidiasis infections are easily treated with topical antifungal preparations. People with persistent/severe cases may require an oral medication, such as over-the-counter (OTC) *clotrimazole* (Lotrimin) or prescription *fluconazole* (Diflucan).

Also: Dark patches of skin that feel velvety and thicker than normal (especially on the neck and under the arms) could be due to *acanthosis nigricans*, a sign of *insulin resistance*, a condition that often precedes diabetes. The skin may also smell bad or itch.

Acanthosis nigricans often improves without treatment when you get your blood sugar under control, so get tested for insulin resistance and glucose tolerance.

DRUG REACTION

Skin symptoms: A widespread red, bumpy and itchy rash involving the trunk, arms, legs and, less often, the face. Other symptoms may include fever, fatigue, facial swelling and enlarged lymph nodes.

Possible underlying cause: A severe reaction to medication known as *drug reaction with eosinophilia and systemic symptoms* (DRESS). (Eosinophilia occurs when there are abnormally high levels of a type of disease-fighting white blood cell.) If the offending medication is not stopped soon enough, patients may experience organ damage. DRESS is fatal in about 5% of cases.

One reason for the high fatality rate is that the rash looks the same as many other less dangerous drug-induced rashes, so a patient (or doctor) might not realize what's happening. Also, the rash may appear weeks to months after starting a new drug. Patients don't realize that they're having a drug reaction.

Drugs that can cause it: Almost any medication but especially antibiotics, seizure medications, *allopurinol* (for gout), *sulfasalazine* (for inflammatory bowel disease) and others.

Next step: Call your doctor immediately if you develop a rash and the symptoms described earlier. You can treat the rash with steroid cream, but the systemic problems will continue if you don't stop the drug or drugs causing the problem. Those who continue to take the offending medication have an increased risk for liver, kidney, lung or heart damage.

HEPATITIS C

Skin symptom: Raised purple rash on the tops of the feet (often on the big toe), lower legs or hands that does not respond to antifungal or dermatitis treatments.

Possible underlying cause: Hepatitis C. This form of viral hepatitis is dangerous because it often causes no symptoms until the liver is severely damaged. Researchers have only recently discovered that patients who have been exposed to the virus will sometimes develop a rash, called *necrolytic acral erythema*, before liver damage has occurred.

Next step: A blood test for hepatitis C. If the result is positive, treatment for hepatitis C, including antiviral drugs, should begin. Zinc supplements also may improve outcomes in people with hepatitis C. This is especially true when there is a deficiency of zinc, which commonly occurs with hepatitis C.

Important: The Centers for Disease Control and Prevention recommends that every baby boomer get tested for hepatitis C. It's now estimated that more than 800,000 Americans have been exposed to the virus but have not been diagnosed.

LUPUS

Skin symptoms: A red and often scaly facial rash on the bridge of the nose and cheeks.

Other symptoms may include fatigue, joint pain and/or dry eyes.

Possible underlying cause: Lupus. A common symptom of this autoimmune disease is a butterfly-shaped rash that covers the cheeks and the bridge of the nose. Some patients develop a rash on other parts of the body—typically areas exposed to the sun, such as the arms, neck and chest.

Next step: See a dermatologist or rheumatologist. He/she will probably order a blood count (to look for lupus-related complications, such as anemia)...a blood test to check for systemic diseases, including kidney, heart and lung disease...and an *antinuclear antibody test* to detect an overactive immune system, which often accompanies lupus.

Treatment for lupus might include immune-suppressant meds, such as *hydroxychloroquine* (Plaquenil), and sometimes steroids to control inflammation. Other treatments will depend on the part of the body that's affected, such as the heart or the lungs. A related condition, *dermatomyositis*, also causes a facial rash and often is misdiagnosed as lupus.

To tell them apart: Dermatomyositis typically causes a bluish-purple rash on the eyelid, which resembles eyeshadow. Sometimes eyelid swelling also occurs. Additional symptoms include a red, scaly rash around the nails and on the knuckles, elbows, knees, chest and back.

REACTIVE ARTHRITIS

Skin symptoms: Small, pimple-like eruptions on the palms and/or soles of the feet. Other symptoms include joint pain and possibly mouth sores.

Possible underlying cause: Reactive arthritis, an autoimmune disease that's triggered by infection, usually one affecting the intestines, genitals or urinary tract.

Reactive arthritis is more likely to affect men than women. It's often caused by *chlamydia* (a sexually transmitted bacterial disease) or infection with *Salmonella* bacteria, commonly transmitted by contaminated food. Reactive arthritis typically occurs two to four weeks after the initial infection.

Besides skin symptoms, most patients develop pain and swelling in the knees, ankles and feet. Also, about 50% of patients develop conjunctivitis, or pink eye.

Next step: Treat the underlying infection and give the reactive arthritis time. Reactive arthritis often goes away within a few months after the infection is treated. Your doctor will prescribe an antibiotic. In the meantime, you can reduce joint pain with *ibuprofen*, aspirin or related drugs.

More from Cindy Owen, MD...

Could Skin Changes Be from Cancer Inside?

It's no surprise that skin cancer causes unusual-looking moles and other changes to the skin. But certain skin changes can be a sign of internal cancers. For example, dermatomyositis and acanthosis nigricans (described earlier) can be signs of internal cancer.

Other possible signs may include a rash that doesn't respond to treatment...or a rash that's accompanied by a fever, muscle aches or other symptoms.

In the case of dermatomyositis, skin changes can occur up to three years before cancer is diagnosed. Ovarian cancer is the most common cancer to be associated with dermatomyositis, but any solid-organ or blood cancer can cause the rash, including malignancies of the breast, lung and colon.

Important: See your dermatologist if you notice any skin change that you can't explain.

4 Secrets to Easier Breathing When You Just Can't Catch Your Breath

Gerard J. Criner, MD, a professor of medicine and director of pulmonary and critical care medicine at Temple Lung Center at Temple University School of Medicine in Philadelphia. He is codirector of the Center for Inflammation, Translational and Clinical Lung Research.

If you can't catch your breath, walking, climbing stairs or simply carrying on a conversation can be a challenge.

When breathing is a struggle, you wouldn't think that exercise is the answer. But it can be a solution for people with *chronic obstructive pulmonary disease* (COPD) or heart failure or even for healthy people who occasionally become short of breath.*

Four better-breathing techniques that really help...

PURSED-LIP BREATHING

When you're feeling short of breath, inhale through your nose for two seconds, then pucker your lips as if you were going to whistle or blow out a candle. Exhale through pursed lips for four seconds.

How it helps: It prolongs the respiratory cycle and gives you more time to empty your lungs. This is particularly important if you have emphysema. With emphysema, air gets trapped in the lungs. The trapped air causes the lungs to overinflate, which reduces the amount of force that they're able to generate. This results in a buildup of carbon dioxide that makes it difficult to breathe.

You may need to do this only when you're more active than usual and short of breath. Or you may breathe better when you do it often.

CHANGING POSITIONS

Simply changing how you stand or sit can improve breathing when you're feeling winded.

How it helps: Certain positions (see below) help muscles around the diaphragm work more efficiently to promote easier breathing.

Examples: While sitting, lean your chest forward...rest your elbows on your knees...and relax your upper-body muscles. When standing, bend forward at the waist and rest your hands on a table or the back of a chair. Or back up to a wall...support yourself with your hips...and lean forward and put your hands on your thighs.

CONTROLLED COUGHING

Your lungs produce excessive mucus when you have COPD. The congestion makes it harder to breathe. It also increases the risk for

*If you don't have COPD, you should see a doctor if you have shortness of breath after only slight activity or while resting, or if shortness of breath wakes you up at night or requires you to sleep propped up to breathe.

pneumonia and other lung infections. A normal, explosive cough is not effective at removing mucus. In fact, out-of-control coughing can cause airways to collapse and trap even more mucus. A controlled cough is more effective (and requires less oxygen and energy). You also can use this technique to help clear mucus from the lungs when you have a cold.

How to do it: Sit on a chair or the edge of your bed with both feet on the floor. Fold your arms around your midsection…breathe in slowly through your nose…then lean forward while pressing your arms against your abdomen. Lightly cough two or three times. Repeat as needed.

Important: Taking slow and gentle breaths through your nose while using this technique will prevent mucus from moving back into the airways.

COLD-AIR ASSISTANCE

This is a quick way to breathe better. When you are short of breath—or doing an activity that you know will lead to breathlessness, such as walking on a treadmill—position a fan so that it blows cool air on your face. You also can splash your face with cold water if you become short of breath.

How it helps: Cool air and water stimulate the trigeminal nerve in the face, which slows respiration and helps ease shortness of breath. That's why the treadmills and exercise bikes used in respiratory-rehabilitation facilities are often equipped with small fans.

More from Gerard J. Criner, MD…

When to Get Breathing Help from a Professional

You can do many breathing exercises on your own without the help of a health professional. For the techniques below, however, it's best to first consult a respiratory therapist (ask your doctor for a referral) to ensure that you know how to do the exercise properly. You can then continue on your own.

•**Paced breathing for endurance.** This technique is useful for people who have COPD and/or heart failure, since it improves lung capacity and heart function.

How it helps: With practice, this technique can increase your cardiorespiratory endurance by 30% to 40%. To perform the exercise, a metronome is set at a rate that's faster than your usual respiratory rate. Your therapist will encourage you to breathe as hard and as fast as you can for, say, about 15 minutes. (Beginners might do it for only a few minutes at a time.)

Example: The metronome may be set for 20 breaths per minute to start, and you may eventually work up to 40 breaths per minute.

You'll notice that breathing becomes easier when you're doing various activities—for instance, when you're exercising, climbing stairs or taking brisk walks.

•**Inspiratory muscle training.** Think of this as a workout for your breathing muscles. It is especially helpful for people with COPD or other lung diseases and those recovering from respiratory failure. People who strengthen these muscles can improve their breathing efficiency by 25% to 30%.

How it helps: For this breathing exercise, you'll use a device known as an inspiratory muscle trainer, which includes a mouthpiece, a one-way valve and resistance settings. When you inhale, the one-way valve closes. You're forced to use effort to breathe against resistance. Then, the valve opens so that you can exhale normally. This breathing exercise is typically performed for 15 minutes twice a day. You can buy these devices online.

Good choice: The Threshold Inspiratory Muscle Trainer, at *FitnessMart.com* for $47.50.**

**Price subject to change.

You Don't Have to Be Overweight to Have Sleep Apnea

Sleep apnea—a chronic condition that involves shallow or missed breaths during sleep—is most common in people whose airways are partially blocked by fat tissue.

However: It can occur in thin people who have narrow jaws or throats, as well as women in midlife whose throat muscles have weakened. If you suspect sleep apnea, talk to your doctor. Sleep apnea is associated with heart problems and other complications.

Julia Schlam Edelman, MD, a clinical instructor at Harvard Medical School, Boston, and a gynecologist in private practice in Middleboro, Massachusetts. She is author of *Successful Sleep Strategies for Women* (Harvard Health).

New Help for Sleep Apnea

When 23 adults with sleep apnea were given 60 milligrams (mg) of *pseudoephedrine* and 10 mg of *domperidone* before bed, all but one reported fewer symptoms, such as loud snoring and daytime fatigue.

Theory: Pseudoephedrine is used to treat nasal congestion, and domperidone is used for acid reflux, so the combination of these drugs may help reduce airway blockages and swollen tissue in the throat that may contribute to sleep apnea.

If you have sleep apnea: Ask your doctor if this drug combination would be effective for you.

Murray Grossan, MD, a Los Angeles–based otolaryngologist in private practice.

How BP Changes Affect Memory

Blood pressure fluctuations may lead to memory loss. In a study of 5,400 adults over age 70, those with the greatest fluctuations in blood pressure performed worse on tests of memory, attention and reaction time than those with more stable levels, even if blood pressure was high. Extreme swings in blood pressure are also associated with brain microbleeds, which may contribute to cognitive decline.

Possible explanation: Unstable blood pressure can disrupt flow of blood to the brain, which could lead to dementia over time.

Simon Mooijaart, MD, PhD, director, Institute for Evidence-Based Medicine in Old Age, Leiden University Medical Center, the Netherlands.

9 Factors Linked to Dementia

Early-onset dementia is linked to nine risk factors, many occurring during a person's teens, a recent study reports.

The most significant risk factor linked to dementia that occurs before the age of 65 is alcohol abuse. The other factors are use of antipsychotic drugs, depression, drug abuse, a father with dementia, poor mental function as a teen, being short, having high blood pressure and stroke. Taken together, these factors accounted for 68% of cases of early-onset dementia.

Study of 488,484 Swedish men by researchers at Umeå University, Sweden, published in *JAMA Internal Medicine.*

DID YOU KNOW THAT...

BP Meds Can Reduce Alzheimer's Risk by 50%?

Patients who took medication for high blood pressure—specifically, *diuretics, angiotensin receptor blockers* (ARBs) or *angiotensin-converting-enzyme* (ACE) *inhibitors*—had 50% lower risk for Alzheimer's in a recent study. Patients who took other blood pressure medications did not show this benefit. Hypertension is a known risk factor for Alzheimer's, so talk to your doctor about the right medication for you.

Sevil Yasar, MD, PhD, assistant professor of medicine at The Johns Hopkins University School of Medicine, Baltimore, and leader of a study of 2,200 people, published in *Neurology.*

Midlife Stress Linked to Late-Life Dementia

Among 800 women tracked for nearly 40 years, those who experienced significant stress (divorce, widowhood, loss of a child or mental illness in a loved one) were 21% more likely to develop Alzheimer's disease.

Why: Stress may cause structural and functional changes in the brain, which may linger for years after a stressful event.

If you're facing midlife stress: Try psychotherapy, meditation and/or yoga.

Lena Johansson, PhD, researcher, University of Gothenburg, Mölndal, Sweden.

Stay Away from Artificial Butter

Artificial butter flavorings can harm brain cells. Many contain the chemical *diacetyl*, which promotes the protein clumps associated with Alzheimer's disease. Make unbuttered popcorn and add salt, herbs or real butter. At the movies, order popcorn without the buttery topping.

Study by researchers at University of Minnesota, Minneapolis, published in *Chemical Research in Toxicology*.

Better Treatment for Early Parkinson's Disease

In a recent study, 251 Parkinson's patients (average age 52) with early motor symptoms, such as tremors, were given either standard medical treatment (the drug *levodopa*) or *neurostimulation* (a therapy involving an implanted device that blocks brain signals that cause motor problems).

Result: Quality of life in the neurostimulation group improved by 26% over two years, compared with a 1% worsening of quality of life in the medical treatment group.

Conclusion: Neurostimulation is an established treatment for advanced Parkinson's but may be effective for early cases as well.

Gunther Deuschl, MD, professor of neurology, University of Kiel, Germany.

New Hope for MS Prevention

In a study of 73 people with early signs of multiple sclerosis (MS), 58% of those given a vaccine that is used to prevent tuberculosis in other parts of the world did not develop MS by the end of the five-year study, compared with 30% of those in a placebo group. More study is under way.

Neurology. Neurology.org

Thoughts Can Move Robotic Arms

Neuroprosthetic limbs can translate brain waves into mechanical movements.

Example: A patient paralyzed from the neck down ate a chocolate bar while guiding a robotic arm with just her thoughts.

The Lancet. TheLancet.com

New Help for OCD

Exposure therapy is more effective for obsessive compulsive disorder (OCD) than adding a second medicine to the antidepressants usually given to patients with the disorder. People with OCD generally are given a *selective serotonin reuptake inhibitor* (SSRI), such as Prozac or Paxil—and if that alone does not help, doctors may prescribe *risperi-done* (Risperdal) as well.

Recent finding: Risperidone is less effective than exposure therapy, in which patients are slowly exposed to things that make them anxious.

Helen Blair Simpson, MD, PhD, professor of clinical psychiatry, Columbia University Medical Center, and director, Anxiety Disorders Clinic, New York State Psychiatric Institute, both in New York City, and leader of a study of 86 OCD patients over five years, published online in *JAMA Psychiatry*

Drinking Wine Guards Against Depression?

People who drank two to seven small glasses of wine each week were 30% less likely to develop depression than nondrinkers.

Possible reason: A compound found in grapes helps protect parts of the brain from inflammation that is linked to depression.

Study of more than 5,500 people ages 55 to 80 led by researchers at University of Navarra in Pamplona, Spain, published online in *BMC Medicine*.

Winter Depression Overdiagnosed

Winter depression is not as common as most people believe. *Seasonal affective disorder* (SAD)—in which people become depressed when the weather is cold and dreary for extended periods—frequently is overdiagnosed, possibly because of people's awareness of the condition and the high frequency of depression in general.

Study of 762 people by researchers at the School of Psychological Science, Oregon State University, Corvallis, published online in *Journal of Affective Disorders*.

Leading Cause of Anxiety and Depression

Ruminating about traumatic life events was found in a recent survey to be a leading cause of anxiety and depression. Such life events, including sexual, physical or emotional abuse, ranked higher than a family history of mental illness, isolation, income and education level.

However: People who dealt with trauma constructively—talking with loved ones versus excessive rumination or turning to alcohol, for example—were less likely to experience anxiety and depression.

Peter Kinderman, PhD, head of the Institute of Psychology, Health and Society, University of Liverpool, UK.

Better Depression Treatment

In a recent finding, among people with both depression and insomnia, 87% of subjects whose insomnia was successfully treated with cognitive behavioral insomnia therapy also recovered from their depression, whether they were taking an antidepressant or not.

Possible explanation: Regular sleep-wake cycles are necessary to regulate neurotransmitters in the brain and stave off depression.

Colleen E. Carney, PhD, director, Sleep and Depression Laboratory, Ryerson University, Toronto, Ontario, Canada.

Suicide Rates Highest in Spring and Summer

Suicide rates are the highest in spring and summer—not during the winter holidays. In contrast to popular thinking, the months of

November, December and January have the lowest number of suicides per day.

Dan Romer, PhD, director of Adolescent Communication Institute of the Annenberg Public Policy Center, University of Pennsylvania, Philadelphia, and leader of a study quoted in *USA Today*.

The Truth About Artificial Sweeteners

Karen Collins, RDN, a registered dietitian nutritionist, speaker and consultant, and nutrition adviser to the Washington, DC–based American Institute for Cancer Research, *AICR.org*. She is also the author of the weekly syndicated newspaper column "AICR HealthTalk" and blogs at *KarenCollinsNutrition.com/smartbytes*. Collins has taught patients how to cut down on sugar intake for more than 25 years.

W e all know that getting too much added sugar carries a slew of health risks—from weight gain and heart disease to diabetes and obesity-linked cancers.

In fact, research shows that most Americans are getting so much sugar in their daily diets that they are increasing their heart attack risk by 20%. But with so many natural and artificial sweeteners to choose from—and new studies coming out all the time that raise questions about their safety—it's tough to know which claims are valid and which are not.

Facts you need to choose the best sweeteners for you…*

TRADITIONAL SWEETENERS

If you are not cutting calories and eat a healthful diet, it's OK to have up to two to three teaspoons of these sugars daily. But if your diet includes high-sugar snacks, cereals, drinks or other processed foods, limit these sugars to a few times a week.

• **Brown and white sugars.** You may think of brown sugar as a more wholesome choice than white sugar. But the fact is, they're both

---

*People with diabetes can use any type of sweetener in their diets but must include it in their total daily carbohydrate limit recommended by their doctors or registered dietitians. Artificial sweeteners themselves have no carbohydrates, but the foods containing them usually do. To cook or bake with artificial sweeteners, check the labels for instructions.

processed—white sugar is derived from sugarcane or sugar beets, while brown sugar is a combination of white sugar and molasses. These sugars also contain roughly the same number of calories—16 calories per teaspoon for white sugar…and 17 for brown sugar.

How safe? When consumed in modest amounts, brown and white sugars are safe for most individuals. Brown sugar is really no more healthful than white sugar, but it does make baked goods moister and adds a hint of caramel flavor. Follow your taste preference.

• **Honey.** Even though honey contains trace amounts of minerals (mainly potassium, calcium and phosphorus), its nutritional value is not significantly different from that of white or brown sugar. Honey is about 25% to 50% sweeter by weight than sugar, so you can use less and still get a nice sweet taste.

How safe? Honey is safe for most adults when consumed in modest amounts. However, honey should never be given to babies under one year of age—it could contain bacterial spores that produce a toxin that causes infant botulism, a serious form of food poisoning. Honey's stickiness also may contribute to cavities in everyone else.

• **Agave (ah-GAH-vay) nectar.** Made from the juice of the agave plant, this sweetener reminds some people of a sweeter, thinner version of honey. Agave and honey have about the same number of calories (21 calories per teaspoon).

How safe? Overall, agave is no more healthful than other types of added sugar. Compared with the same amount of white sugar, agave causes smaller increases in blood sugar, triggering fewer of the metabolic changes that can lead to diabetes and heart disease. However, agave is higher in fructose than other natural sugars, which may not be healthy in large amounts.

• **Molasses.** This syrupy liquid is created from the juice of sugarcane and beet sugar during the refining process. The type of molasses is determined by the degree of boiling that occurs—light molasses comes from the first boiling…dark molasses, which is darker and thicker than the light variety, comes from the second boiling…and blackstrap molasses, which is quite thick and dark, comes from the third boiling.

How safe? Molasses is safe for most people. Dark and blackstrap molasses provide health-protective polyphenol compounds. Blackstrap molasses is also a good source of iron. All types of molasses contain about 20 calories per teaspoon.

LOW- OR NO-CALORIE SWEETENERS

Many people believe almost as a matter of principle that all artificial sweeteners are harmful and should be avoided. But that view is simplistic. *Here is what the science shows about artificial sweetener safety…*

• **Aspartame.** Sold in a light blue packet as NutraSweet or Equal, this artificial sweetener has no calories and is about 200 times sweeter by weight than white or brown sugar. Aspartame is used in soft drinks, chewing gum, pudding and gelatins and hundreds of other products.

How safe? Some individuals get headaches and/or feel dizzy when they ingest too much aspartame. Despite animal studies that have linked aspartame to cancer, no such association has been found in humans. However, a recent study linked consumption of diet soft drinks containing aspartame to an increased risk for non-Hodgkin's lymphoma and multiple myeloma in men. The watchdog group Center for Science in the Public Interest (CSPI) advises against using aspartame. In addition, people with *phenylketonuria* should avoid aspartame completely—this genetic disorder makes it difficult to metabolize *phenylalanine*, one of the protein building blocks used to make the sweetener.

• **Saccharin.** Found in a pink packet and sold as Sweet'N Low, it is 300 to 500 times sweeter than sugar. Saccharin has less than four calories per packet.

How safe? Despite concerns about saccharin causing bladder cancer in male rats, many human studies have shown no link to cancer risk. Even so, CSPI believes the research is inconsistent and recommends against its use. There's some evidence that saccharin can cross the placenta, so some experts advise women to limit it during pregnancy.

• **Stevia.** A highly purified extract made from the leaves of a South American shrub, stevia (sold as stevia, rebiana and under the brand names PureVia and Truvia) has zero calories and is about 250 times sweeter than sugar.

How safe? No health risks have been uncovered in a wide range of studies on stevia, but research is ongoing. Stevia may cause an allergic reaction in people who are allergic to ragweed and could interact with diabetes and blood pressure drugs.

• **Sucralose.** Known as Splenda and sold in a yellow packet, it has four calories per packet and tastes about 600 times sweeter than white or brown sugar. A processed sweetener, sucralose is derived from a molecule of sucrose (table sugar).

How safe? There's no evidence that sucralose harms humans when consumed in small amounts. One recent study suggested that it increases diabetes risk, but this was a small study of obese people looking at how sucralose affected their ability to metabolize a very large load of sugar—about 19 teaspoons consumed all at once. More research is needed on how sucralose may affect metabolism with a more typical diet.

PROCESSED FOOD SWEETENERS

• **High fructose corn syrup (HFCS).** Derived from cornstarch, HFCS is found in a vast and sometimes surprising array of processed foods, ranging from many breads and yogurts to particular brands of applesauce and even macaroni and cheese. Beverages that contain HFCS include a wide variety of soft drinks, sports drinks and even tonic water.

How safe? Most experts have long insisted that there's no research showing that HFCS is any worse than other sweeteners—and, in fact, most HFCS contains only a little more fructose than regular table sugar. However, some studies have now linked HFCS-containing beverages (one or more servings a day) to greater risk for heart disease, diabetes, weight gain and obesity. But these associations may be due to increased calorie consumption from foods that contain HFCS, such as soda, rather than the HFCS itself.

Best: Avoid these beverages and limit processed foods to substantially cut consumption of HFCS and calories.

•**Sugar alcohols.** *Sorbitol, mannitol* and *erythritol* are processed sweeteners that do not actually contain alcohol or sugar. They're about half as sweet as white sugar, with fewer calories. Sugar alcohols are slowly absorbed, so they don't raise blood sugar quickly. A serving of food with less than 5 grams (g) of these sweeteners generally won't affect your blood sugar. Consuming more than 20 g at once can lead to gas, bloating and diarrhea.

Beware the "Salty Six"

Watch out for these salty foods—bread, cold cuts, pizza, poultry, canned soups and sandwiches (bread and cold cuts).

Examples: One slice of white bread may contain 230 milligrams (mg) of salt…three ounces of deli or prepackaged turkey can have 1,050 mg…a four-ounce slice of cheese pizza from a restaurant can contain 760 mg…four ounces of boneless, skinless chicken breast can have 330 mg…one cup of canned chicken noodle soup may contain 940 mg.

Eat fewer processed foods and, when possible, read food labels.

Centers for Disease Control and Prevention data, published in *Harvard Health Letter. Health.Harvard.edu*

A Little Beer May Trigger the Urge for More…

A small taste of beer causes an increase in *dopamine,* a neurotransmitter associated with the brain's reward-and-pleasure centers. That creates a desire for more beer.

Study by researchers at Indiana University School of Medicine, Indianapolis, published in *Neuropsychopharmacology.*

Don't Mix Cocktails with This…

Cocktails containing diet soda can make you 18% more drunk than ones using regular soda. Diet soda has nothing caloric for the stomach to process, so the alcohol hits the bloodstream faster.

Cecile Marczinski, PhD, associate professor of psychology at Northern Kentucky University, Highland Heights, writing in *Health.*

Limit Coffee to Less Than Four Cups a Day

In a recent finding, people who consumed 28 or more cups of coffee a week were 21% more likely to die during the study period than those who drank less coffee. Those under age 55 who drank 28 or more cups were 56% more likely to die.

Reason: Unknown at this time.

Carl J. Lavie, MD, FACC, FACP, professor and director of the Stress Testing Laboratory at John Ochsner Heart and Vascular Institute, New Orleans, and leader of a study published in *Mayo Clinic Proceedings.*

Good News: Coffee Does Not Dehydrate

Contrary to popular belief, drinking coffee doesn't seem to lead to dehydration. In a new study, 50 men drank either four cups of black coffee or four cups of water per day for three days as part of their controlled total fluid intakes, then switched drinks for another three days.

Result: The men's hydration levels were basically the same whether they drank coffee or water.

Reason: Unless it's consumed excessively, coffee has only a relatively mild diuretic effect.

Sophie Killer, PhD, doctoral researcher, School of Sport, Exercise and Health Sciences, Loughborough University, Leicestershire, UK.

FDA Calls for New Labels for This Type of Meat

The FDA has proposed that *mechanically tenderized meat*—in which hundreds of tiny blades break muscle fibers in meat—be labeled as such and include cooking instructions.

Reason: The blades can drive pathogens such as *E. coli* deep inside the meat, where cooking may not kill them. More than 25% of all beef sold in the US is mechanically tenderized. Five E. coli outbreaks attributed to mechanically tenderized beef have sickened 174 people, four of whom died.

Self-defense: Do not eat meat that is rare or medium-rare. Meat should be cooked to an internal temperature of 160°F to be certain that all bacteria have been killed.

USA Today. USAToday.com

Don't Rinse the Chicken...and Other Secrets to Avoiding Food Poisoning

Richard Besser, MD, chief health and medical editor of ABC News. He has served as the acting director of the Centers for Disease Control and Prevention (CDC) and managed the CDC's public health emergency preparedness and emergency response activities. He is also author of *Tell Me the Truth, Doctor: Easy-to-Understand Answers to Your Most Confusing and Critical Health Questions* (Hyperion).

Here's the dilemma—Kale, spinach and other leafy greens are some of the most healthful foods you can eat...but they also are among the most likely sources of food poisoning.

A very real threat: Every year, one in six Americans gets sick after eating contaminated foods. While the symptoms, including upset stomach, abdominal cramps, diarrhea and/or vomiting, usually are not life-threatening, about 3,000 people will die from the illness, according to the Centers for Disease Control and Prevention (CDC).

So how do you get the health benefits of vegetables, fruits and other common foods without running the risk of getting sick? *Here's how you can minimize your risk...*

FRESH PRODUCE

Vegetables account for about one-third of all cases of food poisoning in the US, and leafy greens, such as spinach, lettuce and kale, are the highest-risk produce. That's because leafy greens grow close to the ground and are easily contaminated from irrigation water and livestock runoff. Leafy greens also have shapes and textures that make them harder to clean than other types of produce.

Important: Bagged and prewashed lettuce mixes may be somewhat riskier than "whole" produce because multiple heads of lettuce are used and mixes are handled more during processing. *To minimize risk...*

•**Get a package from the back of the store's refrigerator when buying precut lettuce.** The colder temperature in this location inhibits bacterial growth.

•**Check the expiration date.** While most people are careful to look for the expiration date on dairy, that's not always the case for produce. Packaged fresh produce that's eaten at least five days before the "sell by" date is less likely to cause food poisoning than older produce.

Rinsing produce, including prewashed lettuces, will remove *some* harmful organisms, but not all of them. In addition to rinsing, buy the freshest produce possible, keep it refrigerated and, if possible, cook it thoroughly to kill any bacteria.

POULTRY

Most Americans wouldn't think of preparing a chicken or turkey without rinsing the bird first. The common belief is that rinsing washes away *Salmonella* or other disease-causing microbes. In fact, rinsing poultry is the worst thing you can do. It isn't very effective at removing bacteria—and it sprays potentially contaminated water droplets around the kitchen.

Some harmful organisms can survive for days or even weeks on faucets, countertops, the refrigerator handle, etc. They cause cross-contamination when other foods (or your fingers) touch the invisible hot spots. *To minimize risk...*

•**Always cook poultry** (whether in your kitchen or on the grill) to an internal temperature of 165°F. High temperature—not rinsing—will ensure that the bird is safe.

• **Wash your hands after handling poultry.** Most people remember to wash their hands before handling foods, but it's actually more important to do so afterward to prevent the spread of bacteria.

THE CUTTING BOARD

It's one of the most contaminated surfaces in your kitchen, particularly if you use the same one for all of your food preparation. The bacteria from poultry and other meats are easily transferred to other foods. Wiping a cutting board with a sponge isn't an effective way to remove microbes. Unless it's new or sanitized (put it in the dishwasher or microwave on "high" for one minute), it might actually introduce new organisms.

To minimize risk: Every home should have two cutting boards—one that's used only for poultry/other meats and one that's used only for produce.

Common mistake: Not washing a knife you've used to cut poultry before cutting other foods. Wash it with hot, soapy water or use a clean one.

Plastic or wood? Plastic cutting boards are less porous and easier to clean. Wood boards have natural bacteria-inhibiting properties. Either is acceptable—just keep it clean by using hot, soapy water or sanitize it in the dishwasher.

UNPASTEURIZED DAIRY

According to a CDC study, dairy products (mostly unpasteurized) accounted for 14% of all cases of food poisoning in the US—and the organisms in contaminated dairy are more likely than those in other foods to cause illness that leads to hospitalization.

Some states require all dairy foods to be pasteurized, while others permit the sale of unpasteurized (raw) milk, cheese and other dairy products. *To minimize risk...*

•**Buy *pasteurized* milk, cream, cheese and other dairy products.** One study found that unpasteurized dairy was 150 times more likely to cause a food-borne illness than pasteurized versions.

LEFT-OUT LEFTOVERS

Bacteria need just two things—enough time and a high enough temperature—to multiply. *To minimize risk...*

•**Never eat food that was left out overnight.** This guideline applies even if the food was originally cooked at a high temperature or reheated the next day. The risk for contamination is just too high if food was unrefrigerated for that long.

• **Throw out food that you dipped into after the cooking was completed but didn't refrigerate within two hours.** Let's say you prepared a pot of stew or soup, then had seconds or thirds after it was cooked. If this food wasn't refrigerated within two hours, throw it out. By introducing the spoon multiple times into the pot, you could have introduced harmful organisms that may have multiplied. Some bacteria do grow at cold temperatures but at slower rates. For this reason, you should reuse leftovers within a few days.

DON'T FORGET THE SINK

Multiple studies have revealed that kitchen sinks, including the faucet handles, have extremely high bacterial loads. *To help minimize risk...*

•**Thoroughly wash the sink—and faucet handles.** Use hot, soapy water or a bleach solution—mix one tablespoon of unscented, liquid bleach per one gallon of water, and let stand for five minutes. Rinse well and air dry.

Risky Meats

Meats with the highest risk for food-borne illnessses are chicken and ground beef. Pork, roast beef, most deli meat and beef or pork barbecue are "medium risk."

Least risk for food-borne illness: Chicken nuggets, ham and sausage.

Analysis of more than 33,000 cases of foodborne illness by the Center for Science in the Public Interest, Washington, DC.

Beware Chickens from Farmers' Markets

In one recent finding, 90% of chickens purchased at farmers' markets tested positive for *Campylobacter* and 28% tested positive for *Salmonella*—both bacteria are associated with food poisoning. Smaller farms that produce fewer than 20,000 birds a year and typically supply farmers' markets are not inspected by the Department of Agriculture.

Self-defense: No matter where you purchase chicken, keep it cold until ready for use and always cook it to an internal temperature of 165°F.

Joshua Scheinberg, doctoral student, Pennsylvania State University, University Park, and leader of study published in *The Journal of Food Safety.*

EASY-TO-DO...

Don't Forget to Wipe the Top of Soda Cans

Wipe off the top of a soda can, or rinse it with water, before you drink from it. Cans of soda bought at stores and from machines carried a variety of bacteria on the tops. Cans bought from stores and gas stations had the most germs... those from vending machines had fewer...those bought in 12-packs had the fewest.

Laboratory study arranged by CBS 11, Fort Worth, Texas, reported online at *Consumerist.com*.

2

Medical Insider

What You *Don't Say* to Your Doctor Can Kill You

At a major hospital's emergency department, a 60-year-old patient named May recently told a doctor that she had passed out in the gym locker room after feeling queasy and short of breath during a workout. May answered "yes" to all the doctor's questions. Yes, she had a headache…an upset stomach…shortness of breath—and chest pain.

When the doctor heard chest pain, he linked it in his mind with the patient's fainting (a possible sign of a heart condition) and proceeded to give her the standard evaluation for heart disease. The tests turned up nothing, but overnight the patient developed a 102°F fever and her "upset stomach" became extremely painful.

This time, doctors gave May a full physical exam and blood tests. Results pointed to a gallbladder infection that could have been treated with antibiotics but had become so severe that she now needed an emergency operation. How was the real cause of May's distress missed?

This is a classic example of what can happen when a doctor does not keep an open mind about a patient's health problems—and the patient doesn't do a very good job of describing the ailment. This type of scenario occurs every day in hospitals and doctors' offices across the US.

WHAT GOES WRONG

When you have a doctor's appointment (or go to an emergency department), the diagnosis process starts the moment the physician steps into the examination room. That's why what you say and how you say it are so critical to getting an accurate diagnosis and the best possible medical care.

Leana Wen, MD, director, Patient-Centered Care Research, George Washington University Hospital and co-author, with Joshua Kosowsky, MD, of *When Doctors Don't Listen: How to Avoid Misdiagnoses and Unnecessary Tests* (St. Martin's). *DrLeanaWen.com*

You have probably heard that the average patient has less than 20 seconds (some studies say just 12 seconds) to describe the ailment before being interrupted by the doctor.

What's even more interesting is that the average doctor will have already made a diagnosis during those crucial first seconds. But if he/she hasn't gotten your full medical history, your odds of getting a correct diagnosis dramatically decline.

THE TYRANNY OF THE "CHIEF COMPLAINT"

When doctors do listen during those initial seconds of the visit, they've been taught to organize their thinking around a central focus, or "chief complaint." This is the problem that brought you into the doctor's office—for example, "chest pain," "a sore back" or "a cough that has lasted two weeks."

The chief complaint prompts the doctor to consider a list of possible diagnoses, ask a standard series of questions (for example, "when did it start?"…"what makes it worse?") and then order tests to investigate further.

Even though this approach is logical and efficient, it also can be problematic. Once the doctor focuses on just one possible scenario, he is less likely to look at the whole picture because other information can seem irrelevant. In fact, the chief complaint can actually be a distraction from the real story—a false start that leads the doctor down the wrong path.

In some cases, the basis for an entire diagnostic workup may be a chief complaint given to the first nurse you talk to (or even the receptionist) and may not reflect your greatest concerns.

The chief complaint is also a form of shorthand that doctors use to communicate with one another. If your condition is undiagnosed and you're referred to a specialist, he is likely to base his questions and tests on what he was told was your chief complaint—and you may be stuck in an endless cycle of misdiagnosis.

TALK SO YOUR DOCTOR WILL LISTEN

To prevent this scenario, when you see any doctor—whether it's your primary care physician, an emergency department physician or a specialist—what's most important is to tell your story in a way that will help him truly understand what's happening. *My advice…*

•**Plan what you're going to say beforehand.** If you have a doctor's appointment, write down your complete story and practice beforehand how you'll deliver it with a family member or a friend. While practicing, work out the details that most accurately describe what you are feeling.

•**Don't use medical jargon or diagnose yourself.** Because you probably haven't been trained in medical terms, you may use them incorrectly. In your own words, give a clear, chronological and vivid description of what's going on without a self-diagnosis. For example, instead of saying, "My stomach ulcer pain is an eight out of 10," you might state, "I woke up with a terrible stomachache. I felt like my belly was on fire."

•**Describe how symptoms have impacted your life.** You could say, "I have had such a bad headache that I could not get out of my bed for three days." If a symptom is chronic, describe how it's changed over time. For example, "My joint pain improved for a month, but it has now come back and is worse than ever."

•**Answer your doctor's yes/no questions with details.** Doctors use yes/no questions because it is a quick (though incomplete) way to gather information. What works best for you, the patient, however, is to answer your doctor's questions your way, giving pertinent details.

Example: If your doctor asks, "Do you have pain in your chest?" you might say, "Not pain, exactly…but I felt a kind of dull discomfort right here, around the time I got up. It lasted about an hour, and now I have a throbbing sensation in the same place from time to time."

•**Don't let go of your real concerns.** If you think the doctor is ignoring your concerns, you might say, "I've tried to answer your questions about my chest pain, but I also want to know why I've been feeling so queasy after most meals for the last two weeks."

GET THE INFORMATION YOU NEED

If you want to be fully involved in your medical care, you'll also need to understand the reasoning behind a diagnosis. When making a diagnosis, doctors develop a list of possibilities (known as the "differential diagnosis"). From this list, doctors select one (or more) that seems most likely (called the "working diagnosis"). After you've told your story, ask your doctor what could possibly be wrong and what he thinks your problem is.

Important: If the diagnosis—or anything the doctor says—doesn't make sense to you, ask more questions. For example, you might say, "Does this explain why I've been feeling so tired for weeks?" As the doctor performs a physical exam, participate actively by asking questions such as, "Just what is it we're looking for?"

If the doctor orders tests: Find out why.

Questions might include: Just what will the test show? Will it change treatment? Are there risks? Are there risks in not doing the test? Are there alternatives? Is waiting an option?

AVOIDING MISCOMMUNICATION

Back to May: As mentioned earlier, this patient had a gallbladder infection that was misdiagnosed. This might have been prevented if May had said, "Would a heart problem cause the many other symptoms I'm having, such as an upset stomach and headache?"

Important: If your regular doctor is not open to this type of dialogue, it might be time to find a new one—or if you're in an emergency room, offer to wait until the doctor can spend a little more time with you.

5 Questions Doctors Should Ask

Jamison Starbuck, ND, a naturopathic physician in family practice and a guest lecturer at the University of Montana, both in Missoula. She is past president of the American Association of Naturopathic Physicians and a contributing editor to *The Alternative Advisor: The Complete Guide to Natural Therapies and Alternative Treatments* (Time Life).

When you see a doctor for the first time or visit your longtime doctor just for a routine checkup, if you're like most people, you probably spend no more than a few minutes talking about yourself or your problem. Below are five key questions that I routinely ask my new patients. If you see a new doctor who doesn't ask these types of questions or your own doctor has never inquired about such information, give as much of it as possible to him/her anyway. Your answers may well affect your diagnosis and treatment. If the doctor isn't interested in hearing these details, consider replacing him with a doctor who is. *Questions all doctors should ask…*

Question #1: **What is your health time line?** On my intake form for new patients, I ask for a health history that includes significant events they believe may have affected their health—both emotional events (such as marriage, divorce or loss of a loved one) and medical events (surgeries, accidents or major illnesses) may be listed by the patient. Besides giving me information I can use as a physician, filling out this form arms patients with self-awareness, so they become better prepared to ask questions and give more pertinent details during our appointments.

Question #2: **How are your diet and digestion?** To help assess digestive function and nutrient status, I ask about patients' eating habits and how well they feel they digest their food. It's also useful to learn what foods they crave, what foods they dislike and what they ate in childhood. Additionally, I want to know whether they have daily bowel movements or any pain with digestion and elimination. I've found that many patients don't really know how to eat a balanced diet, and helping them correct that (with specific dietary goals) can lead to huge strides in overall health.

Question #3: **What is your daily fluid intake?** Sometimes, a seemingly mysterious medical problem is simply due to a person getting too much caffeine, alcohol and/or soda (regular or diet). And some people drink zero ounces of plain water daily. These individuals often are surprised to hear (but later thankful when they start to feel better) that I recommend drinking half of one's body weight in ounces of water daily! Low water intake can be hard on the kidneys and heart, in particular.

***Question #4:* How is your sleep?** This includes total hours of sleep time, when they go to bed, when they get up and sleep interruptions. I also want to know where a person sleeps. Surprisingly, many people spend the night in a recliner or in a child's bedroom. Knowing a person's sleep patterns can offer significant clues that help diagnose and treat ailments.

***Question #5:* How is your emotional health?** Are you happy, restless, angry, resentful, peaceful, longing for change or generally content? Emotional issues can worsen or cause physical symptoms.

How to Read Your Blood Test Results

James B. LaValle, RPh, CCN, a clinical pharmacist, nutritionist and founder of LaValle Metabolic Institute, an integrated-care practice in Cincinnati. He is author of *Your Blood Never Lies: How to Read a Blood Test for a Longer, Healthier Life* (Square One). *JimLaValle.com*

Unless your physician tells you there's a problem, you may not give much thought to the blood tests that you receive periodically. But standard blood tests and certain other blood tests that you may request from your doctor can provide valuable—even lifesaving—clues about your health, including explanations for such vexing conditions as short-term memory loss and fatigue.

What you may not realize: If your doctor says that your test results are "normal," this is not the same as "optimal" or even "good."

For example, a total cholesterol reading of 200 milligrams per deciliter (mg/dL) is considered normal, even though the risk of developing heart disease is sometimes higher at this level than it would be if your numbers were lower. Always ask your doctor what your target should be.

Results that you should definitely make note of—and tests you may want to request...*

•**Low potassium.** Low potassium (or *hypokalemia*) is worrisome because it can cause

---

*These blood tests typically are covered by health insurance.

fatigue, constipation and general weakness, along with heart palpitations.

Causes: An imbalance of the hormone insulin often causes low potassium. It also can be due to problems with the adrenal glands or a loss of fluids from vomiting and/or diarrhea. A magnesium deficiency or a high-sodium diet can lead to low potassium, too. It is also a common side effect of certain medications, including diuretics, such as *hydrochlorothiazide*...laxatives...and some types of asthma drugs, such as *albuterol*.

Normal potassium: 3.6 milliequivalents per liter (mEq/L) to 5.2 mEq/L.

Optimal potassium: 4.5 mEq/L to 5.2 mEq/L.

What to do: If your potassium is not optimal, your doctor will probably recommend that you eat more potassium-rich foods, such as fruits (bananas, oranges and cantaloupe)... vegetables (tomatoes and sweet potatoes)... and whole grains (quinoa, buckwheat). You'll also be advised to reduce your sodium intake to less than 2,300 milligrams (mg) daily—high sodium depletes potassium from the body. Additionally, you may be advised to take a magnesium and potassium supplement.

Also: Keep your stress level low. Chronic stress can lead to a high level of the hormone cortisol—which can overwhelm the adrenal glands and lead to low potassium.

•**"Normal" glucose.** Most people know that high blood glucose (126 mg/dL or above) is a warning sign of diabetes. But you may

---

DID YOU KNOW THAT...

Stethoscopes Can Spread Bacteria from One Patient to Another?

Bacteria were found on the part of the stethoscope that touches patients' skin. Some were contaminated with the deadly *methicillin-resistant Staphylococcus aureus* (MRSA).

Self-defense: Ask the doctor to clean the stethoscope with alcohol before using it to examine you.

Study by researchers at University of Geneva Hospitals, Switzerland, published in *Mayo Clinic Proceedings*.

not be aware that slight increases in blood sugar—even when it is still within the so-called normal range—also put you at greater risk.

Surprising: Among 46,000 people who were tracked for 10 years, for every one-point rise in fasting blood glucose over 84 mg/dL, the risk of developing diabetes increased by about 6%. Vascular and kidney damage may begin when glucose reaches 90 mg/dL—a level that's within the normal range.

Causes: High blood glucose usually occurs when the body's cells become resistant to the hormone insulin and/or when the pancreas doesn't produce enough insulin. Obesity and genetic factors are among the main causes.

Normal glucose: 65 mg/dL to 99 mg/dL.

Optimal glucose: 70 mg/dL to 84 mg/dL.

What to do: If your fasting glucose isn't optimal or if tests show that it's rising, try to get the numbers down with regular exercise, weight loss and a healthier diet.

Powerful spice: Add one-quarter teaspoon of cinnamon to your food each day. People who take this small dose can lower their blood glucose by 18% to 29%.

Alternative: A standardized cinnamon extract in capsule form (125 mg to 250 mg, two to three times daily).

• **High homocysteine.** Most physicians will recommend a homocysteine test only for patients with existing heart problems. Everyone should get it. High homocysteine may damage arteries and increase the risk for heart disease and stroke.

Causes: Homocysteine rises if you don't get enough B-complex vitamins or if you're unable to properly metabolize *methionine*, an amino acid that's mainly found in meat, fish and dairy. Vegetarians tend to have higher homocysteine levels. Other causes include a lack of exercise, chronic stress, smoking and too much caffeine.

Normal homocysteine: Less than 15 micromoles per liter (umol/L).

Optimal homocysteine: 8 umol/L or below.

What to do: If your homocysteine level isn't optimal, take a daily B-complex vitamin supplement that has at least 50 mg of vitamin B-6.

Also helpful: A fish oil supplement to reduce inflammation and protect the arteries. Take 1,000 mg, two to three times daily.**

• **Low DHEA.** This is a hormone that's used by the body to manufacture both testosterone and estrogen. It's also an antioxidant that supports the immune system and increases insulin sensitivity and the body's ability to metabolize fats. DHEA is not usually measured in standard blood tests, but all adults should request that their levels be tested.

Low DHEA is a common cause of fatigue, weight gain, depression and decreased libido in men and women of all ages. Over time, it can damage the hippocampus, the "memory center" of the brain.

Causes: It is normal for DHEA to slightly decrease with age. Larger deficiencies can indicate an autoimmune disease (such as rheumatoid arthritis) or chronic stress.

Normal DHEA: Levels of this hormone peak in one's late 20s. Normal levels vary widely with age and gender.

Optimal DHEA: The high end of the normal range is optimal—it reflects a reserve of DHEA.

Examples: 200 micrograms per deciliter (mcg/dL) to 270 mcg/dL for men...and 120 mcg/dL to 180 mcg/dL for women.

What to do: If your DHEA level isn't optimal, managing emotional stress is critical. Get at least eight hours of sleep every night...exercise aerobically for about 30 minutes, three to four times a week...and practice relaxation techniques, such as yoga and meditation.

Also helpful: A daily supplement (25 mg to 50 mg) of DHEA. If you take this supplement, do so only under your doctor's supervision—you'll need regular blood tests to ensure that your DHEA level doesn't get too high.

• **High LDL-P (LDL particle number).** Traditional cholesterol tests look only at triglycerides and total LDL and HDL cholesterol. I advise patients to get a fractionated cholesterol test for a more detailed picture.

Important: Patients with a large number of small LDL particles have an elevated risk for

**Check with your doctor before using fish oil, especially if you take a blood thinner—fish oil can interact with it and certain other medications.

a heart attack even if their overall LDL level is normal. The greater the number of these cholesterol particles, the more likely they are to lodge in the lining of blood vessels and eventually trigger a heart attack.

Causes: Genetics is partly responsible for high LDL and LDL-P. A poor reading can be due to metabolic syndrome, a group of factors that includes abdominal obesity, elevated triglycerides and high blood pressure. A diet high in animal fats and processed foods also can cause an increase in LDL-P.

Normal LDL-P: Less than 1,300 nanomoles per liter (nmol/L).

Optimal LDL-P: Below 1,000 nmol/L on an NMR lipoprofile (this test is the most accurate).

What to do: If your LDL-P level is not optimal (and you have not had a coronary event), I recommend exercise…weight loss…blood pressure and blood sugar management…more antioxidant-rich foods such as vegetables, berries and legumes…and three to five cups of green tea daily—it's a potent antioxidant that minimizes the oxidation of cholesterol molecules, which is important for reducing heart attacks.

Also: Daily supplements of bergamot extract, which has been shown to change the size of cholesterol particles (Earl Grey tea, which is flavored with oil of bergamot, provides a less potent dose)…and aged garlic extract, which has a beneficial effect on multiple cardiovascular risk factors. If these steps do not sufficiently improve your LDL-P level, talk to your doctor about taking a statin and/or niacin.

DID YOU KNOW THAT…

One Drop of Blood Can Be Used for *50 Tests?*

The V-Chip can analyze one drop for insulin, other blood proteins, cholesterol, signs of viral or bacterial infection and more. The device currently is being tested.

Lidong Qin, PhD, principal investigator in the V-Chip project, developed at Methodist Hospital Research Institute and MD Anderson Cancer Center, both in Houston, with preliminary results published in *Nature Communications*.

Don't Let Supplements Sabotage Your Lab Tests: Nutrients and Herbs Can Skew Results

Joseph Lamb, MD, a faculty member of The Institute for Functional Medicine in Federal Way, Washington, and director of intramural clinical research at Metagenics, Inc., in Gig Harbor, Washington. He has also authored numerous articles on nutritional supplements in scientific publications such as *Nutrition Research*.

If you take vitamin and/or herbal supplements, you probably already know that these products can interact—sometimes harmfully—with other types of supplements and medications.

What few people realize: Taking such supplements may also interfere with a wide variety of laboratory tests, including blood work and urine tests.

WHAT CAN HAPPEN

More than half of the adults in the US take one or more dietary supplements every day. And nearly 7 billion lab tests are given each year. In most instances, supplements do not affect the results of lab tests.

However, case reports in the medical literature indicate that certain supplements can…

• **Produce a "false-positive" or "false-negative" test result** that may lead to additional tests and unnecessary treatments.

• **Change your body chemistry in a way that the test accurately reflects**—but leads to incorrect treatment if your doctor doesn't know that the supplement is triggering the change.

SUPPLEMENTS TO WATCH

Commonly used supplements that may affect certain lab tests…

• **Vitamin C.** This vitamin can produce a false-negative reading for a fecal occult blood test, which detects digestive tract bleeding, a possible sign of colon cancer. Vitamin C can interfere with the test's chemical reaction, which signals the presence of hidden blood in the stool. (A fecal occult blood test may be done yearly if you have a family history of colon cancer.)

What to do: Three days before testing, stop taking vitamin C, including multivitamins.

Also important: An iron supplement can produce a false-positive reading on a fecal occult blood test. Excess iron in red blood cells can be mistaken for blood in the stool. Iron supplements also can skew the results of iron tests.

If you are scheduled for a fecal occult (or iron) blood test, be sure to tell your doctor if you're taking iron. (See the next page for advice on the best ways to discuss your supplement use with your doctor.)

• **Riboflavin.** High doses of this B vitamin— usually above the recommended daily intake of 1.3 milligrams (mg) for men or 1.1 mg for women—can turn your urine bright yellow, potentially interfering with any urine test that uses a dipstick indicating a color change.

These lab tests include a urine protein test (to monitor kidney function)…a urine glucose test (to monitor blood sugar levels)…a urine ketone test (for diabetes)…a urine pH test (to monitor the body's acid/alkaline balance)… and a urinalysis itself (which usually doesn't involve a dipstick, but may evaluate the color of the urine).

What to do: Riboflavin is quickly cleared from the body. Don't take a supplement or multivitamin with riboflavin the night before or the morning of a urine test—riboflavin can be safely resumed afterward.

• **Folic acid.** The B vitamin folic acid works in conjunction with another B vitamin (B-12) in many body functions, including cell division. However, a high intake of folic acid can mask one of the telltale laboratory signs of vitamin B-12 deficiency—abnormally large red blood cells—by making the cells appear normal.

A deficiency of vitamin B-12 can cause anemia…neuropathy…and memory loss and other mental difficulties.

What to do: If you are being tested for a B-12 deficiency and take a large dose of folic acid—above 800 micrograms (mcg)—in a supplement or multivitamin, tell your doctor.

Also important: Inform your doctor if you are taking the drug *L-methylfolate* (Deplin). This is a high-dose folate supplement that's sometimes prescribed with an antidepressant to help produce neurotransmitters that regulate mood (including *serotonin, norepinephrine* and *dopamine*).

• **Calcium supplements.** Undigested or unabsorbed calcium in the intestines may cause an artificially high reading on a bone-density scan.

What to do: Avoid calcium supplements and multivitamins that contain calcium for 48 hours before a bone-density scan.

• **Vitamin E, fish oil, ginkgo biloba, hops extract, red clover, ginger and garlic.** These supplements have blood-thinning properties that can cause problems for individuals taking the anticoagulant drug *warfarin* (Coumadin). This medication is prescribed to thin the blood in individuals at risk for blood clots, such as those with heart disease.

To make sure that the medication is working, patients should regularly have their *Prothrombin Time* and *International Normalized Ratio* checked. These tests measure the amount of time it takes for blood to clot. Because the supplements listed above can thin the blood, they can change the results of the tests.

What to do: If you take (or are about to be prescribed warfarin), be sure to tell your doctor if you use one of these blood-thinning supplements. Your doctor will need to closely monitor your prothrombin time and adjust your medication dose accordingly.

• **Dan Shen and Chan Su.** These are Chinese herbs. Dan Shen is used for heart and circulatory problems and Chan Su for sore throats and chest congestion. Both herbs can interfere with the test to determine if a patient's blood level of *digoxin*, a drug prescribed for heart failure or arrhythmias, is within the normal range. This interference can be very dangerous, because too little digoxin is not therapeutic, while too much can be toxic.

What to do: If you're taking digoxin, don't use either of these herbs.

WORK WITH YOUR DOCTOR

The four best strategies to help avoid a false or misinterpreted lab test result caused by a supplement…

•**Inform your practitioner about all the supplements you take.** When you visit your doctor, bring along a written list of all your supplements that can be photocopied. If a supplement contains a unique, multi-ingredient formula, photocopy the package insert or bottle label and attach it to your list.

Mistake to avoid: Do not bring a bag filled with your supplements. If your doctor is writing down a list of your supplements, he'll have less time to attend to other, equally important aspects of your care.

•**Take only quality supplements.** They're less likely to interfere with lab tests. A poorly manufactured supplement may include ingredients not listed on the product label or the amounts could be less (or more) than what is on the label.

To ensure that you're taking a high-quality product…

•**Look for a "GMP Certified" product.** A GMP certification on the label means that "good manufacturing practices" have been verified by an independent third party that checks such important features as the product's strength, composition and purity.

•**Do not purchase anything without a complete listing of ingredients.** Avoid all products with only vague ingredient listings such as "proprietary blend"—neither you nor your practitioner should be in the dark about the contents or dosages of any supplement you're taking.

Fasting May Not Be Necessary Before a Cholesterol Test

Doctors usually recommend that patients fast for at least eight hours before blood is drawn for a lipid profile, which measures cholesterol, lipoproteins and triglycerides. But a recent study found that levels of total cholesterol and HDL (good) cholesterol—the substances that matter most in estimating heart disease risk—varied by less than 2% whether patients fasted for as little as one hour or as long as 16 hours. LDL (bad) cholesterol varied by less than 10% and triglycerides less than 20%.

Note: If a patient is borderline and a doctor is determining whether he/she needs to go on medication, fasting may be advised.

Study of the records of 209,180 people by researchers at Calgary University, Alberta, Canada, published in *Archives of Internal Medicine.*

The Easy Way to Get Your Labs

Rebecca Shannonhouse, editor, *Bottom Line/Health*, 281 Tresser Blvd., Stamford, Connecticut 06901. *Bottom LineHealth.com*

You've no doubt heard that it's a good idea to ask your doctor for copies of any lab tests that you get. Now there's a more direct way of getting those results.

Federal rule: Beginning October 2, 2014, all labs are required to provide test results directly to patients who request them (some labs already do this).

Why this matters: Anywhere from 7% to more than 30% of test results (abnormal and normal) are not reported to patients. It happened to me. I recently noticed a worrisome blood test result that my doctor had overlooked. I caught it because I always ask for copies of my lab tests.

Getting your test results is wise because it gives you "talking points" to discuss with your doctor, explains Trisha Torrey, a patient advocate and founder and director of the Alliance of Professional Health Advocates. *What to do…*

•**Ask for your results directly from the facility that conducted your lab test.** The results will be mailed (or e-mailed) to you within 30 days. In some cases, you may be granted online access or be able to use a smartphone app. If your tests are done at your doctor's office, he/she may tell you how to access the results.

• **Be prepared to put it in writing.** Some facilities that do lab tests will require a written request, while others may not. The exact process will depend on the lab you're using. Some labs may also charge for the service.

Torrey's advice: Because it takes skill to interpret tests, always discuss them with your doctor—even if you receive the results at home.

When Medical Tests Are *Wrong*

Charles B. Inlander, a consumer advocate and health-care consultant based in Fogelsville, Pennsylvania. He was founding president of the nonprofit People's Medical Society, a consumer advocacy organization credited with key improvements in the quality of US health care, and is author or coauthor of more than 20 consumer-health books.

Several years ago, my doctor called to tell me that the results of my PSA test (which measures prostate specific antigen to identify possible prostate cancer) showed levels that were three times higher than normal. As images of my life insurance beneficiaries started to flash before my eyes, my doctor quickly suggested that I get retested because the result might have been a "false-positive" (that is, a mistaken finding of disease that is not present). I was retested at another lab, and the results were normal.

False-positive test results are more common than you might think. Over the course of a lifetime, one in four women will get at least one false alarm from a mammogram. Each year, about 3 million women will get Pap smear results suggesting an abnormality in their cells. Yet only one in 1,000 turns out to be malignant. Blood test results, including those for cholesterol, also can be inaccurate.

What often gets overlooked, however, is the fear and panic that patients suffer due to false-positive test results. According to a recent study, a woman's anxiety and fear can equal that of someone who truly does have breast cancer. And those effects can last for up to three years. So what can you do to protect yourself or a loved one?

My advice…

• **Aim for Monday or Tuesday.** When your doctor orders a test, try to schedule it early in the week. Results from the majority of widely used medical tests can be sent to your doctor within a day. Ask that he/she let you know the results promptly when they are received. If the results suggest a problem, your doctor can order a follow-up or retest by midweek. This eliminates the anxiety of waiting over the weekend or longer if you need to repeat the test or have other follow-up tests.

Helpful: Many hospitals and testing facilities now provide prompt test results (for mammograms, CT scans and MRIs, for example) and follow-up testing if necessary. To save yourself both time and anxiety, check in your area for testing centers, hospitals and labs that offer such services.

• **Follow the rules.** Many false-positive results occur because patients don't follow pre-test instructions. Cholesterol test results may come back too high (in the danger zone) because the patient failed to fast 12 hours prior to the test. Other tests report inaccurate results because patients didn't stop taking certain medications or supplements before the test. Ask your doctor to carefully go over what you should or shouldn't do in the hours or day(s) before the test.

• **Try not to worry.** Sure, it is easier said than done, but remember, false-positive test results are common. When a test result suggests that something is wrong, do your best not to panic. By following the advice above, you can quickly determine if there really is a problem. And most importantly, don't let false-positive test results stop you from getting the medical tests you need. I have continued to have my PSA checked and will do so until a better test comes along!

Protect Yourself from Dirty Endoscopes

Endoscopes sometimes are not properly cleaned. One recent study found that 15% of flexible endoscopes used in gastrointestinal procedures, such as colonoscopies, had unacceptable amounts of biological contamination that could pose an infection risk for patients having these procedures.

Editor's note: To protect yourself, put the name of the medical facility where you will have a procedure and the words "inspection record" in an Internet search engine window to see if violations come up.

Daniel A. Leffler, MD, director of quality improvement, division of gastroenterology, Beth Israel Deaconess Medical Center, Boston.

Be Wary of Low-Price CT Scans

Charles B. Inlander, a consumer advocate and health-care consultant based in Fogelsville, Pennsylvania. He was founding president of the nonprofit People's Medical Society, a consumer advocacy organization credited with key improvements in the quality of US health care, and is author or coauthor of more than 20 consumer-health books.

Certain hospitals and medical facilities are aggressively advertising inexpensive computerized tomography (CT) scans. These scans sometimes cost just a few hundred dollars or less, a fraction of the price that is typically charged. Some even are free. Why? So the medical facility will get your business if any treatment is needed.

A CT scan combines a series of X-ray views of the body taken from many different angles. But it's usually not a good idea to get a CT scan unless your doctor provides a specific medical reason why you need one. Each CT scan you get during your lifetime exposes you to radiation, increasing your risk for cancer. Also, though "precautionary" (not ordered for a specific reason) CT scans often are advertised as offering "peace of mind," they are likely instead to cause unnecessary health scares. The issues they turn up frequently turn out to be false alarms.

Potential exception: A recent study suggests that there could be some benefit to a precautionary chest CT scan for certain long-term heavy smokers. This applies only to people ages 55 to 74 who have smoked a pack or more a day for 30 years or more.

An advertised low-cost CT scan could be worth investigating if your doctor has a legitimate reason to recommend a CT scan and you lack health insurance or you would have to pay a significant amount out of pocket for the scan under the terms of your policy. Contact the hospital recommended by your doctor (and your insurer if you have one) to ask how much you would have to pay for the scan. If it's more than a few hundred dollars, ask your doctor if he/she knows of any way to lower that CT scan cost—many hospitals have programs to help the uninsured and underinsured pay these bills. If not, ask your doctor if he thinks highly of the facility that's been advertising low-cost CT scans. If your doctor cannot recommend the facility, don't use it—there's little point in having a CT scan done at a facility that cannot be trusted to interpret it correctly. Alternatively, call around to other hospitals and medical facilities in your area, and ask them to quote you their prices for the CT scan you need. Rates can vary dramatically.

Is the Drug You're Taking Triggering a Disease?

Armon B. Neel, Jr., PharmD, a certified geriatric pharmacist, adjunct instructor in clinical pharmacy at Mercer University College of Pharmacy and Health Sciences in Atlanta and founder of the Georgia-based Medication-Xpert, LLC, a private practice focused on pharmaceutical care for outpatients and institutional geriatric patients. Dr. Neel is also coauthor of *Are Your Prescriptions Killing You? How to Prevent Dangerous Interactions, Avoid Deadly Side Effects, and Be Healthier with Fewer Drugs* (Atria). *MedicationXpert.com*

When your doctor pulls out his/her prescription pad, you probably assume that your health problem will soon be improving. Sure, there may be a side effect or two—perhaps an occasional upset stomach or a mild headache. But overall you will be better off, right?

Not necessarily. While it's true that many drugs can help relieve symptoms and sometimes even cure certain medical conditions, a number of popular medications actually cause disease—not simply side effects—while treating the original problem.

Here's what happens: Your kidney and liver are the main organs that break down drugs and eliminate them from your body. But these organs weaken as you age. Starting as early as your 20s and 30s, you lose 1% of liver and kidney function every year. As a result, drugs can build up in your body (particularly if you take more than one), become toxic, damage crucial organs such as the heart and brain—and trigger disease.

Older adults are at greatest risk for this problem because the body becomes increasingly less efficient at metabolizing drugs with age. But no one is exempt from the risk.

To protect yourself—or a loved one…

DEMENTIA

Many drugs can cause symptoms, such as short-term memory loss, confusion and agitation, that patients (and physicians) frequently mistake for dementia. The main offenders are *anticholinergic medications*, which treat a variety of conditions by blocking the activity of the neurotransmitter *acetylcholine.*

Hundreds of medications are anticholinergic, and it's very likely that any class of drugs beginning with *anti-* is in this category—for example, antihistamines and antispasmodics. Cholesterol-lowering statins also can bring on dementia-like symptoms.

Other offenders: Beta-blockers (for high blood pressure or cardiac arrhythmias)…*benzodiazepines* (for anxiety)…*narcotics…tricyclic antidepressants…anticonvulsants…muscle relaxants…sleeping pills…fluoroquinolone antibiotics*…heartburn drugs (*H2 receptor antagonists* and *proton-pump inhibitors*)…*antipsychoticsnitrates* (for heart disease)…and *sulfonylurea derivatives* (for diabetes).

My advice: If you or a loved one has been diagnosed with dementia, the patient should immediately undergo a comprehensive medication review—drug-induced dementia usually can be reversed by stopping the offending drug (or drugs). A competent physician or consultant pharmacist can *always* find an alternative drug to use.

Surprising threat: Even general anesthesia can cause weeks or months of dementia-like confusion (and an incorrect diagnosis of Alzheimer's) in an older person, as the drug slowly leaves the body.

The anesthesia is collected in the fat cells in the body, and normal cognition may take months to return. The longer a person is under anesthesia, the longer it takes to recover.

CANCER

Medications known as *biologics* are frequently used to treat autoimmune diseases such as inflammatory bowel disease, or IBD, (including Crohn's disease and ulcerative colitis) and rheumatoid arthritis.

This class of drugs includes *adalimumab* (Humira), *certolizumab* (Cimzia), *etanercept* (Enbrel), *golimumab* (Simponi) and *infliximab* (Remicade).

Important finding: The use of biologics was linked to more than triple the risk for lymphoma, breast, pancreatic and other cancers in a study that was published in *The Journal of the American Medical Association*.

The danger: While these medications may have a role in the treatment of autoimmune diseases, they sometimes are prescribed inappropriately by primary care physicians. For example, a biologic that is intended for IBD might be mistakenly prescribed for irritable bowel syndrome (IBS), a far less serious digestive disorder.

If you are prescribed a biologic for IBD: Before starting the drug, ask for a comprehensive workup to confirm the diagnosis. This may include lab tests, imaging tests (ultrasound, CT or MRI), a biopsy and a stool analysis (to rule out *C. difficile* and other bowel infections that would require an antibiotic). Do *not* take a biologic for IBS.

If you are prescribed a biologic for rheumatoid arthritis: Before starting the medication, ask your doctor for a comprehensive workup to confirm the diagnosis, including lab tests and imaging tests (X-ray, ultrasound or MRI). Do not take a biologic for osteoarthritis. Besides increasing risk of cancer, the suppression of the immune system opens the door for serious bacterial and viral infections.

DIABETES

Many commonly prescribed drugs increase the risk for type 2 diabetes. These medications include statins...beta-blockers...antidepressants ...antipsychotics...steroids...and alpha-blockers, which are prescribed for prostate problems and high blood pressure.

Safer alternatives to discuss with your doctor, consultant pharmacist or other health-care professional...

If you're prescribed a beta-blocker: Ask about using a calcium-channel blocker instead. *Diltiazem* (Tiazac) has the fewest side effects. The 24-hour sustained-release dose provides the best control.

If you're prescribed an antidepressant: Ask about *venlafaxine* (Effexor), a *selective serotonin and norepinephrine reuptake inhibitor* (SSNRI) antidepressant that treats depression and anxiety and has been shown to cause fewer problems for diabetic individuals than any of the older *selective serotonin reuptake inhibitor* (SSRI) drugs.

If you're prescribed an alpha-blocker: For prostate problems, rather than taking the alpha-blocker *tamsulosin* (Flomax), ask about *dutasteride* (Avodart) or *finasteride* (Proscar). For high blood pressure, ask about a calcium-channel blocker drug.

HEART DISEASE

Nonsteroidal anti-inflammatory drugs (or NSAIDs), frequently taken to ease pain due to arthritis, other joint problems or headaches, are widely known to damage the digestive tract. What's less well-known is that NSAIDs have been found to increase the risk for cardiovascular disease.

My advice: No one over the age of 50 with mild-to-moderate pain should use an NSAID.

Fortunately, there is a good alternative. A daily dose of 50 milligrams (mg) of the prescription non-narcotic pain reliever *tramadol* (Ultracet, Ultram) and/or 325 mg of *acetaminophen* (Tylenol) works well and has less risk for adverse effects. Acetaminophen, taken in appropriate doses (less than 3,000 mg daily) without alcohol use, is safe and effective. I also recommend 3 grams (g) to 4 g of fish oil daily—it has been shown to effectively treat joint pain. Talk to your doctor first because fish oil may increase risk for bleeding.

More from Armon B. Neel, Jr., PharmD...

The Very Best Drug Self-Defense

If you're over age 60—especially if you take more than one medication or suffer drug side effects—it's a very good idea to ask your physician to work with a consulting pharmacist who is skilled in medication management. A consulting pharmacist has been trained in drug therapy management and will work with your physician to develop a drug management plan that will avoid harmful drugs. These services are relatively new and may not be covered by insurance, so be sure to check with your provider.

To find a consulting pharmacist in your area, go to the website of the American Society of Consultant Pharmacists, *ASCP.com*, and click on "Find a Senior Care Pharmacist."

Also helpful: Make sure that a drug you've been prescribed does not appear on the "Beers Criteria for Potentially Inappropriate Medication Use in Older Adults." Originally developed by the late Mark Beers, editor of *The Merck Manual of Medical Information*, the list has been recently updated by The American Geriatrics Society. To download the full list for free, go to *AmericanGeriatrics.org/health_care_professionals/clinical_practice/clinical_guidelines_recommendations/2012*.

The Painkiller Trap: Popular Drugs That Can Muddle Your Thinking and Make Your Pain Worse

Jane Ballantyne, MD, a professor in the department of anesthesiology and pain medicine at the University of Washington School of Medicine in Seattle, where she serves as director of the UW Pain Fellowship. She is co-author of *Expert Decision Making on Opioid Treatments* (Oxford University) and has editorial roles on several journals and textbooks, including *Bonica's Management of Pain, 4th Edition* (Lippincott, Williams & Wilkins).

If you have ever suffered from severe pain, you probably know that a strong pain pill can seem like the holy grail. In fact, with chronic pain affecting about one-third of Americans—or roughly 100 million people—it's perhaps no surprise that the most com-

monly prescribed medication in the US is a painkiller, *hydrocodone* (Vicodin).

Frightening trend: Hydrocodone and the other prescription *opioid painkillers* (which are also known as narcotics) have now overtaken heroin and cocaine as the leading cause of fatal overdoses, according to the Centers for Disease Control and Prevention.

WHY THE SHIFT?

Until recently, prescription opioids were used to treat only acute (severe, short-lived) pain, such as pain after surgery or an injury or pain related to cancer.

Now: As doctors have stepped up their efforts to better control pain in all patients, opioids are much more widely prescribed. These powerful medications are now being used to treat *chronic* painful conditions such as low-back pain, chronic headaches and fibromyalgia.

What pain sufferers need to know…

DANGERS OF OPIOIDS

Each day, an estimated 4.3 million Americans take hydrocodone or other widely used opioids, such as *oxycodone* (Oxycontin), *hydromorphone* (Dilaudid), codeine and morphine. For some patients, opioids are prescribed as an alternative to *nonsteroidal anti-inflammatory drugs* (NSAIDs), which are notorious for causing gastrointestinal bleeding and other side effects, including increased risk for heart attack and kidney disease.

Opioids work by mimicking natural pain-relieving chemicals in the body and attaching to receptors that block the transmission of pain messages to and within the brain. These drugs can be highly effective pain relievers, especially for arthritis patients who can't tolerate NSAIDs.

But opioids also have potentially serious side effects, especially when they're used long term (usually defined as more than 90 days). While the effectiveness of the medications often decreases over time (because the patient builds up a tolerance to the drug), the risk for side effects—including constipation, drowsiness or even addiction—*increases* due to the higher and more toxic doses used to overcome tolerance.

Continuous use of these pain medications also can have far-reaching health effects that can include a heightened risk for falls and fractures...slowed breathing...concentration problems...and vision impairment. And these drugs can compromise the immune system, resulting in susceptibility to infection.

Men who take opioids long term are five times more likely to have low testosterone levels, which can curb libido and result in erectile dysfunction. Even at low doses, opioids can diminish alertness and have been shown to increase risk for car accidents by 21%.

BEST NONDRUG ALTERNATIVES

If your doctor suggests taking an opioid for back pain, chronic headaches or migraines, or fibromyalgia, ask him/her about trying the following nondrug treatments first. Opioids should be considered only as a last resort.

•**Back pain.** For long-term low-back pain, exercises that strengthen the abdomen and back (or "core") muscles are *the* most effective treatment. If the pain is so extreme that you can't exercise, over-the-counter painkillers

---

EASY-TO-DO...

Helpful Medication Reminder

Can't remember if you took your medicines? Ask your pharmacist to make daily blister packs containing all your medicines. Not all pharmacies can make the packs—and the ones that do probably will charge extra for them, and that cost will not be reimbursed by insurance. But it may be a worthwhile expense if you want to be sure that you take all prescribed medicines every day and don't accidentally take any pill more than once.

Editor's note: You also can buy a plastic pill organizer at most pharmacies that has compartments for daily pills.

Consumer Reports on Health. ConsumerReports.org

---

sometimes can alleviate the pain enough to start an effective exercise regimen.

Bonus: Exercise can help ease depression, which is common in back pain sufferers. Yoga may also be effective because it stretches the muscles and ligaments in addition to reducing mental stress.

Other possible options: If the approaches described above don't provide adequate relief, you may be a candidate for steroid injections into the spine or joints...a spinal fusion...or disk-replacement surgery. In general, these treatments have less risk for adverse effects than long-term use of opioids.

•**Chronic headaches or migraines.** With chronic headaches or migraines, opioids can worsen pain by causing "rebound" headaches that occur when the drug is overused. Try lifestyle changes, such as daily meditation, and the sparing use of mild painkillers, such as NSAIDs. Supplements, including magnesium and feverfew, also have been shown to relieve headache pain.

•**Fibromyalgia.** With this condition, which has no known cure, opioids have been found to intensify existing pain.

Much better: A review of 46 studies has found aerobic exercise, such as brisk walking or pool aerobics (done two to three times a week for an hour), may reduce system-wide inflammation, which makes it a very effective treatment for fibromyalgia.

If you're in too much pain to do aerobic exercise, a mild painkiller or a nondrug approach, such as massage, may allow you to start.

Cognitive behavioral therapy is yet another good choice. With this treatment, a therapist can help you reframe negative thoughts that may be fueling fibromyalgia pain.

Additional nondrug approaches that may help all of these conditions: Acupuncture, relaxation exercises and heating pads.

Antibiotics That Shouldn't Be Taken with Statins

Some antibiotics should not be taken with statins. *Clarithromycin* and *erythromycin* reduce the metabolism of statins and increase statin concentration in blood, possibly leading to muscle damage and/or kidney damage. While rare, these side effects can be serious. If an antibiotic is needed, statin users should be prescribed one other than clarithromycin or erythromycin when possible.

Amit Garg, MD, PhD, a professor in the department of epidemiology and biostatistics at The University of Western Ontario, London, Canada, and the leader of a study published in *Annals of Internal Medicine*.

Sleep Med Caution

Emergency-room visits related to sleeping medications increased by 220% during a recent five-year period. Adverse reactions to *zolpidem*, the active ingredient in sleep aids Ambien, Ambien CR, Edluar and Zolpimist, include daytime drowsiness, dizziness, hallucinations, agitation and sleepwalking.

Study by researchers from the US Substance Abuse and Mental Health Services Administration (SAMHSA), Rockville, Maryland.

Emergency Surgery on the Weekend May Mean Poorer Results

Ulcerative colitis patients who had surgery on a weekend were 70% more likely to have complications after surgery than those who had surgery on a weekday.

Study of 7,112 emergency operations for Crohn's disease and ulcerative colitis nationwide by researchers at Massachusetts General Hospital, Boston, published online in *Alimentary Pharmacology and Therapeutics*.

Summer Surgery OK

Summer surgery is no riskier than surgery at any other time of year. The "July Effect"—the belief that the arrival of new residents and fellows at teaching hospitals increases the risk for surgical complications—has been proved false.

Study of nearly one million hospitalizations by researchers at Mayo Clinic, Rochester, Minnesota, published in *Journal of Neurosurgery: Spine*.

4,000 Surgical Mistakes

There are at least 4,000 surgical mistakes in the US every year. These include leaving a foreign object such as a sponge or a towel in a patient...performing the wrong procedure... or operating on the wrong side of the body. Mistakes happen most often to patients ages 40 to 49. Doctors ages 40 to 49 are responsible for more than one-third of the errors.

Analysis of national malpractice claims by researchers from Johns Hopkins University School of Medicine, Baltimore, published in *Surgery*.

Antidepressants That Increase Surgery Risks

Patients using *selective serotonin reuptake inhibitors* (or SSRIs), such as Prozac and Paxil, around the time of major surgery had a 10% higher risk for bleeding and death in a recent finding. You may want to stop taking an SSRI for several days before surgery and start again soon after.

Caution: Do not stop SSRI use except under a doctor's guidance.

Andrew D. Auerbach, MD, MPH, professor of medicine in residence, division of hospital medicine, University of California–San Francisco, and the leader of a study published in *JAMA Internal Medicine*.

Statins and Stroke Survival

Stroke victims who take statins in the hospital are more likely to survive than other stroke patients.

Recent finding: Among stroke patients who used statins before and during hospital stays, 6% died, compared with 11% of nonusers.

Study of 12,689 stroke patients by researchers at Kaiser Permanente, Redwood City, California, published in *Neurology*.

#1 Hospital Complaint: Noise

Vineet Arora, MD, associate professor of medicine who studies hospital noise and sleep issues at the University of Chicago.

Hospitals are supposed to help us get well—but too often they can't even make us well-rested. Many hospitals are loud places, even at night, costing patients sleep. And studies have linked patients' insufficient sleep to slower healing, higher blood pressure, increased need for pain medication and elevated levels of delirium and confusion.

It's time to take matters into our own hands! Research has revealed that patients who take action to lower hospital noise not only usually succeed in doing so, they also feel more in control of their situation—and that helps them rest easier, too.

What to do…

•**Ask your nurse if any late-night blood draws or vital sign checks could be safely postponed until morning.** If they can't, be sure to ask the nurse to turn off the lights afterward.

•**Wear earplugs or noise-canceling headphones,** or place a white noise machine next to your bed. Try these out before your hospital stay, if possible, to get used to them.

•**Ask to be transferred to a different room** if you have a roommate who requires late-night visits from a nurse.

•**Get exercise during the day.** Even limited activity could help you sleep deeper at night despite the noise.

•**Use your call button to inform a nurse** of any alarms that sound in your room during the night.

We all need to speak up for our right to quiet!

Sleeping Pills Linked to Falls in Hospital Patients

The fall rate in hospital patients given the sleep medication *zolpidem* (Ambien) was more than four times higher than in patients who did not take the drug. Zolpidem posed greater susceptibility for falls than other risk factors, such as age or cognitive impairment, regardless of the dose.

If you're having trouble sleeping in the hospital: Ask that nighttime interruptions and noise be kept to a minimum and/or bring earplugs.

Timothy I. Morgenthaler, MD, professor of medicine, Center for Sleep Medicine at the Mayo Clinic, Rochester, Minnesota.

Simple Ways to Reduce Delirium Risk in the Hospital

Patients in intensive care units (ICUs) often are subjected to multiple nighttime interruptions involving light and noise, which interfere with sleep. This may delay recovery and lead to short- and long-term confusion and memory problems, hallmarks of delirium, in up to 80% of patients.

Finding: Simple steps such as turning off televisions and minimizing interruptions reduced risk for delirium by 54%. Patients also were given fewer drugs, including sedatives, that can lead to delirium.

Smart: Patients (or their families) should ask the head ICU nurse that efforts be made to reduce noise and interruptions.

Biren Kamdar, MD, physician specializing in critical care medicine, Ronald Reagan University of California–Los Angeles Medical Center.

Statins May Cause Delirium

Statin drugs, which reduce cholesterol, are associated with a 30% increase in risk for postsurgical delirium in people age 65 and older. The result can be long-lasting or even permanent cognitive impairment in the oldest and sickest patients. Factors typically associated with surgery—including general anesthesia, reduced blood pressure and opioids for pain control—may cause statins to raise delirium risk.

Self-defense: Most patients can safely stop taking statins about two days before surgery, then resume taking them the first day after surgery—but always get your doctor's approval.

Donald A. Redelmeier, MD, director of the clinical epidemiology unit at Sunnybrook Health Sciences Centre, University of Toronto, and leader of a study published in *Canadian Medical Association Journal*.

Let the Sun Shine In!

People need 3,000 lux to 5,000 lux (lux is a unit of illumination) during the day to maintain a proper sleep-wake cycle.

Problem: Most hospital patients get less than 200 lux during the day.

Result: Greater fatigue…increased pain… and sometimes a slower recovery.

Self-defense: If possible, hospital patients should spend at least 30 minutes in the morning and another 30 in the afternoon within two feet of a window.

Esther Bernhofer, PhD, RN, a nurse researcher at the Cleveland Clinic's Nursing Institute, Cleveland, Ohio, and lead author of a study published in *Journal of Advanced Nursing*.

Coffee Speeds Recovery After Surgery

Drink three cups of hot black coffee a day, starting as soon after surgery as your doctor allows.

People who drank this amount of coffee had a bowel movement 10 hours sooner than those who drank hot water…spent one day less in the hospital…and were able to return sooner to a diet of solid foods. Major surgery shuts down bowel function, which usually returns two to five days later. Speeding the return of bowel function helps the body resume normal processing of food, which is important for recovery.

Study of 80 patients by researchers at University Hospital, Heidelberg, Germany, published in the *British Journal of Surgery* (BJS).

Ask for an "Enhanced Recovery Program"…

Surgery patients can go home sooner if they follow an enhanced recovery program.

Program basics: Non-narcotic painkillers are used instead of intravenous morphine or other opioid drugs.

Also: Patients are encouraged to consume sports drinks up to two hours before surgery. Hydrated patients require less intravenous fluid. Ask your surgeon for details.

Traci Hedrick, MD, a colorectal surgeon and assistant professor of surgery, and Robert Thiele, MD, is an anesthesiologist/intensivist and assistant professor of anesthesiology, both at University of Virginia, Charlottesville.

To Prevent Postsurgery Scarring...

To reduce scarring after surgery, protect the area from the sun for six months to a year. Use sunscreen or cover the area with clothing. Even minimal exposure to sunlight can cause darker pigmentation within a scar.

During the first few days after surgery: Cleanse the wound carefully, and coat it with a thick layer of petroleum jelly—or follow your doctor's instructions if they are different. Contact your doctor if you have any increased pain or tenderness near the wound.

Mayo Clinic Health Letter. HealthLetter.MayoClinic. com

DID YOU KNOW THAT...

ICU Patients Are at Risk for PTSD?

Up to 35% of hospital intensive care unit (ICU) patients show signs of *post-traumatic stress disorder* (PTSD) as long as two years after being in the hospital. Symptoms include mood swings, nightmares, difficulty sleeping and flashbacks to ICU hallucinations.

If a loved one is in the ICU: Write down what happens every day. The diary will help the patient make sense of his/her memories—real or imaginary—later.

O. Joseph Bienvenu, MD, PhD, associate professor of psychiatry and behavioral sciences at The Johns Hopkins University School of Medicine and director at The Johns Hopkins Anxiety Disorders Clinic, both in Baltimore. He is first author of a study of 520 ICU patients, published in *Psychological Medicine*.

Helpful for Family

Family members who saw resuscitation efforts done on a loved one were much less likely to develop symptoms of post-traumatic stress, anxiety or depression after a relative's death than ones who did not observe revival attempts.

Possible reason: Seeing doctors' efforts reassures the family members that everything possible was done...allows closure for people who want to be with relatives until the very last moment...and may make the otherwise frightening process less mysterious.

Study of 570 people whose family members were treated by emergency medical teams at home by researchers at several emergency centers in France and Texas Tech University Health Sciences Center, El Paso, published in *The New England Journal of Medicine*.

Health-Care Workers Can Refuse to Do CPR

In a recent incident, an employee of an independent-living facility did not perform CPR on an 87-year-old woman who had a heart attack. The facility's rules prevented the employee from doing CPR. Nursing homes and health-care facilities including assisted-living centers have different rules about what kind of medical care they are licensed to provide.

Self-defense: Before deciding on a facility, inquire about its policies.

Charles B. Inlander, a consumer advocate and health-care consultant based in Fogelsville, Pennsylvania. He was founding president of the nonprofit People's Medical Society, a consumer advocacy organization credited with key improvements in the quality of US health care, and is author or coauthor of more than 20 consumer-health books.

3

Quick Fixes for Common Conditions

Do You Really Need an Antibiotic? Foods and Supplements Sometimes Work Just as Well!

Most likely you've been taught that if you have any type of bacterial infection, you need to take an antibiotic. But overuse of antibiotics is increasingly rendering them ineffective and contributing to the rise of deadly drug-resistant superbugs. Not only are new strains of MRSA now emerging, but other types of bacteria, including *Clostridium difficile* and *Salmonella*, are becoming increasingly difficult to treat.

What's more: Antibiotics inhibit the growth of nearly *all* bacteria in the body that they come into contact with (good and bad), often causing annoying side effects such as diarrhea and yeast and intestinal infections.

Time to change your thinking: For many minor infections, natural antibiotics found in foods, supplements and herbs can eliminate harmful microbes just as well as prescription antibiotics—without side effects. Plus, if you do need a prescription antibiotic, natural products can often help these medications work more effectively.

If you think you have an infection: See your doctor.* He/she can tell you whether antibiotics are necessary or if it is safe to try natural products—some may interact with medications you are taking. (A high fever—with or without chills—is one sign you may need an antibiotic.) If you are cleared to try a natural regimen, check back with your doctor if the infection does not improve within 48 hours.

*To find a naturopathic or homeopathic doctor near you, go to *Naturopathic.org* or *HomeopathyUSA.org*.

Joseph Kellerstein, DC, ND, a chiropractor and naturopathic and homeopathic physician who lectures at the Canadian College of Homeopathic Medicine and internationally. He has private practices in Toronto and Oshawa, Ontario, Canada. *DrJoeND.com*

51

PROBIOTICS FOR RESPIRATORY INFECTIONS

You probably already know to take probiotics or eat yogurt to reduce the chance of side effects when you are on antibiotics. What you might not know is that probiotics also can help *prevent* and *treat* infections. And yogurt isn't the only food source. Little-known probiotic-rich alternatives include fermented vegetables (such as sauerkraut and kimchi)…fermented soy foods (such as miso and tempeh)…and kefir, a fermented milk product. When you eat these foods, their beneficial bacteria displace some of the disease-causing bacteria and secrete substances that inhibit or kill harmful germs.

A study found that individuals who took daily supplements of *Lactobacillus reuteri* (a common probiotic) were less than half as likely to take sick days for upper-respiratory or gastrointestinal illnesses than those who took placebos.

Natural approach: Regularly consuming probiotic foods helps prevent and treat infections. If you get recurrent infections and/or frequently use antibiotics, a probiotic supplement may be advised as well. Check with your doctor for the best probiotic and dosage for you.

COLLOIDAL SILVER FOR EAR INFECTIONS, MORE

The antibiotic properties of colloidal silver were first described nearly 2,000 years ago. It comes as a suspension—microscopic bits of silver are suspended in water or a gel-like substance—and can be used for ear, nose, throat and eye infections. Another silver product, silver sulfadiazine cream, is used to prevent and treat skin and wound infections.

Natural approach: Colloidal silver can be used orally or topically, depending on the condition being treated. Use a product that contains "true silver particles" rather than "ionic silver," which may be less effective at killing pathogens.

Caution: Colloidal silver can cause *argyria*, a grayish or bluish skin discoloration that is permanent if you take massive doses (38 grams [g] per day). A standard colloidal silver product has less than 1 milligram (mg) of silver per dose.

OIL OF OREGANO FOR THROAT AND BLADDER INFECTIONS

Oregano contains *carvacrol*, a powerful antimicrobial chemical compound. In a lab study, even low doses of oregano oil inhibited the growth of staph (*Staphylococcus aureus*) as effectively as streptomycin and other antibiotics. I recommend this oil for throat and bladder infections.

Natural approach: Add one or two drops of concentrated oregano oil to one teaspoon of olive or coconut oil to avoid burning your mouth. Take once a day during an infection.

GARLIC FOR H. PYLORI

Garlic has *allicin*, a broad-spectrum antimicrobial agent that fights a variety of bacteria, viruses and fungi. It's been found to be effective against *Helicobacter pylori*, a bacterium linked to stomach ulcers and cancer. Even some antibiotic-resistant strains of H. pylori responded to garlic in studies. And in both World Wars, garlic was used to prevent wound infections.

Natural approach: For prevention and treatment of the infections listed above, take deodorized garlic capsules (such as Vitacost Deodorized Garlic Ultra). They're more convenient—and less smelly—than eating lots of fresh garlic. Follow label directions. For a topical solution for wounds, mix one part garlic juice (found in health-food stores) with three parts water. Apply to gauze and place on skin. Never put garlic juice or crushed garlic directly on the skin—it can cause irritation.

HOMEOPATHY FOR SKIN INFECTIONS

Silica, a homeopathic remedy, helps treat those painful skin infections—such as boils, inflamed acne and skin wounds—that seem to take forever to heal.

Natural approach: Take one pellet (6C concentration) every day for seven to 14 days until the area is about 80% healed. After that, watch the area for a few days to make sure it finishes healing.

Caution: If, at any point, the wound gets very red and inflamed…if redness spreads quickly…or if you have a high fever and/or chills, see your physician *immediately*. Also, see your doctor if the wound does not finish healing after using the silica. These are signs that you may need an antibiotic.

The Best Fruits to Fight Winter Colds

Two compounds, *resveratrol* (in red grapes) and *pterostilbene* (in blueberries), were recently found to help activate a gene that strengthens the immune system. Researchers are not yet sure exactly how much of these foods you need to get this benefit. Until more research is completed, simply make fresh or frozen red grapes and blueberries a regular part of your diet to give your immune system a boost.

Adrian Gombart, PhD, associate professor of biochemistry and biophysics, Oregon State University in Corvallis.

The Power of Meditation

Meditation may cut risk for the common cold and reduce symptoms for those who do get sick. People who practiced *mindfulness-based stress reduction* (MBSR) had 33% fewer colds than people who did not practice MBSR. Also, those who did get colds reported that their colds were less severe and lasted less time.

Study of 149 adults, ages 50 and older, by researchers at University of Wisconsin School of Medicine and Public Health, Madison, published in *Annals of Family Medicine*.

Drink This to Stop a Cold...

Peel and grate about one-half ounce of fresh gingerroot or cut four slices each the size of a quarter. Bring the ginger to a boil in two cups of water, turn down the heat and simmer for 20 minutes. Strain and drink a cup every few hours.

The pungent components in ginger called *gingerols* help fight viruses. If you can handle a little spice, add one-eighth teaspoon of cayenne pepper to one cup of your brewed ginger tea to help clear your sinuses.

Joan Wilen and Lydia Wilen, health investigators based in New York City, who have spent decades collecting "cures from the cupboard." They are authors of *Bottom Line's Treasury of Home Remedies & Natural Cures* (Bottom Line Books) and the free e-letter *Household Magic Daily Tips*. HouseholdMagicDailyTips.com

---

Zinc Shortens the Length of Colds

Using oral zinc lozenges or syrup can end a cold a day and a half sooner than not using zinc. Larger doses bring greater benefits, primarily for adults.

But: Zinc users often report nausea, a bad taste in the mouth and/or loss of smell.

Meta-analysis of 17 trials, including a total of 2,121 participants, by researchers at The Hospital for Sick Children, Toronto, Canada, and McMaster University, Hamilton, Canada, published in *Canadian Medical Association Journal*.

DID YOU KNOW THAT...

There Is a New Warning on Flu Germs?

Flu patients can emit germs as far as *six feet*. This is a much greater distance than previously thought.

Also: People suffering from the worst flu symptoms give off the greatest levels of flu particles into the air.

Study of 94 flu patients by researchers at Wake Forest School of Medicine, Winston-Salem, North Carolina, published in *The Journal of Infectious Diseases*.

Antianxiety Drugs Linked to Pneumonia Risk

In a recent finding, people who took *benzodiazepines,* such as Valium and Xanax—sedatives commonly prescribed for anxiety and insomnia—were 54% more likely to get pneumonia…22% more likely to die within 30 days of being diagnosed with pneumonia…and 32% more likely to die within three years of diagnosis than people who did not take the medications.

Study of almost 5,000 people by researchers at Institute of Cognitive Neuroscience, University College London, published in *Thorax.*

Faster Recovery from the Stomach Flu

Jamison Starbuck, ND, a naturopathic physician in family practice and a guest lecturer at the University of Montana, both in Missoula. She is past president of the American Association of Naturopathic Physicians and a contributing editor to *The Alternative Advisor: The Complete Guide to Natural Therapies and Alternative Treatments* (Time Life).

"We've ALL got the stomach flu," my weary patient announced. Exhausted from caretaking and still not feeling well himself, he was at his wit's end. I was happy to assure him that the illness, which is highly contagious, usually passes within a few days, but with the natural remedies below, he could likely speed up their recoveries by at least a day.

Though commonly known as the "stomach flu," this short-lived gastrointestinal (GI) bug is technically gastroenteritis, a medical term meaning inflammation of the stomach and intestines. It can be caused by bacteria, parasites or a virus—which are spread by human contact as well as contaminated food or water. One of its most common causes, *norovirus,* is often spread when you use a doorknob, for example, that has been touched by someone with the virus on his/her hands, and you then put your fingers (or food you touch) in your mouth. The symptoms of gastroenteritis are well known—nausea, diarrhea, loss of appetite, sometimes vomiting and a mild (99°F) fever. *How to reduce the severity and duration of your misery…**

• **Stick to clear fluids.** At the first sign of gastroenteritis (typically diarrhea), have only chicken, beef or vegetable broth, herbal tea, diluted fruit juice, ginger ale, club soda and water. Consume these liquids either cold, hot or at room temperature—whatever feels most soothing. Avoiding solid foods will decrease both diarrhea and nausea and give your GI tract time to recuperate. When nausea and diarrhea are gone, ease back into eating solid foods with rice, steamed veggies and/or three ounces of chicken or fish.

• **Take a good probiotic.** I recommend a powdered formula containing 3 billion colony forming units (CFUs) of *Lactobacillus acidophilus* and *Bifidobacterium*, taken three times a day. If your probiotic comes in a capsule, open it and dissolve the powder it contains directly in your mouth or in only two ounces of water to avoid the vomiting that can accompany gastroenteritis.

• **Consider chamomile tea.** Lots of herbal teas—such as cinnamon, ginger, chamomile, lemon balm, peppermint and spearmint—soothe nausea and diarrhea. However, I prefer chamomile because it also kills microorganisms, decreases inflammation and reduces intestinal gas. For gastroenteritis, I recommend drinking 32 to 48 ounces of chamomile tea daily. People who are allergic to plants in the daisy family—daisy, ragweed, marigold, chrysanthemum—should avoid chamomile.

• **Use natural antiseptics.** Two natural antiseptics can quicken your body's process of shedding an unwanted stomach bug. Oregon graperoot is an antimicrobial, and activated charcoal binds to microorganisms so they can be eliminated via the stool. Use these medicines separately, or the charcoal will also sweep the Oregon graperoot out of your body.

*If you are frail, elderly or have a compromised immune system…or if vomiting or diarrhea lasts more than 48 hours, see your physician.

My advice: Take one-eighth teaspoon of Oregon graperoot tincture in four ounces water, followed two hours later by two charcoal capsules, opened and mixed with four ounces of water. Do this until you get four doses of each medicine in 24 hours. Consult a pediatrician before giving Oregon graperoot and/or activated charcoal to children.

Common Chemicals That Increase Food Allergies

Chemicals called *dichlorophenols*, used to chlorinate public water and found in insect- and weed-control products, can reduce food tolerance and cause food allergies in some people. Avoiding tap water is likely not enough. Limit your exposure to dichlorophenols by buying organic produce and avoiding areas where pesticides have been applied.

Elina Jerschow, MD, MSc, allergist, American College of Allergy, Asthma and Immunology, and leader of a study of 2,211 participants in the US National Health and Nutrition Examination Survey, published in *Annals of Allergy, Asthma and Immunology.*

No More Allergy Shots?

In a recent finding, putting allergens under the tongue in a water solution, known as *sublingual immunotherapy*, improved asthma symptoms by more than 40%, including runny nose and eye inflammation. The FDA has not yet approved sublingual immunotherapy, but it is widely used in Europe and some US doctors are prescribing it.

Meta-analysis of 5,131 patients, ages four to 74, by researchers at Johns Hopkins University, Baltimore, and published in *The Journal of the American Medical Association.*

A Tick Bite Can Trigger a Meat Allergy

People bitten by the *lone star tick*, so named because of the white spot on the female's back, may develop an allergy to meat. While the tick bite may have occurred weeks or even months earlier, symptoms start only four to six hours after eating beef, pork or lamb. Reactions can range from vomiting and abdominal cramps to life-threatening anaphylaxis. Cases have spread as far north as Maine and as far west as Texas and Oklahoma.

NPR.org and *CDC.gov.*

Foods to Avoid If You Have Severe Headaches

Foods containing the amino acid *tyramine* or certain other chemicals can bring on headaches or make them worse. If you have serious headaches, try eliminating from your diet aged, dried and fermented meats, such as pepperoni and salami…aged cheeses, such as blue, Brie, cheddar and provolone…fermented soy products, such as miso, soy sauce and teriyaki sauce…beans…sauerkraut…pickles… olives…alcoholic beverages such as Chianti, sherry, Burgundy, vermouth, ale and beer, which all contain tyramine…and foods containing *monosodium glutamate*, *nitrites* and *sulfites*.

Recommendations from the National Headache Foundation, Chicago.

Coffee for Migraine Relief

Samantha Brody, ND, LAc, a naturopathic doctor, licensed acupuncturist and owner of Evergreen Natural Health Center in Portland, Oregon. She has lectured extensively to lay and professional audiences across the country. *DrSamantha.com*

What if you could stop a migraine in its tracks? Many people can with a simple home remedy that's readily available.

Here's why: The pain of a migraine headache is usually caused by dilated or widened blood vessels, pressing against nerves.

Home remedy: Drinking coffee can constrict those blood vessels, relieving pain.

If you are skeptical, consider this research. A 2012 review of 19 studies involving more than 7,000 people showed that a dose of 100 milligrams (mg) or more of caffeine (the typical amount in a cup of coffee) boosted pain relief in headache sufferers taking painkillers. I've found that this approach also can help relieve pain without the use of medication.

What to do: At the first sign of a headache, drink an eight-ounce cup of coffee (or about two cups of black tea). If the remedy is going to help, you should experience pain relief in about 20 minutes.

Coffee is most likely to work if you don't ordinarily drink it or consume other caffeine-containing beverages, such as tea or energy drinks.

For even greater relief: Try adding an ice pack to your neck or head for a few minutes to further constrict dilated vessels.

Red flags: If you have insomnia, high blood pressure, anxiety or chronic fatigue—all of which coffee can worsen—this remedy probably isn't for you. Also, for some people, caffeine can trigger a migraine.

The Migraine Brain

The brains of migraine suffers look different from those of people without migraines. People with migraines have a smaller and thinner cortex (outer layer of the brain) in areas that process pain, making these people more vulnerable to migraines.

Massimo Filippi, MD, professor, neurology, University Vita-Salute's San Raffaele Scientific Institute, Milan, Italy, and senior researcher of a study published online in *Radiology*.

Nasal Allergies Linked to Migraine Frequency

People with migraine headaches who also have allergies such as hay fever were 33% more likely to suffer from frequent migraines than people who had no allergies in a recent study.

Theory: Treating allergy symptoms may relieve migraine symptoms. Talk to your doctor.

Vincent Martin, MD, professor of medicine and co-director of the Headache and Facial Pain Program at University of Cincinnati, is the lead author of a study based on questionnaires from 6,000 people with migraines, published in *Cephalalgia*.

Gurgles, Burps and Pops: How to Silence Embarrassing Body Noises

Richard O'Brien, MD, associate professor of emergency medicine at The Commonwealth Medical College, Scranton, Pennsylvania. He is an emergency physician and a spokesperson for the American College of Emergency Physicians (*ACEP.org*).

Have you ever wondered why joints pop or your nose whistles? Or whether that embarrassing sound was loud enough that others could hear it? (The body's involuntary noises usually sound much louder to the perpetrator than to bystanders.) You also might wonder if you need to worry about any of this sonic activity.

Common body noises—and how to quiet them…

FLATULENCE

Passing gas is great fun if you happen to be a 10-year-old boy. It's not so amusing for the rest of us, particularly when it "slips" at the wrong time—a likely occurrence because the average adult passes gas up to 20 times a day.

What it means: The tight anal muscle that allows us to control what comes out (and when it comes out) also accounts for the sound. The outward rush of air causes the tissues to vibrate. The more air that comes out and the greater the pressure, the louder it's likely to be.

Gas is partly caused by emissions from intestinal bacteria triggered by certain foods such as beans, broccoli, asparagus and onions. It also may be caused by foods that your body cannot tolerate, such as dairy products or gluten. But it's mainly due to swallowed air. In one study, researchers "tagged" room air with radioactive particles, then looked for the presence of these particles in the intestinal gas of test subjects. They found that most of the expelled gas consisted of the tagged particles.

Helpful: You can control flatulence by reducing the amount of air that you swallow—by eating more slowly, taking smaller bites and not chewing gum. Also, avoid carbonated beverages. The carbon dioxide gas that gives beer and sodas their "fizz" has to go somewhere—and out it comes.

Over-the-counter products such as Beano can help prevent gas. Take it along with your first bites of gassy foods. Or have a cup of fennel seed tea (available at health-food stores) after a meal for a simple, effective remedy.

BURPING

The same air that produces intestinal gas can travel in the other direction and produce a loud belch. It travels upward from the stomach and through the esophagus. The sound that you hear is caused by movements of the upper esophageal sphincter.

What it means: If you don't burp often and it doesn't hurt when you burp, don't give it a second thought. If it bothers you, you can try to swallow less air (see above). You also should curtail your consumption of carbonated beverages.

Peppermint oil (10 to 15 drops in one-quarter cup cold water) is a quick remedy for burping.

Caution: If you burp a lot or the burps cause a burning sensation or a foul taste, you could have *gastroesophageal reflux disease* (GERD), a potentially dangerous condition in which stomach acids surge upward into the esophagus.

People with GERD tend to have more symptoms in the morning because the body's secretion of stomach acid is highest at night. They also might have voice hoarseness because the vocal cords are at the same level as the stomach during sleep.

The over-the-counter medicines for GERD, such as *omeprazole* (Prilosec), *esomeprazole* (Nexium) and TUMS, will help relieve symptoms, but they shouldn't be used for long periods without checking with your doctor.

STOMACH RUMBLING

The scientific term for stomach growls, gurgles and rumbles is *borborygmus*. It tends to get louder when you're hungry, and it has a disconcerting tendency to occur during silences in conversations.

What it means: The stomach isn't merely a storage tank. The muscular walls are frequently expanding and contracting. At the same time, the contents of the stomach—primarily food and fluids, along with air—do a lot of sloshing. They generate sound waves that are clearly audible.

A stomach growl doesn't always mean that you're hungry. It does mean that there's empty space in the stomach. Just as a half-full bottle makes more noise than a full one when it's shaken, the stomach is noisier when it doesn't contain enough food to dampen the sounds.

One way to stop your stomach from gurgling is to have a small banana (which helps absorb stomach acids) and a glass of water. Or try a granola bar, a handful of crackers, some trail mix or a cup of herbal tea.

JOINT POPS

It's normal for joints to snap, crackle and pop, particularly in older adults. The percussive sounds don't mean that you're a candidate for surgery. They usually are just a result of pressure, friction and suction.

What it means: The joints that do the most popping—the knees, shoulders, hips and jaw—are ball-and-socket joints. A ball-shape surface at the end of one bone fits snuggly into a hollow depression on the one next to it.

The bone ends are coated with a sheen of a thick, clear liquid called synovial fluid. This lubricating fluid on one end clings to the fluid on the next—and makes a distinct snapping sound when you move the joint and the fluids pull apart. "Cracking" the knuckles is a similar phenomenon.

There's also more "slop" in the joints as you get older. The ends don't fit together as tightly as they used to. The misalignment can produce snapping or popping sounds. As long as the pops aren't accompanied by pain, they're unlikely to be a problem.

Important: If you have noisy joints and other symptoms such as pain and swelling, see your doctor. You could have torn tissues (for example, in the knee), tendon damage or arthritis, all of which can cause popping.

NOSE WHISTLES

When I was a kid, I had bad allergies that caused me to whistle through my nose all the time.

What it means: You have a too-narrow nasal opening. This usually is due to congestion from allergies and colds.

Simply blowing your nose may eliminate the whistle. If this doesn't help, try using an over-the-counter saline nasal spray (such as Ocean) twice a day as directed on the label. This nasal moisturizer will provide natural, nonmedicating dryness relief, shrinking nasal membranes and thus opening up the "whistling" passage. Nasal decongestant sprays that contain *oxymetazoline* (such as Afrin) work, but use them only for a day or two—they can cause increased, "rebound" congestion if you use them regularly for more than three days.

Drink Milk to Prevent Cavities

Of course you want to avoid a sugary breakfast, but if you do have one, drink milk afterward. It reduces plaque and may prevent damage to tooth enamel that leads to cavities.

But: Combining milk with a sugary product, such as a sweetened breakfast cereal, does not have the same effect—milk has to be drunk last to reap the plaque-fighting benefit.

Study by researchers at University of Illinois at Chicago College of Dentistry, published in *The Journal of the American Dental Association.*

EASY-TO-DO...

Heartburn Cure in Your Pantry

If you have a bout of heartburn and you've run out of antacids or prefer a safe, natural route to feeling better, here's what to do. Take a teaspoon or two of uncooked oat flakes, and chew thoroughly before swallowing. Oatmeal absorbs the stomach acid that can cause the burning pain.

Joan Wilen and Lydia Wilen, health investigators based in New York City, who have spent decades collecting "cures from the cupboard." They are authors of *Bottom Line's Treasury of Home Remedies & Natural Cures* (Bottom Line Books) and the free e-letter *Household Magic Daily Tips.* HouseholdMagicDailyTips.com

---

Healthy Drinks That Can Harm Your Teeth

The acids in fruits and vegetables used in smoothies may weaken tooth enamel.

Best: Use a straw when drinking a smoothie...rinse your mouth with water afterward... wait an hour before brushing your teeth to give tooth enamel time to recover.

Graham Chadwick, PhD, FDS, senior clinical lecturer and honorary consultant in restorative dentistry at University of Dundee, Nethergate, Scotland, quoted in *Good Housekeeping.*

Do Healthy Wisdom Teeth Need to Be Pulled?

Healthy teeth should not be pulled out simply to avoid possible difficulties in the future. Wisdom tooth extraction is surgery and—like any surgery—can cause infection, nerve damage or other problems.

Better: Have your wisdom teeth monitored by a dentist—not by an oral surgeon (who may be inclined to do surgery)—and extracted only if there is persistent pain or discomfort or a clear indication of problems.

Examples: Recurrent inflammation...abscess (pocket of pus caused by infection)...impacted teeth (not enough room to emerge) that have cysts around them...teeth that are damaging neighboring teeth.

Jay W. Friedman, DDS, MPH, dental consultant based in Los Angeles and author of *The Intelligent Consumer's Complete Guide to Dental Health* (AuthorHouse).

How to Get Yourself to Floss Daily

Victor Zeines, DDS, a holistic dentist with practices in New York City and Woodstock, New York. He is a founder of The Institute for Holistic Dentistry and author of several books, including *Healthy Mouth, Healthy Body: The Natural Dental Program for Total Wellness* (Xlibris). *NatDent.com*

Just can't get in the habit of flossing every day? You know it's good for your gums and teeth and can help prevent bad breath, but consider this: Scientists recently discovered bacteria linked to gum disease in the brains of Alzheimer's patients...and research shows that people with gum disease are more likely to get heart disease and diabetes. *If this doesn't have you reaching for the dental floss right now, here are some other tricks to get you on track...*

• **Get gross.** The following advice may seem extreme, but it works—tape a photo showing the ravages of periodontal disease (search for one online) in a prominent place in your bathroom. After your first month of daily flossing, replace it with an image of a healthy white smile as positive reinforcement.

• **Try different flosses**—one variety is not more effective than another. The point is to find a floss that you're comfortable with so that you'll be more likely to use it regularly. In general, there are two types—multifilament (nylon) and single filament (plastic/rubber). Multifilament floss has been around for a long time and is cheaper. It comes unwaxed or waxed. Single filament uses newer technology—it doesn't rip, tear or fray and glides very easily between the teeth even though it isn't waxed. These products are available in a wide variety of flavors, including mint, cinnamon, cranberry and tea tree oil. Try a bunch!

• **Floss while you are doing something else** —while in the shower, watching TV or reading the newspaper.

• **Floss the correct way.** I recommend flossing after eating and when you brush. It really doesn't matter if you floss before or after brushing, as long as you do a thorough job.

To floss correctly: Bring the string down gently along the side of one tooth, then back up. Do the same on the adjacent tooth, and work your way around the entire mouth. If you have restorative work, like crowns, pull the floss out sideways instead.

Quick Tricks to Eliminate Garlic Breath

When you eat garlic, the sulfuric compounds get into your mouth and also seep into your lungs, causing garlic breath. To eliminate the odor, eat the parsley, basil, thyme, cilantro, mint or dill that decorates your plate. Or sip milk before or during a meal with garlic—the water in the milk acts like a mouth rinse, and the fat neutralizes sulfur. You can also drink green tea or add mushrooms to your meal—they both are rich in polyphenols that counteract garlic's effect on breath. Natural enzymes in apples, berries, pineapple and kiwi break down sulfuric compounds so have fruit for dessert.

Joan Wilen and Lydia Wilen, health investigators based in New York City, who have spent decades collecting "cures from the cupboard." They are authors of *Bottom Line's Treasury of Home Remedies & Natural Cures* (Bottom Line Books) and the free e-letter *Household Magic Daily Tips. HouseholdMagicDailyTips.com*

Can't Stop Rubbing Your Eyes?

Frequent rubbing of your eyes could damage the cornea and even lead to *astigmatism,* a condition in which a part of the eye is irregularly shaped, resulting in blurred or distorted vision. Rubbing your eyes also can eventually lead to wrinkles and an aged look around your eyes.

If your eyes are dry or itchy, rubbing may bring temporary relief but will also increase redness and swelling and cause you to rub the irritated area even more. An ophthalmologist can evaluate and treat symptoms so that you can stop rubbing. Eyedrops, such as *azelastine hydrochloride* (Optivar), often are prescribed.

Robert Latkany, MD, director, Dry Eye Clinic, New York Eye and Ear Infirmary, New York City. *DryEye Doctor.com*

Eyes Can Get Sunburned, Too

Photokeratitis, which is also known as snow blindness, happens when intense ultraviolet light—often reflected off the water, sand or snow—burns the cornea, the transparent tissue covering the front of the eye. This recently happened to CNN's Anderson Cooper. Most people recover in two or three days. But photokeratitis can be so painful that sufferers cannot open their eyes and feel as if they have gone blind.

Self-defense: Wear sunglasses that block at least 99% of both UVA and UVB light.

Anne Sumers, MD, ophthalmologist, Ridgeway, New Jersey, and spokesperson for the American Academy of Ophthalmology, quoted in *USA Today.*

How Painkillers Harm Your Hearing

In a recent finding, women who regularly took *ibuprofen* (such as Advil or Motrin) or *acetaminophen* (Tylenol) at least twice a week had up to a 24% higher risk for hearing loss than women who used the painkillers infrequently. Other studies have found similar effects in men. These pain relievers may damage the cochlea in the inner ear by reducing blood flow or depleting antioxidants.

Self-defense: Limit painkillers to occasional short-term use—but talk to your doctor before making any changes in your medications.

Study of more than 62,000 women by researchers at Harvard Medical School, Boston, published in *American Journal of Epidemiology.*

How to Talk to Someone with Hearing Loss

If you're speaking with someone who has hearing loss, don't shout. Instead, speak in a normal voice. Also, do not lean into the person's ear—many people with hearing loss read lips, so they need to see what you are saying. Try to eliminate any background noise that can interfere with hearing, such as a TV program or an air conditioner. And in a group meeting, try to have one general conversation rather than several overlapping ones. If someone does not hear what you say after you try two or three times, rephrase your comment and try again. Finally, do not say, "Never mind. It doesn't matter." It matters to the person who can't hear.

Katherine Bouton, author of *Shouting Won't Help: Why I—and 50 Million Other Americans—Can't Hear You* (Picador).

Antibiotics May Relieve Chronic Low-Back Pain

Nearly half the people whose back pain is caused by a herniated disk later develop a bacterial infection. For those people, a 100-day course of the antibiotic *amoxicillin* reduced pain by up to 80% in a recent study. If you have had severe low-back pain for at least three months…have a damaged vertebra and swelling…and other treatment options have failed, ask your doctor whether an extended course of antibiotics is worth trying.

Study of 61 people with back pain by researchers at University of Southern Denmark, Odense, published in *European Spine Journal.*

Natural Help for Back Pain

Back pain can be helped by topical herbal remedies with fewer side effects. The remedies—*capsaicin* (cayenne) and a *wintergreen/peppermint oil combination*—are available over the counter. Apply the product to the painful area three times a day, following directions on the package insert. The remedies have shown promising results, but direct testing comparing the herbal remedies to standard painkillers is needed.

Charles H. Hennekens, MD, DrPH, the first Sir Richard Doll Professor and senior academic adviser to the dean in the Charles E. Schmidt College of Medicine at Florida Atlantic University, Boca Raton.

How to Avoid "Text Neck"

Spending too much time leaning your head forward and down while looking at your phone or other mobile device puts excessive strain on the spine, causing "text neck." Avoid the pain and discomfort by holding your cell phone higher…and taking frequent breaks.

Chris Cornett, MD, orthopaedic surgeon and spine specialist, department of surgery and rehabilitation, University of Nebraska Medical Center, Omaha.

You May Not Need Surgery for a Torn Meniscus!

A tear in this C-shaped piece of knee cartilage commonly occurs in people with osteoarthritis and often is treated with surgery.

Recent finding: Among patients age 45 and older who had a torn meniscus, along with knee arthritis and pain, those assigned to physical therapy alone had improvements in pain and physical function after six months that were similar to those who received arthroscopic surgery and physical therapy.

Jeffrey N. Katz, MD, codirector, Brigham Spine Center, Brigham and Women's Hospital, and professor, Harvard Medical School, both in Boston.

How to Care for a Sprained Ankle

Don't try to "walk off" a sprained ankle.

Better: Get off the injured foot, prop it up, wrap it in a compression bandage and apply ice over the bandage 20 minutes per hour for the first 24 hours. Do not take a nonsteroidal anti-inflammatory drug such as *ibuprofen* within the first 48 hours of the injury—it could slow the healing process. If you need something for pain, consider *acetaminophen.* Have a doctor determine the extent of the injury and the treatment needed.

Recommendations from National Athletic Trainers Association, reported in *The New York Times.*

Better Gout Control

Painful gout attacks are commonly thought to occur mainly in the big toe joint.

Discovery: In a study of 46 adults, researchers found that those whose gout first appeared in a knee, elbow or other joint had at least twice the risk for further flare-ups than those whose gout originated in the big toe. The reason for this association is not yet known.

If you have gout: Talk to your doctor about taking medication that reduces uric acid, such as *allopurinol*, to help decrease your risk for flare-ups.

Eric Matteson, MD, rheumatology chair, Mayo Clinic, Rochester, Minnesota.

How to Fall Down Without Getting Hurt: Tricks from an Oscar-Winning Stuntman

Hal Needham, who appeared as a stuntman in more than 4,000 television episodes and more than 300 feature films. He also directed movies including *The Cannonball Run*. In 2012, he became only the second stunt performer to receive an honorary Oscar for his work. He is author of *Stuntman! My Car-Crashing, Plane-Jumping, Bone-Breaking, Death-Defying Hollywood Life* (Little, Brown).

When we fall, our natural instinct is to reach out for the ground with our hands. Unfortunately, that only increases our odds of injury—our hands, wrists and arms are full of small bones that are easily broken. *Instead, when you realize you are falling…*

1. Buckle both your knees. This can in essence lower the height that your upper body falls by as much as one foot or two, significantly reducing the impact when you hit the ground. In a forward fall, it might result in bruised knees,

but that's better than a broken bone in the upper body.

Helpful: In a backward fall, tuck your head into your chest as you buckle your knees—try to turn yourself into a ball.

2. Throw one arm across your chest whether you're falling forward or backward. Do this with enough force that it turns your body to one side. It doesn't matter which arm you use.

3. Rotate the rest of your body in the direction that you threw your arm, increasing your spin. If you can rotate enough, you will come down mainly on your backside, a well-padded part of the body unlikely to experience a serious injury.

Trouble is, while stuntmen know exactly when and where they're going to fall, real-world falls usually take people by surprise. It can be difficult to overcome instinct and put this falling strategy into action in the split second before hitting the ground.

Practice can help. If you have access to a thick gym mat and you don't have health issues that make it risky, try out this falling technique until it feels natural.

Asthma Drug Helps Relieve Chronic Hives

Antihistamines may not work for people who have *idiopathic hives*—hives with no known cause.

Recent study: Three injections of the asthma drug *omalizumab* (Xolair) reduced the amount of itching in patients resistant to antihistamines by up to 71%. The most common side effects were headache and sore throat.

Marcus Maurer, MD, research director and professor of dermatology and allergy at Charité-Universitätsmedizin, Berlin, Germany, and lead author of a study of 323 patients, published in *The New England Journal of Medicine*.

Blow Away the Itch from Poison Ivy and Oak

If you have poison ivy or oak, use a blow-dryer to blow warm air on the itchy area for about five minutes. The heat and pressure stimulate the mast cells of the immune system to release all their itch-causing histamines—and you get an hour's relief from the itching.

Amy Rothenberg, ND, naturopathic physician and co-director of New England School of Homeopathy, Amherst, Massachusetts, quoted in *Bottom Line's Speed Healing* (Bottom Line Books).

Don't Rely on Clothing for Sun Protection

Cotton shirts don't offer sufficient protection from the sun. They have an *ultraviolet protection factor* (UPF)—the equivalent of SPF—of no more than eight. That drops to two if the shirt gets wet. Do not rely on clothing for sun protection unless it is made for that purpose. Some long-sleeved shirts made of a spandex-and-nylon mix have a UPF rating of 50+. Also, use sunscreen, and reapply often.

Health. Health.com

Give Yourself a Natural Face-Lift: Take Years Off Your Looks

Eudene Harry, MD, medical director of Oasis for Optimal Health in Orlando, Florida. She is board-certified in both emergency and holistic medicine and serves as medical director for the Women's Wellness Society, a national group that focuses on women's health. She is author of *Live Younger in 8 Simple Steps: A Practical Guide to Slowing Down the Aging Process from the Inside Out* (Harry). *DrHarryMD.com*

It's a fact of life that our skin becomes more wrinkled as we age. But you may be surprised to learn that our skin starts changing as early as *age 30* for both women and men.

What happens: The cells that make up the skin divide more slowly with age, so the top layer of skin gets about 10% thinner every decade. The result? You guessed it—more wrinkles as well as more bruises...an uneven skin tone...and sagging skin. Of course, you can "refresh" your appearance with Botox and skin fillers, but even "inexpensive" cosmetic procedures cost hundreds of dollars.

A better option: Natural skin care. Used properly, natural approaches can take years off your appearance.

STEP 1: TWEAK YOUR DIET

While you might think that skin-care products are the logical choice to smooth wrinkled skin, it's wise to first work from the "inside out" to give your skin the nutrients it needs to look its best.

Increasing laboratory evidence and positive reports from patients suggest that the following foods promote younger-looking skin...

• **High-sulfur foods.** Sulfur is known to be one of the "building blocks" of *collagen*, a protein that strengthens skin and gives it elasticity. Fortunately, sulfur is found in a number of foods.

My advice: At least once a day, eat sulfur-rich foods.

Good choices: Eggs, chives, legumes (such as black, white or kidney beans) and fish that is high in omega-3 fatty acids (such as salmon and sardines).

• **Grape juice or red wine.** These contain *flavonoids* known as *proanthocyanidins* and proteins called *tenascins*—both help to make the skin smoother and more elastic.

My advice: Enjoy a daily glass of grape juice—or red wine if your doctor says daily alcohol consumption is appropriate for you. Both are high in proanthocyanidins.

In addition, a grape seed extract supplement (typical dose 200 milligrams [mg] once a day) is beneficial, but check first with your doctor if you take medication, especially a blood thinner—the supplement may interact with certain drugs.

•**Soy foods.** Tofu, soy milk and other foods derived from soy can make skin appear significantly younger. This is mainly due to *genistein,* an antioxidant in soy that slows skin aging and increases collagen. Genistein and other compounds are linked to increased skin elasticity and plumpness. These compounds give the skin a "glow" that makes it appear younger.

My advice: Have one or more daily servings of soy foods.

Good choices: Edamame (steamed soy beans) and miso (a fermented paste used in cooking). Check first with your doctor if you have breast cancer or kidney disease or take any medication. Soy may be harmful for some breast cancer and kidney disease patients...it may also interact with certain drugs, including blood thinners and some antidepressants.

Also: To help keep skin hydrated, drink eight eight-ounce glasses of water each day.

STEP 2: USE THE RIGHT SKIN-CARE PRODUCTS

Skin-care products can help smooth wrinkles and provide other benefits, but there are so many on the market that most people are confused about which to use. *Best choices for younger-looking skin...*

•**Topical vitamin C.** About 80% of the dermis (the second layer of skin) consists of that all important protein collagen. Because collagen production declines with age, it's a good idea to promote collagen production any way you can.

That's where vitamin C enters the picture. The body uses vitamin C to produce collagen, but whatever is consumed orally doesn't reach adequate concentrations in the skin to boost collagen. That's why you need to apply it *topically.*

My advice: Use skin-care products (such as lotions and sunscreens) that have *ascorbic acid* (vitamin C)—the best form of the vitamin for absorption as well as collagen production and sun protection. Studies show that topical vitamin C can reduce the appearance of fine lines and wrinkles in as little as three months.

To save money: Buy powdered vitamin C at a health-food store, and mix in a small pinch each time you use a moisturizer/sunscreen that does not contain the vitamin.

•**Retinoic acid.** This is a form of vitamin A that is added to hundreds of over-the-counter (OTC) skin-care products. It is also available by prescription. Retinoic acid increases cellular turnover, the rate at which cells divide. This makes the skin appear brighter, smoother and plumper.

My advice: Use OTC *retinol cream* once daily. Apply it at night because it temporarily increases the skin's sensitivity to sun. Most products have a concentration of 1% or less. Prescription-strength retinoic acid usually is not necessary.

•**Moisturizer.** *Everyone* should use this as they age. Adding moisture to skin cells makes them expand, which improves skin volume and texture. Moisturizers protect the skin from environmental factors (heat, dryness and pollution) that undermine skin health.

My advice: Use moisturizer with sunscreen at least twice a day. I recommend a vitamin C–enhanced moisturizer that includes green-tea extract. Both ingredients improve the skin's ability to absorb the moisturizer. Compounds in green tea also reduce skin inflammation and sun-related skin damage. Soy moisturizers may provide similar benefits.

Also important: Exfoliation, an effective form of *controlled trauma* that stimulates the skin to produce more collagen. Every week or two, use a gentle facial scrub with fine grains and a soft facial brush. This practice also removes the dead skin cells that can dull your complexion.

Sensitive skin sometimes cannot tolerate even a mild scrub. An ultrasonic brush, such as Clarisonic ($100 to $200 online*), with a hydrating cleanser is a good alternative.

A chemical peel once or twice a year is another good way to remove dead skin cells. OTC peels contain *glycolic acid, lactic acid* or *salicylic acid,* usually in a concentration of about 5% to 10%. Peels should also contain moisturizing ingredients to minimize irritation. If you're new to chemical peels, talk with your dermatologist before using one of these products, since they can irritate skin, especially sensitive skin.

*Price subject to change.

Why Sugar Makes You Look Older

In a recent study, people were asked to guess the age of volunteers. Researchers observed that every 0.18-gram increase in the volunteers' blood sugar level was associated with a five-month increase in perceived age.

Possible reason: Glucose can damage the skin's collagen and elastin, causing wrinkles and sagging.

Study by researchers from Unilever Discover, Colworth House, Sharnbrook, Bedfordshire, UK, and Leiden University Medical Center, the Netherlands, published in *AGE: Journal of the American Aging Association*.

Antiaging Secret from the Kitchen

Men who consumed more than two teaspoons of olive oil daily showed fewer signs of sun-related aging than men who consumed smaller amounts, a recent study shows.

Theory: The monounsaturated fatty acids in olive oil may protect the body against damage by free radicals.

Study by researchers at University of Paris and Research Center on Human Skin, founded by Chanel, Neuilly sur Seine, France, published in *PLOS ONE*.

Help for Dark Circles

Under-eye bags, puffiness and dark circles are hereditary, so if your parents had them, you probably will, too. Skin becomes thinner as we age, so tiny blood vessels around the eyes become more visible. Eye creams with caffeine, such as 100% Pure Organic Coffee Bean Eye Cream and Garnier Skin Renew Anti-Puff Eye Roller, temporarily constrict these blood vessels and help hide dark circles and puffiness. Lack of sleep and fluid reten-

tion can trigger puffiness. You should address any problem that can cause you to retain fluids, such as a kidney or thyroid condition or too much salt in your diet. Sinus conditions or allergies also can cause under-eye bags or dark circles. Elevating the head of your bed a few inches will help drain fluids from your face.

For a more permanent solution, a cosmetic dermatologist can inject dermal fillers, such as Juvederm or Restylane, to fill hollows under the eye. Eyelid surgery, or *blepharoplasty*, can tighten sagging skin that causes puffiness.

Neal Schultz, MD, dermatologist in private practice, New York City. *NealSchultzMD.com*

No More "Swimming-Pool" Hair

The greenish tint in hair is not caused by chlorine in pools but by copper oxide and copper sulfate in the water. The copper comes from old brass fittings, gas-heater coils, algaecides and the water supply itself. To make it harder for copper to penetrate hair, use a conditioner or leave-in treatment containing silicone polymers such as *dimethicone* or *cyclomethicone*…or apply sesame or olive oil before swimming. After you get out of the pool, rinse hair with plain water. You can wash your hair with one-half cup of vinegar to remove copper oxide. One-half cup of tomato juice or lemon juice also will work.

Nicole Rogers, MD, dermatologist at Tulane Medical School, New Orleans, quoted in *The Wall Street Journal*.

Easy Ways to Strengthen Fingernails

Research suggests that biotin, a B vitamin, can help strengthen weak or brittle nails. Take one 2.5-milligram (mg) tablet daily. It has no known harmful effects and is available at most drugstores and online. Because nails grow so slowly, it can take six months or longer to work.

Caution: If you take medications such as statins regularly, talk to your doctor before taking biotin.

Other ways to keep nails from cracking…

• **Coat them with hand cream** throughout the day, especially after exposure to water.

• **Wear rubber gloves** when washing dishes or cleaning.

• **Use only acetone-free polish remover.**

Rochelle Torgerson, MD, PhD, assistant professor of dermatology, Mayo Medical School, Mayo Clinic, Rochester, Minnesota.

Tongue Trick Stops Nervous Cough

Why is it that the minute we have to be quiet, like during a play or a speech, we cough? A theatrical stage manager we know gave us this advice. To stop a nervous cough, press hard on the roof of your mouth with your tongue or your index finger. Your cough should stop immediately!

Joan Wilen and Lydia Wilen, health investigators based in New York City who have spent decades collecting "cures from the cupboard." They are authors of *Bottom Line's Treasury of Home Remedies & Natural Cures* (Bottom Line Books) and the free e-letter *Household Magic Daily Tips. HouseholdMagicDailyTips.com*

Stressed? Fish Oil May Help

In a recent study, adults took a daily dose of either fish oil or olive oil for two months, then had their responses to a mildly stressful situation measured.

The result: Those who had taken fish oil showed less heart-rate and nerve response to stress than those who had taken olive oil, possibly due to the omega-3 fatty acids in fish oil.

If you're under stress: Talk to your doctor about taking a daily fish oil supplement.

Important: Be sure to mention any blood thinners or other medications you take—fish oil may interact with them.

Jason Carter, PhD, chair of kinesiology and integrative physiology, Michigan Technological University, Houghton.

Natural Remedy for Anxiety

The light, soothing fragrance of lavender oil has long been used in aromatherapy to ease anxiety and insomnia. You also can try a lavender oil supplement. For example, Calm Aid by Nature's Way contains *Silexan*, a type of lavender oil shown in clinical studies to ease anxiety as effectively as the *benzodiazepine* drug *lorazepam* (Ativan). Those who took the supplement also reported better sleep quality. I recommend taking one 80-milligram (mg) softgel in the morning with a glass of water. Side effects are rare but can include nausea, constipation and headache. Check with your doctor before trying.

Holly Lucille, ND, RN, naturopathic doctor based in West Hollywood, California. *DrHollyLucille.com*

Food for a Better Mood

Trans fats, alcohol and too much sugar can make you sad and anxious. Replace all sugary beverages with water or unsweetened drinks…processed foods with natural foods such as fruits, vegetables, nuts and fish…and simple carbohydrates (such as table sugar and white bread) with complex carbohydrates, such as whole-grain breads, pastas and cereals. Also, drink no more than two caffeinated drinks a day. And increase your healthy fat intake with olive, canola and vegetable oils, fish, avocado, flaxseeds and nuts.

Mind, Mood & Memory.

Red Light Fights Afternoon Sleepiness

Fatigue is common for many people from about 2 pm to 4 pm. According to a recent study, exposure to red light in the afternoon boosts alertness. Blue light also has some positive effect.

Study by researchers at Lighting Research Center, The Light and Health Program, Rensselaer Polytechnic Institute, Troy, New York, published in Physiology & Behavior.

Salt Your Feet to Fall Asleep

Lindsey Duncan, ND, a naturopathic doctor and nutritionist in Austin, Texas. With more than 28 years of clinical experience, he uses a variety of natural therapies. He is also founder of Genesis Today, Inc., a supplement and natural-food product company.

A little-known secret to getting a good night's sleep is keeping the pH of your body *alkaline* rather than *acidic*.

Problem: The typical diet (too much processed food, red meat, dairy, fried food, sugar, salt, coffee and alcohol) and lifestyle (constant stress) acidify the body—a major reason why so many people don't get a good night's sleep. An acidic body chemistry creates tension, making it difficult to fall asleep. But an alkaline body chemistry creates a relaxed feeling.

Home remedy: Try a saltwater foot soak. Scientists haven't looked at this practice, but my clinical experience shows that it works.

What to do: Before bed, soak your feet for 20 minutes in hot water and sea salt, which is the best source of minerals to alkalinize and relax the body.

For an average size foot bath, add about one-half cup of sea salt to the water. If you're soaking your feet in a regular bathroom tub, use about one to two cups of salt. There are many types of sea salt, each with different beneficial minerals. I prefer Dead Sea salt, which has a high concentration of magnesium to relax the nervous system and other minerals (available online and in health-food stores).

Note: The water temperature for your foot soak should be as hot as your feet can bear—but not hot enough to break a sweat above your lip or to cause a burn. To keep the water hot for 20 minutes, add more hot water during the soak.

Caution: If you have diabetes, check with your doctor before doing this. *Neuropathy*, a complication of diabetes that can cause loss of feeling in the feet, could prevent you from noticing that the water is too hot.

For a Better Night's Sleep, Paint Your Bedroom This Color...

People who slept in blue rooms got more sleep—an average of seven hours and 52 minutes a night—than people who slept in rooms of any other color.

Possible reason: The color blue is associated with calmness and is thought to help reduce blood pressure and heart rate.

Study of 2,000 bedrooms in the UK by Travelodge, Parsippany, New Jersey. Travelodge.com

Lycopene for Longer Sleep

People who got less than five hours of sleep a night had lower intake of *lycopene* than those who slept longer in a recent finding. Lycopene-rich foods include red- and orange-colored fruits and vegetables such as tomatoes, watermelon, pink grapefruit and red cabbage.

Study of more than 9,000 people by researchers at Perelman School of Medicine, University of Pennsylvania, Philadelphia, published in Appetite.

Best Bedtime Snack for Better Zs...

The best snack for restful sleep is peanut butter on toast...or a small serving of fruit and yogurt.

Reason: The protein in these snacks contains the amino acid *tryptophan*. The carbohydrates make tryptophan more available to your brain, where the relaxation neurotransmitter *serotonin* is produced.

Tasneem Bhatia, MD, medical director and founder, Atlanta Center for Holistic & Integrative Medicine, writing in *Prevention*.

Smartphone Apps That Help You Sleep Better

Sleep Cycle ($1,* iOS) uses the iPhone's sensors to monitor movements and record your sleep patterns, from light sleep to deep sleep. It provides a daily graph that shows how well you managed to stay in deep sleep. *Sleepbot* (free, Android, iOS) also tracks sleep patterns and has a sound-monitoring function to see if there are noises that disturb your sleep. *Simply Rain* ($1, iOS) plays soothing rain sounds. *Sleep Pillow Sounds* ($2, iOS) plays sounds of rain, water, crackling fires or waves on the

*Prices subject to change.

shore. *Relax and Sleep* (free, Android) has a wide range of sounds, including a rocking chair and a cat purring.

The New York Times. NYTimes.com

Hand-Washing Alert!

More than 10% of adults in the US don't wash their hands after using the toilet. And almost 22.8% don't use soap. The Centers for Disease Control and Prevention recommends washing hands thoroughly with soap and water for 20 seconds.

Study of 3,749 adults by researchers at Michigan State University, East Lansing, published in *Journal of Environmental Health*.

Got a Hangover? Try Honey

The fructose in honey helps the body metabolize alcohol more quickly. Try a spoonful—or other fructose-rich substances, such as 100% fruit juice if you're suffering from a hangover.

Reid B. Blackwelder, MD, family physician, Kingsport, Tennessee, quoted in *Redbook*.

4

Easy Fitness & Weight Loss

Unleash the Power of Your Brain to Lose Weight Once and for All

Think about all of the changes that you make when you are trying to lose weight. You alter your food choices, serving sizes and daily calories. The pounds do come off—but only to come back on again.

Reason: You haven't made the most important change of all—to your brain. There could be an imbalance in the brain's circuitry. The areas that trigger impulsive behavior have been strengthened from years of bad habits, while the areas that control rational decision-making have been weakened.

Everyone knows the weight-loss basics. The challenge is to restore mental balance so that you automatically make healthier choices for yourself. *What to do…*

LOOK AT YOUR FEELINGS

When you wish to eat, ask yourself whether you really are hungry. Pay attention to your stomach. Is it full or empty? Ask yourself, Do I really need food right now?

People often eat for reasons that have nothing to do with hunger. We eat when we're upset, frustrated, bored, etc. The act of eating is a distraction from uncomfortable feelings and a coping mechanism that makes the feelings less intense.

Studies have shown that mood significantly affects food choices. One study published in *American Demographics* found that people gravitate toward ice cream and cookies when they're sad…potato chips when they're

---

Rudolph E. Tanzi, PhD, the Joseph P. and Rose F. Kennedy Professor of Child Neurology and Mental Retardation at Harvard University as well as director of the Genetics and Aging Research Unit at Massachusetts General Hospital, both in Boston. He has a special on PBS, *Super Brain* with Dr. Rudy Tanzi. He is coauthor, with Deepak Chopra, MD, of *Super Brain: Unleashing the Explosive Power of Your Mind to Maximize Health, Happiness, and Spiritual Well-Being* (Harmony).

bored…and pizza or steak when they're feeling happy.

My advice: Before you eat anything, seriously ask yourself why you want it. If you haven't eaten for several hours, you're probably just hungry. But if you're craving a snack even though you ate recently, you're probably dealing with emotional hunger. Ask yourself, *How am I feeling about the world today?… What's my mood?…What do I really need at this particular moment?…Does my stomach feel empty?*

When you eat only when you're hungry and you don't use food for an emotional fix, you've achieved *homeostasis*, a type of mind-body balance in which you desire only what you need.

Imagine a single cell floating in a petri dish. It doesn't think about food. It takes in nutrients when it needs them and stops when it has had enough. The cell is in a perfect state of homeostasis.

You can achieve the same harmony by being self-aware, or mindful.

What to do: Suppose that you come home from work and already are anticipating the taste of chocolate. Do not go straight to the pantry. Instead, run through the mindful list. If you determine that you are experiencing only emotional hunger, take three very deep breaths and smile. This simple exercise can make the craving go away. It also works if you've already started eating and don't want to overeat.

DON'T RESIST

It's human nature to crave what you can't have, so forcing yourself to resist may not be the answer. Whatever you resist persists. So if you've gone through your mindful eating list and still feel like eating, don't fight the feeling. Even if you know that you tend to eat more on those days when nothing's going right, it's better to lose the battle than to lose the war.

Instead of resisting, try to reshape your brain. Focus on awareness, not resistance.

Example: You're standing in front of the refrigerator, staring at a slice of pecan pie. You go through your mindful checklist and realize that you're not really hungry, but it's been a

lousy day and that pecan pie sure will make you feel better. Go ahead and eat it, but be mindful of why you are eating it. This will train your brain about when and how you wish to eat.

Maintaining a healthy weight is a lifelong endeavor. You cannot spend your entire life fighting urges. What you can do is gradually become more aware of your feelings…know when you're weak…and learn not to depend on food to get you through. Along the way, you will train your brain to eat healthier.

EAT MUCH MORE SLOWLY

Many people race through meals. By the time they realize that they are full and the appropriate message is sent to the brain, they've already consumed hundreds of extra calories—and later feel bloated and uncomfortable.

In a recent study, researchers found that people who ate quickly consumed 55% more food per minute than those who ate slowly. In the study, people who ate slowly consumed two ounces of food per minute. Those who ate a little more quickly consumed 2.5 ounces per minute…and those who really gobbled their food consumed 3.1 ounces per minute.

Hunger and eating involve a balancing act between two hormones. While you're eating, the hormone that stimulates appetite, *ghrelin*, starts to decline. At the same time, the hormone that suppresses appetite, *leptin*, starts to rise. The hormones work together to control how much you eat. But they take time to work. If you're a fast eater, they can't keep up—and you wind up consuming more calories than your body needs.

My advice: Eat slowly and mindfully. Enjoy each bite of food. Notice the smell, texture and taste. Don't take another bite until you've thoroughly chewed the previous bite.

DID YOU KNOW THAT…

You Should Take at Least 20 Minutes to Eat a Meal?

That is about how long it takes for hormones to send the appropriate signals to the brain that you've had enough.

Foods That Rev Up Your Metabolism: Drop Those Extra Pounds and Get an Energy Boost to Boot!

Ridha Arem, MD, an endocrinologist, director of the Texas Thyroid Institute and clinical professor of medicine at Baylor College of Medicine, both in Houston. He is a former chief of endocrinology and metabolism at Houston's Ben Taub General Hospital and is author of *The Thyroid Solution Diet* (Atria). *AremWellness.com*

Forget about calories! Most people who are trying to lose weight worry too much about calories and not enough about the *actual* cause of those extra pounds.

The real culprit: Out-of-balance hormones.

Best approach for controlling weight: A diet that rebalances the body's hormones. Carefully chosen foods and food combinations rebalance levels and/or efficiency of metabolism-regulating hormones, including *ghrelin*, *leptin* and *thyroid hormone*. You'll burn more calories, and your body will be less likely to store calories as fat. *Here's how…*

TWEAKING THE BEST DIETS

Hands down, the Mediterranean diet is one of the healthiest diets out there. With its emphasis on plant-based foods (such as vegetables, fruits, grains and nuts) and healthful fats (from fatty fish and olive oil), it is good for your heart and helps control blood sugar levels.

But for more efficient weight loss, you need to go a step further. That's where the *Protein-Rich Oriental Diet*, developed by Korean researchers, enters the picture. With its heavy focus on high-protein foods, this diet has been found to provide twice the weight loss offered by calorie restriction alone.

To achieve and maintain an optimal body weight: The diet I designed includes elements of both these diets—as well as some important additional tweaks such as timing your meals (see next page) and consuming a *mix of proteins* in order to get the full complement of amino acids, which is essential for increasing metabolism and controlling hunger. On my diet, you will eat a combination of at least two proteins, good fats and vegetables at each meal. *For example…*

- **Fish, turkey and chicken contain all of the essential amino acids that are in red meat,** but with fewer calories and less saturated fat. They're particularly rich in *arginine*, an amino acid that increases the speed at which your body burns calories.

My advice: Aim for six to eight ounces of these foods as the primary protein for dinner. You also can include these foods at breakfast and lunch as one of your protein choices. (If you're not a fish lover, see next page.)

- **Reduced-fat cottage cheese, ricotta, yogurt and goat cheese.** Certain forms of dairy are filled with *branched-chain amino acids*, which help quell appetite and increase the ability of *mitochondria* (the energy-producing components of cells) to burn fat.

My advice: Each day, eat about a half-cup of low-fat or nonfat dairy as a protein.

- **High-protein beans, lentils and grains,** such as black beans, kidney beans, quinoa and brown rice. Consume one of these protein sources (three-fourths cup to one cup) at lunch—usually combined with a small serving of fish or lean meat. In addition to packing plenty of protein and fiber, these foods provide large amounts of amino acids that will help you get fitter and have more energy.

- **Egg whites** contain all of the amino acids that you need for efficient weight loss, and they are my favorite choice as a protein for breakfast. An egg-white omelet with onions, mushrooms and other vegetables can be prepared in just a few minutes. Limit your intake of egg yolks due to their cholesterol.

LOW-GLYCEMIC CARBS

Carbohydrates that are digested quickly—mainly refined and processed foods such as juices, white rice and French fries—increase insulin and fat storage. Carbohydrates with a lower glycemic score are absorbed more slowly and don't cause unhealthy changes in insulin or fat storage.

Good choices: Whole oats, chickpeas and fruit (see next page) at breakfast and lunch, and vegetables at each meal.

MORE FIBER

The fiber in such foods as beans and vegetables reduces appetite and slows digestion, important for preventing insulin "spikes." Research shows that people of normal weight tend to eat significantly more fiber than those who are overweight or obese.

For efficient weight loss: Get 35 grams (g) of fiber daily.

Fruit is also a good source of fiber. Just be sure that you choose fresh fruit that's low in natural sugar (*fructose*).

Good choices: Raspberries, strawberries, papayas, apples and cranberries. Avoid fruit at dinner to make it the lowest glycemic meal.

GREEN TEA

Green tea is high in *epigallocatechin gallate* (EGCG), a substance that can decrease the accumulation of body fat. It also increases insulin sensitivity and improves an obesity-related condition known as *metabolic syndrome*. Consume a few cups every day. Do not sweeten the tea with honey or other sweeteners—they are among the main causes of high insulin and weight gain.

FISH OIL SUPPLEMENTS

The omega-3 fatty acids in fish increase the rate at which calories are burned. However, even if you eat fish every day, it doesn't contain enough omega-3s for long-term weight control.

Solution: Take a daily supplement with 600 milligrams (mg) of EPA and 400 mg of DHA—the main types of omega-3s. Check first with your doctor if you take blood thinners or diabetes medication, since fish oil may interact with these drugs.

NOT JUST FOR WEIGHT LOSS

A hormone-balancing eating plan can rev up your metabolism even if you don't need to lose weight, giving you more energy and mental focus. If you aren't overweight and you follow this eating plan, you may lose a pound or two, but mostly you'll simply feel a whole lot better.

More from Ridha Arem, MD...

Timing of Your Meals Matters, Too!

When you eat is almost as important as what you eat…

• **Plan on eating four or five daily meals**—breakfast between 6 am and 8 am…an optional (and light) late-morning snack…lunch between 11 am and 12:30 pm…a mid-afternoon snack… and supper between 5 pm and 7 pm.

• **Plan your meals so that you get more protein at supper.** It will stimulate the release of growth hormone, which burns fat while you sleep.

• **Avoid having any food three hours before bedtime.** Eating late in the evening causes increases in blood sugar and insulin that can lead to weight gain—even if you consume a lower-calorie diet (1,200 to 1,500 calories a day).

Mixed Drinks Can Make You Hungry

Sweet alcoholic drinks, such as rum-and-cola and fancy cocktails, not only have more calories than beer or wine, they also cause your blood sugar to spike higher than beer or wine. The drop in blood sugar that follows leaves you hungry.

Health. Health.com

DID YOU KNOW THAT...

Cookie Addiction Is Real?

If you have trouble putting down the Oreos, take heart. Lab animals that ate the cookies had brain activity similar to that which ordinarily occurs with drug use.

Connecticut College. *ConnColl.edu*

Menu Trick Helps People Eat Less

In a recent finding, when diners were shown menus that listed the amount of brisk walking they would need to do to work off each dish, they were less likely to overeat than diners whose menus listed only calorie counts or had no health information. Calorie counts alone had no effect—diners ordered the same number of calories whether or not calories were listed.

Study of 300 men and women, ages 18 to 30, by researchers at Texas Christian University, Fort Worth, presented at the Experimental Biology 2013 conference, Boston.

Weight-Loss Tip: Two Large Meals a Day

Individuals with type 2 diabetes lost more weight when they ate two large meals a day (breakfast and lunch—no dinner) than similar people who ate six small meals with the same number of calories.

Study by researchers at Institute for Clinical and Experimental Medicine in Prague, Czech Republic, presented at the 2013 American Diabetes Association Meeting in Chicago.

Best Time to Eat Lunch for Maximum Weight Loss

People who ate lunch before 3:00 pm lost an average of 22 pounds in 20 weeks, versus 17 pounds for those who ate lunch after 3:00. Both groups consumed the same number of calories each day.

Study of 420 obese people by researchers at University of Murcia in Spain and Brigham and Women's Hospital and Tufts University, both in Boston, published in *International Journal of Obesity*.

Challenging Your Mind Helps You Eat Better

People who took a hard computer-based quiz were less likely to crave unhealthy snacks than those given an easier test.

Theory: An intellectually challenging distraction can cut off desire before it takes over behavior, thus lessening the chance that you will reach for junk food.

Study by researchers at Leiden University, the Netherlands, published in *Journal of Personality and Social Psychology*.

Scare Off the Pounds

Watching a 90-minute horror movie can burn an average of 113 calories, a recent finding reports. That's as many calories as you would burn if you ran a 10-minute mile. The adrenaline spikes raise your metabolic rate. Researchers found the best calorie-burning flick to be *The Shining*, scaring 184 calories away...followed by *Jaws* (161 calories) and *The Exorcist* (158).

Study by researchers at University of Westminster, London, UK, reported in *Health*.

The Unhealthy "Healthy" Snack

Joan Salge Blake, RD, LDN, clinical associate professor at Boston University's Sargent College of Health and Rehabilitation Sciences and author of *Nutrition & You* (Benjamin Cummings).

Kale chips? Brown-rice crackers? Bean tortilla chips? Are these snacks really healthier for us?

Don't count on it. People do glance at the front of the package and see healthy-sounding ingredients. But most don't read the list of ingredients and nutrition facts on the side of the package.

If they did, they would discover that many "healthy" snacks have similar amounts of fat, calories and sodium as mainstream treats. A one-ounce serving of Doritos Nacho Cheese tortilla chips has 140 calories, 8 grams (g) of fat and 210 milligrams (mg) of sodium. That isn't very different from 140 calories, 7 g of fat and 140 mg of sodium for a one-ounce serving of Beanitos Nacho Cheese bean (not corn) tortilla chips.

Faux-healthy snacks are legitimately slimming in one way, though—they make our wallets lighter. One brand of kale chips costs about $8 for a 2.5-ounce bag.

If you really want a healthy snack, skip the pricey processed ones made from fruits and vegetables and simply eat fruits and vegetables, suggests Blake. As she puts it, "Mother Nature won't try to fool you."

If fruits and vegetables aren't your idea of a treat, Blake recommends old-fashioned, inexpensive popcorn, which is quite healthful—it is rich in antioxidants and fiber. Just don't load it up with too much salt and butter.

A Few Extra Pounds May Be Good

When more than 9,000 adults over age 50 were tracked for 16 years, those with a body mass index (BMI) of 25 to 29.9 (overweight but not obese) lived longer, on average, than those who were obese or started at a normal weight but steadily added pounds.

Why: A few extra pounds in older people may be a buffer against weight loss associated with illnesses such as cancer.

If you're a little overweight: Work at keeping your weight stable.

Hui Zheng, PhD, assistant professor of sociology, The Ohio State University, Columbus.

This 7-Minute Workout Really Works!

Chris Jordan, CSCS, director of exercise physiology at Human Performance Institute in Orlando, Florida. Jordan designed the exercise programming portion of the Corporate Athlete Course, which was described in an article—which he coauthored with Brett Klika—in *American College of Sports Medicine's Health & Fitness Journal. HPInstitute.com*

Don't have the time to exercise? Then here's the workout for you! It is a series of 12 resistance and aerobic exercises that can be completed in seven minutes. It's a tough seven minutes. The exercises are easy to learn, but they will push your body to the limit.

HOW IT WORKS

We designed the following workout for "corporate athletes"—busy adults without a lot of free time or access to a health club. The exercises can be done at home or in a hotel room because the only "equipment" that's required is the weight of your body and a sturdy chair.

This approach, known as *high-intensity circuit training*, is effective for weight loss as well as metabolic and cardiovascular health. Workouts that are done at high intensity—during which the heart will beat at up to 80% to 90% of its maximum rate—cause changes in the muscles that are comparable to the changes produced by lengthier workouts at moderate intensity.

You don't need a heart monitor to determine exercise intensity. I recommend the talk test. If you can speak an entire sentence while exercising, you're not pushing hard enough. If you can't speak at all, you're working too hard. You're in the right zone when you can speak a few words before pausing for breath.

On an exertion scale of one to 10—with one being at rest, and 10 being almost impossible—the workout should be an eight or a nine. This can be a very tough workout. No one should do it without getting a physical and the go-ahead from a doctor.

EASE INTO IT

If you're not already an athlete, start slowly. While you're learning and getting in shape, you might take a little longer than seven minutes to complete all 12 of the exercises. Your goal is to get the time down to seven minutes using correct form and technique for each exercise in the routine. Do the seven-minute workout every other day.

You may need to go to your local fitness center and get guidance from a certified fitness professional. When you get stronger, you can do the seven-minute workout two or three times in a row if you wish for the ultimate 15-to-20-minute workout.

It's important to do the exercises in the order listed.

Reason: The workout includes total-body exercises, which are more aerobic in nature, and exercises that give the lower- and upper-body muscles some time to recover. When you're doing a leg exercise, the muscles in the upper body have a chance to rest. When you're working the upper body, the legs have the opportunity to rest. These intervals of exertion and rest help make the workout so effective.

THE EXERCISES

Aim to perform 15 to 20 repetitions of each exercise over a period of 30 seconds, but don't compromise form and technique for repetitions. When you finish one exercise, don't rest. Immediately start the next one.

Caution: If you have high blood pressure or heart disease, skip the isometric exercises (wall-sit, plank and side plank). These movements involve extended muscle contractions that can impede blood flow. A trainer can suggest safer alternatives.

• **Jumping jacks.** Start the routine with a classic jumping jack—with your feet shoulder-width apart, arms at your sides, jump slightly and spread your legs while bringing your arms together over your head until your hands almost touch. Jump again as you bring your feet back to the starting position while lowering your hands to your sides.

Helpful: If you are uncomfortable doing jumping jacks, you can run or walk in place.

• **Wall-sit.** Start out standing with your back against a wall. Bend your knees, and slide down until your thighs are parallel to the floor. Hold the position for 30 seconds.

• **Push-up.** Support your body on your hands and toes, your palms about shoulder-width apart. Lower your upper body toward the floor until the elbows form a 90° angle. Then raise your body. If you want, you can start out on your knees and progress to a full push-up as you gain more strength.

• **Abdominal crunch.** Lie on your back, with your knees bent, your feet flat on the floor and your arms extended toward your knees. Using the abdominal muscles, lift your head and shoulders a few inches off the floor. Then lower your head/shoulders back down.

• **Step-up.** Leading with your left leg, step onto a sturdy chair. (If you aren't sure of your strength or balance, you can substitute something that's lower than a chair, such as a step or a low bench.) Use the strength of your left leg to bring your other foot up onto the chair. Then step off the chair, leading with your left leg. Repeat the movement alternating legs each time.

• **Squat.** Stand with your feet shoulder-width apart and your arms at your sides. Bend your knees, and squat until your thighs are parallel to the floor. While lowering your body, extend your arms in front of your body. Keep your knees over your toes. Then rise to the starting position.

● **Triceps dip on chair.** Sit on the edge of a sturdy chair (or step or low bench), with the heels of your hands on either side of your butt. Slide off the seat so that your weight is supported on your hands. Your legs will be extended forward. Bend your elbows, and lower your behind toward the floor. When your waist is a few inches lower than the seat of the chair, push up with your arms until your elbows are straight. Keep your shoulders flat, not shrugged.

● **Plank.** Lie facedown on the floor while supporting your weight on your toes and forearms. Hold the position, keeping your body straight for 30 seconds.

● **High knees/running in place.** This exercise combines a running motion with exaggerated knee lifts. While "running," raise your knees as high as you comfortably can, without compromising your rhythm or balance. Stay on your toes, not your heels.

●**Lunge.** While keeping your upper body straight, lunge forward with one leg. Lower your hips until both knees are bent at a 90° angle. Push back with the leading leg until your body returns to the starting position. Then step forward with the other leg and repeat.

● **Push-up and rotation.** Assume the normal push-up position. As you come up, rotate your body so that your right arm rises overhead. Return to the starting posi-

tion, and lower yourself. Do another push-up, this time extending the other arm. Do this for 30 seconds, alternating sides.

● **Side plank.** Lie on your side, with one forearm under your shoulder. Your upper leg will be directly on top of the lower leg, with your knees straight. Raise your hips until your body forms a straight line from the ankles to the shoulders. Hold the position for 30 seconds, then repeat on the other side.

---

4 Dangerous Fitness Myths: Half-Truths Can Turn Your Exercise Regimen into an Injury Trap

Wayne L. Westcott, PhD, an instructor of exercise science at Quincy College in Massachusetts as well as a strength-training consultant for the American Council on Exercise, the American Senior Fitness Association and the National Youth Sports Safety Foundation. He is also author, with Thomas R. Baechle, EdD, of *Strength Training Past 50* (Human Kinetics).

D on't believe everything you hear when you are trying to get in shape or stay in shape. There are plenty of myths and half-truths.

Among the most dangerous fitness myths to avoid…

Fitness Myth #1: **A little pain means you're getting maximum benefit from your workout.** Despite the popular cliché "no pain, no gain," you should never feel prolonged, stabbing or sharp pain during a workout or continue to exercise when something hurts.

The risk: Pain means damage. It could be a warning sign that you have overstressed or overstretched a muscle, tendon or ligament. It also can indicate joint damage. People who continue to exercise when they hurt risk more serious injuries, such as torn muscles or tendinitis (inflammation of a tendon).

Exception: A little soreness after exercise means that you have had a good workout. When you exercise hard, the muscles develop microscopic tears that lead to rebuilding of tissue and an increase in strength. If you are very sore, however, you have overworked your muscles.

Warning: Don't believe the myth that you can exercise longer and harder if you take an anti-inflammatory pain reliever, such as *ibuprofen* (Motrin), before going to the gym. Taking a preworkout anti-inflammatory may reduce muscle performance and prevent you from feeling an injury while working out.

Important: If you have arthritis or another painful condition that requires daily treatment with aspirin, ibuprofen or another anti-inflammatory medication, ask your doctor if it's safe to take the drug prior to workouts. The combination of exercise and anti-inflammatories might increase the risk for damage to the gastrointestinal lining, according to recent research.

Fitness Myth #2: **You should stretch before exercising.** Trainers used to advise everyone to stretch before lifting weights, going for a run, etc. Do not do it.

The risk: Tendons and ligaments take longer to warm up than muscles. People who stretch when they are "cold" are more likely to suffer from muscle and tendon strains and other injuries than people who begin their workouts with a progressive warm-up. Static stretches, in which you stretch a muscle to a point of tension and hold the stretch for a certain period of time, can be particularly harmful before a workout.

Recent finding: Research also has shown that people who do static stretches prior to working out can't exercise as long and may have reduced muscle strength.

Exception: You can start a workout with dynamic stretches, slow movements that mimic the exercise patterns you're about to do. Before taking a run, for example, you could do some fast walking and slow jogging. This type of stretching is safe and prepares the muscles for exercise.

Also: Stretch after vigorous activity. That's when muscles and tendons have the best blood flow and elasticity, and you're less likely to get injured. *Good postworkout stretches…*

• **Figure Four.** Sit on the floor with both legs out in front of you. Bend your left leg, placing the sole of your left foot against your right inner thigh. With your right hand, reach for your right ankle and hold for 30 seconds. Perform twice on each side to stretch your hamstrings and calves.

• **Letter T.** Lie faceup on the floor with your arms in a T-position. Slowly cross your left leg over your body, allowing your torso to rotate so that your left foot is near your right hand. Keep your leg as straight as possible. Hold for 20 seconds. Perform twice on each side to stretch your hips and lower back.

Fitness Myth #3: **Do not rest during workouts.** You have probably heard that the best strength-training workouts involve non-stop action, with no rest (or very little rest) between exercises.

The risk: Failing to rest will cause muscle fatigue and poor form, a common cause of injuries. Also, you won't fully train the muscles because they need time to recover.

When you're working the same muscles, you need to rest 30 to 90 seconds between sets.

Example: Do eight to 12 biceps curls… take a 30- to 90-second break…then curl the weight again.

Exception: With circuit training, you move quickly from one exercise to the next. You might do a biceps exercise, then a leg exercise, then return to the biceps. Even though you're constantly moving (and getting a good cardiovascular workout), you're allowing one group of muscles to rest while you work a different part of the body.

Fitness Myth #4: **High-heat exercise can work the muscles more.** Some people believe that high-temperature workouts—including "hot" yoga, spinning and others in which the room temperature may be 90°F or even hotter—make the muscles more limber and improve the body's ability to remove toxins.

I do not recommend it. For the average person, exercising in high temperatures will reduce their performance because the body has to work harder to fend off the heat.

The risk: It forces the heart to do double-duty—not only to bring oxygen to the muscles and remove wastes that accumulate during exercise, but also to pump more blood to the skin to dissipate the extra heat. If you're tempted to try high-heat workouts, ask your doctor first.

More from Wayne L. Westcott, PhD...

Save Your Back

Core-strengthening exercises help prevent low-back pain by strengthening abdominal and back muscles. However, one of the most popular of these workouts, which involves lying on your back and simultaneously raising both legs in the air, causes a pronounced arch in the low back that can trigger—or worsen—low-back pain.

Better: Bicycle maneuver. Lie with your lower back pressed against the floor, your hands clasped behind your head and your knees bent. Simultaneously lift your head and shoulders off the floor. Bring your left knee to your right elbow, while straightening your right leg. Using a bicycle-pedaling motion, alternate sides. Extend your legs as far as you comfortably can without arching your back.

Typical number of reps: 10 to 15 times on each leg with slow and controlled movements.

Why You Shouldn't Take Pain Meds *Before* Exercise

Many athletes take *ibuprofen*—found in Advil and other medicines—or another *nonsteroidal anti-inflammatory drug* (NSAID) before workouts because they think it will help them exercise more strenuously and prevent muscle soreness afterward.

But: NSAIDs—which can cause damage to the lining of the gastrointestinal (GI) tract—should not be combined with strenuous exercise, which also can cause short-term damage to the GI lining.

Recent finding: Men who took ibuprofen before a workout showed higher intestinal permeability than men who did not—which

means that toxins and other bacterial by-products may get into their blood.

Self-defense: If you feel that you need medicine in order to exercise without discomfort, try *acetaminophen*, which does not have the GI effects of NSAIDs. Or ask your doctor for a recommendation.

Study done by researchers at ORBIS Medical Center, Maastricht, the Netherlands, published in *Medicine & Science in Sports & Exercise.*

Add Weights to a Walk?

Adding hand (or ankle) weights to your walks will cause only a modest increase in the calories that you burn but may lead to injury since they change your center of gravity and subsequently your gait. Hand weights can cause damage to ligaments, tendons and muscles in the shoulders and upper arms, and ankle weights can lead to knee, hip and back injuries.

What's more, walking with hand weights, either small dumbbells or wrist weights, provides little in the way of toning benefit but increases the natural momentum of the walker's swinging arms, and this overswinging can be harmful.

If you want to step up your walks, increase your pace and distance.

Mel Cave, DPT, director of physical therapy, Somers Orthopaedic Surgery & Sports Medicine Group, Carmel, New York.

Walking Provides the Same Benefits as Running

Both running and walking reduce the likelihood of diabetes, high blood pressure and heart disease.

But: You have to expend the same amount of calories walking as you would running.

Example: You would need to walk for 45 minutes to burn 225 calories...you would need to run for only 21 minutes.

Health. Health.com

A Personal Trainer for Olympians Shares His Favorite Stretches: They Help Nagging Back, Hip or Knee Pain

Joel Harper, a New York City–based personal trainer whose clients include several Olympic medalists. The creator of the PBS DVD *Firming After 50*, he designed all of the personal workout chapters for Drs. Mehmet C. Oz and Michael F. Roizen's YOU series of books and accompanying workout DVDs. *JoelHarperFitness.com*

You may not be surprised if you feel a little stiff or achy after doing something you ordinarily don't do—such as sleeping on one side all night long…playing an especially tough tennis match or round of golf…or hunching over a computer for long hours.

What does surprise most people is the long-term effect of *habitually* doing any of these things. The result is out-of-balance muscles—an often hidden trigger of chronic pain and tightness in the back, knees, hips, shoulders and/or ankles.

Muscle imbalances don't happen overnight, but if certain activities are repeated day in and day out, the pain often goes undiagnosed and may drive sufferers to take potentially dangerous medications or even get surgery.

Joel Harper, a leading New York City–based personal trainer, knows how harmful muscle imbalances can be and has created specific muscle-balancing stretches for the Olympic medalists and other clients he works with. *Here are the habits that most often cause muscle imbalances—and the simple daily exercises that help…**

•**Sleeping on the same side every night.** This habit compresses one shoulder and hip.

The fix: Remind yourself when you go to bed that you want to start alternating sleeping sides throughout the night. After a while, your habit may change. Also, do the passive spinal twist below each morning upon waking to elongate the muscles on both sides of your body.

*It's always wise to consult a doctor before doing any new exercises.

What to do: While lying on your back in bed, interlock your fingers behind your head. Keep your elbows out, and lift your knees into a 90-degree angle. Then, keeping your torso flat and level, gently drop both of your knees to one side as far as you comfortably can, while looking straight up, and take five deep breaths. Repeat on the other side. If you notice more tightness on one side, repeat the stretch on that side for a few more breaths.

Also: Place a pillow between your knees when sleeping to help keep your hips and spine aligned.

•**Too much sitting.** Sitting for hours on end at a desk, while traveling or even on the couch tightens the hip flexors (the muscles that contract when lifting your knees to your chest) and weakens the opposing muscles of the buttocks, or "glutes." As a result, your pelvis tilts downward, stressing your lower back muscles.

The fix: Walk around for at least five minutes every few hours. Also, try the seated airplane stretch.

What to do: Sit in a chair with your feet flat on the floor. Then, place your right ankle on your quad, about an inch above your left knee. Next, rest your right elbow on top of your right knee and place your right hand on your right ankle. Gently lean forward, until you feel a comfortable stretch, while looking ahead, not down, and keeping your back straight. Hold for 30 seconds, then switch sides.

•**Repeated one-sided activities.** Stand shirtless in front of a full-length mirror. If one shoulder appears slightly lower than the other, it may be because you always keep your computer mouse on the same side…favor your right or left leg when crossing your legs…or always wear a purse, backpack or other bag on the same side. These activities cause a muscle imbalance in which your back becomes overworked on one side but underused on the other. Sports in which one side is dominant, such as tennis, golf or bowling, also can cause this type of muscle imbalance.

The fix: Alternate the shoulder on which you carry your bag, the way you cross your legs and, yes, even the side of the computer where you place your mouse (this will help

79

you become ambidextrous). Then, try a stretch for your chest.

What to do: With your fingers interlocked behind your head and your elbows out, slightly move your hands away from your head and hold for five deep inhalations. Do this a few times each day. Look straight ahead during this stretch.

If you play a racket sport or enjoy another sport in which one side is dominant, incorporate strengthening moves for the opposite side when you're not playing.

Also helpful: Consider taking up a new activity that uses muscles on both sides more equally, such as swimming, yoga or tai chi.

A Fruit That Gives Muscle Aches the Boot

Muscle soreness is the big downside of working out.

Good news: When athletes drank 16 ounces of watermelon juice an hour before exercise, they had less muscle soreness than when they did not drink it.

Theory: Watermelon contains *L-citrulline*, an amino acid that boosts blood flow and oxygen in muscles, reducing pain.

To ease sore muscles: Try eating some watermelon (or drinking the juice if you have a juicer).

Encarna Aguayo, PhD, associate professor of food technology, Technical University of Cartagena, Spain.

Fabulous Foot Stretches

By strengthening and stretching your feet, you can improve coordination, balance and stability.

What to do: Without shoes, move your foot in circles, first one way and then the other, then side to side, moving only your foot and ankle, not your leg…do toe curls—flex toes as much as possible and then uncurl them…with your foot flat on the floor, lift your big toe without lifting the other toes, then try lifting the others without lifting the big toe…use your feet to pick up items such as marbles or pencils…spread your toes apart like a fan…roll a small rubber ball or golf ball under the sole of your foot to massage it.

University of California, Berkeley Wellness Letter. BerkeleyWellness.com

No More Heartburn After a Workout

Prevent heartburn after a workout by avoiding fatty and greasy foods before working out…and waiting a few hours after eating to exercise.

Also: Sip water slowly during and after your workout to avoid filling your stomach with water and air.

If you still get heartburn: Try taking an over-the-counter medicine, such as Pepcid or Zantac, 30 minutes before your workout…or talk to your doctor.

William D. Chey, MD, professor of internal medicine, University of Michigan, Ann Arbor, quoted in *Shape*.

EASY-TO-DO…

Short Bouts of Activity Just as Good for You as Going to the Gym!

One- and two-minute increments of short-term activity, such as pacing while talking on the phone, doing housework, pushing a lawn mower or doing sit-ups or push-ups during TV commercials, may lower blood pressure and cholesterol and improve health as effectively as a structured exercise approach, a recent study reports. Aim for 30 minutes of activity a day.

Study of 6,000 adults by researchers at Oregon State University, Corvallis, published in *American Journal of Health Promotion*.

5

Natural Solutions

Surprising Food Cures: For High Cholesterol, Memory Loss, More

Everyone knows that some foods are healthier than others. What's not always clear is which foods are best for specific problems. When it comes to "food cures," most of what you read is questionable.

Here is what the science really shows…

HIGH CHOLESTEROL

In the past, oats (particularly oat bran) were touted as the best food for lowering LDL "bad" cholesterol. Oats help because they're high in soluble fiber, which helped lower my cholesterol by nearly 70 points. But they are not the only plaque-fighters in town.

Best food: **Benecol spread**…Lifetime Low Fat Cheese…Heart Wise Orange Juice…and other foods enriched with *phytosterols*, plant-based compounds that can lower LDL by up to 14%.

What to do: For people with high cholesterol, the National Cholesterol Education Program recommends 2 grams (g) of phytosterols daily. Serving sizes will vary, depending on the food. One tablespoon of Benecol spread will provide a little less than 1 g.

Also helpful: Avocado. It increases HDL, the "good" cholesterol that helps fight heart disease. One study found that people who added avocado to their diets had an increase in HDL of 11% in just one week.

CANCER

Many people think of broccoli and other cruciferous vegetables as the best cancer-fighting

---

David Grotto, RD, LDN, a registered dietitian and founder and president of Nutrition Housecall, LLC, a Chicago-based nutrition consulting firm that provides nutrition communications, lecturing and consulting services, along with personalized, at-home diet and lifestyle counseling. He is also author of *The Best Things You Can Eat* (Da Capo Lifelong). *DavidGrotto.com*

foods. These are excellent choices…but they're not the best.

***Best food:* Black beans.** They're high in *anthocyanins* and *triterpenoids*, potent antioxidants that can reduce cell-damaging inflammation and possibly increase the destruction of abnormal cells.

All beans with vivid colors—such as kidney beans (red), pinto beans (brown) and adzuki beans (deep red)—contain these cancer-fighting compounds.

What to do: Eat at least three cups of cooked beans a week. One study found that people who ate beans more than twice a week were 47% less likely to develop colon cancer than those who ate them less than once a week.

Also helpful: Tomatoes in all forms, including ketchup and tomato paste. Tomatoes are rich in *lycopene*, a compound that appears to reduce the risk for prostate cancer. Cooked tomatoes actually provide more lycopene than fresh. But don't overdo ketchup—it's loaded with sugar and salt.

MEMORY LOSS

If names are escaping you or you're always losing your keys, you may need to enhance your diet.

***Best food:* Blueberries.** Multiple studies have shown that patients at risk for dementia have improvements in memory when they eat more blueberries. The berries have *flavonoids* and other antioxidants that reduce inflammation. In the brain, inflammation can lead to a decline in memory and other types of cognitive functions.

What to do: Eat one cup of blueberries at least twice a week. If you don't like blueberries, you can substitute strawberries, raspberries and/or cranberries.

HYPOGLYCEMIA

This is a dangerous condition commonly associated with diabetes in which blood sugar falls below 70 milligrams per deciliter (mg/dL). It can happen periodically to some people with diabetes when the drugs used to treat the condition, such as insulin, work too well and cause an excessive drop in blood sugar.

***Best food:* Apricots.** Seven to eight dried apricot halves provide 15 g of a fast-acting carbohydrate when you have a crash in blood sugar. Fresh apricots also will help, but the carbohydrates (sugars) aren't as concentrated. And dried apricots are easy to store and take with you.

What to do: Eat seven or eight dried apricot halves as soon as you notice the symptoms of hypoglycemia, such as fatigue, dizziness, sweating and irritability.

Also helpful: Anything sugary, including a small amount of jelly beans. When your blood sugar is "crashing," you need sugar immediately. Toby Smithson, RD, LDN, a nutritionist who has had diabetes for 40 years, always carries jelly beans. They are even mentioned on the American Diabetes Association website.

Other sources of fast-acting sugars include honey and fruit juices.

STOMACH PAIN

Maybe you ate too much…or life's stresses affect your stomach first. You could take an antacid, but it doesn't always help and often causes side effects, including constipation or diarrhea.

***Best food:* Hot peppers.** You would not think that tongue-torching hot peppers would be good for your insides, but they are. They contain *capsaicin*, a proven pain reliever that works on the inside as well as externally.

One study, which looked at 30 patients with *dyspepsia* (stomach upset), found that those who consumed about one-half teaspoon of dried red pepper daily for five weeks had a 60% reduction in symptoms. Hot peppers also seemed to help with heartburn.

What to do: To help prevent stomach trouble, eat meals daily that contain "heat"—from chili powder, hot peppers, hot curry and the like. Or add a small amount of cayenne pepper to hot water for a spicy tea.

GUM DISEASE

Periodontal (gum) disease is the leading cause of tooth loss. Research shows that this infection and/or inflammation of the gums also can lead to heart disease.

***Best food:* Kefir.** This fermented milk is high in calcium (good for tooth enamel). It also contains the beneficial probiotic organism *Lactobacillus*, which secretes hydrogen peroxide and other substances that help kill the bacteria that cause gum disease.

What to do: Drink kefir in place of regular milk. Two or more one-cup servings daily have been linked to a reduced risk for tooth loss.

Also helpful: Live-culture yogurt. Many brands contain Lactobacillus.

Important: If you have any of these conditions, be sure to see your doctor.

---

6 Herbs That Slow Aging

Donald R. Yance, CN, MH, RH (AHG), clinical master herbalist and certified nutritionist. Yance is medical director at the Mederi Centre for Natural Healing in Ashland, Oregon...founder and president of the Mederi Foundation, a not-for-profit organization for professional education and clinical research in collaborative medicine...and president and formulator of Natura Health Products. He is author of *Adaptogens in Medical Herbalism* (Healing Arts) and *Herbal Medicine, Healing & Cancer* (Keats). *DonnieYance.com*

You can't escape aging. But many Americans are aging prematurely. *Surprising fact*: The US ranks 42nd out of 191 countries in life expectancy, according to the Census Bureau and the National Center for Health Statistics.

The leading cause of this rapid, premature aging is chronic stress. Stress is any factor, positive or negative, that requires the body to make a response or change to adapt. It can be psychological stress, including the modern addiction to nonstop stimulation and speed. Or it can be physiological stress—such as eating a highly processed diet...sitting for hours every day...absorbing toxins from food, water and air...and spending time in artificial light.

Chronic stress overwhelms the body's *homeostasis*, its inborn ability to adapt to stress and stay balanced, strong and healthy. The result?

Your hormonal and immune systems are weakened. Inflammation flares up, damaging cells. Daily energy decreases, fatigue increases and you can't manage life as effectively. You suffer from one or more illnesses, take several medications and find yourself in a downward spiral of worsening health. Even though you might live to be 75 or older, you're surviving, not thriving.

We can reduce stress by making lifestyle changes such as eating better and exercising. You also can help beat stress and slow aging with *adaptogens*. These powerful herbs balance and strengthen the hormonal and immune systems...give you more energy...and repair cellular damage, thereby increasing the body's ability to adapt to chronic stress.

Important: Adaptogens are generally safe, but always talk with your doctor before taking any supplement.

Six of the most powerful adaptogens...

ASHWAGANDHA

This adaptogen from Ayurveda (the ancient system of natural healing from India) can help with a wide range of conditions.

Main actions: It is energizing and improves sleep, and it can help with arthritis, anxiety, depression, dementia and various respiratory disorders, including asthma, bronchitis and emphysema.

Important benefit: It is uniquely useful for cancer—some researchers claim that it can help kill cancer cells...reduce the toxicity of chemotherapy (and prevent resistance to chemotherapeutic drugs)...relieve cancer-caused fatigue...and prevent recurrence.

ELEUTHERO

This is the most well-researched adaptogen (with more than 3,000 published studies). It often is called the "king" of adaptogens. (It was introduced in the US as "Siberian ginseng," but it is not a ginseng.)

Main actions: Along with providing energy and vitality, eleuthero protects the body against the ill effects of any kind of stress, such as extremes of heat or cold, excessive exercise and radiation. More than any other adaptogen, it helps normalize any type of physiological abnormality—including high or low blood pressure...and high or low blood sugar.

Important benefit: Eleuthero is a superb *ergogenic* (performance-enhancing) aid that can help anyone involved in sports improve strength and endurance and recover from injury.

GINSENG

Used as a traditional medicine in Asia for more than 5,000 years and the subject of more than 500 scientific papers, ginseng has two primary species—Panax ginseng (Korean or Asian ginseng) and Panax quinquefolius (also known as American ginseng).

Main actions: Ginseng is antifatigue and antiaging. It increases muscle strength and endurance and improves reaction times. It also strengthens the immune system and the heart and helps regulate blood sugar.

Important benefits: American ginseng can be beneficial for recovering from the common cold, pneumonia or bronchitis (particularly if you have a dry cough)…and chronic stress accompanied by depression or anxiety.

Korean or Asian ginseng is helpful for increasing physical performance, especially endurance and energy. It is effective for restoring adrenal function and neurological health such as learning and memory.

RHAPONTICUM

This herb contains more *anabolic* (strengthening and muscle-building) compounds than any other plant. It is my number-one favorite herb for increasing stamina and strength.

Main actions: It normalizes the central nervous and cardiovascular systems…improves sleep, appetite and mood…and increases the ability to work and function under stressful conditions.

Important benefit: This herb is wonderful for anyone recovering from injury, trauma or surgery.

RHODIOLA

Rhodiola has gained popularity over the past few years as studies show that it rivals eleuthero and ginseng as an adaptogen. It is widely used by Russian athletes to increase energy.

Main actions: Rhodiola increases blood supply to the muscles and the brain, enhancing physical and mental performance, including memory. It normalizes the cardiovascular system and protects the heart from stress. It also strengthens immunity.

Red flag: Don't use rhodiola alone—it is extremely astringent and drying. It is best used along with other adaptogens in a formula.

SCHISANDRA

This herb has a long history of use as an adaptogen in China, Russia, Japan, Korea and Tibet. The fruit is commonly used, but the seed is more powerful.

Main actions: Schisandra can treat stress-triggered fatigue…protect and detoxify the liver…and treat insomnia, depression and vision problems. It can also enhance athletic performance.

Important benefit: This adaptogen may help night vision—one study showed it improved adaptation to darkness by 90%.

COMBINATIONS ARE BEST

Any one herb has limitations in its healing properties. But a combination or a formula of adaptogenic herbs overcomes those limitations—because the adaptogens act in concert, making them more powerful.

This concept of synergy—multiple herbs acting together are more effective than one herb acting alone—is key to the effectiveness of the herbal formulas of traditional Chinese medicine (TCM) and Ayurveda. Both these ancient forms of medicine often employ a dozen or more herbs in their formulas.

But it's not only the combination of herbs that makes them effective—it's also the quality of the herbs. There are many more poor-quality adaptogens on the market than high-quality (or even mediocre-quality).

My advice: Look for an herbalist or herbal company that knows all about the source and content of the herbs it uses.

Example: Herbalist & Alchemist, a company that grows most of the herbs used in its products.

Or find a product sold to health practitioners, who then sell it to their patients—this type of product is more likely to be high-quality.

Example: MediHerb, from the company Standard Process.

Herbal formulas from my company, Natura Health Products, also meet these criteria for high quality.

You Can Have a Much Younger Body and Mind: A Few Simple Changes Can Turn Back the Clock

Mike Moreno, MD, who practices family medicine in San Diego, where he is on the board of the San Diego Chapter of the American Academy of Family Physicians. He is also author of *The 17 Day Plan to Stop Aging* (Free Press). *DrMikeDiet.com*

What is it that allows some people to remain robust and healthy well into their 80s and 90s while others become frail or virtually incapacitated? It's not just luck. New studies indicate that aging is largely determined by controllable factors.

Case in point: Millions of people have chronic inflammation, which has been linked to practically every "age-related" disease, including arthritis, heart disease and dementia.

Inflammation can usually be controlled with stress management, a healthful diet, weight loss (if needed) and other lifestyle changes, but there are other, even simpler, steps that can strengthen your body and brain so that they perform at the levels of a much younger person.

To turn back your biological clock…

CHALLENGE YOUR LUNGS

You should not be short of breath when you climb a flight of stairs or have sex, but many adults find that they have more trouble breathing as they age—even if they don't have asthma or other lung diseases.

Why: The lungs tend to lose elasticity over time, particularly if you smoke or live in an area with high air pollution. "Stiff" lungs cannot move air efficiently and cause breathing difficulty.

Simple thing you can do: Breathe slowly in and out through a drinking straw for two to three minutes, once or twice daily. Breathe only through your mouth, not your nose. This stretches the lungs, increases lung capacity and improves lung function.

Helpful: Start with an extra-wide straw, and go to a regular straw as you get used to breathing this way.

DRINK THYME TEA

When the lungs do not expand and contract normally (see above), or when the tissues are unusually dry, you're more likely to get colds or other infections, including pneumonia. The herb thyme contains *thymol*, an antioxidant that may help prevent colds, bronchitis and pneumonia and soothe various chronic respiratory problems such as asthma, allergies and emphysema.

Simple thing you can do: Add a cup of thyme tea to your daily routine. If you have a chronic or acute respiratory illness, drink two cups of thyme tea daily—one in the morning and one at night.

To make thyme tea: Steep one tablespoon of dried thyme (or two tablespoons of fresh thyme) in two cups of hot water for five minutes, or use thyme tea bags (available at most health-food stores).

If you take a blood thinner: Talk to your doctor before using thyme—it can increase risk for bleeding. Also, if you're allergic to oregano, you're probably allergic to thyme.

Another simple step: Drink at least six to eight eight-ounce glasses of water every day. This helps loosen lung mucus and flushes out irritants, such as bacteria and viruses.

LOWER YOUR HEART RATE

Heart disease is the leading cause of death in the US. The average American would live at least a decade longer if his/her heart pumped blood more efficiently.

Elite athletes typically have a resting heart rate of about 40 beats per minute, which is about half as fast as the average adult's resting heart rate. This reduced heart rate translates into lower blood pressure, healthier arteries and a much lower rate of heart disease. But you don't have to be an athlete to lower your heart rate—you just have to get a reasonable amount of aerobic exercise.

Simple thing you can do: Aim for a resting heart rate of 50 to 70 beats a minute—a good range for most adults. To do this, get 30 minutes of aerobic exercise, five days a week.

Good aerobic workouts include fast walking, bicycling and swimming. Even if you're not in great shape, regular workouts will lower your resting heart rate.

To check your pulse: Put your index and middle fingers on the carotid artery in your neck, and count the beats for 15 seconds, then multiply by four. Check your pulse before, during and after exercise.

WALK JUST A *LITTLE* FASTER

A study recently published in *The Journal of the American Medical Association* found that people who walked faster (at least 2.25 miles per hour) lived longer than those who walked more slowly.

Why: Faster walking not only lowers your heart rate and blood pressure but also improves cholesterol and inhibits blood clots, the cause of most heart attacks.

Simple thing you can do: You don't have to be a speed-walker, but every time you go for a walk, or even when you're walking during the normal course of your day, increase your speed and distance slightly.

Time yourself and measure your distance to monitor your progress, and create new goals every two weeks. Walk as fast as you can but at a speed that still allows you to talk without gasping, or if you're alone, you should be able to whistle. You'll notice improvements in stamina and overall energy within about two to three weeks.

TRY THIS FOR BETTER MEMORY

A study found that people who got even moderate amounts of exercise—either leisurely 30-minute workouts, five days a week, or more intense 20-minute workouts, three times a week—had better memories than those who exercised less.

Why: Physical activity increases oxygen to the brain and boosts levels of neurotransmitters that improve mood as well as memory.

Simple thing you can do: Try an aerobic dance class, such as Zumba or salsa, or power yoga. These activities provide the physical activity needed to boost memory...and learning and remembering complicated routines will

EASY-TO-DO...
Shake Up Your Mental Routines

In a study of about 3,000 older adults, those who performed mentally challenging tasks, such as memorizing a shopping list or surfing the Internet to research a complex topic, were found to have cognitive skills that were the typical equivalent of someone 10 years younger. You'll get the same benefit from other activities that promote thinking and concentration.

Why: These tasks trigger the development of new neurons in the brain, which boost cognitive function.

Simple thing you can do: Try to change your mental routines daily.

Fun ideas: If you're right-handed, use your left hand to write a note. Study the license number of the car in front of you, and see if you can remember it five minutes later. Listen to a type of music that's new to you. Rearrange your kitchen cabinets so that you have to think about where to find things. Overall, don't let your brain get into the rut of performing the same tasks over and over.

activate brain circuits and promote the growth of new brain cells for further brain benefit.

Bottom line: Just keep moving—even housecleaning and yard work count. *More on boosting brain function below...*

FIGHT BRAIN INFLAMMATION

You've probably heard that good oral hygiene can reduce the risk for heart disease. A new study suggests that it also can promote brain health. Researchers found that men and women over age 60 who had the lowest levels of oral bacteria did better on cognitive tests involving memory and calculations than those who had more bacteria.

Why: Bacteria associated with gum disease also cause inflammation in the brain. This low-level inflammation can damage cells in the brain and affect cognitive function.

Simple thing you can do: Brush your teeth after every meal—and floss twice a day. I also recommend using an antiseptic mouthwash, which helps eliminate bacteria.

Take a Walk and Call Me in the Morning: Exercise Can Work Better Than Drugs for Stroke, Pain, More

Jordan D. Metzl, MD, a sports medicine physician at the Hospital for Special Surgery in New York City. The author of *The Exercise Cure: A Doctor's All-Natural, No-Pill Prescription for Better Health & Longer Life* (Rodale), Dr. Metzl maintains practices in New York City and Greenwich, Connecticut, and is a medical columnist for *Triathlete Magazine*. He has run in 31 marathons and finished 11 Ironman competitions.

A recent study made international headlines when it found that exercise was just as effective as—or sometimes even outperformed—drugs when treating such conditions as heart disease and stroke.

The details: After examining about 300 medical trials involving more than 330,000 patients, Harvard researchers found that frequent exercise and powerful drugs, such as beta-blockers and blood thinners, provided very similar results. And in the case of stroke recovery, regular workouts were actually more effective than taking anticoagulant medications.

A troubling fact: Only one-third of clinicians "prescribe" exercise, which could not only boost the health of Americans significantly but also save the average patient thousands of dollars a year in medical costs.

My recommendations for condition-specific routines that contribute to a healthy, disease-free future...*

HEART ATTACK AND STROKE

Drugs such as *beta-blockers* help treat heart disease, but side effects can include fatigue, dizziness, an upset stomach and cold hands. Meanwhile, a single 40-minute session of aer-

*Be sure to check with your doctor before starting any fitness program. If your condition is severe, he/she may initially want you to use exercise as an adjunct to medication, not as a replacement. Never stop taking a prescribed drug without talking to your doctor. Caution: With any of these workouts, seek immediate medical attention if you experience chest pain, shortness of breath, nausea, blurred vision or significant bone or muscle pain while exercising.

obic exercise has been shown to lower blood pressure for 24 hours in hypertensive patients, and regular workouts can reduce both systolic (top number) and diastolic (bottom number) blood pressure by five to 10 points. Consistent exercise also can improve cholesterol levels.

Why exercise works: The heart is a muscle, and cardiovascular exercise forces it to pump longer and eventually makes it stronger, preventing the buildup of plaques that can rupture and lead to a heart attack or stroke. Many heart attack and stroke survivors are afraid to exercise, but it's crucial that they move past this fear. Survivors who exercise require less medication...need fewer major surgeries such as bypasses...and are 25% less likely to die from a second heart attack than their couch potato counterparts.

What to do: Five times a week, do 30 to 40 minutes of cardiovascular exercise at a "Zone 2" level of exertion (see next page). You have lots of choices for this exercise. Options include very fast walking, jogging, swimming, using an elliptical machine or recumbent bike, or taking an aerobics class. Pick an activity you enjoy to help you stay committed. After just six weeks, you'll likely have lower blood pressure, and by three months, your cholesterol levels should be improved.

Note: People with heart failure, a condition in which the heart cannot pump enough blood to the rest of the body, should avoid resistance exercises, such as push-ups and heavy weight lifting, that force muscles to work against an immovable or very heavy object. Such activities can put an excessive burden on the heart and cause further injury to it.

DEPRESSION

Exercise really is nature's antidepressant. Several studies have shown that working out is just as effective, if not more so, than medication when it comes to treating mild-to-moderate depression. Exercise also can help reduce the amount of medication needed to treat severe cases of depression...and even prevent depression in some people.

One Norwegian study that tracked about 39,000 people for two years found that those who reported doing moderate-to-high physical activity, including daily brisk walks for more than 30 minutes, scored significantly lower on depression and anxiety tests compared with nonexercisers.

There are so many effective antidepressant drugs, but they are frequently accompanied by bothersome side effects, including sexual dysfunction, nausea, fatigue and weight gain. And while most of these drugs can take a month to work, a single exercise session can trigger an immediate lift in mood, and consistent aerobic exercise will make an even more lasting positive impact.

What to do: The key is to boost your heart rate high enough to trigger the release of *endorphins*, feel-good chemicals that elicit a state of relaxed calm. Spend 30 to 45 minutes at a "Zone 3" level of exertion (see below), three to five days a week, to benefit.

You also may want to try exercising outdoors. A study published in *Environmental Science & Technology* found that outdoor exercise produces stronger feelings of revitalization, a bigger boost of energy and a greater reduction in depression and anger than exercising indoors.

Strength training also is effective in treating depression, as lifting weights releases endorphins and builds a sense of empowerment. For a tailored strength-training program, ask your doctor to recommend a physical therapist or personal trainer.

If it's difficult to motivate yourself to exercise when you're depressed, relying on a personal trainer—or a "workout buddy"—can help.

BACK PAIN

Back pain strikes roughly half of Americans. Pain medications are available, but many are addictive and merely mask the symptoms rather than address the underlying problem. Muscle relaxants cause drowsiness...overuse of *nonsteroidal anti-inflammatory drugs* (NSAIDs), such as ibuprofen, can lead to ulcers...and steroid injections, which can be given only a few times per year, can cause infection or nerve damage and long-term side effects such as osteoporosis or high blood pressure.

What to do: There's a very powerful low-tech solution—a foam roller. Widely available at sporting goods stores, these cylindrical rollers have a record of preventing and relieving back pain. With the cylinder on the floor, move various muscles (your hamstrings, quadriceps and lower back) back and forth over the foam roller slowly. Roll each area for one to two minutes. If you hit an especially tender spot, pause and roll slowly or hover in place until you feel a release. The entire routine should take about 10 minutes.

Note: Rolling muscles can feel uncomfortable and even painful at first. But the more painful it is, the more that muscle needs to be rolled. Frequency eases discomfort.

In addition to rolling your muscles, start a back- and core-strengthening program. Avoid using heavy weights, especially within an hour of waking—that's when your muscles are tighter and you're more likely to strain a muscle.

Instead, opt for higher repetitions (three sets of 15) with lighter weights (three to five pounds for women and eight to 10 pounds for men) to build endurance in your back and core, which is more protective than sheer strength.

A good core-strengthening exercise: The plank. In a push-up position, bend your elbows and rest your weight on your forearms (your body should form a straight line from shoulders to ankles). Pull your navel into your spine, and contract your abdominal muscles for 30 seconds, building up to a minute or two at a time. Perform the plank once a day.

THE 3 EXERCISE EXERTION ZONES

There are three main levels of exertion that are based on how easy it is for you to talk...

Zone 1: Talking is easy while moving. An example of Zone 1 exertion might be a moderate-paced walk.

Zone 2: Talking is tough but manageable. In Zone 2, there should be a little huffing and puffing but no gasping for air.

Zone 3: Carrying on a conversation is quite difficult at this level of exertion due to panting.

Starve Cancer to Death with the Ketogenic Diet

Thomas N. Seyfried, PhD, a professor of biology at Boston College and author of *Cancer as a Metabolic Disease: On the Origin, Management, and Prevention of Cancer* (Wiley). His numerous scientific articles have appeared in *Nature Medicine, Science, The Lancet Oncology, Proceedings of the National Academy of Sciences, Journal of Oncology, Cancer Letters, Journal of Neurochemistry* and many other medical and scientific journals.

A 65-year-old woman with brain cancer had surgery to remove the tumor, but the operation could not remove it all. The woman started following the *ketogenic diet*—a diet very high in fat, moderate in protein and very low in carbohydrate. She also had chemotherapy and radiation. After six weeks on the diet, a brain scan showed that the tumor had disappeared. A brain scan five months later showed it was still gone. However, the patient stopped the diet—and a scan three months later showed that the tumor had returned.

Yes, a special diet called the ketogenic diet can fight cancer. It is being used to manage brain cancer and advanced (metastatic) cancer, which is when the disease has spread beyond the original tumor to other parts of the body (such as breast cancer that spreads to the liver and bones). It may be effective in fighting most, if not all, cancers, but it must be done under the supervision of an experienced oncological nutritionist.

Here, what you need to know about this little-known therapy for cancer...

HOW IT WORKS

The ketogenic diet is very high in fat—the ratio is 4 grams (g) of fat to 1 g of protein/carbohydrate. It has long been used to control epilepsy and is offered as an epilepsy treatment at hundreds of hospitals and clinics around the world, including The Johns Hopkins Epilepsy Center, Mayo Clinic and Mattel Children's Hospital at UCLA.

It eases epilepsy by stabilizing neurons (brain cells). It does so by reducing glucose (blood sugar), the main fuel used by neurons, and increasing *ketones (beta-hydroxybutyric acid* and *acetoacetic acid)*, a by-product of fat metabolism used by neurons when glucose levels are low. Reducing glucose and increasing ketones play key roles in fighting cancer as well.

The typical American diet is about 50% to 60% carbohydrate (fruits, vegetables, breads, cereals, milk and milk products, and added sugars in sweetened foods and beverages). The body turns carbohydrate into glucose, which is used for energy.

Cancer cells gorge on glucose. Eating a ketogenic diet deprives them of this primary fuel, starving the cells, which stop growing or die. Also, ketones are a fuel usable by normal cells but not by cancer cells, so this, too, helps stop cancer growth. *In addition, the diet...*

• **Puts you into a metabolic state similar to that of fasting**—and fasting has repeatedly been shown to arrest cancer.

• **Lowers levels of insulin** (the glucose-regulating hormone) and insulin-like growth factor—both of which drive tumor growth.

CASE HISTORIES

The first case report about the ketogenic diet for cancer appeared in *Journal of the American College of Nutrition* in 1995. The ketogenic diet was used by two children with advanced, inoperable brain cancer who had undergone extensive, life-threatening radiation and chemotherapy. They both responded remarkably well to the diet.

A case report that I coauthored, published in *Nutrition & Metabolism* in 2010, told the story (see beginning of this article) of the 65-year-old woman with *glioblastoma multiforme*—the most common and most aggressive type of brain tumor, with a median survival of only about 12 months after diagnosis. Standard treatment—surgery to remove as much of the tumor as possible, plus radiation and/or chemotherapy—lengthens average survival time only a few months beyond that of people who aren't treated.

My viewpoint: In animal research, the ketogenic diet is the only therapeutic approach that deprives tumors of their primary fuel...stops tumor cells from invading other areas...stops the process of *angiogenesis* (blood supply to tumors)…and reduces inflammation, which drives cancer. The diet also could reduce the need for anticonvulsant and anti-inflammatory medications in brain cancer patients.

Considering how ineffective the current standard of care is for brain cancer (and for metastatic cancer), the ketogenic diet could be an attractive option for many cancer patients.

WORKING WITH AN EXPERT

The ketogenic diet for cancer is not a diet you should undertake on your own after reading a book or similar self-help materials. It requires the assistance of an oncological nutritionist or other health professional who is familiar with the use of the regimen in cancer patients. Ask your oncologist for a referral.

The most important aspects of the ketogenic diet include…

•**Measuring glucose and ketone levels.** For the management of cancer, blood glucose levels should fall between 55 milligrams per deciliter (mg/dL) and 65 mg/dL, and ketone levels between 3 millimoles (mmol) and 5 mmol. In order to monitor those levels—and adjust your diet accordingly—you need to use methods similar to those used by patients with diabetes. These methods include glucose testing several times a day with a finger stick and glucose strip…daily urine testing for ketones…and (more accurate) home blood testing for ketones, perhaps done weekly.

•**Starting with a water-only fast.** If you are in relatively good health (aside from the cancer, of course), it is best to start the ketogenic diet with a water-only fast for 48 to 72 hours, which will quickly put you in ketosis—the production of a therapeutic level of ketones. This fast should be guided by a health professional.

If you are fragile or in poor health, you can skip the water fast and initiate ketosis with the ketogenic diet, reducing carbohydrates to less than 12 g a day. This should produce ketosis within two or three weeks.

•**Macronutrient ratios and recipes.** Working with a nutritionist, you will find the fat/protein/carbohydrate ratio that works best for you to lower glucose and increase ketones…and the recipes and meal plan that consistently deliver those ratios. A food diary, a food scale and the use of a "KetoCalculator" (available on websites including *FlexibleKetogenic.com*) are necessary tools to implement the ketogenic diet.

Helpful: The oncological nutritionist Miriam Kalamian, EdM, MS, CNS, managed her own son's brain tumor with the ketogenic diet, and she counsels cancer patients around the world in the implementation of the diet. You can find more information on her website, *DietaryTherapies.com*.

CLINICAL TRIALS

Currently,* there are several clinical trials testing the ketogenic diet for cancer.

•**Brain cancer.** There are trials at Michigan State University and in Germany and Israel testing the diet's efficacy as a complementary treatment with radiation for recurrent glioblastoma…and by itself to improve the quality of life and survival time in patients with brain cancer. Michigan State University currently is recruiting patients for its trial.

Contact: Ken Schwartz, MD, 517-975-9547, e-mail: *Ken.Schwartz@hc.msu.edu*.

•**Pancreatic cancer.** A trial at Holden Comprehensive Cancer Center at University of Iowa is recruiting patients with pancreatic cancer for a trial using the ketogenic diet along with radiation and chemotherapy.

Contact: Heather Brown, RN, BAN, 319-384-7912, e-mail: *Heather-Brown@uiowa.edu*.

•**Lung cancer.** The University of Iowa also is recruiting lung cancer patients for a similar trial. The contact information is the same as for the trial on pancreatic cancer (see above).

You can find out more about these trials at *ClinicalTrials.gov*. Enter "Ketogenic Diet" into the search engine at the site for a complete listing of cancer trials and trials testing the ketogenic diet for other conditions, including ALS, Parkinson's disease and obesity.

More from Thomas N. Seyfried, PhD…

Can the Diet Prevent Cancer?

Cancer survivors and people with a family history of cancer may wonder if they

*At time of press.

should go on the ketogenic diet as a preventive measure. It is not necessary for people to follow the diet if they do not have cancer. A six-to-seven-day water-only fast done once or twice a year—*always under a doctor's supervision*—can be effective in reducing the risk for recurrent cancer in survivors and in those individuals with a family history of cancer. Fasting reduces glucose and elevates ketones.

Breath Test for Lung Cancer

New research suggests that breath temperature could serve as a marker for lung cancer. More studies are under way.

European Respiratory Society.

Coffee: More Good News

An analysis of more than 3,000 adults found that drinking one to three cups of caffeinated coffee daily reduced liver cancer risk by at least 40%.

Theory: Coffee has been shown to reduce the risk for diabetes, which has been linked to liver cancer.

Carlo La Vecchia, MD, head of epidemiology, Istituto di Ricerche Farmacologiche Mario Negri, Milan, Italy.

DID YOU KNOW THAT...

Stress May Cause Cancer to Spread?

The *ATF3 gene* is activated in response to stressful conditions and can cause immune cells to act erratically and give cancer an escape route from a tumor to other areas of the body.

Study by researchers at The Ohio State University, Columbus, published in *The Journal of Clinical Investigation*.

Trying to Quit Smoking? Load Up on Veggies and Fruit

People who ate the most fruits and vegetables were three times more likely to succeed at stop-smoking programs.

Possible reason: The high fiber and water content of produce fills the stomach—and because hunger is triggered by hormones such as the ones that cause nicotine cravings, it can be mistaken for the urge to smoke.

Study of 1,000 smokers by researchers from University at Buffalo, New York.

Tea That Works as Well as Some BP Meds!

In a recent finding, people with prehypertension or mild hypertension who drank three cups of hibiscus tea a day for six weeks had a 7.2-point drop in their systolic pressure (the top number), compared with a one-point drop for people who drank a placebo beverage. The higher a person's blood pressure was at the start of the study, the more benefit hibiscus tea provided.

Hibiscus has a fruity, tart taste. It is rich in antioxidants, including *anthocyanins, flavones, flavonols* and *phenolic acids*.

Study of people ages 30 to 70 by researchers at HNRCA Antioxidants Research Laboratory, Tufts University, Boston, reported in *Tufts University Health & Nutrition Letter*.

Lower BP with Yogurt

Yogurt may lower your risk of developing high blood pressure. People who consumed at least 2% of their daily calories from yogurt were 31% less likely to develop high blood pressure during a 14-year period than those who ate less or no yogurt. The 2% level is the equivalent of at least one six-ounce serving of yogurt every three days.

Study of data on 2,197 adults without high blood pressure, 913 of whom developed it over a 14-year period, by researchers from Jean Mayer USDA Human Nutrition Research Center on Aging, Tufts University, and Massachusetts General Hospital, both in Boston, published in *Hypertension*.

These Muffins Lower Blood Pressure

Adults with hypertension who ate muffins or bagels laced with 30 grams (g)—about three tablespoons—of flaxseed daily for six months had an average drop in blood pressure of 15 points in the top (systolic) reading and seven points in the bottom (diastolic) number.

Why: Flaxseed has omega-3s, which may help lower blood pressure.

Grant Pierce, MD, executive director of research, St. Boniface Hospital, Winnipeg, Manitoba, Canada.

Vegetarians Have Lower Risk for Heart Disease

People who don't eat meat are 32% less likely to be hospitalized or die from heart disease than people who eat meat.

Possible reason: Vegetarians tend to have lower blood pressure and cholesterol levels than meat eaters.

Francesca Crowe, PhD, nutritional epidemiologist, Oxford University, England, and leader of a study of 44,561 people, published in *The American Journal of Clinical Nutrition*.

Omega-3s for Longer Life

In a recent finding, people over age 65 with the highest blood levels of omega-3 fatty acids were 27% less likely to die of any cause during the study period…40% less likely to die of coronary heart disease…and 45% less likely to die of an arrhythmia than people with the lowest levels of omega-3s. Overall, those with the highest omega-3 levels lived an average of 2.2 years longer than those with the lowest levels.

Study of 2,692 people, average age 74, by researchers at Harvard School of Public Health, Boston, published in *Annals of Internal Medicine*.

Recent Finding: Berberine Can Lower Cholesterol by 30%

Berberine is a natural substance extracted from barberry, goldenseal, Oregon grape and other plants. It can be tried before going on cholesterol-lowering statin drugs, or it can be taken by statin users who need further cholesterol reductions.

Typical dosage: 500 milligrams (mg) to 1,000 mg daily. Consult your physician before starting any supplement.

Jacob Schor, ND, a naturopathic physician and primary health-care provider, Denver Naturopathic Clinic, Denver. He is author of a review of berberine published in *Natural Medicine Journal*.

Easy Ways Heart Patients Can Lower Risk for Death *by 55%!*

When cardiac patients talked with nurses and doctors about their treatment and other concerns…did relaxation exercises…and/or participated in music therapy during their hospitalization or rehabilitation, they were 55% less likely to die or have another cardiovascular event after two years, in a recent study.

How heart patients can get this type of support: Ask health-care providers more questions about their treatment…and seek out activities, such as music or exercise programs, group psychotherapy and meditation.

Zoi Aggelopoulou, PhD, RN, head of continuing education, NIMTS Veterans Hospital of Athens, Greece.

Olive Oil Can Keep Strokes Away

People who consistently added olive oil to their food in cooking and salad dressings were 41% less likely to suffer from an ischemic stroke than people who did not use olive oil, a recent study found. An *ischemic stroke*, in which blood flow to a part of the brain is blocked, is the most common kind of stroke.

Cécilia Samieri, PhD, researcher, department of epidemiology, Université Bordeaux Segalen, France, and leader of two studies on olive oil consumption and stroke risk, published in *Neurology*.

New Stroke Fighter: Red Peppers

Eating red peppers and other vitamin C–rich fruits and veggies may reduce your risk for *intracerebral hemorrhagic stroke* (a blood vessel rupture in the brain). What's so special about red peppers? At 190 milligrams (mg) per cup, they contain three times more vitamin C than an orange. Other good sources of vitamin C—broccoli and strawberries. Researchers believe that this vitamin may reduce stroke risk by regulating blood pressure and strengthening collagen, which promotes healthy blood vessels.

Stéphane Vannier, MD, neurologist at Pontchaillou University Hospital, Rennes, France, from research being presented at the annual meeting of the American Academy of Neurology.

How Pasta Can Cut Stroke Risk

For every 7 grams (g) of fiber daily, the risk for a first-time stroke decreased by 7%, in a recent analysis. One serving of whole-wheat pasta or two servings of fruits and vegetables contain about 7 g of fiber. Other high fiber sources include brown rice, spelt, quinoa and other whole-grain foods…almonds and other nuts…lentils and other dried beans.

Recommended daily fiber intake: People age 50 or younger, 38 g (men) and 25 g (women)…over age 50, 30 g (men) and 21 g (women).

Victoria J. Burley, PhD, senior lecturer in nutritional epidemiology at University of Leeds, England, and coauthor of an analysis of eight studies, published in *Stroke*.

Lower Stroke Risk with a Cup of This—or This…

Coffee and green tea were both found in a recent 13-year study of more than 83,000 adults (ages 45 to 74) to lower stroke risk.

Findings: People who drank at least one cup of coffee daily had about a 20% lower risk for stroke than those who seldom drank coffee. For green tea drinkers, a 14% reduction in stroke risk was found in those who consumed two to three cups daily versus those who rarely drank it.

A possible explanation: Coffee's glucose-lowering *chlorogenic acid* and green tea's antioxidant, anti-inflammatory *catechins* might provide the protective effect.

Yoshihiro Kokubo, MD, PhD, chief doctor, department of preventive cardiology, National Cerebral and Cardiovascular Center, Osaka, Japan.

Better Stroke Recovery

When 128 adult stroke survivors were divided into two groups, those who took a brisk outdoor walk for 30 minutes three times per week for three months reported a 16.7% greater improvement in their general health and ability to perform everyday physical activities, compared with those who had therapeutic massage but did no exercise. The walking group also was able to walk farther during a six-minute endurance test, indicating better mobility and physical fitness. Those who walked for 20 minutes daily also showed improvement.

Carron Gordon, PhD, lecturer in physical therapy, The University of the West Indies, Mona, Jamaica.

Easy Way to Reduce Risk for Dangerous Aneurysms

People who eat more than two servings of fruit daily are 25% less likely to develop *abdominal aortic aneurysms* (or AAAs) than people who eat little or no fruit—and they are 43% less likely to have aneurysms that rupture. If an AAA ruptures, life-threatening bleeding will occur.

Otto Stackelberg, MD, a PhD student at Institute of Environmental Medicine, Karolinska Institute, Stockholm, and lead author of a study of 80,426 people, published in *Circulation*.

Fight Diabetes Naturally: 3 Proven Nondrug Remedies

Bill Gottlieb, CHC, a health coach certified by the American Association of Drugless Practitioners. He also is author of 13 health books that have sold more than two million copies and former editor in chief of Rodale Books and Prevention Magazine Health Books. Based in northern California, he is author of *Defeat High Blood Sugar Naturally! Super-Supplements and Super-Foods Selected by America's Best Alternative Doctors* (Online Publishing & Marketing). *BillGottliebHealth.com*

Scientific research and the experience of doctors and other health professionals show that supplements and superfoods can be even more effective than drugs when it comes to preventing and treating diabetes. I reviewed thousands of scientific studies and talked to more than 60 health professionals about these glucose-controlling natural remedies. One is magnesium. Studies show that magnesium significantly reduces the risk for diabetes. (*Note*: High doses of magnesium can cause diarrhea.)

Here are three additional standout natural remedies…

Caution: If you are taking insulin or other medications to control diabetes, talk to your doctor before taking any supplement or changing your diet.

GYMNEMA

Gymnema has served as the standard anti-diabetes recommendation for the past 2,000 years from practitioners of *Ayurveda*, the ancient system of natural healing from India. Derived from a vinelike plant found in the tropical forests of southern and central India, the herb also is called gurmar, or "sugar destroyer"—if you chew on the leaf of the plant, you temporarily will lose your ability to taste sweets.

Modern science has figured out the molecular interactions underlying this strange phenomenon. The gymnemic acids in the herb have a structure similar to glucose molecules, filling up glucose receptor sites on the taste buds. They also fill up sugar receptors in the intestine, blocking the absorption of glucose.

And gymnemic acids stimulate (and even may regenerate) the cells of the pancreas that manufacture insulin, the hormone that ushers glucose out of the bloodstream and into cells.

Standout research: Studies published in *Journal of Ethnopharmacology* showed that three months of taking a unique gymnema extract, formulated over several decades by two Indian scientists, reduced fasting blood glucose (a blood sample is taken after an overnight fast) by 23% in people with *type 2 diabetes* (defined as fasting blood sugar levels of 126 milligrams per deciliter [mg/dL] or higher). People with *prediabetes* (defined as those with blood sugar levels of 100 mg/dL to 125 mg/dL) had a 30% reduction.

Important: The newest (and more powerful) version of this extract is called ProBeta, which is available at *PharmaTerra.com*. A naturopathic physician who uses ProBeta with his patients told me that the supplement can lower fasting glucose in the 200s down to the 120s or 130s after five to six months of use.

Typical daily dosage: ProBeta—two capsules, two to three times a day. Other types of gymnema—400 milligrams (mg), three times a day.

APPLE CIDER VINEGAR

Numerous studies have proved that apple cider vinegar works to control type 2 diabetes. Several of the studies were conducted by Carol Johnston, PhD, RD, a professor of nutrition at Arizona State University.

Standout scientific research: Dr. Johnston's studies showed that an intake of apple cider vinegar with a meal lowered insulin resistance (the inability of cells to use insulin) by an average of 64% in people with prediabetes and type 2 diabetes...improved insulin sensitivity (the ability of cells to use insulin) by up to 34%...and lowered postmeal spikes in blood sugar by an average of 20%. Research conducted in Greece, Sweden, Japan and the Middle East has confirmed many of Dr. Johnston's findings.

How it works: The acetic acid in vinegar—the compound that gives vinegar its tart flavor and pungent odor—blunts the activity of disaccharidase enzymes that help break down the type of carbohydrates found in starchy foods such as potatoes, rice, bread and pasta. As a result, those foods are digested and absorbed more slowly, lowering blood glucose and insulin levels.

Suggested daily intake: Two tablespoons right before or early in the meal. (More is not more effective.)

If you're using vinegar in a salad dressing, the ideal ratio for blood sugar control is two tablespoons of vinegar to one tablespoon of oil. Eat the salad early in the meal so that it disrupts the carb-digesting enzymes before they get a chance to work. Or dip premeal whole-grain bread in a vinaigrette dressing.

SOY FOODS

A new 10-year study published in *Journal of the American Society of Nephrology* found that the mortality rate for people with diabetes and kidney disease was more than 31%. Statistically, that makes kidney disease the number-one risk factor for death in people with diabetes.

Fortunately, researchers have found that there is a simple way to counter kidney disease in diabetes—eat more soy foods.

Standout scientific research: Dozens of scientific studies show that soy is a nutritional ally for diabetes patients with kidney disease. But the best and most recent of these studies, published in *Diabetes Care*, shows that eating lots of soy can help reverse signs of kidney disease, reduce risk factors for heart disease—and reduce blood sugar, too.

The study involved 41 diabetes patients with kidney disease, divided into two groups. One group ate a diet with protein from 70% animal and 30% vegetable sources. The other group ate a diet with protein from 35% animal sources, 35% textured soy protein and 30% vegetable proteins. After four years, patients eating the soy-rich diet had lower levels of several biomarkers for kidney disease. (In another, smaller experiment, the same researchers found that soy improved biomarkers for kidney disease in just seven weeks.) In fact, the health of the participants' kidneys actually improved, a finding that surprised the researchers, since *diabetic nephropathy*

95

(diabetes-caused kidney disease) is considered to be a progressive, irreversible disease.

Those eating soy also had lower fasting blood sugar, lower LDL cholesterol, lower total cholesterol, lower triglycerides and lower *C-reactive protein*, a biomarker for chronic inflammation.

How it works: Substituting soy for animal protein may ease stress on the delicate filters of the kidneys. Soy itself also stops the overproduction of cells in the kidney that clog the filters…boosts the production of *nitric oxide*, which improves blood flow in the kidneys… and normalizes the movement of minerals within the kidneys, thus improving filtration.

Suggested daily intake: The diabetes patients in the study ate 16 grams (g) of soy protein daily.

Examples: Four ounces of tofu provide 13 g of soy protein…one soy burger has 13 g…one-quarter cup of soy nuts, 11 g…one-half cup of shelled edamame (edible soybeans in the pod), 11 g…one cup of soy milk, 6 g.

WHAT'S WRONG WITH DIABETES DRUGS?

Doctors typically try to control high blood sugar with a glucose-lowering medication such as *metformin* (Glucophage), a drug most experts consider safe. But other diabetes drugs may not be safe.

Example #1: Recent studies show that *sitagliptin* (Januvia) and *exenatide* (Byetta) double the risk for hospitalization for *pancreatitis* (inflamed pancreas) and triple the risk for pancreatic cancer.

Example #2: *Pioglitazone* (Actos) can triple the risk for eye problems and vision loss, double the risk for bone fractures in women and double the risk for bladder cancer.

Catch-Up Sleep Helps Stave Off Diabetes

When a group of 19 nondiabetic men who usually sleep about six hours a night during the week spent three days in a sleep lab where they slept 10 hours every night, their in-

sulin sensitivity improved, lowering their risk for type 2 diabetes. Regular sleep, just like good eating habits, keeps insulin levels balanced.

If you get less than seven hours of sleep a night during the week: Plan to get more sleep every night, but if you can't, get more on weekends.

Peter Liu, MD, PhD, principal investigator, division of endocrinology, metabolism & nutrition, Los Angeles Biomedical Research Institute, Harbor-UCLA Medical Center.

Tasty Fruit Protects Against Metabolic Syndrome

Metabolic syndrome is a cluster of symptoms that includes increased blood pressure, high blood sugar, excess body fat around the waist, low HDL and high blood triglycerides, all linked to inflammation. The syndrome raises the risk for heart disease, stroke and type 2 diabetes.

Study finding: Obesity-prone rats that were fed red, green and black grapes for 90 days had significantly lower inflammation markers, especially in liver and abdominal fat tissue.

Best: Eat 15 to 20 grapes per day.

E. Mitchell Seymour, PhD, a research investigator, department of cardiac surgery, University of Michigan.

Walnuts May Cut Diabetes Risk

Women who ate at least eight ounces of walnuts a month were 24% less likely to develop type 2 diabetes than women who ate none, in a recent finding.

Possible reason: Walnuts are especially rich in polyunsaturated fats, which may help prevent diabetes. They also have high amounts of dietary fiber, antioxidants and other beneficial substances. These results most likely apply to men, too.

Frank Hu, MD, PhD, professor of nutrition and epidemiology, Harvard School of Public Health, and professor of medicine, Harvard Medical School, both in Boston. He is senior author of a study on walnuts and diabetes published in *Journal of Nutrition*.

More Red Meat Means Higher Diabetes Risk

People who increased their red-meat consumption by more than half a serving a day over a four-year period had a 48% higher risk for type 2 diabetes in the following four years. People who reduced their consumption by at least half a serving daily had a 14% lower risk for type 2 diabetes.

Red-meat consumption has been linked to diabetes before, but this is the first analysis to observe the results of increases or decreases in consumption over time.

Analysis of three studies involving a total of more than 149,000 people by researchers at National University of Singapore, published online by *JAMA Internal Medicine*.

Surprising Link to Diabetes

Women who had low levels of the hormone *melatonin* were twice as likely to develop type 2 diabetes as women with high levels. It is not yet clear if low melatonin causes type 2 diabetes, so taking melatonin supplements is not yet recommended.

Study of 370 women who developed type 2 diabetes from 2000 to 2012 by researchers at Brigham and Women's Hospital, Boston, published in *The Journal of the American Medical Association*.

Brown Rice Lowers Risk for Diabetes

Eating brown rice twice a week can lower risk for type 2 diabetes by 11%. Brown rice has more fiber and magnesium than white rice and does not cause a significant rise in post-meal blood sugar.

If you don't like the taste of brown rice: Try mixing brown and white rice together until you become more accustomed to the taste of brown rice.

Qi Sun, MD, ScD, assistant professor, department of nutrition, Harvard School of Public Health, Boston, and leader of a study of 197,228 people, published in *Archives of Internal Medicine*.

Supplement Fights Off Diabetes

Adults with type 2 diabetes who took 250 milligrams (mg) daily of the polyphenol *resveratrol* (along with diabetes medications) for three months had significantly more improvement in their systolic (or top number) blood pressure readings, blood glucose and total cholesterol levels compared with those who took only diabetes medications.

If you have type 2 diabetes: Ask your doctor if a resveratrol supplement is right for you.

MJ Nanjan, PhD, professor, JSS College of Pharmacy, Ootacamund, Tamil Nadu, India.

Coffee and Tea Are Good for the Liver

Caffeine has been found to stimulate the metabolization of lipids (fats) stored in liver cells and decrease the fatty liver of mice. People at risk for or diagnosed with nonalcoholic fatty liver disease could benefit from drinking up to four cups of coffee or tea a day.

Study by researchers at Duke-NUS Graduate Medical School's Cardiovascular and Metabolic Disorders Program, Singapore, and Duke University School of Medicine, Durham, North Carolina, published in *Hepatology*.

The Secret Thief of Good Health: It's Slowly Stealing Your Muscles, Your Strength—and Maybe Even Your Life

Michael J. Grossman, MD, a specialist in antiaging and regenerative medicine. Dr. Grossman is medical director of BodyLogicMD of Irvine, California, which focuses on bioidentical hormones, nutritional support and stress reduction. He is author of *The Vitality Connection: Ten Practical Ways to Optimize Health and Reverse the Aging Process* (Vitality). *DrMichaelGrossman.com*

You probably know all about osteoporosis, the gradual, age-related loss of bone.

What you may not know: There also is an age-related loss of muscle mass, strength and function—a condition called *sarcopenia*. And it is a problem for all of us as we age.

EASY-TO-DO...

Have a Beer for Your Health!

Good news for brewski lovers—researchers are finding that beer, like wine, is an excellent source of health-promoting *flavonoids*. Beer also provides a good amount of B vitamins and bone-strengthening *silicon*—and may even reduce risk for kidney stones by a whopping 41%!

Just go easy: No more than one (12-ounce) glass for women per day and two for men. The darker the beer, the more flavonoids you get!

Sandra Woodruff, MS, RD, LDN, registered dietitian and nutrition consultant located in Tallahassee, Florida.

Sarcopenia generally starts at age 40. By the time you're 50, you're losing 1% to 2% of your muscle mass every year. And as you lose muscle, you lose strength.

For instance: Starting in your 40s, leg strength typically drops by 10% to 15% per decade until you're 70, after which it declines by 25% to 40% per decade.

But you don't have to become physically debilitated to suffer the devastating effects of muscle loss. When you have less muscle, you have more fat—and fat cells produce inflammatory compounds that drive many deadly chronic diseases, such as heart disease and cancer.

The good news: Starting today, there are many actions you can take to slow, stop and even reverse sarcopenia...

WHAT YOU NEED TO KNOW

When sarcopenia is at its worst—what some experts call pathological sarcopenia—you become weak, walk slowly, fall easily, are less likely to recover from an illness and are more likely to die from any cause. That degree of sarcopenia afflicts 14% of people ages 65 to 75 and 45% of those 85 and older.

Sarcopenia is linked to a 77% increased risk for cardiovascular disease. It's also linked to higher death rates in breast cancer survivors and older people with lymphoma.

With less muscle, you burn less glucose (blood sugar), so it becomes harder to prevent, control or reverse type 2 diabetes, a disease of chronically high blood sugar that can plague your life with complications such as vision loss, nerve pain and kidney failure. Diabetes also doubles your risk for heart attack, stroke and Alzheimer's disease.

Studies also link sarcopenia to triple the risk for osteoporosis, a fourfold increase in postoperative infections and extreme menopausal symptoms.

NUTRITION

The right diet and supplements can fight muscle loss...

•**Eat protein-rich food daily.** Increasing the amount of protein in your diet not only can help stop the breakdown of muscle, but it also helps build new muscle.

Scientific evidence: In a three-year study, published in *The American Journal of Clinical Nutrition*, older people who ate the most protein lost 40% less muscle compared with people who ate the least.

My advice: Every day, eat at least four ounces of protein-rich food, such as lean beef, fish, chicken or turkey. A four-ounce serving is about the size of a deck of cards.

Helpful: Whey protein, from milk, is rich in *branched-chain amino acids.* These three amino acids (*leucine, isoleucine* and *valine*) comprise 35% of muscle protein and are uniquely effective in building muscle. Look for a protein powder derived from *whey protein*, and use at least one scoop daily in a smoothie or shake. You also can get some of these amino acids by eating Greek yogurt, nuts, seeds, cheese and hard-boiled eggs.

• **Take a vitamin D supplement.** Vitamin D is widely known to stop bone loss, but it also stops muscle loss.

Scientific evidence: A study published in *Journal of Internal Medicine* linked low blood levels of vitamin D to a four-fold increase in the risk for frailty, a problem of old age that includes pathological sarcopenia.

Vitamin D works to protect the muscles by decreasing chronic, low-grade inflammation, which contributes to the breakdown and loss of muscle protein.

Unfortunately, an estimated nine out of 10 Americans have suboptimal blood levels of vitamin D, below 30 nanograms per milliliter (ng/mL). A simple blood test can reveal your vitamin D level. Research shows that people with a blood level of 55 ng/mL or higher of vitamin D have 50% less heart disease and cancer than people with a blood level of 20 ng/ml or below. It also reduces the risk of falling by 19%.

My advice: I recommend the same 55 ng/mL level to control muscle loss. To achieve that level, most people need to take a daily vitamin D supplement that supplies 3,000 international units (IU) to 5,000 IU.

• **Take fish oil.** Like vitamin D, fish oil works to protect muscle by reducing the chronic inflammation that damages muscle cells.

Scientific evidence: In one study in *The American Journal of Clinical Nutrition*, women who participated in strength-training and also took fish oil had much stronger muscles after three months than women who did only strength-training.

My advice: To protect and build muscle, I recommend a supplement containing 1,000 milligrams (mg) of omega-3 fatty acids, with 400 mg of EPA and 300 mg of DHA. Take it twice daily.

• **Consider creatine.** Creatine is an amino acid–like compound found mostly in red meat, pork and fish, such as salmon, tuna and herring. More than 70 clinical studies show that regularly taking a creatine supplement can help build muscle and increase strength.

However: The nutrient works to build muscle only if you are exercising—without that regular challenge to the muscles, supplemental creatine has no effect.

My advice: If you are exercising regularly, take 3 grams (g) of creatine daily.

EXERCISE

Regular exercise is one of the best ways to stop or even reverse muscle loss. You need both aerobic exercise and resistance exercise (which stresses the muscles, causing them to get stronger). *My advice…*

• **For aerobics, use your lower and upper body.** Walking is a good exercise, but it builds only lower-body strength. Also include aerobic exercise that uses the lower and upper body, such as tennis, ballroom dancing or working out on an elliptical machine. Try to participate in 30 to 60 minutes of aerobic exercise five or more days a week.

• **For resistance training, work all your muscles.** I recommend resistance exercise three times a week, concentrating on the different muscle groups at each session—chest and triceps…back and biceps…and legs and shoulders. If you don't like weight-lifting, try another form of resistance exercise, such as resistance bands.

HORMONES

As you age, you lose bone, muscle—and hormones. And many of those hormones, in particular testosterone, are crucial for building muscle in both men and women. (Women manufacture testosterone in the ovaries and adrenal glands.) *Estrogen* and *dehydroepiandrosterone* (DHEA) also play a role in creating and maintaining muscle.

My advice: Find a doctor who is trained in antiaging medicine and *bioidentical hormone replacement therapy* (BHRT), which uses compounds that are identical to the hormones that your body manufactures rather than synthetics. Ask the doctor to test your hormone levels and determine if BHRT is right for you.

Little-Known Therapy for Knee Osteoarthritis

Sugar injections may help knee osteoarthritis that has not responded to physical therapy or to *nonsteroidal anti-inflammatory drugs* (NSAIDs). The reason *dextrose prolotherapy*—an injection of a sugar solution into and around the knee joint to relieve pain and stiffness—helps is not known. The shots may trigger a healing response.

To find an experienced prolotherapist: Visit the website of the American Association of Orthopaedic Medicine (*AAOMed.org*, under "Patients," click on "Find Experienced Orthopaedic Doctors").

Sugar injections typically are not covered by insurance.

David Rabago, MD, assistant professor and associate research director of department of family medicine, University of Wisconsin, Madison, and leader of a study in *Annals of Family Medicine*.

The Amazing Pain-Relieving Diet: Ease Your Aches with These Tasty Foods

Heather Tick, MD, the Gunn-Loke Endowed professor for integrative pain medicine at the University of Washington, Seattle, where she is a clinical associate professor in the department of family medicine and the department of anesthesiology and pain medicine. She is author of *Holistic Pain Relief: Dr. Tick's Breakthrough Strategies to Manage and Eliminate Pain* (New World Library).

It's no joke to say that pain really hurts us—because it makes us less productive, less happy and less able to spring back from other conditions. And it leads millions of Americans to a steady intake of dangerous and, in many cases, counterproductive drugs, such as powerful painkillers, antidepressants and narcotics.

Chronic pain (that which lasts for longer than six months) can occur anywhere in the body—in the muscles…joints…head…stomach…bladder…and so on. And though some people find it hard to believe, there are more Americans affected by pain—whether it is from arthritis, headaches, nerve damage or some other condition—than diabetes, heart disease and cancer combined.

What's the answer? Fortunately, there are a variety of highly effective, evidence-based ways to turn your diet into a pain-fighting machine.

HEAL YOUR DIGESTIVE TRACT

Pain anywhere in the body is almost always accompanied, and made worse, by inflammation. The inflammatory response, which includes the release of pain-causing chemicals, can persist in the body for decades, even when you don't have redness or other visible signs.

Common cause: A damaged mucosa in the innermost lining of the intestines. The damage can be caused from food sensitivities…a poor diet with too much sugar or processed foods…or a bacterial imbalance, among many other factors. A weakened mucosal lining can allow toxic molecules to enter the body, where they then trigger persistent inflammation.

If you suffer from chronic pain—particularly pain that's accompanied by intermittent bouts of constipation and/or diarrhea—your first step should be to heal the damaged intestinal tissue. *To do this...*

• **Eat a variety of fermented foods.** They are rich in *probiotics*, which will help the mucosa heal. Most people know that live-culture yogurt is one good source of probiotics...but yogurt alone doesn't supply enough. You can and should get more probiotics by eating one or more daily servings of fermented foods such as sauerkraut or kimchi (Asian pickled cabbage).

Because highly processed fermented foods—such as canned sauerkraut—will not give you the live probiotics you need, select a product that requires refrigeration even in the grocery store. You also can take a probiotic supplement, which is especially important for people who take antibiotics or who don't eat many fermented foods.

• **Cut way back on sugar.** A high- or even moderate-sugar diet, which includes the "simple sugars" in refined carbohydrates such as bread and other baked goods as well as white rice, many breakfast cereals and most juices, increases levels of *cytokines*, immune cells that cause inflammation.

• **Limit red meat.** Red meat, especially the organic, grass-fed kind, does have valuable nutrients and can be part of a healthy diet. But eaten in excess (more than three ounces daily), red meat increases inflammation. If you eat more than the amount above, cut back. At least half of each meal should be foods grown in the ground—such as vegetables, nuts and seeds. One-quarter should be whole grains, and the rest should be protein, which doesn't always mean animal protein. Other good protein sources include lentils, beans and tempeh.

EAT OTHER FOODS THAT TURN OFF THE FIRE

Avoiding inflammatory foods is only half the equation—the other half, if you want to reduce pain, is to eat foods that can reduce the inflammation in your body.

If you are expecting an exotic recommendation here, sorry—because what you really need to eat to reduce inflammation in your body is lots and lots of vegetables—raw, steamed, sautéed, baked or roasted. Vegetables contain *cellulose*, a type of fiber that binds to fats and some inflammatory substances and carries them out of the body in the stools. The antioxidants in vegetables, such as the *lycopene* in tomatoes and the *indole-3-carbinol* in crucifers such as broccoli, cabbage and Brussels sprouts, further reduce inflammation.

This part of your pain-reduction strategy is pretty simple, really: There is not a vegetable on the planet that will worsen your pain...and most of them, if not all, will help reduce your pain. For easy, general dietary guidelines, just follow the well-known, traditional Mediterranean-style diet plan, which includes plenty of vegetables, fish (fish oil is anti-inflammatory), small amounts of red meat and olive oil.

Helpful: It's advisable to avoid sweets, but make an exception for an ounce or two of dark chocolate daily. Chocolate that contains at least 70% cocoa is very high in antioxidants. It reduces inflammation, improves brain circulation and lowers blood pressure, according to research. And because it's a sweet treat, it will make it easier for you to say "no" to the nasty stuff like cake, cookies and ice cream.

DON'T FORGET SPICES

Turmeric and ginger are great spices for pain relief and can replace salty and sugary flavor enhancers. Ginger tea is a tasty pain fighter. Also, garlic and onions are high in sulphur, which helps in healing.

COFFEE: YES...BUT

Even though some people can stop a migraine by drinking a cup of coffee when their symptoms first start, too much coffee (the amount varies from person to person) can have a negative effect on other types of pain. It increases the body's output of *adrenaline*, the stress hormone, as well as inflammation. It also masks fatigue, so you're more likely to push yourself too hard.

Dr. Tick recommends: Do not drink more than one or two cups of coffee daily. I love coffee, but limit myself to that amount...and I give it up for about a week once every three months. This stops me from getting addicted. Reducing coffee gradually over several days also helps prevent a caffeine-withdrawal headache.

Reflexology Really Works for Pain

Reflexology can reduce pain by 40% and may be as effective as drugs, a recent study claims. Reflexology involves applying pressure to specific points on the hands, feet or ears—that is believed to stimulate the body's production of pain-relieving *endorphins* in the brain and spinal cord.

Study of reflexology by researchers at University of Portsmouth, England, published in *Complementary Therapies in Clinical Practice*.

Common Vitamin Slows Alzheimer's Symptoms

When people with mild-to-moderate Alzheimer's took a high dose of vitamin E —2,000 international units (IU) daily—they had slower declines in activities of daily living, such as dressing and bathing without help, than people who didn't take the vitamin or took the Alzheimer's drug *memantine* (Namenda). Vitamin E provided just over a six-month delay in the disease's progression over a two-year period.

Note: A doctor should be consulted before this therapy is tried—vitamin E may increase risk for bleeding and/or interact with various medications.

Maurice Dysken, MD, geriatric psychiatrist, Minneapolis VA Health Care System, Minnesota.

More Good News About Cocoa

Polyphenols in cocoa may protect against brain conditions such as Alzheimer's and Parkinson's diseases by activating the *brain-derived neurotrophic factor* (BDNF) *pathway*, which is vital for the survival of neurons.

Study by researchers at University of L'Aquila, Italy, Temple University, Philadelphia, and other universities, published in *Journal of Cellular Biochemistry*.

White Wine Has Health Benefits, Too

Red wine has more heart-healthy *polyphenols*, which provide antioxidant protection and ease inflammation, than white wine, but white has more brain-saving compounds called *hydroxycinnamates* than red.

Caution: Men should have no more than two five-ounce glasses of wine a day…women should have no more than one glass a day.

Men's Health. MensHealth.com

Fight Dementia by Learning a Second Language

In a study of people with dementia, bilingual people developed dementia about five years later than people who spoke just one language.

Possible reason: Switching from one language to another in the course of routine communication helps to stimulate the brain.

Study of the medical records of 648 people, average age 66, by researchers at University of Edinburgh, Scotland, and Nizam's Institute of Medical Sciences, Hyderabad, India, published in *Neurology*.

Help for Depression: The "Positive" Memory Strategy

The *method-of-loci strategy* teaches people who suffer from depression to associate vivid positive memories with physical objects or locations—such as buildings they see every day on their way to work, for example. This technique makes it easier for depressed individuals to call up self-affirming memories that boost their mood long-term. Tips for learning this strategy are available online—type "method of loci" into any search engine.

Study of depressed patients by researchers at Medical Research Council Cognition and Brain Sciences Unit, Cambridge, UK, published in the journal *Clinical Psychological Science*.

Better Stress Buster

When adults used a skill called *cognitive reappraisal* (reframing a situation), depression eased when the stress was beyond their control (such as a sick spouse). But if the stress was controllable (such as job duties), the technique made depression worse.

Reason: You may need to take action to address the root causes of stressful situations, if possible, instead of simply changing your emotional response to them.

Allison Troy, PhD, assistant professor of psychology, Franklin & Marshall College, Lancaster, Pennsylvania.

A Tea That Fights Depression

People who consumed two to three cups of green tea daily were about 40% less likely to report feeling depressed than those who drank one cup a day or less, in a recent finding.

Possible reason: The antioxidants in green tea may help reduce levels of *cortisol*, a stress hormone associated with depression. Fresh-brewed green tea delivers more antioxidants than bottled tea.

Studies of green tea by researchers at Tohoku University, Sendai, Japan, published in *The American Journal of Clinical Nutrition*, and Rutgers University, New Brunswick, New Jersey, published in *Cancer Epidemiology, Biomarkers & Prevention*.

The Color of Your Night-Light May Affect Your Mood

Light-sensitive cells in the eye send signals to mood-regulating parts of the brain.

Recent finding: Depression-like symptoms in animals exposed to dim white or blue light at night were twice as great as in animals exposed to red or no light.

Implications for humans: Reduce exposure to blue/green or white light starting two to three hours before bedtime. Use night-lights and bedside clocks that emit dim red light.

Randy J. Nelson, PhD, professor and chair of neuroscience at The Ohio State University Wexner Medical Center, Columbus, and author of a study published in *The Journal of Neuroscience*.

EASY-TO-DO...

Eat Yogurt to Boost Your Mood

Probiotic foods that contain healthy gut bacteria, such as yogurt, were recently found in a meta-analysis to help relieve chronic fatigue, depression and other mood disorders.

Theory: "Good" bacteria help produce serotonin and other beneficial brain chemicals.

Researchers are still studying exactly how much yogurt you need to get these benefits.

Ted Dinan, MD, PhD, professor of psychiatry, University College Cork, Ireland.

Does Dark Chocolate Have Less Sugar Than Regular?

Don't assume that dark or "semi-sweet" chocolate contains less sugar than regular chocolate, even when it is marketed with terms that imply less sugar.

Examples: Hershey's Milk Chocolate has 15 grams (g) of sugar per ounce...Hershey's Special Dark chocolate has 14 g, a tiny difference. Three kinds of Hershey's chips—Milk Chocolate, Special Dark, and Semi-Sweet—all contain the same amount of sugar.

Self-defense: Favor brands with much less sugar, such as Ghirardelli 72% cacao, which contains 7 g of sugar per ounce.

Cathy Charles, coauthor of *Gluten-Free Baking with the Culinary Institute of America* (Adams Media Corp.) and the upcoming *Nutritional Baking* (Culinary Institute/Wiley).

Better Than Meat! Proteins You Should Be Eating...

Dawn Jackson Blatner, RD, a registered dietitian in private practice in Chicago. She is author of *The Flexitarian Diet: The Mostly Vegetarian Way to Lose Weight, Be Healthier, Prevent Disease, and Add Years to Your Life* (McGraw-Hill) and the nutrition consultant for the Chicago Cubs. As a flexitarian expert, she gets most of her protein from plants. *DawnJacksonBlatner.com*

When it comes to getting enough muscle-building protein, most people do just fine by having a juicy steak, a generous chicken breast or a tasty fish fillet a few times a week.

The problem is, most Americans need to get more protein from other foods and a little less from animals, since research suggests a more plant-based diet reduces the risk for chronic health problems, such as heart disease, diabetes, cancer and obesity. Balancing animal protein (from meat, for example) with protein from plants and other foods is one of the simplest ways to improve your diet. Of course, you don't have to be a vegetarian or vegan to enjoy meat-free protein foods.* *My favorite options...*

FOR BREAKFAST

If you want protein in the morning, you may reach for some eggs and sausage. But not so fast! *Here are some other great ideas...*

• **Quinoa.** Often used as a dinner side dish, quinoa also can be eaten as a great nutty-tasting grain for breakfast. Technically a seed, quinoa wins points for being a high-protein whole grain with 8 g per cooked cup. It's also naturally gluten-free—a bonus for those who can't safely eat most oatmeal, since oats may be contaminated in the field or through processing with gluten-containing foods.

For a great protein-packed breakfast: Have a bowl of quinoa with chopped fruit and nuts...or top it with sautéed spinach and a poached egg. To make things easier, there's nothing wrong with buying precooked, frozen quinoa—it is now sold at lots of markets.

• **Cottage cheese.** It is not a plant-based food, but it's an excellent source of protein. In fact, you may be surprised to find out that a half cup of 1% milk fat cottage cheese contains more than twice as much protein (14 g) as an egg.

Caution: Most cottage cheese is high in sodium, so be sure to stick to the low-sodium variety if you are on a low-sodium diet.

Not a fan of curds? Puree it. Make "whipped cottage cheese" in your blender and flavor it with cinnamon for a delicious spread to smear on apple slices or add chives and basil for a veggie dip.

FOR LUNCH OR DINNER

Want a quick and easy protein for lunch or dinner? Tofu or beans are excellent choices, but you may want to try something new. *Here's what I suggest...*

• **Split peas.** A bowl of delicious split pea soup will add some variety. Dried peas have four times more protein than brown rice—

---

*Adults over age 19 should consume 0.37 grams (g) of protein per pound of body weight, according to the Institute of Medicine (IOM). *Example*: If you weigh 150 pounds, you need about 55 g of protein daily.

and four times more fiber. If you don't want to cook your own split pea soup, certain prepared varieties are worth trying.

Good choices: Fantastic Foods Split Pea Soup Mix and Tabatchnick Split Pea Soup.

•**Spinach.** Most people don't realize that cooked spinach—at 4 g per half cup—offers more protein than most other vegetables. Not only that, spinach is incredibly nutrient-dense—it contains antioxidant vitamins A, C and E and is a rich plant source of iron and calcium.

To get a lot of spinach, buy it frozen. Since frozen spinach is precooked, it's easier to eat more—toss it into soups, pasta sauce, bean burritos or lasagna—than if you are downing it raw in, say, a salad. Frozen spinach is picked at peak season before freezing, so it retains its nutrients for months. And it's a great value!

FOR SNACKS

You already know that nuts are excellent protein-rich snacks. *Some other options you may want to try...*

•**Edamame.** These young green soybeans are a versatile protein source. One-half cup of frozen edamame contains 6 g of protein...and a quarter cup of roasted soybeans has an impressive 15 g (roasting concentrates the protein by removing the water). Soy foods contain phytochemicals that may help slow or protect against certain cancers.

•**Hummus.** Here's a great way to spice up the hefty protein kick you get from beans.

What to do: Blend two 15.5-ounce cans of rinsed, drained garbanzo beans with one-quarter cup each tahini, lemon juice and water. Add one tablespoon each of olive oil and Frank's RedHot Cayenne Pepper Sauce (or any brand of pepper sauce you like). Cayenne pepper contains pain-alleviating capsaicin. Then finish it off with one clove of minced garlic and one-half teaspoon of sea salt. Use it as hearty dip with whole-grain pita bread or veggies...and maybe some tabouli. It's scrumptious!

How to Trick Picky Eaters

Karen Larson, editor of *Bottom Line/Personal*, 281 Tresser Blvd., Stamford, Connecticut 06901. *BottomLine Personal.com*

When I met my husband, I could count on one hand the fruits and vegetables that he was willing to eat. He's gotten better over the years, but he still falls well short of the recommended five servings a day. When I push him to do better, it has the opposite effect—he simply refuses.

I knew just who to turn to for help—food expert, Missy Chase Lapine. She has written a series of Sneaky Chef books on how to hide healthy ingredients in favorite foods.

Lapine's husband was very much like mine in that he seemed to intentionally eat more of the foods that were bad for him. So Lapine stopped trying to persuade him and started tricking him. She turned vegetables into a smooth purée using a food processor—and then added the purée to his favorite dishes.

Lapine's husband loves barbecue chicken, so she puréed cauliflower and zucchini and mixed it into his barbecue sauce. To make the purée, she first steamed the cauliflower until very tender (about 10 minutes). The zucchini was peeled and puréed raw with a little lemon juice, then it was blended with the cauliflower purée.

Her husband loves guacamole, so she added a purée of raw baby spinach, steamed broccoli and baby peas. And he loves pasta, so she added a purée of eight vegetables (sweet potato, carrot, cauliflower, zucchini, red bell pepper, celery, squash and onion) to his tomato sauce.

He never realized that these recipes had changed. I guess when it comes to vegetables, honesty isn't always the best policy.

Lamb: A Highly Nutritious Red Meat

Lamb is a good source of omega-3 fatty acids, which may protect against heart disease and stroke...and is rich in iron, which can boost energy and help prevent anemia. Choose lean cuts of lamb from the leg, loin and shank.

Reader's Digest. RD.com

DID YOU KNOW THAT...

Chicken Thighs Are More Nutritious Than Breasts?

Chicken thighs have twice as much iron and nearly three times as much zinc—which boosts the immune system—as chicken breasts. Skinless thighs contain only one more gram of fat per serving than skinless breasts—and are less likely to dry out during cooking. Thighs cost less, too.

Prevention. Prevention.com

Calcium Supplements May Reduce Mortality One Study Finds

Contrary to recent research finding that calcium supplements increase risk for heart disease, a new study found that women who took up to 1,000 milligrams (mg) of calcium a day were 22% less likely to die over a 10-year period than women who didn't take the supplements. Calcium supplements had no statistically significant effect on men in this study. Always check with your doctor before starting any supplement.

Study of 9,033 people by researchers from the Canadian Multicentre Osteoporosis Study Research Group, published in *The Journal of Clinical Endocrinology & Metabolism.*

Calcium Tea

One cup of stinging nettle tea provides 2,000 milligrams (mg) of calcium, compared with 300 mg in a cup of milk. Put one ounce of dried nettles in 32 ounces of water, and let it steep for four to 10 hours. Stinging nettle is available at health-food stores.

Jennifer Adler, MS, CN, certified nutritionist and natural foods chef, writing in *Speed Healing* (Bottom Line Books).

6

It's Personal

Great Sex for Women: How to Revive Your Sex Drive

iminished libido—little or no sexual desire—is the most common sexual complaint among older women. But repeated attempts by the pharmaceutical industry to solve the problem with one or another form of "female Viagra" have failed.

My viewpoint: Reviving a mature woman's sex drive requires addressing multiple factors. *These include…*

• Balancing hormones—which play a key role in both physical and mental aspects of arousal—particularly during the hormonal changes of perimenopause and menopause.

• Treating the pelvic problems of aging, such as vaginal atrophy and dryness, which can cause painful sex.

Here are natural ways to boost libido that consistently work for the mature women in my medical practice. Choose one or even two based on your particular needs. If you still have problems, consult a licensed naturopathic physician.

HORMONE HELP

Several herbs and herbal combinations can help balance a mature woman's hormones. *Two of my favorites…*

• **Maca.** This powerful Peruvian herb is a good choice for women going through perimenopause or menopause because it is rich in plant sterols that balance and strengthen the entire hormonal system. The herb not only increases sex drive but also improves perimenopausal and menopausal symptoms such as hot

---

Laurie Steelsmith, ND, LAc, a licensed naturopathic physician and acupuncturist with a 20-year private practice in Honolulu. Dr. Steelsmith is a coauthor of *Great Sex, Naturally: Every Woman's Guide to Enhancing Her Sexuality Through the Secrets of Natural Medicine* (Hay House). *NaturalChoicesforWomen.com*

flashes, night sweats and insomnia. Additionally, it supports the adrenal glands, reducing levels of energy-depleting stress hormones.

Typical dose: 1,000 milligrams (mg), twice daily.

• **Two Immortals.** This herbal formula from Traditional Chinese Medicine builds two types of *chi*, or life-energy—*yin* (feminine) chi and *yang* (masculine) chi—thereby enhancing a woman's libido, which requires both nurturing (yin) and stimulation (yang).

It also helps to balance hormones and control some symptoms of perimenopause (irregular menstrual bleeding and cramping) and menopause (hot flashes).

Many of my patients take it for six months to a year to rebuild their vitality.

Typical dose: Many companies manufacture the supplement, and dosages vary—follow the dosage recommendation on the label.

SUPER-SEX SUPPLEMENTS

Two nutritional supplements are particularly effective at stimulating sexuality…

• **L-arginine.** This amino acid works by boosting *nitric oxide*, a compound that promotes blood flow—including blood flow to your genitals.

A study in *Journal of Sex & Marital Therapy* showed that more than 70% of women who took a supplement that contains L-arginine (ArginMax for Women) experienced increased sexual desire…more frequent sex and orgasm …enhanced clitoral stimulation…decreased vaginal dryness…and improved overall sexual satisfaction.

Typical dose: 3,000 mg daily.

Caution: Talk to your doctor before you take L-arginine, especially if you have low blood pressure, herpes, gastric ulcer, liver disease or kidney disease.

• **PEA (phenylethylamine).** Called the "love supplement," PEA boosts the neurotransmitter *dopamine*, enhancing feelings of well-being, joy and pleasure.

Typical dose: 60 mg once a day. (Higher doses can cause overstimulation, insomnia or anxiety.)

Caution: Don't take PEA if you are nursing, pregnant or take an MAOI antidepressant medication such as *selegiline* (Eldepryl).

You also can boost PEA by exercising regularly, eating dark chocolate and taking a blue-green algae called *spirulina*.

APHRODISIACS

Two aphrodisiacs are particularly effective for mature women because—by relaxing your body and improving your mood—they slowly and gently boost your libido.

• **Cordyceps.** This mushroom is considered a potent sexual tonic in Traditional Chinese Medicine. It enhances both yin and yang chi, making it an ideal aphrodisiac for women.

Typical dose: 500 mg, twice daily.

What works best: Pills made by a hot-water extraction process that pulls out the herb's most active constituents, such as the cordyceps supplement from JHS Natural Products (*JHSNP.com*).

• **Ginkgo biloba.** Often recommended for memory loss because it improves blood supply to the brain, ginkgo also promotes blood flow to the vulva and vagina. Studies show that it may help restore libido in women taking antidepressants, which can destroy sex drive.

Typical dose: 40 mg, three times a day. The label should read, "Standardized extract of 24% ginkgo *flavonglycosides* (or *flavone glycosides*)."

STATIN WARNING

Cholesterol-lowering statin drugs—taken by millions of older women—can lower libido, probably by damaging mitochondria, energy-generating structures inside cells. If you take a statin and notice a decrease in libido, talk to your doctor about your options.

VAGINAL WEIGHT-TRAINING

The *pubococcygeal* (PC) muscle—a bowl-shaped "hammock" of pelvic muscle that contracts rhythmically when you have an orgasm and also supports your genital organs and bladder—is crucial to sexual pleasure.

New approach: Using a vaginal weight (a small, round weight inside an oval tube that is inserted into the vagina like a tampon) is the best way to strengthen the PC muscle, enhancing erotic sensation and sexual response.

What to do: To start, insert the tube for one to five minutes, twice daily, squeezing your PC muscle repeatedly to hold the tube in place. You can do this standing or lying down. Gradually work up to 20 minutes, twice daily, using progressively heavier weights. Do this for three months. You can order a set of vaginal weights at *Vagacare.com*.

Cost: About $30.*

Other benefits: Regular use of vaginal weights can help prevent and treat urinary incontinence and prevent prolapse of the bladder or uterus.

VAGINAL DRYNESS AND PAINFUL INTERCOURSE

Enjoyable sex requires vaginal tissue that is healthy and well-hydrated. But the midlife drop in estrogen levels causes a decrease of blood flow to the vagina, which can lead to vaginal atrophy and dryness. *A simple remedy…*

• **Vitamin E.** The unique lubricating properties of vitamin E make it especially effective.

What to do: Pierce a soft 400 international units (IU) vitamin E gel capsule with a pin, squeeze the oil onto your finger, and apply it to the outside of the vagina and inside about an inch. Or use a vitamin E vaginal suppository. Apply the gel or insert the suppository nightly at bedtime for at least two weeks. Taper use to three times a week.

*Price subject to change.

EASY-TO-DO…

Use Better Lubricants

To prevent dryness during intercourse, use a lubricant that mimics natural body fluids, such as Good Clean Love (*GoodCleanLove.com*) or Pre-Seed (available in drugstores).

Recent finding: 36% of women who used massage oil or baby oil as lubricants developed yeast infections…women who used petroleum jelly had twice the risk for bacterial infection.

Study of 141 women by researchers at David Geffen School of Medicine, University of California, Los Angeles, published in *Obstetrics & Gynecology*, with additional reporting from *Good Housekeeping*.

Size Does Matter…

Women who viewed life-size images of men with penises of various sizes tended to rate those who were well-endowed as more attractive.

But: Size became less important past a certain length—about three inches—indicating that proportion also plays a role.

Study of 105 women by researchers in the department of biology, University of Ottawa, Canada, published in *Proceedings of the National Academy of Science.*

How to Prevent Erectile Dysfunction

Sheldon Marks, MD, associate clinical professor of urology at The University of Arizona College of Medicine, Tucson, and adjunct assistant professor of urology at Tufts University School of Medicine in Boston. He is the medical director for the International Center for Vasectomy Reversal (*DadsAgain.com*), directs the men's health and erectile dysfunction community at *WebMD.com* and serves as the integrative urologist for *DrWeil.com*. Dr. Marks is also author of *Prostate & Cancer* (Da Capo).

Erectile dysfunction (ED) drugs have become so popular in the US—about 20% of American men over age 45 have used them—that the most obvious and safest solution to the problem is now being largely overlooked.

What works best for ED: Instead of taking a medication that can bring on side effects ranging from vision problems to headaches, it is much smarter to prevent the condition from developing.

Good news: Recent research shows that there are simple yet effective techniques to prevent ED. Men who already suffer from ED can improve their symptoms, too, by addressing these health issues.

THE NEW THINKING

While doctors have long known that ED can sometimes be caused by emotional factors, such as depression, there is now a growing

109

body of evidence that shows how closely this problem is related to the same physical problems that can lead to heart disease, high blood pressure (hypertension) and stroke.

Example: The main artery in the penis is only about 0.02 inches in diameter. A man with *atherosclerosis* (plaques in the arteries) will often develop impotence years or even decades before he's diagnosed with cardiovascular disease.

What men need to know about the underlying causes of ED…

BELLY FAT

Men who are overweight or obese have a high risk of developing ED, particularly if they also have diabetes, hypertension or heart disease—all of which can damage the blood vessels and/or nerves that are needed for erections.

The risk is even higher in men who have excessive belly fat. That's because fat that accumulates in the abdomen, known as *visceral fat*, converts testosterone to estrogen. Men with a low testosterone-to-estrogen ratio frequently suffer from ED. Low energy is another warning sign.

What to do: Men who have excessive belly fat should lose weight. If weight loss does not eliminate the ED, it then makes sense to get a hormone test. Your doctor can check your testosterone-estrogen ratio with blood and/or saliva tests. Men with this hormone imbalance often improve when taking an *aromatase inhibitor* (such as Arimidex). This class of medications blocks the conversion of testosterone to estrogen.

Important: I do not recommend testosterone supplements because they could disrupt the balance between testosterone and estrogen, creating more visceral fat.

GUM DISEASE

Scientists have known for years that men with periodontal (gum) disease tend to have more cardiovascular disease, but gum problems also have recently been linked to an increased risk for ED.

It's possible that bacteria from infected gums can get into the bloodstream and cause inflammation in the arteries in the penis. Inflammation can, in turn, accelerate arterial obstructions that can lead to ED as well as heart disease.

What to do: Take better care of your gums with daily brushing and flossing. *Important:* Dentists recommend brushing for at least two minutes twice daily—most people do not brush for nearly that long.

HEART DISEASE

There's now strong evidence showing that ED is often a marker for undiagnosed heart disease.

Here's what happens: When the narrow arteries in the penis become blocked by plaque (leading to ED), this is a good indicator that arteries in the heart also could be obstructed. It's crucial to recognize that arterial blockage in the heart can occur long before a man develops chest pain, shortness of breath or other cardiovascular symptoms.

What to do: I advise men with ED to see a cardiologist first. They should assume, until testing proves otherwise, that ED is an early sign of heart disease. You'll probably be given an echo stress test. With this test, you'll use a treadmill or bicycle while a technician monitors your heartbeat and uses ultrasound to show the heart's movements.

If you have early-stage heart disease, you can save your life—and your sex life—with a combination of lifestyle changes (such as regular exercise) and, if necessary, medication to lower cholesterol.

HIGH BLOOD PRESSURE

Both high blood pressure and the drugs used to treat it are among the most common causes of ED.

If you have high blood pressure, damage to the arteries from excessive blood pressure can interfere with erections. Unfortunately, the problem can get worse if you take blood pressure medication.

What to do: In addition to reducing high blood pressure—by lifestyle changes (such as getting more exercise, dropping some pounds if you're overweight and eating less salt) and taking medications, if needed—tell your doctor right away if you're suffering from ED. He/she might be able to switch you to a different antihypertensive medication that doesn't itself cause you to have ED. Every man responds to blood pressure drugs differently.

Worth noting: Prescription antidepressants are notorious for causing ED in some men. As with blood pressure drugs, switching to a different antidepressant is sometimes enough to resolve the problem. Drugs for male pattern baldness, such as *finasteride* (Propecia), also may cause ED.

SLEEP APNEA

Sleep apnea is a condition in which breathing intermittently stops and starts during sleep. It causes a decrease in oxygen in the blood and an increase in carbon dioxide that can lead to hypertension, heart disease—and ED.

Obesity is among the main causes of sleep apnea. Apnea also can be caused, or increased, by excessive consumption of alcohol, medications (such as sedatives) and smoking.

What to do: If you are a loud snorer or your partner reports that you frequently gasp or snort during sleep, you might have sleep apnea. Other symptoms include morning headaches and extreme daytime fatigue.

Ask your doctor if you should have a sleep test. If you are diagnosed with sleep apnea, you'll probably be advised to lose weight if you're overweight and perhaps be prescribed treatment such as a *CPAP* (continuous positive airway pressure) device. It delivers pressurized air to the nose and/or mouth while you sleep and can sometimes eliminate both apnea and ED.

Why "The Pill" May Increase Glaucoma Risk

In a recent finding, women who took oral contraceptives for at least three years had twice the risk for glaucoma as women who took contraceptives for a shorter time or did not take them at all.

Possible reason: Birth control pills reduce estrogen—and estrogen is believed to protect the retina. Women who take or have taken birth control pills should consider getting an annual eye exam for glaucoma.

Shan Lin, MD, professor of clinical ophthalmology, University of California, San Francisco, School of Medicine, and leader of a study presented at the annual meeting of the American Academy of Ophthalmology in New Orleans.

TV Watching Lowers Sperm Count

The more TV a man watches, the lower his sperm count. Men who watched television for more than 20 hours a week had 44% lower sperm concentration than men who did not watch TV. Sperm concentration fell as TV viewing increased. Men who engaged in the most moderate-to-vigorous physical activity had the highest sperm counts.

Study of 222 male college students, ages 18 to 22, by researchers at Harvard School of Public Health, Boston, published in *British Journal of Sports Medicine*.

Testosterone Supplements Decrease Male Fertility

In a recent finding, testosterone supplements, often taken by men to improve their sex drive or fuel muscle growth, impeded sperm production. But the effect was not permanent. Most men who stopped taking testosterone supplements saw a jump in their sperm count. Average sperm concentration in semen went from 1.8 million per milliliter to 34 million per milliliter within one to six months.

Study of 1,500 men, average age 35, by researchers at University of Alabama, Birmingham, presented at the annual meeting of the American Urological Association in San Diego.

For Better Sperm Health...

Walnuts improve sperm quality in younger men. Men ages 21 to 35 who ate 2.5 ounces of walnuts daily for 12 weeks had improvements in sperm motility. While a diet rich in antioxidants helped preserve sperm quality in middle-aged and older men. Men over age 44 who had higher intakes of vitamins C and E and the mineral zinc produced sperm with less DNA damage than men with lower intakes of these substances. And, physically active men had better-formed and faster-swimming sperm than sedentary men.

Roundup of studies from UCLA and UC Berkeley, and studies published in *European Journal of Applied Physiology* and *British Journal of Sports Medicine*, reported in *University of California, Berkeley Wellness Letter.*

The Don'ts of Online Dating

●**Don't count the first date.** It's a nerve-racking experience that can turn even the most extroverted person inside out. Go on a second or third date to see if you really click.

●**Don't give up dating altogether after a few bad dates.** Take a break for a week or even a month. Then adjust your profile, choose a new photo and pick a new dating website for a fresh new start.

Also: Search by what interests you. A shared interest in hiking, wine tasting or skydiving means that you will have plenty to talk about.

Men's Health. MensHealth.com

Absence Does Make the Heart Grow Fonder, but...

Dating couples in long-distance relationships tend to share more personal feelings and thoughts than couples who are geographically close. Physically separated people tend

to idealize their partners' behavior, making them feel closer.

But: These good feelings can lead to problems when the couples reunite—the positive illusions created by distance disappear, and couples may become bogged down in everyday, mundane issues that they did not discuss when they were apart.

Study of dating couples by researchers at City University of Hong Kong and Cornell University, Ithaca, New York, published in *Journal of Communication.*

No More Hot Flashes!

In a study of more than 6,000 menopausal women, those who ate the most fruit and a Mediterranean-style diet with vegetables, whole grains, fish and healthy fats, such as olive oil, were less likely to experience hot flashes and night sweats than those who did not closely follow this diet.

Theory: Diets high in fat and sugar can increase blood sugar levels, which can trigger hot flashes.

Gerrie-Cor Herber-Gast, PhD, research fellow, School of Population Health at The University of Queensland, Australia.

Don't Let Your Bladder Run Your Life! Natural Help for Women and Men

Holly Lucille, ND, RN, a naturopathic doctor based in West Hollywood, California. She is author of *Creating and Maintaining Balance: A Woman's Guide to Safe, Natural Hormone Health* (Impakt Health) and serves on the Institute for Natural Medicine Board of Directors. *DrHollyLucille.com*

Women and men who scout out restrooms wherever they are may think that others don't have to worry so much about their bladders. But that's not true.

Eye-opening statistic: One in every five adults over age 40 has overactive bladder... and after the age of 65, a whopping one in every three adults is affected. If you regularly have a strong and sudden urge to urinate and/or need to hit the john eight or more times a day (or more than once at night), chances are you have the condition, too.

Men with prostate enlargement and post-menopausal women (due to their low estrogen levels) are at increased risk of having overactive bladder. Urinary tract infections, use of certain medications (such as antidepressants and drugs to treat high blood pressure and insomnia) and even constipation also can cause or worsen the condition.

But there is a bright side. Research is now uncovering several surprisingly simple natural approaches that are highly effective for many people who have overactive bladder. *Among the best...**

START WITH YOUR DIET

Most people don't connect a bladder problem to their diets. But there is a strong link. *My advice...*

• **Take a hard line with irritants.** Alcohol, caffeine and artificial sweeteners can exacerbate the feeling of urgency caused by overactive bladder. Cutting back on these items is a good first step, but they often creep back into one's diet over time.

What helps: Keep it simple—completely avoid alcohol, caffeine (all forms, including coffee, tea and caffeine-containing foods such as chocolate) and artificial sweeteners. Stick to decaffeinated coffee and herbal teas, and use agave and stevia as sweeteners.

Many individuals also are sensitive to certain foods, such as corn, wheat, dairy, eggs and peanuts. They often trigger an immune reaction that contributes to overall inflammation in the body, including in the bladder. If your symptoms of urinary urgency and/or frequency increase after eating one of these (or any other) foods, your body may be having an inflammatory response that is also affecting your bladder. Eliminate these foods from your diet.

---

*Talk to your doctor before trying any of these herbal remedies, especially if you take medication or have a chronic health condition. You may want to consult a naturopathic doctor. To find one near you, check *Naturopathic.org*.

• **Keep your gut healthy.** The scientific evidence is still in the early stages, but research now suggests that *leaky gut syndrome*, in which excess bacterial or fungal growth harms the mucosal membrane in the intestines, is at the root of several health problems, including overactive bladder.

The theory is that an imbalance of microbes, a condition known as *dysbiosis*, can irritate the walls of the bladder just as it does in the gut.

What helps: *Probiotics* and *oregano oil capsules*. Probiotics replenish "good" bacteria, and oregano oil has antibacterial properties that help cleanse "bad" bacteria and fungi from the gut.

• **Drink up!** People with overactive bladder often cut way back on their fluid intake because they already make so many trips to the bathroom. But when you don't drink enough fluids, urine tends to have an irritating effect because it becomes more concentrated. This increases urgency.

What helps: Drink half your body weight in ounces of water or herbal tea daily. Do not drink any fluids after 5 pm to help prevent bathroom runs during the night.

THE RIGHT SUPPLEMENTS

Cranberry supplements (or unsweetened cranberry juice) can be helpful for bladder infections, but they're usually not the best choice for overactive bladder. *My advice...*

• **Try pumpkin seed extract.** These capsules help tone and strengthen the tissue of your pelvic-floor muscles, which gives you better bladder control.

Typical dosage: 500 milligrams (mg) daily.

• **Consider Angelica archangelica extract.** This herb has gotten positive reviews from researchers who have investigated it as a therapy for overactive bladder.

Recent finding: When 43 men with overactive bladder took 300 mg of the herb daily, they had increased bladder capacity and made fewer trips to the bathroom.

Typical dosage: 100 mg daily.

OTHER WAYS TO
KEEP YOUR BLADDER HEALTHY

• **Kegel exercises,** which help strengthen the pelvic-floor muscles, are essential for getting control of overactive bladder symptoms. Unfortunately, most people who try doing Kegels end up doing them the wrong way.

How to do Kegels: Three to five times a day, contract your pelvic-floor muscles (the ones you use to stop and start the flow of urine), hold for a count of 10, then relax completely for a count of 10. Repeat 10 times. If you're a woman and aren't sure if you're contracting the right muscles, there is a possible solution.

New option for women: A medical device called Apex acts as an automatic Kegel exerciser. It is inserted into the vagina and electrically stimulates the correct muscles ($249* at *InControlMedical.com*—cost may be covered by some insurance plans). Check with your doctor to see if this would be an appropriate aid for you.

Even though there's no handy device to help men do Kegels, the exercises usually reduce urgency when they're performed regularly.

Kegels can easily be part of anyone's daily routine—do them while waiting at a red light, after going to the bathroom or while watching TV.

• **Try acupuncture.** An increasing body of evidence shows that this therapy helps relieve overactive bladder symptoms. For example, in a study of 74 women with the condition, bladder capacity, urgency and frequency of urination significantly improved after four weekly bladder-specific acupuncture sessions.

• **Go for biofeedback.** Small electrodes are used to monitor the muscles involved in bladder control so that an individualized exercise program can be created. Biofeedback is noninvasive and is most effective when used along with other treatments. To find a board-certified provider, consult the Biofeedback Certification International Alliance, *BCIA.org*.

*Price subject to change.

New Treatment for UTIs on the Way

Recurring urinary tract infections (UTIs) in women may be caused by a strain of *E. coli* that can flourish in both the gut and bladder. This strain can migrate back and forth despite repeated treatments—and even get stronger, causing recurring infections. The discovery may lead to new and better treatments for women who suffer recurrent infections.

Study of urinary tract infections by researchers at Washington University, St. Louis, published in *Science Translational Medicine.*

How to Keep Your Bladder Healthy

Jamison Starbuck, ND, a naturopathic physician in family practice and a guest lecturer at the University of Montana, both in Missoula. She is past president of the American Association of Naturopathic Physicians and a contributing editor to *The Alternative Advisor: The Complete Guide to Natural Therapies and Alternative Treatments* (Time Life).

If you're age 50 or older and haven't had a bladder infection, count yourself very lucky. The reality is that bladder infections are among the most common complaints of the AARP crowd.

Here's why: With age, women—and men—are at increased risk because tissues in the bladder weaken, making it more difficult for it to fully empty...so bacteria have more time to proliferate and cause a urinary tract infection (UTI). As we age, our immune systems also don't work as well.

Interestingly, the symptoms of bladder infection become less apparent with age. Instead of the burning, cramping pain and bloody urine that generally go along with a UTI in younger people, only a modest increase in urinary frequency and a dark urine color may indicate a bladder infection once you're middle-aged or older. After about age 70, confusion, agitation, balance problems and falling may be a physician's only clues of a bladder infection.

Fortunately, there are some highly effective natural approaches to help prevent UTIs. *My favorite UTI-fighting strategies…*

•**Stay hydrated.** You must drink a minimum of two quarts of plain water daily—no matter what other beverages you consume. If you take a prescription medication, you may need even more water. Diuretics and some other drugs will make you lose water, so you'll need to drink more than usual. Discuss this with your pharmacist.

•**Use good hygiene.** OK, you might find this is a little embarrassing, but make sure that you wipe from front to back after a bowel movement...wash your genitals before and after sex…and change your undergarments regularly, particularly if you have incontinence or are sedentary (small amounts of stool on a person's underwear can increase infection risk).

•**Load up on cranberry.** Everyone knows that cranberry is supposed to be good for the bladder, but recent research made some people doubt its effectiveness. One study found that cranberry may not be very effective at preventing UTIs. But do not write off cranberry. The same research showed that compounds in cranberry do prevent infections by making it difficult for bacteria to stick to the walls of the bladder. Because most brands of cranberry juice (perhaps the most convenient form of the fruit) have added sugar to make them less tart, I usually advise people who develop more than one bladder infection a year to take 600 milligrams (mg) of a freeze-dried cranberry extract daily.

Caution: People with a history of calcium oxalate kidney stones or who take *warfarin* (Coumadin) or regularly use aspirin should avoid cranberry—it can increase stone risk and interact with these medications.

•**Get more probiotics.** These beneficial bacteria found in yogurt and other cultured foods, such as kefir and miso, reduce risk for bladder infection. Eat one cup of plain yogurt, kefir or miso soup daily or take a probiotic supplement.

•**Do Kegel exercises.** Women—and men—listen up! Strong pelvic muscles allow for more complete bladder emptying and reduce infection risk.

What to do: At least once daily, contract and release the muscles of your pelvic floor (the ones that stop urine flow) 10 times while seated or standing.

Vaginal Suppository for Chronic Yeast Infection

In a recent finding, women who placed one probiotic tablet directly in their vaginas at night for seven nights…then every three nights for three weeks…and then once a week after that had an 87% reduction in yeast infections. The suppository approach may help women for whom conventional therapy has not worked —ask your doctor.

Laurie Cullen, ND, naturopathic physician and associate professor of clinical medicine at Bastyr University, Kenmore, Washington, commenting on a recent Italian study quoted in *Prevention*.

For a Better Gynecological Appointment…

Don't get a "Brazilian" bikini wax before a gynecological appointment. Waxing a large part of the pubic area often causes redness and inflammation, which can make it harder for the doctor to provide an accurate exam.

Hilda Hutcherson, MD, obstetrician and gynecologist, Columbia University Medical Center in New York City, writing in *Redbook*.

Vital: Regular Pap Smears After Age 50

In a British study of 1,341 women, those who were not screened for cervical cancer after age 50 were six times more likely to be diagnosed with the disease later in life. Plus, women whose screening results were normal had a lower-than-average risk for cervical cancer into their 80s. Pap smears now are advised every three years until age 65 in the US.

Anne F. Rositch, PhD, MPH, assistant professor of epidemiology and public health, University of Maryland School of Medicine, Baltimore.

Single Dose of HPV Vaccine May Be Sufficient

A single dose of the HPV vaccine may be enough to protect women against cervical cancer. Officially, three doses of the vaccine are recommended. However, researchers have found antibodies to the human papillomavirus, which causes HPV, in women who received only two vaccinations six months apart...and in women who received only a single vaccination.

Mahboobeh Safaeian, PhD, investigator, division of cancer epidemiology and genetics, National Cancer Institute, Bethesda, Maryland, and leader of a study published in *Cancer Prevention Research*.

New Treatment for Advanced Ovarian Cancer?

In a recent finding, ovarian cancer patients given the drug *pazopanib* (Votrient) stayed in remission almost six months longer than women who did not receive the medication. Ovarian cancer has a current cure rate of only 20% to 25%, and two-thirds of patients will experience a relapse despite successful initial treatment and chemotherapy. Side effects of the drug include hypertension, diarrhea, nausea, headache and fatigue.

Study of 940 ovarian cancer patients over 24 months by researchers at Kliniken Essen-Mitte, Essen, Germany, presented at the American Society of Clinical Oncology annual meeting.

Study Finds Most Uterine Cancers Are Preventable

Regular physical activity—at least 30 minutes each day—and maintaining a healthy weight can prevent nearly 60% of cancers of the lining of the uterus, a recent study reports. Dietary choices also matter—drinking one cup of coffee a day, regular or decaf, can reduce risk by 7%...but eating lots of sugary foods and processed grains can raise cancer risk.

Study published by American Institute for Cancer Research and World Cancer Research Fund International.

Common Pelvic Surgery Often Fails

Pelvic organ prolapse, when the uterus, bladder, rectum or other pelvic organs fall out of place, affects about one in four women during their lifetime, often after childbirth. The most common treatment is *abdominal sacrocolpopexy*, a surgical procedure in which tissue or synthetic mesh is attached to the top of the vagina.

Recent finding: In nearly one in three women who had the procedure, symptoms returned within seven years...and about 17% needed additional surgery.

Study of 215 women for seven years by researchers at University of Utah School of Medicine, Salt Lake City, published in *The Journal of the American Medical Association*.

Negative for the Breast Cancer Gene? Why You Still May Be at Risk...

It was originally thought that women who come from families with *BRCA mutations* but who test negative for any BRCA mutations had the same risk for breast cancer as the general population.

Recent finding: Women from such families with negative BRCA2 mutation had *four times* the risk for breast cancer as the general population.

Gareth Evans, MD, honorary professor of medical genetics and a cancer epidemiologist at The University of Manchester in England and lead author of a study of 800 families, published in *Cancer Epidemiology, Biomarkers & Prevention*.

Take a Walk to Reduce Breast Cancer Risk

An hour walk each day lowered breast cancer risk by 14% among postmenopausal women. And women who did at least one hour of strenuous physical activity daily had 25% lower risk for breast cancer. Physical activity is thought to lower risk by reducing hormones...improving weight control, glucose metabolism and insulin sensitivity...and lowering inflammation.

Alpa Patel, PhD, strategic director of the Cancer Prevention Study-3 (CPS-3) for the American Cancer Society, Atlanta, and leader of a study of 73,615 postmenopausal women, reported in *Cancer Epidemiology, Biomarkers & Prevention*.

Exercise—at Any Age—Cuts Risk for Breast Cancer

In a study of more than 3,000 women (both premenopausal and postmenopausal), those who did 10 hours of moderate exercise per week—including walking and gardening—had a 30% lower risk for breast cancer than those who were sedentary.

Theory: Besides reducing body fat, exercise may increase antioxidant capacity and enhance cell repair.

Lauren McCullough, PhD, epidemiologist, The University of North Carolina at Chapel Hill.

Tomatoes vs. Breast Cancer

In a recent study, postmenopausal women at increased risk for breast cancer ate about 25 milligrams (mg) of *lycopene* (the amount in one cup of tomato juice) every day. After 10 weeks, they had increased blood levels of the protein *adiponectin*, which has been linked to reduced breast cancer risk. Besides tomatoes, other good sources of lycopene include apricots, watermelon and papaya. Cooked tomatoes have even more lycopene than raw, so also enjoy tomato soup or red pasta sauce.

Adana Llanos, PhD, MPH, assistant professor of epidemiology, Rutgers, The State University of New Jersey, New Brunswick.

BP Meds and Breast Cancer Risk

Blood pressure medication may increase risk for breast cancer.

Recent finding: Women who took calcium-channel blockers for 10 years or longer had more than double the risk for breast cancer, compared with women who did not take these medications. No risk was found for short-term use of the drug (less than 10 years) or for any other antihypertensive medication.

Christopher Li, MD, PhD, an epidemiologist specializing in breast cancer at Fred Hutchinson Cancer Research Center, Seattle, and lead author of a study of nearly 3,000 women, published in *JAMA Internal Medicine.*

How High Cholesterol Impacts Breast Cancer

The molecule *27HC,* a derivative of cholesterol, mimics estrogen, a hormone that increases breast cancer risk and reduces the effectiveness of anti-estrogen treatments for breast cancer including *aromatase inhibitors* and *tamoxifen.* Women with breast cancer and high cholesterol should talk to their doctors about lowering cholesterol with statins and/or dietary changes.

Donald McDonnell, PhD, chairman of the department of pharmacology and cancer biology at Duke University School of Medicine, Durham, North Carolina. He is lead author of a study published in *Science.*

Get This Type of Scan for Better Breast Cancer Detection

Mammograms using *digital radiography* (DR) are slightly more effective than the computer radiography (CR) mammograms for detecting breast cancer.

Recent finding: DR detected 4.9 cancers per 1,000 mammograms, while CR detected 3.4.

Study of 816,000 mammograms that were carried out on 688,000 women, ages 50 to 74, by researchers at several cancer care centers in Ontario, Canada, published in *Radiology.*

Less Invasive Breast Cancer Treatment May Be Better for Some

Over a 14-year study period, early-stage breast cancer patients 50 years old and older who chose a lumpectomy plus radiation were 13% less likely to die from breast cancer and 19% less likely to die from any cause than similar women who had more invasive mastectomies.

Study of 112,154 women by researchers at Duke Cancer Institute, Durham, North Carolina, and the Cancer Prevention Institute of California, Fremont, published in *Cancer.*

More Effective Breast Cancer Treatment

Women at risk for *hormone receptor-positive breast cancer* may benefit from taking *tamoxifen* or *raloxifene.* Tamoxifen was more effective than raloxifene but also increased the incidence of endometrial cancer and cataracts. Both medications increase risk for blood clots. Talk to your doctor.

Heidi D. Nelson, MD, MPH, research professor, departments of medical informatics and clinical epidemiology and medicine, Oregon Health & Science University, Portland. She analyzed treatment recommendations from the US Preventive Services Task Force that were published in *Annals of Internal Medicine.*

Fish Oil vs. Prostate Cancer

Geovanni Espinosa, ND, LAc, CNS, director, Integrative Urology Center, New York University Langone Medical Center, New York City.

In my opinion, recent research indicating that fish oil increases prostate cancer risk is weak. First, the study does not show that fish oil causes prostate cancer. The finding suggests only an association—in analyzing reams of health data on a group of men, the researchers found that men with prostate cancer were more likely to have high blood levels of the omega-3 fatty acids found in fish oil. But just why this might be the case isn't known.

Interestingly, in the media coverage, it was not widely reported that the same researchers inexplicably found a reduced risk for prostate cancer in men whose diets included more trans fats (the harmful type found in margarine) and omega-6 fatty acids (another dangerous fat, which is implicated in some cancers)!

It's crucial to be skeptical of new, headline-grabbing studies and to look at the preponderance of evidence. Clearly, there are multiple, high-quality studies indicating that fish oil (from one's diet and supplements) has a wide range of health benefits, such as reducing risk for heart disease, stroke—and prostate cancer. I take fish oil—and will continue to use it. My suggestion to you is to be sure to discuss any supplement you take with a nutritionally oriented doctor, but don't make any changes based on this study alone.

Better Prostate Cancer Screening

Two new tests help men avoid unnecessary treatments for prostate cancer. The *PCA3 test* measures urinary levels of prostate cancer gene 3, found only in cancerous prostate cells. Men with higher-than-normal PSA levels should ask for a PCA3 test before getting a biopsy. A PCA3 score of 25 or lower means that a biopsy likely is not needed. The *Prolaris test* uses cancer cells taken during a biopsy to determine how aggressive a tumor is. This helps doctors pursue the best course of treatment.

Prevention. Prevention.com

New Guidelines for PSA Testing?

Prostate specific antigen (PSA) screening is highly controversial because it can lead to unnecessary treatment that may result in complications, including impotence and incontinence. In a recent study of 21,000 middle-aged men, a single midlife PSA test accurately identified men who would die of prostate cancer within 20 to 30 years.

Takeaway: Most men should get a baseline PSA test at age 45 (those with a strong family history might begin sooner). Men with low PSA levels (at or below 1.0 ng/mL) at baseline should have two additional PSA tests—one in their early 50s and another at age 60. Men with a baseline PSA level above 1.0 ng/mL should have more PSA tests, every two to four years until age 70.

Andrew Vickers, PhD, attending research methodologist, Memorial Sloan-Kettering Cancer Center, New York City.

Shorter Prostate Cancer Treatment Works as Well as Longer Therapy

In a recent finding, men with high-risk prostate cancer who were treated with testosterone-blocking hormone for 18 months had essentially the same survival rate as those who were treated with the same hormone for 36 months. Shortening hormone treatment can reduce side effects, which include impotence, fatigue and a general decline in vitality.

Study of 630 prostate cancer patients by researchers at Centre Hospitalier Universitaire de Sherbrooke, Quebec, Canada, presented at a symposium of the American Society of Clinical Oncology in Orlando, Florida.

Prostate Drug Safer Than Believed

Finasteride does not increase the risk for high-grade prostate cancer as previously thought. Instead, a recent study shows that it reduces the size of the prostate by about 30%, making it easier for doctors to find aggressive cancer when doing biopsies. If you are at high risk for prostate cancer—for example, you have a family history of the disease—ask your doctor about taking the drug.

Ian Murchie Thompson, Jr., MD, director of the Cancer Therapy and Research Center at University of Texas Medicine Health Science Center at San Antonio. He led an 18-year follow-up study published in The New England Journal of Medicine.

Too Much Radiation Given for Bone Pain?

Radiation may be administered to patients with advanced prostate cancer who are experiencing pain because the cancer has spread to the bone. This type of treatment is different from radiation to treat prostate cancer and prolong survival. The majority of patients get pain relief from just one radiation treatment.

But: More than half of patients studied received more than 10 treatments.

Patients should speak to their doctors about starting with just one treatment and monitoring their pain level.

Justin E. Bekelman, MD, assistant professor of radiation oncology at Perelman School of Medicine at University of Pennsylvania, Philadelphia, and leader of a study published in The Journal of the American Medical Association.

T Level "Sweet Spot"

An analysis of the health records of 3,690 men ages 70 to 89 found that those with the lowest testosterone levels had the highest risk for death. And those with the highest levels of testosterone had the next highest death risk. Men who had testosterone levels in the middle range (9.8 nmol/L to 15.8 nmol/L) tended to live the longest.

Bu Beng Yeap, MD, PhD, endocrinologist and professor in medicine, The University of Western Australia, Perth.

Hormone Troubles in Men

Jamison Starbuck, ND, a naturopathic physician in family practice and a guest lecturer at the University of Montana, both in Missoula. She is past president of the American Association of Naturopathic Physicians and a contributing editor to The Alternative Advisor: The Complete Guide to Natural Therapies and Alternative Treatments (Time Life).

Out-of-whack hormones can turn women's lives upside down. But hormones are just as important to men's health as they are to women's. You see, a man's hormones—like *cortisol, DHEA, norepinephrine, testosterone* and, yes, even *estrogen* and *progesterone*—affect everything from mood, sleep and memory to inflammation, heart disease risk and overall energy levels. Both men and women have the same hormones. It's just that the levels change depending on your gender, and they often change significantly throughout life. So if you are a middle-aged or older man and are not satisfied with your overall health, your hormones may be the culprit.

Start by asking yourself several basic questions: How well do you sleep? Do you eat well and get enough fluids? How often do you exercise? Do you have any chronic pain? How often are you happy? How do you feel about your sex life? If your assessment comes up short in any of these areas, consider the following suggestions, which I've found to be quite helpful with my middle-aged male patients…*

• **Keep your liver healthy.** Your liver is vital to your hormone health because steroid hormones (reproductive and adrenal) are made from cholesterol, which is produced primarily in the liver. For that reason, I advise most men (there are some exceptions, such as men who have had heart attacks) to avoid statin drugs if at all possible. One reason for this advice is that statins can drive cholesterol too low for adequate hormone production, and studies show that cholesterol that's too low is as dangerous to long-term health as elevated cholesterol.

If it's possible, get your total cholesterol under 200 milligrams per deciliter (mg/dL) with diet and exercise (see below). To promote the health of your liver, eat lots of leafy greens… root vegetables, such as beets and carrots… healthy oils (two tablespoons daily), such as olive, coconut and fish oils…fresh fruit…and some lean meats.

• **Don't shirk exercise.** It's simply a fact that adrenal and reproductive hormone levels are improved with regular, moderate exercise. I recommend one hour of brisk walking daily. If you're unable to do this, consider swimming, pilates or hiking.

• **Try botanicals.** *Urtica dioica* (also known as stinging nettle) has a long history of use as an anti-inflammatory for the male urinary tract and as a treatment for prostate enlargement. I usually recommend 250 milligrams (mg) of Urtica dioica root a day.

Caution: If you have prostate cancer, talk to your doctor before taking Urtica to ensure that the herb is safe for you. *Eleutherococcus senticosus* (sometimes found labeled as Siberian ginseng) helps the body adapt to stress and is useful in treating fatigue, concentration problems and mild depression. This herb is best absorbed in tincture form, typically one-quarter teaspoon in water, 15 minutes before or after meals, twice daily for three months.

*If you have any chronic health conditions or take medications, talk to your physician before trying the herbs in this article.

If these simple changes aren't enough, get help. You may not need an endocrinologist—many naturopathic physicians and conventional family doctors are skilled at hormone evaluation and treatment. Just be sure to inquire about the doctor's experience, training and treatment style.

Peyronie's Drug Gets FDA Nod

Men with *Peyronie's disease* develop a lump in the penis that causes abnormal curvature and pain upon erection and difficulty with intercourse. *Collagenase clostridium histolyticum* (Xiaflex) recently became the first FDA-approved nonsurgical treatment for Peyronie's disease. The drug, prescribed for men whose curvature is at least 30 degrees upon erection, is believed to break down the collagen that causes the penile curvature.

Consult a health-care professional who has been trained to administer the drug—it can trigger adverse effects such as injury to the penis.

Andrea Fischer, spokesperson, FDA, Silver Spring, Maryland.

DID YOU KNOW THAT…

Magnesium May Reduce Risk for Colon Cancer?

For every 100-milligram-a-day increase in magnesium from food (the amount in about one cup of beans or two potatoes), the risk for colon polyps dropped by 19%. Foods high in magnesium include wheat bran, nuts, spinach, soybeans, white potatoes, pinto beans, brown rice, lentils and bananas.

Study of 1,477 people by researchers at Imperial College London, published in *Tufts University Health & Nutrition Letter*.

Family History of Colon Cancer? You May Benefit from Calcium

People with variations in one of two genes had a 39% lower risk for precancerous colon and rectal lesions if they consumed at least 1,000 milligrams (mg) of calcium a day from food and supplements, a recent study found. People with variations in both genes reduced their risk by 69%.

Caution: Some studies have linked high calcium consumption to increased risk for other health problems. Talk to your doctor.

Xiangzhu Zhu, MD, MPH, a staff scientist, division of epidemiology, Vanderbilt Epidemiology Center, Nashville, and leader of a study of 5,810 people, presented at a recent meeting of the American Association for Cancer Research.

Women Smokers at Greater Risk for Colon Cancer Than Men Smokers

In a recent finding, women who smoked or who had ever smoked had nearly 20% higher risk for colon cancer than women who never smoked. Men who smoked had an 8% higher risk for colon cancer than men who never smoked.

Study of data on more than 600,000 people ages 19 to 67 over 14 years by researchers in the department of community medicine, University of Tromsø, Norway, published in *Cancer Epidemiology, Biomarkers & Prevention.*

Easier Colonoscopy Preparation

A new colon-prep solution consists of only two five-ounce servings—much less than the two to four liters of salty-tasting fluid that patients usually drink before a colonoscopy. Patients take the first five-ounce dose of the new prep, Prepopik, the evening before the procedure, and the other five ounces five hours before the colonoscopy. Each dose is followed by several eight-ounce servings of a clear liquid such as water or clear broth to prevent electrolyte imbalances. Ask your doctor whether the new preparation is appropriate for you.

Mayo Clinic Health Letter. HealthLetter.MayoClinic. com

New At-Home Colon Cancer Test: It's Prep-Free!

In a recent study, the *Fecal Immunochemical Test* (FIT), an inexpensive stool test, detected 79% of cancers. The standard fecal occult blood test detects up to 50% of cancers, and colonoscopy detects more than 95%. FIT may be appropriate for people who are unwilling to undergo the bowel preparation the night before a colonoscopy…or are afraid of an invasive procedure.

Jeffrey Lee, MD, a gastroenterology fellow at University of California, San Francisco, and leader of an analysis of 19 studies of FIT screening, published in *Annals of Internal Medicine.*

Two Pairs of Eyes Better Than One During Colonoscopy

A study found that when a nurse watched the screen along with the doctor during a colonoscopy, the average number of polyps detected per patient was 28% higher than when the doctor did it alone. The detection rate was higher for all types and locations of polyps when there were two observers—perhaps because the physician performs a more careful exam to avoid the embarrassment of a missed lesion.

Before your colonoscopy: Ask whether a nurse, endoscopy technician or gastroenterology fellow can also watch the screen during the procedure.

Harry R. Aslanian, MD, associate professor of medicine, Yale School of Medicine, New Haven, Connecticut.

How to Pick the Best Doctor for Your Colonoscopy

Choose a doctor with an *adenoma detection rate* (ADR) of at least 20%—that is, the doctor should be able to detect adenomas (precancerous polyps) in one of five patients getting a colonoscopy (the current recommended national benchmark). Even higher ADRs may become standard with the use of high-definition scopes and training to detect very subtle and flat polyps. Before scheduling a colonoscopy, ask the doctor for his/her ADR.

Michael Wallace, MD, MPH, professor of medicine, division of gastroenterology and hepatology, Mayo Clinic, Jacksonville, Florida.

Colon Cancer Alert

Using current screening guidelines, about one in 10 colon malignancies was missed among people with a family history of advanced colon polyps (precursors of colon cancer), in a recent study.

If you have a first-degree relative (a parent, sibling or child) who had advanced polyps diagnosed at any age: Talk to your doctor about getting screened more often than the current recommendation (once every five years beginning at age 40).

N. Jewel Samadder, MD, assistant professor of medicine, Huntsman Cancer Institute, University of Utah, Salt Lake City.

New Blood Test for IBS

Among 221 adults who had acute gastroenteritis and were screened with a new blood test, those with *irritable bowel syndrome* (IBS) were identified by a biomarker (antibodies to a protein called *vinculin*).

Implication: The test will help distinguish between IBS and inflammatory bowel disease (IBD), two conditions that have similar symptoms but very different treatments.

IBS is currently diagnosed by frequency of symptoms. The blood test should be available soon.

Mark Pimentel, MD, director, GI Motility Program, Cedars-Sinai Medical Center, Los Angeles.

Better Care for IBS

In a recent study of 45 adults who had *irritable bowel syndrome with diarrhea* (IBS-D)—but not celiac disease—those who ate a gluten-free diet for a month had significantly fewer bowel movements per day than those whose diets included gluten (a protein found in wheat, barley and rye).

Possible explanation: Gluten can irritate the lining of the small intestine, even in people who do not have celiac disease.

Michael Camilleri, MD, professor of medicine, pharmacology and physiology at Mayo Clinic in Rochester, Minnesota.

Standing Is a Hemorrhoid Risk

Standing for long periods of time is a common cause of hemorrhoids, as blood above the rectum exerts pressure on the rectal and anal areas. You can help ease this pressure by sitting down for five minutes every hour or two.

Constipation, diarrhea, obesity and frequent straining when having a bowel movement also can cause hemorrhoids.

Hemorrhoids can lead to persistent bleeding, pain, burning and itching and fecal soiling and leakage. Creams or ointments usually are effective for small hemorrhoids, but larger hemorrhoids may need treatment. The best treatment (which is painless) involves using infrared coagulation to shrink the hemorrhoidal tissue. Surgery may be required for large hemorrhoids.

Michael S. Epstein, MD, gastroenterologist and founder of Digestive Disorders Associates, Annapolis, Maryland. DDA.net

---

EASY-TO-DO...

Quick Trick for Drinking Less

Drink wine from a narrow glass, and place it on a table before pouring if you are trying to reduce your consumption. This results in pouring 9% to 12% less. People tend to drink more wine when using wide glasses and holding a glass while pouring the wine into it.

Study of 73 people who drank at least one glass of wine per day by researchers at Iowa State University, Ames, and Cornell University, Ithaca, New York, published in Substance Use & Misuse.

New Treatment for Alcoholism

The drug *gabapentin*, which has been approved for treating seizures and neuropathic pain, may help alcoholics cut down or quit drinking. It is not metabolized by the liver—which often is damaged from alcohol abuse—and has no evidence of abuse potential. Ask your doctor for details on when its use might be appropriate.

Barbara J. Mason, PhD, codirector of Pearson Center for Alcoholism and Addiction Research, The Scripps Research Institute, La Jolla, California. She led a study published online in JAMA Internal Medicine.

Baldness Drug May Quench Excessive Drinking

Finasteride (Propecia, Proscar), used for male pattern baldness and enlarged prostate, has been found to decrease tolerance for alcohol in men who have persistent sexual side effects after taking it. In a study of 83 men who took the drug, 65% of those who had at least one drink weekly reported drinking less after taking finasteride. Nearly 30% became abstinent.

Michael S. Irwig, MD, associate professor of medicine, The George Washington University School of Medicine & Health Sciences, Washington, DC.

7

Moneywise

Financial Paperwork Overload: What to Keep, What to Toss, What to Store on Your Computer

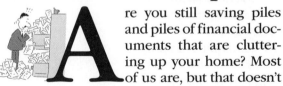re you still saving piles and piles of financial documents that are cluttering up your home? Most of us are, but that doesn't mean you need to. You can get rid of much of that space-hogging mess with the help of your computer and a few simple strategies.

Here is how to decide when you need to keep paperwork…when to shred it…and when saving digital copies is a viable option…

WHAT TO KEEP

***Keep:* Tax returns and supporting paperwork,** including receipts from tax-deductible purchases, for at least three years, or up to seven years in special situations. The IRS generally has three years to launch an audit, but

that window opens to six years when income is underreported by 25% or more…or seven years when a loss from worthless securities or bad debt is reported.

After three (or up to seven) years, shred most of the supporting documents, but keep the return itself, plus any W-2s and documents detailing retirement account contributions. Save these until you start receiving Social Security payments and withdrawing money from your retirement plan. They could come in handy if there's a dispute about your Social Security or retirement plan contributions.

Digital storage: The IRS now accepts digital copies of returns and supporting documents in audits—but these digital copies must have been saved in a fashion that renders them

Nanette Duffey, member of the National Association of Professional Organizers. She has the professional daily money manager designation from the American Association of Daily Money Managers. She is a former finance manager for General Electric and founder of Organized Instincts, LLC, an organizing and daily money-management company located in Kennesaw, Georgia. *OrganizedInstincts.com*

unalterable. The IRS has not been 100% clear about what forms of electronic documents meet this criteria—though a PDF should—so the safest policy is to keep paper files and use digital copies only as backup in case the originals are lost. Digital storage is fine for items saved beyond three to seven years. (See below for tips on how to store digitally.)

Keep: **Investment account statements and trade confirmations,** but toss monthly and quarterly ones when year-end statements arrive. Keep year-end statements as long as you are a customer of the investment company. *Two exceptions...*

•Keep paperwork that shows the initial price paid for an investment until you sell that investment, then transfer this paperwork to the selling year's tax file and deal with it as discussed in the section on tax paperwork above. This is especially important for investments made prior to 2012, before investment companies were required to maintain cost-basis information for clients.

•Keep paperwork related to nondeductible IRA contributions—those that you already paid taxes on—until you withdraw that money from your IRA. Otherwise you accidentally might pay taxes on the same money twice.

Digital storage: Most investment-related paperwork can be scanned and stored in a digital form if you prefer. (Original stock and savings bond certificates should be retained, however.)

Keep: **Financial documents related to your home and other real estate** at least as long as you own the property and ideally a few years longer. The more maintenance records you keep in the years after you sell, the better the odds that you could defend yourself against a lawsuit from the home's next owner that the house had a problem that you failed to disclose. The key records to save include mortgage documents signed at closing...federal truth-in-lending disclosure statements... recent homeowners' insurance contracts...title insurance documents...warranty deeds...receipts from work done on the home...home inspectors reports...and any additional paperwork received at closing.

Digital storage: Digital files usually are fine, but keep originals of anything that is notarized or that has an official seal.

Keep: **Insurance contracts and policy amendments as long as the policies are in effect.** Dispose of these when the policy ends or a new contract takes effect. If there are outstanding claims or any possibility that a claim might be made later for damage incurred during the prior contract term...or you are not yet certain that work done to satisfy an earlier claim was sufficient...then save the contract until these situations are resolved.

Digital storage: Digital copies are fine.

WHAT TO TOSS

Toss: **Sales receipts and bank ATM slips** after confirming that transactions have been reported correctly on credit card and bank statements. *Exceptions...*

•Keep receipts for big-ticket purchases, purchases where warranty or rebate claims might be made and purchases that might be returned. Dispose of these when the rebate or warranty period expires or the return window closes.

•Keep receipts from purchases related to home improvements, business spending, health care, gifts to charities or rental properties you own. File these with your tax paperwork, and keep them for at least three years after you sell the house in case you need them to establish a higher cost basis on the home or up to seven years to justify a tax deduction.

•Keep receipts related to auto maintenance and repairs as long as you own the vehicle. These could establish that you have lived up to the terms of the car's warranty or help you convince a buyer that you've taken good care of the car when you sell it.

Digital storage: Digital copies of receipts usually are acceptable, but check over the terms of any warranty, rebate or return programs to make sure that original documents are not specified.

Warning: If you save printed receipts, do not store them in a hot attic. Register receipts often are printed on thermal paper, which can be rendered illegible by heat.

Toss: **Utility bills when the following month's bill comes in showing that your**

prior payment was received. If you wish to track utility usage over time, record information from each bill on one list rather than save the bills themselves.

Exception: Save utility bills with your tax documents if you have a home office or rent out the property. They could be tax-deductible.

Digital storage: Paper copies are safest if your utility bills are tax-deductible.

More from Nanette Duffey…

Top Tech for Digital Document Storage

If you opt to store some of your financial documents in digital form, it pays to choose technology that will make the digital conversion process simple—and make your digital documents easy to sort through later.

The typical household all-in-one printer/scanner is fine for scanning the occasional page, but it's much too slow to scan years of financial documents. *Better products, programs and services for creating and organizing digital financial documents…*

• **Buy a scanner that processes at least eight pages per minute…**that can scan both sides of the page at the same time…and that can handle undersized items, like receipts. Nice options include the Fujitsu ScanSnap line of scanners—the ScanSnap S1300i is sufficient for most households ($295 list price,* *Fujitsu. com*)…and the NeatDesk desktop scanner and digital filing system ($399.95, *Neat.com*). NeatDesk doesn't just scan documents—it also features software that automatically organizes them for you.

• **When you scan documents, convert them to PDF format.** PDF offers excellent legibility and searchability without taking up a lot of memory. It's also a widely used, nonproprietary format, which means that it's unlikely to become unusable in the years ahead and leave you struggling to find a way to open your old documents.

Ideally you should store the PDFs with both an online storage service and a storage device in your home. Storing to two locations makes it

*Prices subject to change.

extremely unlikely that your documents will be lost. Prices for digital storage have fallen rapidly over recent years, so redundant storage is not cost prohibitive anymore. Carbonite (from $59.99 per year at *Carbonite.com*) and Mozy (starting at about $70 per year at *Mozy.com*) are two companies that offer secure off-site digital document storage for a reasonable price.

• **External hard drives are the safest, most cost-effective choice for digital storage in the home.** Drives providing one terabyte of storage—all you're likely to need—made by leading makers Western Digital (*WDC.com*) and Seagate (*Seagate.com*) now can be found for $80 or less. *A free service that could make digital storage of future financial documents easier…*

• Shoeboxed (*Shoeboxed.com*) is an app for Apple and Android smartphones that saves digital copies of receipts (and other small pieces of paper) when you photograph them with your phone's camera.

Free Sites to Manage Your Finances

At Planwise (*PlanWise.com*), you first enter your current bank account balance, income, debt and expenses. Then you add information on goals, such as buying a home, and the site shows how each of these large expenses will affect your finances months or years in the future…FindaBetterBank (*FindaBetter Bank.com*) lets you pick the aspects of banking most important to you, such as interest or mobile banking, then creates a list of checking accounts that meet your desires…SigFig (*SigFig.com*) shows you a summary of your balances, gains and losses, account fees and more, after you link your investment accounts to the site…and Jemstep (*Jemstep.com*) helps you to plan for retirement—it summarizes all of your retirement account information, estimates your income at retirement and suggests ways to increase it.

Kiplinger's Personal Finance. Kiplinger.com

Watch Out for These Financial Traps If You're Divorced or Remarrying

Eric A. Manterfield, an attorney specializing in estate planning, family business succession planning and probate litigation with Krieg DeVault, an Indianapolis-based law firm. He served as adjunct professor of estate planning at Indiana University School of Law for 30 years and is author of "Estate Planning for Couples in a Second Marriage," a paper published in *Journal of Practical Estate Planning* that later was reprinted in book form (American Law Institute). *KriegDeVault.com*

I t's hard enough to tackle standard estate-planning issues, but a divorce or remarriage further complicates the task. *Here's what you need to know if you've been through one of these life events recently, or might be in the future...*

DIVORCE: ACCOUNTS & POLICIES

Your former or soon-to-be former spouse likely was named as a beneficiary on many of your investment accounts, retirement accounts, life insurance policies and annuities. If you're like most divorced people, you no longer want him/her to receive these assets after your death. Contact account and policy providers to find out how to update these beneficiary designations.

Do this before filing for divorce, if possible, so that your spouse won't inherit if you die before the divorce is finalized. In some states, once you (or your spouse) file for divorce, an *Automatic Temporary Restraining Order* (ATRO) might prevent you from updating beneficiary designations until the divorce is final. You won't be allowed to remove your spouse as beneficiary from most pension and retirement plans without the spouse's consent until after the divorce is complete. This is true of qualified pensions and retirement plans, including 401(k)s, but not of IRAs (though your spouse might legally own some or all of your IRA if you live in a community property state).

Update your health-care and financial powers of attorney as soon as the divorce process begins as well. Fail to do this, and it might fall to your former spouse to make life-and-death decisions or important financial choices for you should you become incapacitated.

DIVORCE: WILLS & TRUSTS

You may not want to bother updating your will and living trusts—in most states, the law covering the court process called probate automatically disqualifies an ex-spouse as a beneficiary in these documents. Ask your divorce or estate-planning attorney whether your state does this.

Some people decide to remove their former spouses from their wills and trusts anyway, because they want them out of their estate plans for emotional reasons or they're concerned that these laws could change in the future.

If you funded an irrevocable trust that names your ex or soon-to-be ex as beneficiary, not only will this ex not be automatically removed as beneficiary upon divorce, it might not be possible to remove him/her at all. There's a reason that it's called an irrevocable trust. Ask your estate-planning attorney whether you have any options with such a trust, but don't be optimistic.

Warning: If you are granted ownership of jointly held property in your divorce settlement, this ruling does not automatically update ownership status of these assets. It's up to you to remove your ex as co-owner. Contact the insurance or investment firm managing the asset, or ask your estate-planning attorney or divorce attorney how to do this.

REMARRIAGE

When people remarry, it's fairly common for each partner to enter the union with substantial assets. The primary estate-planning issue becomes which partner will control which assets. Usually they decide that each will maintain control of assets that he/she brought into the marriage, while assets accumulated during the marriage will be shared—but reality can get more complicated.

Without proper estate planning, the assets of the first spouse to die will pass to the surviving spouse, which could result in eventual distributions that the first spouse would not condone if he/she were still alive. For example, the surviving spouse could pass the first spouse's assets to the surviving spouse's own kids or a favorite charity rather than to the departed spouse's children, as intended. Even a cherished family heirloom could pass outside the family.

Ways to prepare, starting with one that gives you the least control...

Tell your new spouse which heirs you would like to eventually inherit your assets and trust the new spouse to follow through on all your intentions.

Potential complication: Even if you trust this spouse completely, he/she later might go against your intentions, particularly if he/she remarries or has kids from a prior relationship who experience financial problems.

Set up a trust to receive the assets of the first spouse to pass away. The surviving spouse could receive income from this trust, but the first spouse's chosen heirs would inherit the assets upon the second spouse's death.

Potential complications: The income from this trust might not be sufficient for the surviving spouse's needs.

Also, this trust would receive only assets that the first spouse to die owns in his/her own name, not those owned jointly with the surviving spouse and not those that list the surviving spouse (or anyone else) on beneficiary-designation forms, which can lead to unintended consequences if the first spouse to pass away thought other major assets would be transferred to the trust as well.

Ask an estate-planning attorney to help you draft a contract between spouses detailing how assets will be divided among heirs upon the second spouse's death. Include this contract in both partners' wills or revocable trusts. This can provide the surviving spouse with greater access to resources than the trust option mentioned above while still protecting the intentions of the first spouse to die.

Potential complications: These contracts must be drafted carefully to avoid loopholes that could undermine their intent. For example, the wording must prohibit large wealth transfers by the surviving spouse during his/her lifetime. Hire an experienced estate-planning attorney to draft the contract, not a friend or relative who happens to be a lawyer. This strategy tends not to work well with marketable securities, which can become comingled with assets belonging to the surviving spouse (or the surviving spouse's next spouse if he/she remarries again), making it very difficult to confirm that the contract is being honored.

Consider using the trust option for most assets—but first speak with a financial planner to make sure that the assets that the surviving spouse receives from the trust will be sufficient for his/her needs and confirm with your attorney that the assets that you expect to go into this trust will indeed do so upon your death. Use the contract option for identifiable assets such as a family business that can't easily become comingled.

Be aware of spousal minimum share rules. Most states have laws requiring a surviving spouse to receive a minimum share of his/her deceased spouse's estate, often one-third or one-half. When people remarry, they often wish to leave the lion's share of their assets to their kids from their first marriage instead, particularly if the new spouse has considerable assets of his own. *Two ways around spousal minimum share rules...*

• **The spouse's minimum share can be waived through a prenuptial agreement.**

• **Assets can be made payable directly to the children.** List your children from your first marriage as named beneficiaries on some of your financial accounts, insurance policies or other assets...or title accounts and assets as jointly held with these children. These assets will not be included in your estate, so in most states, they will not be included in calculations of the surviving spouse's minimum share. Speak with an estate-planning attorney to confirm that this is true in your state.

What You Must Talk About Before the Wedding

First off, find out how your future spouse handles money—pay attention to how and where he/she spends it. And be sure to reveal everything about your own finances, including income, debts and retirement accounts—and explain your strengths and weaknesses with money. Each of you should also get copies of credit reports from the three major credit bureaus and share them. If you both work, plan to live on one salary and save as much as possible of the second one. If your partner was married before, find out about any financial obligations to the former spouse or children of that marriage.

Bill Hardekopf, CEO of *LowCards.com*, which tracks credit cards, Birmingham, Alabama, and author of *The Credit Card Guidebook* (Lulu).

Consumer Protection for Overseas Money Transfers

Recent rules governing wire and electronic transfers stipulate more disclosure from those providing the transfer service. Providers must tell consumers the exchange rate being used, the amount of fees and taxes, and how much money the recipient will receive. Providers also must give the consumers a receipt including the information already disclosed…and also saying when the money will be available and whom the sender can contact in case of a problem. Finally, consumers can cancel a transfer and get a full refund as long as the request is made within 30 minutes—although different rules may apply to recurring or preauthorized transfers and under certain circumstances.

FDIC Consumer News. FDIC.gov/ConsumerNews

DID YOU KNOW THAT...

The Average Checking Account Has 30 Possible Fees?

And banks don't always disclose their fees clearly.

Worst banks for fee disclosure: Comerica Bank, KeyBank, USAA Federal Savings Bank and M&T Bank.

Top-rated banks: Capital One, Citibank, Compass Bank and JPMorgan Chase Bank.

WalletHub.com's 2014 Checking Account Transparency Report.

Beware of Account Inactivity Fees!

Inactivity fees can eat into your holdings in accounts that you do not use often. Some banks and credit unions charge monthly fees when accounts are dormant for six months or more.

Example: Evantage Bank's Mega Money Market Account recently paid 0.9% interest on balances up to $35,000*…but the bank charges $10 per statement cycle if an account is not used.

Best: Ask if your institution charges an inactivity fee and how to avoid it.

Examples: Direct deposits of as little as $1 a month may avoid the fees…or simply calling to inquire about the account may be enough.

Caution: Inactivity fees are not limited to banks and credit unions. About one-third of prepaid debit cards charge a monthly inactivity fee if the card is not used for 90 days.

Kiplinger's Personal Finance. Kiplinger.com

*Rates and prices subject to change.

Checking Account Fees at Record Highs

Banks now charge noncustomers an average of $2.77 to use ATMs, up from $2.60

in 2013, making the total cost $4.35 when you include the fee that your own bank charges when you use another bank's machine. If you use an out-of-network ATM weekly, that's $226.20 a year.

Bankrate.com's *2014 Checking Survey* of 10 banks in each of the 25 largest US markets.

Is Your Name in This Database Designed to Protect Banks?

Little-known check-fraud databases are ensnaring more than a million low-income Americans who have made minor financial mistakes such as bouncing a check. These databases, designed to protect banks against fraud, prevent individuals from getting loans and opening bank accounts.

Roundup of experts in banking, reported in *The New York Times*.

Free Money from Banks

Some banks are offering cash or cash equivalents to people who open specific new accounts during specified periods of time.

Examples: Chase gives a $150 bonus for a new Total Checking account with minimum deposit and direct deposit.* KeyBank, Santander and others also have cash offers. EverBank offers a 1.4% six-month bonus rate on its Yield Pledge checking account to first-time checking customers. BankDirect offers several airline-mileage awards—for example, Mileage Checking with Interest gives 10,000 American Airlines AAdvantage miles if you direct-deposit at least $2,000 monthly for six consecutive months.

GoBankingRates.com
*Offers and rates subject to change.

Getting Bank Loans Is Now Easier!

What you can expect for different types of loans…

• **Auto loans**—consumers with credit scores that are below 620 can qualify for longer (60-to-72-month) loans, although the loans have high single-digit interest rates.

• **Home-equity loans**—lenders are allowing consumers to borrow up to 85% of the value of their homes, up from a maximum of 80%.

• **Home mortgages**—in areas where prices have stabilized, the required down payments for 30-year fixed mortgages are dropping from 20% to between 10% and 15%.

Greg McBride, CFA, chief financial analyst for *Bank rate.com*, a personal finance website based in North Palm Beach, Florida.

Some Credit Unions Match Competitors' Interest Rates

Always ask a credit union or bank if it will beat a competitor's rate. *Some examples of recent offers…*

AOD Federal, Bynum, Alabama, pays borrowers $100 if it can't match an auto loan rate.* Campus USA, Gainesville, Florida, says it will try to match CD rates. Freedom First in Salem, Virginia, says it will beat competitor rates on auto loans. Georgia Guard in Macon will usually match rates on CDs. OSU Federal, Corvallis, Oregon, asks for a chance to match rates. Savannah Federal Credit Union, Savannah, matches reasonable rates on loans and savings accounts. SODES Federal, Aberdeen, South Dakota, matches rates on some secured loans for qualified customers.

GoBankingRates.com
*Offers and rates subject to change.

What to Check Before Applying for a Loan

Check the accuracy of your employment and salary history when applying for a loan or a job. Potential lenders and employers can gain access to this information through employee-data reporting firms such as Equifax Workforce Solutions and First Advantage. Under the Fair Credit Reporting Act, you are entitled to receive a report with this information annually from each firm, and you can dispute any incorrect information.

Contact Equifax Workforce Solutions for the Employment Data Report, (866-604-6570, *TheWorkNumber.com)*...or contact First Advantage for the Background Check Report, (888-215-3727, *FADV.com)*.

Persis Yu, JD, staff attorney with National Consumer Law Center, Boston. NCLC.org

Free FICO Credit Scores

Free FICO credit scores now are available for some holders of credit cards issued by Discover, First National Bank of Omaha and Barclaycard US. These are the actual FICO scores used by lenders to grant or deny credit and assign interest rates—not the so-called "educational" credit scores sold to customers under such names as PLUS and VantageScore. Those scores are used by few if any businesses.

FICO is allowing its actual scores to be given to consumers because Congress is considering a law giving consumers a legal right to their actual credit scores—which now generally are available only in special circumstances, for instance when someone is turned down for credit or gets less money than he/she applied for. Ask your credit card issuer for details on FICO score availability.

ConsumerReports.org and *CreditCards.com.*

Watch Out for the $1 Credit Score

Ed Mierzwinski, consumer program director and senior fellow for the nonprofit US Public Interest Research Group, Washington, DC.

Credit-reporting bureaus have a new way to coax us into paying big bucks for a monthly credit-monitoring service by charging only $1 for our credit score. Experian, Equifax and TransUnion have historically marketed their credit-monitoring services as "free," even though these services actually cost as much as $21.95 a month.* The bureaus provided a brief free-trial period—often seven days—before the charges started. The Credit Card Accountability Responsibility and Disclosure Act of 2009 cracked down on their use of the word "free," requiring them to more clearly disclose the recurring charges.

Now Experian and TransUnion are sidestepping the crackdown on the word "free" by offering credit scores and an accompanying credit report for $1. People who sign up are charged a monthly fee—$21.95 at Experian and $17.95 at TransUnion—unless they cancel the service within seven days. That is stated on the website, but most people don't read every word on a web page and may just focus on the big banner headline that highlights the $1 price.

Warning: Even the credit bureau's seven-day grace period before the recurring charges start might not be what it seems. As Experian states on its website, "The credit monitoring benefit may only be available for five days during your trial period since enrollment can take up to 48 hours."

The reality is that you can get three free credit reports (which will give your credit history but not your credit score) each year from *AnnualCreditReport.com,* a website created by Congress that is run by the three national credit bureaus. You can stagger your three reports so that you get one every four months. And if you suspect that you are a victim of ID theft, you can get one, for free, under a

*Prices subject to change.

different part of the law (*Consumer.FTC.gov*, click on "Privacy & Identity," then on "Repairing Identity Theft.")

Stay-at-Home Spouses Can Get Credit Cards Again

Housewives and house husbands who have been unable to qualify for credit cards previously should try again. A recent rule change has greatly improved their odds of approval.

Up until 2011, stay-at-home spouses had no more trouble obtaining credit cards than anyone else. But an amendment to the Credit Card Accountability Responsibility and Disclosure Act (CARD Act) enacted that year blocked card issuers from offering credit to applicants with limited income. The amendment was meant to prevent consumers from accumulating high-interest-rate credit card debt that they couldn't afford to repay. But the way the amendment was worded, it also prevented issuers from offering credit cards to homemakers—even if their spouses' income put them in an excellent position to pay their bills.

This so-called "anti-housewife" rule was finally amended in 2013, and credit card issuers are once again allowed to factor in third-party income to which the applicant has access, such as a spouse's income.

John Ulzheimer, president of The Ulzheimer Group, LLC, an Atlanta–based company offering credit-related consulting services. Ulzheimer is also author of The Smart Consumer's Guide to Good Credit *(Allworth).* JohnUlzheimer.com

---

DID YOU KNOW THAT...

Banks Can Take Your Money Without Asking?

Any loan you take from a bank establishes a debtor-creditor relationship. If you do not make good on your promise to repay your debt, the bank can seize money in your deposit account to the extent of what you owe.

GoBankingRates.com

Sneaky Rewards-Card Rules

Odysseas Papadimitriou, founder and CEO of Evolution Finance, Inc., the Arlington, Virginia–based parent company of CardHub.com, *an online marketplace for comparing credit cards, prepaid cards and gift cards.*

If you charge a pricey purchase on a rewards credit card, you probably expect to earn a lot of rewards points. But it doesn't always work out that way. Legislation that took effect in 2010 requires card issuers to be up-front about most card fees and terms—but those consumer protections don't apply to rewards programs that offer cash back, points, airline miles or similar perks. Issuers still can change program terms with little or no notice and hide confusing rewards rules in the small print.

Rewards-card issuers can unilaterally declare that rewards points or miles suddenly are worth less than in the past. They quietly can add new rules that allow points or miles to expire. And they can impose rules that cause rewards balances to be forfeited when consumers make missteps, such as being late with consecutive payments. *What to do...*

• **Choose rewards cards issued by banks that tend to be transparent with rewards-programs terms.** These include Capital One, Bank of America and US Bank, according to our recent survey. Avoid those such as Barclays Bank that tend to make their rewards programs difficult to understand.

• **Read rewards-program terms carefully, including any footnotes.** Read any program updates that are mailed to you as well.

• **Lean toward cash-back cards over rewards cards that offer points or airline miles.** Issuers cannot devalue the cash you already have accumulated in a cash-back card rewards account.

• **If you are late with a payment or make some other misstep** with a rewards card on which you have accumulated a sizable rewards balance, contact the card issuer to see whether you have put your rewards balance at risk. If you have, ask what you can do to minimize the negative consequences.

•**Redeem rewards balances before canceling rewards cards.** Fail to do so, and those rewards likely will be lost.

Surprising Credit Card Fact

A credit card payment must be at least 30 days past due before the issuer can legally report it to a credit bureau.

John Ulzheimer, president of The Ulzheimer Group. *JohnUlzheimer.com*

Enjoy Longer Periods of 0% Interest on Credit Card Balance Transfers

Offers of 0% interest—frequently for 15 or 18 months rather than the standard 12 months—have now become more widespread among major credit card issuers. Consumers generally must have credit scores at least in the mid-700s to qualify, and nearly all of the cards impose a transfer fee, typically 3% to 5%.

Exception: The Slate card from Chase Visa offers 0% interest for 15 months on balance transfers and on new purchases, with no transfer fee.

Bill Hardekopf, CEO of *LowCards.com*, which tracks credit cards, Birmingham, Alabama, and author of *The Credit Card Guidebook* (Lulu).

Rent Out Your Home for Extra Cash

Scott Shatford, founder of *RentingYourPlace.com*, which helps property owners maximize their rental income on Airbnb. He is author of *The Airbnb Expert's Playbook* (Amazon Digital Services) and creator of AirDnA, a tool that offers Airbnb analytics for more than 2,500 global cities. He has used Airbnb to rent his own home and rental properties.

Thanks to the website Airbnb, more home owners are earning extra cash by taking in guests. This site has over one million listings worldwide, allowing property owners to earn money by renting out a second home…spare rooms in their primary residence…or their entire primary residence when they are out of town.

But many home owners worry that inviting strangers into their homes could be an invitation to disaster. A guest could steal or damage their property or even do them physical harm.

What you need to know to successfully rent out your home or a room on Airbnb…

ATTRACTING GUESTS

Airbnb (*Airbnb.com*) is not the only short-term property rental website—competitors include *HomeAway.com* and *VRBO.com*—but it is the best choice. It can market rental properties to literally millions of potential guests…it's the easiest home-rental site to use…it does not impose any upfront or annual fees (hosts pay 3% of their rental income)…and it offers the strongest safety features, including free insurance (see page 136) and "Verified ID"—most guests must provide Airbnb a copy of a passport or driver's license or verify personal information in other ways.

To rent out your place…

•**Advertise yourself, not just your property.** Include a friendly picture of yourself in your listing and personal details, such as your hobbies. Potential guests are much more likely to rent from you if they form a positive first impression of you.

•**Set a low initial rate.** When you're starting out, price your property around 25% below the rates charged by the most comparable Airbnb properties in your area. This gives guests a reason to take a chance on your unproven property rather than rent a nearby property that already has numerous glowing reviews. A low price also increases the odds that guests will feel they got their money's worth and post positive reviews of your property. Those positive reviews will attract future guests...even after you have raised your price.

• **Target peak-demand weeks.** If your plan is to rent out your primary residence when you're away on vacation, take your vacations when lodging in your area is in greatest demand. *To identify these weeks, consider...*

• Do other Airbnb properties and hotels in your area charge higher rates during particular weeks?

• Is there a festival, marathon, sports game or other event that annually draws large numbers of visitors to your area?

• When do area colleges have their homecoming, graduation and parents' weekends?

• **Don't oversell your home.** Giving an overly rosy picture of your property will lead to disappointed guests. Disappointed guests are likely to post negative reviews. *Examples:* Don't say your home is on the beach if it is actually two blocks away...don't call the property tranquil if it is on a busy road.

Use the listings of highly rated Airbnb properties in your area as a template for what to mention in your listing.

The photos you include should tell an honest story as well. For instance, don't take a picture of the beautiful view from your rooftop if the view from the inside of your home is far less impressive.

• **Clean, then clean again.** Some guests have very high standards for cleanliness. Better to spend extra time cleaning than receive a negative review.

• **Form a personal connection.** Greet your guests in person when they arrive, if possible. Check in with them during their visit to see if there's anything they need. Send a note thanking them for their visit. These connections will help guests see you as a person, not just a property owner, which increases the odds that they will take good care of your property and give you a good review.

SAFETY AND SECURITY

Airbnb does not disclose statistics about how often rentals go wrong, but theft and serious property damage appear to be rare. There were more than 10 million Airbnb rentals last year, yet mentions of major problems are uncommon on social media and in the press. I've never had a single problem in more than 50 rentals at my private home and 500 rentals at my full-time rental properties—not so much as a broken dish.

Still, it is prudent to be cautious...

• **Install digital door locks.** With these you can give guests a code that they can use to enter, then you can change the code after their visit. That is safer than handing over a key, which a guest could have copied in order to sneak in later. Digital locks cost $100 to $300.

• **Rent only to guests who have excellent reviews and "verified IDs."** A guest who has received uniformly glowing feedback after five or more rentals is unlikely to cause problems. Guests with "Verified ID" badges on their profiles almost certainly are who they claim.

Also: Read what the guest has written about himself/herself in his profile...what he has written about Airbnb properties he previously has visited...and what the owners of those prior Airbnb properties have written about this guest.

• **Exchange e-mails with a potential guest.** Try to get a feel for this person and anyone he will be traveling with. Families and retirees tend to be especially low-risk guests.

• **Lock up portable valuables, or store them off-site.** Buy a safe...rent a bank security-deposit box...or store items of particular value with a friend or relative.

LEGALITY

Many cities and some towns have laws that restrict property owners' right to rent out their homes on a short-term basis or require them to pay hotel taxes if they do so. Call your town's or city's zoning or development office to ask about applicable laws in your area. Or enter the terms "Airbnb," "legal" and the name of your town into a search engine to see if a local newspaper or other reliable source has written anything on the subject.

In practice, however, these laws are almost never enforced even when they exist...unless neighbors complain.

Also worth noting...

•**Even if local laws restrict your right to rent out your property on a short-term basis,** you probably can rent out a room in your property while you are on hand.

•**Homeowner's associations (and condo or co-op boards)** often have rules blocking short-term rentals. These groups may enforce rules strictly.

•**Tenants often are prohibited by the terms of their rental contracts from subletting** their dwellings without the property owner's permission.

More from Scott Shatford...

Airbnb Insurance

Homeowner's insurance often does not cover claims related to paying guests. Airbnb recently addressed this concern—starting January 2015, the company began providing $1 million in liability insurance at no extra charge to protect property owners should a guest be injured or killed. That's in addition to the $1 million in coverage it already supplies for property theft and/or damage stemming from rentals.

This greatly reduces insurance concerns, but...

•**The liability component of Airbnb's coverage is new and untested.** If you want to be certain that you are well-covered—or if you rent out your home through a service other than Airbnb—consider purchasing coverage designed specifically for properties that are rented out on a short-term basis. Providers include CBIZ Insurance Services (*CBIZ.com*) and Peers Marketplace (*Peers.org*).

•**Cash and securities are not covered by Airbnb's million-dollar theft insurance.** Coverage for jewelry, collectibles, artwork and certain other high-end items is limited. Airbnb's coverage also does not protect property owners from losses due to identity theft if a guest gets hold of, say, credit card account information, Social Security numbers or other sensitive information.

•**There have been reports of homeowner's insurance companies threatening to cancel the coverage of homes that are rented out.** Ask your insurer if renting out your property through Airbnb will affect your coverage—and get the answer in writing.

Where Homes Sell in One Day!

Homes are selling very quickly in some communities in Florida and California, where the inventory of homes is small and the prices are far below what they were in 2005 or 2006. In other markets, time to sale also is going down.

MarketWatch.com

Short Sales Still Offer Deep Discounts

Even with rising house prices, short sales offer deep discounts, compared with the cost of a nondistressed home. Some cities are particular bargains in these kinds of sales, where the house is sold for less than what the owner owes on the mortgage.

Recent examples: In Santa Barbara, California, average short-sale price was $283,825, a discount of 42.7% from nondistressed sales (that's a savings of $211,420)...Phoenix, average short sale $149,094, a discount of 37.8%...Las Vegas, average short sale $124,555, a discount of 33.4%...in Cleveland, average REO (bank-owned) price $57,782, a discount of 56%...Charlotte, North Carolina, average REO price was $111,260, a discount of 43%.

Consult a real estate agent with experience in sales of distressed properties.

MarketWatch.com

Bidding Wars Are Back! How to Win If You're Buying a Home...or Selling One

Robert Irwin, who has more than 40 years of experience as a real estate broker and investor. Based in Westlake Village, California, he is author of several books about real estate, including *Tips and Traps When Buying a Home* (McGraw-Hill). *RobertIrwin.com*

R ecently, one simple four-bedroom tract house in Dublin, California, attracted 40 offers from would-be buyers. The winning bid was an amazing $100,000 above the $399,000 asking price.

Yes, bidding wars are back. Seven years after the collapse of the US housing market, prices are rising...shoppers are showing up...and in many areas, bidders are competing for homes that are in short supply. More than two-thirds of US homes recently for sale received multiple offers, according to the online real estate brokerage *Redfin.com*.

Here's what potential buyers need to know now—plus tips for sellers...

• **Set a walk-away number in advance.** Before you even make your initial offer, decide how high you are willing to increase your offer if a bidding war breaks out. Without this walk-away number set in your mind, it's easy to get caught up in trying to win and bid more than the property is worth.

Helpful: Focus your home search on just one or two neighborhoods. Visit open houses frequently in these neighborhoods, and use *Zillow.com* and *Trulia.com* to track actual sale prices for homes that are comparable to what you're looking for.

• **Promise to come up with more cash if the appraisal comes in low.** Real estate offers usually are contingent on the property being appraised for at least the purchase price. If the appraisal comes in lower, the buyer's financing is likely to fall through. Trouble is, appraisers base their judgments on past transactions, so appraisals often fall short of aggressive offers. Agents representing sellers realize this and worry that their best offers will evaporate.

One powerful way to make your offer stand out is to include an agreement to pay a larger share of the purchase price in cash, if necessary, to prevent the appraisal clause from quashing the deal. Of course, you can do this only if you can come up with tens of thousands of dollars in a hurry on top of the money you already have set aside for your down payment.

Example: A man bidding $250,000 on a home added an agreement to increase the cash portion of his offer by up to $50,000, if necessary, to obtain a loan. His offer was accepted, even though there were higher bids.

Alternative: If you can afford to make a cash offer on a home rather than take out a loan, you can eliminate the appraisal clause and other mortgage-related contingencies from your offer entirely. That will make you even more attractive to sellers.

If you're bidding on a house worth less than $300,000, you might be up against big real estate investors offering cash. However, these bidders want bargains and so are not always willing to engage in bidding wars.

• **Address the seller's nonmonetary priorities.** Have your agent ask the listing agent if the seller has any concerns related to the home sale beyond getting as much money as possible. Address these concerns in your offer.

Examples: The seller might be worried that construction of the new home that he/she is planning to move to won't be completed on schedule. You could offer to rent back the home that you are buying to the seller for a month or two, if necessary. If the seller is especially proud of his/her garden, you could promise to maintain it with great care. If the seller is downsizing and can't fit all his old furniture into his new home, you could offer to buy some of the furniture at a relatively modest price.

●**Write the seller a letter praising his home.** State how much you love the home, how perfectly it meets your needs and how well you intend to take care of it. Include this letter with your offer.

Helpful: If the seller's agent mentioned an aspect of the property that the seller particularly loved, include this feature in your letter.

●**Consider arranging for a preacceptance home inspection if a seller sets an extended window for offers.** Would-be buyers who want to stand out from other bidders in competitive markets sometimes waive the home-inspection contingency in their offers—the right to back out of the deal if an inspector finds problems with the home. This may get a seller's attention, but it's not worth the risk.

However, there is one situation when waiving a home-inspection contingency can make sense. Sellers sometimes announce that they won't choose an offer for a week or 10 days, in hopes of drawing many offers and starting a bidding war. Would-be buyers can take advantage of this delay by having a home inspection done before making an offer. If the home inspection comes back relatively clean, the would-be buyers can safely waive the home-inspection contingency. This home inspection will cost you $300 to $500,* however—money that's wasted if the seller chooses another offer. So use this strategy only in very competitive markets and for a very special property.

●**Don't agree to automatically "escalate" your offer.** If you're looking for a house in a very competitive market, your agent might encourage you to include an escalation clause in your offer. This clause is an agreement to increase your initial offer enough to top any other offer that the seller receives by some predetermined amount—say, $1,000 or $5,000.

In practice, such clauses often lead to paying more than a home's true value. If another would-be buyer falls in love with the home and overbids, your escalation clause might

*Prices subject to change.

force you to overbid by even more. If another would-be buyer makes a bid that includes a steep purchase price but has other details that make that price worth less than it appears, your escalation clause might force you to bid above the high price without taking these other details into account.

Example: A bidder offers $400,000 but also demands that the seller make $35,000 in repairs to the home or contributions to closing costs. The true value of that offer is just $365,000, but your escalation clause probably would increase your offer above $400,000 regardless—potentially far above the true value of the property.

Of course, you could put a cap on your escalation clause—but such a cap would only tip off the seller to exactly how much you're willing to spend to obtain the property.

●**Find a "vest pocket" deal, and skip the bidding wars.** Tell a handful (or more) of real estate agents that you're very interested in a particular neighborhood or in a type of property—and that you have not signed on with a buyer's agent. The best agents to approach are the ones who seem to do the most business in your favorite neighborhoods, based on the "Home for Sale" signs. You might find an agent who has a vest pocket property—a home for sale that has not been posted to the Multiple Listing Service (MLS) and therefore is unknown to other potential buyers. Agents occasionally keep a choice property or two off the MLS in hopes of finding a buyer themselves. That way, they can claim the whole commission for the sale rather than split it with a buyer's agent.

More from Robert Irwin...

5 Tips for Sellers

Home sellers have the upper hand in many real estate markets these days, but that doesn't mean they should just sit back and wait for the offers to roll in.

Here are five ways that sellers in hot markets can increase the odds that their property will ignite a bidding war and get the most money out of the situation if it does...

1. Set your asking price roughly 5% below market. A low asking price usually draws in more bidders and can lead to a higher final sale price in a hot market.

2. Hold an open house for agents only. Each agent who learns about your property could tell several potential bidders about it. Mention that free food will be offered, and you'll get a great agent turnout. Open houses for the general public tend not to attract serious bidders.

3. Fix any cosmetic problems. Many more potential bidders will fall in love with a beautiful home than a fixer-upper.

4. Don't accept any offers for 10 to 14 days. This gives as many potential buyers as possible a chance to see the property. Set a deadline for offers after that period ends.

5. Tell at least the top three or four bidders that you have received multiple bids. Ask for their best offers.

Mortgage Preapprovals Are Vanishing

Mortgage preapprovals—documents that state the maximum-size home loan that a buyer can get as well as the likely interest rate—accounted for just 4% of purchase mortgages originated by the top 25 lenders recently. Preapprovals traditionally have helped buyers compete with people offering cash for a home—by showing that they already have a mortgage lined up. Preapprovals are in decline because of reduced competition among mortgage lenders for new clients...and because lower-than-expected appraisals have led lenders to insist that buyers put up extra cash, resulting in buyers walking away before a preapproval is completed. Banks say that they continue to do prequalifications, informing borrowers—often verbally—what size loan they probably can qualify for. But these do not give buyers much leverage in bidding for a house that has several offers.

MarketWatch.com

Save Hundreds by Negotiating Mortgage Fees

You can now save hundreds of dollars by negotiating mortgage fees.

Biggest chances for leverage: Application or processing fee, which some brokers will waive. You also can save by calling several attorneys to get their costs for a closing—rates vary, and some lawyers charge a flat fee while others bill by the hour. Shop around, but do not try to negotiate third-party fees, such as appraisal costs and the charge for running a credit report—those are not negotiable.

Roundup of experts in mortgage financing, reported at *FoxBusiness.com*.

Interest-Only Mortgages

Interest-only mortgages are making a comeback but carry significant risks. Borrowers pay interest but no principal during the first few years of the loan.

However: Lenders often require high down payments for interest-only loans...sometimes charge higher interest rates...and may make rates adjustable, so payments rise when interest rates do.

MarketWatch.com

New Rules for ARMs

New adjustable-rate-mortgage (ARM) rules made the loans safer but harder to get. The rules (effective January 2014) require lenders to consider what the rate will be after it is adjusted when deciding whether a potential borrower will be able to repay the loan. ARMs become more expensive as their interest rates rise—so monthly payments go up.

Keith Gumbinger, vice president of HSH Associates, publisher of mortgage and real estate information, Riverdale, New Jersey. *HSH.com*

Low Interest Rates for These Types of Mortgages...

Ten-year fixed-rate home mortgages offer low interest rates and are gaining popularity. You still can get an ultra-low rate of around 3% on a 10-year loan,* which can save a lot of money.

Example: On a home with $100,000 left in principal to pay, refinancing at 4% for 30 years will cost you $71,869 in interest with $477 in monthly payments...while a 3% loan for 10 years costs just $15,873 in interest but has monthly payments of $965.

Keith Gumbinger, vice president of HSH Associates, publisher of mortgage and real estate information, Riverdale, New Jersey. *HSH.com*

*Rate subject to change.

Court Makes Reverse Mortgages Safer

Ira Rheingold, executive director of the National Association of Consumer Advocates, Washington, DC. *ConsumerAdvocates.org*

There will be no more foreclosure for widows and widowers whose spouses took out reverse mortgages (which allow home owners who are age 62 or older to borrow money against the home's value and not have to pay it back unless they move).

The US Department of Housing and Urban Development (HUD) has contended that if only one spouse is named as the borrower on a reverse mortgage, the death of that spouse means that the survivor must either pay off the reverse mortgage or lose the home. But the US District Court for the District of Columbia recently ruled that federal laws protect surviving spouses from these foreclosures. That ruling will apply nationwide unless it's successfully appealed in a higher court. Many married couples have listed only the older spouse as a bor-

rower on the reverse mortgage because this netted them more money from the lender.

Bottom line: Surviving spouses who are not listed on reverse mortgages should be allowed to stay in their homes—pending a possible HUD appeal. But in light of the court decision, lenders are less likely to offer more money if only one spouse is listed as the borrower.

EASY-TO-DO...

Cut the Cost of Title Insurance by 50%

Ask about a "reissue rate" for title insurance when you are refinancing your home. Reissue rates—the extension of a current policy at reduced rates—also may be offered if you buy a home from someone who has lived there for 10 years or less. Ask your real estate agent or title company for details.

AARP Bulletin. AARP.org/bulletin

Vacation Home Bargains: Prices Are Down 25% or More

Robert Irwin, who has more than 40 years of experience as a real estate broker and investor. Based in Westlake Village, California, he is author of several books about real estate, including *Tips and Traps When Selling a Home* (McGraw-Hill). *RobertIrwin.com*

The residential real estate market is roaring back as homes sell at their fastest pace in five years. But in one segment of the housing market, bargains still abound—vacation homes.

In some areas where vacation homes are popular and plentiful, median sale prices remain 25% or more below their peaks.

Vacation homes are expensive discretionary purchases, and historically buyers don't start snapping them up again after a recession until there's no doubt that the economy is firmly back on its feet. There also is a significant supply of vacation homes currently on the market, helping depress prices.

Buyers tend to get the best deals on vacation homes in the off-season—so unless you're in the market for a winter ski cabin, this fall and winter might very well be one of your few remaining chances to get a great price on a vacation property.

But be aware that buying a vacation home differs from buying a primary residence in some crucial ways. *Here's what you need to know…*

WHAT TO BUY

Four key considerations when selecting a vacation property…

•**Vacation homes immediately adjacent to desired features are the safest investments.** Developers always can build more homes near the beach or the golf course—it's the properties right next to these things that are in limited supply, and so they are the most likely to at least hold their value and potentially even gain in value. And if there are no properties between you and your stunning view, you don't have to worry that one of your neighbors will expand his house or allow a tree to grow in a way that blocks that view.

Properties right next to amenities inevitably cost more than those a short distance away. If that strains your budget, opt for a smaller home right next to the amenity rather than a larger one farther away…or opt for a home next to the amenity in a slightly less upscale area.

•**Older vacation homes can become upkeep nightmares.** Ask vacation home owners about their biggest complaint, and most will say maintenance. Having two homes means maintaining two homes, and upkeep issues can be magnified in a vacation home because it likely is unoccupied much of the time. A drip or leak could cause extensive damage before it's spotted. A broken furnace might not be noticed until the home's pipes have frozen and burst. The older the vacation home, the more maintenance issues there are likely to be.

Helpful: To minimize maintenance issues, have a neighbor or caretaker look in on the property when you are not around, or buy a vacation condo rather than a freestanding house.

•**The distance from your primary residence to your vacation property will play a major role in determining your satisfaction with it.** If the total travel time is longer than four to five hours, you might not use or appreciate the property as much as you expect.

•**Peak season probably is not the only time you'll visit.** You might love a ski chalet in the winter or a beach house in the summer, but it usually is best to buy a second home in an area that has some appeal during multiple seasons. The cost of buying a vacation home might curtail your ability to do other traveling, so it should be someplace that you enjoy visiting whenever you feel like getting away from your primary residence.

FEES, RULES AND INSURANCE

Discuss zoning rules with the town or the county building department before buying if you hope to expand or rebuild your vacation home. Vacation home areas often have particularly strict zoning laws to prevent landowners from hindering access to an amenity (such as the shore), altering the character of the region or overdeveloping the land around a popular amenity.

Also, ask at the town offices if there are any special fees or requirements that apply to the property because of its location.

Examples: The owner of a small cabin in the woods might be required to pay a special fire-control fee…the owner of a waterfront property might be required to install a special high-end septic system the next time the septic system needs to be replaced.

Also, investigate insurance costs before you settle on a vacation home area. Homeowners insurance rates have been rising rapidly in many hurricane-prone waterfront communities along the Atlantic and Gulf coasts. And some policies now feature huge hurricane deductibles equal to 10% of the home's value.

If a property is in an area at risk for floods, you might need to purchase a separate flood insurance policy as well—standard homeowners insurance does not normally cover flooding. The federal government is phasing out its subsidies of flood insurance, so this policy could cost thousands of dollars a year on top of your homeowners insurance rates.

PRICING AND FINANCING

It isn't always easy to determine what a vacation home is worth. Recent sales of homes that seem comparable based on their size and neighborhood might not be truly comparable at all. With vacation properties, differences in things such as views or water access can result in substantial differences in value.

● **Drive by properties mentioned as comparables,** if possible, to confirm that their views and/or water access truly are similar to the property you're considering. Work with a real estate agent who is not just familiar with the area, but who also has extensive experience in the purchases and sales of vacation homes such as the one you hope to buy.

● **Be very cautious about buying a vacation home unless you can do so by paying cash or nearly all cash**—especially if you already have a sizable mortgage on your primary residence. Paying two mortgages—plus the maintenance and taxes on two properties—can become a crushing financial burden. But some vacation home buyers might choose to take out a mortgage, even though they could afford to pay cash, to take advantage of today's still relatively low interest rates. If so, get quotes from at least three or four lenders or brokers—rates and terms offered on second-home mortgages can vary dramatically.

TAXES AND RENTAL INCOME

If you use your vacation home as a second home, not a rental property, you might be able to deduct your mortgage interest and property taxes just as you do with your primary residence.

Some vacation home buyers intend to defray the cost of ownership by renting out the property when they're not using it. This rarely works as well as they hope.

Many vacation homes are highly seasonal and command attractive rental rates only 10 to 12 weeks each year—and that's during the weeks when you probably want to use the property yourself.

If you don't live very near your vacation home, you probably will have to pay a property-management company to handle tenant selection and coordinate maintenance. Expect this company to claim 12% to 25% of your gross rental receipts.

Meanwhile, tenants often don't take very good care of rental properties, leading to high upkeep costs.

Renting out a vacation home can complicate your taxes, too. You might have to pay income tax on the money paid to you as rent. The rules are complex. Talk to a qualified accountant.

8 College Admissions Myths...and What It Really Takes to Get In

Michele Hernandez, EdD, a former Dartmouth College admissions officer who currently is president of Hernandez College Consulting, a college admissions consulting service based in Weybridge, Vermont. She is cofounder of Application Boot Camp, a four-day college admissions program offered each August to students entering their senior year of high school. She is author of several books on college admissions, including *A Is for Admission: The Insider's Guide to Getting into the Ivy League and Other Top Colleges* (Grand Central). *ApplicationBootCamp.com*

Many high school students and their parents do not fully understand the college admissions process. They believe myths that can hurt a student's chances of getting into his/her school of choice...or cause students to waste time and money applying to schools that really are not within reach.

Myth: **A college sent me a letter (or an e-mail) asking me to apply, so I'm likely to get in.**

Reality: Letters and e-mails encouraging application are very widely distributed. Colleges want as many students as possible to apply—even students who have no realistic chance of acceptance. The more applicants they reject, the more selective and desirable the institutions seem in college rankings.

Myth: **I need a long list of extracurricular activities and interests to get into a top school.**

Reality: Colleges no longer seek out students who have long and varied lists of projects and activities. These days, they prefer students who have specialized interests that they've pursued extensively. Students should emphasize one or two areas in which they have the greatest interest and show how they have gone above and beyond in these areas.

Myth: **As long as my essay is well-written, the topic is relatively unimportant.**

Reality: The main essay of a college application should revolve around the student's primary scholarly passion. That is what colleges want to know about most, so writing about anything else is a wasted opportunity.

Many of the other common essay topics are best avoided. Essays about how working for a charity changed the student's life come off as clichéd and phony...essays about what the student learned from an important role model might help that role model get into the college, but they don't do much for the essay writer.

Helpful: After the essay is written, go over it to improve it—10 to 15 times. Good essays don't happen in the first draft.

Myth: **My high school doesn't rank students, so colleges will not know where I stand.**

Reality: High schools that don't rank their students usually still calculate a "GPA distribution." Colleges use this data to determine where applicants stand in their classes. Unfortunately, few students know that this GPA distribution exists, much less where they stand on it. In my experience, many students overestimate their class standing and apply mainly to schools at which they have little hope of acceptance. I've had students from high schools that don't rank tell me that they're at the top of their class...only to learn from their high school's GPA distribution that they're not even in the top 10%.

A high schooler who is told that his school does not rank students should ask his guidance counselor for a copy of the official high school profile that has all the information colleges are privy to. It's a public document that students are entitled to see.

Helpful: Also ask the guidance counselor if the school uses Naviance, a computer program that tracks the college applications and acceptances of the school's graduates. If so, this program can be used to gauge where students from the high school must fall along the school's GPA distribution in order to have a realistic chance of being accepted at a particular college.

Myth: **High SAT scores will get me into a top college.**

Reality: Low SAT scores can cost an applicant a shot at a top college, but high scores alone won't guarantee entry. Top schools usually turn down applicants who have high SAT scores but less than stellar GPAs. And Ivy League schools reject plenty of students who have perfect SAT scores.

Myth: **Attending a private high school improves my odds of getting into a good college.**

Reality: There was a time when prestigious private high schools served as feeder schools for top colleges and universities, greatly improving students' chances of acceptance, but those times are past. These days, acceptance rates are almost identical for students applying from public high schools and those applying from private schools. Attending a private high school still could be beneficial for students who require the small class size or other resources offered by the private schools to thrive...or for those who live in public school districts with very poor schools.

Students applying to college from parochial high schools actually are at a slight statistical disadvantage compared with other applicants, likely because parochial school students take classes such as theology that do not match up well with the courses that colleges and universities tend to look for on transcripts. (Graduating from a parochial school can be advantageous when applying to a religious university or college such as Boston College, Georgetown, Notre Dame or Villanova.)

Home-schooled students typically are at a slight disadvantage, too, as they often do not take as many AP or achievement tests or win as many statewide honors as students of similar ability who are not home schooled.

Myth: **I'll wow them in my interview to make up for my low scores/grades.**

Reality: College interviews don't count for much—they're a small part of the admissions process. A great interview might help a borderline candidate get in to a school, but it won't make enough of a difference for a subpar candidate.

Myth: **I should wait to apply—rather than apply for early decision—if I can use the extra time to improve my GPA.**

Reality: The odds of admission are so much better during the early decision process—three to six times better at many schools—that it's definitely worth applying for early decision to the student's top-choice school, even if that means the student's GPA is a bit lower than it might be in a few months.

Example: At University of Pennsylvania, half the class is filled during the early decision process—even though only one-tenth as many students apply for early decision as apply during the standard admission process.

There's almost no risk that applying for early decision will hurt a student's chances of getting into a school. If the student had any chance of acceptance, he will at worst be deferred, not rejected. A deferred student's odds of acceptance during the standard application process only are improved by the fact that he applied early—it tells the school that it's the student's top choice.

The early application advantage is not as dramatic at schools offering "early action" rather than early decision, but there still is some upside. (With early action, students are not required to attend if accepted.)

Some Colleges Lie About Statistics

Recently, *Forbes* removed four universities from its list of the country's best colleges because the schools lied about students' SAT and ACT scores. To get the most accurate information about a college or university, enter the college's name and the words "common data set" in a search engine—there are a lot of numbers, so you will find many things to compare.

Michele Hernandez, EdD, president of Hernandez College Consulting, Weybridge, Vermont.

How to Pay for College Now That Loan Rates Are Soaring

Mark Kantrowitz, senior vice president and publisher of the college finance website group Edvisors Network and founder of the college financial-aid site *FinAid.org* and the college scholarship site *FastWeb. com.* He is author of *Secrets to Winning a Scholarship* (CreateSpace). *Edvisors.com*

A college education could amount to hundreds of thousands of dollars in tuition bills over four years.

College loans are the traditional way to make up any shortfall, but they might no longer be the best option. The interest rates on subsidized Stafford loans for undergraduates in 2014–2015 rose to 4.66% from 3.86% in 2013–2014. (Rates drop down to 4.29% if loans are disbursed between July 1, 2015 and July 1, 2016.) Rates on private student loans sometimes top 10%, depending on the borrower's credit scores.*

A growing number of credit unions are offering loans for college expenses—sometimes at attractive rates—but these loans' repayment

*Rates and prices as of September 2, 2015.

DID YOU KNOW THAT...

People Who Spend Money on This Are Happiest?

People who spend money on food and travel usually are more adventurous and happier than people who buy material objects. About 60% of so-called experiential consumers report overall satisfaction with life, compared with about 40% of those who favor buying objects.

Studies by researchers at San Francisco State University, and University of Colorado.

terms are much less flexible than with federal college loans, which often offer deferment, forbearance or other options to borrowers who cannot afford to make payments.

Here's a look at six alternative options that could help families pay for college…

RISKIER OPTIONS

These three college payment options carry significant potential financial downside, but are worth considering if handled with care.

• **Home-equity loans/lines of credit.** Borrowing against the equity in your home could provide cash for college at rates lower than those now charged by most student loans—and the interest portion of the home loan is tax-deductible. Home-equity line-of-credit (HELOC) loans recently were available with variable rates of roughly 4.6%, while home-equity loans recently offered 6% fixed rates.

Downside: Fail to repay the money you borrow, and you could lose your home. As with other private loans, repayment terms are much less flexible than with federal college loans. The variable rates on HELOCs make them appropriate only for borrowers who are confident that they can repay within three to five years.

Reason: If today's low interest rates rebound significantly over the next five to 10 years, your HELOC payments could increase enough to become unmanageable.

Alternative: Investigate cash-out mortgage refinancing if you're considering refinancing anyway. This would reset your mortgage rate to today's low rates and let you pull money out of your home to pay for college. The interest portion of mortgage bills is tax-deductible. On the downside, it could leave you paying off college bills for up to the next 30 years.

Warning: Proceeds that come from a home-equity loan (as opposed to a line of credit) or a cash-out refinance will count as an asset on financial-aid applications.

• **Loans from permanent life insurance policies.** Whole and universal life policyholders typically can borrow against the value of their policies. The interest rates charged on these loans often fall between 4% and 6%, but refer to your contract or check with your insurer for details.

Downside: The insurance policy's death benefit will be reduced if the loan is not repaid before the policyholder dies. Also, money borrowed from an insurance policy typically must be reported on college financial-aid forms as income. (To avoid this problem, use life insurance to pay only for the senior year. At that point, no further financial-aid forms will be submitted.) This option isn't worth pursuing unless you already have significant equity in a permanent life insurance policy.

• **0% introductory offers on credit cards.** Some credit cards offer new cardholders 0% rates on new purchases during the first 12 to 18 months. Charge tuition payments on such a card, and you essentially get a 12-to-18-month interest-free loan. When that 0% rate nears its end, you might be able to roll the balance onto a different card that offers a 0% rate on balance transfers, extending your interest-free loan for perhaps another 12 to 18 months.

Downside: You can't be certain that you will be able to transfer debt from one 0% offer to another each time a 0% introductory rate expires. Eventually, there might not be any 0% balance-transfer credit card offers available to you, which could leave you paying steep credit card interest rates of 15% or higher on any balance that you can't pay off immediately. So this strategy works best if you have assets that you could tap into to pay off credit card debt at the end of the 0% period if necessary.

If you're late with a credit card payment or break some other card-issuer rule, you might be required to pay an ultra-steep penalty rate of as much as 30%. The lower your credit scores, the more difficult it will be to obtain 0% offers.

Other problems with using credit cards to charge tuition payments: You may have to pay a transaction fee (often called a convenience fee) of 2% or 3% on top of tuition, especially if the college uses a third party to process their credit card payments. And your monthly payments usually are a percentage of the outstanding balance, so they start off higher and gradually reduce. This is in contrast to student loans, which either have level payments throughout the life of the loan or start off low and gradually increase.

Warning: Some parents charge tuition bills on rewards credit cards to earn cash back or airline miles. Before doing this, contact the card issuer to confirm that tuition payments indeed qualify for rewards—some issuers specifically exclude tuition payment from their rewards programs...and some colleges don't accept credit card payments at all.

LESS RISKY OPTIONS

These three college payment options do not carry substantially more financial risk than more common ways of paying for college.

• **The military.** Students who enlist in the Reserve Officers' Training Corps (ROTC) are eligible for scholarships that can pay a significant portion of their tuition, college fees and textbook expenses (and an option to pay for room and board in place of tuition, if you qualify). For more information, call 800-USA-ROTC (Army)...800-USA-NAVY...866-423-7682 (Air Force)...or 800-MARINES...or visit *FinAid. org/military*.

There also are college financial-aid programs for military veterans who enroll in college, such as the Montgomery G.I. Bill (*Benefits. va.gov/GIBill*).

Note: ROTC scholarships require a commitment to military service after graduation.

• **Scholarships, grants and 0%-interest loans from businesses or nonprofits.** Thousands of nonprofit and for-profit organizations offer money for college. Examples can be found at *FastWeb.com* or *StudentScholarshipSearch. com*.

Also do a web search for the phrase "0% student loans" to find no-interest loan programs. These are separate from the 0%-interest loans you might be offered directly by a college or university, which would be included in the financial-aid package you received.

Downside: There is lots of competition for these scholarships and interest-free loans, and some have very specific eligibility requirements. Still, applying could be worth your while—one of every eight students in bachelor's degree programs who applies to multiple scholarship programs receives at least some free money for college, an average of $2,800.

These programs often have late-April/early-May deadlines.

• **Installment plans for tuition.** Many colleges permit students to divide their tuition bills into monthly payments (either nine, 10 or 12 monthly payments, depending on the program). These plans typically do not charge interest, but a flat fee of perhaps $50 to $100 might be imposed. It's a useful option for families who come up a bit short of the amount required in August.

Downside: Miss a monthly payment, and the student might not be allowed to attend classes or graduate until the college receives its money.

Improve Your Child's Chances of a College Scholarship

FoxBusiness.com

Scholarship awards totaling $3 billion are made annually, with the average being $2,000 to $3,000 a year.

To boost your chances: Apply for as many scholarships as you qualify for, not just a few large ones. Be sure you do qualify to avoid wasting your time—for example, check on what "need-based" means in each case. Look for local organizations and businesses that offer award money.

Research the groups offering scholarships and the previous winners for ideas on how to tweak your essay or interview to make it compelling. Use essays to tell stories interestingly without repeating information from your résumé. Edit essays carefully—many applicants are disqualified because of spelling and grammar errors.

If an interview is required: Research the interviewer's background and connection to the scholarship program so that you show knowledge and create rapport.

Best Scholarship Search Engines

Scholarships.com provides the best possibilities overall but also has many ads and mismatches...The College Board's BigFuture (*BigFuture.CollegeBoard.org*) is fast, ad-free and screens out most promotional scholarships but lists scholarships only alphabetically—not by deadline or relevance...Cappex (*Cappex.com*) offers useful information on competition for awards and the effort needed to apply—but registering results in a large number of recruiting e-mails...Chegg (*Chegg.com*) has the best-designed website, with an easy-to-use interface, but very few matches to local or specialized scholarships...and FastWeb (*FastWeb.com*) clearly labels promotional scholarships but has ads and mostly recommends national scholarships.

Try all these sites to get a comprehensive sense of available scholarships, both national and local or specialized.

Roundup of college-aid experts, reported at CNN *Money.com.*

Some Colleges Trick Students

Maura Dundon, JD, senior policy counsel at the Center for Responsible Lending, Washington, DC. Formerly, Dundon was an attorney in the enforcement division of the Consumer Financial Protection Bureau. *Responsible Lending.org*

Look out for deceptive promises, high-pressure sales tactics and expensive student loans if you or someone in your family is thinking of attending certain for-profit colleges. Overall, there are an estimated 3,000 for-profit colleges across the US—their convenient class hours and easy admissions policies make them attractive to working adults, laid-off workers who want to beef up their educa-

tions and young people who hope to get into vocational careers.

But some of these colleges charge about six times as much for tuition as comparable public colleges for a two-year degree and have very high dropout rates because of the expense and student dissatisfaction with the quality of programs. Half of the students enrolled at 30 of the largest for-profit schools left within four months without getting a degree or diploma.

The federal Consumer Financial Protection Bureau began an investigation during the fall of 2013 into suspected fraud at two leading for-profit college groups—Corinthian Colleges and ITT Educational Services—in response to hundreds of complaints. The bureau recently sued ITT Educational, accusing it of predatory lending. Meanwhile, attorneys general in 12 states are investigating Education Management Corporation. This doesn't mean that all for-profit colleges have problems. *But investigators warn about the possibility of...*

• **Predatory loans.** Some for-profit colleges make it very easy to borrow tuition money, including no interest payments while students still are in school. But the interest rates and fees on some loans can total as much as 20%, and the terms often are unclear.

• **Promises of a better job after graduation.** Some schools routinely inflate their job-placement rates and overstate relationships with big employers to encourage prospective students to enroll. Some students find that their degrees do not qualify them to work in the professions they were supposed to prepare them for. Oftentimes, a nearby community college may offer you the same or a better degree for a fraction of the cost.

Should Parents Pay for College?

The more college money parents provide, the lower their children's grades tend to be.

But: Students whose parents pay their way are more likely to graduate—many students who leave college do so for financial reasons.

Study based on two nationally representative data sets collected by the National Center for Educational Statistics and by researchers at University of California, Merced, published in *American Sociological Review*.

Reduce Out-of-State Tuition Charges at Top State Schools

Many state universities offer in-state rates to out-of-state students that they want to recruit—typically those with GPAs of 3.75 or above. Some schools have reciprocal agreements with ones in other states that include reduced tuition for out-of-state students. If you live in a nearby county, ask whether you qualify for in-state tuition—some schools offer waivers or scholarships to students who live nearby but in a different state. Ask the school if it offers waivers under special circumstances.

Example: University of Alaska does not charge out-of-state costs to those who enroll in the state's 529 college savings plan.

Also: Think about moving to the school's state—you usually must do so at least a year in advance. Check the College Board's list of state requirements at *CollegeBoard.org*. Average cost of out-of-state tuition for the 2014–2015 school year was $22,958, more than twice the cost of in-state tuition and fees.

Bankrate.com

Free Tuition After 4 Years

Free tuition after four years is being offered by some colleges in recognition of the fact that the majority of students take more than four years to graduate. But the guarantees often have many restrictions.

Example: Students may be required to declare a major as freshmen, stick to it for all

four years and give up studying abroad. The plans do not cover more than tuition—students staying longer than four years still must pay dorm and living costs.

Here's a twist: Ball State University in Indiana pays students who finish on time a $500 bonus.*

DailyFinance.com
*Rate subject to change.

Are Need-Blind Colleges Lying?

Mark Kantrowitz, senior vice president and publisher of the college finance website group Edvisors Network and founder of the college financial-aid site *FinAid.org* and the college scholarship site *FastWeb.com*. He is author of *Secrets to Winning a Scholarship* (CreateSpace). *Edvisors.com*

Officials at The George Washington University recently acknowledged that the school's admissions policy is not truly "need-blind," as it had previously claimed. Some applicants slated for acceptance instead were wait-listed because they required financial aid.

At last count, 99 of the country's approximately 6,000 colleges and universities claimed to be need-blind—to not consider applicants' aid requirements when deciding who gets in. But GW probably isn't alone in breaking its own need-blind admissions rules—and even when need-blind policies are followed, there usually are loopholes. For example, of those 99 "need-blind" schools, only five extend the need-blind policy to students on their waiting lists. In other words, when a need-blind college places an applicant on its waiting list, that student's financial-aid requirements very likely will be a factor in determining whether that student eventually gets in. The only exceptions are Amherst, Babson, Bard, Baylor and Wellesley.

And of the 99 need-blind schools, only 62 guarantee that they will provide all the aid students require to enroll. At the other 37, students might very well be accepted only to discover that they can't afford to attend.

What to do: Students who can comfortably afford to attend college without financial aid might consider not applying for aid. Being able to pay the full tuition could improve their odds of getting in—even if the school claims to be need-blind. Students who cannot comfortably afford to forgo grants and loans should apply for aid, however. There's no point in getting in and then not being able to afford to attend.

Warning: Some students claim not to need financial aid when applying to colleges in order to improve their odds of getting in, then try to apply for aid in future years. But most schools allow students who initially claimed to not require aid to later request it only if they can show that their finances dramatically worsened in the interim.

Student Loan Debt Relief

Firms that offer student loan "debt relief" charge exorbitant fees for access to government programs that can be used for free. These firms, which have proliferated, sometimes charge initial fees as high as $1,600 and monthly fees of $20 to $50.

What to do: Review debt-relief options at *StudentAid.ed.gov/repay-loans* or *StudentLoan BorrowerAssistance.org*.

Deanne Loonin, an attorney with the nonprofit National Consumer Law Center, based in Boston, which had a "secret shopper" contact 10 student loan relief companies and which reviewed the websites of 10 more companies.

DID YOU KNOW THAT...

Public-College Tuition Hikes Have Slowed?

Tuition rose by an average of 2.9% for public-college in-state students for the 2014-2015 school year. Tuition averaged $9,139 for in-state students, and $22,958 for out-of-state students, an increase of 3.3%. At private four-year colleges, rates went up 3.7%, to $31,231.

Trends in Higher Education, College Board.

"Surprise Defaults" on Student Loans

Rohit Chopra, student loan ombudsman at the Consumer Financial Protection Bureau, Washington, DC. *ConsumerFinance.gov*

Student-loan borrowers often face "surprise defaults" even when their loan payments are up-to-date, according to a report by the Consumer Financial Protection Bureau.

Many private student-loan contracts include an option for lenders to demand the full balance when a borrower's co-signer—commonly a parent or other relative—has died or filed for bankruptcy. Lenders often automatically place these loans into default, an action that may trigger a negative credit report.

Having a student loan co-signed, which can help the borrower obtain a lower interest rate, is an increasingly common practice.

What to do: If you have a private student loan or you are a co-signer of such a loan, seek to get a "co-signer release," which allows the borrower to drop the co-signer after a certain number of consecutive, timely payments and a credit check.

To complain about student loan practices, contact the Consumer Financial Protection Bureau ombudsman's office at 855-411-2372 or go to *ConsumerFinance.gov/complaint*.

College Refunds If a Child Drops Out

The earlier in the school year that a student decides to leave a college, the better the chance of at least a partial tuition refund—but school rules vary. For students who received financial aid, federal grants for completed semesters may not have to be paid back, but other grants may need to be returned. Most schools will refund dormitory fees—less a per diem for days that the student lived on campus—but usually will not give back a housing deposit. Savings in 529 plans usually can be transferred to other close relatives, such as a sibling, but some college savings accounts have strict time limits.

Self-defense: Request exit counseling from the school's finance department to determine what you must pay.

Roundup of experts in college financing, reported in The Wall Street Journal.

Cash for Relocating

Recent grads can get cash for relocating through the Rural Opportunity Zone program. In exchange for moving to a designated rural county, graduates receive money to be used toward loan repayment.

Examples: Moving to one of 54 rural counties in Kansas can bring up to $3,000 per year for up to five years.* Moving to Niagara Falls, New York, is worth $7,000 over two years to a limited number of recent graduates.

Search "rural opportunity zone" and a state's name to find programs available there.

Kiplinger's Personal Finance. Kiplinger.com

*Rates subject to change.

Why Are Contracts So Complex?

Alan Siegel, coauthor with Irene Etzkorn, of *Simple: Conquering the Crisis of Complexity* (Twelve). The book argues that most businesses could increase profitability by decreasing complexity.

Have you looked at a contract lately—whether it's from a bank or an insurer or a car-rental company? Easy to understand? Not!

But we can do something about that.

Today's consumers have more power to influence corporate policies than they realize because of the Internet. When many consumers complain about a corporate policy on Twitter or Facebook, the corporation tends to take notice. Online consumer discontent recently caused Capital One to back off contract terms that would permit its employees to visit customers' homes and workplaces in pursuit of late payments.

You don't need to start a social-media campaign to spur corporate change. *Two websites that can help you quickly bring unnecessary complexity and other issues to companies' attention…*

• ***PlanetFeedback.com*** provides a forum for consumers to offer constructive criticism to companies. (Other consumer-complaint sites feature mainly unproductive venting.) Companies monitor this site and typically respond to valid complaints.

• ***ExecutiveBomb.com*** provides e-mail addresses and even direct phone numbers for highly placed executives at thousands of companies. It could help you bypass low-level customer service employees and reach someone who has the power to enact real change.

8

Insurance Now

The Obamacare Marketplace Maze: Figure Out Your Health Insurance Options

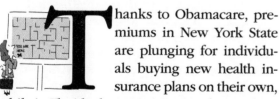

Thanks to Obamacare, premiums in New York State are plunging for individuals buying new health insurance plans on their own, while in Florida they are rising. And, insurance plan options are numerous in California, but they're scarce in Maine.

After years of debate and planning, the health insurance marketplaces that have been created as part of the Affordable Care Act, also known as Obamacare, have finally launched. Coverage took effect starting January 1, 2014. But confusion over the plans and uncertainty about how to compare them persist.

WHO IS AFFECTED BY THE NEW MARKETPLACES?

The insurance marketplaces—also known as exchanges—are designed as online shopping malls for people who do not have access to Medicare, Medicaid or quality health coverage through an employer.

Also, people considering early retirement might want to explore the exchanges, where plans may be less expensive than COBRA temporary health coverage or previously available insurance plans.

To compare estimated costs for a new exchange plan versus your employer plan, go to the Kaiser Family Foundation's website, *KFF. org/interactive/subsidy-calculator*.

Joe Touschner, former senior health policy analyst at the Center for Children and Families, Georgetown University, Washington, DC. He has conducted extensive research on the health insurance marketplaces created by the Affordable Care Act. Touschner also previously served as assistant director for state government affairs for the American Academy of Physician Assistants.

Additional helpful advice…

EVALUATING ALL OF YOUR ALTERNATIVES

In some states, such as California and Colorado, consumers are able to choose among dozens of plans, while in other states there may be fewer than 10. Either way, price isn't the only difference among them. *There also are key differences in…*

•**The share of health costs that plans pass along to consumers.** Policies are grouped into four tiers—bronze, silver, gold and platinum. (Less expensive but more limited "catastrophic plans" also are available to people younger than age 30.) The higher the tier, the lower the share of medical costs that the policyholder has to pay out-of-pocket—and the higher the premiums are likely to be.

What to do: If you are fairly healthy and have no reason to believe that you will have significant health-care costs, a bronze or silver plan that keeps premiums relatively low is a reasonable choice. If there is a strong possibility that you will require extensive medical care, it might make sense to pay more for a gold or platinum plan that pays a larger share of medical bills.

But whatever tier you select, your annual maximum out-of-pocket limit for 2015 (not including the premiums) is $6,600 for an individual plan or $13,200 for a family plan—or less than that for people who qualify for subsidies because they earn less than 250% of the federal poverty level and sign up for a silver plan. (Insurers can set lower out-of-pocket maximums on specific plans if they choose, and some states might mandate lower maximums on high-end plans—platinum plans in California have maximums of $4,000, or $8,000 for families.)

Note: The maximum out-of-pocket cost limit for any individual Marketplace plan for 2016 can be no more than $6,850 for an individual plan and $13,700 for a family plan.

•**Where plan members can seek treatment.** Many plans limit policyholders to a list of "in-network" physicians and hospitals. This seems to be particularly common in California. Policyholders who go outside the network in nonemergency situations might receive little or no coverage.

What to do: It may not pose big problems for most people to sign up for a plan with a limited provider network—such plans might feature significantly lower premiums. But first consider whether the health-care providers you use and the leading hospitals in your region are included in the plan's network—and how important that is to you.

•**The benefits that the plan provides.** Covered benefits vary much less than among policies available in the past, because all marketplace plans are required to at least provide 10 "essential health benefits" that range from hospital care and prescription drugs to pediatric dental and vision care and mental-health care. But there is leeway that can lead to variations in how well specific plans cover specific health services, even if those plans are in the same tier.

What to do: Before signing up for the lowest-cost option in a tier, consider how well that plan and others in the tier cover any specific ongoing treatments or health services you require.

THE TRUTH ABOUT HEALTH INSURANCE RATES

Whether health insurance rates in your state for people obtaining their own insurance go up or down overall depends largely on how high or low they were to start with—and how much coverage plans in your state have provided in the past. In New York, for instance, which has had a highly regulated individual health insurance market and very high rates, premiums are falling sharply. That's because under the new rules, which penalize people who don't obtain coverage, there is a bigger proportion of healthier individuals buying insurance than before, and that means lower costs to insurers and greater competition among insurers.

But if you live in a state such as Florida or Texas that has had less stringent rules and lower rates, premiums are rising overall. The higher premiums largely reflect the requirements for more extensive coverage, including more mandated benefits and consumer protections. In other words, people who previously bought bare-bones coverage may be paying more—but they get more insurance coverage as well.

Rates vary from state to state under Obamacare, and even within states, but most studies have concluded that rate differences among states are significantly less than in the past.

Still, statewide insurance rates don't tell the complete story. Whether your insurance rates rise or fall under Obamacare also depends on factors such as your age, health status, gender, income and community.

Examples: Individuals who are over age 50, people with preexisting health conditions and women and households earning less than 400% of the federal poverty level might have seen their premiums fall or remain relatively unchanged under the new rules, even if rates went up in their state overall. About 48% of people buying insurance on their own qualify for a tax credit on their premiums, according to a Kaiser Family Foundation study.

INDIVIDUAL VS. FAMILY PLANS

Traditionally, family health insurance plans have cost less than the sum of the cost of individual policies for the same family members. But under Obamacare, for most families, a family plan purchased through an exchange would cost exactly the same as buying individual policies for all the family members.

Exception: If there are more than three children younger than age 21 in the family, there is no extra charge for the additional kids if you buy a family plan. So in that case, a family plan probably is the best option because the total premiums would be lower than if you bought separate plans.

For small families, a major variable will be maximum out-of-pocket expenses, which are twice as high for family plans as for individual plans. In general, if multiple members of a family have potentially costly health issues, a family plan likely will do a better job of limiting out-of-pocket costs. If only one family member has significant health costs, an individual plan could be the way to go.

CAN YOU KEEP YOUR CURRENT POLICY?

Starting in 2014, all newly issued nongroup health insurance policies have to conform to Obamacare's "essential benefits" rules. However, if you have a nongroup policy that took effect on or before March 23, 2010, and that policy has not substantially changed since then, you might have the option of continuing that policy rather than buying a new policy. Your insurance company should inform you whether your current policy has this "grandfathered" status and can be continued. If you haven't received a notice about this from your insurer, contact it for details.

Confused About Obamacare? Who Isn't?! Clear Answers to Your Questions

Kathleen D. Stoll, JD, director of health policy for Families USA, a nonprofit organization that advocates for affordable health care, Washington, DC. She previously served as special assistant for health and welfare issues for the House Ways and Means Committee. *FamiliesUSA.org*

After years of discussion and amid continuing controversy, some of the most important parts of the Affordable Care Act took effect in 2014. Yet many people still aren't clear on how these elements of "Obamacare" affect them.

To help make clear what is happening, we asked Kathleen D. Stoll, JD, director of health policy for Families USA, to answer 11 crucial questions…

ELIGIBILITY

• **I read that my state decided not to set up a health insurance marketplace. Will there be any marketplace available to me?** Yes. All states and Washington, DC, have marketplaces (also called "exchanges") of insurance plans from private insurers. Some marketplaces are run by the states themselves…others by the federal government…and still others by a state/federal partnership. All of the marketplaces help consumers compare plans and find financial assistance, if they are eligible, to help pay for coverage.

However, it is possible that differences in funding will result in less in-person support for consumers in states where the marketplaces are run by the federal government.

•**I have Medicare. How do these health marketplaces affect me?** They do not affect your coverage. Medicare recipients are not eligible for coverage through the marketplaces.

•**I obtain health insurance through my employer. Do I have to shop for insurance through these marketplaces?** No. You can continue with your employer's coverage. But if it offers limited benefits and/or little help with premiums, you might have the option of buying coverage through a marketplace instead. The marketplaces provide details about what to ask your employer to determine if its group health coverage is so limited that you qualify for this option.

•**I heard that some small businesses are dropping their current insurance plans and leaving it up to their employees to shop for their own plans in the marketplace. Is that true?** Employers with more than 50 employees that do not provide insurance plans face penalties. Instead of dropping coverage, some employers are switching plans, using the marketplaces to compare small group plans. To help pay for the cost of insurance, tax credits are available to some small businesses.

COVERAGE

•**What will the plans in the new marketplaces include?** Health insurance plans sold to individuals and small businesses both inside and outside the new marketplaces have to provide at least "essential benefits." This means that all policies include prescription drug coverage, preventive services, maternity care, mental health services and other components currently missing from many individual insurance plans. And plans can't arbitrarily limit or cap the coverage received. Also, plans

have to meet rules about providing adequate networks of medical providers.

•**Is it true that there are only four health insurance plans?** That is not true in most states, if any. All the health marketplaces divide plans into four tiers—bronze, silver, gold and platinum—but that's just to make it easy for consumers to determine quality of coverage. In most states, there are a number of different plans within each of these tiers, likely from multiple insurers.

Plans must meet a certain actuarial value to qualify for a given ranking—that is, they must pay a predetermined percentage of total average costs for covered benefits—but even within a tier, plans could have different costs and benefits. For example, one plan might have relatively high deductibles and low co-pays, while another might offer the reverse.

The online marketplaces are supposed to list each plan's costs and benefits in a consistent format and clear language to make the plans easy to compare.

•**My son is 20. Why should he have to pay for a plan meant for older people?** He doesn't have to. There are certain low-cost, high-deductible plans available only to people under age 30. These are much less expensive than more comprehensive plans. But with high deductibles and less financial protection, these plans are appropriate only for people who have sufficient financial resources to pay hefty medical bills out-of-pocket. Also keep in mind that under the new law, children are now allowed to remain on their parents' health plans until age 26.

•**If I use a marketplace, do I have to shop online for coverage?** Not necessarily. The marketplaces offer shopping assistance through toll-free phone numbers and in person in many communities.

•**I looked for the marketplace online but couldn't find it. Where is it?** Visit *Healthcare. gov/Marketplace.*

TAX CREDITS

Nearly 26 million Americans are eligible for tax credits to help them pay the cost of health insurance.

•**Do I have to be poor to qualify for these health insurance tax credits?** Many middle-class families qualify. The limit has been set at 400% of the federal poverty level (FPL). In 2015, that's an annual income of $46,680 for an individual…$62,960 for a couple…or $95,400 for a family of four. However, your tax credit decreases the closer you get to these limits.

The tax credits are based on the price of a typical silver-tier plan in the state. Families receiving tax credits can opt for pricier gold or platinum plans…or pay even less in premiums if they are willing to accept the more limited benefits of a bronze plan.

People don't have to do this math on their own. The marketplaces guide users through the process.

•**The subsidy is in the form of a tax credit. Does that mean I won't receive it until I file my tax return?** No. People can elect to get credits in advance, but in that case, the government pays the amount of the credit directly to the insurer and you pay only the remaining portion of your premiums.

More from Kathleen D. Stoll, JD…

Obamacare Basics

Since October 1, 2013, individuals and small businesses have been able to compare and sign up for health insurance policies through new online marketplaces. These policies took effect January 1, 2014.

Among the people who benefit the most are those who have health problems but lack access to group coverage. Insurers are no longer allowed to refuse coverage or charge higher premiums based on preexisting conditions.

Also benefiting are people from ages 50 to 64 who lack group coverage, including early retirees. Insurers still are allowed to charge older applicants more than younger ones, but they no longer are able to charge older applicants the prohibitively high rates that they often imposed in the past.

Americans who choose not to obtain health insurance have to pay a penalty. That penalty is $325 or 2% of income, whichever is greater, in 2015, but the penalty will climb in future years, to $695 or 2.5% of income by 2016.

Long-Term-Care Insurance Scams

Some providers claim falsely that a policy will cover all of the buyer's needs or will prevent the buyer from becoming a financial burden to his/her family. And some agents sell costly policies to people who cannot afford the high premiums or sell multiple, overlapping policies when only one is needed.

Self-defense: If you have a policy, get a second opinion from a trusted financial adviser on any recommended changes. If you are a first-time buyer, interview at least three agents…check the experience of each one in the long-term-care field…and turn down anyone who is impatient or pushy.

Roundup of experts in long-term-care insurance, reported at *Bankrate.com.*

Scams Tied to the Affordable Care Act

Crooks posing as federal employees phone victims and say that they will soon receive health insurance cards under a provision of the act—but must give a bank account number and routing number first. Another version of the scam claims that new Medicare cards are being mailed out in connection with the law. But the act does not mandate a new insurance card, and no new Medicare cards are being mailed.

What to do: Realize that government agencies already have your personal information on file—no one will call and ask you for it. Do not be fooled if your caller-ID shows a call coming from a seemingly legitimate agency—scammers use technology that lets them display any number or name they wish. And never reply to an unsolicited e-mail that supposedly comes from a government agency—they are never legitimate.

AARP.org

Do You Work for a Small Business (or Own One)? What You Need to Know About Obamacare

Victoria Braden, president and CEO of Braden Benefit Strategies, Inc., a group health insurance consulting firm located in Johns Creek, Georgia, that works with employers that have fewer than 300 employees. *BradenBenefits.com*

An alarm company in suburban Atlanta and its 36 employees face the possibility of changing health insurance plans three times in the space of four months, in response to rising rates and changing rules. Many other small companies are in the same boat—but not all of them realize it.

The landscape is now changing dramatically because of the Affordable Care Act (ACA), known as Obamacare, which imposes penalties on individuals who fail to obtain health insurance and on large companies that fail to provide insurance to their employees (though these large-company penalties have been delayed until 2015). But companies with 50 or fewer employees face no penalties. That has convinced some small-business owners and employees that Obamacare does not affect them. They are in for a shock. Obamacare is bringing big choices and changes to small-business health insurance.

Six things you need to know if you own a small business or work for one...

•**Small-business owners no longer determine the number of hours an employee must work to qualify for health benefits.** Starting in 2014, any employee who works at least 30 hours per week, on average, must be offered whatever health insurance benefits are offered to the company's full-time employees. Business owners previously set this benefits bar wherever they chose, often at 32 or 36 hours.

Some employers have responded to this new rule by scaling back certain employee schedules to 28 or 29 hours per week.

•**The new health insurance rules don't necessarily apply to your plan starting January 1, 2014.** Starting in 2014, health insurance plans are required to cap out-of-pocket expenses at $6,600 ($13,200 for families)...small group health insurance plans—that is, plans for businesses with between two and 49 employees—generally must cap deductibles at no more than $2,050 a year ($4,100 for families)... and coverage must include a broad range of "essential health benefits," such as maternity, mental-health and pediatric services including oral and vision care.

Exceptions: "Self-funded" insurance plans are not required to comply with many Obamacare rules (see below). Group insurance plans established prior to March 23, 2010, that have not had significant changes since that date might not have to comply with the new rules, either. Employers can ask their insurance companies whether their plans qualify as "grandfathered." Employees can ask their company benefits administrators if and when the new health insurance rules apply to them.

• **Employers no longer need to worry that an older or unhealthy employee will push up the companies' health insurance rates.** In the past, just one or two expensive-to-insure employees could push a small business's rates through the roof. But starting with plans that take effect in 2014, the age and health status of employees and their covered dependents will not affect the rates.

Bonus: This might reduce one of the roadblocks faced by older job hunters.

• **Employees of small businesses in most states aren't able to shop for coverage as extensively as originally promised.** Starting October 1, 2014, small companies are able to shop for insurance through a Small Business Health Options Program (SHOP) exchange—comparable to the much publicized Obama-care individual insurance exchanges, also known as insurance marketplaces. Coverage purchased through these exchanges took effect as early as January 1, 2014. But the SHOP exchanges aren't what small businesses were told to expect when the Obamacare plan was unveiled.

The original idea was that a small-business owner could select a level of coverage—say, bronze or silver—and decide how much money to contribute toward that coverage for each eligible employee. His/her employees would then choose among a number of insurance companies and plans available at that level through the SHOP exchange. But it turns out that the number of insurance companies most employees are choosing among is…one. The requirement that multiple insurance companies be offered has been delayed until at least 2016.

Small-business owners should investigate the SHOP option even without the employee-choice component. As many small-business owners know, Obamacare offers a tax credit to small companies that provide their employees with access to health insurance if those companies fall below certain staffing levels and average wage limits, among other requirements. But not all small-business owners realize that this tax credit is available only if the company buys its health insurance through a SHOP exchange or a SHOP-recognized health insurance company.

Speak with your tax adviser or contact the government's Health Insurance Marketplace for Small Employers (800-706-7893) to find out if your company could qualify for these tax credits.

• **Rates are likely to rise for many small businesses.** The new rules and requirements imposed on small-business insurance plans by Obamacare come at a cost—higher premiums than were charged for previous bare-bones plans. Early indications are that rates could increase by 30% or more for many companies, though this will vary by state and company. Some of that rate increase probably will be passed along to employees in the form of higher premiums.

Employees might receive better coverage, however. And small businesses that have a significant number of employees or covered dependents who are past age 50 and/or unhealthy actually could see their rates decline. So could some small businesses that already provide coverage that offers the now-required essential benefits and relatively low deductibles.

• **Self-funding is coming to small-business health insurance.** When organizations "self-fund," they serve as their own insurers, paying employee medical bills rather than purchasing outside health insurance to do so. (The administration of a self-funded plan still is likely to be outsourced.) Self-funding has become popular among large companies because it frees them from certain taxes and Obamacare rules.

Small businesses historically have stayed away from self-funding because a single major health problem can ravage a small company's bottom line. But insurers increasingly offer hybrid options that feature catastrophic coverage to protect self-funded small companies if they incur greater-than-expected medical costs.

Helpful: Self-funding does make particular sense for companies with workforces that are young and healthy.

More from Victoria Braden…

When Lack of Employer Health Insurance Is Preferable

Some small-business employees will be better off if their employers don't offer health insurance. If your household income for 2015 falls below 400% of the federal poverty level—that is, if your income is below $46,680 for an individual...$62,960 for a married couple...or $111,640 for a family of five, for example (these figures will increase slightly with inflation)—you're likely to qualify for a tax credit to help pay for health coverage purchased through the new Obamacare individual insurance marketplaces. The tax credit could make individual health coverage more affordable than employer-provided health insurance.

There's a catch—you will not be eligible for Obamacare's individual insurance tax credit if you have access to an "affordable" employer-provided health insurance plan.

But the fact is, many small employers feel that they can't eliminate their health insurance plans, even if both they and most of their employees would save money if they did. The most skilled, highest-paid and hardest-to-replace workers often earn too much to qualify for a tax credit in the individual market, and these employees likely would defect to other companies in large numbers if their current employers dropped their health plans.

New Health Insurance Rule

Employees cannot be made to wait more than 90 days for health insurance when starting a new job under a new Affordable Care Act rule. But there are exceptions when workers are subject to other requirements before their employment becomes permanent.

Examples: Obtaining a job-related license ...passing the bar exam.

When licensing is required, employees must be given health insurance within 90 days of the date they obtain the license.

The Kiplinger Letter.

EASY-TO-DO...

Don't Let Your Doctor Charge Co-Pays for Preventive Care

Many doctors are mistakenly charging co-pays for preventive care services. Under the Affordable Care Act, these services *must* be covered by your insurer with no out-of-pocket expense to you, even for the high-deductible plans. That includes annual physicals...colonoscopies...flu shots...mammograms...and vaccinations. The rule does not apply if the doctor is out of network or your plan existed on or before passage of the law on March 23, 2010, and has not substantially changed.

Adam J. Schafer, Montana's deputy commissioner of securities and insurance.

Beware of Out-of-Network Rip-Offs

Charles B. Inlander, a consumer advocate and health-care consultant based in Fogelsville, Pennsylvania. He was founding president of the nonprofit People's Medical Society, a consumer advocacy organization credited with key improvements in the quality of US health care, and is author or coauthor of more than 20 consumer-health books.

If you have a Medicare Advantage Plan or some other individual or employer-provided health insurance that requires you to pay a higher percentage of fees for a doctor or hospital that is out of your insurer's network, this is a definite case of "buyer beware." More and more out-of-network providers are charging consumers exorbitant amounts for their services, a recent report points out. In one instance, a patient was charged $60,000 for a gallbladder surgery after the insurer had paid the doctor only $2,000—the going rate for this operation when performed by an in-network surgeon. The doctors and hospitals can get away with such huge fees because there are no regulations on how much a patient can be charged if he/she is insured by a company that has no agreement with the provider. To top it off, even if the hospital is in the network, the doctor providing the services there may not be and can charge whatever he wants!

Fortunately, there are some steps you can take to avoid receiving a wallet-emptying bill from an out-of-network provider. *My advice to you…*

• **Know before you go.** Unless it's an emergency, it's crucial for you to ask any doctor or hospital before receiving care whether the services will be considered "in network."

Caution: Do not rely on the insurance company's printed lists of providers. Many are outdated—and protect the insurers and doctors with small-print disclaimers. If a provider is not in the network, ask that provider in advance for the exact amount you will be charged for the services.

Insider tip: If you are traveling and need out-of-network medical care, do not assume that your insurer will consider it an emergency and pay the entire bill—even if you're treated in an emergency room. Make sure the hospital or doctor you see submits documentation to your insurer noting that your care was truly an emergency. Otherwise, you will be liable for the out-of-network balance.

• **Strike a deal.** Sometimes, going to an out-of-network provider is your only good choice. For example, perhaps you need a type of surgery or other treatment that is available only from an out-of-network doctor. In these cases, you may be able to negotiate with your insurance company.

Insider tip: If your insurance is provided through your employer, your company's human resources department often can negotiate on your behalf with the insurer for full coverage of specific out-of-network services in which a compelling case can be made. If you want to see an out-of-network provider for routine care, you also can try to strike a deal with him on your out-of-pocket costs before you receive the care.

• **Take advantage of "special arrangements."** Most insurers, including Medicare Advantage Plans, have made special in-network arrangements with renowned medical centers, such as the Cleveland Clinic or Mayo Clinic, that are outside their normal service areas. Ask your insurer for a "list of covered facilities," and check to see whether there are any restrictions—for example, you may need a referral from an in-network doctor. Also make sure that all services and doctors at those facilities will be covered.

More Doctors Are Taking New Medicare Patients

In recent years, some doctors had stopped taking on new Medicare patients because of Medicare payment caps and paperwork. But now 90% of office-based physicians accept new Medicare patients, a rate similar to those taking privately insured patients.

Roundup of experts in Medicare, reported in *USA Today.*

Retiree Health Insurance Fading

Only 25% of employers now provide financial assistance to help retirees under age 65 with medical costs, versus 60% in the 1980s. Many companies that still offer retiree health benefits are giving employees fixed amounts to find policies on their own or are raising co-pays and deductibles.

If you plan to retire before age 65: Ask your benefits department what the company offers and what changes are likely before you become eligible for Medicare.

MarketWatch.com

Relocate for Health Insurance?

Twenty-eight percent of Americans say that they would consider moving to a new state or county for better and/or cheaper health insurance—and more than 40% of 18-to-29-year-olds would think about it. Among low-income people, with annual household incomes less than $30,000, one-third would consider moving for health insurance reasons.

Health Insurance Pulse, a monthly survey from *Bankrate.com* that is conducted by Princeton Survey Research Associates International.

Insurer Says "No"? What to Do

Charles B. Inlander, a consumer advocate and health-care consultant based in Fogelsville, Pennsylvania. He was founding president of the nonprofit People's Medical Society, a consumer advocacy organization credited with key improvements in the quality of US health care, and is author or coauthor of more than 20 consumer-health books.

Here's a sobering statistic—each year, more than 200 million (yes, you read that right) claims are refused by insurance companies and Medicare. Sometimes these denials can be chalked up to mistakes made by doctors and hospitals in filing incomplete claims and errors made by the insurance company itself. But many claims are turned down for "medical" reasons, meaning the insurance company does not believe that a treatment or procedure is medically necessary...or the treatment is considered experimental (not enough evidence supports its effectiveness). *In these cases, you'll have better odds of getting that denial reversed if you...*

•**Read your policy!** It's amazing how many people have never read—or even scanned—their health insurance policies to see what's covered. Well, if you have a claim denied, it's time to look at the policy to see whether that particular denial matches what's there in black and white. If the policy states that the insurer does not pay for a service, such as genetic tests for breast cancer predisposition (a service that's sometimes not covered), little can be done. But even if the policy says that the procedure you're considering is covered, it's wise to make absolutely sure!

Insider tip: Insurance companies can alter what is covered at any time, so call your insurer before getting any invasive test or extensive or new medical procedure to make sure there have been no changes.

•**Get to the bottom of the "no."** If a claim is denied, your doctor or other health-care provider may not know why. So cut to the chase and call the insurer to find out the exact reason for denial. It could be as simple as the doctor or hospital using the wrong payment code or not completing the insurance submission properly.

Insider tip: Keep a log of whom you spoke with and what that person said. Keep copies of any correspondence with doctors, hospitals and insurers that's related to a denied claim. You'll need all this if you decide to file an appeal.

•**Move fast!** By law, every insurer must have a process to appeal when a claim is denied. Call your insurance company, and ask for its "insurance appeal procedure" and find out to whom the paperwork should be submitted. But don't dawdle. Time limits for making an appeal can be as short as 60 days, depending on the company.

Insider tip: Have your doctor and/or a hospital social worker assigned to insurance claims (if a hospital is involved) submit supporting documentation. Your doctor(s) should also submit a special "letter of medical necessity" to the insurer explaining, in great detail, why the claim should be accepted. Most appeals are won with this type of documentation. If you have Medicare, there is an extensive appeal process. To read more about it, go to *Medicare.gov* (click on "Claims & Appeals") or call 800-633-4227.

•**Don't back down.** Even if your appeal is denied, you can file an appeal to that denial with your state's insurance department. An outside panel of experts will review your case.

Insider tip: It helps to submit to the state appeals group any articles from medical journals and other documentation that support why the test, procedure or medication was necessary for your care. A little research can go a long way!

Appealing a Medicare Claim

Appealing a denial of a Medicare claim has a good chance of succeeding, although it can be slow and time-consuming. Government reviewers at the first level of the appeals process reversed denials in 40% of cases involving Medicare Part A…53% involving Part B…and 44% relating to durable medical equipment. Before appealing, talk with the doctor, hospital and Medicare to see if the denial was caused by something that can be easily corrected, such as wrong coding. If that does not work, read the appeal rules on the back of your quarterly Medicare summary notice. Appeals range from reconsideration by a Medicare contractor to going to US District Court. There are special rules for Medicare Advantage plans and Part D prescription-drug appeals. To get help with an appeal, contact your local State Health Insurance Assistance Program (SHIP). For information, go to *SHIPTalk.org*.

Roundup of experts in Medicare appeals, reported in Kiplinger's Retirement Report. Kiplinger.com

What Disability Insurers Don't Want You to Know

Linda Nee, owner of Disability Claims Solutions, Inc., a consulting service based in Portland, Maine, that assists insurance customers in the US, UK and Canada with disability claims. From 1994 until 2002, Nee worked as a lead customer specialist for the insurer Unum. She was fired after becoming a whistle-blower and speaking with news program Dateline NBC about the company's practices. Unum was later fined $15 million by the insurance commissioners of 48 states for its unfair claims practices. LindaNee.WordPress.com

The Social Security disability program replaces only a small fraction of the typical disabled worker's earnings. Dis-

ability insurance obtained through an employer, a professional association or an individual policy can provide a more substantial financial cushion—but this insurance is loaded with caveats and limitations that most people don't consider until it's too late. In fact, employer-sponsored group disability coverage should never be counted on for long-term financial security, as these policies contain provisions that often allow insurers to terminate legitimate claims long before the claimant reaches age 65. *Here are important but poorly understood details about disability insurance…*

GROUP DISABILITY

If you receive your disability insurance through an employer or a professional association…

• **Your coverage is based on your ability to work in your current occupation, not your current job.** You won't receive benefits if there are jobs in your current profession that you would still be capable of doing.

Example: A retail manager's current job requires him to lift 50-pound boxes. He likely will not receive benefits if a back injury prevents him from lifting those boxes—the insurance company will argue that the Department of Labor's official description of the retail manager occupation does not list heavy lifting as a requirement.

• **Your policy won't replace as much of your predisability income as you might expect.** Policy provisions typically claim to replace 60% of base salary, but even that overestimates their benefits. These policies usually contain "offset provisions" that allow the insurance company to subtract from the 60% any money that you receive from Social Security disability, workers' compensation, state disability programs, retirement and pension plans and perhaps even injury settlements related to your disability.

Warning: Don't try to escape the Social Security disability offset by not applying for Social Security disability benefits. While policies typically do not contain provisions requiring claimants to apply for Social Security disability, they usually do contain language that allows the insurer to reduce your benefits based on its estimate of the benefits that you would have received.

• **Coverage for mental and nervous conditions usually is capped at just 24 months of benefits.** This is true even if your mental-health providers have not released you to return to work after 24 months.

• **You can't sue for punitive damages even if the insurance company acts in bad faith— and you might have trouble suing at all.** Employer-sponsored disability policies are covered by the Employment Retirement Income Security Act of 1974 (ERISA). ERISA lawsuits are extremely time-consuming for attorneys and offer no possibility of obtaining punitive damages from the insurer. The most you can win is the benefits that you should have received in the first place. With such a limited upside, it can be difficult to find an attorney willing to take the case—and without an attorney, ERISA claimants have very little chance of success.

Exception: Many attorneys will consider claims if the policy offers relatively hefty benefits of $3,000 or more per month, and there are some attorneys who will litigate less lucrative ERISA claims as well. Expect your attorney to claim 30% of unpaid back benefits plus 40% of all future benefits.

• **Benefits will be paid beyond 24 months only if your disability prevents you from working in any occupation.** For the first 24 months, policies typically pay benefits if you can't work in your current occupation. But after that time, benefits usually continue only if the disability is severe enough to preclude employment in any occupation for which you have training, education or experience. Many approved claims no longer pay out after this initial 24-month "own-occupation" period.

What's more, access to group health coverage often is linked to disability coverage—if your benefits end after 24 months, your right to remain on the company health plan might end then as well. Employees can use COBRA health insurance coverage to remain on their company plans for up to 18 months beyond that, but that requires paying for the coverage out-of-pocket, something many families cannot afford.

• **Your employer likely selected a disability insurance provider based on price—but if it selects a provider that tends to treat claimants unfairly, it's you who will pay the price.** Some insurance companies truly attempt to be fair with claimants, while others seem to regularly reject legitimate claims, knowing how difficult it is for claimants to appeal.

INDIVIDUAL DISABILITY

If you purchase disability insurance on your own…

• **Self-employed professionals should expect to be asked for massive amounts of financial data when submitting a claim for benefits.** The insurer might demand five to six years of past tax returns and 12 months of monthly profit-and-loss statements for your business to determine how much you should be paid. If your business doesn't create monthly profit-and-loss statements, you may be asked to compile them retroactively. (If you aren't self-employed, you will be asked to submit two years' worth of tax returns.)

• **Most individual policies offer reduced benefits or no benefits at all if you still are capable of working in any profession— even a profession very different from your current one.** It's worth paying extra for what is called own-occupation disability coverage. Read the contract carefully to make sure that you are buying true own-occupation coverage and not modified own-occupation coverage, which might reduce or eliminate your benefits if you do later work in another profession. Also read how the policy defines your "own occupation." Some use intentionally broad definitions of this to avoid paying claims later.

• **Waiting to make a claim increases the odds that your claim will be rejected.** The insurer might argue that the delay "prejudiced the investigation," making it impossible to determine if and when you really were disabled. Make a claim as soon as your doctor recommends that you stop working. You do not need to wait until the end of the policy's elimination period—the number of days that you have to wait for your first check—to file your application.

12 Hidden Discounts on Car Insurance Save $200 a Year or More

Amy Danise, editorial director at *Insure.com*, an independent website that provides articles and tools to aid consumers in making insurance decisions. It recently conducted a study of nearly 25,000 auto insurance discounts nationwide.

D o you have a master's degree? Are you married? Do your children get good grades? Strange as it may seem, answering yes to any of these questions—or other seemingly unrelated questions—might earn you a discount on your auto insurance policy.

You may know that insurers often offer discounts to policyholders who take defensive-driving classes or install antitheft devices in their cars. But those are just two of the many discounts available—including some that are completely unrelated to your vehicle or your driving skills.

These discounts sometimes subtract 15% to 20% or more from collision, liability, comprehensive and/or overall premiums. Policyholders usually are allowed to combine discounts to increase their savings, though total discounts often are capped, sometimes at around 25%. The average auto insurance policy costs around $800 a year, so that 25% off represents an annual savings of $200—possibly more if your coverage is especially expensive.

Don't assume that your insurer will automatically apply all of the available discounts. It's often up to the policyholder to inform the insurer that he/she qualifies. That's especially likely if you didn't qualify for a discount when you initially signed up for the coverage but do now.

The discounts vary dramatically in type and size from insurer to insurer, and even from state to state with the same insurer.

If any of the discounts listed here fit your situation, call your insurer to find out whether it's available and, if so, whether you currently are receiving it. When you shop around for your next auto insurance policy, ask insurers which discounts are available to you and make sure that their price reflects the discounts.

Among the discounts...*

1. Good-student discount. If there's a high school or college student in your family, your auto insurance probably is pretty pricey—young drivers are charged steep rates. But if one or more of the students on your insurance policy does well in school, there might be a way to trim your bill. More than 75% of insurers offer discounts to students under age 25 who get good grades. Good students tend to be safe drivers.

Rules vary, but a 3.0 GPA often is required. In some cases, the student must maintain this GPA...in others, he need only achieve it in the most recent semester to qualify for the discount in the following policy period.

Average savings: 16%.

2. Marriage discount. Tying the knot can make you eligible for a discount with about 40% of all auto insurers. Insurers have found that married people tend to be safer drivers than unmarried ones. In some instances, even civil unions qualify.

Average savings: 14%.

3. Low annual mileage discount. The fewer miles you drive, the lower your odds of getting into an accident. Your insurer likely asked you to estimate the length of your daily commute and/or the number of miles you drive each year when you applied for coverage. But perhaps you overestimated these distances or perhaps you're driving less now than you were then. Calculate your commute and annual mileage. If you drive substantially less than the national average of 15,000 miles

*Offers and rates subject to change.

a year, call your insurer to confirm that you're receiving any discounts you're due.

Average savings: 11% for car owners who drive less than 5,000 to 8,000 miles per year. Smaller discounts may be available to car owners who drive more than this but less than 15,000 miles per year.

4. Farm-vehicle discount. Around 40% of all auto insurers offer discounts based on "use" of the vehicle, such as farm use. The odds of getting into an accident with another vehicle are much lower when a vehicle is driven primarily on a farm.

Average savings: 10%.

5. Facebook "like" discount. The Allstate Esurance website offers a discount to residents of Texas and Arizona who "like" Esurance on Facebook.

Savings: 10%.

6. Membership discounts. Insurers often offer discounts to members of clubs and associations with which they have partnered. These could include professional associations, workers' unions, large employers or membership organizations such as AARP or AAA. You even could qualify for savings based on the college you attended or the fraternity or sorority you belonged to decades ago.

Examples: Geico offers a discount of up to 8% to members of Mensa, the high-IQ organization, and up to 8% to active and retired federal employees. Country Financial offers up to 10% off for full-time teachers of kindergarten through 12th grade and up to 5% for emergency first responders. Allstate's Esurance offers up to 15% to students and alumni of the Pacific-12 collegiate athletic conference schools who reside in Arizona, Colorado, Oregon and Utah.

7. Up-front payment discount. About half of all insurers offer a discount for paying premiums in full at the start of the policy period rather than in monthly installments. The savings can be significant, so if you can afford to pay in advance, it's often worth doing so.

Average savings: 9%.

8. Bundled-policy discount. Insurers often offer discounts to customers who purchase both auto and homeowner's insurance from the same company. But many people don't realize that this bundling discount also might be available if you combine auto insurance with renter's insurance, life insurance or some other type of insurance.

Average savings: 9%.

9. Advance-purchase discount. More than 25% of auto insurers offer a discount to existing customers who renew their coverage seven to 10 days before the old policy expires, though this varies.

Examples: In Florida, Travelers, Allstate, Progressive, Safeco and Infinity are among the insurers offering this discount. Some insurers extend this discount to new customers who sign up for coverage well before their current policy with a different insurer expires.

Average savings: 8%.

10. Owning a home. Insurers have found that home owners are less risky as customers because they tend to act more responsibly and are less likely to file claims.

Average savings: 6%.

11. Automatic-payment discount. Around one-third of insurers offer discounts to customers who agree to have their premiums automatically withdrawn from their bank accounts.

Average savings: 4%.

12. An advanced-degree discount. A small number of insurers offer discounts to customers who have earned master's degrees or PhDs.

Average savings: 4%.

DID YOU KNOW THAT...

These Traffic Violations Raise Your Insurance the Most?

DWI/DUI, driving while impaired or driving under the influence, can lead to a 25% premium hike. Reckless driving raises insurance costs by 15% to 20%. Speeding raises rates about 10%, although some insurers will waive your first speeding ticket if you were within 10 miles per hour of the limit. Running a red light can bring a 10% rate increase. Driving without a valid license also can raise your rate 10%.

Bankrate.com

9

Tax Hotline

7 Tricky Tax Return Questions Answered! Don't Get Tripped Up by the New Rules

Each new year brings tricky changes in the tax code, creating confusion when it comes time to fill out your tax forms and do tax planning. Soaring stock prices and rising real estate values could further complicate these tasks as many taxpayers deal with the effects of outsized capital gains.

Seven questions that taxpayers are asking about 2015 taxes...

TAX CHANGES

•**Am I going to have to pay a tax penalty under the Affordable Care Act if I don't have health insurance? I don't see anything about that on the tax forms.**

If you didn't obtain health insurance or enroll in Medicare by April 30, 2015, you likely will face a penalty on your 2015 taxes.

Meanwhile, taxpayers who do sign up for coverage through an Obamacare marketplace might qualify for tax credits to help them pay for coverage. Visit *HealthCare.gov* to see whether you qualify. These credits typically will be paid by the government directly to the health insurance provider, but if your income does not match the income estimate you provide when signing up for coverage, you might owe additional taxes or receive an additional credit when you file your 2015 taxes.

•**Has anything changed about the taxation of my retirement accounts?**

Gregg R. Wind, CPA, a partner with Wind & Stern, LLP, a Los Angeles–based accounting firm. He has more than 25 years of experience as a CPA, is former vice chair of the California Society of Certified Public Accountants and is a former member of the governing council of the American Institute of Certified Public Accountants. *WSCPAs.com*

165

Starting in 2014, distributions made directly from a tax-deferred IRA to a charity are no longer income tax–free unless the legislators decide to restore this rule. In the past, some IRA owners used this charity option to satisfy required minimum distribution (RMD) rules without incurring income taxes.

• **I have a home office, and I heard something about a new option for tax deductions called "safe harbor." Is it a good option?**

The IRS is offering taxpayers who have tax-deductible home offices the option of simply deducting $5 per square foot of home office space up to 300 square feet, rather than completing Form 8829, *Expenses for Business Use of Your Home*. This deduction would be reported on line 30 of Schedule C (Form 1040). You still can use Form 8829 to calculate your home-office deduction if you prefer.

It's worth calculating your deduction both ways to see which results in a larger tax savings. Or just compare the $5-per-square-foot deduction to the amount you deducted on a recent year's Form 8829. Assuming that your mortgage, insurance rates, utility bills and other home-office expenses didn't change much from 2014 to 2015, that should give you a pretty good idea of which option is preferable for you.

• **I heard that the IRS changed the rules for Flexible Spending Accounts (FSAs) and that I now won't lose money that was remaining in my account at the end of last year. Is that true?**

The IRS now lets employers offer employees the option to carry over a balance of as much as $500 from one year to the next—but this provision is not automatic. You can take advantage of this provision only if your employer has already amended its plan documents to allow it. And there's still a chance that money remaining in your FSA from 2015 might not be lost even if your plan does not offer the carryover option. FSAs are allowed to have grace periods of up to two and a half months for all of your FSA balance, so leftover 2015 FSA funds could be accessible as late as March 15, 2016.

Caution: Employers can't offer both the $500 carryover and the two-and-a-half-month grace period—check to see which one, if either, your employer offers.

CAPITAL GAINS

• **I finally sold a house that I had been renting out for a few years while I waited for home prices to rebound. Do I have to pay capital gains tax on the sale?**

Home prices have rebounded recently, so many people who had put off selling houses after the real estate bubble burst finally unloaded them. Problem is, not all of those people had been living in those homes recently. Some who were forced to relocate for career reasons or to enter a nursing home were instead renting out their former homes or letting them stand vacant while waiting for the real estate market to recover. The tax code exemption that allows home sellers to avoid paying capital gains taxes on the first $250,000 in profits from the sale of a home ($500,000 if married and filing jointly) applies only to principal residences. To take advantage, you must have used the home as your primary residence for at least two years during the five years preceding the sale. These two years do not need to be consecutive, and you can claim the capital gains tax exclusion from the sale of a home no more than once every two years. (The two-year requirement is reduced to one year for people who move into nursing homes, and these people are allowed to consider the house their primary residence even when they are living in the nursing home.)

You might qualify for a partial exclusion of capital gains even if you didn't live in the home for two of the past five years if the sale of the home was due to a change in job location, a health issue, a divorce or certain other reasons. For details, see IRS Publication 523, *Selling Your Home*.

• **My stocks are doing very well. Will I have to pay a big capital gains tax bill?**

That depends on whether you sell your investment, whether you own shares in individual stocks or mutual funds and, thanks to new tax rules, how high your income is this year.

Capital gains on individual stocks are taxed in the year in which the appreciated investments are sold, not necessarily in the year in which the gains occur. If you hold on to most of your shares, you shouldn't face a big capital gains tax bill on your 2015 taxes no matter how well those investments did.

However, mutual fund investors sometimes face big capital gains tax bills even when they don't sell their mutual fund shares. This happens if the fund managers sell appreciated securities from the funds' underlying holdings.

Tax preparers are hearing lots of questions about capital gains this year, in part because stocks have appreciated strongly, but also in part because new tax rules have increased capital gains taxes for high earners.

If your modified adjusted gross income (MAGI) is more than $200,000 ($250,000 if married and filing jointly), you now may face an additional 3.8% Medicare surtax on a portion of your investment income (including long-term capital gains and dividends after subtracting investment expenses). Go to *IRS. gov*, and search for "NIIT" for more details.

If your taxable income is more than $400,000 ($450,000 for married couples filing jointly), your capital gains tax has increased, too, from 15% to 20%. (High earners also face higher income tax rates and a new 0.9% Medicare surtax on salaries and self-employment income.)

If you sell highly appreciated investments, consider offsetting these gains by selling investments that have lost money, too. That's a particularly good idea if the new high-earner capital gains taxes and/or Medicare surtaxes apply. If you are not in a rush to sell a highly appreciated asset, consider postponing the sale until a future calendar year when you fall below the high-earner tax thresholds.

SPEEDY REFUNDS

● **What's the quickest way to get my tax refund?**

Tax preparers hear this question a lot. The best way to speed up a refund is to eFile the return and request direct-deposit of the refund into a bank account. Your refund should reach you in around seven business days.

Warning: Double-check that you or your tax preparer entered your bank account number correctly on your tax return. It might be impossible to recover the money if your tax refund is mistakenly sent to someone else's bank account.

A Handful of Tax Savings

Forbes.com

Most taxpayers can expect to get modest savings for 2015. This is a result of inflation adjustments to income tax brackets and to other tax provisions. (The projections are unofficial estimates based on a government inflation index as analyzed by tax publisher CCH.)

Examples: A married couple filing jointly with total taxable income of $100,000 can expect to pay $125.50 less in 2015 than in 2014 because of tax-bracket indexing. A single filer with income of $50,000 can expect to pay $62.50 less. The standard deduction will increase by $200 (from $12,400 to $12,600) for married couples filing jointly and $100 for single taxpayers (from $6,200 to $6,300). The personal exemption amount rises by $50, to $4,000. The estate and gift-tax lifetime exemption rises to $5.43 million (double that for a married couple) from $5.34 million. The annual gift-tax exclusion will remain at $14,000, same as in 2014. The $5,500 limit ($6,500 for people who are age 50 or older) on IRA contributions also remains the same. The alternative minimum tax (AMT) exemption is $83,400 for joint filers, up from $82,100, and $53,600, up from $52,800, for single filers.

Taxpayer Victories (and Defeats) Can Save You $$$

Barbara Weltman, Esq., an attorney in Vero Beach, Florida, author of *J.K. Lasser's 1001 Deductions & Tax Breaks* (Wiley) and publisher of *Big Ideas for Small Business*, a free monthly e-letter. *BarbaraWeltman.com*

There are many ways that taxpayers trigger challenges from the IRS—including mailing mistakes and errors involving fine print. Whether the taxpayer wins or the IRS does, these disputes provide lessons that could reduce your taxes or at least save you from a stressful battle…

A PAPERWORK MISTAKE MAY NOT COST YOU A TAX BREAK

In 2002, Mark and Jennifer Ambrose's home on a farm in Auburn, New York, was destroyed by a Christmas fire. Mark immediately reported the fire to his insurance company and met with the adjuster two days later.

However, the Ambroses did not file a personal property inventory (called a "proof of loss" document) within the required 60 days, and the insurance company would not pay the claim because of this. The couple sued the insurance company in state court but lost. Then they deducted a casualty loss of $167,619 that was not reimbursed by insurance.

IRS Position: Failure to file the insurance document was the same as not submitting a claim, which is a prerequisite to claiming a tax deduction.

Court of Federal Claims Ruling: The deduction is allowed because the report of the fire to the insurer was a "claim" for tax law purposes. The fact that the insurer denied the claim because the home owner didn't provide all of the required proof does not prevent a tax deduction.

Lesson: Even though you should submit all required documents to your insurer for a theft or casualty loss, if you slip up, you may not be out of luck for tax purposes.

Mark D. Ambrose, Court of Federal Claims, 2012-2 USTC

DIVORCE AGREEMENT APPLIES TO TAX FILING

When Gary and Denise Scalone of Rochester, New York, got divorced, Denise retained physical custody of their child. In the legal separation agreement, a document signed by both Gary and Denise, she promised to file IRS Form 8332, *Release/Revocation of Release of Claim to Exemption for Child by Custodial Parent,* with her tax return every year to allow Gary to claim the exemption for the child—that is, she agreed not to claim the exemption herself. She didn't sign Form 8332 for 2006, but he claimed the exemption nonetheless, attaching a copy of the relevant page from the separation agreement to his tax return (which is permitted for taxpayers who divorced before 2009).

IRS Position: The IRS denied Gary's dependency exemption on the grounds that the document attached to his tax return failed to include the required Social Security numbers for him and the custodial parent, Denise, and so could not be treated as an acceptable substitute for Form 8332.

Tax Court Ruling: Gary's exemption claim is allowed because the language in the separation agreement signed by both parties was unequivocal—he could claim the exemption, and she could not.

Lesson: Taxpayers don't always have to be meticulous in following the fine print in IRS rules every step of the way.

Gary L. Scalone, Tax Court Summary Opinion 2012-40

RELIANCE ON A TAX PREPARER IS NOT ENOUGH

For his 2004 tax return, Anthony Tesoriero wanted a filing extension, which his CPA prepared and left in a pile on the CPA's desk for a secretary to mail by regular mail. When Tesoriero's return was filed in August 2005, the IRS notified him that it was late—no extension request had been received.

IRS Position: The taxpayer could not rely on the presumption that the extension had been filed. It was not sent by registered or certified mail or an authorized private-delivery service.

Tax Court Ruling: Reliance on a tax return preparer to file for an extension is not an acceptable excuse to avoid a late-filing penalty when the extension isn't filed. Testimony about the CPA's office procedures was not sufficient to prove that the extension request was mailed.

Lesson: Always verify that a filing extension has been submitted. This can be done, for example, with a receipt for certified mail.

Anthony Tesoriero, Tax Court Memo 2012-261

USE THE RIGHT DELIVERY SERVICE

Marcius and Andrea Scaggs wanted to file a petition in Tax Court to contest an IRS notice of deficiency on their taxes—there is a 90-day limit to file after such a notice is mailed by the IRS. They mailed the petition using FedEx Express Saver third business day. The 90 days ended on July 7, but their petition was received on July 12. The couple said it was timely because it was filed using FedEx.

IRS Position: The "timely mailed, timely received" rule did not apply here because not all FedEx services are on the list of approved private-delivery services, which include FedEx Priority Overnight, FedEx Standard Overnight, FedEx 2 Day, FedEx International Priority and FedEx International First but not FedEx Express Saver.

Tax Court Ruling: Using the wrong delivery service prevented the timely filing of the return. When mailing near a deadline, only an IRS-approved type of service is allowed under the timely mailed, timely received rule.

Lesson: When filing a paper return close to the filing deadline, use only the US Postal Service or an IRS-approved version of private-delivery service to avoid late-filing penalties —or file electronically. The approved services are listed under "Private Delivery Services" in the instructions to IRS Form 1040.

Marcius J. Scaggs, Tax Court Memo 2012-258

WHEN A CHURCH DONATION CAN'T BE DEDUCTED

David Durden and his wife, Veronda, took a charitable contribution deduction on their 2007 tax return for $25,171 in gifts to their church. Except for five small checks, all of the other contributions were in amounts of $250 or more.

IRS Position: The deduction (except for the small checks) is disallowed because there was no written acknowledgment from the church for the donations at the time the return was filed. Canceled checks are not enough.

Tax Court Ruling: The charitable contribution deduction for checks of $250 or more is denied for lack of substantiation. Even though proper donations were made, the taxpayers' failure to obtain the correct written acknowledgment in a timely fashion meant that the checks could not be deducted. The couple got acknowledgments in 2009 after the IRS notified them of the disallowance of their deduction, but it was too late.

Lesson: Obtain proper substantiation for the type of assets donated. Details of the rules can be found in IRS Publication 526, Charitable Contributions.

David P. Durden, Tax Court Memo 2012-140

Financial Aid and Tax Breaks for Caregiving

Jim Miller, an advocate for older Americans, who writes "Savvy Senior," a weekly information column syndicated in more than 400 newspapers nationwide. Based in Norman, Oklahoma, he also offers a free senior news service at *SavvySenior.org*.

If you're hiring someone to take care of an elderly family member—or even doing it yourself—you may be in a precarious position. For many families, caregiving can quickly grow into a heavy financial burden, especially if you've had to quit your job to provide care. However, there are a number of government programs and tax breaks that can help you financially. *Here are some options to explore…*

State assistance: Many states help low-income seniors pay for in-home care services, including paying family members for care. These programs—which go by various names such as "cash and counseling" or "consumer-directed"—vary greatly depending on where you live and, in some states, on whether the senior is on Medicaid. To find out what's available in your state, contact your local Medicaid office.

Veterans benefits: In some communities, veterans who need assistance with daily living activities can enroll in the Veteran-Directed Home and Community Based Services program. This program provides a flexible stipend, which can be used to pay family members for home caregiving. Information about these programs is available at *VA.gov/geriatrics*.

A VA benefit available only to wartime veterans and their spouses is Aid and Attendance, which helps pay for in-home care as well as assisted living and nursing home care. This benefit also can be used to pay family caregivers. To be eligible, the person must need assistance with daily living activities such as bathing, dressing and going to the bathroom. And the person's annual income must be less than $13,794 as a surviving spouse…$21,446 for a single veteran…or $25,448 for a married couple—after medical expenses. The person's assets must be less than $80,000 excluding a home and car.

To learn more about these VA benefits, go to *VA.gov/geriatrics* or contact your regional VA office or your local veterans service organization.

Tax breaks: If you pay more than half of your elderly relative's yearly expenses and his gross income was below $4,000 in 2015, not counting Social Security, you can claim him as a dependent on your taxes and reduce your taxable income by $4,000 in 2015. For more information, see IRS Publication 501, *Exemptions, Standard Deduction, and Filing Information*, at *IRS.gov/publications* or call 800-829-3676 to ask for a copy.

If you can't claim your relative as a dependent, you still may be able to get a tax break if you're paying more than half his living expenses, including medical and long-term-care costs, and what you're paying exceeds 10% (or 7.5% if you're 65 or older) of your adjusted gross income. You can include your own medical expenses in calculating the total. See IRS Publication 502, *Medical and Dental Expenses* (*IRS.gov/publications*) for details.

Long-term-care insurance: If your relative has long-term-care insurance, check whether it covers in-home care. Some policies permit family members to be paid, although that may exclude people who live in the same household.

Family funds: If your relative has savings or other assets, discuss the possibility that he could pay for his own care. If he plans to pay a family member to provide care, consult with an attorney about drafting a short written contract that details the terms of the work and payment arrangements so that everyone involved knows what to expect.

Other assistance: To look for financial assistance programs that your relative or you may be eligible for, visit *BenefitsCheckup.org*, a free, web-based service that helps low-income seniors and their families identify federal, state and private benefits programs that can help with prescription drug costs, health care, utilities and other basic needs.

Tax-Free Income from Your Home

Rent out your home for fewer than 15 days in a year, and the income is tax-free and not reportable to the IRS. This can be especially beneficial for homes near the sites of major sports events. Ask your accountant for more information.

Bill Woodward, CPA, Elliott Davis, accounting, tax and consulting firm with offices in Augusta, Georgia, and Atlanta, quoted in *The Wall Street Journal*.

Could You Use Your Dog as a Tax Deduction?

Service-dog costs are tax deductible as a medical expense. And guard dogs—for example, for junkyards—can be business deductions. Under some circumstances, if an animal earns money for you—perhaps your dog was in a pet-food commercial—costs associated with the animal's training or care may be tax deductible.

Roundup of experts in tax deductions, reported in *The Wall Street Journal*.

Will Your Tax Preparer Get You in Trouble? If He Makes a Mistake, *You* Pay the Price

Scott M. Estill, JD, a former senior trial attorney for the IRS who currently is of counsel to Estill & Long, LLC, a tax law firm based in Denver, Colorado. He is author of *Tax This! An Insider's Guide to Standing Up to the IRS*, currently in its ninth edition (Self-Council). *EstillandLong.com*

Each year, taxpayers turn to professionals for help in preparing 82 million tax returns, partly to avoid running into trouble with the IRS and state tax agencies. However, in various instances, some of those 1.2 million tax preparers get us into trouble instead.

Tax rules are so complex—and the typical return contains so many details—that even skilled preparers can make mistakes that trigger audits.

Example: When the Government Accountability Office examined the work of 19 randomly selected tax preparers in 2006, it found that six had significantly overestimated refunds due and almost all had made mistakes of some kind.

When preparers make mistakes, it's their clients who pay the price. A taxpayer is legally responsible for his/her return, even when it is a tax preparer who erred (although the IRS can pursue action against unethical preparers, too).

And an IRS or a state-tax audit isn't the only danger we face when we go to a tax preparer—there also is the risk that the preparer might overcharge us.

Example: In 2010, tax attorney Roni Deutch, founder of a nationwide chain of tax-preparation offices, was sued for $34 million by the state of California for allegedly defrauding thousands of customers by making false promises about her ability to help them reduce debts they owed to the IRS. The chain eventually closed, and Deutch surrendered her law license.

You must be careful when choosing your preparer...

SELECT THE RIGHT ONE

Five ways to reduce the risk that you will pick a preparer who gets you into trouble...

• **Check IRS and state databases for indications of past problems.** The IRS often pays special attention to returns filed by preparers who have shown a willingness to play fast and loose with rules before. Taxpayers who hope to avoid audits would do well to avoid such preparers.

EASY TO DO...

Avoid the Most Common Tax Return Mistakes

Entering the wrong Social Security number... putting the right information on the wrong line... forgetting to sign and date forms before mailing them...failing to claim dependents or claiming ones you are not entitled to claim...not filing a return because you have very low income—this may cost you the earned income credit (a credit for people in lower- and middle-income brackets)...failing to report stocks sold at a loss—the IRS will assume the entire sale price was profit... improperly reporting the taxable amount of an IRA or a retirement-plan distribution...and errors on Schedule E, which is used to report rental property, royalties, partnership income and expenses, estate income and expenses, and S-Corp income and expenses.

Finally, mistakes are often made due to waiting until the last minute to file. Be sure to give yourself enough time.

Roundup of experts on tax filing, reported at *DailyFinance. com*.

The websites of many state boards of accountancy permit visitors to search through lists of certified public accountants (CPAs) for ethical or malpractice violations. The website of the National Association of State Boards of Accountancy includes links to the state boards (*NASBA.org/stateboards*).

The IRS Office of Professional Responsibility also reports sanctions and other penalties imposed on CPAs, tax attorneys and enrolled agents. Type the name of a tax preparer into the search box at *IRS.gov* to see if red flags such as these pop up.

However, these databases are unlikely to include storefront seasonal tax preparers, many of whom are not CPAs, enrolled agents or attorneys. There are no federal rules preventing people with no certification and little or no training from acting as professional tax preparers, though a few states do require licenses.

•**Ask preparers if they will pay the penalties and interest if they make mistakes that lead to a costly audit.** Reputable tax preparers are likely to do this—and it gives them excellent motivation to avoid mistakes. Ask to have this confirmed in writing.

•**Make sure that the preparer asks you about the level of aggressiveness you are looking for.** Some taxpayers stress the need to minimize the odds of an audit…while others care more about lowering the tax bite as much as possible. A preparer who doesn't ask you about this might not pay enough attention to his/her clients' audit tolerance.

•**Watch out for refund guarantees.** Don't work with any tax preparer who promises to get you a refund (or a refund of a certain size) before he has started doing your returns. He might have to take significant chances and cut corners to make good on his promise.

•**If you own a rental property or small business, choose a tax preparer who has extensive experience with these.** Returns featuring a Schedule E, *Supplemental Income and Loss* (the form that covers rental real estate, among other topics), and/or a Schedule C, *Profit or Loss from Business*, are particularly likely to attract attention from the IRS, in part because these forms are so complex

that mistakes are common. If your return will include one of these forms, find a preparer who each year handles dozens of returns that include the form.

Helpful: Obtain targeted referrals. If you own rental property, do not simply ask your neighbor who does his/her taxes, ask an experienced area real estate agent or real estate attorney for a recommendation. If you have a small business, ask other small-business owners or your business's attorney.

DOUBLE-CHECK YOUR RETURNS

When the preparer gives you a completed return for your signature…

•**Check for major differences from last year's return.** Don't assume that the preparer did everything right. Pull out the prior year's return, and compare it with this year's line for line. Give some thought to any major differences—lines that are blank one year but not the other…lines where the amount has changed by thousands of dollars. Is there an obvious reason why this figure changed so much? If nothing comes to mind, call the preparer, tell him what line of the return you're looking at and ask him to explain the change. (Tax forms can differ slightly from year to year, so make sure that the lines you're comparing cover the same topic before calling.)

•**Question any unclear tax credits.** The IRS pays special attention to tax credits that are claimed on returns. If you're not 100% certain why you qualify for a credit that your preparer has you claiming, confirm with him that you're on safe ground doing so before signing.

Tax credits are reported on the second side of Form 1040. As of 2014, they were on lines 47–53, 64–66 and 70–71. Claiming the Earned Income Credit (EIC)—line 64a as of 2014—is particularly likely to attract IRS attention because it so often is claimed improperly.

GUARD AGAINST OVERBILLING

Three ways to weed out tax preparers who might try to take financial advantage of you…

•**Choose a preparer who provides a cost estimate up front.** Many preparers will supply estimates of their bills based on the forms that the client's return is likely to require. Some preparers even list fixed per-form prices on their websites.

• **Make sure that your refund is sent to you.** Confirm that the routing and account numbers on lines 74b and 74d of Form 1040 are for your bank account. Be extremely suspicious if your tax preparer has tried to route your refund to his account. This shouldn't occur unless the preparer has given you a refund anticipation loan—and these loans charge such horrible interest rates that you should not agree to take one.

• **Steer clear of percentage-based billing.** A tax preparer who charges based on a percentage of the client's refund has an incentive to be overly aggressive.

Tax-Prep Software: Desktop vs. Online

The desktop tax-preparation programs tend to cost more, but they are more flexible than online programs. A single purchase lets you prepare and file multiple returns, and it is easier to use a desktop program to move back and forth between the return itself and the interviews that the program uses to gather data from you. Online versions allow you to work on your return from any Internet-connected computer and store your return on a secure server in the cloud.

Each of the three major programs, whether used online or as a desktop program, has its own strength: TurboTax is easiest to use, requiring only a few clicks to import a lot of financial information…H&R Block offers the greatest reassurance—the firm's staff will represent you at no charge if you are audited… TaxAct is the least expensive but requires you to type in more information than the other programs and does not offer a desktop version for Macs.

The New York Times. NYTimes.com

When Not to File an Amended Return

Edward Mendlowitz, CPA, a partner at the accounting firm WithumSmith+Brown, New Brunswick, New Jersey. He is author of 20 books including *Getting Your Affairs in Order* (iUniverse).

Do you ever have second thoughts regarding tax returns you filed months ago? Despite those second thoughts, it is not always worth the effort and expense to file an amended tax return when you realize that you made a mistake. *Three examples of when not to file an amended return…*

• **Your additional deductions and credits would result in a small refund.** Weigh the cost of what you would get back versus your accountant's fee to prepare an amended return. (But note that accountants don't charge for an amended return if they made the mistake.) Even if you use tax software and can do it yourself, an amended return draws unwanted attention because the IRS takes a second look at the entire return. In my experience, that increases the chance that the IRS will do an audit or at least request additional documentation to substantiate what has been reported.

• **You made a simple math error.**

Example: You listed all your dividend income correctly but wrote down the wrong total on the first page of your return. In cases of math errors such as this, the IRS automatically will correct the error and notify you…and you won't suffer any consequences except some interest if you owe additional tax because of the mistake.

• **You omitted a W-2 or a 1099 form.** The IRS will process your return anyway and will contact you if more information or specific documents are needed.

Important: File an amended return right away if you made mistakes that could result in owing additional tax. This will limit interest and penalty charges that might accrue.

New Ways to Track Your Tax Refund

The *IRS2Go* app for smartphones lets you check your refund status anytime. It's free for Apple and Android. You must enter your Social Security number, filing status and expected refund to use it. The IRS automated toll-free phone line, 800-829-1954, is dedicated to refund status updates.

Also: You can track your refund at *IRS.gov.* If the IRS says a refund was mailed at least 28 days ago and you have not received it, you can use the website to trace the check.

Barbara Weltman, Esq., an attorney in Vero Beach, Florida, author of *J.K. Lasser's 1001 Deductions & Tax Breaks* (Wiley) and publisher of *Big Ideas for Small Business,* a free monthly e-letter. *BarbaraWeltman.com*

IRS Whistle-Blower Awards Have Been Cut

Awards for tax whistle-blowers have been cut under the automatic federal spending reductions. The cutback on IRS payouts reduces the minimum reward to 13.6% from 15% of the additional tax and penalties that the IRS recovers as a result of information the whistle-blower supplied.

Forbes.com

DID YOU KNOW THAT...

IRS Audits Are Down?

In 2014, the IRS audited less than 1% of all returns filed. If you made less than $200,000, your chance of being audited was just 0.65%...between $500,000 and $1 million, 3.62%...and more than $1 million, up to 16.22%.

Bankrate.com

Don't Fall for This "IRS" Phone Scam

One realistic-seeming IRS phone scam demands immediate payment for a phony tax bill—and uses the last four digits of victims' Social Security numbers. The caller ID is "spoofed" to seem as though the call comes from the IRS. Thieves sometimes send victims a false e-mail as well—using the IRS logo and format. The scammers say that if victims do not pay immediately, they can be arrested or deported or lose their business or driver's license. But the IRS initiates taxpayer contact only by US mail, never by phone or e-mail... and the agency does not work directly with police or immigration officials.

Self-defense: If you get any initial call claiming to be from the IRS, hang up and report the scam to the Treasury Inspector General for Tax Administration, 800-366-4484. If you get an e-mail, forward it to *Phishing@IRS.gov* without opening any attachments—they may contain malware.

CBSNews.com

10

Investment Forecast

What's the Next Apple? Innovative Companies to Invest in Now

ichael Lippert loves companies that shake things up. They don't just amble along. Instead, they innovate, transform and sprint ahead. Their products and services reshape global industries and change the way we live and behave. And they have the potential to grow tremendously.

That's why, the mutual fund manager says, you need to find just a few of these companies over the course of your investing life to achieve market-beating returns.

In the past, companies that shook up their industries have included stock market winners such as Apple, Netflix, Priceline.com and Whole Foods, all of which the Baron Opportunity Fund, run by Lippert, began investing in years ago.

We asked Lippert which modest-sized companies today could become the innovation stars of tomorrow...

THE BIGGEST TRENDS

Innovation is not confined to companies with the next popular high-tech gadget. There also are highly innovative companies in sectors such as health care, financial services and industrial manufacturing. The companies that I look for must have the potential to grow fast enough to double their size—and their share prices—within the next five years regardless of how the economy is doing or what goes on in Washington, DC. They can do this because these companies are all tapping into major consumer and business trends.

While some trends, such as the proliferation of mobile communications and online social networking, are well-known among investors,

Michael Lippert, CFA, JD, vice president at Baron Capital, Inc., New York City, and manager of the Baron Opportunity Fund (BIOPX). Over the past decade, his fund had annualized gains of 10.47%, compared with 8.08% for the Standard & Poor's 500 stock index. *BaronFunds.com*

175

others get less media attention but are becoming just as pervasive in our lives. These include the growing popularity of genetic testing…digital money replacing paper money…the everyday use of satellite data for maps and driving directions…and the shift to cheaper, environmentally friendly food packaging.

Innovative companies don't just profit from trends—they also are heavily influencing them with revolutionary products and services. Think how Amazon disrupted the way we shop for retail items…and how Whole Foods turned organic food into a mainstream supermarket experience. These businesses aren't content to just create a successful product or business model and stick with it. They keep reinventing themselves in order to push into more and more new markets and attract consumers and business clients who must have what they are selling.

Investing in companies that are so innovative does carry risks. Many aren't household names yet, and because they take big chances, their stock prices can be very volatile. Also, these stocks aren't meant to be held in your portfolio forever. When companies get very large, they often become less daring because they have so many employees and so much market share to protect. Their ability to innovate diminishes.

Example: I sold all of my fund's Apple holdings back in 2012, several months after the death of its brilliant founder and innovator, Steve Jobs. Apple hasn't released a truly transformative product since the iPad premiered in 2010, and in 2013 it said it would return $100 billion to shareholders in the form of dividends and stock buybacks rather than use the money for new acquisitions or for research and development.

MY FAVORITE STOCKS

The following stocks look attractive now…

•**Berry Plastics (BERY).** Glass, metal and traditional plastic packaging are increasingly expensive and regarded as harmful to the environment. This Evansville, Indiana, packaging company serves more than 13,000 clients including Burger King, Colgate-Palmolive, Pillsbury, Hershey's and Procter & Gamble.

Among its many patented products: Its new plastic Versalite cup, which has insulation characteristics that are far superior to Styrofoam and paper, is expected to shake up the disposable-cup market.

Recent share price: $36.09.*

•**DigitalGlobe (DGI)** is the world's largest provider of commercial high-resolution Earth-imagery products and services. Its five satellites collect geospatial data on millions of square miles of Earth every day, allowing clients to view conditions and changes in the planet's landscape that can help save lives, evaluate geopolitical and business risks, and optimize natural resources and infrastructure planning. Although more than half of the company's annual revenue comes from US government defense and intelligence agencies, DigitalGlobe is rapidly diversifying. Major clients include the government of India…AutoNavi, which is China's digital map and navigation giant…and Google, which licenses images for Google Earth and Maps. The company, based in Longmont, Colorado, recently purchased its major competitor, GeoEye, creating a US monopoly with little international competition.

Recent share price: $34.60.

•**Guidewire Software (GWRE)** provides computer software systems for just one industry—property and casualty insurance. By specializing in that industry, Guidewire, which was established in 2001 and began offering publicly traded shares of stock last year, is able to convince insurers to replace their outdated systems for tasks ranging from underwriting and policy administration to billing and claims management. Guidewire, based in Foster City, California, has more than 100 clients, including such major players as Amica, Nationwide, Hartford Mutual Insurance Companies and Zurich Insurance, but it has barely penetrated the $15-billion-a-year market for insurance software and information-technology services, leaving plenty of room for growth. Most of the 7,000 major insurers around the world still use homegrown software. Guidewire also is expanding its consulting services, analyzing insurance customer and company performance data to help improve pricing and efficiency in writing policies, dispatching adjusters and settling claims.

*Prices as of April 2, 2015.

Recent share price: $52.53.

•**Illumina (ILMN)** is the leading manufacturer of instruments, test kits and supplies used by scientists and research laboratories for DNA analysis and genetic testing, including screening for cancer and prenatal testing. The San Diego–based company often is referred to as the Apple of the genomics industry. About 90% of the world's DNA sequencing is now done on Illumina machines, and the company is trying to become a one-stop shop for all genetic research needs. This is the largest position in my portfolio because I think Illumina will play a major role as the health-care industry around the world moves toward personalized medicine, which involves designing drugs to target specific mutations of diseases based on a person's own DNA.

Recent share price: $183.01.

How to Make Money Like Warren Buffet…Whether the Market Goes Up, Down or Sideways

John Reese, founder and CEO of *Validea.com*, which provides stock research and model portfolios based on the methods of legendary investors, and CEO of the investment advisory firm Validea Capital Management, New York City.

How do you invest in a tempting but volatile stock market? Try emulating Warren Buffett, the legendary investor and CEO of Berkshire Hathaway. He ignores the broad market and instead uses stringent criteria to pick high-quality companies whose stocks are selling at a discount. That strategy provides you with the opportunity for long-term gains but affords some protection should the market retreat.

To help you find Buffett-like picks, we spoke with John Reese, who has made a career out of analyzing investments by Buffett and other legendary investors…

BORING YET RELIABLE

My computer stock-screening method incorporates more than 40 years of Warren Buffett's annual reports and other research on how he selects his boring-yet-reliable stocks. Since its 2003 inception, my 10-stock Buffett portfolio has had a cumulative return of 154.68% (an average of 8.6% annually) versus 94.72% (6.1% annually) for the Standard & Poor's 500 stock index. Over the same period, Buffett's own Berkshire Hathaway stock had a total return of 159%. But small investors have somewhat of an advantage now. Buffett has stated candidly that his company and its investment portfolio are so large that he can no longer invest in stellar small companies and achieve the outsized returns of the past. As a small investor, however, you can own shares in and potentially profit from these companies. *My Buffett stock-screen criteria include…*

•**Protection from losses.** Buffett invests in companies that have strong brand-name products whose sales hold up well in troubled times. In downturns, these stocks typically fall by much less than the S&P 500.

•**Predictable growth.** Buffett searches for companies that dominate their industries and can increase their earnings year after year for decades.

•**Little or no long-term debt.** This gives businesses enormous financial flexibility, especially in the next several years, when rising interest rates will make interest payments burdensome.

•**Shareholder-friendly management.** Buffett likes CEOs who make moves that benefit investors, such as buying back shares with excess corporate cash and making shrewd acquisitions.

•**An economic moat.** This is Buffett's term for some kind of lasting advantage that a company has over its competitors, such as a patent on a product, a unique business model or a trusted name.

MY FAVORITE BUFFETT-LIKE STOCKS

•**Bed Bath & Beyond (BBBY).** Buffett loves investing in businesses offering strong profits and steady growth that are suffering a temporary setback and depressed stock price.

This company, with nearly 1,500 stores and more than $12 billion in annual sales, controls an estimated 9% of the total domestic home-furnishings market.

Buffett would focus on the long-term picture: Bed Bath & Beyond is a company whose stock is trading at a substantial discount to that of retailers such as Costco and Target…enough free cash flow to spend about $800 million in each of the next three years to buy back another 15% of its stock…and smart management that has positioned the company for additional expansion with the construction of a major e-commerce fulfillment center in Georgia.

Recent share price: $76.80.*

•**C.H. Robinson Worldwide (CHRW).** This shipping logistics and freight company handles more than 10 million shipments and earns more than $13 billion in revenue without owning a single truck, plane, ship or train. Instead, the company uses its supply-chain expertise to contract with tens of thousands of mom-and-pop operations (more than 95% of US trucking companies operate fewer than 20 trucks). The company's immense network and buying power allow it to negotiate lower prices for clients than competitors are able to offer. Earnings have increased every year for the past decade at an annualized rate of about 17%.

Recent share price: $71.33.

•**FactSet Research Systems (FDS)** often tops my Buffett-inspired stock screen, but with just a $5.85 billion market capitalization, it is far too small to attract Buffett's attention. The company provides global financial and economic data to thousands of investment professionals. FactSet, which charges about $50,000 annually for the basic Internet subscription, has carved out a lucrative niche in the highly competitive financial-information industry by aggregating and repackaging data from more than 50 research firms and providing its own proprietary research that helps money managers analyze client portfolios. Buffett is drawn to industries with solid long-term prospects, and the insatiable appetite investors have for financial data is only going to increase. Although the company's US business

*Prices as of April 2, 2015.

can fluctuate with employment trends on Wall Street and the amount of assets clients oversee, management has buffered slumps by diversifying internationally. Overseas clients constitute one-third of its revenue.

Recent share price: $159.99.

•**Hormel Foods (HRL).** Buffett is a fan of powerful global brands, and it does not get much more iconic than this 122-year-old lunch giant. Hormel Foods leads the meat-oriented packaged-food sector with products such as Dinty Moore beef stew, Country Crock side dishes, Hormel Chili and Spam. While Spam may be the butt of jokes, a can is purchased somewhere in the world every three seconds of every day. Hormel, which earned $9 billion in revenues last year, has such reliable cash flow that it has been able to increase its annual dividend for 48 consecutive years. In down markets, its stock typically has fallen less than half as much as the S&P 500. In 2013, Hormel took a big step in broadening its lineup by acquiring Skippy peanut butter for $700 million. Skippy, which is the leading peanut butter in China, provides Hormel with a strong platform to grow international sales.

Recent share price: $57.42.

•**Varian Medical Systems (VAR)**, the leading manufacturer of systems for treating cancer with radiation therapy, sells to hospitals, cancer clinics and health agencies. It has perhaps the strongest economic moat of any company in my Buffett screen, controlling roughly 60% of the global market for linear accelerators —large machines that beam high-energy X-rays into tumors. There are steep barriers for competitors because this type of business requires extensive regulatory approval, and customer retention is high. The machinery is so expensive that hospitals would rather upgrade than buy a competing system. Despite the reduction in hospital budgets during the recession and concerns about cuts in Medicare reimbursement rates for radiation procedures, Varian hasn't had a down year in revenues or earnings for more than a decade. And it can expect reliable growth for many years.

Recent share price: $93.79.

Are You Prepared for a Stock Market Plunge?

Janet Briaud, CFP, CEO of Briaud Financial Advisors in Bryan, Texas, for almost 30 years. Her firm oversees $450 million in portfolio assets. Briaud has been named by *Barron's* as one of the top 100 independent financial advisers in the US. *Briaud.com*

Scott Rothbort, president of LakeView Asset Management, LLC, an investment advisory firm for high-net-worth clients, in Millburn, New Jersey. He also is professor of finance for the Stillman School of Business of Seton Hall University, South Orange, New Jersey. *LakeViewAsset.com*

Kelley Wright, chief investment officer and portfolio manager at IQ Trends Private Client Asset Management, Carlsbad, California. Wright is also managing editor of the dividend-stock investing newsletter *Investment Quality Trends. IQTrends.com*

Todd Rosenbluth, senior director overseeing mutual funds for S&P Capital IQ, an equity research firm that provides investment research and analytical tools to more than 4,000 investment banks, private-equity firms and financial-services clients, New York City. *CapitalIQ.com*

It may be days, weeks, months or even years away, but inevitably the stock market will descend, as many analysts warn and as history has shown.

How big that drop will be and how long it will last are open to debate. In fact, a large number of analysts contend that the bull market still has plenty of pep, which would mean that you don't have to take extreme defensive steps for a while.

But even so, it's important to think about your own financial situation and how it could be affected by an extended pullback, especially because the traditional strategy of shifting toward bonds or bond funds may not work as well this time as in the past. Interest rates are so low that they could surge—hurting bond prices badly. That could happen in the next few years as the economy strengthens and the unemployment rate drops.

We asked four top market strategists to each describe his/her favorite way to start preparing so that you can cushion your portfolio once a stock market pullback begins...

CASH IN ALL YOUR STOCKS
Janet Briaud

Does the idea of selling off all of your stock holdings now and possibly sidestepping another drop of more than 50% like the one in the 2008–09 financial crisis sound attractive? This is, of course, a radical approach, and if the market continues to rise, people who take this approach would miss out on future profits. But if you have saved up enough money that you could live off of a very modest yield from short-term savings and some bonds (possibly with the help of Social Security and a pension), it might be a viable option. This works best for people whose stocks are mostly in tax-protected retirement accounts, such as 401(k)s and traditional IRAs and Roth IRAs, so that the sale of stocks does not trigger capital gains taxes.

For taxable savings accounts, you might want to stretch out the sales over a period of a few years. That way, you can avoid realizing so much in capital gains from the stock sales in any given year that you push yourself into a much higher tax bracket.

As you sell the stocks, you might want to use some of the cash proceeds from those sales to help pay off outstanding credit card balances, car loans and other debts that have high interest rates.

Other than paying off bills, there are a variety of ways that you could invest the bulk of the cash proceeds from the stock sales, but if you want to be supersafe, consider a mix of savings and/or money market accounts for short-term use, certificates of deposit (CDs) and US Treasury securities. Two-year CDs offer up to 1.23% currently*...five-year CDs pay up to 1.76%...and 30-year Treasuries pay around 1.9%—so depending on how much of your money you put into the bonds, you may end up with an overall yield in the 2% range.

That's very little, but at least it's ahead of the current inflation rate. During a prolonged period of weak stock prices, you wouldn't have to worry about having to liquidate investments at the worst possible time. With this strategy, if there is a major stock market pullback, you can, of course, move back into the market at bargain prices. Also, as interest rates rise, you can invest proceeds from maturing CDs in higher-yielding CDs and Treasuries. Even if the value of your Treasuries drops as a result of rising interest rates, you won't suffer losses if you don't sell the Treasuries early, and you

*Rates and prices as of April 2, 2015.

will continue to get their guaranteed 3% yield year after year.

PRUNE YOUR PORTFOLIO
Scott Rothbort

If you are not in a position—or of a mind—to cash in all your stocks, you might want to consider paring back your stock holdings, especially the riskiest ones.

Start by reducing your allocations to areas of the market that are most vulnerable to a big sell-off—either because they are overvalued right now (the home-builder, utility and oil-service sectors, in my opinion) or because they sell for hundreds of dollars per share, making them seem pricey. Panicky investors tend to dump these first. Next, reevaluate the potential of stocks you still own that have had a substantial run-up over the past year.

Example: My shares of Boston Beer Company (SAM), the largest microbrewery in the US, rose 69% in the two years ending April 2, 2015. Premium beers are a fast-growing niche, and I think the stock has more upside. But to be prudent, I'm selling an amount equal to my initial investment. That way, in the worst-case scenario—a plunging market—I give up some profit, but I always at least break even.

SHIFT TO SAFER STOCKS
Kelley Wright

In addition to paring back on your riskiest stocks, you might want to shift to much safer ones. Look for stocks of companies that pay decent dividends that have increased year after year even throughout recessions…have products or services that are so ingrained in business and consumer life that they have been able to survive and profit no matter how bad the economy gets…and have held up well in market declines and always bounced back, beating the Standard & Poor's 500 stock index over the long run.

Examples of stocks to buy and/or keep…

•**Air Products and Chemicals (APD),** which is in 50 countries, is the dominant global manufacturer of industrial gases essential to the production of products as diverse as beer, golf balls, rubber gloves and rockets.

Recent yield: 2.1%.

Recent share price: $151.04.

•**Automatic Data Processing (ADP)** is among a handful of US companies with a triple-A credit rating, and it is a leading provider of outsourcing services, including managing payrolls and employee records for more than a half-million businesses.

Recent yield: 2.3%.

Recent share price: $85.92.

•**Archer Daniels Midland Company (ADM)** is one of the world's largest processors of corn, wheat and other agricultural products and a top producer of vegetable oil, ethanol and animal-feed ingredients.

Recent yield: 2.4%.

Recent share price: $47.35.

•**ConocoPhillips (COP),** the third-largest US oil company, has secured future growth with recent large discoveries in the Gulf of Mexico and major operations in the growing US shale oil-drilling industry.

Recent yield: 4.6%.

Recent share price: $63.18.

•**Genuine Parts Company (GPC)** distributes automotive and industrial replacement parts throughout North America and supplies auto-repair shops through its NAPA brand. The company's very consistent cash flow has allowed it to raise annual dividend payouts 57 years in a row.

Recent yield: 2.6%.

Recent share price: $92.73.

•**PepsiCo (PEP)** has well-known brands including Pepsi, Mountain Dew, Gatorade, Tropicana, Lay's, Doritos and Quaker. It will continue to prosper in developed markets, along with competitors such as Coca-Cola and Kraft, and has barely begun to penetrate some of the world's largest emerging markets.

Recent yield: 2.7%.

Recent share price: $95.69.

FOCUS ON CAUTIOUS FUNDS
Todd Rosenbluth

Rather than concentrating on individual stocks—even relatively safe ones—you might want to ride out a prolonged pullback with cautious mutual funds. They give you an opportunity to profit when the market is rising but offer substantial protection in declines. They often hold a significant amount of cash when their managers believe that the market is overvalued and/or that they can't find stocks they believe are worth investing in. And these funds' portfolios have a low "beta," a common measure of a fund's sensitivity to market movements as compared with the S&P 500.

Cautious funds to consider…

• **Copley Fund (COPLX),** a conservative large-cap value fund with a beta of 0.50 (versus 1 for the S&P 500), lost just 15.6% in the 2008 market plunge, compared with a 37% drop for the S&P 500.

10-year annualized performance: 4.8%.

• **T. Rowe Price Capital Appreciation Fund (PRWCX),** a large-cap fund that has both growth and value stocks, has suffered an annual loss in only two of the past 25 years.

10-year annualized performance: 9.2%.

• **Yacktman Focused Fund (YAFFX)** looks for large, high-quality businesses with cheap stock prices. Its performance puts it in the top 1% of funds in its category over the past 10 years, outperforming the S&P 500 by an annual average of five percentage points.

10-year annualized performance: 10.6%.

Big Dividends from Small Stocks

Thomas E. Browne, Jr., CFA, a portfolio manager at Keeley Asset Management Corp. He manages Keeley Mid Cap Dividend Value Fund (KMDVX) and the Keeley Small Cap Dividend Value Fund (KSDVX), whose five-year annualized return of 14.7% ranks in the top 11% of its category. *KeeleyFunds.com*

S ome of the better opportunities today among stocks that pay attractive dividends are found in small and midsized companies. In part, that is because investors seeking income and safety have bid up prices of large dividend-paying companies so high that they've now lost much of their appeal. Meanwhile, there are many smaller compa-

nies whose stocks offer attractive yields—the trick is predicting which can sustain or even increase their dividends.

We asked dividend-stock expert Thomas E. Browne, Jr., how he chooses both small- and mid-cap stocks for steady income and capital appreciation…

SEEK
TOP PERFORMERS

The funds I manage invest in companies that my team believes will consistently pay dividends over long periods. The ability and willingness to do this provides evidence that a company has a strong balance sheet and management committed to rewarding shareholders. Over the past two decades, the stocks in the Russell 2000 small-cap index that pay dividends have outperformed those that don't by an average of four percentage points a year…and with less volatility. *To find a place in my fund portfolios, a company should…*

• **Have a strong market share in a niche industry with a long-term advantage over its competitors.**

• **Generate enough cash flow to be able to invest in its business** and have enough left over to maintain and increase its dividend.

I currently hold shares in two types of dividend payers…

GROUP 1: HIGH YIELDS

These businesses offer moderate growth potential but attractive yields…

• **AutoLiv (ALV)** is the world's largest maker of car-safety equipment, a lucrative niche that the company protects with numerous patents on airbag and electronic-detection systems.

The stock is attractively priced because investors are worried about the company's exposure to struggling European economies. But I think this Swedish company will continue to generate substantial cash flow.

Reasons: Developed markets are adopting next-generation driving-safety systems (for example, devices that sound an automatic warning when a driver drifts out of his/her lane) and emerging markets are upgrading their minimal safety standards.

Recent yield: 1.9%.*

• **Ryman Hospitality Properties (RHP)** is a real estate investment trust (REIT) that owns the Gaylord Hotels properties and the media and entertainment assets associated with the hotels. The company recently sold the contracts to manage those assets to Marriott International. This transaction should improve convention bookings and occupancy rates at the hotels as well as fuel cash-flow growth.

Recent yield: 4.3%.

GROUP 2: FAST-GROWING DIVIDENDS

These companies offer modest or even low yields, but they have the ability and inclination to substantially increase dividends and plan to increase dividends more rapidly each year.

• **BancorpSouth (BXS),** headquartered in Tupelo, Mississippi, is a banking and financial services company with 292 locations in nine states. The company has lagged behind its peers in resolving its credit problems but finally seems to be getting there. In addition, a new CEO seems to be able to operate the bank more efficiently. The company increased its quarterly dividend by 50% to 7.5 cents in July 2014.

Recent yield: 1.3%.

• **Bristow Group (BRS)** is the leading provider of helicopter services to offshore operations of energy companies. The company likely will see double-digit growth in earnings for many years because global oil and gas production in countries ranging from Brazil to Russia increasingly comes from deep-water facilities that require constant shuttling of crew and supplies. The company's dividend likely will grow

*Yields as of April 2, 2015.

182

at a rate of 10% or more annually for the next five years.

Recent yield: 2.4%.

• **Iron Mountain (IRM)** is the leading global provider of archival services for physical records. It operates more than 1,000 facilities in 32 countries and serves more than 156,000 customers. While its earnings and cash-flow growth are modest, its dividend growth could be dramatic if it is successful in converting its corporate structure into a REIT. Its current annual dividend of $1.90 per share, recently yielding 5.2%, could nearly double.

• **Lincoln National Corp. (LNC)** offers life insurance and investment products such as variable annuities to wealthy older investors. The number of Americans over age 65 will grow to 72 million by 2030, compared with 40 million in 2010. Many will want the guaranteed returns that annuities provide. The company, which manages $215 billion in assets, raised its quarterly dividend by 25% in 2014.

Recent yield: 1.4%.

Reinvestment Strategy

Focus on small companies that make it easy to reinvest in their stocks. Typically, it is big companies that offer dividend reinvestment plans (DRIPs), which allow investors to buy shares and reinvest dividends without brokerage fees. But some small companies that offer DRIPs provide greater opportunities for earnings growth and stock price gains.

Favorites now: Federal Signal Corp. (FSS), which provides security equipment…Midsouth Bancorp (MSL)…and auto-parts firm Modine Manufacturing (MOD).

Charles B. Carlson, CFA, CEO of Horizon Investment Services, located in Hammond, Indiana, and Chicago. *HorizonInvestment.com*

The Best and Worst Stocks When Interest Rates Rise

Pat Dorsey, CFA, chief investment strategist at The Sanibel Captiva Trust Company, a wealth-management firm with more than $1 billion in assets, Sanibel, Florida. Formerly the director of equity research at research firm Morningstar, Inc., he is author of *The Little Book That Builds Wealth* and *The Five Rules for Successful Stock Investing* (both from Wiley). *SanCapTrustCo.com*

Will rising interest rates in the next few years deflate the stock market? But the stock market actually has done quite well in some past periods of rising rates. And certain kinds of stocks could do especially well.

We asked noted investment strategist and market trends researcher Pat Dorsey for his take on the market outlook and what kinds of stocks he thinks may benefit the most—and what kinds may suffer the most—from higher interest rates…

DANGER LEVELS FAR OFF

When the long-term interest rates get high enough, they will slow economic growth and eventually kill the bull market in stocks—that's what almost always happens in economic cycles. But in my view, the recent volatility in the stock market is an overreaction because we still are in the very earliest stages of a rising-rate environment—not anywhere near dangerous levels.

The interest rate on 10-year Treasury bonds, a key benchmark, is a very low 1.9% (as of April 2, 2015).

What most investors don't realize: In the past, the Standard & Poor's 500 stock index has gained an average of 1.7% a month during rising interest rate periods when 10-year Treasury yields were between 3% and 4%. Historically, investors tend not to lose confidence in stocks until rates hit 6%, which we likely won't see until beyond 2016. At that level, higher interest rates become a drag on the economy as they discourage consumer and business borrowing—and they lure many more investors away from stocks into bonds.

What about short-term interest rates? The Federal Reserve has more direct control over those than it does over long-term rates, and one day—when inflation is accelerating above its very low current levels—the Fed will start raising short-term rates again to keep the economy from overheating. But contrary to what many people think, even that will not necessarily spell the end of stock gains. In fact, a gradual rise in short-term rates, such as the Fed undertook from June 2004 to June 2006, could allow stocks to continue gaining for a while. During that stretch of 17 rate increases, the S&P 500 rose 11%.

HOW TO INVEST NOW

How do higher interest rates affect individual companies? Slow-growing businesses and those that need to borrow lots of money may struggle and see their stock prices sag. On the other hand, cyclical businesses such as technology and asset-management companies, which do best in fast-growing economies, as well as companies that generate enormous cash flow and can earn increasingly higher interest income on their cash will see higher profits.

Types of companies that are likely winners…

WINNER: CASH-RICH COMPANIES

Many businesses started hoarding cash after the 2008 recession, fearing another credit crunch. With higher interest rates, these companies can earn better money on their cash and increase their profits. Companies that naturally accumulate large amounts of cash because of the nature of their businesses also benefit. *Examples…*

•**Property and casualty insurers benefit from the "float"**—those enormous cash reserves that result from the premiums they collect each month but have not yet had to pay out in claims. For example, the float from the insurance divisions of Berkshire Hathaway (BRK.B), the company led by Warren Buffett, has accumulated to about $60 billion. Insurance premiums also have been heading up, and they typically go even higher when inflation starts to rise.

•**Payroll processors benefit from interest income on a different kind of float.** Businesses outsource their payroll services to processors such as Paychex (PAYX), which serves more than a half million employees at small and medium-sized businesses in the US. Paychex's float is created by the lag time between collecting payroll money and issuing paychecks. Also, a stronger economy means companies add more employees. That will help Paychex's revenues and profits.

WINNER: TECH GIANTS

Large-cap technology stocks typically are market leaders when interest rates are rising. That's because the companies sell more software and equipment as consumers and businesses typically increase their tech spending in a growing economy...and they earn higher interest rates on their massive cash reserves.

Examples: Apple (AAPL) has about $33 billion in cash...Microsoft (MSFT), $90 billion ...and Cisco Systems (CSCO), $53 billion.

WINNER: FUTURES EXCHANGE

As interest rates rise, more and more investors will want to protect their portfolios against rising rates by using futures and other derivatives that allow them, for example, to bet against falling bond prices.

Example: CME Group (CME) owns the Chicago Mercantile Exchange, the country's largest exchange for trading futures. Increased trading volume would boost investor interest in the company.

WINNER: FINANCIAL-SERVICES FIRMS

Brokerage and banking stocks tend to do the best of any market sector in the initial phases of interest rate increases.

Examples: Both Charles Schwab (SCHW) and Wells Fargo (WFC) are likely to profit for the next year or two from the fast-growing spread between the short-term interest rates that they pay depositors and the long-term interest rates at which they can lend money. In addition, many Schwab investors are likely to dump their bond funds, whose values are dropping as bond yields rise, and move money into the stock market. That permits the company to collect more financial advisory and stock-trading fees. Wells Fargo also is a major mortgage lender and should benefit from the rising demand for mortgage loans in the next year, which will more than offset a sharp drop

in refinancing. More buyers will jump into the housing market when they realize that fixed-rate mortgages and housing prices are likely to keep climbing.

STOCK LOSERS

As yields on 10-year Treasuries rise, certain types of companies typically have been hurt. *They include...*

• **Highly leveraged businesses such as telecommunications firms, utilities and real estate investment trusts (REITs).** They need to take on substantial debt in order to support expansion. In fact, REITs are prohibited by law from retaining more than 10% of their annual earnings, which makes them heavily dependent on loans to acquire new properties. Rising rates will increase the burden of these companies' debt payments, cut into their profitability and hurt their stock prices.

• **Blue-chip dividend payers.** Investors have poured into the stocks of these companies as an alternate source of fixed income in recent years because their hefty annual dividends, consistent cash flow and relatively low volatility made them attractive. But many of the stocks now are richly valued, and their dividend yields compare less favorably to rising yields on Treasuries.

This doesn't mean that you should dump all your dividend stocks, but you need to review their long-term potential and whether they still make sense as a bond substitute.

Example: The spice and seasonings leader McCormick & Company (MKC) is a consistent slow grower that controls half of its entire market in North America and has paid a dividend to investors for more than 85 years. But its annual yield was recently 2.1%, and I think McCormick stock, with a three-year annualized return of 14%, offers very little growth potential in coming years.

• **Companies that rely on low-cost loans to spur consumer demand** such as auto manufacturers and home builders. They eventually will see less demand and lower profits as interest rates rise. This won't happen right away because both car loans and fixed-rate mortgage loans still are quite affordable. But the stock prices of many of these companies have had big run-ups, and investors already are worried that higher rates could slow the housing recovery as well as the market for new automobiles.

For the Daring Investor: Tiny Tech

John Bichelmeyer, CFA, manager of the Buffalo Emerging Opportunities Fund (BUFOX), whose five-year annualized performance of 18.8% ranks in the top 5% of its category. *BuffaloFunds.com*

The smallest companies offer the greatest potential for investors because they tend to grow much faster than larger businesses. And as the US economy improves, investors are more willing to bet on stocks with total stock market values of less than $1 billion—or even microcaps, which have the lowest market capitalizations—even though they can be far more volatile. Microcaps have gained an annualized 17% over the past three years through April 2, 2015 based on the Russell Microcap Index, versus 15.7% for the Standard & Poor's 500 stock index.

The best tiny stocks today can be found in growth industries such as technology that are being propelled by trends likely to last for several years…

• **Trend—With health insurance and government reimbursements shrinking, hospitals are seeking help to improve efficiency and reduce expenses.**

Favorite stock: Omnicell (OMCL) provides software and automated dispensing equipment to improve distribution of medications to doctors and patients in hospitals.

Three-year annualized performance: 31.4%.*

• **Trend—Companies always seek ways to harness the power of the data they collect.** A more scientific approach to product pricing can have a meaningful impact on profitability.

Favorite stock: Pros Holdings (PRO) provides computer software that helps businesses

*Performance as of April 2, 2015.

mine vast databases to improve pricing and increase profits.

Three-year annualized performance: 10.4%.

Bet on Big Banks: Why They're Set to Soar

Richard Bove, vice president of equity research specializing in the financial services sector at Rafferty Capital Markets, Garden City, New York. *RaffCap.com*

Big banks are those companies whose stock prices plummeted the most after the financial crisis hit in 2008. The six biggest have piled up more than $100 billion in legal costs. One of them, Bank of America, has been booted from the Dow Jones Industrial Average. And big banks are widely cast as the villains of the 2007–2009 Great Recession. So what's the verdict on big banks now? Their stock prices, which have jumped overall by 131% since the market hit bottom in March 2009, could soar for years. Two of them, Bank of America and Citigroup, could double within several years.

The reason why: The biggest threats—trillions of dollars in toxic mortgage loans and the continuing doubts about whether financial institutions could survive another economic meltdown—have been contained. Home foreclosures have fallen recently, and 94% of major banks passed the Federal Reserve's 2013 stress test. Most important, the industry is making a staggering amount of money, aided by steady growth in the economy.

Two attractive bank stocks now: Bank of America (BAC), whose stock price plunged 90% before rebounding some, has done an excellent job of shoring up its balance sheet and won Federal Reserve approval to buy back as much as $5 billion in its stock shares…and Citigroup (C), whose stock plunged 95%, is cutting expenses by $900 million and is generating loan demand faster than other US banks because of its big presence overseas.

Be Bold!
Try Biotech

Jason Browne, chief investment officer at FundX Investment Group, San Francisco, which manages more than $1 billion in investor assets. *FundX.com*

The stocks of biotechnology companies, which use biological substances such as enzymes and proteins from living cells as components for new medications, were up 65% for the year ending April 2, 2015. Although biotech stocks are volatile, they likely will continue to surge. That's because an unusually high number of new biotech drugs are being approved for commercial sale by the FDA. In 2012, 39 biotech drugs received approval, the most in nearly two decades. There likely will be about 35 approvals annually through 2016.

The value of biotech companies also is being bid up by acquisition-minded global pharmaceutical giants seeking to fill their pipelines with the new products that the biotechs can provide. Valuations of biotech stocks are high compared with the Standard & Poor's 500 stock index but remain reasonable for companies likely to grow their earnings per share by 40% annually for the next several years.

Biotechs tend to focus on chronic or life-threatening illnesses such as cancer for which the government and private insurers continue to pay well for effective treatments.

Putting just 5% of your stock portfolio in biotechs can boost overall returns over time. But because these stocks' individual potential can be complicated to evaluate, most people should invest through a fund.

My favorites: Fidelity Select Biotechnology Portfolio (FBIOX), which focuses on more established, large-cap biotech companies (*10-year annualized performance:* 19.7%*)…and SPDR S&P Biotech ETF (XBI), a low-cost exchange-traded fund launched in 2006 that keeps about two-thirds of its portfolio in small- and micro-cap stocks (*five-year annualized performance:* 31.1%).

*Performance as of April 2, 2015.

Favorite Anticancer
Stocks

John McCamant, editor of *Medical Technology Stock Letter*, Berkeley, California.

Out of more than 500 investment newsletters, the model stock portfolio that performed the best in 2013 was one zeroing in on biopharmaceutical stocks that develop treatments for diseases such as cancer. That narrow focus by the *Medical Technology Stock Letter* makes its investment advice potentially risky, although the portfolio's value more than tripled in 2013. Below, the newsletter's editor, John McCamant, lists some of his favorite anticancer stocks…

• **Nektar Therapeutics (NKTR).** Injectable chemotherapy drugs deliver peak concentrations to tumors but tend to diffuse quickly. Repeated dosages are necessary, and that causes extensive side effects. Nektar has created a technology called PEGylation that can be used to combine cancer-fighting drugs and other drugs with a polymer that releases the drugs at lower, more consistent dosages in the body for longer periods of time. The company already receives tens of millions of dollars in royalties from successful reformulations of FDA-approved drugs. Nektar soared 53% in 2013 and 32% in 2014, although it plunged about 25% in 2015 through April 2.

Recent share price: $11.*

• **Isis Pharmaceuticals (ISIS)** has created an injectable drug that uses a technology called "antisense." It targets specific genes in cancer cells to stop their development. Isis has more than 30 compounds in clinical trials using antisense—they have proved so promising that the stock has gained 620% over the past three years. It has the potential to go much higher. Antisense is proving effective in fighting cancers and other diseases that have defied conventional treatments.

Recent share price: $61.63

*Prices as of April 2, 2015.

Health-Care Stocks to Consider

Earnings of managed-care companies that help run Medicaid programs likely will increase by 15% or more a year for the next several years. About half the states are expanding Medicaid programs under the Affordable Care Act.

Stocks likely to benefit: Centene Corp. (CNC)…Molina Healthcare (MOH)…WellCare Health Plans (WCG).

Marshall Gordon, senior research analyst for health care at ClearBridge Investments, a global equity manager with more than $70 billion in assets under management, New York City.

Ebola Drugs Investment Opportunity

Several small biotech firms are racing to develop drugs for Ebola. Inovio Pharmaceuticals, Inc. (INO), is developing a DNA-based vaccine that helps activate the body's immune responses. A Tekmira Pharmaceuticals Corp. (TKMR) drug targets several of the protein-coding genes of the virus and has been approved for isolated cases of Ebola. Both companies' drugs have been successful on animals.

Jason Kolbert, a senior managing director and lead health-care analyst at The Maxim Group, a wealth-management firm, New York City.

Time to Invest in Electric Utility Stocks?

Stocks of electric companies are cheaper than those of other energy providers because of fears that more stringent environmental regulations and restrictions will hurt profitability. But numerous electric companies have made significant strides in shifting to renewable sources and natural gas.

Favorites: NextEra Energy (NEE)…Westar Energy Inc. (WR).

Richard J. Moroney, CFA, chief investment officer and portfolio manager at Horizon Investment Services, which has more than $150 million in assets under management, Hammond, Indiana. He is editor of the *Dow Theory Forecasts* newsletter. *DowTheory.com*

Stock Opportunity: Drinking-Water Suppliers

Public demand for clean water is soaring, plus water utilities will profit from "fracking," a technique used by the energy industry that pumps high-pressure water into the ground to crack shale rock and release oil and natural gas.

Companies most likely to benefit: American Water Works (AWK) is the largest publicly traded water utility in the US…Aqua America (WTR) is the second largest.

Timothy Winter, CFA, based in St. Louis, an equity analyst specializing in the utility industry for Gabelli & Co., Rye, New York. *Gabelli.com*

Favorite Uranium-Mining Companies

Since the 2011 nuclear plant disaster in Japan, uranium prices have dropped more than 30%. But Prime Minister Shinzo Abe's energy policy calls for bringing Japan's shuttered nuclear reactors back online, and China has 29 reactors under construction, 51 more planned and an additional 120 proposed.

Small companies likely to benefit: Paladin Energy (PALAY)…Denison Mines (DNN).

David Talbot, vice president and senior mining analyst at Dundee Capital Markets in Toronto, Canada. *DundeeCapitalMarkets.com*

Sector to Watch: Cruise Line Companies

Lower fuel costs, increased bookings by retirees and growing demand in countries including China and Brazil are boosting profits.

Most likely to benefit: The two companies that dominate the industry—Carnival Corp. (CCL), the world's largest cruise line, with 10 global brands and 101 ships…and Royal Caribbean Cruises Ltd. (RCL), which operates a younger, more modern fleet of 41 ships and targets high-end consumers.

Jaime M. Katz, CFA, an equity analyst specializing in leisure stocks for Morningstar, Inc., Chicago, which tracks about 479,000 investment offerings. *Morningstar.com*

Infrastructure Funds Set to Benefit

Firms that own, operate and/or build things ranging from toll roads to energy pipelines are poised to benefit from increased consumer travel needs…public works projects that have been deferred…and expanding industries such as drilling for oil in shale rock deposits.

Fund to consider: Macquarie Global Infrastructure Total Return (MGU).

Michael Joyce, CFA, CFP, president of the investment advisory firm Joyce Payne Partners, Richmond. *JoycePaynePartners.com*

Upscale Hotel Stocks Attractive

Corporate spending on travel for business may soon rebound to prerecession levels, and room supply is low due to minimal new hotel construction. The stocks are relatively cheap, having lagged in the broad real estate recovery.

Stocks most likely to benefit: Hyatt Hotels (H)…Starwood Hotels & Resorts (HOT).

Jeff Kolitch, a vice president at Baron Capital and portfolio manager of the Baron Real Estate Fund (BREFX), New York City. Its three-year annualized return of 24% ranks in the top 1% of its category. *BaronFunds.com*

Consider Stocks of Local TV Broadcasting Companies

The broadcasters, which own groups of local stations that carry programming from major networks, should benefit from soaring fees paid by cable- and satellite-TV providers that carry the stations…and from a recovery in sales.

Companies most likely to benefit: Nexstar Broadcasting Group (NXST)…Sinclair Broadcast Group (SBGI).

Eric Green, CFA, a senior managing partner and director of research at Penn Capital Management, which oversees more than $7 billion in assets, Philadelphia. *PennCapital.com*

Looking Good: 3-D Printer Companies

The new technology uses software to create a precise, 3-D virtual model of an object—then actually builds it using an industrial printer that squirts and molds layers of quick-setting material—typically plastic or metal.

Worldwide sales of 3-D printers and supplies are expected to reach $6.5 billion by 2019.

Most likely to benefit: Stratasys (SSYS)... 3D Systems Corp. (DDD).

Paul Goodwin, a stock analyst at Cabot Wealth Advisory, an investment advisory firm, Salem, Massachusetts. *Cabot.net*

Stock Opportunity: Paper Companies

Paper companies have reinvigorated themselves, finding new markets, such as producing cardboard shipping boxes for Internet retailers...and making paper food containers to replace plastics and Styrofoam.

Favorites: International Paper Co. (IP)... Packaging Corporation of America (PKG)... Rock-Tenn Company (RKT).

Todd Wenning, an equity analyst who specializes in the paper industry at Morningstar, Inc. Chicago, which tracks about 479,000 investment offerings. *Morningstar.com*

How to Use Options to Protect Your Portfolio

Sheryl Garrett, CFP, founder of Garrett Planning Network, an international network of fee-only planners based in Shawnee Mission, Kansas. She is author of *Just Give Me the Answer$: Expert Advisors Address Your Most Pressing Financial Questions* (Kaplan Business) and *Personal Finance Workbook for Dummies* (Wiley). *GarrettPlanning.com*

How do you protect your stock portfolio from a possible crash when the market is hitting record highs? One option is to use an options strategy. Specifically, it involves a "protective put option contract."

An option contract gives you the right to buy or sell shares of a stock or exchange-traded fund (ETF) at a specific price in the future regardless of the actual price on that date.

With a put option, if a stock you own sinks, at least you know exactly what your lowest selling price could be months from now.

What you get: You are effectively setting a limit on the maximum amount you can lose if your shares fall below the option contract's preset price, also known as the "strike price."

Example: You own 500 shares of the SPDR S&P 500 ETF (SPY), an ETF tracking the Standard & Poor's 500 stock index, selling for $206 per share in April 2015, worth a total of $103,000 at that time. You are worried that the next several months could be scary for the market and that you can't stomach a loss of more than 10%, or $10,300. In this case, you could ask for January 2016 protective put option contracts that allow you to sell your holdings for $185 per share (10% below the current price) at any point up to the expiration of the option contracts. (You typically can buy an option with an expiration date anywhere from a week to 18 months.) Even if your ETF drops by, say, 50%, the most you will lose is $10,500 rather than $51,500.

What happens if the market rises in the future and your ETF's value is above the initial $206 per share? Since your contracts don't obligate you to sell your shares, you simply let your put options expire and enjoy the profit. Of course, the drawback is that if your ETF still is trading at $206 per share or slightly below when the options expire, you paid for coverage that you didn't really need.

How much options cost: You pay the seller a "premium," which varies depending on not just the length of time and number of shares but also factors such as the current volatility of the market and how much your stock or ETF is trading for. In April 2015, the premium in the above example would be about $6 per share, or a total of $3,000.

Also, your brokerage firm will charge a commission to assist you in buying a put. (Buying it electronically without assistance involves a much smaller fee.)

Commissions are $8 at Fidelity, $9 at Schwab and $10 at TD Ameritrade and E-Trade.* In

*Prices subject to change.

addition, you usually are charged 75 cents per contract. A contract covers 100 shares.

The brokerage firm will match your request with a seller through an options exchange, typically the Chicago Board Options Exchange. (You can research available options yourself at *CBOE.com*.)

Preferred Stock ETFs

Preferred stock ETFs are less volatile than junk bond funds while offering similar high-yield income. A surge in interest rates in May and June 2013 caused a benchmark index of junk (high-yield) bonds to drop by about 5%. But preferreds, which are stock/bond hybrids, lost about 3%.

Favorite: iShares S&P US Preferred Stock Index (PFF).

Five-year annualized performance: 7.8%.*

Doug Fabian, president of Fabian Wealth Strategies, an investment advisory firm specializing in portfolios of ETFs, Costa Mesa, California. He is host of the syndicated radio show *Doug Fabian's Wealth Strategies. FabianWealth.com*

*Rate as of April 2, 2015.

Invest in IPOs via ETFs

There were 273 initial public offerings in 2014, the most since 2000. Exchange-traded funds (ETFs) enable investors to invest in a wide array of IPOs.

Attractive IPO ETFs now: First Trust US IPO Index (FPX), the largest, holds the 100 biggest offerings for up to 1,000 trading days… Renaissance IPO ETF (IPO) is a new fund that owns about 50 stocks.

Eric Dutram, an ETF strategist at Zacks Investment Research, an independent equity research firm based in Chicago. *Zacks.com*

Low-Volatility Funds Smooth Out the Market's Bumpy Ride

Tom Lydon, president of Global Trends Investments, Irvine, California. He is editor of *ETFTrends.com* and author of *iMoney: Profitable ETF Strategies for Every Investor* (FT Press).

Stock investors currently have their pick of roughly three dozen "low-volatility" funds.

These mutual funds and exchange-traded funds (ETFs) invest in companies whose stock price fluctuations tend to be less severe than those of the overall market. The companies typically offer consistent earnings and cash flow and include utilities and consumer-staple businesses. Over the past 35 years, low-volatility stocks have beaten the broad market by one percentage point annually, on average, although they often lag in bull markets.

Low-volatility funds have become popular, attracting approximately $11 billion in assets from investors, but you should evaluate them carefully. About half of these funds are so new that they haven't been tested in volatile times. And some of them carry high fees and don't live up to the promise that they will limit losses in down markets.

Two attractive low-volatility ETFs with 0.25% expense ratios…

•**Powershares S&P 500 Low Volatility Portfolio ETF (SPLV),** which lost just 4% in the third quarter of 2011, holds the 100 stocks in the S&P 500 with the lowest volatility over the past year and rebalances each quarter. *InvescoPowerShares.com*

•**iShares MSCI Emerging Markets Minimum Volatility ETF (EEMV)** chooses about 200 stocks for low volatility from an overall emerging-markets stock index. It lost 5.1% in the second quarter of 2013, versus a 9.3% drop for the diversified emerging-markets fund category overall. *iShares.com*

Betting on Rising Rates

David Fry, founder and publisher of *ETF Digest*, Carson City, Nevada, and author of *Create Your Own ETF Hedge Fund: A Do-It-Yourself ETF Strategy for Private Wealth Management* (Wiley). *ETFDigest.com*

Rather than hide from the effects of rising interest rates, which cause bond prices to fall, daring investors can bet on a certain kind of investment to benefit as interest rates ratchet up.

The investment? Inverse-bond exchange-traded funds (ETFs).

How they work: Inverse-bond ETFs buy derivatives and futures contracts designed to produce the opposite daily return of major bond indexes. For example, if the Barclays US Treasury Index, a popular gauge of intermediate-term Treasury securities decreases by 1%, the corresponding inverse-bond ETF should rise by 1%. These ETFs are best used to hedge an existing investment in bonds, but they also can be used to profit from a bet on rising rates.

Caution: There are leveraged versions of these inverse-bond ETFs that are designed to rise much more than interest rates do.

Example: The Direxion Daily 20+ Year Treasury Bear 3x ETF seeks to provide 300% of the inverse (opposite) performance of the NYSE 20 Year Plus Treasury Bond Index. Such funds are very risky. The Direxion ETF has gained as much as 28% in some three-month periods but lost nearly 60% in others.

Inverse-bond ETFs to consider now: Pro Shares Short 7-10 Year Treasury ETF (TBX)… ProShares Short 20+ Year Treasury ETF (TBF) …and ProShares Short Investment Grade Corporate Bond ETF (IGS).

Great Mutual Funds

Janet M. Brown, president of FundX Investment Group in San Francisco, and managing editor of the *NoLoad FundX* newsletter. Based on risk-adjusted returns for its model portfolio, the publication has been ranked by *The Hulbert Financial Digest* as a top-performing mutual fund investment newsletter for more than three decades. *FundX.com*

After years of a bull market, mutual funds face greater challenges when they try to sort winning stocks from losers and stragglers. *Here, mutual fund strategist Janet M. Brown tells which funds are likely to stand out from the crowd…*

MANY STOCKS ARE PRICEY

The bull market has been remarkably resilient since the 2007–2009 recession ended, and it easily could last a while longer as the economy continues its steady but slow recovery. That said, I think that the overall market is fairly valued right now and that many stocks are quite pricey.

Companies that will benefit the most are those with cheap valuations that have lagged in the multiyear rally and whose financial performance can surprise investors. Certain fund managers are especially good at spotting these bargain stocks. *Some of my favorite no-load funds…*

CORE FUNDS

These funds are adept at finding bargain-priced large-cap stocks and can constitute a major portion of a typical portfolio.

●**Sound Shore Fund (SSHFX).** For the past 30 years, this fund has diligently dug up out-of-favor stocks of profitable businesses that have manageable debts and the ability to overcome short-term problems. In 2014, the fund's careful selection of battered health-care companies and financial-services firms paid off with a gain of 11.8%.

Performance: 15.3%.* *SoundShoreFund. com*

●**Oakmark Global Fund (OAKGX).** If you would rather not figure out what percentages of your portfolio to devote to US versus foreign

*Performance figures based on five-year annualized returns through April 2, 2015.

stocks, this fund decides for you. It invests in a company only if its share price is 40% below what the fund managers believe it really is worth. The fund's recent holdings included the Swiss financial firm Julius Baer Gruppe and US-based MasterCard.

Performance: 12.4%. *Oakmark.com*

FOREIGN FUNDS

These funds, which invest in foreign stocks, add diversity to your portfolio. Right now, I especially like funds that invest in developed foreign markets, particularly European countries, because their stocks still look cheap and the region is recovering from a prolonged recession. These markets could rally for many years.

• **Dodge & Cox\International Stock Fund (DODFX)** has about 40% of its assets in Europe. European nations have gotten crippling government debt under better control, and the euro no longer appears to be on the brink of disaster. The fund managers look for bargain-priced stocks and hold on to them for years.

Performance: 9.9%. *DodgeandCox.com*

• **Oakmark International Small Cap Fund (OAKEX).** Led by award-winning manager David G. Herro, whose stellar Oakmark International Fund recently was closed to most new investors through brokerage firms, this fund hunts for bargain-priced small- and mid-cap foreign stocks that get very little attention from Wall Street.

Performance: 9.8%. *Oakmark.com*

• **SPDR Euro Stoxx 50 ETF (FEZ).** This exchange-traded fund (ETF) invests in stocks of about 50 of the largest companies in 12 of the eurozone nations. After having had a weak decade, it should do well as the eurozone continues to recover.

Performance: 5.3%. *SPDRS.com*

SMALL-CAP/MID-CAP FUNDS

If you can handle volatility, these funds, which invest in companies with market capitalizations of less than $10 billion, can deliver a big pop to your portfolio. The companies they invest in can grow faster than their large-cap counterparts. But because they tend to have only one or two products or operate in niche markets, they also carry greater risk.

Funds with substantial investments in small technology companies are especially attractive now because these firms tend to grow very quickly when the economy improves.

The funds below seek companies that are growing significantly faster than the overall market.

• **Primecap Odyssey Aggressive Growth Fund (POAGX)** ranks in the top 1% of its category over the past five years. It is managed by the same team that has produced stellar results at Vanguard with the large-cap funds Primecap and Capital Opportunity. The managers use a more aggressive version of their strategy here, looking for companies that they judge to have great long-term growth potential but whose share prices are temporarily depressed.

Performance: 22.2%. *OdysseyFunds.com*

• **Hodges Small Cap Fund (HDPSX)** is a "contrarian" fund that seeks out small companies whose potential is underappreciated by most analysts and investors. Examples include Cracker Barrel Old Country Store and Spirit Airlines. The companies tend to have strong catalysts, such as opportunities for expansion, that could sharply push up their stock prices in the next 12 to 18 months.

Performance: 21.3%. *HodgesFund.com*

SINGLE SECTOR/COUNTRY

A fund that focuses on a single sector or country can be very volatile but can pay off big. Certain biotechnology funds—especially those that invest in companies that use biological substances such as enzymes and proteins from living cells as components to create new medications—are especially attractive now.

• **Janus Global Life Sciences (JAGLX)** invests in almost all of the largest biotech companies. But it also tempers risk by keeping one-third of the portfolio in slower-growth, more stable health-care companies. The fund invests about 20% of its assets overseas, which gives it access to undervalued biotechs that many investors don't know about.

Performance: 27.2%. *Janus.com*

• **PowerShares Golden Dragon China ETF (PGJ).** Funds that invest in shares of Chinese companies catering to that nation's consumer market are attractive now. That's because the

Chinese government is in the midst of a massive economic transformation that shifts the focus from exporting to building a stronger consumer economy and a more advanced technology sector. This ETF tracks the performance of about 70 fast-growing technology and consumer-oriented Chinese stocks.

Performance: 4.9%. *InvescoPowerShares. com*

Stock Market Disaster Insurance

Bear market funds rise if the market sinks but suffer if the market does well. The funds short (bet against) stock indexes and individual stocks.

Worth considering now: Federated Prudent Bear Fund (BEARX), whose sales commission is waived by some discount brokers…Pimco StocksPLUS AR Short Strategy Fund (PSSDX).

The funds should make up no more than 5% of your stock portfolio.

David Snowball, PhD, founder and publisher of *MutualFundObserver.com*, Rock Island, Illinois.

Dividend Bargains

Todd Rosenbluth, senior director overseeing mutual funds for S&P Capital IQ, an equity research firm, New York City. *CapitalIQ.com*

In the past few years, with interest rates so low, investors have flocked to mutual funds that focus on dividend-paying stocks as a way to squeeze out income. But not all dividend-focused funds are created equal.

Today it's best to seek funds that concentrate on stocks whose dividends are most likely to grow substantially rather than stocks with the greatest yields. That way, as interest rates rise (as they're expected to do) and the economy improves, these funds will offer some protection against inflation.

If, instead, you stick with the highest-yielding stock funds, you are taking a greater risk. Some of the companies they invest in are paying out more in dividends than their earnings justify, so these dividends could be pruned back or even eliminated. And some are large, slow-growth businesses such as telecommunications firms and utilities. As interest rates rise, investors may abandon these in favor of bonds with higher yields.

In contrast, some of today's stocks with great dividend-growth potential still are bargains, and they typically are in sectors that take off in a stronger economy, such as technology, energy and materials. *Consider…*

• **Nichols Equity Income Fund (NSEIX)** seeks small- and midsize companies that have annual earnings growth of 10% or more.

• **TCW Dividend Focused Fund (TGIGX),** an aggressive fund, looks for large, undervalued companies with clear catalysts to increase earnings.

• **Vanguard Dividend Growth Fund (VDIGX)** mixes high-quality companies that have long histories of annual dividend increases with firms that are starting to raise dividends.

How to Get More Cash from Your Investments

Robert M. Brinker, CFS, publisher of the monthly investment letter *Brinker Fixed Income Advisor*, Littleton, Colorado. According to *The Hulbert Financial Digest*, it is the top-performing fixed-income newsletter over the past five years. *BrinkerAdvisor.com*

Neil George, former editor of *Lifetime Income Report* and *Income on Demand* at Agora Financial, a publisher of financial and other types of books and newsletters in Baltimore. He also served as chief economist for Mercantile Bank and Mark Twain Bank (now part of US Bank). *NeilGeorge.com*

For investors who want their portfolios to generate income, getting the yields they need has become tricky—especially if they don't want to take big risks. Interest rates still are near historically low levels, and when they rise in the next few years, as they are expected to, most bonds and bond funds will lose value, as they did last year for the first time since 1999. Also, many dividend-paying stocks have become less attractive because their share prices have risen so much.

But there still are ways to get yields of 2% to 3%…3% to 5%…and even higher if you know where to look and are willing to take on a little more risk.

We asked two top fixed-income experts how our readers can get the best yields now…

FOR CONSERVATIVE INVESTORS
Robert M. Brinker, CFS

Right now, conservative investors should stay away from Treasuries, mortgage-related bonds and long-term bonds, all of which are most likely to be hurt as the Federal Reserve continues to scale back its substantial bond-buying program. I'm also avoiding dividend stocks for income because they present too much risk. Although dividends from a stable company such as General Electric have been yielding 3%, GE shares lost more than 50% of their value in 2008. A sharp pullback could happen again even with strong companies. Instead, I prefer the simplicity and diversification of bond funds whose managers keep their durations low (duration is a measure of a bond's sensitivity to interest rate fluctuations) and have the flexibility to find decent yields with low risks. *My favorites…*

YIELDS OVER 2%

• **Vanguard Short-Term Investment-Grade Fund (VFSTX).** This fund has lost money only twice in the past 31 years (–0.08% in 1994 and –4.7% in 2008). The fund has been exceptionally stable…has some of the lowest fees in its category…and is widely diversified among domestic and foreign holdings.

Recent yield: 1.85%.

Performance: 2.67%.*

YIELDS FROM 3% TO 5%

• **Fidelity Floating Rate High Income Fund (FFRHX).** This fund invests in securities that are similar to junk bonds but are safer because they have lower default rates. It buys loans that major banks have made to corporations with

*Performance figures are average annualized returns for the five years through April 2, 2015.

194

"junk" credit ratings, typically BB or lower. The yields on these loans are higher than ones from investment-grade bonds. In addition, floating-rate funds tend to do well in periods of rising interest rates because of another feature—the yields on their bank loans are structured to re-set every 30 to 90 days, so if rates go up, you are not stuck with a lower-yielding investment. This fund takes a more conservative approach than its peers and has one of the lowest levels of volatility in its category.

Recent yield: 3.57%.

Performance: 4.25%.

• **Osterweis Strategic Income Fund (OSTIX).** I'm avoiding many junk-bond funds because yields are at historic lows and not worth the higher risk of default. But this fund is a noteworthy exception, even though it is riskier than the two funds described above. Manager Carl Kaufman buys short-term junk bonds issued by companies that generate strong annual cash flow. That way he can be confident they can pay their debts over the next two years. The fund returned 1.26% in 2014 and 6.5% annualized over the past decade.

Recent yield: 5.06%.

Performance: 6.22%.

• **Campus Crest Communities (CCG).** Like MLPs, real estate investment trusts (REITs) are required to distribute most of their taxable income to their shareholders, typically from the rents they collect on their properties, which results in high, steady annual dividends. But unlike the shares of MLPs, shares of many REITs lost value in 2013 as investors worried that rising interest rates would make it more expensive for REITs to borrow capital in order to expand their real estate holdings. Campus Crest shares dropped nearly 18% in 2013, but I think it is a major buying opportunity even as interest rates continue to rise. The company owns about 80 residential properties near major universities, which have a chronic shortage of student housing.

Recent yield: 5%.

Recent share price: $6.85.

GREATER RISKS, GREATER REWARDS
Neil George

Investors willing to take on the risk of owning individual investments rather than mutual funds often can find much higher annual yields. But you need to look past conventional picks such as dividend stocks in the utilities and telecommunication sectors, which have become pricey. I'm finding more value in businesses that trade like stocks but have beneficial tax structures that require them to pass along most of their income to shareholders. *My recent favorites…*

YIELDS OVER 5%

• **Cheniere Energy Partners (CQP).** Master limited partnerships (MLPs) such as Cheniere are corporate structures that are common in the energy sector. They trade like ordinary stocks, but in exchange for tax advantages, they must distribute most of their taxable income to shareholders annually in the form of dividends. Cheniere owns storage terminals, pipeline connections and liquefaction facilities for liquid natural gas exports from the US Gulf Coast. It has 20-year contracts with major energy players that ensure the stability of its dividend.

Recent yield: 5.7%.

Recent share price: $30.69.

YIELDS ABOVE 7%

• **Compass Diversified Holdings (CODI).** This holding company acts like a private-equity investor, acquiring controlling interests in established, highly profitable businesses that dominate niche industries.

Example: Compass owns a company that makes premium safes for banks and another that supplies outdoor equipment, such as hydration packs and protective gear, to the US military and law-enforcement agencies.

Recent yield: 8.4%.

Recent share price: $16.86.

• **BlackRock Kelso Capital (BKCC).** Business-development companies (BDCs) such as this one are tax-advantaged companies that function as aggressive venture-capital funds. They make high-interest loans to small, private companies and startups, many of which have trouble getting conventional loans from banks. They also provide managerial expertise and sometimes take an ownership stake. If that sounds risky, it is, but many BDCs offer eye-popping dividends. BlackRock Kelso has stakes in nearly 150 companies, including kitchen supplier Sur La Table and American Piping Products.

Recent yield: 10.3%.

Recent share price: $9.07.

Cash-Rich Stock Funds

Ronald W. Rogé, CFP, CEO of R.W. Rogé & Co., a financial advisory firm managing more than $200 million in assets, Bohemia, New York. *RWRoge.com*

One of the best ways you can cushion your portfolio against a stock market plunge is to hold assets in cash. But if you shift to—or stick with—cash at the wrong time, you miss the possibility of further gains in the stock market, which hit record highs recently. So you might want to depend on mutual fund pros to decide when—and to what degree—to turn to cash and then when to shift assets back into the market. Some of the best fund managers have been good at doing this.

It's not that the fund managers try to exactly time the ups and downs of the market. Instead, they follow a disciplined approach of investing in stocks only when stocks clearly are at bargain prices. If no stocks meet the managers' stringent criteria, they allow cash to build, even if that means their fund performance lags the overall market for years at a time until buying opportunities emerge.

My favorite cash-heavy funds…

• **Yacktman Fund (YACKX)** has 17% of its assets in cash, an indication of how few undervalued large-cap stocks there are that meet fund manager Donald Yacktman's criteria. The fund's performance is in the top 2% of its category over the past 10 years as of April 2, 2015, gaining an annualized 10.2% versus 8.1% for the Standard & Poor's 500 stock index.

•**FPA Crescent (FPACX),** which can invest in a mix of stocks of all sizes and bonds too, has steadily increased its cash holdings over the past five years. Cash now totals about one-third of assets as a result of fund manager Steven Romick slashing his bond holdings but maintaining about half of the portfolio in stocks. Over the past decade, the fund gained an annualized 8.1% matching the performance of the S&P 500 with one-third less risk.

A New Kind of Treasury Bond

Marilyn Cohen, CEO, Envision Capital Management, which manages bond portfolios, Los Angeles. She also is author of *Surviving the Bond Bear Market* (Wiley). *EnvisionCap.com*

Uncle Sam is making some bonds more flexible. The US Treasury introduced a new type of government bond with an interest rate that can rise after investors buy the bond. That feature makes the investment more attractive now, as investors expect today's extremely low interest rates to be on the rise in coming years.

The new type of bond, called floating-rate notes (FRNs), was introduced in January 2014. Initially, FRNs have two-year maturities. And the interest rate will be reset weekly, somewhat above the interest rate for three-month Treasury bills, which was recently at 0.03%.* FRNs might serve as an alternative to money-market funds for very risk-averse investors. In-

*Rate as of April 2, 2015

EASY-TO-DO...

Municipal Bonds to Avoid

Avoid municipal bonds from cities with heavily underfinanced pension loads.

Most at risk: Chicago...Fresno...Portland, Oregon...and Providence.

Safer bets: Indianapolis, San Francisco and Washington, DC.

Recently, Stockton, California, suspended interest payments to investors in muni bonds that it issued to pay for city worker pensions. It also proposed returning as little as 20% of the principal to the bondholders.

Marilyn Cohen, CEO, Envision Capital Management, which manages bond portfolios, Los Angeles. She also is author of *Surviving the Bond Bear Market* (Wiley). *Envision Cap.com*

vestors will be able to use the TreasuryDirect program (*TreasuryDirect.gov*) to buy FRNs in amounts of at least $100.

FRNs are the first new type of security from the Treasury since 1997, when Treasury Inflation-Protected Securities (TIPS) were introduced, and the first with a floating rate, although corporations have issued FRNs for years. The interest on both FRNs and TIPS is exempt from state and local taxes.

The idea of rates that adjust has caught on with investors. For example, one of the most popular nongovernment bond investments recently has been floating-rate bank-loan funds, which fared relatively well in June 2013 when many other kinds of bond funds suffered because interest rates jumped. Interest rates on the loans that the funds invest in typically reset every 90 days.

11

Savvy Shopper

How to Save $5,000 a Year on Expenses Everyone Has

Most consumers spend more than they have to for the following seven commonly used products and services. In some cases, lower-cost options have only recently become available and are not yet widely known. In others, sellers intentionally put up roadblocks that make it challenging to get the best prices. *Smart ways to save money on…*

•**Cellular service.** If you have a cellular service contract and/or obtain your service through a well-known provider, you're almost certainly overpaying—possibly by more than 50%. The typical smartphone owner now pays upward of $110 a month for service, even though he/she could obtain virtually the same service for less than $50. That's an overpay-

ment of more than $1,400 over the course of a two-year contract.

What to do: Sign up for a pay-as-you-go plan without a contract—through a lesser-known, low-cost provider. These companies purchase access to the same cellular networks that the major providers use, so quality of coverage should not suffer. *Great options…*

•Straight Talk features unlimited talk and texts plus 3 gigabytes of data for $45 per month.* (You will be switched to a slower data speed if you exceed that limit, but that's unlikely—90% of smartphone users use less than two gigabytes a month.) Customers can choose which cellular network will provide access—all of the major networks are available. *StraightTalk.com*

*Prices, rates and offers subject to change.

Clark Howard, host of *The Clark Howard Show*, a syndicated radio program about saving money. He is author of *Clark Howard's Living Large for the Long Haul: Consumer-Tested Ways to Overhaul Your Finances, Increase Your Savings, and Get Your Life Back on Track* (Avery). *ClarkHoward.com*

•GoSmartMobile offers unlimited talk and texts plus five gigabytes of data for $40 per month. It operates on the T-Mobile cellular network (either the 2G or 3G network, depending on the plan selected). *GoSmartMobile.com*

•Republic Wireless features unlimited talk, texts and data for $25 per month on the 3G network or $40 per month on the 4G network. It operates on the Sprint cellular network and on Wi-Fi when available. *RepublicWireless.com*

The only significant downside—you probably won't get a subsidized phone. But smartphones now can be had for $100 to $200 or less.

Annual savings: $750 to $1,000.

•**Cable TV.** Read the small print the next time you see a great bargain advertised by a cable, satellite or fiber-optic TV service provider—the offer probably is available only to new customers. New customers often pay as little as $50 to $60 a month for services that would cost an existing customer $90 to $100 or more. Providers think that they don't have to offer existing customers a good deal because few people bother to change TV service after they've signed up.

What to do: Every two years or so, call every company offering TV service in your area other than the company you currently are using. In addition to the local cable company, this includes DirecTV, Dish Network and any telephone company offering fiber-optic TV service in your area. Ask for the best new-customer rates and inducements they can offer you to sign up. Then call your current TV provider and say that you want to cancel your service. That should get you transferred to a customer-retention representative empowered to offer you much better terms than the other phone reps could. You even might be offered terms comparable to what a new customer would get—but only if you can cite a specific deal offered to you by a competitor. You probably won't do nearly as well if you haven't bothered to shop around first. If your current provider won't match a competitor's terms, go ahead and switch.

Annual savings: $300 to $500.

•**Car loans.** Approximately 80% of car buyers who finance their vehicles get financing through the dealership—and pay hundreds or thousands of dollars more than they should as a result.

What to do: Shop for a car loan before you shop for a car. Many credit unions offer rates below 2% to qualified borrowers, for example. Dealerships sometimes offer very competitive rates, too—but only to consumers who already have a low rate in hand from another lender. Car buyers who have not already obtained a loan offer often pay around three percentage points more than necessary.

Savings: Three percentage points add up to about $1,300 more in additional loan payments on a four-year $20,000 loan.

•**Bank accounts.** Many large banks have been quietly adding new charges and increasing existing fees. And many small banks that didn't previously charge steep fees have been absorbed into large bank chains that do. This has left bank customers paying $5 to $10 or more each month for the right to have a checking account, something that used to be free.

What to do: Contact credit unions and small local banks to see if they offer truly free checking accounts that meet your needs. Only 25% of big banks still offer free checking with no strings attached, but about 70% of credit unions still do so. You even might be able to earn as much as 2.5% interest on your checking account if you're willing to jump through a few hoops, such as using your debit card to make at least 10 or 12 purchases each month. To find a credit union in your area, go to *My CreditUnion.gov*.

Annual savings: Frequently $60 to $120 or more.

•**Auto and homeowner's insurance.** Most people just renew their current coverage every year rather than shop around for better rates. That has left most policyholders paying more than they need to—sometimes as much as 50% more.

What to do: Every year, use an insurance-shopping website such as *Insure.com*, *InsWeb.com* or *NetQuote.com* to find the best rates available to you or contact an insurance broker. You might save hundreds of dollars in just a few minutes. Shopping around is especially likely to produce sizable savings if you have had one at-fault auto accident, speeding ticket or claim against your homeowner's insurance policy in the past few years.

Annual savings: If you slash 10% to 20% from both your auto and homeowner's insurance bills, that might add up to $150 to $400 a year.

●**Cars.** Used vehicles haven't been a particularly good deal lately, leading many drivers to ante up for pricey new cars. But used cars are likely to be good deals once again starting this year.

The financial crisis of 2007–2008 slammed the brakes on new-car sales and, especially, new-car leases. Because fewer new cars were sold late last decade, fewer used cars reached the market early this decade—and that lack of supply led to high used-car prices. But car buying and leasing rebounded strongly starting with the 2011 model year. Most auto leases last three years, so those 2011s reached the used-car market in big numbers in 2014, finally tilting the used-car supply/demand balance somewhat back in buyers' favor.

What to do: Watch for good deals on used 2012s this year if you're in the market for a car. Prices could be as little as half what you might have paid for the same car new three years ago, even though three-year-old cars often have less than 50,000 miles on their odometers and perhaps even time left on their warranties. If you can wait a little longer to buy, the used-car market is likely to swing even further in buyers' favor in 2016.

Savings: You could save thousands of dollars buying used instead of new.

●**Airfare.** Most people first choose a vacation destination and the dates they would like to travel and only then shop for the best available price on airline tickets. If you follow that strategy, you're likely to pay roughly twice as much as necessary for airfare.

What to do: Rather than choose a particular destination and dates, let airfare deals play a role in determining when and where you travel. Use discount travel sites such as *Kayak. com*, *AirGorilla.com* and *HipMunk.com* to find low fares to appealing destinations. With Kayak, you enter the airport that you would depart from, and the lowest rates to destinations around the world appear on a map.

Example: I am treating my staff to a trip to Italy in March this year for just $635 per round-trip ticket. Had I decided first to take them to Italy for a specific week, it's unlikely I would have found tickets for less than $1,000.

Estimated annual savings: Up to 50% or more of your airfare budget.

Pay Attention to Alerts from Cell Phone Companies

New alerts from cell phone companies let customers know that they are in danger of being charged more than the normal price of their plans. The Federal Communications Commission now requires companies to let consumers know when they approach, reach and exceed limits on voice, data, text and international roaming charges.

If you get an alert: Pay close attention to your usage so that you do not incur extra charges.

DailyFinance.com

EASY-TO-DO...

No Need to Charge Cell Phones Fully

Keeping them at or near a 100% charge costs more money and does not make them work better. Cell phones—and laptops, too—generally use lithium-based batteries, and those batteries are designed to work best in a charge range of 40% to 80%. Repeatedly letting the batteries drop too low can potentially make them impossible to charge at all—but keeping them charged above 80% does not make the devices they power work better.

Roundup of experts in battery performance, reported at *DailyFinance.com*.

Secure Your Old Phone Before Selling It or Donating It

Prior to selling or donating your old cell phone, remove any SD or Micro SD memory card. Also, take out the SIM card, which gives your phone its number and identifies it on your cellular network—you may need a pin or straightened paperclip to pop it out. Then wipe the phone's built-in memory, and return it to the factory settings. To do this in iOS, choose "Settings/General/Reset/Erase All Contents and Settings." In Android, search in "Settings" for words such as "Backup & Reset"—exact language varies by manufacturer. In a Windows Phone, go to "Settings/About/Reset Your Phone."

CBSNews.com

Protect Yourself from Moving Companies

Get recommendations for moving companies from friends, family members or real estate agents you trust. Do not rely on ads—some companies promote super-low prices, then charge more on arrival and threaten to auction possessions if the inflated charges are not paid. Verify a company's licensing—go to *ProtectYourMove.gov* for information. Check for complaints at the same website and with the Better Business Bureau (at *BBB.org*). Also search the company's name online to find customer reviews. Get information on protecting your rights from *ProtectYourMove.gov* and the American Moving & Storage Association (*Moving.org*).

If you find a problem after the move: Contact the mover immediately. If you think you have been defrauded, contact your state attorney general or consumer protection agency. Call the police if the mover is holding your possessions and making demands.

Consumer Reports. ConsumerReports.org

Apps That Cut the Cost of Eating Out

Y*elp* has a "deals" feature to find discounts and freebies at nearby restaurants...*Foursquare* points to local dining establishments offering discounts and can be used as a digital loyalty card at some locations...*Forks* offers instant coupons for fast-food chains and local restaurants, plus a customer loyalty program...*Scoutmob* is focused on supporting local businesses that offer discounts in the 13 cities where it is available...and *Blackboard Eats* provides users with special offers and discounts of up to 30% off meals in Los Angeles, New York City, San Francisco and Chicago.*

GoBankingRates.com

*Offer subject to change.

Growing the Right Vegetables Saves $$$$

Niki Jabbour, a food gardener and garden writer based outside Halifax, Nova Scotia. Jabbour is author of *The Year-Round Vegetable Gardener: How to Grow Your Own Food 365 Days a Year, No Matter Where You Live* (Storey) and host of *The Weekend Gardener*, a call-in radio show that can be heard online at *News957.com* Sundays 11 am to 1 pm, eastern time. *NikiJabbour.com*

Having a green thumb can save you some green. Growing your own vegetables will lower your grocery bills—potentially by hundreds of dollars a year—and put fresher, tastier produce on your table.

Choose your veggies carefully if saving money is your goal. Some, such as artichokes and cauliflower, are tricky to grow or susceptible to pests and diseases that can reduce yields and quash savings. Others, such as onions and potatoes, are so inexpensive in stores that growing your own won't save you much money.

Easy-to-grow garden vegetables that offer big savings...

•**Salad greens** such as arugula, Swiss chard and spinach can cost $4 to $5 for a bag sufficient for perhaps two salads when bought in a market. Or for $2 to $2.50, you can buy a packet of seeds that can produce enough greens for daily salads starting 40 to 50 days after the initial planting and continuing until the first frost.

Sample savings: If your garden produces five months' worth of daily salads and you previously had been spending $2 per day on greens for those salads, your savings would be approximately $300.*

To guarantee an extended supply of fresh greens, plant a small number of seeds each week throughout the growing season rather than all the seeds at once. When you require only a small quantity of greens, harvest just the outer leaves so that the plant can continue growing. Arugula, Swiss chard, spinach and most other greens are easy to grow. They need only four to six hours of sun each day. They do best in soil at least six inches deep with good drainage. Keep the soil moist until the seeds germinate.

• **Heirloom cherry tomatoes** can cost $4 to $5 per pint in a farmers' market. Or you can grow them yourself from a packet of seeds costing $2 to $2.50 (or from starter plants costing perhaps $2 to $3 for four). Under favorable conditions, each plant could yield 20 pints or more of heirloom (nonhybrid) cherry tomatoes.

Sample savings: If you have four plants that produce 20 pints of heirloom cherry tomatoes apiece, that's the equivalent of $320 worth of produce if you had been paying $4 a pint.

Heirloom cherry tomatoes are a better money saver than larger heirloom tomato varieties because they tend to have a longer growing season and larger overall crop. They're easy to grow but require at least six hours a day of sunlight to thrive.

• **Heirloom green beans** (also called string beans or snap beans) can cost $6 or $7 per pound in farmers' markets. Or you can grow them yourself from a packet of seeds costing $2 to $2.50. Each plant could produce several pounds of beans.

*Prices and sample savings in this article are estimates. Your actual savings will vary significantly depending on the size of your garden, the amount of sunlight your plants receive, the quality of your soil and other factors.

EASY-TO-DO...

Find a Cereal That's Good for You

Look for a whole grain as the first ingredient—whole wheat, whole corn or brown rice. Look for at least 3 grams (g) of fiber per serving. Also, pick a cereal with no more than 6 g of sugar per serving.

Samantha B. Cassetty, RD, nutrition director, Good Housekeeping Research Institute, quoted in *Good Housekeeping.*

Sample savings: If you grow 20 plants and each produces three pounds of beans, that's around $350 in savings if you would have paid $6 a pound at a farmers' market.

Green beans are very easy to grow but prefer full sunlight. Favor green beans that grow on a vine rather than on a bush—they will yield two to three times as many beans per square foot of garden space. You will need to provide poles or trellises for the vines to climb.

• **Herbs including basil, parsley, chives, thyme and rosemary** can cost $2 to $3 for a few sprigs if you buy them fresh. Or for that same $2 to $3, you could buy a four-pack of starter herb plants at a nursery. Each of those plants could produce 50 times as much as that supermarket package, for savings in the hundreds if you use fresh herbs frequently.

Sample savings: If you grow four herb plants and each provides 50 times as much as that $2 container of fresh herb sprigs in the market, that's nearly $400 in potential savings—though realistically few people buy that many herbs.

Herbs generally require at least four to six hours of sunlight per day. Clip flower buds when they appear—your herbs won't be as flavorful if the plants flower, and flowering stops growth. If your plants produce more herbs than you can use, freeze the excess for winter use.

To freeze: Place one spoonful or two of chopped herbs in each compartment of an ice-cube tray. Top with water to cover the herbs. Freeze.

How to Buy a Mattress (and Still Sleep at Night): 7 Traps to Avoid

Ronald Czarnecki, a former manager of multiple mattress stores in the Pacific Northwest. He is author of *Shop for Sleep and Survive the Bite: How to Shop for a Mattress and Save Money in the Cold White Sea of Deception* (CreateSpace).

Mattresses might be soft to sleep on, but they are notoriously hard to buy. Various stores sell very similar mattresses under different names, thwarting attempts to compare prices. Salespeople often steer shoppers toward ultraexpensive products, and the manufacturers highlight features that consumers can't easily evaluate. As a result, many shoppers pay hundreds of dollars more than necessary—or end up sleeping for years on mattresses that they hate.

Beware of these traps…

Trap #1: **It is very difficult to compare mattress prices from store to store.** With the exception of certain specialty mattresses, each retailer typically uses product names and numbers that you won't find anywhere else. This is true even when the mattresses are virtually identical, aside from cosmetic changes involving fabric colors and quilting patterns.

What to do: When you find a mattress that feels comfortable (see below for evaluating comfort), jot down every available piece of information about what's inside the mattress. Include the coil count and coil wire gauge… dimensions including the height…firmness (based on your judgment of where it falls on a one-to-10 firmness scale with one the firmest)…materials used…how the sleep surface is described…and what position the list price occupies compared with other mattresses at the store from the same manufacturer. When you visit other mattress retailers, examine mattresses that fall in the same general position in the manufacturer's price scale until you find one that matches up very closely. Start there and compare coil counts, firmness and other characteristics of various models until you find one that seems to match. Lie on this mattress, if possible, to confirm that it feels about the same as the one you tried earlier.

Tell the salesperson that you found the corresponding mattress at the other store, and ask if he/she can beat the other store's price. If the second store has the lower price, you could return to the earlier store and try the same tactic. Most mattress stores and many furniture stores will negotiate. Their list prices tend to be double their cost, so it is perfectly reasonable to try to negotiate a price 20% to 40% off list price (which could mean a savings of $400 off a $1,000 mattress). Department stores often won't negotiate, but they sometimes will honor their price-match guarantee if the customer shows that a mattress at another store is essentially identical despite different names. And the department store might offer a better deal on shipping and better return options if you're not satisfied, both important considerations.

Reasonable price: You should be able to find a good queen-size mattress for $700 to $1,000—for guest rooms, $500 to $800.*

Trap #2: **"Pillow top" softness may not last.** So-called pillow-top mattresses feel great when you lie on them at the store. They have thick, soft layers of fiber and/or foam above the mattress springs. Trouble is, these thick layers soon will develop deep, annoying body indentations. The heavier you and/or your partner, the faster this will happen.

If you love the soft pillow-top feel, opt for a "plush top" instead. These have perhaps two to three inches of foam and fiber, rather than the four to six inches of a pillow top—and they will be less likely to develop deep body indentations. Plush tops also tend to be $100 to $300 less expensive than pillow tops.

Helpful: If there are two separate "tape edges"—ropelike lines—running around the mattress above and below the foam layers, it is called a pillow top.

Trap #3: **Warranties and satisfaction guarantees are less impressive than they seem.** If you voice concern about whether a mattress is right for you, the salesperson might assure you that there's no need to worry because the store offers a satisfaction guarantee.

*Prices subject to change.

Quiz the salesperson about this guarantee. Can you get cash back or only exchange the mattress for a different one—and how much time do you have to return it? Is there a restocking fee for returns? What about a pick-up charge or additional shipping charge for the replacement mattress? And if you purchase a mattress during a sale, will you be able to exchange it for one of similar list price or only for a lesser one with a list price similar to the sale price you initially paid?

Caution: Manufacturers' mattress warranties cover only major defects. They won't permit you to return the mattress because you don't find it comfortable. Mattresses generally should be replaced every eight to 10 years.

Trap #4: **New foundations often are unnecessary.** If you buy a mattress, expect the salesperson to push you to buy the matching foundation (what used to be called a box spring) as well. You might be told that this foundation will extend the life of your mattress or make it more comfortable or that not buying it will void the mattress warranty. None of this is likely to be true.

Unlike the old-fashioned mattresses, many modern mattresses do not require you to flip them over from time to time, and these no-flip mattresses don't require springs beneath them at all. Today's "box springs" really are just simple wood-and-wire frames covered in fabric. These foundations cost retailers very little, yet they're often sold for hundreds of dollars.

If your old foundation has no obvious problems such as sagging or cracking and is the same size as the new mattress, you can continue to use it. If you have an old spring-type box that flexes when you push down on it, you don't want to use it with a new "no-flip" single-sided mattress.

If you have a platform bed or a bed with slats that are spaced no more than two inches apart, you can skip the box spring entirely—assuming that the resulting mattress height is not too low. If you do need a new foundation, purchase the one that's matched (brand-wise) to your new mattress. Don't feel that you need to match the fabrics. A lower-priced foundation of the correct size should be fine if you're buying a single-sided mattress.

Trap #5: **A higher coil count doesn't necessarily mean higher quality.** For spring mattresses, mattress salespeople often stress high coil count—more springs per square inch—as they steer shoppers toward high-end models. It's true that having more coils is better than having fewer coils, all else being equal, but all else is not equal when it comes to coils. Coils might be made from different materials or in different ways.

Example: A mattress with independent coils—coils each made from a separate piece of wire—is likely to do a better job of conforming to the contours of your spine than a mattress with coils made from continuous strands of wire, even if the coil count isn't as high. Independent coils also do a much better job of isolating movement, a big plus for those who share a bed.

Trap #6: **Delivery and removal charges.** Ask about delivery charges before you agree to buy a mattress. Some retailers provide free delivery, but others see it as a way to slip one last sneaky fee into the deal.

Also ask whether removal of the old mattress is included in delivery—there is sometimes an additional charge for this. Include any delivery and pick-up fees when you compare prices at different stores.

Trap #7: **An expensive specialty mattress might have drawbacks.** Solid foam and dual-zone, air-filled mattresses look great in ads and can feel great when you lie on them—but there might be concerns that the salesperson won't mention. *For instance…*

• Memory foam mattresses such as those made by Tempur-Pedic do a wonderful job of conforming to the contours of the body and providing support—but they also make some sleepers feel too hot.

If you want foam but are a warm sleeper, consider a natural latex foam mattress, which sleeps cooler. Some synthetic foam mattresses have gel embedded in them to keep sleepers cooler, but these mattresses are extremely heavy and difficult to move.

• Dual-zone, air-filled mattresses such as Sleep Number by Select Comfort provide separate firmness controls for each side of the bed. But humidity and perspiration tend to build up around the internal air bladders of even the best-made air-filled mattresses. Mildew and mold can spread if the bladders are not cleaned frequently using liquid detergent.

These mattresses can be opened up for cleaning and for ventilation—but make sure that the mattress is completely dry before closing it up.

More from Ronald Czarnecki...

The Best Way to Test a Mattress

Lie on a mattress for at least 10 to 15 minutes in the showroom to make sure that it feels comfortable—and that it properly supports your spine.

Doctors used to recommend firm mattresses for back health, but they've since concluded that firm mattresses actually provide poor spine support. Backs do best in beds that allow the spine to be straight and supported as you sleep. When you lie on your side on a too firm mattress, your shoulders and hips don't sink in far enough for your spine to stay straight...and when you lie on your back, your hips don't sink in far enough for the mattress to support your lower back. A medium-firm mattress is the best choice for the vast majority of sleepers.

The mattress industry uses terms like "firm," "medium-firm," "plush" and "pillow-soft." But it may be more helpful to use a one-to-10 firmness scale with one as the firmest and four-to-six as medium. Ask the salesperson where each mattress falls on this firmness scale so that you can learn what firmness number you like best. Then you can specify this number when comparing other mattresses.

Exception to the medium-firmness rule: Side-sleepers prone to hip or shoulder discomfort might do better on a soft mattress.

Helpful: Bring someone along on your shopping trip to make sure that your spine is straight as you lie on your side...and to confirm that there's no gap between your lower back and the mattress when you lie on your back.

Great Eyeglasses for Half the Price

Clark Howard, host of *The Clark Howard Show*, a syndicated radio program about saving money. He is author of *Clark Howard's Living Large for the Long Haul: Consumer-Tested Ways to Overhaul Your Finances, Increase Your Savings, and Get Your Life Back on Track* (Avery). *ClarkHoward.com*

A pair of eyeglasses can cost hundreds of dollars, but there's no need to pay anywhere near that much. Quality eyeglasses can be bought online for less than $15 a pair for standard prescriptions*...and even complicated prescriptions generally can be filled at various websites for $30 to $100, including the frames and lenses.

Even if you prefer not to buy eyewear online, there still are places you can shop where your price is likely to be less than $200 for glasses that might cost $400 or more elsewhere.

Here, Clark Howard explains what eyeglass wearers need to know...

CONSIDER BUYING ONLINE

The Internet sellers including Zenni Optical (*ZenniOptical.com*)...EyeBuyDirect (*EyeBuyDirect.com*)...and Goggles4u (*Goggles4u.com*) offer well-made prescription eyeglasses, including both lenses and frames, for as little as $6.95. Shipping might add $5 or so to your order. Features such as thin lenses, tinted lenses, antiglare coatings, bifocals and progressive lenses—lenses that offer multiple lens powers without the lines of bifocals—usually cost extra. Many frame choices cost more than the base price as well. Still, even a challenging prescription with extras and upgrades typically costs less than $100.

The online eyeglass deals can get better if you use a coupon code. Google "coupon" and either "eyeglasses" or the name of the online seller you're considering...or go to *RetailMeNot.com* to find these codes. Typical codes provide 15% to 20% off for first-time customers...free shipping...free antiglare coating...and more savings. Once you buy from an online eyeglass seller, you're likely to receive even better coupon offers in your e-mail.

*Prices subject to change.

Example: I got two pairs for the price of one.

Downside of buying eyeglasses online...

• **It is more challenging to find frames that fit your face and look good on you.** The websites do provide tips for selecting frames that fit, but you should look at the numbers on the temples of your current glasses for help with sizing information, assuming that they fit well.

Most of these sites also let shoppers upload a photo of their face and then superimpose different frames to see which look best.

• **Some shoppers complain that they have had trouble resolving problems with eyeglasses purchased online,** and there have been reports of some unreliable eyeglass sites. Personally, I've had only one problem in all my years of ordering eyeglasses online, and it was resolved to my satisfaction. Do be cautious about ordering eyewear from sites not mentioned in this article, however, unless you get positive reviews of those sites from friends, publications or review sites that you consider reliable.

• **Internet sellers cannot provide an eye exam.** You will have to see a local optometrist or ophthalmologist to confirm that your eyes are healthy and to obtain a prescription. Such exams can cost $100 or above, though this could be partially covered by your health insurance. Or save money by getting your exam at a Walmart Vision Center or Costco Optical, where rates can be as much as 50% lower.

Helpful: Eyeglass prescription forms typically do not list "pupillary distance" (PD), the distance between your pupils, center to center, in millimeters (mm). (Most adults have a PD between 54 mm and 74 mm.) Ask for this when you get your exam—you will need it to order glasses online. The online glasses sites do provide do-it-yourself PD measurement guidance, but a professional measurement is more accurate.

• **Your glasses might take one to two weeks to arrive, sometimes longer.** If you need glasses in a hurry, it might be worth paying the higher prices charged by a provider that can make lenses while you wait, such as LensCrafters.

• **Progressive lenses are particularly complicated to make and to match to the wearer,** increasing the odds of problems that could be difficult to correct if the glasses are ordered online. Buying glasses with progressive lenses from a local eyeglass store also allows you to work with that professional to find the progressive lenses best-suited to your needs—for example, some have expanded intermediate zones for computer use...others, expanded near-zones for reading.

• **Even if you prefer not to order your primary eyeglasses online,** this still is a good way to get backup glasses so that you don't have to overpay for replacements if your primary glasses are lost or broken. A woman I work with tends to misplace her eyeglasses, so she orders eight pairs of very inexpensive glasses from Zenni each time she gets a new prescription. For around $60, she never has to worry about not being able to find her eyewear.

Alternate strategy: Buy frames online, and get your lenses locally.

DEALS ON FRAMES

Warby Parker (*WarbyParker.com*) is a good option if you want to save money but also want trendy frames. It does not offer bifocals, however.

Warby Parker prices start at $95, shipping included, for glasses featuring stylish frames. Warby Parker mainly sells through the Internet, but it does have showrooms in nine cities and retail stores in New York City and San Francisco, with an optometrist and opticians available. If you don't live near one of these locations, you can use the company's virtual try-on feature that allows you to see how different frames would look on your face (select frames, then click the "Virtual Try-On" button)...or try out up to five frames (without lenses) for up to five days without cost or obligation through Warby Parker's "home try-on program" (select frames, then click the "+ Add to Home Try-On" button).

The company offers a 100%-satisfaction, no-questions-asked, 30-day return policy that even covers return shipping. There's a one-year no-scratch guarantee on the lenses, too.

BEST IN-PERSON OPTIONS

If you prefer to purchase eyeglasses from a bricks-and-mortar store that provides high-quality in-person customer service, buy your glasses at Costco. Eyeglasses cost an average of $150 there, which is more than you would pay online but significantly less than you would pay for comparable glasses at almost any other store—so much less that buying a single pair of eyeglasses can more than cover Costco's $55 annual membership fee. Another option is to have Costco install new lenses in your current frames or frames that you bought online, though there is a small additional fee for not buying your frames there.

If you are not satisfied with your Costco glasses, you can return them at any time for a full refund without limitations. Certain types of lenses, such as lenses that provide a wider field of vision for progressive lenses, might not be offered at Costco.

Alternative: The company For Eyes Optical also has prices below typical retail at its more than 140 locations (800-367-3937, *For Eyes.com*). It's appropriate if you are not near a Costco or don't want to pay an annual membership fee.

If neither chain is in your area and you don't want to order glasses online, buy from an independent optometrist, ophthalmologist or optician rather than another chain. Most chains tend to charge higher prices and offer worse service than the independents.

Printer Ink Is Not Just Used Up by Printing

Printer ink also is used to clean print heads and for other maintenance chores—and the difference between a printer that uses a lot of ink for those purposes and one that does not use much can be $100 or more per year.

What to do: If you print only from time to time, consider a Brother printer—it uses little

ink in intermittent usage. Leave the printer's power on to avoid starting a maintenance cycle every time you use the unit—inkjets use little power, and the ink savings should more than make up for the added energy cost. For less critical work, print in draft mode. Avoid printing a lot of large photos, especially in high-quality mode. Do not change cartridges until you must.

ConsumerReports.org

Items That Usually Are *Not* a Good Deal at Drugstores

Batteries can cost 70% less at warehouse clubs than at drugstores.* Cleaning products cost less at big-box stores and even less at dollar stores. Photo prints cost less through online services, as little as nine cents each, compared with 50 cents at a drugstore. Greeting cards may cost $4 at a drugstore, 50 cents at dollar stores. Office and school supplies also cost less at dollar stores. Over-the-counter medicines cost less at warehouse clubs, even compared with the drugstore's own brands. Pregnancy tests can cost a dollar at dollar stores and are just as accurate as $10 drugstore ones. Prescription drugs may cost much less at warehouse clubs than at drugstores—$7 at Costco compared with $126 at CVS in one case ($119 savings). Toys and games cost less at *Amazon.com* and elsewhere online.

Roundup of experts on retail pricing, reported at *Kiplinger.com*.

*Rates and prices subject to change.

Save on Health and Beauty Products

Save on health and beauty products by buying them at Harmon, Target and Walmart. Drugstores had the highest prices (as much as

53% higher) on shampoo, toothpaste, deodorant and other personal-care products. Prices at supermarkets came in second.

Consumer Reports Money Adviser. ConsumerReports. org

Return Beauty Products You Don't Like

Many merchants will take cosmetics back, even if you have opened and tried them. CVS, Kohl's, Rite Aid and other merchants will accept returns with a receipt. Ask about the store's policy before making a purchase.

AARP Bulletin. AARP.org/bulletin

Lipstick May Contain Metal in Toxic Amounts!

In a recent finding, daily use of lipstick and/or lip gloss may have exposed women to excessive amounts of the metal chromium, which is associated with stomach cancer. Also, 75% of products tested contained lead. Currently, there is no way for consumers to find out a product's metal content—so apply lip coloring less frequently and/or in smaller amounts.

S. Katharine Hammond, PhD, professor of environmental health sciences, School of Public Health, University of California-Berkeley, and coauthor of a study of 32 lipsticks and lip glosses, published in *Environmental Health Perspectives.*

Vitamin D Pills May Have Too Much Vitamin D

In a recent analysis by *ConsumerLab.com,* some had up to 80% more than the labeled amount. High blood levels of vitamin D can

increase risk for heart and kidney diseases and even death. At appropriate levels, vitamin D can reduce the risk for cardiovascular disease, diabetes, osteoporosis and Alzheimer's.

Among the vitamin D supplements that passed recent tests: Simply Right (Sam's Club), 2,000 international units (IU)…Spring Valley (Walmart and Rexall), both 1,000 IU.

Tod Cooperman, MD, president of ConsumerLab. com, an independent publisher of information on dietary supplements, White Plains, New York.

Save on Medicine by Shopping Around

You can save $749/month on medicine by shopping around. In a recent finding, out-of-pocket costs for a one-month supply of five popular medicines varied by that much among pharmacies around the US. The drugs studied were Actos for diabetes, the antidepressant Lexapro, the statin Lipitor, the blood thinner Plavix and the asthma drug Singulair. Someone buying the five medications from the highest-priced pharmacies would pay $749 more per month than someone buying them from the lowest-cost ones. Prices varied by pharmacy and region—but overall, Costco had the lowest retail prices and CVS had the highest.

Consumer Reports. ConsumerReports.org

DID YOU KNOW THAT...

Supplements May Have Harmful Ingredients?

Since 2009, the FDA has recalled more than 275 dietary supplements because they contained unapproved or possibly harmful ingredients. The biggest offenders are supplements marketed for sexual enhancement, muscle building and weight loss.

University of California, Berkeley, Wellness Letter. Berkeley Wellness.com

The Lowdown on Layaway Plans

Beware of fees and conditions on holiday layaway plans. These plans, which typically require you to put down 10% to 20% on a purchase and then pay off the rest over an eight-to-12-week period, can trip you up if you don't read the fine print.

Example: If you do not make all payments and pick up your items by mid-December, most stores will refund your money but charge you a cancellation fee.

Edgar Dworsky, creator of Consumer World. Previously, he served as a Massachusetts assistant attorney general. *ConsumerWorld.org*

EASY-TO-DO...

Ask Stores to Sub Out-of-Stock Sale Items

Rather than requesting a rain check during a sale—which requires you to come back another time—see if the store will let you have an equivalent or better item at the advertised sale price. Some retailers automatically designate substitute items—look for signs or ask customer service. If no item has been picked by the store, find one yourself and ask an employee or a manager if you can have it at the sale price.

ConsumerReports.org

Good News: Products That Have Gone Down in Price!

Camcorders have dropped 15% in price. Cookware has fallen by 20% because of competition from celebrity-chef product lines. Digital cameras are 10% less expensive now and have better lenses than smartphones and tablets—resulting in sharper pictures. Food processors cost 10% less. So do paper shredders—look for them at big-box stores for add-

ed savings. Tablets are selling for 15% lower prices—but not ones made by Apple or Samsung. TVs cost 10% less, and ones with larger screens have gone down the most in price.

Consumer Reports Money Adviser. ConsumerReports.org

Save $1,000 a Year by Buying Products with Your Neighbors

Collect e-mail addresses of neighbors who want to participate in the discount group until you have 20 to 30 households. Then contact firms that provide services such as lawn mowing and snow plowing...and companies that offer fuel and products such as oil, propane and mulch...and negotiate group discounts. Everyone still gets an individual account with direct billing.

Potential savings: $1,000 a year per household or more.

Consumer Reports Money Adviser. ConsumerReports.org

Get Discounts from Companies When You Invest in Their Stock

Some companies offer savings and discounts when you invest in their stock. While this should not be the major factor when making an investment decision, it is a sign that a company appreciates its shareholders. In some instances, you could even save enough to cover the cost of your initial investment.

Attractive stocks that come with extras: Carnival Corporation (CCL) and Royal Caribbean Cruises (RCL)—a shipboard credit of up to $250 on cruises for shareholders with 100 or more shares*...Crimson Wine Group (CWGL)—a 20% discount on wines from its

*Offers subject to change.

vineyards in California, Oregon and Washington...Ford Motor Company (F)—special pricing offers on Ford and Lincoln cars and trucks, typically just over the dealer's invoice price, for investors who own at least 100 shares of stock...IBM (IBM)—Lenova offers discounts on its entire product line, including ThinkPad notebooks.

Paul Mladjenovic, CFP, CEO, *RavingCapitalist.com*, Fort Lee, New Jersey, and author of *Stock Investing for Dummies* (Wiley).

Companies Reward Fans with Freebies

To be eligible for freebies, "like" companies on Facebook...follow them on Twitter... and sign up for fan-focused contests promoted on these and other social-media sites. Also, write positive reviews in online forums such as Yelp—companies watch these sites and sometimes reward favorable remarks.

Example: Spas have been known to give complimentary treatments—such as a $65 tub soak treatment—after fans have raved about them on Yelp.

If you particularly like one specific brand, write to the company explaining why—many will respond by thanking you and sending free gifts, coupons or samples.

Roundup of experts on making connections with companies, reported at *GoBankingRates.com*.

A Sampling of Birthday Freebies

The restaurants Acapulco and El Torito offer a free birthday entrée*...Baja Fresh, a free birthday burrito...Baskin-Robbins, free ice cream...BJ's, a free dessert...Black Angus, a free steak dinner...Denny's and IHOP, a free breakfast meal...and Red Robin and Fud-

*Offers subject to change and may vary by location.

druckers, a free burger. You may have to buy something or sign up for a free e-mail newsletter to get something free. The stores Aveda, Benefit Cosmetics, Old Navy and Sephora offer birthday treats or surprises.

Coupons or other birthday offers: American Eagle, Anthropologie, Benihana, CVS, Payless Shoes, DSW Shoes and Victoria's Secret all give birthday discounts.

Many other businesses offer birthday specials of some sort—ask at your favorite places.

GoBankingRates.com

You May Get Sued for Negative Online Reviews

Some companies go after people who post unflattering comments—typically accusing them of defamation. Even if you post anonymously, a company may be able to find you through the review site. Making a false statement that damages a company's reputation increases the chance of being sued. If you get a threatening letter from a company that you have reviewed, hire a lawyer. Depending on your policy, your homeowner's insurance may cover legal fees and any damages if you are found liable. Check with your insurer. And review your state's rules involving defamation lawsuits of this type at a website called *AntiSlapp.org*—about half the states have protections for online reviewers.

Roundup of experts in legal issues involving online postings, reported at *MarketWatch.com*.

Advertising Phrases That Dupe Many Consumers

Up to makes people imagine that they will get the maximum discount—which may not be true...*Doctor-recommended* may mean that a physician was paid to make a recommendation—but what matters is whether your own doctor recommends a product for you... *For pennies a day* and similar phrases make a costly item seem inexpensive by breaking down the price into tiny amounts...and *Don't be taken in by* warns consumers of scammers in an industry—but the company issuing the warning may be the scammer.

Consumer Reports Money Adviser. ConsumerReports. org

Retailers Keep Track of Shoppers' Returns

Best Buy, J.C. Penney, Victoria's Secret, The Home Depot, Nike and other stores maintain return-tracking databases. Retailers say they need the databases to fight theft and fraud. But consumer advocates say that the databases—whose existence often is not disclosed by retailers—invade consumer privacy.

To see what return information retailers have on you: Request a copy of your *Return Activity Report* from *TheRetailEquation.com*.

Experts in retailers' data practices and consumer protection, reported in *USA Today*.

EASY-TO-DO...

How to Cash in an Unwanted Gift Card

Several websites buy gift cards for cash—*ABC GiftCards.com*, *Cardpool.com* and *GiftCards. com.** One site—*GiftCardGranny.com*—lets you compare offers from several places. Offers vary, ranging from 50% to 90% of a card's value. The best offers usually are for gas-station, retail-chain and grocery cards. Some sites give higher offers if you exchange a card for something other than cash—for example, *Amazon.com* credit. Follow the directions on the site where you choose to make the transaction. You may be able to enter the card number online or may have to ship the card to the buyer. Site fees vary depending on what you are selling and how you want to be paid—read each site's instructions carefully.

Kiplinger's Personal Finance. Kiplinger.com

*Offers and rates subject to change.

Attention Consumers: Fight Back with Facebook (and Twitter)— Fix Problems Fast

Natalie Petouhoff, PhD, a social-media marketing consultant based in Los Angeles. She is an adjunct professor and program director of social-media executive education at UCLA Anderson School of Management and author of *Like My Stuff: How to Get 750 Million Members to Buy Your Products on Facebook* (Adams Media) *DrNatalieNews.com*

When United Airlines baggage handlers broke Dave Carroll's guitar, the musician called their customer service phone number and then traded e-mails with company representatives for nine months—but United refused to pay for the damage. So Carroll composed a music video titled *United Breaks Guitars* and posted it on YouTube. Millions of people all over the world started watching it. Less than a week later, United backed down and offered to cover Carroll's guitar repair costs and give him $1,200 in flight vouchers.

When we call customer service, no one hears about our problem except the phone rep we speak with. That makes it easy for the company to ignore us. When we complain through social media such as Facebook, Twitter or YouTube, however, many other potential customers might hear about our problem, greatly increasing the company's incentive to resolve the issue in a fair manner.

More and more companies are realizing that social media is a potent consumer weapon that could hurt them and so cannot be ignored. Comcast, Delta Air Lines, JetBlue, L.L.Bean, Nike, Southwest Airlines, UPS and Zappos are among the companies that have geared up to respond quickly to social-media complaints.

Example: Delta agents told me nothing could be done when a flight delay threatened to make me late for a speaking engagement. I sent a Tweet about my problem to Delta's customer service department from my smartphone, and 13 minutes later, I was booked on a flight that got me to my destination on time.

Rather than rely on a single social-media tool to obtain customer service, it pays to make your voice heard in more than one place…

• **Send the company a Tweet reading:** "I'm having trouble with [one of the company's products or services]—is there anything you can do to help me? #fail". Twitter is a great place to start when you're trying to obtain customer service because it's quick and easy. Tweets are brief—140 characters or fewer—and can be sent from a computer or cell phone.

Visit *Twitter.com*, and follow the directions to sign up for an account if you haven't already. Then track down the Twitter "handle" of the company you are trying to reach by searching on Twitter or by doing an online search for the company's name and the word "Twitter." (Add the phrase "customer service" to this search if the company appears to have multiple Twitter handles.) Start your message, which will be available to all Twitter users, with this handle.

Example: "@Comcastcares I am having trouble with my cable installation—can you help me? #fail".

Politeness pays here even if you are very upset. Ranting increases the odds that the company—and other Twitter users—will dismiss you as a crank.

Do include "#fail" at the end of complaint Tweets. This "hashtag" is used on Twitter and elsewhere to indicate that the message involves a problem or mistake. Some customer service departments make a special effort to respond promptly to messages ending in "#fail". (If you make a YouTube video about the problem, include a link in your Tweet.)

If the company's customer service department does monitor Twitter, you could hear back within a few minutes or a few hours—response times vary widely. If so, you might be asked to provide additional details via Twitter's "Direct Message" feature. To send a Direct Message, click the gear icon in the top right of the Twitter home page, select "Direct Messages" from the drop-down menu, click "New Message" and type the Twitter handle of the recipient in the address box.

• **Contact customer service via live chat.** If your Tweet does not trigger a prompt response, check the company's website to see if you can chat online with customer service. Online chat is not as powerful as Twitter, because no one besides the company rep will see your complaint, but when available, it's usually a preferable option to calling the customer service phone number. Wait times are typically shorter with live chat, and there's no need to navigate tricky phone trees or struggle with difficult accents. Calmly explain your problem, and propose a fair solution, either through live chat or on the phone.

• **Make a YouTube video showing the absurdity or frustration of your situation,** particularly if your problem is visually dramatic.

Example: Your luggage arrives at baggage claim looking like it was mauled by bears. Use your smartphone or digital camera to film it as it travels around the carousel, then film opening the bag to reveal the damage inside.

Post a video on YouTube featuring this footage. Consider adding audio of your struggle to sort out the issue with the company's unhelpful phone reps.

Warning: Recording phone conversations without the other party's consent is illegal in many states, but a recording of just your side of the conversation is legal and potentially effective. Repeat back the absurd things the phone rep tells you to confirm them and get them on your recording—"So you are telling me my lifetime warranty expired?"

Keep this YouTube video brief, and include the product name or company name in its title.

• **Post an account of your problem on your Facebook page, Google+ page and/or blog** if you still haven't obtained satisfaction. If you don't have a blog or a page on these social-media sites, search online for the name of the company together with the word "forum" or "complaints" to see if there are independent websites where the company's customers discuss their experiences and post your story there. (Consumer complaint sites such as *RipoffReport.com* and *PissedConsumer.com* are less likely to be monitored by company representatives.)

This post should explain your problem and the struggles you've had getting the company to address it. It should ask, "Has anyone else had this happen? Did you get it resolved?" (If you made a YouTube video, include a link to it in the post.) A fellow consumer might have a suggestion about how to get the company to help. Or your post might trigger a wave of attention and discussion that gets the company's attention.

•**Tweet your problem to consumer reporters.** If a member of the media starts making inquiries, it will greatly increase the odds that the company will seek to resolve your complaint.

Twitter is the best way to reach most consumer reporters these days. Read local newspapers and watch local TV news to learn the names of reporters who cover consumer issues in your area, then do a search online for those reporters' names and the word "Twitter" to find their Twitter handles. Tweet a brief description of your problem to them followed by the question "Can you help me with this?"

How to Win Sweepstakes on Facebook and Twitter: Tricks from the Contest Queen

Carolyn Wilman, editor of the *ContestQueen.com* website and author of *You Can't Win If You Don't Enter* (BookSurge). Wilman runs sweepstakes seminars in the US and Canada. She also consults with businesses about running effective sweepstakes.

Sweepstakes have now entered the Internet era—entries are submitted online through company websites or, increasingly, through companies' Facebook, Twitter and Pinterest social-media pages.

This means that you can use Internet tools to search for appealing promotional giveaways and use form-filling programs such as Roboform Everywhere to dramatically reduce the time that it takes to enter (a free version is available or you can pay $10 annually for additional features,* *Roboform.com*).

*Prices subject to change.

Prizes for online sweepstakes can be significant. For example, the cable channel HGTV gives away a house each year in its Dream Home Giveaway (*HGTV.com/dream-home*).

To take full advantage of online sweepstakes, you must know how to find the best ones for you and how to increase your odds of winning…

FINDING SWEEPSTAKES

The sweepstakes aggregator websites, such as *Online-Sweepstakes.com* and *PowerSweep staking.com*, provide links to hundreds of current sweepstakes. They also filter out most of the scams. My site, *ContestQueen.com*, includes links to dozens of resources (from the "Resources" menu, choose "U.S. Resources," then "Find Sweepstakes," followed by "Sweepstakes Aggregates" or "Sweepstakes Newsletters"). Settle on one or two resources that you find easy to use. *Also…*

•**Set up a Google Alert for the word "sweepstakes" together with your state or city.** This should turn up regional sweepstakes, which typically attract fewer entrants and thus offer better odds than national drawings. Set up a second Google Alert for the phrase "open only to residents of [YOUR STATE]" as well.

To set up a Google Alert: Go to *Google.com/ alerts*. In the box, enter the words you want to get e-mail notifications for. Then click "Show Options" and "Create Alert." You will receive e-mail alerts whenever web pages containing your keywords appear.

•**Sign up for the e-newsletters of companies and brands that you especially like, too**—these sometimes include sweepstakes. (Have all these sent to an e-mail address that you've set up specifically for sweepstakes so that your main e-mail account isn't flooded with contest-related e-mails or spam.)

•**Consider subscribing to a sweepstakes e-newsletter.** Many of them specialize in sweepstakes not found on the sweepstakes aggregators such as mail-in or regional sweepstakes. *SweepingAmerica.com* specializes in mail-in and text sweepstakes ($75 annually for weekly e-mails plus alerts), and *IWinCon tests.com* specializes in short-entry-period and regional giveaways, which, as pointed out above, tend to attract fewer entrants and thus offer better odds of winning ($20 annually for weekly e-mails).

WINNING TIPS

Winning strategies for today's social-media–based sweepstakes…

•**Facebook features more sweepstakes than any other social-media site.** To enter, you typically must "Like" the page of the company or brand offering the sweepstakes, then fill out a short online entry form.

Example: Kraft and Procter & Gamble frequently run Facebook sweepstakes—but you usually will find them on the Facebook pages of these companies' brands and products, not on their general corporate pages.

Strategy: Read all Facebook sweepstakes' rules carefully—sometimes you can earn extra entries, thereby increasing your odds of winning, by sharing the promotion with your Facebook friends.

•**Sweepstakes on Twitter often are very short-term**—many close within a few hours. Short entry periods mean fewer entries and better odds of winning. The prizes tend to be modest, however—the value might be just $20 to $50. Twitter sweepstakes typically are very easy to enter—usually just a matter of retweeting the sweepstakes tweet or answering a single question.

Example: Book publishers, movie theater chains and movie studios frequently give away books and movie tickets through Twitter sweepstakes.

Strategy: The main secret to winning Twitter sweepstakes is locating them before they close—aggregator sites often don't list them in time. Follow businesses you like that have run Twitter sweepstakes in the past, then skim their Twitter feeds on a smartphone whenever you have a moment that would otherwise go to waste, such as when standing in line at the store.

•**Pinterest sweepstakes often require entrants to create special Pinterest pages** or follow complex rules. That can hold down the number of entrants, increasing your odds of winning—but it also means that entering could take hours.

Strategy: Skim the sweepstakes rules to determine whether the winner will be selected by judges evaluating entrants' Pinterest pages or by a random drawing. If it is a random drawing, there's no need to invest a lot of time in your entry.

Example: Mrs. T's Pierogies recently ran a "Re-Pin to Win" Pinterest sweepstakes with a grand prize of $1,000 and a year's supply of pierogies. The winner was selected by random drawing.

Hidden Treasures at Yard Sales

Terry Kovel, author of more than 100 books, including *Kovel's Antiques & Collectibles Price Guide* (Black Dog and Leventhal). Her nationally syndicated newspaper column appears in more than 150 newspapers. *Kovels.com*

Prices for antiques and collectibles finally are rebounding from the recession, improving the odds that garage sale finds can be flipped for a profit. Below are six often-overlooked garage sale items that are increasing in value.

Helpful: If you're not sure what an item looks like, do an online search for it and the year.

•**Printed cloth handkerchiefs from the 1970s and earlier.** Handkerchiefs tend to sell for pennies at garage sales, but those with nice patterns and colors have value to quilters. Particularly distinctive examples even can be framed as art. The finest examples are hand-hemmed and made of fine linen or cotton.

Example: A child's handkerchief from the 1970s featuring the picture of a comic duck sells for $18.*

Similar: Scarves from designers such as Hermès or Marimekko may be sold for very little at garage sales but can be worth hundreds, particularly if the pattern is rare and beautiful.

*Prices are from 2013 auctions and shows.

• **Williamsburg-style wood furniture from the 1950s and early 1960s.** This furniture isn't trendy—it has an old-fashioned colonial look—but it is timeless and made completely from solid wood. That sets it apart from so much of today's wood furniture, which may be laminated particleboard and has pressed-board backs and drawer bottoms. Pieces from respected makers such as Baker, Beacon Hill and Kittinger are climbing in value as furniture buyers seek quality and durability.

Example: 1960s mahogany library steps by Kittinger brings $550.

• **Psychedelic posters from the late 1960s and early 1970s.** Those that feature colorful psychedelic graphics, cite specific concert dates and have pinholes in the corners tend to be worth the most. A lack of pinholes (or other signs of age and use) might mean that the poster is a modern reproduction.

Example: A Peter Max poster from 1968 called "Love" sells for $316.

• **Fisher-Price toys.** Kids have been enjoying Fisher-Price products for generations—and they're often handed down from generation to generation. Look for ones in pristine condition to have value.

Example: A Fisher-Price Doggy Racer with no plastic parts, in excellent condition, brings $390.

Also, keep an eye out for Fisher-Price "Little People" from the 1980s or earlier. In excellent condition, they can bring $2 each...wooden ones $5 or more. You sometimes find bags containing dozens of them at garage sales for $1 or so.

• **Modern Swedish glass.** Glass from Swedish glassworks Kosta and Orrefors (both now part of Orrefors Kosta Boda) has quietly been increasing in value of late. It typically is contemporary in style—whether it is a bowl or an art piece—and much heavier than other glass.

Look closely at the bottom of any stylish, well-made glass item you discover in garage sales—these makers usually etch their names into their products but generally in extremely tiny, easy-to-miss print.

Example: A rare five-inch-by-eight-inch sculpture of a head by Kosta sells for $5,625 to a serious collector.

• **Decorative garden items.** Bird feeders, birdhouses, fountains and iron garden sets have become increasingly more valuable.

Example: A vintage set of two chairs with a cat design on the back brings $4,000.

Helpful: People who have garage sales sometimes forget to include yard items—they just stock their sale with stuff from their attics and basements. Take a peek into the backyard. If you see a nice garden item, ask if it's for sale, too.

12

Richer Retirement

7 Fun Jobs for Retirees

You may have retired, but you still can get a job—and have fun doing that job! *Here are seven options to consider...*

• **National Park Service employees** get paid to work in spectacular natural or historical settings. They work at the gift shops and entrance gates, give talks to guests, maintain trails and perform all the other tasks that keep the National Park system running. These jobs tend to be seasonal—don't expect many openings until spring. Age is not an issue. More than one-third of National Park employees are over age 50. Salaries typically are between $12 and $15 an hour,* sometimes higher. Lodging might be provided as well.

To learn more: Visit the National Park Service website (*NPS.gov*) or *USAJobs.gov* to find openings. Private website *CoolWorks.com* lists

National Park job openings, too (select "National Park Jobs" from the "Find a Job" menu).

• **English language teachers** are in heavy demand in Asia and elsewhere. It is a great opportunity to get paid to live abroad. Some of these positions pay only travel expenses, lodging and a small stipend, but others pay $50,000 a year or more. A one-year commitment often is required. Passing a certificate program on teaching English as a second language can improve your odds of landing good jobs in this field, but it's not required.

To learn more: Visit the sites of Teach English as a Foreign Language (*TEFL.net*) or Transitions Abroad (*TransitionsAbroad.com*).

• **Adjunct professors** share their expertise while working in an intellectually stimulating environment. Impressive academic credentials usually are required to land an adjunct

---

Nancy Collamer, a career coach in Old Greenwich, Connecticut. She is author of *Second-Act Careers: 50+ Ways to Profit from Your Passions During Semi-Retirement* (Ten Speed) and founder of *MyLifeStyleCareer.com*.

*Rates and prices subject to change.

professor position at a prestigious college—but at junior colleges, community colleges and technical colleges, these jobs are within reach of many retirees. If you had a successful career in marketing, for example, a local community college might hire you to teach a marketing course. Adjunct professors typically earn a few thousand dollars per course taught at four-year colleges but often just $1,000 to $2,000 per course at two-year colleges.

To learn more: Visit the websites of two-year and technical colleges in your region to see if they are looking for an instructor in your area of expertise.

• **Caretakers** take care of homes or other properties while their owners are away. Retirees are in particular demand as caretakers because property owners consider them mature and responsible. Often all a caretaker has to do is live in the property and care for it as any resident would—having someone there reduces the odds of break-ins or that a major maintenance issue will go unnoticed.

Caretaking doesn't tend to pay very much—sometimes nothing at all—but it can be a great way to reduce retirement travel costs by staying in interesting properties in interesting locations with no out-of-pocket housing costs. (Income should be provided if the caretaker is asked to perform significant maintenance or groundskeeping.)

To learn more: Subscribe to *The Caretaking Gazette*, which lists caretaking opportunities worldwide ($29.95/year, *Caretaker.org*).

• **Inn sitters** take care of inns and bed-and-breakfasts while their owners are away. Duties might include handling guest check-ins and checkouts, cooking breakfast and cleaning up rooms. Compensation varies greatly depending on the inn sitter's level of experience and other factors, but experienced inn sitters or inn-sitting couples often earn $100 to $200 a day plus lodging and perhaps travel expenses.

To learn more: Ask innkeepers and B&B owners whether they ever hire inn sitters. The website of the Interim Innkeepers Network provides some additional details (*InterimInnkeepers.net*).

• **Stadium ushers** help fans find their seats on game days. The job doesn't pay much—often little more than minimum wage—but it's a way to get paid to attend sporting events. Usher jobs can be difficult to land with top teams, but the odds can be better at minor league stadiums or at baseball spring-training facilities in Florida and Arizona.

To learn more: Visit the websites of local teams and stadiums to find openings, or call the team offices.

• **Museum docents** serve as guides, helping visitors to understand the museum exhibits. Docent jobs typically are unpaid, but they can be an enjoyable opportunity to share your passion for a topic and further your knowledge of it by attending museum lectures, events, exhibitions and training programs for free. (Some museums offer extensive training programs for their docents.)

To learn more: Call local museums, and ask about their docent or volunteer programs. Or visit a museum's website, and look for a section labeled "Volunteer" or "Docent Program."

DID YOU KNOW THAT...

Motor Homes Cost More Than Many Realize?

The purchase price—an average of $100,000 for a motor coach*—is only the beginning. The purchase is taxable, and there may be annual state and county taxes in addition to the initial sales tax. A service plan may cost 2.5% of the vehicle's value, and insurance will be several thousand dollars a year. Many average only six to eight miles per gallon of gas, so a 20,000-mile cross-country road trip will cost $6,000 to $8,000 in fuel. Day rates for parking can run $20 to $70. And, monthly rates including power, water and sewer hookup can be $850. Finally, if you are not a full-time traveler, you may have to pay $100/month or more for outside storage.

Helpful: Before buying an RV, rent one for a week to get a taste of living in it.

Kiplinger's Retirement Report.

*Prices and rates subject to change.

How a Job Impacts Your Retirement Benefits

Kiplinger's Retirement Report. Kiplinger.com

If you want to return to work after retirement, find out how the job will affect your retirement benefits. Social Security is not reduced if you are past "full" retirement age. But if you are within the year in which you reach that age, you forfeit $1 of benefits for every $3 you earn above the $41,880 earnings limit up to the month of your birthday…and if you are taking benefits earlier than your full-retirement year, you forfeit $1 for every $2 of earned income over the $15,720 earnings limit. However, at full retirement age, your Social Security benefit will be adjusted upward to take into account the amounts that were withheld.

If you receive annuity or pension payments: They will continue if you go back to work—but you may be able to stop periodic withdrawals from a variable annuity's investment portfolio if you wish. In retirement accounts, you can again contribute to an IRA or a 401(k) if you meet eligibility and age requirements…and you won't have to take required minimum distributions (RMDs) from your employer's 401(k) as long as you work there. Consult a financial adviser. Social Security, annuity and retirement account rules are complex and vary widely.

Daring Strategy to Protect Your Nest Egg

Michael Kitces, CFP, partner and director of research for Pinnacle Advisory Group, a private wealth-management firm in Columbia, Maryland, that oversees more than $1 billion in client assets. *PinnacleAdvisory.com*

Most retirees may have it backward when it comes to making a nest egg last through their retirement.

Here's why: Common wisdom says that to protect your retirement assets you should *slowly scale back* your exposure to stocks throughout your retirement years.

But the truth is, it may be safer and smarter to *slash* your stock holdings as you near retirement or in early retirement, then slowly *increase* the allocation to stocks over time during retirement.

That's the startling conclusion of top financial planner Michael Kitces, CFP, who says this counterintuitive strategy reduces the possibility of running out of money.

We asked Kitces why this approach may be more effective and how our readers could use it in their own retirement planning…

CUSHIONING THE CRASH

Before the 2008 stock market crash, many investors were heavily overweighted in stocks on the eve of their retirement or relatively early in retirement. When the market crash came, many suffered devastating losses.

Fearful of further losses, they became more conservative, selling their stocks at terribly low prices and missing out on much of the enormous five-year rebound. They also tended to cut way back on their spending—scrimping when they probably wished they could have been enjoying their first few years of retirement.

This was more than just bad luck and unfortunate timing. Many prospective retirees were overlooking something very important—how you fare in trying to preserve and extend your money over a typical 30-year or longer retirement is heavily driven by the "sequence" of investment returns you get, especially in the years right before and after you stop working. As a result, strategies with a heavy stock allocation early in retirement may leave you too vulnerable to a stock market crash. Even if there is no dramatic crash, if you retire at the start of a prolonged period of mediocre returns, you may face severe constraints on your spending in your later years.

RETHINKING THE MIX

A recent research study that Wade D. Pfau and I published provides an alternative. We used computer simulations (see next page) to see how various mixes of stocks and bonds that change throughout retirement could help determine how long a retiree's money would last.

217

What we found is that if you maintain a 60% stock/40% bond allocation throughout retirement—the sort of strategy recommended by many advisers—you have a 93% chance of never running out of money. That doesn't sound too bad. If you trim your stocks during retirement as you get older—for instance, cutting 1% per year and finishing at 30%—the situation is the same, also with a 93% chance of success.

However, reversing this pattern—starting with a 30% stock/70% bond split and finishing with a 60% stock/40% bond split—produced a better outcome, a 95% probability of never running out of money. Although this may not seem like a huge difference, it is a very significant one when it comes to helping most people prolong their assets, especially since it involves allocating less to stocks for most of your retirement, including when your portfolio may be largest and most prone to disaster (at the start of your retirement).

WORST-CASE SCENARIOS

In addition, when we looked at some of the worst-case scenarios from the simulations, this "increasing-stock-allocation" portfolio still would produce enough money to last an average of more than two years longer than the traditional "decreasing-stock-allocation" portfolio.

This also may not sound like a monumental difference when you are middle-aged and in good health. But imagine that you are in your late 80s, and you realize that you're almost out of money. It's especially frightening at an advanced age when you have far fewer options for generating income. To put it mildly, in retirement planning, it pays to skew the odds in your favor as much as possible.

Our strategy can be useful even if you are already retired, as long as you might live for another 20 years or more. It also was a superior strategy using a higher initial spending rate (5% instead of 4%) and when the assumed average returns were much lower (3.4% for stocks and 1.5% for bonds).

However, if your spending rises too high relative to your returns, your only choice becomes owning a lot of stocks throughout retirement and praying things go well. (At that point, the only way to reduce risk and prolong retirement is to spend less!)

Why it works: If there is a big stock market crash and/or bear market around the year in which you retire, owning much less in stocks means that you take much less of an immediate hit. In the ensuing years, as you gradually raise your stock allocation, you're essentially loading up on stocks when they're cheap. If, on the other hand, the stock market soars around your retirement year, owning much less in stocks may mean that you don't leave as large of an inheritance, but you'll still be on track to make your money last until age 95.

TO MAKE IT WORK

To make this strategy work, you need to carry it out in the following way…

• **Decrease your stock allocation when you retire (or in the years leading up to retirement).** Our research suggests that you need only about 30% of your stock portfolio in stocks the day you retire (as long as you are ready to gradually increase later).

Note: Many investors are nervous about increasing their bond exposure right now, given the potential for bond values to decline as interest rates rise, as they are likely to do in the next several years. But the key here is that the bonds we used—US Treasuries with maturities from three to 10 years—still aren't nearly as risky as the stock component of the portfolio. Owning less in bonds and more in stocks still is the greater retirement risk. Bond risks can be further managed by using individual bonds in a bond ladder, rather than bond funds, or buying shorter-term bonds (which lose less when rates rise) and waiting to reinvest at higher rates in the future.

• **Upon retirement, start increasing your stock allocation by one percentage point a year.** If you enter retirement with a 30% stock/70% bond portfolio, after the first year, rebalance to 31% stocks/69% bonds…the second year, 32% stocks/68% bonds…and so on.

You also can help manage year-to-year volatility by keeping one year's worth of living expenses in cash, perhaps in a high-yield online savings account, and using money from whichever investment has fared best to replenish it.

218

You may want to reassess your need for an increasing-stock-allocation strategy once you reach what you estimate to be the latter half of your retirement. If your portfolio is much larger than you expected at this point, you can do one of the following—decide to become more conservative and dial back on stocks...continue increasing your stock allocation annually but start withdrawing more each year...or plan on leaving a bigger inheritance for your heirs.

Important: No retirement strategy is foolproof. Retirement strategies of all sorts still are subject to the risk that investment returns in the future are even worse than any disasters we have ever seen in history, so there always is a possibility that a few further adjustments will be necessary. If one of those true economic disaster scenarios unfolds, you can either tighten your belt and draw down less annually for a period of time, especially in down years for the stock market...or try to further diversify your portfolio, for instance, with foreign and small-cap stocks.

HOW THE RETIREMENT STUDY WAS CONDUCTED

Here's how financial planner Michael Kitces describes his groundbreaking retirement investment study...

To do our analysis, we started by using two simple asset classes—large-capitalization stocks (the kind of big companies found in the Standard & Poor's 500 stock index) and intermediate-term US Treasuries that mature in three to 10 years. We tested a number of situations, including average returns consistent with history and lower-return environments where stocks alone or both stocks and bonds are less rewarding.

We ran these criteria through computer simulations to consider thousands of possible market-performance scenarios for a 30-year period, allowing us to evaluate the risk to a retirement plan and the implications of good and bad markets and various sequences of returns. We assumed that retirees would start out spending either 4% or 5% of their initial portfolio and would adjust that dollar amount each subsequent year for inflation (so "real" spending remained consistent for life).

Little-Known "Saver's Credit"

The "saver's credit" for lower-income workers can help qualified people reach retirement goals. Using the federal credit, someone who saves $2,000 in their 401(k), IRA, 403(b) or 457 account will get government matching funds of as much as 50 cents on the dollar, up to a maximum of $1,000. The credit must be requested on IRS Form 8880, *Credit for Qualified Retirement Savings Contributions.*

To be eligible for 2015, single filers must have income of no higher than $30,500...heads of household, no more than $45,750...married filing jointly, no more than $61,000. Full-time students are not eligible for the credit.

What to do: Visit *IRS.gov*, and search for the form by number.

Clark Howard's Living Large for the Long Haul (Avery). *ClarkHoward.com*

Tax Bonus from New Retirement Account

Barbara Weltman, Esq., an attorney in Vero Beach, Florida, author of *J.K. Lasser's 1001 Deductions & Tax Breaks* (Wiley) and publisher of *Big Ideas for Small Business*, a free monthly e-letter. *BarbaraWeltman.com*

You may be able to get a tax bonus for the myRA retirement accounts that President Barack Obama announced in his State of the Union address in January 2014.

The new type of workplace account does not offer an employer-match or up-front tax deductions, but depending on your adjusted gross income (AGI), you may qualify for a saver's tax credit ranging from 10% to 50% of your after-tax contributions to the account. For instance, married couples filing jointly with AGIs up to $36,500 in 2015 may qualify for a 50% credit and those with AGIs up to $61,000 may qualify for a 10% credit.

The only investment option for myRA accounts is based on the federal employee Thrift

Savings Plan Government Securities Investment Fund, which returned 2.31% in 2014. The account balance cannot go down in value, but annual returns are not expected to get much higher.

The government-backed myRA accounts, whose investment gains and withdrawals are tax-free, will be available to you this year if your employer chooses to take part in the initial pilot program.

Employees in households with incomes up to $191,000 (or individuals with incomes up to $129,000) can take part with initial investments as low as $25 and subsequent payroll deductions as low as $5. You can contribute up to $5,500 this year ($6,500 if you are age 50 or older) in all your IRAs, including a myRA account.

You can save up to $15,000 in a myRA for a maximum of 30 years before you must roll the account over to a Roth IRA.

Beware of Promises of "Free" IRA Accounts

The Financial Industry Regulatory Authority (FINRA) recently warned brokerage firms to stop using misleading language in advertising for their retirement accounts.

Example: E*Trade has a "No Annual Fee" IRA.

While these offers may save you a $25 maintenance fee, your account still is subject to charges that can add up to thousands of dollars.

Allan S. Roth, CFP, CPA, president of Wealth Logic, a financial advisory firm overseeing more than $1 billion in assets, Colorado Springs. He is author of *How a Second Grader Beats Wall Street* (Wiley). *DaretoBeDull.com*

State Tax Treatment of IRAs Varies Widely

Withdrawals from traditional IRAs and other tax-deferred retirement accounts generally are taxable at the state level but are not taxed by these seven states that do not have income tax—Alaska, Florida, Nevada, South Dakota, Texas, Washington State and Wyoming. Some other states exempt at least a portion of the withdrawals from tax—but in some of those, you must be above a specified age to receive the exemption. The US tax code allows taxpayers to deduct IRA contributions up to a certain amount, but some states do not allow that deduction on state returns. Rules vary widely and change frequently.

What to do: Consult a knowledgeable accountant or financial planner.

Roundup of experts in IRA taxation reported at *MarketWatch.com.*

IRA Beneficiary Mistakes to Avoid

Forgetting to update the beneficiary form after a major life event, such as a divorce or remarriage—your IRA could go to someone with whom you no longer have a relationship...naming your estate as beneficiary, either on purpose or by failing to choose a beneficiary—this can trigger unfavorable tax consequences and may make your IRA subject to creditors after your death...naming a child who is not good with money as beneficiary—ask the custodian (the financial institution that holds the assets of the IRA) whether it offers a restrictive beneficiary endorsement that gives beneficiaries earnings each year, but not principal...and forgetting to name a guardian when leaving the IRA to an underage child—a court then will name a guardian, who could be an estranged spouse or someone else you would not choose.

Rules governing IRA beneficiaries are complicated—consult a knowledgeable financial adviser.

Roundup of experts on IRAs, reported at *Bankrate. com.*

Don't Forget Social Security

Consider counting Social Security as an asset category when deciding how to plan for retirement. Social Security benefits are, in effect, fixed-income investments. You can estimate how long you will live and how much Social Security you will collect during that time, then include the amount in your asset allocation. This will have the effect of boosting your allocation to stocks.

Example: If you have a $700,000 investment portfolio and expect to collect $300,000 in Social Security, your total portfolio would be $1 million. If you wanted to put a total of 50% in fixed-income investments, you would invest just $200,000 in bonds—and $500,000 in equities.

Caution: Some financial advisers say that this approach puts too much retirement income at risk. Discuss options with your financial adviser.

Roundup of experts in retirement planning and investing, reported at *MarketWatch.com*.

If You're Disabled: How to Get the Social Security Benefits You Deserve

Ronald A. Marks, a recently retired US administrative law judge who served as chief judge for the Cleveland Social Security Disability Hearing Office and later as judge of the Social Security Disability Appeals Council/Decision Review Board in Falls Church, Virginia. He continues to consult with law firms about Social Security disability issues and is author of *Navigating the Social Security Disability Maze* (Golden Oriole).

Applications for Social Security disability benefits have surged to all-time highs in recent years, driven in part by an increase in claims involving chronic pain and emotional difficulties.

Approvals also have soared, but don't expect it to be easy to get money out of the program if you become disabled. Approximately two-thirds of initial claims are rejected, forcing most applicants to endure a lengthy and complex multilevel appeals process.

What you need to know if you or your loved one makes a Social Security disability claim…

ELIGIBILITY

To determine whether your major health problem qualifies for Social Security disability benefits, go to *SSA.gov,* then search for "Listing of Impairments," which provides details about qualifying conditions. You might have to consult with your doctor to determine if your disability meets the criteria.

You generally will be eligible only if you have a health problem that is expected to prevent you from working in your current line of work (or any other line of work that you have been in over the past 15 years) for at least one year…and/or you have a terminal condition. There's no such thing as a partial disability benefit—if you're fit enough to work part-time, your application will be refused. Do not apply while you still are working with the intention of quitting if your application is approved—if you're working, your application will be denied.

Your skill set and age are factors as well. Your application will be denied if your work history suggests that you have the skills to perform a less physically demanding job that your disability does not prevent you from doing. (Applicants over age 50 are less likely than those under age 50 to be required to seek employment in a new profession that still is within their abilities.)

ESTABLISHING YOUR DISABILITY

If your disability is something like chronic pain that is difficult to prove, the judge who rules on your application will be evaluating not just your medical records but also your credibility. *To be seen as credible…*

•**Provide consistent answers.** You will be asked the same questions time and again throughout this process. How far can you walk without pain? How much can you lift?

How often does the pain occur? The more consistent your answers, the more you will be believed.

•**Provide answers consistent with information in government databases.** Do not claim that you haven't been able to drive for months if you just registered a new vehicle. Don't claim that you haven't been able to walk more than a few steps without pain for months if you recently renewed a hunting license.

•**Admit to some abilities.** Applicants who claim that they can't make a move without agonizing pain tend to be viewed with greater skepticism than those who concede that they still can do some things and/or that the pain is worse some days than others.

•**Encourage your doctors to include your description of your pain and limitations in your medical file before you apply for benefits.** Doctors don't always write such things in their notes—but they usually will if the patient explains that it could help him/her make a disability claim.

•**Watch for back and leg pain traps during consulting exams.** If the judge asks you to see a doctor other than your own to confirm your back or leg pain, expect this doctor to watch you with a very critical eye—including before and after the exam.

Example: The doctor (or a nurse) might observe you climbing up onto the examining table before the exam or getting into your car after the exam and note if your movements don't seem as restricted as you claim.

HIRE A REPRESENTATIVE

You can hire a representative to help you with your Social Security disability claim. This might be an attorney specializing in Social Security disability or a nonattorney Social Security disability advocate. Either is fine—experience with the Social Security disability system is what matters most, not a law degree.

Your local SSA office might be able to provide a list of representatives in your area or point you to a local organization that can. Otherwise, search on the web for the name of your state or city, plus the terms "Social Security," "disability" and "representative."

It's probably worth hiring a representative at the start of the application process if your disability is something difficult to prove such as chronic pain or emotional issues. If your disability is obvious to anyone who has access to your medical records, it might be worth initially working without a representative to avoid paying a fee. You still can hire a representative later if your initial application and first appeal are denied.

Choose someone who at a minimum has handled several dozen cases over multiple years. Also, a qualified, experienced representative should have one or more paralegals or assistants.

By law, representatives can charge only $6,000 or 25% of the retroactive benefits you receive (that is, 25% of the initial benefits check covering the months from the onset of your disability until your benefits are approved), whichever is less. You should not be asked to pay this fee in advance, nor should you have to pay if your application is denied.

Ask the representative about expenses, too. They shouldn't amount to more than a few hundred dollars. The only significant expense should be the acquisition of your medical records—don't work with a representative who passes along the cost of basic office expenses or paralegal help.

More from Ronald A. Marks...

How to Apply (and Appeal)

There are two separate Social Security disability programs...

•**Social Security Disability Income (SSDI)** benefits are calculated much like Social Security retirement benefits—the size of your monthly check is based on your earnings history. The average monthly benefit is $1,165 in 2015. Spouses, ex-spouses, widows and/or minor children can qualify as well. The benefits are automatically converted to retirement benefits when you reach "full" retirement age.

•**Supplemental Security Income (SSI)** benefits are more like welfare. This program is for disabled people who have limited work histories and very limited assets—less than $2,000 ($3,000 for married couples) excluding a home, car and a few other assets. Someone can qualify for both SSDI and SSI benefits at the same time, but the SSDI income will count as income in SSI calculations, so this is likely only if the SSDI benefits are quite low. The current SSI benefit is $733 per month.

How to apply for disability benefits: In person often is the best option, particularly if your disability will be apparent to the Social Security employee with whom you meet.

Phone usually is not the best option to apply for benefits, although calling the Social Security Administration (SSA) at 800-772-1213 can make sense if you have a serious health problem but still are trying to work. Explain your situation, and say that you would like to learn more about Social Security disability in case you decide to apply later. The employee you speak with should complete a form about your call. If you later apply for benefits, having this in your file will help you establish that you've been struggling with the health problem for some time.

Online applications are best avoided. The judge who rules on your application might conclude that your ability to fill out a form online means that you're healthy enough to do "sedentary work," which requires mainly sitting in a chair and using a computer—especially if you also have an active account on Facebook or some other significant Internet presence. If you're younger than age 50, the ability to do sedentary work likely will render you ineligible for benefits. If you're age 50 or older, the ability to do sedentary work likely will render you ineligible for benefits if you have done sedentary work before or have the education and training to do it.

How to appeal if your initial application is denied: Pay special attention to appeal deadlines mentioned on the denial notice— miss just one, and you might have to begin the whole process again. The denial notice should provide directions about how to appeal...or go to the *SSA.gov* website, then search "Appeal Our Recent Medical Decision" for instructions.

Retirement Assets Can Count for Mortgages

Retirees on fixed incomes sometimes have trouble refinancing or getting a new mortgage because they cannot show enough work-related income to repay the loan. But Freddie Mac—the government-sponsored entity that guarantees mortgages—now lets lenders take retirement account assets into consideration when retirees seek to take out a mortgage or refinance. IRAs, 401(k)s, lump-sum distributions and annuities all may be considered. The assets to be used for the mortgage or refinance cannot be subject to an early-withdrawal penalty or be used for current income.

What to do: Ask several different lenders whether they are using these new guidelines. Any of the 2,000 lenders that sell mortgages to Freddie Mac can make the option available. Ask your financial adviser for more information.

Roundup of experts in mortgage financing, reported at *Kiplinger.com*.

Discounts for Grown-Ups: Start Saving at Age 55

David Smidt, founder and president, *SeniorDiscounts.com*, a website based in Albuquerque, New Mexico, that tracks discounts available to people age 50 and older.

It's no secret that some businesses, museums, parks and zoos offer discounts to seniors. But many shoppers are surprised to discover that they don't necessarily need to be "senior citizens" to qualify—some of these discounts are available to people who are as young as 55.

The wide range of businesses offering senior discounts may come as a surprise, too. In addition to getting discounts at restaurants and retailers, you might get a discount on a round of golf, a plumber's services or even a highway toll. But in most cases, you need to know to ask for senior discounts—few businesses offer them unless they're specifically requested by the customer.

Opportunities to save...*

RETAIL STORES

Among the senior discounts available at retail stores...

•**Ace Hardware.** Many locations offer a 10% senior discount every day.

Age requirement: 60.

•**Dressbarn.** This budget-minded women's wear chain offers senior discounts one day each week at most locations. Details vary by location, but the typical offer is a 10% discount on either Tuesdays or Wednesdays. Ask at your local Dressbarn for details.

Age requirement: Varies by location, but sometimes as young as 55.

•**Goodwill.** Goodwill is a nonprofit organization that sells mostly secondhand apparel, furniture, housewares, books and other merchandise for very reasonable prices. Most locations offer a 10%-to-20% senior discount on certain days of the week. Ask for details at your local Goodwill.

Age requirement: Varies by location, but often 55.

•**Hallmark.** Most locations offer a 10% senior discount on regularly priced merchandise. At some locations, this discount is available only one day each week.

Age requirement: Varies by location, but often 55.

•**Kohl's.** The department store chain offers seniors a 15% discount on non-sale merchandise every Wednesday.

Age requirement: 55.

RESTAURANTS

Senior discounts are fairly common at mom-and-pop diners and family-style restaurants. Many fast-food chains including Burger King,

*Always confirm senior discount terms before making a purchase. These discounts might not be available on all merchandise or services. In some cases, they cannot be combined with other discounts or coupons. Other restrictions might apply as well, and discount terms might change without warning and vary by store.

Chick-fil-A, Church's Chicken, Dairy Queen, Mrs. Fields Cookies, Subway, TCBY and Wendy's offer seniors discounts or specials, too—often either 10% off or a bargain-priced beverage. The fast-food senior discounts tend to vary by location within each chain, so don't assume that the discount you get at one Burger King or Subway will be the same at the one down the road.

Other senior discounts available at restaurant chains...

•**International House of Pancakes (IHOP).** Many locations offer 10% senior discounts and/or special senior menus featuring discounted prices and smaller portions. Some locations of IHOP also offer half-price dinners for seniors one night each week.

Age requirement: Varies, but sometimes as young as 55.

•**Dunkin' Donuts.** Many locations offer seniors reduced prices on coffee and other types of beverages. And some offer a free donut or 10% off the entire purchase.

Age requirement: Varies by location, but sometimes as young as 55.

•**Elephant Bar Restaurants.** Sign up for the Senior Explorer VIP Card, which provides 20% off future food purchases at this midpriced American and Asian chain. There are numerous restrictions, however—beverages are not included in the discount, nor are meals for dining partners under age 60, specials or meals on certain holidays.

Age requirement: 60.

•**El Pollo Loco.** This chain specializing in grilled chicken and Mexican entrées offers a 10% senior discount.

Age requirement: Varies by location, but often 55.

ENTERTAINMENT

Seniors sometimes qualify for discounts on popular pastimes, including the following...

•**Golfing.** Many public and private golf courses provide senior discounts. These discounts occasionally are restricted to weekday hours when most nonretirees are working. Savings can be as much as 20% to 50%. Call courses in your area for details.

• **Skiing.** Ski slopes often offer senior discounts on lift tickets and season passes, typically starting at age 60 or 65, but the savings might increase with age. By age 70 or 80, you might be able to ski virtually for free.

Example: At Killington in Vermont, skiers age 65 and older can save $400 on an unlimited season pass. They can save $14 on a one-day lift ticket. Skiers age 80 and older can ski all season for just $59. *Killington.com*

UNEXPECTED SAVINGS

• **New Jersey E-ZPass.** Drivers age 65 and older who sign up for a New Jersey E-ZPass account can fill out a special form to receive discounts on certain New Jersey highway and Delaware River crossing tolls. You don't have to be a New Jersey resident to sign up for a New Jersey E-ZPass. The discount often is 10% and is restricted to off-peak hours. For details, visit *EZPassNJ.com*, select "E-ZPass Information," then "Plan Descriptions." Scroll down to the "Senior Citizens Discount Plan" section.

• **Pet-adoption organizations and veterinarians.** Many municipal and private pet-adoption facilities provide discounted or free spaying or neutering for pets adopted by seniors. Some veterinarians offer senior discounts as well—that is, discounts for older pet owners, not for older pets. Call local vets' offices.

• **Plumbers, heating and air-conditioning contractors and landscapers.** An increasing number of local home-care professionals have begun offering senior discounts.

Check your local Yellow Pages in search of ads mentioning senior discounts. Or enter the type of service provider you require, your city or region, and the phrase "senior discount" into an online search engine to see what comes up.

EASY TO DO...

Retire on $30,000 a Year in These Great Places

Daytona/Deltona/Ormond Beach, Florida, has a median home price of $108,900* and easy access to outdoor activities. Pocatello, Idaho, has a median price of $127,500 and offers skiing, hiking, biking, horseback riding and water sports. Bangor, Maine, has a median price of $110,400, with plenty of hiking trails and water activities. Greenville, South Carolina, has a median price of $127,600 and the cultural attractions of a city. Grand Rapids, Michigan, has a median price of $114,200 and offers music, art and a chance to watch the Grand Rapids Griffins hockey team.

Gabrielle Redford, editorial project manager, AARP, which asked experts to identify the best areas for retirement on $30,000 a year based on property taxes and lifestyle factors, published in *AARP The Magazine*.

*Prices subject to change.

Worst States for Retirement

Worst states for retirement based on tax burden (income, sales, property and other taxes), crime rates, access to medical care and cost of living... *Oregon* ranked lowest on the list due to a higher-than-average crime rate, high state and local taxes, high cost of living and a cold average annual temperature. *Alaska* was next worst on the list. It is the coldest state in the US and has very high living costs. *Washington* has a high rate of crime and high living costs, a low average temperature and a high tax burden, even though it does not levy an income tax. *California* has one of the nation's highest costs of living and a very high tax burden. *Wisconsin* has higher-than-average living costs and taxes and low average temperatures. *Maine* has a high cost of living, some of the nation's highest state and local taxes and low temperatures.

Bankrate.com

Planned Multigenerational Communities

Planned multigenerational communities give special attention to residents 55 and older but are not age-restricted—so parents can live near adult children or so aging baby boomers, who are notorious for keeping a youthful perspective on life, can be close to younger people.

Example: One planned community in Seattle includes an independent and assisted-living facility that shares the courtyard and amenities with non–age-restricted apartments.

Developments of this type are likely to increase as baby boomers continue to age.

Roundup of experts in housing, reported at *Market Watch.com.*

Before You Sign That Retirement-Community Contract...

Bradley J. Frigon, JD, president-elect of the National Academy of Elder Law Attorneys. He practices law in Englewood, Colorado, and is an adjunct professor of law at Stetson University. *BJFLaw.com*

Living in a retirement community typically costs thousands of dollars per month and potentially hundreds of thousands of dollars in up-front entrance fees as well.

But what, precisely, do you get for all that money? And will you or your heirs get the entrance fee back if you pass away, change your mind or require specialized care that the complex can't provide?

The answers depend on terms buried deep in the contract you sign. Unfortunately, few people bother to read their retirement-community contracts closely. Hire an elder-law attorney to review the contract before signing, or at the very least, ask a retirement-community representative to point you toward the

sections of the contract that clarify key issues, including...

•**Are entrance fees refundable? And under what circumstances?** For-profit retirement communities traditionally have "fee-for-service" contracts, in which entrance fees are fully refundable upon the resale of the unit. Nonprofit retirement communities are more likely to have "life-care" contracts, in which entrance fees are partially refundable at first but become completely nonrefundable after a few years. This can vary, however, and is sometimes negotiable.

•**Is this a Medicaid-certified facility?** If so, Medicaid will pay for your continued stay should you run through your assets.

•**Which expenses are included in your basic monthly fee (or "daily rate"), and which cost extra?** For example, what nursing and skilled-care expenses are included? What meals, housekeeping services, over-the-counter medicines and health-care products? And what utilities, such as phone or cable-TV?

•**Will your monthly fees increase if your care needs do?** In general, your monthly fees should not increase dramatically if you sign a "life-care" contract (though they probably will increase with inflation). They likely will if you sign a "fee-for-service" contract and later require more extensive care.

Say "No!" to a Nursing Home: Stay Safe and Comfortable at Home

Wendy A. Jordan, a Certified Aging-in-Place Specialist (CAPS), designated by the National Association of Home Builders. Located in Washington, DC, Jordan is the author of numerous books on residential design and remodeling, including *Universal Design for the Home: Great-Looking, Great-Living Design for All Ages, Abilities, and Circumstances* (Quarry). She also writes for various trade and consumer magazines.

Wouldn't you love to stay in your own home as you get older? Well, thanks to a new trend called "aging in place" (AIP), thousands of aging baby boomers and older people are comfortably, economically and safely remaining at home—avoiding the high cost and upheaval of moving to assisted-living facilities or nursing homes.

What's involved: Homes are now being cost-effectively and stylishly modified for individuals living with vision, balance, mobility or other health concerns. Renovations are done so that the space doesn't feel sterile and the home is functional for anyone, regardless of age or health condition. For example, an able-bodied person can be comfortable in the same environment as a spouse in a wheelchair...and children can spend time at their grandparents' home without ever noticing anything "different" about the space.

AIP features include skylights and well-placed task lighting for people with diminished vision...open showers for individuals in wheelchairs...easy-to-turn lever doorknobs and faucets for arthritis sufferers and much more. People need not wait to renovate until they have retired or been diagnosed with a chronic condition—many home owners are proactively retrofitting their living spaces.

Bonus: AIP saves money. The average cost of a private room in a nursing home is currently $6,965 a month or $83,580 a year. Of course renovations cost money as well, but while some are more complicated and costly, many are fairly simple and inexpensive. Plus, making a home more comfortable, functional and safe adds to its resale value, especially when modifications are done stylishly.

Products to check out now...*

•**Better lighting.** Vision inevitably deteriorates with age. Adequate lighting throughout the house helps prevent falls and run-ins with walls, corners and doors. Central ceiling fixtures, wall sconces with translucent shades and skylights are all good choices. Motion-activated lighting is helpful during middle-of-the-night trips to the bathroom. Task lighting in the bathroom, kitchen and reading nooks

*Most of these items are widely available at home-improvement and plumbing-supply stores. For proper installation, consult an occupational therapist or Certified Aging in Place Specialist (CAPS)—architects, designers, contractors and health-care consultants who have special training in modifying homes for older individuals. To find a CAPS in your area, go to *NAHB.org/directory*.

should be directed from the side, versus overhead, to avoid glare. Rocker light switches are easier to use than traditional flip switches, and when positioned 42 to 48 inches above the floor, they are accessible to everyone, including someone in a wheelchair.

•**Easy-to-reach cabinets and drawers.** Vision difficulties, limited range of motion or the constraints of a wheelchair make it extremely difficult to locate and reach items in the back of a typical pantry, cabinet or drawer. Customized shelving and ready-made inserts (these can be cut to fit a drawer) that easily pull out bring items in the deeper parts of cabinets, drawers and pantries within reach with a minimum of bending and lifting. Pop-up shelves work well for heavy items such as kitchen mixers or blenders—a lift mechanism does all the work.

Check: *Rev-A-Shelf.com...ShelfGenie.com.*

•**Accessible sinks.** Wheelchair users need plenty of clearance below sinks (typical sinks might have a vanity or plumbing underneath). They also need sinks that are a minimum of 27 to 29 inches and a maximum of 34 inches off the floor so that faucets are within reach. Since standard counter height is 36 inches, the slightly shorter height often works fine for non–wheelchair users.

Rear-mounted pipes, four-legged consoles and wall-mounted sinks are all good alternatives. There are many stylish sinks that meet these requirements. Faucets installed on the side of the sink enhance accessibility, and lever-style handles offer better grip than knobs (the same goes for doorknobs).

•**Elevated toilets.** At 17 to 19 inches high (a few inches higher than a standard toilet), "comfort height" or "chair height" toilets are often more comfortable for anyone to use, regardless of health condition. For people with painful joints or arthritis, they require less bending at the knee, and wheelchair users find them easier to get on and off of. They come in a range of designs, from utilitarian to trendy, and need not cost more than standard-height models.

•**Grab bars.** Used to maintain balance or offer something to grasp in case of a slip, grab bars have traditionally had an institutional look. But today's grab bars come in beautiful finishes, such as brushed nickel and bronze.

They can be installed next to the toilet and inside and outside the tub and shower area but also in the kitchen, hallways, entryways and other living spaces.

Note: A towel bar is not the same thing as a grab bar—the latter is designed to be weight bearing and must be anchored into blocking (a secure mount). If they are in the right location, your contractor can attach grab bars to wall studs. Otherwise, a contractor can open the wall and install mounts for grab bars.

• **Open showers.** Wheelchair users need a wide entry and turnaround space in the shower. A flat entry promotes safe access for anyone who has balance, vision or mobility concerns. With no raised threshold to avoid overflow, the floor of the shower should be gently angled toward the drain. To guard against slipping, the floor should have a nonskid surface. Honed-finish ceramic tiles and tiles with non-slip coating are good choices. Small tiles (four inches or smaller) are preferred—the extra grout lines also help prevent skids.

An AIP shower needs a bench or seat...and multiple showerheads (an overhead fixture as well as a handheld), ideally with heat-control function to avoid accidental burns. The faucet, handheld showerhead and grab bar should be reachable from the seat. These accessories come in a wide range of prices and styles and don't take up as much room as you would think.

For people who prefer baths, wide, flat tub ledges provide seating for safe transfer into the tub. And faucets can be offset for easier transition in and out of the tub. Another option is a walk-in tub, with a hinged door for easy, safe entry. Walk-in tubs come in a variety of sizes. Prices vary widely.

EASY-TO-DO...
Make Your Bathroom Safer

Highly glazed ceramic floor tile can be slippery. Consider replacing it with slip-resistant tiles or tiles with a surface that mimics natural stone. Also, opt for smaller tiles because smaller tiles mean more grout, and grout is less slippery.

Alternative: Rubber or vinyl flooring.

Also: Install screw-mounted grab bars—suction cups can come away from the wall. Attach to the wall studs, not just drywall. And it's best if the bars run horizontally, not vertically or at an angle, as your hand could slip.

Sheila Barton, LCSW, social worker at Mount Sinai School of Medicine, New York City, writing in *Focus on Healthy Aging.*

Hiring an In-Home Caregiver? What You Must Know

Jullie Gray, LICSW, CMC, principal of Aging Wisdom, a geriatric-care-management company located in Bellevue, Washington. Gray is a certified care manager and licensed independent clinical social worker with three decades of experience working with older adults. Gray served as 2013 president of the nonprofit National Association of Professional Geriatric Care Managers and has been an instructor at the University of Washington's School of Social Work. *AgingWisdom.com*

The vast majority of Americans would rather remain in their homes than move to an assisted-living facility, according to surveys done by AARP. Hiring an in-home caregiver could make it possible to remain at home even after you no longer can live fully independently—but this is a trade-off in challenges compared with a nursing home–type facility. The experience can be pretty horrible, in fact, if you don't take the right steps.

Here's how to choose and manage an in-home caregiver...

ASSESSING YOUR NEEDS

As a first step, it is very worthwhile to have a professional geriatric care manager assess the senior's needs. For example, does the senior mainly need companionship during the day? Housekeeping? Meals prepared and served? Medication doled out? Does he/she need help with activities of daily living, such as toileting, bathing and dressing? Are there health issues that require trained assistance, such as giving injections to a person with diabetes or assistance with physical therapy exercises? Do you need an aide who can drive—on outings, errands and to doctor appointments...and will you provide a car or will you require the use of the aide's car? (The care manager also will be able to recommend caregiver agencies and/or caregivers.)

This assessment usually takes about two hours at $100 to $150 an hour.* The National Association of Professional Geriatric Care Managers (*CareManager.org*) can help you find a care manager in your area. Or ask local senior centers, Area Agency on Aging offices or the senior's doctor if he/she can recommend agencies or care providers.

HIRE THROUGH AN AGENCY

In-home caregivers can be hired directly or through an agency, but agencies are the safer and simpler option.

Hiring in-home help directly might save you a few dollars an hour, but in general, the savings are significant only for people who hire an undocumented immigrant and/or don't pay the required taxes. Doing either of these things could lead to legal problems for both of you. (If you hire someone directly, that person will be your employee, creating insurance and tax obligations—you are required to pay payroll taxes, obtain the worker's liability insurance and file employer tax forms with the state and federal governments.)

Hiring directly also means that you will have to conduct a background check on this person yourself and find a replacement on short notice if he/she is sick, needs time off, quits or is fired. Hiring an undocumented immigrant also makes it virtually impossible to run a full background check on the caregiver. That's a big risk when you consider that this person essentially will be unsupervised in the senior's home.

A reputable agency should handle all of these issues for you.

When you speak with an agency, ask the following...

•**Are you licensed by the state?** Some, though not all, states require licensing—your

*Prices subject to change.

local Area Agency on Aging office should know if yours does.

•**Are you a member of the American Association for Homecare?** Belonging to this professional association suggests a commitment to professionalism (*AAHomeCare.org*).

Also ask about the process for requesting a new caregiver if the first one assigned doesn't work out or is sick. You should be able to do this relatively quickly and easily.

Make sure the senior meets any potential caregivers during the interview process so that he will be more welcoming when you actually make a hire.

MAKING THE CAREGIVING RELATIONSHIP WORK

•**Be very clear with the caregiver about all your expectations.** Explain precisely what you want him or her to do. Are there specific household or personal tasks that should be prioritized? Is social interaction for the senior a priority?

Lack of communication about needs and expectations is a common cause of problems. If you want something done, ask. If you don't like how something is being done, give instructive feedback.

•**Lock up all valuables, or move the valuables to the home of a trusted relative before allowing a caregiver to work in your home.** Secure any checkbooks, credit cards and documents that contain Social Security numbers or other personal data, too, and keep a close eye on accounts and credit reports for any signs of identity theft. These measures are important even if you eventually come to know and trust a caregiver.

•**Plan ahead for backup.** It is best to hire multiple caregivers on a rotating schedule—possibly one for weekdays and one for weekends—when your caregiving needs are truly full-time. Even if you hire a live-in, no one can work 24/7. And even if the caregiver tells you that he wants to work every day to make more money, everyone needs days off for vacation, sick days and doctor visits. It will be easiest on your senior, both physically and emotionally, if his care is consistently provided by caregivers he knows and who are adequately trained in his needs.

• **Visit randomly.** Close friends and relatives of the senior should drop in without warning occasionally when the caregiver is working to make sure that he is doing his job and that the senior is happy and safe in his care.

WHAT WILL THIS COST?

Extensive in-home support is expensive. In-home care costs an average of $18 an hour—around $19 if "personal care" such as help bathing, dressing and/or using the bathroom is required. These hourly rates vary by region and can easily reach $25 or more per hour in high cost-of-living areas. Agencies typically have four-hour minimums per day. Round-the-clock live-in assistance averages around $350 a day, nearly three times the price of the typical assisted-living facility. There might be additional onetime costs associated with remaining in the home as well, such as modifying the house to allow wheelchair access, installing an easy-access bathtub and grab bars throughout the home or adding a bedroom for a live-in caregiver.

9 Things Your Mother's Nursing Home Won't Tell You

Robert Kane, MD, director of the Center on Aging at University of Minnesota, Minneapolis. Dr. Kane holds an endowed chair in the department of long-term care and aging at University of Minnesota School of Public Health, where he previously served as dean. He is author of *The Good Caregiver: A One-of-a-Kind Compassionate Resource for Anyone Caring for an Aging Loved One* (Avery).

You trust your parent's nursing home to take care of him or her. Unfortunately, some homes do not deserve this trust. Nine secrets you need to know about nursing homes—public and private...

1. You would lose your taste for this facility if you visited during mealtime. Mealtimes are when nursing home employees are

under the greatest stress. Some residents have meals served in their rooms, but most eat in a dining room. Try to look in on a meal—if employees are interacting with residents in a friendly and respectful manner, they probably treat residents well all the time.

2. Our nurses aren't really our nurses. When nursing homes can't find enough permanent nurses, they arrange for "agency nurses" to fill the manpower gaps. These agency nurses work for staffing agencies, not the nursing home, and they rarely stay long enough at a home to form a bond with the residents or get to know their needs.

Most facilities use agency nurses from time to time, but it's a bad sign if more than 15% to 20% of a home's manpower is provided by agency nurses. The facility should provide this statistic upon request.

3. Our physical therapy facilities and staff fall well short of our claims. Insist on touring the physical therapy department especially if your parent requires rehab. Does the equipment look modern and extensive? Ask your parent's doctors if any special rehab equipment would be helpful, and confirm that this is present. Also ask whether the nursing home's physical therapists are on staff or on contract—facilities with physical therapists on staff likely have made a greater commitment to rehab services.

4. We have less than four stars in the overall rating. The Medicare system's website includes the Nursing Home Compare database (*Medicare.gov/nursinghomecompare*), which grades every Medicare- or Medicaid-certified nursing home using a star system, with five stars indicating the best. Avoid facilities with an overall rating lower than four stars if you can afford to do so.

5. Our activities schedule is simply for show—the main activity here is sitting and staring. Every nursing home has an "activities schedule" that inevitably lists an impressive array of things for residents to do each day. Look in on one or two of these activities next time you visit your parent. Is the activity really taking place? How many residents are participating? Does it look like they are having fun? Be concerned if the main activity of most residents appears to be clustering around the nurses' station in wheelchairs staring into space or at a TV. (Residents sitting around is perfectly fine—if they are chatting together, playing cards or interacting in some other way.)

6. Trust your nose. Some subpar nursing homes manage to make their facilities *look* presentable for visitors, but getting them to *smell* pleasant is the tougher challenge. Walk down a few corridors where doors to patient rooms are open and take a whiff. A bad facility might reek of urine, feces or large amounts of Lysol.

7. We cannot provide what our residents really desire—privacy. The contentment of nursing home residents is closely correlated with their ability to obtain privacy, according to our research. Unfortunately, many homes provide mostly shared rooms. It doesn't really cost that much more to build nursing homes with private rooms—it's just a matter of adding a few extra walls—but many nursing homes were constructed before the importance of single rooms was widely recognized.

Helpful: If single rooms are not available in your parent's price range, consider how much privacy the facility's shared rooms offer. Some feature sturdy partitions...others just thin curtains or nothing at all between beds.

8. The more you visit, the better the care your parent will receive. Residents whose families visit often typically receive significantly more attentive care from nursing home employees than residents who rarely receive guests. If you live far away, perhaps a friend or relative can visit regularly.

Helpful: Each time you visit, ask a question or two of a staff member. This sends the message that you are paying close attention to your parent's care. But always be polite, and don't let these questions become excessive or frivolous—you want the staff to consider you involved, not annoying.

9. We can kick your parent out at any time. Nursing homes cannot legally expel residents because they've run out of savings and must resort to Medicaid to pay. But nursing homes are allowed to send away residents who have come to require more care than the home can provide. Some disreputable facilities expel residents who run out of money by claiming that their care needs have increased.

If this happens to your parent, you could contact your state's long-term-care ombudsman to make a complaint. (Find your state's ombudsman at the website *LTCOmbudsman. org*.) But even if the ombudsman agrees that the facility cannot kick out your parent, you probably don't want your parent staying in a nursing home that would act this way, assuming that you can afford other options.

More from Robert Kane, MD...

What Your Mother's Hospital Isn't Telling You About Nursing Homes

If your parent requires nursing home care following a hospital stay, there is a good chance that the hospital discharge planner will give you just a few days to choose a nursing home. The longer your parent stays in the hospital, the less profit the hospital makes. (Medicare and health insurance plans typically pay a predetermined fixed amount for the treatment of a particular health problem, with no additional payments for longer-than-average stays.)

What most families don't realize is that they can push back when discharge planners try to push their parents out the door. If you haven't selected a nursing home yet, tell the discharge planner that you require more time and that you will file an appeal with Medicare if he/she doesn't relax the deadline. The threat alone often is enough to make discharge planners back down—they don't like the paperwork hassles associated with appeals. If not, file the appeal. Even if your appeal is rejected, the appeals process will buy you some additional time.

Helpful: The hospital's patient advocate should be able to provide details about how to file this appeal. Or hire a long-term-care case manager who can help with filing the appeal and selecting a nursing home. You will have to pay this case manager a few hundred dollars, but it's money well-spent. Your local Area Agency on Aging might be able to help you find a local case manager.

Don't Be a Victim of Nursing Home Theft

Robyn Grant, director of public policy and advocacy at the National Consumer Voice for Quality Long-Term Care, a nonprofit organization. *TheConsumerVoice.org*

Nursing home residents often entrust a portion of their savings to the facility's care so that the facility can handle their funds like a bank and make purchases on their behalf. Unfortunately, oversight of this money often is lax. A recent study by *USA Today* uncovered more than 1,500 cases of theft from such savings during a three-year period. And that's probably just the tip of the iceberg—most thefts of this type likely go undetected.

To evaluate the risk at a nursing home that you or your loved one is in or is considering, first see if similar thefts have been uncovered there. To do this, visit *Medicare.gov/nursinghomecompare*, select "Download the Nursing Home Compare database" under "Additional Information."

Also, ask a nursing home representative the following questions: "Who manages residents' trust funds?"…"What vetting was done on this employee—was a criminal background check conducted?"…and "Do independent auditors periodically review these trust funds?" Be wary if the nursing home representative's answers seem evasive or insufficient.

When money is deposited with a nursing home, the home is required to provide a quarterly statement listing all transactions. Scan all purchases and withdrawals listed on this statement, then request receipts for any that seem questionable. Confirm that the account is earning interest, as required.

Occasionally request an account statement between the quarterly statements—the nursing home must supply these upon request. Unexpected statement requests send the message that someone is paying attention to the account, a strong deterrent to theft.

Speak with a nursing home administrator about questions or concerns you have after reading account statements. Consider moving the money to a bank account if you are not 100% confident in the home's management of these assets. If you suspect that money has been misused, contact your state's long-term-care ombudsman, the state survey agency, the Medicare Fraud Control unit of your state's Attorney General's office and/or the police.

DID YOU KNOW THAT...

Most Americans Don't Want to Live Past 100?

Of the people recently surveyed, 69% said that they want to live to between the ages of 70 and 100, with the ideal age cited as 90. More than half of those surveyed would not want medical treatment that would extend their lives to 120 years. The current US average life span is 78.7 years.

Survey of 2,012 adults by Pew Research Center, Religion & Public Life Project, Washington, DC.

13

Happy Travels

How Not to Get Sick on a Cruise (A Stomach Virus Is the Least of Your Worries)

Norovirus outbreaks on cruise ships are sure to receive media attention, but passengers' odds of contracting this unpleasant gastrointestinal ailment actually are very low. Only a few thousand of the roughly 10 million cruise passengers who depart from US ports each year catch it, according to data compiled by the Centers for Disease Control's Vessel Sanitation Program. In fact, we're no more likely to catch Norovirus on a cruise ship than in any other crowded location—we just hear about cruise ship outbreaks most often because cruise lines are required to report them.

With all the attention paid to the Norovirus, other more serious and more common cruise health issues often are ignored. *To stay healthy on a cruise...*

•**Bring copies of key medical records.** Large cruise ships generally have high-quality doctors and well-equipped medical facilities. What they might not have is fast access to your medical records in an emergency (although the ability of cruise ship doctors to obtain digital copies of medical records from sea is improving).

Self-defense: Bring copies of key medical records with you onto the ship. This includes copies of prescriptions for medications that you currently are taking, paperwork related to recent or ongoing medical conditions, your doctor's contact information and—if you've had any heart problems—a copy of your most

James Windeck, MD, a retired physician who formerly worked as a cruise ship doctor for the Royal Caribbean cruise line. He also is a frequent cruise passenger and author of *Cruise Ship Doctor* (Amazon Digital Services).

recent electrocardiogram (EKG). Be sure a travel companion knows where this information is.

Also, be sure to bring sufficient quantities of any prescription and over-the-counter medications you currently use—more than you think you'll need. The ship's pharmacy might have these in stock, but it probably won't accept Medicare or health insurance in payment, and its prices likely will be several times what you would pay onshore.

•**Control your eating and drinking.** Overconsumption of food and alcohol is extremely common on cruises, and it can lead to gastrointestinal distress or worse—binge eating and drinking have been linked to increased risk for heart attack.

•**Choose a large ship if you're prone to seasickness (or if you're not certain whether you're prone to seasickness).** Ships with passenger capacities of roughly 3,000 or more are so massive that you would barely feel them moving even in a big storm, greatly reducing the risk for seasickness. Larger ships also tend to have more extensive medical facilities.

•**Purchase travel health insurance that will cover emergency evacuation if your cruise leaves US waters.** This is particularly important if your ship calls at ports in parts of the world where the medical care is not as good as in the US. Websites *SquareMouth. com* and *InsureMyTrip.com* can help you find and compare these policies.

RISKS ON SHORE

Significant portions of the typical cruise vacation take place off the ship—and that's where many cruise health risks can be found…

•**Don't rent a motor scooter unless you have extensive experience riding on them.** Scooter rentals are common in many cruise ship ports, but scooters are dangerous for novices, particularly in parts of the world where road conditions are poor and traffic rules lax. Of course, you should always wear a helmet.

•**Be picky about restaurants.** When cruise ship passengers get food poisoning, it's usually because of something they ate onshore, not aboard ship. Many restaurants and roadside food stands in common cruise destinations such as the Caribbean pay insufficient attention to cleanliness and food safety.

Lean toward restaurants where you can walk into the kitchen to confirm that the staff is wearing gloves—even better if you see them washing their hands—an indication that the restaurant takes food safety seriously. Drink only bottled or canned beverages, and make sure that the cap still is on the bottle when it arrives at your table.

•**If you're flying to the cruise departure point, be sure to move around the plane.** Remaining in one's seat for the duration of a long airline flight significantly increases the risk for blood clots. Such clots can be fatal if they reach the lungs—particularly if this happens aboard a cruise ship, where medical care is less extensive than in a hospital. Simply strolling around the aircraft's cabin every few hours greatly reduces this risk.

Hidden Costs of a Cruise

Roundup of experts on cruise costs, reported at *AARP.org*.

B everages usually cost extra on cruises, and you are not allowed to bring your own alcohol—but you usually can take soda and bottled water aboard. An unlimited-drinks package could save you money.

The gratuities are added automatically onboard—usually $10 to $12 per day per passenger.* Bar bills often have 15% added. You can adjust the tip amount up or down at the purser's desk.

Shore excursions almost always cost more when you set them up on the ship than when booked through local operators.

Gourmet dining and treats can cost you a lot more than standard offerings—there may even be additional charges for name-brand ice cream and specialty coffee drinks.

Spas and fitness classes can be expensive onboard—a $22 pedicure at home can cost

*Prices and rates subject to change.

$70 on the boat ($48 more!), $119 for a massage, $10 to $15 for a fitness class.

What to do: Ask in advance about extra charges, and budget for the ones you are willing to pay for.

Cruise Complaints

Nearly one in five cruise passengers experiences at least one problem on his/her cruise, a recent report says. The problems were mostly related to customer service, the stateroom, food, and the quality of embarkation and debarkation. The lowest-ranking cruise lines in the survey were Carnival and Norwegian. The highest-ranked line in the survey by far was Disney, which performed especially well in the entertainment and food categories, trailed by Royal Caribbean and Holland America. For more on the *2013 Cruise Line Satisfaction Report,* go to *JDPower.com* and type "cruise" in the search box.

J.D. Power *2013 Cruise Line Satisfaction Report,* based on responses from 3,003 customers who traveled on a cruise line.

VIP Treatment at Universal Studios

You don't have to be a celebrity to be a VIP at Universal Studios in California. Purchase Universal's VIP ticket for $299 per person per day,* and skip to the head of any line in the park...enjoy valet parking, breakfast in a luxury lounge and a gourmet lunch...and have special access to Universal's back lot. Disney currently has no plans to add VIP tickets—but VIP guides are available starting at $360 an hour for up to 10 people (minimum six hours).

The New York Times. NYTimes.com

*Prices subject to change.

These Cities Have the Tastiest Burgers?

The tastiest burgers are served at Vortex Bar & Grill in Atlanta, according to Zagat's. Rounding out the top 10 are Hopdoddy Burger Bar in Austin, Texas...Linwoods in Owings Mills, Maryland...Mr. Bartley's in Boston...Kuma's Corner in Chicago...Maple & Motor in Dallas/Fort Worth...Crave Real Burgers in Castle Rock, Colorado...Le Tub Saloon in Hollywood, Florida...Hubcap Grill in Houston...and LBS: A Burger Joint in Las Vegas.

Study of burger spots in or near 20 US cities by Zagat's.

What "All-Inclusive" Vacations Do *Not* Include

Robert Firpo-Cappiello, editor in chief of *Budget Travel,* a travel publication based in New York City. *BudgetTravel.com*

If you pay for an all-inclusive resort stay, a cruise or a vacation package, you might assume that everything is included. You might be wrong.

Check details carefully before booking, and ask whether the following cost extra...

•**High-quality liquor and wine.** Resorts and cruise lines often boast that you can drink as much as you like without paying extra. They don't mention that in some cases, only the cheapest or midlevel brands of wine, beer and liquor are included, and you will have to pay per drink if you want better quality. In some cases, all alcoholic drinks cost extra, and only drinks such as juice and soda are included.

•**Upgrades and so-called VIP areas.** Special beaches, pools and other facilities may be set aside only for guests willing to pay extra. If there are multiple eateries on the cruise ship or resort grounds, some of those with the best food might not be included in the all-inclusive price.

- **Resort fees.** Some all-inclusive packages tack on a "resort fee" as high as 16% and that, they say, covers services such as Wi-Fi access, towels and/or housekeeping service—essentially, run-of-the-mill services that you would expect at any hotel.

- **Excursions.** Cruise lines usually offer passengers off-ship activities. Many resorts offer special trips outside the resort grounds, such as zip-lining through a nearby forest or taking a guided bike tour. These extras typically are not included in the price.

- **Spa treatments.** Massages, facials, manicures and other spa services might be supplied by third-party providers, and so they may not be covered by the all-inclusive price that you were charged.

- **Tips.** Sometimes gratuities are included… sometimes employees expect to be tipped… and sometimes a required gratuity of perhaps 15% is tacked onto bills without warning.

When to Use a Travel Agent

Travel agents can be very helpful when you want to arrange a complicated or unique itinerary…you want someone to call if things go wrong during your trip…you are pressed for time when setting up the trip or just want to avoid the overload of complex online information…or you are looking for a customized experience.

Examples: A food-focused trip including private cooking classes overseas…a chance to interact with local families in several places… recommendations of restaurants that tourists rarely know about.

Find a good travel agent by getting referrals from people you know. Another way is to interview several agents about what you want to do and to find out if any of them has the knowledge and connections to arrange the kind of trip you want to take. You also can

ask to speak with previous clients about their experiences.

Roundup of experts in the travel industry, reported at MarketWatch.com.

Little-Known Travel Strategies

Call the airline for seats instead of booking online—phone agents may have access to special deals (there may be a customer service fee). If you search online but don't buy, switch browsers or clear your computer's cookies and cache before going back or you may be shown a higher fare as a returning customer. If you are a frequent-flier member, check the program's site with and without entering your member number to see whether you get different prices. If you like train travel, consider Amtrak's 15-day, $459 go-anywhere deal.*

For hotel rooms, phone hotels directly for the best room rates—do not book online or through a toll-free phone number. If you want to search hotels online, use *Venere.com* and *Booking.com* for the widest choice.

Beware of travel offers on Facebook—many are scams. And when trying to decide where to travel, look at countries not often visited by Americans (Holland, Poland, Sicily, Belgium) and ones where the local currency has fallen in value.

Roundup of experts on travel, reported at MarketWatch.com.

*Price subject to change.

Best Sites for Booking Flights

Pintrips.com compares flights from multiple airline sites and provides up-to-date fares. *RouteHappy.com* scores each route based on the age and type of plane, in-flight entertainment options, legroom, traveler feedback and more.

Also: The app *CheapAir* (free, iOS) uses voice commands to provide travelers with itinerary and flight options.

Travel + Leisure. TravelandLeisure.com

Example: Recently, a flight from Oakland to Phoenix cost $111.22 if bought at least 21 days in advance…but $234.89—or 111% more—when bought within a week of departure.

Savings by buying early: $123.67.

Analysis by Travel Leaders Corporate, travel-management company, Miami, reported in *USA Today*.

Buy Airline Tickets Early?

It doesn't always pay to buy airline tickets early. In one recent study, flights between New York City and Chicago, Boston and Los Angeles cost more when booked 21 days in advance than when booked 14 to 20 days before departure. But those are the exceptions. On 21 of the 25 routes studied, average prices were lowest at least 21 days in advance…higher 14 to 20 days in advance…still higher seven to 13 days in advance…and highest within a week of departure.

DID YOU KNOW THAT…

More Frequent-Flier Seats Are Available?

Frequent-flier seats are becoming more plentiful five to 15 days before departure at certain airlines. In a survey of 25 major airlines, this last-minute approach worked especially well for airlines that generally make frequent-flier redemption most frustrating, including American, Delta and US Airways. These airlines used to hold last-minute seats for late-booking business travelers paying high fares, but businesses are booking cheaper airline seats now.

Jay Sorensen, president of IdeaWorksCompany, a consulting firm that specializes in loyalty marketing and frequent-flier programs, Shorewood, Wisconsin. *IdeaWorksCompany.com*

Don't Pay Extra for Coach Seats

Airlines hold back 30% to 40% of coach seats for elite-level frequent-flier customers or people with special needs—or to raise extra money by charging more for them—(typically ranging from about $39 to $99). Travelers checking in online may find only middle seats or ones available at an extra charge listed as available—even though many seats really remain unassigned.

If you do not want to pay extra: Choose the best available seat when you buy your ticket, and then check back at the airline's website repeatedly. Many so-called preferred seats are opened up to regular customers 24 hours to seven days before departure.

Roundup of frequent travelers and airline spokespeople, reported in *The Wall Street Journal*.

Shrinking Airplane Lavatories

Airlines are shrinking lavatories so that they can add more seats. A new lavatory design on one airline allows the addition of four seats in the coach section. Delta Air Lines is among the first to have the smaller lavatories.

The Wall Street Journal. WSJ.com

Fight Airline Change Fees

George Hobica, founder of *AirfareWatchdog.com*.

Airline change fees have been changing for the worse. Switching flights or canceling reservations now often costs around $200 per ticket*—more for international flights. A friend was recently hit with change fees when a truck accident shut down the highway to the airport, causing her to miss her flight. A helpful agent waived her fees, but such leniency is becoming rare. I don't want you to get stuck with change fees. *Here's what to do now…*

• **Choose your airline carefully.** Book on Southwest Airlines if you think your plans may change—Southwest doesn't impose these fees. Alaska Airlines doesn't either if changes are made 60 or more days before departure. Virgin America waives change fees when tickets are purchased using the premium version of the airline's Visa Signature card.

• **Check the cost of a refundable ticket.** These can be very expensive but not always.

Example: American Airlines offers "Choice Essential" status for an additional $58, which also offers priority boarding and one fee-free checked bag.

• **Know the change-fee loopholes.** Airlines must waive these fees if they make substantial changes to a flight's schedule or itinerary after the ticket is booked or if the customer cancels within 24 hours of booking. (American Airlines instead allows customers to hold seats without payment for 24 hours.) Airlines also generally waive these fees if a member of the traveling party dies and for passengers with frequent-flier elite status traveling on rewards tickets.

*Price subject to change.

TSA PreCheck Speeds Airport Security

The Transportation Security Administration (TSA) PreCheck program charges $85* for a five-year membership to route prescreened travelers to a separate, faster security line. Pre-Check members can bypass some procedures, such as removing shoes. In addition to the fee, the program requires fingerprinting and a background check. *TSA.gov/tsa-precheck*

Money. Money.com

*Price subject to change.

Great New Airline Services!

American Airlines will deliver bags anywhere within a 40-mile radius of the airport within four hours of landing for $29.95 per bag*—in addition to the $25 checked-bag fee. Qantas sells a permanent luggage tag for $29.95, or 6,500 frequent-flier points, that synchronizes bags with boarding-pass information, making check-in faster and losses less likely. Southwest planes offer 19 channels of live TV free for passengers to watch on their own devices. At Korean Air, winter travelers heading for tropical destinations can check their heavy coats free for five days—extra days are $2 each. Spanish airline Vueling guarantees its international passengers a vacant seat beside them if they choose the "Excellence" fare. The upgrade includes preferential boarding and refreshments.

Travel + Leisure. TravelandLeisure.com

*Prices subject to change.

Healthier at the Airport

The goal is to lure more people to airports for connections because airports collect passenger facility charges from airlines when travelers stop over.

Examples: San Francisco International has a medical clinic for vaccinations and treatment of colds and a yoga room...there are half-mile walking paths laid out in Indianapolis, Cleveland, St. Louis and Dallas-Fort Worth. Many airports have added healthier food options as well. Also, many airport hotels allow travelers to take advantage of their fitness centers for a fee. A day pass to the fitness center and spa at the Grand Hyatt within Dallas/Fort Worth Airport is $30.* To see if you can exercise at the airport or close by during your next layover, visit *AirportGym.com.*

The Wall Street Journal. WSJ.com

*Price subject to change.

To Be Safer in Case of a Plane Crash...

To stay safer in the event of a plane crash, sit in an exit row if possible or within one row of an exit so that you can get out easily in an emergency. Or sit in the rear of the plane—seats close to the tail are safest. Keep your seat belt on throughout the flight. During severe turbulence, put your head on the back of the seat in front of you and place your hands on your head to reduce the risk for injury. Buy an extra seat if you are traveling with a child, and bring a child seat approved for air travel for him/her to sit in. Stay alert, especially during takeoff and landing—do not drink alcohol.

Reader's Digest. RD.com

Is That Duct Tape on the Wing?

Air travelers are sometimes startled to see what appears to be duct tape holding their plane's wing together. In truth, duct tape is used only inside the plane and on noncritical components, such as to temporarily secure loose carpeting. If you see what appears to be duct tape on the wing, you're actually looking at something called speed tape, a very heavy-duty aluminum bonding tape used to temporarily patch noncritical external parts until a more permanent fix can be made. Speed tape is designed to withstand extremes of temperature and wind—in fact, it's sometimes called "600-mile-per-hour tape."

The Federal Aviation Administration does restrict how speed tape can and can't be used, and it is never used for anything critical to flight. Usually it's used as a temporary way to cover small scrapes, punctures or other superficial damage or perhaps to secure an external panel that has a weak latch.

Patrick Smith, a first officer with a large US airline who has been flying professionally since 1990. He is author of Cockpit Confidential *(Sourcebooks) and founder of the website* AskthePilot.com.

Zipcar at More Major Airports

The popular urban car-sharing service Zipcar is now available at more than 30 airports in the US and in Toronto. Zipcar lets people who pay membership fees rent a car for as little as a half hour and unlock and drive a rented car without going through a rental office.

More information: *Zipcar.com.*

USA Today. USAToday.com

Beware of Rental Cars with High Mileage

Some rental cars have as much as 50,000 miles, which has led to complaints about problems such as dead batteries and weak shock absorbers.

What to do: Request a vehicle with less than 30,000 miles.

Also: Demand a replacement car if you spot worn-down tire treads…squeaky or ineffective windshield wipers…or brakes that squeal, slip or feel soft and spongy (check the brakes by pressing hard a few times while driving on the lot).

Jeremy Acevedo, an analyst for *Edmunds.com,* an auto-information provider in Santa Monica, California. He formerly worked as an agent and manager for a national rental-car company.

Rental Car Rip-Off: Steep Fees for Road and Bridge Tolls

Rental car companies such as Avis and Hertz are offering automatic toll-paying devices such as E-ZPass and FasTrak. But some companies charge as much as $4.95 per day* even if you don't use the device (that's $34.65 for a week)…and they charge the regular cash rate for all tolls, not the discounted rate that device owners often get.

Self-defense: Decline the device and pay cash.

Christopher Elliott, a consumer advocate specializing in the travel industry. His latest book is *How to Be the World's Smartest Traveler* (National Geographic). Elliott.org

*Price subject to change.

Where to Find Bus and Train Schedules

Searching for buses and trains online is becoming easier, thanks to several new sites. *Wanderu* lets you search among multiple trains and bus companies in the Northeast—it does not sell tickets but provides links to the firms' sites. *Bustripping* will search bus companies throughout the US as well as limited routes in Europe and Canada. You can filter searches by time, price and operator. The site is new and currently is building partnerships. It does not

yet include major carriers such as Greyhound. Other sites are in planning or start-up stages, and existing sites are changing rapidly.

The New York Times. NYTimes.com

Save Hundreds on Vacation Lodging

Pauline Frommer, a nationally syndicated newspaper columnist and radio talk-show host. She is a member of the Frommer guidebook family.

You can save hundreds, perhaps even thousands, of dollars by exchanging homes instead of staying at a hotel.

Example: Seven nights at a hotel costing $150 a night is $1,050. Swapping homes costs almost nothing. *Three tips for a successful swap…*

1. Pay a membership fee. You likely will have more success finding the right exchange if you choose a company that charges a fee. These organizations provide better customer support…their users are more serious about exchanging…and a fee is likely to weed out scammers. Bigger also is better in this field, as the companies with the most members offer the most potential swaps. So look at *HomeExchange.com, LoveHomeSwap.com* and *Intervac-HomeExchange.com.* Fees generally range from about $8 to $20 a month,* based on a yearlong membership.

2. Check the national makeup of the home-exchange company. If you have your heart set on going to, say, Norway, look at the membership statistics of the clubs to find one with a lot of Norwegian members. You even may want to go with a company based in that country. (Do an Internet search of the country name plus "home exchange.")

3. Exchange with people like yourself. If you're a family, trade with another family so that you'll be stepping into a child-friendly home. Or if you're fastidious and you don't want to worry about kids tracking dirt into your home, trade with other child-free swappers.

*Prices subject to change.

Share a Hotel Room to Save Money

The free website *Easynest.com* lets travelers connect with people interested in splitting the cost of a double-occupancy hotel room. People who want to share a room ("guests") can post a message on Easynest explaining where they are headed and when...and then wait for someone who already has booked a hotel in that area (the "host") to contact them through the site. The guest and host negotiate costs and other details directly.

USA Today. USAToday.com

"Standby" Upgrades for Hotel Rooms and Airline Seats on the Rise

These offers for hotel rooms usually are made just after you make a reservation or at check-in. A typical "standby" offer to upgrade to a bigger room at the hotel chains Hilton, Hyatt, InterContinental, Carlson and Fairmont costs an extra $10 to $30 a night,* and the overall price ends up being 25% to 40% less than booking the better room in the first place. Accepting the offer doesn't guarantee that you will get the room—it depends on availability. (You pay the extra only if you do get an upgrade.)

Among the airlines, Delta offers "same-day standby" upgrades, providing space is available and your ticket is eligible, ranging from $50 for flights up to 500 miles and $330 for flights longer than 3,000 miles...Alaska Airlines upgrades cost from $50 to $100 within 24 hours of the flight's departure...and United uses "personalized" pricing based on factors including the passenger's frequent-flier status, seat availability and the date of ticket purchase.

The New York Times. NYTimes.com

*Prices subject to change.

Extra Fees at Hotels

Hotels are creating extra fees just like airlines. Convention, resort and luxury hotels are especially likely to charge travelers extra for amenities, such as use of a business center, in-room safes and parking valets. Before booking a room, ask whether there are additional fees.

*Joe Sharkey, author and columnist for *The New York Times*.*

"Smoke-Free" Hotel Rooms Still Contain Smoke

When a hotel allows smoking anywhere, the smoke gets into all the rooms—in the air and onto surfaces—through ventilation systems and under doors.

To avoid smoke: Stay only in hotels that do not allow smoking at all.

Study of 30 California hotels where smoking is allowed and 10 where it is not by researchers at San Diego State University, published in *Tobacco Control*.

Later Sunday Checkout Times

Later Sunday checkout times are being offered by some hotels as a free benefit for guests—because there are fewer check-ins on Sunday and many guests prefer to sleep late.

Examples: Westin has a free 3 pm Sunday checkout at all its properties…Novotel hotels have free Sunday checkouts as late as 5 pm…and Radisson Blu offers free checkouts as late as 6 pm on any day, depending on room availability.

USA Today. USAToday.com

Better Room Service

To get the best from room service—insist that sauces be put in separate bowls with lids so that they do not leak onto other foods on your plate…ask that ice cream and other chilled desserts be placed in a container of ice…ask if there are specials that are not on the printed menu…say just how you want your food cooked—not only meat, fish and vegetables but also pasta…ask if the tip is included…and before the server leaves your room, be sure you have everything you need—including napkins, salt and pepper, butter, jam, cream, sugar, lemon and ice.

Nancy Dunnan, editor of *TravelSmart. TravelSmart Newsletter.com*

No-Frills Hotel Room Service

Some high-end hotels are delivering meals on paper trays or in brown paper bags—saving the labor costs of cleaning tables, dishes and utensils.

Examples: Public Chicago promises gourmet meals in less than 10 minutes, delivered

in bags hung on the room's doorknob. Hilton Worldwide is testing the brown-bag idea at some Hilton and DoubleTree locations. The Four Seasons in Washington, DC, has a 15-minute express menu—breakfast comes on brown paper trays…lunch and dinner in plastic stackable containers in clear plastic bags.

USA Today. USAToday.com

Borrow Handy Items from Hotels and Airlines

You can borrow iPads, beauty items, games and more from airlines and hotels while you travel. Several airlines, including Southwest, now lend iPads to travelers on select flights. Hyatt hotels let guests borrow humidifiers and personal-grooming items, such as curling irons, robes and more. Candlewood Suites locations lend customers kitchenware, such as blenders and Crock-Pots, as well as board games. Kimpton hotels have a lending program that includes beds and bowls for your pets—and if you do not have a pet but want one, you can borrow a goldfish at some locations. Some hotels near golf courses lend clubs to guests. And individual hotels may have special lending arrangements. Ask what items are available when booking a room or when you arrive.

Roundup of travel executives at *MarketWatch.com*.

Hotel-Guest Satisfaction Is Way Up

Hotel-guest satisfaction is the highest it's been in eight years. There has been a 27-point improvement since 2012—to an industry average of 784 on a 1,000-point scale.

Satisfaction increased in all seven factors studied: Reservations, check-in and checkout, guest room, food and beverages, hotel services, hotel facilities, and costs and fees. The biggest improvements were in reservations, check-in and checkout, and costs and fees.

Top-scoring hotels by category: Luxury—Four Seasons…upper upscale—Kimpton…upscale—Hilton Garden Inn…midscale full service—Holiday Inn…midscale—Drury…economy/budget—Microtel…upper extended stay—Homewood Suites…extended stay—Candlewood Suites.

J.D. Power 2014 North America Hotel Guest Satisfaction Index Study. *JDPower.com*

The Vacation Apartment You're Renting May Be Illegal

The rules for short-term rentals vary from city to city and may be complex.

Examples: Austin, Texas, requires licenses, collects taxes and enforces a limit to the percentage of housing stock that can be used for short-term rentals. San Francisco prohibits renting out any apartment or house for fewer than 30 days. New York City bans rentals for fewer than 30 days in buildings with three or more units unless the person renting out the room is present throughout the stay. Outside the US, cities such as Paris have their own restrictions.

Best: Trust your instinct when renting. If you are asked to pretend to be a relative or not to talk to the doorman, take that as a warning sign.

Travel + Leisure. TravelandLeisure.com

Stupid Travel Mistakes

William McCarthy, former commanding officer of the NYPD Bomb Squad and president of the security consulting company, Threat Research, Inc., Alexandria, Virginia.

It is shocking how stupid we are when we travel. We're not prepared if disaster strikes, whether it's a terrorist attack or a natural disaster. *Here's what we must do…*

•**Rethink your shoes.** Many people wear slip-on shoes—loafers, sandals or even flip-flops—onto planes because these are easy to slip on and off at security checkpoints. But such shoes are likely to fall off if you're forced to run from danger. Lace-up shoes with rubber soles are a wiser choice.

•**Carry a key-chain flashlight.** Carrying a key-chain LED flashlight (*typical cost:* $5*) could be the difference between finding your way out of a darkened building or becoming lost and trapped.

A smartphone's flashlight function is not an adequate substitute, because using this would deplete the phone's battery—a very bad idea in an emergency.

•**Prepare for the possibility that your cell phone could be lost or stolen during an emergency.** Carry a short list of important phone numbers. Numbers worth jotting down include those of close family members, the concierge at your hotel, acquaintances who live in the area you're visiting and the US embassy if you're traveling overseas.

•**Play the disaster game.** While waiting in an airport terminal or a train station, think about what you would do if disaster struck. This game could be a whole lot more rewarding than the Sudoku you might otherwise play on a smartphone.

More helpful travel advice: Carry a single dose of aspirin in case you get chest pain, and in non–English speaking countries, be sure to take along a matchbook from your hotel to show to someone who needs to know where you are staying.

*Price subject to change.

Travel Can Boost Your Sex Life

Couples who took trips together had better relationships and better sex than ones who did not, a recent survey found. Nearly two-thirds of those surveyed said that a weekend getaway is more likely than a present to increase romance. Twenty-eight percent said their sex life got better after they traveled together...and 40% of those said the improvement was permanent.

Survey of 1,100 US adults by Edge Research, Arlington, Virginia, reported in *USA Today*.

Food-Safety Tips When Traveling Outside the US

Wash your hands often and before eating or handling food. Avoid eating uncooked fruits and vegetables—they may not have been washed...or they may have been washed with contaminated water. Eat food that's steaming hot and not left to sit at buffets, markets, etc. Make sure that eggs, meat, fish and shellfish are fully cooked. Avoid unpasteurized dairy products, including cheese and creamy dressings. Drink beverages made with boiled water, such as coffee and tea. Avoid ice cubes, which may have been made with contaminated water. Bring water to a boil for 10 minutes, and then allow it to cool before drinking. Use bottled or boiled water to brush your teeth. Keep your mouth closed in the shower and while swimming. Be sure to pack Imodium A-D tablets.

Mayo Clinic Health Letter. HealthLetter.MayoClinic. com

Better Travel with Food Allergies

If you are allergic to certain foods and travel frequently...

• **Learn how to say "I am allergic" in the language of your destination**—*Je suis allergique* in French...*Soy alérgico* in Spanish...*Ich bin allergisch* in German. (You can download allergen-free dining translation cards for $2.99 at *GlutenFreePassport.com*.)

• **Use the local language to say what you are allergic to.** Dairy, milk, eggs are *aux laitages, au lait, aux œufs* in French...*a los productos lácteos, a la leche, a los huevos* in Spanish...and *milchprodukte, milch, eier* in German.

• **Eat only foods that you recognize as safe.** When in doubt, do not eat it.

• **Order special airline meals in advance.**

• **Bring plenty of snacks that you know you can eat.**

• **Tell restaurants and hotels of your special dietary requirements.**

• **Take along medicine for a food-related emergency.**

GlutenFree Passport, a health-education company that's located in Chicago, London, England, and Manly, Australia.

14

Fun Times

Great Gadgets for Golfers—When You Need a Little Help with Your Game

I f you just love golf but struggle with arthritis, back pain or any other condition that limits your mobility, help is available through a wide variety of nifty golf accessories and adaptive equipment...

GRIPPING AIDS

These make holding the club much easier.

• **Bionic Golf Gloves** are designed with extra padding in the palm and finger joints that can improve grip and require less effort.

Cost: $16.99 to $29.99 each glove.* (877-524-6642, *BionicGloves.com*)

• **Powerglove** has a small strap attached to the glove that loops around the club grip to secure it in your hand and keep it from slipping during the swing.

Cost: $19.95 per glove. (800-836-3760, *Power glove.com*)

• **Oversized grips** make gripping clubs easier and also are very good at absorbing shock when you don't hit the ball. Oversized grips usually are one-sixteenth-inch or one-eighth-inch larger in diameter than a standard grip and cost around $10 per grip. You can find these grips (and have them installed) at your local golf store or pro shop.

• **Quantum Grip** is a grip-and-glove-combination product, which incorporates Velcro material recessed in the golf club grip and a companion golf glove that has mating Velcro material in the palm. This ensures gripping

*Prices subject to change.

Jim Miller, an advocate for older Americans who writes "Savvy Senior," a weekly information column syndicated in more than 400 newspapers nationwide. Based in Norman, Oklahoma, he also offers a free senior news service at *SavvySenior.org*.

245

power and prevents the club from slipping in your hand.

Cost: $19.95 per grip or $139.65 for a set of seven, plus $39.95 per glove. (805-549-0495, *QuantumGrip.com*)

BENDING SUBSTITUTES

A number of innovative gadgets can eliminate the repetitive bending and stooping that golf entails. To find dozens of these, visit *Upright Golf.com* (319-268-0939). *Some of the best…*

• **Upright Putting Pack** includes the Upright Claw, a small, plastic, four-finger gripping tool that screws into the hole on the end of the putter grip…and the Marker Mag, which is a small magnetically treated sticker that adheres to the bottom of your putter head…and a magnetic ball marker that you can rub on the putting green to release the magnetic hold.

Cost: $11.99.

• **Upright Golf Stick** is a modified golf shaft with a plastic tee-and-ball-holder device attached to the end of it that allows you to insert the tee in the ground…place the ball on the tee…and retrieve the tee.

Cost: $44.99.

ERGONOMIC CARTS

Ergonomically designed golf carts can help you transport your golf bag and clubs around the course.

Two options…

• **Bag Boy TriSwivel** is a three-wheel push cart with a 360-degree rotating front wheel for easy maneuverability.

Cost: $250.

Bag Boy also offers a padded cart seat accessory for $50 that attaches to the push-cart wheel base so that you can sit down to take a rest. (800-955-2269, *BagBoyCompany.com*)

• **SoloRider** offers specialized electric carts for people with more severe mobility problems. The carts enable golfers to play golf from a seated or standing-but-supported position. These single-rider golf carts have hand controls and a swivel seat with an electric stand-up mechanism. The carts are lightweight and precisely balanced so that they can be driven right onto tees and greens without damaging

the course. Federal ADA laws require that all publicly owned golf courses allow them.

Cost: $9,450, plus a $500 shipping fee. (800-898-3353, *SoloRider.com*)

Playing Sports Makes You Smarter

Men who played sports exhibited better cognitive performance and longer attention spans than people who were less active in a recent study.

Study from researchers at University of Granada, Spain, published in *PLOS ONE*.

Take Yourself Out to the Ball Game for Less

To save at ball games, search team websites for special promotions, such as $1 hot dogs—the average hot dog price is $4, so a special-promotion night can save a family of four $12 on food. Better yet, bring your own snacks—many ballparks allow this. Also, look for family-pack offers for select games—they may include tickets, food, beverages and souvenirs. Or go to minor-league games, which are inexpensive. Watch for free-ticket promotions—businesses often give tickets away to people who buy a certain product or test-drive a car. Or wait until the last minute, and buy tickets from someone selling them at the stadium—most sellers are legitimate and sell at reduced prices.

Caution: Be sure to know and obey team resale regulations.

Andrea Woroch, consumer money-saving expert. *AndreaWoroch.com*

EASY-TO-DO...

How to Pay Less for Concerts and Ball Games

To pay less for concerts and ball games, wait to buy e-tickets. Prices almost always drop in the days before an event.

Even users of reduced-price Groupon deals might not get the lowest prices—one recent deal at Groupon was for Yankees seats at $22 apiece, but similar seats have sold for as little as $3 on game day.

Baseball fans who buy 30 days in advance can pay an average of 43.3% more...fans who buy 14 days in advance pay an average of 33.5% more.

If you must see a certain event on a specific day or in a specific seating area, pay the going rate. But if you can be flexible and you don't mind limited seat selection, wait until the last minute to buy.

MarketWatch.com

Problems with Paperless Event Tickets

Paperless tickets are becoming increasingly common as a way to prevent scalping. But they can be inconvenient. For example, they are tied to the specific credit card used to buy them, so you must take the card to the event. If you give a ticket as a gift, you may need to escort the recipient to the gate. And if a group buys a block of tickets, they may need to wait outside until everyone arrives. Finally, resale may not be allowed—or if it is, it must be done through the ticket company's website.

Self-defense: Check the fine print when buying paperless tickets to find out the restrictions on them. Some states now are considering banning or restricting the tickets because of consumer complaints.

Kiplinger's Personal Finance. Kiplinger.com

Great TV Series You've Never Heard Of

Alan Sepinwall, TV critic for *HitFix.com* and previously for the *Newark Star-Ledger*. He is author of *The Revolution Was Televised: The Cops, Crooks, Slingers, and Slayers Who Changed TV Drama Forever* (Touchstone).

Hit TV shows such as *Downton Abbey* and original series such as *House of Cards* attract a lot of attention on the Internet-streaming services Netflix Instant and Amazon Prime. But these services, which allow subscribers to view programs on computers, TVs and other devices, also are a great place to find and watch shows that most people missed when they originally aired, as well as shows from Canada and England that never aired widely in the US.

Some wonderful but little-watched shows...

DRAMAS

• **Cracker** is a British crime drama from the mid-1990s starring Robby Coltrane, who would later play the gentle giant Hagrid in the Harry Potter films. Here he is cast as Dr. Eddie Fitzgerald, a brilliant but self-destructive criminal psychologist. Television has given us many dark, tormented lead characters in recent years, but rarely are the roles this well-written and acted. (Amazon Prime)

• **Sleeper Cell** is a thriller about an FBI agent who goes undercover to stop a terrorist attack in Los Angeles. It's tense, exciting and quite thoughtful about the underlying issues. *Sleeper Cell* is somewhat similar to the hit show *24*—only its ratings were nowhere near as strong when it ran on Showtime. (Amazon Prime and Netflix Instant)

• **Terriers** is a crime drama about a recovering alcoholic former police officer who joins forces with his petty-criminal friend to run an unlicensed private eye business. It sounds like a million other shows when you read that description. The difference is that Terriers is wonderfully executed. The actors playing the private eyes—Donal Logue and Michael Raymond-James—have amazing chemistry. The show lasted only one 13-episode season on FX in 2010 before it was canceled, but it is

247

13 episodes of great TV. (Amazon Prime and Netflix Instant)

COMEDIES

• **Slings & Arrows** is a Canadian comedy about the crew of a theater company. The humor is smart and universal, not insidery and self-congratulatory like that of other shows about show business. It aired in Canada from 2003 to 2006. (Amazon Prime)

• **Sports Night** is a comedy/drama set behind the scenes at a sports news program. It ran on ABC from 1998–2000. It was witty, intelligent and even touching at times, yet it never resulted in strong ratings. The quality trailed off a bit in the second season, as creator/writer Aaron Sorkin spread himself a bit thin writing the first season of *The West Wing* at the same time, but season one is definitely worth seeing. (Amazon Prime)

OTHER

• **Firefly** lasted just one season on Fox in 2002–2003, perhaps because it didn't fit comfortably into a single genre. It's essentially a Western set in outer space—and most Western fans are not sci-fi fans. That's a shame, because *Firefly* is a fun, exciting adventure. It was directed by Joss Whedon before he became famous for directing *The Avengers* and starred Nathan Fillion before he became famous for playing the title role in ABC's *Castle*. (Amazon Prime)

Your Playlist Can Change Your Life

Galina Mindlin, MD, PhD, assistant clinical professor of psychiatry at Columbia University and supervising attending physician in the department of psychiatry at St. Luke's Roosevelt Hospital Center. She is clinical/executive director of the Brain Music Therapy Center in New York City and coauthor of *Your Playlist Can Change Your Life* (Sourcebooks). *BrainMusicTreatment.com*

Music can improve our productivity, boost our mood and even help us eat less—but only if we choose our playlist wisely. *Here's how to select music for...*

• **Relaxing.** Don't assume that the slowest songs are best for relaxation—the most relaxing tempo for you will be the one that's in sync with your brain waves.

Keep a list of songs that seem to calm you and with which you have an emotional connection, then use the website *TempoTap.com* to determine their beats per minute (BPM) or enter the song title and "BPM" into a search engine. If many songs on your list have similar BPM, that's probably the tempo that's in sync with your brain waves. Enter that number, "BPM" and "songs" into a search engine to turn up additional options for your personal relaxation playlist.

Albums featuring the sounds of nature, such as ocean waves, waterfalls and rain, also can help set aside the day's problems and help you relax.

• **Falling asleep.** People tend to put on very slow, calm songs when they want to sleep. It's more effective to start with music that matches the current pace of your mind, then ease your way into slower music. So paradoxically, the first song you listen to when you want to calm down from a hectic day might have a tempo of 100 BPM or more. The calm songs should come later.

Examples: Slow-paced songs for the final minutes before sleep include The Tokens' "The Lion Sleeps Tonight" (at 61 BPM)...Etta James's "At Last" (60 BPM)...and Ray Charles's "Georgia on My Mind" (64 BPM).

• **Getting out of a crabby mood.** The very best mood boosters are songs that transport us back to a happy place and time in our life. What songs did you dance to at your wedding? What songs were on the radio or on your turntable during the happiest year of your life?

• **Waking up.** Songs with a relatively fast tempo—upward of 100 BPM—can help our minds get into gear in the morning.

Examples: "I'm Too Sexy" by Right Said Fred (120 BPM) and "Seaside Rendezvous" by Queen (168 BPM).

• **Eating.** Slow songs that make us feel happy are best for mealtime—particularly instrumentals. Music with a slow tempo encourages us to eat slower, reducing the odds that we will overeat. Instrumentals reduce the risk of overeating as well—lyrics are particularly distracting to our minds, and distracted people sometimes overeat simply because they don't realize how much they have already consumed. Music that makes us feel happy is a smart choice for meals because unhappy people are more likely to indulge in unhealthy comfort foods to cheer themselves up.

Examples of instrumentals: Slow-paced selections from Beethoven, Mozart and Bach.

• **Staying awake.** Very fast-paced music can be more effective than caffeine for remaining sharp when driving at night or when performing mindless or repetitive tasks. The website *RunningMusicMix.com* is one place to locate songs with high BPM.

Examples: Many songs from the techno, dance and hip-hop genres have very high BPM. Or try Lindy Hop swing jazz (140 to 200 BPM). Other popular songs with high BPM include The Coasters' "Charlie Brown" (131 BPM)…and Charlie Daniels's "Devil Went Down to Georgia" (136 BPM).

How to Get More from Your eReader

Michael Kozlowski, editor in chief of *GoodeReader. com*, based in Vancouver, British Columbia. It is the largest independent website devoted to eReaders and eBooks.

The Amazon Kindle, Barnes & Noble Nook, Sony Reader and other eReaders allow their owners to carry a library of digital books, magazines and other printed content with them wherever they go.

Most have special screens featuring "e Ink" (or comparable technology) that's much easier to read than tablet and computer screens, even in direct sunlight. Such screens require far less power than tablet screens, too, so eReaders often can go a month or two between battery charges. And because eBooks usually are cheaper than printed books, eReaders can be money savers for people who buy lots of

---

EASY-TO-DO...

How to Share Media Services with Friends and Family

Friends and family can share media services under some circumstances—even when the services are designated members-only. Netflix charges $8.99 per month* to allow streaming to two devices and $3 to add two more. HBO Go provides one household log-in for the service (cost varies by cable provider)—the company does not specify how many people may share the account.

CNNMoney.com

*Prices subject to change.

---

books, quickly paying back their price tags of typically $70 to $200.

But eReaders also have a big limitation—while tablets, smartphones and laptops are all very versatile, most eReaders are designed primarily to purchase books and magazines from the online store of the company that makes the eReader. *Still, there are other things eReaders can do…*

• **Download books for free from libraries.** Many local libraries now feature a digital download section on their websites or on partner websites. Anyone with a library card can choose from a wide selection of eBooks for free. Visit your library's site for details or call a librarian for guidance.

Helpful: Sony's eReader is adept at downloading library eBooks—it comes with the necessary software installed.

Sites including Project Gutenberg (*Gutenberg.org*) and Open Culture (*OpenCulture.com*) also provide free downloads of certain titles, mostly classic works that are now in the public domain.

• **Access the Internet or e-mail.** Most eReaders include web browsers. These tend to struggle with graphics-intensive web pages, but they generally do a reasonable, if somewhat slow, job loading text-oriented pages. Some eReaders make browsers challenging to locate. Your eReader's user's guide has details.

Example: On a Kindle, the browser is buried in the "Experimental" menu. To find it, press the Home button, select "Experimental," then choose "Basic Web," followed by "Enter URL."

•**Play games.** There are games designed for eReaders. Text-based games such as Sudoku and Scrabble and slow-paced games such as Monopoly tend to work better on eReaders than fast-paced or graphics-intensive games. Visit your eReader's store to find game options. Most cost only a few dollars or less.

Example: In the Amazon Kindle online store (*Amazon.com/Kindle-eBooks*), search for "Puzzles & Games."

•**"Push" Internet content onto your eReader.** If you find an interesting article or blog post on the Internet, you can transfer it to your eReader. That way you can read it when you aren't near your computer—and read it on your eReader's easy-to-read screen rather than on a computer screen.

Start by creating an Instapaper (*Instapaper. com*) or Readability (*Readability.com*) account. These free online services let you click a "Read Later" bookmark to highlight online content that you wish to transfer to your eReader (or simply read later on your computer). If your eReader is a Kindle, these services can automatically transfer this content to your eReader via Wi-Fi.

With other eReaders, you will have to download the content to your computer, then transfer it to your eReader manually via a USB cable. A free online service called Calibre can help convert online content to eReader-friendly formats (*Calibre-ebook.com*).

Tricks to Great Pix with Your Smartphone

Dan Burkholder, a professional photographer and photography teacher who has taught at the School of the Art Institute of Chicago, the International Center of Photography in New York, University of Texas at San Antonio and elsewhere. Based in Palenville, New York, he is author of *iPhone Artistry* (Pixiq). *DanBurkholder.com*

The digital cameras built into today's smartphones are capable of taking high-quality photos. But snapping pictures with a smartphone is quite a bit different from doing so with a conventional camera. *To take great smartphone photos…*

•**Don't use the zoom.** The vast majority of smartphones don't have zoom lenses but offer a zoom function. When you use the zoom function, your smartphone's camera just enlarges the pixels in the middle of the frame and discards those around the edges. Unlike true optical zoom, this doesn't capture any additional detail, and your photo could look pixilated if you zoom in too far.

Rather than using the zoom function, the best way to "zoom" with a smartphone camera is to get closer before taking the shot. If that isn't possible, take the picture without zooming, then use a photo-editing program or app to crop the photo later (enlarging the part you want). The result is essentially the same as using the digital zoom on the smartphone, but this way you have the larger image saved so that you're not stuck with the pixilated image if you zoom in too far.

Helpful: If you expect to crop a smartphone photo later, go into the phone's camera settings or main settings menu and adjust the resolution as high as possible before taking the picture. The highest resolution often isn't the default setting because higher resolutions can lead to long processing delays between shots.

•**Take special steps in low-light situations.** Many of today's smartphone cameras tend to struggle in low light. Using the flash is typically a poor solution—smartphone LED flashes often produce a very harsh tone.

Three options for better low-light smartphone photos…

•Snap pictures from multiple angles with and without the flash, time permitting. Keep the one that comes out best. If there is an image-stabilizer option in your phone's camera settings menu, turn it on before taking low-light photos. Digital image stabilization can degrade image quality, however, so it might not make sense to leave it on when it isn't needed.

•Load a long-exposure app onto your smartphone. A long exposure allows more light to reach your camera's sensor. A good long-exposure app also may include image stabilization to reduce the odds that the long exposure will lead to blurriness, a common problem. Using a tripod also can reduce blurriness.

Good examples of apps include *Slow Camera Shutter Plus Pro*, a long-exposure app for iPhones and iPads (free through *iTunes**), and *Night Camera*, one of the leading options for Android (free on *Play.Google.com*).

•Buy a smartphone that performs unusually well in low light.

•**Be gentle with the shutter button.** Tap your smartphone's onscreen shutter-release button too aggressively and you'll jar the phone slightly, causing a blurred shot. Instead, press your finger lightly and smoothly on the button.

Helpful: The volume buttons on recent-model iPhones (and some other smartphones) can be used as a shutter release, too. That can come in handy when you have to hold the phone at an odd angle to get the shot and can't comfortably tap the screen. In fact, the volume buttons on a pair of earbuds connected to an iPhone can serve as shutter releases, too. Using the earbud button avoids any risk that snapping the picture will jar the phone, because you're not tapping the phone at all.

•**Brace your elbow against your torso.** Smartphones are not equipped with optical viewfinders—the LCD screen serves as the viewfinder. But to see this screen, you must hold the smartphone at some distance away from your face, and that could cause blurred pictures if you can't hold your arms perfectly steady.

If your shots often are blurry, reduce arm shake by bracing your elbow against your body before snapping a picture. Better yet,

*Prices subject to change.

hold the phone with both hands and brace both elbows.

•**Wipe off the lens before snapping a picture.** Unlike most cameras, smartphone cameras don't have lens covers. Their lenses often get dusty or dirty in our pockets or purses or get smudged when we handle the phone. A quick wipe with a clean, microfiber cloth or lens wipe can prevent this from ruining a shot. You even can use the hem of a cotton T-shirt.

•**Load other useful photo apps onto your phone.** When you buy a regular camera, you're generally stuck with the software that the manufacturer includes in the camera. When you buy a smartphone, you can load some wonderful camera apps onto it, improving its programming.

In addition to the exposure apps mentioned earlier, examples include…

•*Snapseed* (free, iPhone or Android) for editing smartphone photos after you've taken them. Unlike other free photo-editing apps, it lets you make localized changes to photos.

Example: If the tone of one face in a photo doesn't look quite right, you can adjust just that face without changing the tone of other parts of the photo.

•*Camera+* ($1.99, iPhone) and *ProCamera* ($3.99, iPhone) offer image stabilization, delay timers and expanded control over light levels, among other perks.

•*AutoStitch Panorama* ($1.99, iPhone) lets users snap several overlapping pictures, then combine them together into one large, seamless image. There are other photo-stitching apps, but this one lets you join photos in multiple configurations, not just side-by-side in a long, thin panorama.

ADD-ON LENSES

The Sony QX10 is an attachment that turns a standard Android or Apple smartphone into a high-quality camera complete with 10x optical zoom lens, 18-megapixel image sensor and high-quality image stabilization. There is also a QX100 model that offers a higher-end sensor and lens as well as other perks, but for twice the price. ($199.99, *Store.Sony.com*)

Protect Photos with Free Online Storage

Flickr gives users 1,000 GB of storage at the site—more than 500,000 photos. Shoebox provides unlimited storage, although at lower resolution.

Also: Burn photos to DVDs—one disc holds about 1,000 images. You can make the DVD yourself or have it done for $10 to $20* by an online service such as Shutterfly.

To digitize old prints: ScanDigital, GoPhoto, DigMyPics and similar services will scan hard copies for 39 to 88 cents apiece. You can archive the scans online or store them on DVD.

Roundup of experts in photo printing, reported at *CNNMoney.com.*

*Prices subject to change.

How to Grill a Wicked Good Burger

Andy Husbands, chef/owner of Tremont 647, a restaurant in Boston's South End that specializes in American cuisine. He is coauthor of *Wicked Good Burgers: Fearless Recipes and Uncompromising Techniques for the Ultimate Patty* (Fair Winds). *Tremont647.com*

It's fairly easy to grill a decent hamburger—but grilling a really great one takes a few tricks…

1. Choose a fairly fatty meat. Chuck with 20% fat is ideal. Less fatty meat lacks juiciness and cohesion—your burgers might fall apart and will taste dry.

Alternative: If you have a meat grinder, consider combining a chuck roll (the typical meat for burgers) with either skirt steak or short ribs in a roughly 50/50 ratio—these cuts add a nice beefy flavor. But if you do grind meat, chill it to nearly the point of freezing before doing so. That helps the grinder cut the meat properly. Also, ground beef's fat and flavor start to melt away when it becomes warm.

EASY-TO-DO…

How to Garden Even When You Have Allergies

If you love to garden but suffer from allergies, garden after 10 am, when pollen counts are not at their highest, and take frequent breaks to avoid lengthy exposure to allergens. Also, be sure to cover up— wear gloves and long sleeves and tuck long pants into socks…a mask and goggles or wraparound sunglasses…and a wide-brimmed hat. Take a shower as soon as you are inside, and put a cold compress on your eyes. Store gardening clothes separately or wash them immediately.

Boyan Hadjiev, MD, adult and pediatric allergy, asthma and sinusitis specialist in private practice in New York City.

---

2. Mix "fifth dimension powder" into the meat. This gives burgers a savory flavor that makes you want another bite and then another! Combine six tablespoons porcini powder… two tablespoons portabella powder…two tablespoons Worcestershire powder…two tablespoons onion powder…and two tablespoons of garlic powder. Use one tablespoon of the mixture per pound of meat. The powders can be purchased at specialty stores or online at *Amazon.com.*

3. Form flat patties. Make loose balls of meat six to eight ounces in size, then flatten these balls into patties about a half-inch thick. Don't pack these patties very tight, and don't leave the center thicker than the edges—thick-in-the-middle patties don't cook evenly. Next, use two fingers to press a dimple roughly one-quarter-inch deep into the middle of one side of each patty. This divot prevents the burger from puffing up in the middle as it cooks. Preformed burgers are great in a pinch, but burgers formed by hand are juicier.

4. Build a hardwood charcoal fire. This sort of charcoal doesn't just impart a smoky flavor, it also burns hotter than the typical gas grill or charcoal briquette fire. High heat—ideally 600°F to 800°F—sears the outside of meat before the inside becomes overcooked. That sear is what gives great grilled meat its wonderful caramelized flavor. To check if the grill is hot enough, hold your hand about five inches above the grill. The grill is ready when you can't stand the heat for three to five seconds.

Helpful: Form a charcoal fire off-center in your grill. That way you can move the patties away from the highest heat later, if necessary, to have them cook further without burning.

5. Season the patties liberally on both sides with kosher salt and cracked pepper right before you grill them. Season too soon, and the salt will tighten and dry out the meat.

6. Let the patties cook virtually undisturbed for two to three minutes. Peek gently underneath after two minutes. If the patties lift easily off the grill and are golden brown underneath, it's time to flip them. If not, let them continue to cook for up to an additional minute. Do not poke, prod or push down on patties as they cook—that just pushes juice and flavor out of the meat.

7. Use a meat thermometer to monitor temperature after flipping the patties. Cook to 160°F for safety.

Helpful: Consider buying a Thermapen, a digital meat thermometer favored by professional chefs for its fast, accurate readings ($96,* *ThermoWorks.com*).

8. Let cooked burgers sit for five minutes before eating. "Resting" burgers allows their juices to distribute throughout the meat. That way the juice—and the flavor—won't spill out onto your plate when you take the first bite.

*Price subject to change.

Guilt-Free Chocolates: Delicious...Easy to Make ...and Good for You!

Ellie Krieger, RD, host of *Healthy Appetite*, which runs on the Food Network. She is a winner of the James Beard Foundation Award for "Best Cookbook with a Healthy Focus." Her most recent cookbook is *Weeknight Wonders: Delicious Healthy Dinners in 30 Minutes or Less* (Houghton Mifflin Harcourt). *EllieKrieger.com*

Yearning for candy but concerned about its effects on your health? Indulge guilt-free by making healthful chocolate candy at home. You will have full control over the ingredients and portion size, so you can get maximum flavor and health benefits with minimal sugar and calories. You probably will spend less than you would at a fancy chocolate shop. And it's easy to do.

You can whip up decadent-tasting treats that actually are good for you by using just three key ingredients...

•**Top-quality dark chocolate.** Chocolate is derived from the cacao bean, which is high in heart-protective *flavonoids* (antioxidant-containing plant pigments), as well as iron, magnesium, phosphorus, potassium, zinc, copper and manganese. The higher the cocoa percentage in the chocolate, the more antioxidants it has—but also the more bitter the taste. To reap the health benefits with optimal taste, choose dark chocolate containing 60% to 70% cacao. I generally use Scharffen Berger... Ghirardelli...or Green and Black's. You can get it in bar form or as chips—60%-to-70% dark is comparable to "bittersweet" chocolate.

•**Dried fruits.** Yes, dried fruits are high in sugar—but it is naturally occurring sugar, not the refined type. And the drying process concentrates the minerals and the antioxidants. Look for dried fruits with no sugar added.

•**Nuts.** Nuts provide healthful monounsaturated fats and omega-3 fatty acids that help reduce LDL cholesterol and triglycerides and also modulate the blood sugar spike that you otherwise would get from the candy. What's more, nuts fight inflammation, thanks to the antioxidant vitamin E and their soluble fiber.

EASIEST CHOCOLATE CANDY RECIPES

For all these simple treats, start by melting chocolate. Place chopped chocolate in a microwave-safe bowl, and heat on high for 30 seconds, then stir. Repeat the 30-second heating-then-stir process until the chocolate is mostly melted but you still can see a lump or two—at that point, some stirring and the residual heat will finish the melting job for you.

For a flavor boost, sprinkle flaky salt, such as fleur de sel, over any of the following while the chocolate is still liquid.

Chocolate-dipped fruit: Dip dried apricots, figs and other fruits in melted dark chocolate, covering one-quarter to one-half of each piece of fruit. Place on waxed paper to cool.

Super-nutty bark: Melt dark chocolate, spread it about one-quarter-inch thick with a spatula on a parchment-lined baking sheet, and top with different types of chopped nuts. Let set, then break into bite-size pieces.

Chunky chocolate squares: Melt dark chocolate. Stir in a combination of chopped nuts and chopped dried fruits—for instance, pistachios plus apricots...peanuts plus raisins...walnuts plus blueberries...hazelnuts plus figs. Pour the mixture into a square baking dish lined with waxed paper. Refrigerate until firm, then cut into squares.

SOPHISTICATED PALATE PLEASERS

When you are ready to try something a bit more complex, give these a whirl...

Cherry Almond Chocolate Clusters

1 cup roasted almonds, coarsely chopped
½ cup dried cherries, coarsely chopped
6 ounces dark chocolate, finely chopped

In a medium bowl, toss together the almonds and cherries. Line a baking sheet with waxed paper. Melt half of the chocolate in the top of a double boiler or in a small, shallow bowl over a saucepan containing barely simmering water over low heat. (Make sure that the water is at least two inches below the bottom of the top pan or bowl.) Stir until melted. Remove the double boiler from the heat, and stir in the rest of the chocolate until melted. Remove the top pan from the bottom pan, and set it aside. Replace the simmering water in the bottom pan with warm tap water. Put the pan of melted chocolate on top of the bottom pan—this will keep the chocolate at the right temperature while you make the clusters. Stir the fruit/nut mixture into the chocolate.

Spoon out heaping tablespoon-size clusters of the chocolate mixture onto the baking sheet, placing them about one inch apart. Place the baking sheet in the refrigerator to cool and set for about 20 minutes, then remove from the refrigerator. Store and serve at room temperature. Makes 12 servings, about 150 calories a serving.

Fig and Ginger Truffles

2 cups dried black Mission figs or other dried figs (about 8 ounces), stems removed
¼ cup crystallized ginger (about 2 ounces)
1 Tablespoon honey
½ teaspoon ground cinnamon
2½ ounces dark chocolate, chopped

Put the figs, ginger, honey and cinnamon in a food processor, and process for about 45 seconds until they are finely chopped and begin to stick together. Roll the fig mixture with your hands into heaping teaspoon-size balls, and set them on a baking sheet or plate lined with waxed paper. Place half of the chocolate in the top of a double boiler or in a small shallow bowl over a saucepan containing barely simmering water over low heat. (Make sure that the water is at least two inches below the bottom of the top pan or bowl.) Stir until melted. Remove the saucepan from the heat, and add the remaining chocolate. Stir until all the chocolate is melted.

Remove the bowl with the chocolate from the pan. Roll the fig balls into the melted chocolate, one or two at a time, until all are covered. Place them on the waxed paper. Refrigerate for 15 minutes. Remove from the refrigerator. Store and serve at room temperature. Makes 16 truffles, each about 65 calories.

DID YOU KNOW THAT...

There Are a Handful of New Roller Coasters to Ride?

Thunderbolt at Coney Island, New York, has a 125-foot lift hill and reaches speeds of 65 miles per hour. *Goliath* at Six Flags Great America in Gurnee, Illinois, has a near-vertical 85-degree, 180-foot drop and will reach speeds of 72 mph. *Banshee* at Kings Island in Mason, Ohio, has more than 4,000 feet of track with seven inversions and reaches speeds of 68 mph. *Seven Dwarfs Mine Train* at the Magic Kingdom in Lake Buena Vista, Florida, is a family-style coaster featuring a musical journey inside and outside caverns in mine cars that swing. *Harry Potter and the Escape from Gringotts* at Universal Studios Florida in Orlando is an indoor coaster that takes riders through the vaults of the Goblin-run bank.

USAToday. USAToday.com

15

A Smooth Ride

The Right Way to Pump Your Gas…and 6 Other Tips to Save Money and Protect Your Car

Gasoline plays a big role in daily life for many of us, fueling our journeys and costing us money. And over the years, many myths have developed about gas and how to spend less on it.

Here we set the record straight…

• **Common belief.** If you allow your gas tank to reach empty, accumulated sediment on the bottom of the tank could get sucked into the fuel system and damage your engine.

False: There is a minimal amount of sediment in the bottom of most gas tanks. Also, the fuel pump in your tank has a filter screen, as do the valves leading into your engine, to catch any debris.

• **Common belief.** It's OK to top off your tank at the gas station with a few extra squirts after the automatic fuel nozzle clicks off.

False: It's a waste of money because some of the additional gas you're forcing into your tank may be drawn into the nozzle's vapor recovery system and rerouted back into the station's storage tanks instead of your car. Moreover, if the fuel level in your car gets too high, it can spill into the vapor hoses at the top of your tank and leak into the evaporative emission control system. That won't do permanent damage, but it will cause your engine to temporarily falter and run poorly when you are driving, and it could trigger your "Check Engine" light.

John Kelly, program manager of the automotive technology department at Weber State University, Ogden, Utah. He is certified by the National Institute for Automotive Service Excellence as a Master Automobile Technician and Advanced Engine Performance Specialist. *Weber.edu/automotive*

•**Common belief.** Brand-name gas stations carry better gas than what you get at off-brand stations.

True: What distinguishes the two dozen pricier "top-tier" brands, which include BP, Chevron, Conoco, Costco, Exxon, Mobil, Phillips 66, Shell, Texaco and others, is higher levels of detergent additives in both regular and premium gas. These additives help reduce carbon deposits that build up on your engine's fuel injectors, intake valves and combustion chambers.

If you use generic gasoline, it's a good idea to fill your tank with a brand-name gas a few times each year, especially in older cars. You could see reduced emissions and a slight improvement in power and performance—but don't expect to get better gas mileage. Whether they have a big brand name or not, all gas stations in the US are governed by stringent regulations regarding the quality, storage and pumping of fuel, and stations typically get their gas from the same or similar refineries.

•**Common belief.** Using the wrong octane fuel will void portions of the warranty on your car.

True: Running low-octane fuel regularly in an engine built for premium can result in sluggish performance, lower fuel economy and, in worst-case scenarios, physically damage the engine. The knocking caused by low-octane gas puts pressure on the pistons and valves.

•**Common belief.** Premium gas helps your vehicle even if the owner's manual says it's not necessary.

Generally false: You typically get no better performance, gas mileage, longevity or other benefits from premium gas unless your car requires it. "Premium" is a marketing term that simply indicates that the gas has a higher octane level, meaning that it takes more compression inside the engine to ignite it.

Certain luxury and sports cars have powerful, high-performance engines that need premium-grade gas (91 or 93 octane) because regular gas (87 octane) tends to ignite too quickly for their engines. That creates an improper fuel-air mixture that disrupts the proper working of the engine and causes a knocking or pinging sound.

Exception: Older (model year 1995 and earlier), heavier cars made for regular gas may experience knocking under severe engine strain such as towing big loads up mountain passes. Using premium gas may stop the knocking and improve engine performance.

•**Common belief.** Certain fuel additives from auto-parts stores can improve gas mileage.

False: The Environmental Protection Agency has tested hundreds of these products over the years specifically for their better mileage claims. It has not found any that make a significant difference.

•**Common belief.** The higher the ethanol mix, the worse your mileage.

True: Since 2007, Congress has required oil companies to blend ethanol, an alcohol distilled from corn, into gasoline. Most fuel sold in the US is "E10," meaning that it may contain as much as 10% ethanol. Vehicles typically get three to four fewer miles per gallon on E10 than on straight gasoline. Gas stations do not reveal the exact amount of ethanol in their E10 blends, but some actually use far less than 10% ethanol. This is the reason you may get better mileage using fuel from one station than from another.

More from John Kelly...

Storing Gas for Your Lawn Mower, Snowblower, More

Knowing how to use gasoline in your lawn mower, snowblower and other gas-powered equipment can make a big difference in the engine's performance. *What to do…*

•**Keep containers of gasoline no longer than 30 days.** Both premium and regular gas degrade rather quickly into a thicker, varnish-like substance. Not only does this old gas burn less effectively hurting engine performance but it can clog up your gas lines, filters and carburetor channels.

Helpful: If you are going to keep gas in a container for more than 30 days, add a fuel-stabilizer product called Sta-Bil, available in most auto-parts stores.

Cost: Less than $10 for 10 ounces.* One ounce protects 2.5 gallons of gasoline for up to one year.

You don't need Sta-Bil for two-cycle engines, such as those in hedge trimmers, that burn a mixture of gasoline and oil because the oil works as a stabilizer.

• **Before you stow four-cycle equipment for the season,** fill the tank with fuel and stabilizer, and run the equipment for 10 minutes. The old method was to run the equipment on straight gas until it conked out, but that still can leave some unstabilized fuel sitting in the engine for months.

• **Use low-octane gas in your equipment.** Putting in premium gas will not make the equipment run more smoothly or powerfully. However, as with your car, I would be sure to run a tank of top-tier gasoline at least once each season to help clean any carbon deposits building up inside the engines.

*Price subject to change.

Best Used Cars for Teenagers

The following cars are safe, reliable and easy for inexperienced drivers to handle. All prices are averages for vehicles bought from a dealer and are subject to change. Chevrolet Malibu, $12,925 for a 2009, or $14,483 for a 2010. Hyundai Sonata, $9,917 for a 2008, $11,167 for a 2009 or $13,317 for a 2010. Mazda6, $10,800 for a 2009 or $12,625 for a 2010. Ford Focus, $10,388 for a 2009 or $12,313 for a 2010. Volkswagen Jetta, $13,831 for a 2009.

Consumer Reports. ConsumerReports.org

What Car Do People Keep the Longest?

The car Americans keep the longest is a Volvo. Volvos averaged 7.05 years before being turned in…Jaguar, 7 years…Buick, 6.92 years… Mitsubishi, 6.92 years…Lincoln, 6.79 years.

247WallSt.com

Car Deposit Smarts

Many people think they can get a deposit back from a car dealer within three days of signing a contract—but that is not always true. You can cancel the sales agreement, but unless a refundable deposit is stipulated in the contract, you may not be able to get it back. You can get the deposit back if the deal is contingent on your getting financing and you can't (and if this clause is written into the agreement)…the dealer commits fraud or misrepresentation…or the dealer cannot get the vehicle specified.

Make the deposit with a credit card so that you can ask the card company to dispute the charge. Also, if you are entitled to a refund and the dealer refuses, contact your state consumer agency (*USA.gov/directory/stateconsumer*).

Consumer Reports Money Adviser.

EASY-TO-DO…

Best Ways to Avoid a Used-Car Scam

Private-sale used-car scams typically include one or more of these warning signs…

• **Very low prices**—use *Edmunds.com* or *Kelley Blue Book* (*KBB.com*) to get an idea of reasonable private-party pricing.

• **The seller and the car are in different places**—this may or may not be legitimate, but you need to be able to inspect the car in person before agreeing to buy.

• **Changing stories,** such as a sudden shift in terms or the seller wanting to move the deal from one website to another, usually indicate a scam.

• **Asking for money up-front or through a wire-transfer service**—this is a common way thieves operate…money should change hands only when you can leave with the car.

Money.MSN.com

How to Buy a Car at Costco

The Costco Auto Program acts as a middleman for buyers and dealers. The program works by prenegotiating discounted vehicle prices with local dealers, then brings dealer and buyer together to finalize the deal. Prices tend to be good—about $1,000 less* than the *Kelley Blue Book* price—although not necessarily the lowest you can get. But the arrangement can be good for Costco members who prefer not to haggle and still want a reasonably low price. The Costco deal is best for models that dealers already have on their lots, not premium or unusual cars or ones with limited availability—and not for special-order vehicles.

For more information: *CostcoAuto.com. Money.MSN.com*
*Price subject to change.

Avoid These Car Loans

Many people getting car-title loans—high-cost, short-term loans that use the titles of the borrower's car as collateral—can't afford to pay off the loan in full. The loans usually are offered for 30 days, after which a borrower who can't repay must keep paying more fees and interest or risk losing the car. The average borrower renews eight times, paying $2,142 in interest for $951 in credit. These loans are offered in 21 states and are based on a car's value, not the borrower's ability to repay.

Study by Center for Responsible Lending and Consumer Federation of America, reported in *The New York Times.*

When Hybrid-Car Owners Must Pay Extra...

Some hybrid-car owners must pay extra taxes to make up for the gasoline taxes that owners of fuel-efficient hybrid and electric cars don't pay at the pump. Several states charge extra fees or levy special taxes. Washington State charges $100/year* for all-electric vehicles. Similar levies are being considered in other states.

USA Today. USAToday.com
*Price subject to change.

When Your Car Warranty Is Up...

If your car suffers a major failure soon after the warranty is up, you still may be able to get the manufacturer to cover the repair...

•**Search online for reports of the problem.** Check the database of the National Highway Traffic Safety Administration (*SaferCar.gov*) for complaints and technical service bulletins.

•**Keep repair records**—the more evidence you have that you took good care of the vehicle, the better.

•**Go on social-media sites such as Twitter to discuss your problem**—manufacturers watch those sites carefully.

•**Be persistent but polite**—try to get the dealer on your side in talks with the vehicle manufacturer.

Consensus of car owners and manufacturers' representatives, reported in *The Wall Street Journal.*

Best Car Warranties Now

Hyundai has a basic warranty good for five years or 60,000 miles...a power-train warranty—for the original owner only—good for

10 years or 100,000 miles…and free roadside assistance for five years.* Mitsubishi has basic power-train and roadside-assistance warranties similar to those from Hyundai. Kia also has the same basic power-train and roadside-assistance warranties. Volvo warranties last for four years or 50,000 miles, with corrosion protection for 12 years and four years of roadside service. Buick offers a six-year or 70,000-mile warranty, plus transferable power-train warranty…corrosion protection for six years…and six years of roadside assistance.

Bankrate.com

*Offers subject to change.

Auto Leasing Is Back: Secrets to Getting the Best Deal

Phil Reed, senior consumer advice editor at *Edmunds.com*, an automotive information website. He is author of *Strategies for Smart Car Buyers* (Edmunds).

Leasing a car instead of buying suddenly is hot. Around 25% of the new cars being driven off dealer lots now are leased, not purchased, because attractive lease terms once again are available.

Unfortunately, many lessees are not getting those attractive deals. The car-leasing process has some complex aspects and unfamiliar terminology, and some dealerships take unfair advantage of the resulting consumer confusion.

Warning: Advertised lease specials often are not as appealing as they seem. Manufacturers sometimes keep the monthly lease payments in these offers low by allowing just 10,000 miles per year, rather than the usual 12,000, or by requiring steep down payments.

Example: Audi's advertised lease specials often ask for $4,000 down, much more than lessees normally pay.

To get a good lease deal…

• Select a vehicle with a high residual value. The size of your lease payments will be based in part on how close the vehicle's "re-sidual value" (the amount the vehicle is worth when you turn it in at lease end) is to its "capitalized cost" (the initial sales price).

Examples: Toyota, Honda, BMW and Mercedes-Benz vehicles generally hold their value quite well. Most American-brand vehicles tend not to hold their value as well. Those that do are the Jeep Wrangler and Ford Focus.

• E-mail or call the Internet department of three to five dealerships in your area that sell the vehicle you want. Explain that you are "shopping for a lease payment" on this vehicle. This phrasing lets dealerships know that you are contacting their competitors, too, improving the odds that they will give you a competitive price. (Don't let those advertised lease deals convince you that lease terms are not negotiable—they are.) Ask them to e-mail a quote to you. Say that you won't visit the dealership until you have agreed to terms. Arriving on a dealer lot without a deal in hand greatly reduces your leverage.

Exception: It's OK to visit a dealer lot to test-drive a vehicle, but don't let the salesperson talk you into his/her office.

When you request quotes, indicate lease length, mileage allowance, money-down preferences and the options packages that you want. Also ask whether taxes will be included in the quote—they usually are not.

Helpful: Not sure what details to tell the dealership to include in their quote? Three years at 12,000 miles per year and around $1,000 down usually are the best lease options. Lease for longer than three years, and by the end, you might not be driving a car that seems new and is trouble-free. Most car owners drive around 12,000 miles a year—though it is fine to specify 10,000 miles per year if you're sure you won't drive more than this.

• Ask the dealerships that quote you the lowest monthly payments to e-mail you a "work sheet." This work sheet puts the details of the lease offer on paper. Some dealerships might be hesitant to e-mail a work sheet, but almost all will do so when pressed.

• Compare the "capitalized cost" charged in the lease offer to the vehicle's market value. *To do this…*

259

Locate the *True Market Value* and *Dealer Invoice Price* of the vehicle on the Edmunds website. (On *Edmunds.com*, at the very top of the page, select the make, model, options and year of the car, then scan down the page.) Note that the True Market Value might be below the invoice price if, for example, there is a manufacturer's rebate on the car.

If the capitalized cost listed on the lease-offer work sheet is higher than this True Market Value, subtract the Dealer Invoice Price from this capitalized cost.

E-mail or call the dealership and say, "I see this lease is based on a capitalized cost of $X above (or below, if that is the case) invoice. My research suggests that this car currently is selling at $Y above (or below) invoice (subtract the Dealer Invoice from the True Market Value to find this second figure—in many cases, these numbers will be quite close). I'm looking for a dealership that will lease to me at that figure." Try this first with the dealership that offered the lowest monthly payments, but try the others, too, if the first won't give you a capitalized cost very close to True Market Value.

• **Check the "money factor" listed on the work sheet.** This sometimes is called "lease factor," "lease rate" or just "factor." It is the lease equivalent of the interest rate on a car loan—but it is presented in a confusing way that makes it very difficult for lessees to tell if they're getting a good rate.

To convert a money factor to an interest rate, multiply by 2,400.

Example: A 0.00125 money factor converts to 3% (0.00125 x 2,400 = 3%). If the resulting figure is higher than the going rate on a car loan, you might be paying too much. This usually isn't something that the dealership can negotiate—money factor is set by the bank or leasing company. Still, a high money factor could suggest that the bank or leasing company considers you a risky borrower. If that doesn't seem right and you're not in a rush to get a new car, obtain copies of your credit reports (available at *AnnualCredit Report.com*) and scan for errors that could be lowering your score before leasing.

• **If you are trading in a car and there is a location of the national used-car chain** CarMax near you, take your car there for a quote.** If the dealership you're leasing from won't match CarMax's quote on the trade-in, go ahead and sell the car to CarMax. Or sell directly to another buyer through Craigslist if you're willing to take the time to do so. You then can use the money as a down payment.

Rent Out Your Car If You Aren't Using It

Rent out your car when you don't need it or rent a car from someone nearby when you do need one. The biggest peer-to-peer rental service is *RelayRides*, which has tens of thousands of members who rent cars in 1,000 cities. Other sites are regional, such as *Getaround* in San Francisco…Portland, Oregon…Chicago…San Diego…and Austin, Texas. The car-sharing service handles insurance and billing. Check costs, terms and conditions at the sites carefully.

USA Today. USAToday.com

Replace These Car Parts to Boost Gas Mileage

The *mass airflow sensor* measures air entering the engine and sends information to the engine computer, which handles fuel injection and other functions. When the sensor gets dirty, the information may be wrong. Replacement is easy to do yourself. The *oxygen sensor* monitors oxygen flow for efficient fuel-burning. It sends data to the engine computer, which adjusts fuel injection. A faulty sensor may mean bad data. Replacement of this part is also easy. *Spark plugs* ignite the car's air/fuel mixture—new ones are more efficient. Replacement is moderately easy. The *air filter* processes air coming into the engine—a dirty one reduces gas mileage, especially on older cars. Replacement is easy.

Bankrate.com

DID YOU KNOW THAT...

Texting Is as Dangerous as Drunk Driving?

Both of these behaviors led to the same degree of slowed braking time and increased speeding in a recent study.

Study by several Australian universities, published in *Traffic Injury Prevention*.

Save Money on Your Daily Commute

A trip-tracking device known as Automatic (*Automatic.com*, $99.95*) plugs into your car and alerts you on your smartphone when you are using the most fuel. It suggests ways to change your driving habits for more efficient driving, and the company says that this can reduce fuel consumption by 30%.

Other ways to save: Get the free *Waze* app to find out how slowly traffic is moving so that you can look for faster routes…share the cost of gas by carpooling with the help of an app-based service such as *Lyft*—its drivers undergo strict background checks.

ABCNews.com

*Price subject to change.

Adults More Likely to Text While Driving Than Teens

Almost half of all adults report texting while driving, versus 43% of teens.

Comparison of two surveys of more than 1,000 adults and 1,200 teens ages 15 to 19 by AT&T.

Break the Texting Habit Now!

Larry Rosen, PhD, a psychology professor at California State University, Dominguez Hills, and author of *iDisorder: Understanding Our Obsession with Technology and Overcoming Its Hold on Us* (Palgrave Macmillan).

Why are so many people willing to risk their lives—and the lives of people in other vehicles—to read or send text messages that almost always could have waited until they parked their cars? Because people are obsessed. Their anxieties about being out of contact overwhelm their common sense.

If you suffer from this problem (or a family member does), try this strategy. Check messages immediately before starting a drive, then set your phone's alarm to sound in 15 or 20 minutes—however long you tend to be able to go before anxiety about missed messages becomes too much to bear. If you're still on the road when this alarm sounds, find a safe, legal place to pull over and let yourself check your messages. Then reset the alarm, put the phone back down and resume your drive. Having an alarm set like this can reassure an anxious mind that any messages missed will be dealt with very soon.

Slowly extend the alarm time until you can complete your daily commute or other oft-made trips without stopping. You'll make the world safer for yourself—and the rest of us!

Fast Music = More Driving Errors for Teens

Teen risk for traffic violations increases when they listen to fast music. When teenagers were allowed to drive while listening to music with fast-paced vocals, about 98% of them made driving errors, such as speeding. When they listened to a softer, easy-listening background, driver errors declined by 20%.

Study of 85 teens by researchers at Ben-Gurion University of the Negev, Beer-Sheva, Israel, published in *Accident Analysis & Prevention*.

261

Signs an Older Person Should Give Up Driving

Signs that it is time to discuss an elderly person's driving include scrapes on the person's car, a garage door or a mailbox. If you notice these signs, ride with the driver to evaluate how well he/she drives and whether it is time to give up driving. In a recent analysis, 17% of traffic deaths in the US involved people age 65 and older who made up only 13% of the population, according to the US Department of Transportation.

Survey conducted by Liberty Mutual Insurance of 1,007 adults ages 40 to 65 with at least one parent who drives, reported in *USA Today*.

New Crash Test Results

Nearly one-quarter of front-end collisions that cause serious or fatal injuries involve a corner of the car striking an object.

Some of the cars that earned poor ratings on the new test: Nissan Quest...Chrysler Town & Country...Dodge Grand Caravan... and Ford Escape.

Some of the best ratings: Honda CR-V... Chrysler 200...and Subaru Forester, Impreza and XV Crosstrek.

More information: IIHS.org/ratings.

Russ Rader, a senior vice president at Insurance Institute for Highway Safety, Arlington, Virginia, an independent, nonprofit organization that created and conducted the new test.

An App That Helps Teen Drivers

Help your teenage driver gain more experience behind the wheel with a new app called *Time to Drive*. Your teen turns on the app before starting to drive, and it maps the driving route, keeps track of hard stops, records driving conditions and logs the time on the highway, in bad weather, driving at night, etc., so you can be sure that your teen is getting experience with all conditions. Currently available for iPhone for $3.99.* A version is in development for the Android operating system.

Arthur Goodwin, senior research associate, Highway Safety Research Center, University of North Carolina, Chapel Hill.

*Price subject to change.

Vehicles More Likely to Be Stolen

Large SUVs and pickups are more likely to be stolen than other vehicles. The four-wheel-drive Ford F-250 crew cab has the highest theft rate, with owners submitting nearly six times more theft claims than owners of other types of vehicles.

Insurance Institute for Highway Safety/Highway Loss Data Institute. *IIHS.org*

EASY-TO-DO...

Document *Any* Car Accident Carefully

Document even a minor car accident carefully. In modern cars with significant computer and electronic components, the extent of damage may not show up for weeks.

What to do: Report even minor incidents to your insurance company. Use your smartphone to record information for a claim, using free apps such as *WreckCheck*. Insist that the car be repaired by a dealership specializing in your make, not by your insurer's preferred all-makes repair shop.

What to do if your car is totaled: Use the prices at *KBB.com* to negotiate with your insurer for payment for a comparable car.

Roundup of experts in car repair, reported at *Money.CNN.com*.

16

Family Life

"Movie Therapy" Cuts Divorce Rates in Half: How Films Can Help Keep Your Marriage Strong

L et's face it. Many couples going through rough patches in their wedded bliss balk at turning to couples' therapy to get help. But what if watching a handful of movies together in the comfort of one's own home could help prevent problems from getting to that point?

*A **new** approach:** Having couples watch movies and then discuss the on-screen relationship issues afterward can sometimes be just as effective as more traditional relation-

*This approach is not a substitute for formal couples' therapy but may obviate the need for it—especially if the partners use it as a way to help keep their relationships healthy.

ship-strengthening interventions, according to research recently conducted at the University of Rochester.

Even if your marriage isn't troubled: Watching films and answering targeted questions can help you identify ways that you can make a good relationship even better.

Here is how this fascinating research unfolded...

5 FILMS = A BETTER RELATIONSHIP

Even though couples' therapy can be helpful when there's an emotional impasse, many people are uncomfortable discussing intimate problems with a stranger. On top of that, therapy sessions can sometimes go on for weeks or months, and it can cost an arm and a leg if it's not covered by your health insurance.

Ronald Rogge, PhD, an associate professor in the department of clinical and social sciences in psychology at the University of Rochester, New York. His main research interests include the complexities of couplehood and the early years of marriage. Dr. Rogge is the lead author of a movie-relationships study that appeared in the *Journal of Consulting and Clinical Psychology*.

263

To find out whether there might be a way to head off relationship problems before they become too serious, researchers divided 174 couples who had been together for about three years (though not necessarily engaged or married for all that time) into four groups.

Two of the groups participated in one of two forms of relationship-strengthening programs for about a month (one type focusing on empathy and acceptance…the other type zeroing in on communication styles). Those in the third group watched and discussed five movies over the course of about a month. The fourth group was a control—the participants didn't watch movies or attend counseling.

Surprising result: Three years later, the movie watchers were half as likely to separate or divorce as those in the control group. In fact, their divorce and separation rates (11% over three years) were the same as those who participated in either the empathy or communication programs.

Important: Even though the couples in the study had not been together very long, researchers suspect that movie therapy also can help long-term relationships if the partners are willing to put in the work and communicate openly with one another.

HOW IT WORKS

Sometimes, relationships get torn apart by weighty conflicts over money, sex or how to raise the children. But other times, everyday interactions fuel the discontent. Maybe your partner interrupts your stories…leaves dishes in the sink…or nags about your driving. Any of this sound familiar?

The good thing about movie-watching is that it can jump-start conversations about virtually any issue that's tripping up your relationship. Plus, it's fun to do.

And if the thought of enduring hours of saccharine-sweet "chick flicks" makes you wince, relax.

Sure, *Love Story* and a few other sappy movies are on the researchers' suggested list of films to watch. But there also are films you might never expect—great old classics like *Gone With the Wind, Barefoot in the Park* and *The Out-of-Towners.* There are plenty of complex, critically acclaimed films, too—such as *American Beauty, Children of a Lesser God* and *On Golden Pond.* If you're looking for a little humor, there are even such choices as *Meet the Fockers, The Big Wedding* and *The Five-Year Engagement.*

To get started…

• **Pick your flicks.** You and your partner need to agree to watch a movie together once a week and choose ones that you both find interesting. Check over the preselected list at *Couples-Research.com* for ideas.

When you watch, look at how the characters interact. Pay particular attention to the scenes that reflect your relationship—it might be flashes of temper, a condescending voice or frequent interruptions. These are the issues you'll want to talk about later.

• **Watch the films together.** It defeats the purpose if you watch a movie at separate times or in separate rooms—or don't even watch the same movie. Treat it like a date night. Watch the movie all the way through with a minimum of interruptions. Watch for those scenes that make you laugh (or groan or nod your head) when they hit close to home.

• **Talk it over.** After the movie's done, walk through some of the issues within its plot.

Some of the researchers' post-movie questions: What problems did the couple face? Are they similar to issues in your own life? Did the couples communicate well or poorly? Did they try to understand each other, or did they go on the attack? How did they handle conflicts or differences of opinion? For the complete list of discussion points to help you have your own conversations, go to *Couples-Research.com.*

• **Consider joining the study.** Couples in the study watched one movie each week followed up by a 45-minute discussion over a period of about a month. You can do this on your own, or you can use the above website to sign up for the online study. Couples who participate in the study will be asked to complete a short survey, watch five movies of their choosing in about a month's time and have 30- to 45-minute discussions after each movie they watch.

You'll be given individual feedback from the researchers conducting the survey on different parts of your relationship…and, at the end of the month, on changes that occurred within your relationship. There's no charge to participate.

Small Gestures Mean a Lot

Harry Reis, PhD, professor of psychology at University of Rochester, who studied 175 recently wed couples.

Grand romantic gestures and declarations of everlasting love are not the secrets to marital bliss—it's the couples who regularly do small tasks for one another who are most likely to be happy. For married people, these small but frequent gestures serve as ongoing confirmation that our partners still care. We never really know what's going on in another person's mind. These gestures show that our partner is thinking of our needs.

One somewhat surprising finding: While women usually are credited with being the relationship experts, it turns out that husbands tend to do these small gestures much more often than wives. That might be because while women tend to be very comfortable saying, "I love you," many men are more comfortable doing small things to show their love.

When it comes to selecting appropriate gestures, what matters is that we do things that our partners truly appreciate. Your husband may know that you dislike filling the gas tank, but if you want to reciprocate, you may be better off giving him a back rub!

DID YOU KNOW THAT...

Marriage Can Hurt Your Heart?

Longtime married couples who have mixed feelings toward each other had the highest rate of *coronary artery calcification* (a predictor of coronary artery disease), according to a recent study of 136 couples married for an average of 36 years.

Reason: Constant ambivalent feelings create stress, which can raise blood pressure.

Bert Uchino, PhD, professor of psychology, The University of Utah, Salt Lake City.

How to Love Life Again After Losing a Spouse

Becky Aikman, a New York–based journalist and author of *Saturday Night Widows: The Adventures of Six Friends Remaking Their Lives* (Broadway), the memoir of a group that Aikman founded to help herself and five other widows focus on happiness rather than grief. The former *BusinessWeek* editor lost her husband to cancer in 2004 after 20 years of marriage. *BeckyAikman.com*

Becky Aikman was in her 40s when she lost her husband to cancer. She formed a group with five other widows.

Their goal: To learn to live again after the worst thing that ever happened to them.

In the process, they found that some of the traditional thinking about loss and recovery wasn't helpful.

Here, advice for rebuilding your life—when you feel ready to do so—in the months or years after the death of your husband or wife…

AVOID COMMON TRAPS

Beware the missteps that can stand in the way of remaking your life…

•**Don't put off rebuilding because you haven't yet experienced the stages of grief.** In the late 1960s, a psychiatrist named Elisabeth Kübler-Ross popularized the idea that the grieving process has five predictable stages—denial, anger, bargaining, depression and acceptance.

These "five stages of grief" have become so ingrained in our culture that some widows and widowers believe they can't be truly ready to move on with their lives if they haven't yet passed through each of them. In fact, these stages were never intended to apply to grieving spouses but only to those who were dying themselves.

People who lose a spouse often experience waves of emotion separated by periods of feeling relatively normal. Over time, the waves become less extreme and less frequent until the widow or widower feels ready to reengage with humanity.

•**Be wary of support groups.** These groups are supposed to help widows and widowers cope with their grief by talking about it with others. Trouble is, spending time with other

265

grieving people and focusing your attention on your grief can make you sadder.

Give one of these groups a try if you think talking about your grief might help. But if you discover that it isn't for you, don't feel that your recovery depends on your continued attendance at these meetings.

• **Make decisions based on what you want your life to look like in the future,** not on maintaining the life you had before. It can be very difficult to give up the plans we made with our late partners, but those plans might no longer be appropriate for us.

Example: Some widows hang onto the family home, even though they no longer need the space, and then feel isolated living in communities full of families. Many who move into smaller homes closer to other singles are glad they did.

FRIENDS

It might make sense to alter whom you socialize with or how you arrange to spend time with them…

• **Be proactive about making plans with friends.** You can't just sit at home waiting for friends to call with things for you to do. Your friends might go out of their way to extend invitations in the months immediately after your spouse passes away, but those invitations are likely to eventually dry up as your friends return to their normal patterns and forget that you're sitting home alone. It's up to you to contact them to make plans. Do this days or weeks in advance, when possible, to reduce the odds that they already will have made plans.

• **Construct a new circle of single friends.** If you and your late spouse were like a lot of married couples, you probably socialized predominately with other married couples. You might start to feel like a fifth wheel if couples remain your only friends. If other members of your circle have also lost their spouses, make a particular effort to socialize with them. If you don't have unattached friends, ask your friends if they have other friends who have lost their partners or are otherwise unmarried and suggest that they be invited to get-togethers, too.

• **Get over any guilt about new romantic relationships.** Widows and widowers often worry that seeing someone new implies that their departed spouse wasn't really the love of their life. This isn't true—researchers have found that it's people who were very deeply in love with their departed spouses who are most likely to find love again.

ACTIVITIES

Certain pursuits are particularly worthwhile when you're trying to recover from the loss of a spouse.

• **Seek new experiences.** Explore new hobbies. Visit new places. Take classes in subjects you know little about.

Examples: I attended the opera, took architecture tours and joined a group of friends on a spa trip, all things I don't normally do.

Doing new things is not just enjoyable—it also helps widows and widowers gain confidence in their ability to face new challenges. That can be very empowering for people worried that they might not have it in them to remake their lives after decades of marriage and routine.

• **Cook well for yourself.** Losing a spouse can mean losing the person who cooked for you…or losing the individual for whom you cooked. In either case, the outcome often is a dramatic decline in the quality of the surviving spouse's meals. (And, when the survivor is the cook, he/she often concludes that it isn't worth preparing elaborate meals that no one else will eat.)

Dining out can be challenging, too. Many newly widowed people find it uncomfortable and boring to eat alone in restaurants.

But if you stop eating well after the loss of a spouse, you deny yourself an important source of pleasure when you need it most. Your health might suffer, too, if you resort to junk food.

What to do: Make cooking good food a priority, even if you're the only one who will eat it. If your late spouse was the cook in the family, enroll in cooking classes. Not only can these classes teach you to cook well for yourself, but you also might meet new friends.

• **Travel with tour groups.** Travel is an excellent way to have new and enjoyable experiences, but many people find it awkward to travel alone, and not having someone to share travel experiences with can detract from the fun.

If you travel with a tour group, you'll have people with whom you can share the adventure. You might even form lasting friendships with other members of the group.

Helpful: Before signing up for a trip, call the tour operator to confirm that a significant number of the members of the group are single. It can be uncomfortable to be the only one traveling alone in a group.

The Secrets of Happy Families: Rethink the Family Dinner, Tell Stories, More

Bruce Feiler, a *New York Times* columnist and six-time best-selling author based in Brooklyn, New York. His books include *The Council of Dads: A Story of Family, Friendship & Learning How to Live* and *The Secrets of Happy Families* (both from William Morrow). *Bruce Feiler.com*

It's hard for stressed-out modern families to feel like effective, close-knit teams these days. *New York Times* columnist Bruce Feiler—himself part of a two-career couple with twin eight-year-old daughters, aging parents and a large extended family—wanted to find ways to make his family life richer and reduce tensions.

He looked to unexpected sources, gathering and adapting innovative ideas about team-building and problem-solving from corporate boardrooms, university campuses and even the US military.

We asked Feiler for the strategies he found most helpful. He says incorporating just one or two of these ideas can make a significant difference in family closeness…

RETHINK THE FAMILY DINNER

Eating dinner together has long been shown to unify families and reduce behavioral problems in children. But fewer and fewer families are actually eating dinner together. And nearly everything in my life conspired against regular nighttime meals—from longer working hours for my wife and me to more extracurricular activities for the kids.

The Columbia University Center for Addiction and Substance Abuse has studied the role of family dinners in uniting families. It found that most of the benefits are derived from just 10 minutes of connection time during the meal—and you could get the same results at any meal. It's really about coming together as a family.

What my family does: We like to have a family-bonding experience over food every day. Sometimes, we opt for a family breakfast or a family dessert in the evening depending on our schedules.

Important: Adults tend to take up around two-thirds of the conversation. Family meals are most effective in building cohesion if you let your kids speak for at least half the time.

TELL FAMILY STORIES

Researchers at Emory University who studied myth and ritual in American families created the "Do You Know (DYK) Scale," widely regarded as one of the best single predictors of children's emotional health and happiness. It asks 20 questions about family history, such as "Do you know where your parents met?" and "Do you know of an illness or something really terrible that happened in your family?" Children who provided the most comprehensive answers to the test had a stronger sense that they controlled their lives and a deeper belief that their families functioned well. You can find the complete listing of questions at *TheMustardSeedHouse.com/tag/do-you-know-scale.*

What my family does: We tell stories of our family history that convey our values and emotional toughness. Kids need to know that they are part of something bigger and more important than just the ups and downs of their own daily needs and behavior. We don't try to shield our children from struggles or failures that have occurred in our family's past.

For example, one of our family's most memorable stories was my diagnosis with a rare and potentially deadly form of cancer at 43. Wracked with worry that my daughters would grow up without a father figure, I wrote a letter to six of my closest friends, asking them to be there for my daughters if I died. Each man represented a different era of my life and had different characteristics and values that I hoped to pass on to my girls. My "council of dads" are not just my friends now but also my daughters' friends, and they enrich all of our lives.

STRIKE THE WORD "YOU" FROM FAMILY SQUABBLES

William Ury, a senior fellow at the Harvard Negotiation Project, gets called in to handle some of the toughest disputes in the world, including nuclear-test-ban treaties and major labor strikes. Ury and other conflict experts sometimes make headway over deadlocked issues by simply changing up their language. For example, using the pronoun "you" throws the blame for a dispute on the other party. Rephrasing issues with the pronoun "we" can force both sides to acknowledge that there's a joint problem and to seek joint solutions.

What my family does: Instead of telling my wife, "I waited for an hour, and you never called," I say, "I waited for an hour. We need to improve our scheduling and communication during the day." *Other big-league negotiating ideas we adapted…*

•**Keep your facial expressions neutral and especially avoid rolling your eyes.** Eye rolling conveys not just impatience or annoyance but contempt.

•**Walk away from fights after three minutes.** Beyond that, family members just repeat themselves at higher and higher decibels. Instead, I separate my bickering daughters until both cool down. Then I ask each girl to come up with a few alternative solutions to the conflict before she speaks again. This way they move from rigid positions in an argument to starting with new options that they can shape together.

REARRANGE YOUR FAMILY ROOM FURNITURE

Sally Augustin, PhD, the founder of Design with Science, is well-known in the corporate world as a "place coach." One of the country's leading environmental psychologists, she redesigns workplaces so that employees can relate better. I realized that many of her ideas were applicable to home life.

What my family does: We circled the furniture so that it resembled an O shape (seating in a circular pattern) rather than the more alienating L-shape (two sofas at a right angle) or V-shape (a sofa flanked by two chairs). If O-shaped layouts aren't possible or offend your decorating tastes, use ottomans or other portable seating that can be easily repositioned during family gatherings. We also use plush surfaces for tense conversations. Sitting on chairs with soft cushions makes people more flexible and conciliatory than hard-backed surfaces.

KEEP EVERYONE VERY BUSY DURING FAMILY GET-TOGETHERS

Many extended families dread these gatherings because the focus is too often on sitting around, watching TV, drinking or gossiping. I was having trouble finding good advice about how to create camaraderie among disparate individuals until I ran across groundbreaking research done by the US military's special forces unit, the Green Berets. They use a constant cycle of games and exercises to promote cooperation and team-building among recruits.

What my family does: We never rest when the extended family gets together each July 4th on Cape Cod and then again on Labor Day off the coast of Georgia. At "Camp Feiler," as it is known, we have a watermelon seed–spitting contest, make homemade ice cream and play touch football or Frisbee, complete with team colors, cheers and flags. While these activities may seem hokey, friendly competition is very effective at uniting different generations and personalities in our families and allowing moments of genuine connection.

Important: Conclude all family gatherings with an emotional ritual. What happens last is often what's most deeply remembered. Camp Feiler ends with an elaborate family play. The children take the lead roles…aunts and uncles wear silly costumes…and my mother paints the backdrop on the stage

Caffeinated Drinks Linked to Low Baby Weight

In one recent finding, every 100 milligrams (mg) of caffeine (roughly equal to one eight-ounce cup of coffee) that a pregnant woman drank daily was associated with an infant losing up to one ounce of birth weight.

Study of nearly 60,000 pregnancies by researchers at Norwegian Institute of Public Health, Oslo, published in *BMC Medicine*.

DID YOU KNOW THAT...

Crib Bumper Pads Have Been Banned in Some States?

Maryland decided to ban the sale of bumper pads after an 18-month investigation found that they offered no significant benefit and could cause babies to be trapped, strangled or suffocated. Chicago has banned the sale of the pads, and most states do not allow their use in child-care facilities.

USA Today. USAToday.com

Breakfast Makes Kids Smarter

In a recent finding, six-year-olds who did not eat breakfast daily scored 4.6 points lower, on average, on verbal and performance IQ tests than children who ate breakfast every day. Both the nutritional and social aspects of breakfast are important—eating after a full

night of fasting supplies fuel to the brain…and social interaction at breakfast may promote brain development.

Study of 1,269 children by researchers at University of Pennsylvania School of Nursing, Philadelphia, published in *Early Human Development*.

Children's Headaches Probably Not Caused by Vision Problems

Parents often believe that children who develop headaches need glasses.

But: Most headaches in children go away over time whether or not they get glasses.

Study of 158 children by researchers at Albany Medical Center, New York, presented at the 116th annual meeting of the American Academy of Ophthalmology in Chicago.

TV Myth Debunked

Sitting close to a TV or computer screen does not damage kids' eyes as previously thought. But close viewing can cause headaches and temporarily blurred vision.

Mark Borchert, MD, division head, Vision Center at Children's Hospital Los Angeles.

Kids in the US More Prone to Allergies Than Those Outside the US

American children born outside the US are 48% less likely to have asthma, eczema, hay fever, food allergies and other allergic conditions than American children born in the US.

And: Foreign-born children who live in the US for 10 years or more are more than three

269

times as likely to have allergies as similar children living in the US for two years or less.

Study of 80,000 children by researchers at St. Luke's-Roosevelt Hospital Center in New York City, published online in *JAMA Pediatrics*.

Eyedrops and Nasal Sprays Pose Danger to Kids

Between 1985 and 2012 (latest data available), at least 96 children between the ages of one month and five years ingested over-the-counter eyedrops and nasal sprays, even though the products are packaged as childproof. When ingested, they can trigger nausea, vomiting, lethargy, increased heart rate, decreased respiration and other problems. If you think that your child has ingested one of these products, seek immediate emergency medical care.

US Food and Drug Administration, Silver Spring, Maryland. *FDA.gov*

Keep Meds Safe from Kids!

The accidental ingestion of medicine sends more than 64,000 children to emergency rooms each year.

But: Kids rarely get these medicines from drawers or bathroom medicine cabinets. In cases where the source of medication was known, 27% of pills came from the floor or were otherwise misplaced…20% came from a purse, bag or wallet…another 20% had been left out on counters, dressers or tables.

Self-defense: If you are concerned that you might forget to take pills you cannot easily see, use a cell phone alarm or other reminder to alert you when it is time for your medication.

Study done by Safe Kids Worldwide, Washington, DC. *SafeKids.org*

Cough and Cold Medicine Caution

Do not give cough and cold medicine to kids under age four—even if the products are labeled as being for children. More than 40% of parents say that they give their children under age four cough medicine or multisymptom cough and cold medicine. But these medicines do not reduce the time an infection lasts—and they can cause serious side effects in young children, including uneven heart rate, sleep problems, confusion, hallucinations, nausea and constipation. Products marketed as being for children have been labeled since 2008 as not for kids under age four—but the information usually is in small print and is easy to miss.

C.S. Mott Children's Hospital National Poll on Children's Health at University of Michigan, Ann Arbor.

Amusement Rides Do Cause Injury

About 20 kids a day are hurt on amusement rides between May and September in the US, according to a recent report. Most of the injuries are not serious—just bumps and bruises—but about 67 kids a year are injured badly enough to be hospitalized. The report didn't include how many children died because fatalities aren't tracked by hospital injury reports.

Gary A. Smith, MD, who conducted research for the Center for Injury Research and Policy at Nationwide Children's Hospital, Columbus, Ohio, quoted at *NBC News.com*.

Training Guidelines for Young Athletes

Weekly training hours of young athletes, ages eight to 18, should not exceed their age.

Example: A 10- year-old should train for no more than 10 hours a week.

Recent finding: Those who spent more hours than their age in training during a given week were 70% more likely to have serious overuse injuries such as stress fractures, elbow ligament injuries and damaged cartilage.

Study of 1,206 athletes who had 859 documented injuries by researchers at Loyola University Medical Center, Maywood, Illinois, and Ann & Robert H. Lurie Children's Hospital of Chicago, presented at a recent meeting of the American Medical Society for Sports Medicine in San Diego.

DID YOU KNOW THAT...

Identity Theft Is More Common with Children Than Adults?

Identity theft of children is 51 times higher than with adults. Ten percent of kids have had their Social Security numbers used by someone else.

Reason: Kids' information is held in places with little cyber security, such as schools and doctors' offices.

Self-defense: Contact each of the credit-reporting agencies—Equifax, Experian and Trans-Union—and file a child-identity inquiry. If evidence of fraud is found, follow the agency's procedures to have the errors corrected. Also, place a free 90-day fraud alert on the child's files, and order a credit freeze (generally $5 to $10*). Report the fraud to the Federal Trade Commission (*FTC.gov/complaint*) and your local police department.

Lisa Schifferle, attorney, Federal Trade Commission, Washington, DC, quoted in *Real Simple*.

*Prices subject to change.

Financial Risks from Computer-Savvy Kids

If your family shares a computer or has multiple computers connected to the same router, young users may compromise family financial data and bring malware into the house—10% of home networks were infected in the second

quarter of 2013 (latest data available). For protection, make sure that your wireless router is password-protected...remind all household members of the danger of downloading anything without first checking it out...and tell everyone to avoid clicking links in e-mails that are supposedly from banks or phone carriers but are more likely to be phishing scams.

Ellen E. Schultz, "Conquering Retirement" columnist, *The Wall Street Journal.*

Still Supporting Your Grown Kids?

Tom Healy, a consultant who helps companies recruit and retain younger workers.

Generation Y has reached adulthood—they're in their 20s and 30s. But two-thirds of this generation continue to depend on their parents for regular financial support. Two-thirds! And that does not even include help from grandparents.

So how can we provide financial support to our Gen Y kids in a way that helps them grow into true adults, rather than trapping them in a cycle of dependence? *Three suggestions...*

• **Insist on a plan of action.** Your love for your child is unconditional, but your financial support shouldn't be. Get details about how the money will be spent and how, specifically, it will lead to self-sufficiency. Don't accept, "I need the money for bills." Insist on something such as, "I need the money to help with the rent until I land a better job and find a roommate." Gen Y needs to learn that in the real world, we get paid for our efforts and our results, not just because we're short of funds.

• **Set a cutoff date.** Be clear about when assistance will end. This prevents dependence from becoming a habit and allows you to cap the drain on your savings.

• **Tell your story.** Gen Y sees what their parents have, but not the effort they put in to earn it. Reminisce (do not lecture!) with your child about the sacrifices you made and challenges you faced. Maybe you didn't take a vacation in your 20s. Maybe you didn't eat in restaurants to save for the down payment on your home. If you've shared these stories with your child before, try again—the odds of the message getting through are better now that Gen Y is older.

Mistakes Parents Make That Push Adult Children Away

Jeffrey Jensen Arnett, PhD, a research professor in the department of psychology at Clark University, Worcester, Massachusetts. He is coauthor, with Elizabeth Fishel, of *When Will My Grown-Up Kid Grow Up?* (Workman). *JeffreyArnett.com*

Our children will always be our children, but once they turn 18 or leave home, they also are adults with lives increasingly separate from our own. It is a challenge for parents to step back while also staying connected to their grown-up kids.

Much of the angst between parents and adult children stems from the tug-of-war over whose life it is. There often is a disconnect between parents who still want to shape their grown-up kids' future course and the kids who are determined to live their lives their own way.

For loving parents, their grown children's trials and errors, including failed projects and teary breakups, can be anguishing. It can be wrenching to let go of the old parental omnipotence and not be able to fix everything. But when grown kids cope with these ups and downs, they develop into resilient, self-sufficient people with the confidence that comes from standing on their own feet.

Seven "don'ts" to keep in mind when dealing with grown children…

MONEY AND CAREER

It takes a long time these days for grown kids to achieve financial independence, and my research shows that money issues are the number-one topic of conflict between parents and kids 18 to 29 years old.

• **Do not use your financial support to control your adult kids.** If you are supplying money to your adult child, you certainly can set ground rules about how that money is used—but you should not threaten to withdraw your support if the adult child doesn't make life changes unrelated to finances.

Example: It's reasonable to tell your adult child that money you're providing cannot be spent on a vacation—but don't tell him that it can't be spent on a vacation unless he leaves the girlfriend you don't like.

• **Don't push your kids to take a job in a field that pays well but that they don't like.** Not only might they hold their unhappiness with the hated job against you, their lack of passion for the field could inhibit their career growth.

Also: Do not make snide comments about the job prospects of your college-age child's field of study or the earnings potential of his line of work. It is reasonable to discuss career and earnings outlooks with your kids before they choose a college major, field of graduate study or first job. But trying to control the big decision of what field your adult child will choose is sure to stir up resentment. Keep in mind that although college majors do vary in their future earnings, getting a college degree, in any area, is the most important goal for enhancing lifelong career prospects.

• **Don't insist that your kids find their own way after college rather than return home.** These days, many adult children live at home for a short time. Almost always, their return home is temporary because they prefer to live independently as soon as they can afford to do so.

Helpful: Agree on a division of household responsibilities. Your adult child is now an adult member of the household and should do an adult share of the housework, laundry and cooking.

COMMUNICATION

Most adult children like talking to their parents and enjoy having a more adultlike relationship than they did in their teens. *But…*

• **Don't ask probing questions about your children's lives.** If they want to share something personal, they will. Adult children vary a lot in how much they want their parents to know about their lives and how much they want to confide in them.

Take special care not to raise subjects that your adult child has historically been disinclined to discuss. Resist the urge to ask follow-up questions on the rare occasions when your child does raise one of these subjects.

Example: Many adult children prefer not to discuss their love lives with their parents.

• **Don't overdo it.** Today's technology makes it cheap and easy to stay in contact with loved ones, and many adult children and their parents are in contact with one another nearly every day. However, for some grown kids, that's a bit too much togetherness at a time when they are striving to become self-sufficient. In general, it's best to follow your adult children's lead on communications. If they contact you weekly via text message, then contact them weekly via text message, too. Text messaging might not be your preferred communication method, but it's a great way to touch base with today's young adults without seeming pushy. You can always slip in a phone call now and then.

Helpful: Don't feel offended if kids go a few days without answering your text message or voice mail. It doesn't mean that they don't care. It could just mean that they are busy—or that they're not that eager to discuss that particular topic.

ROMANCE

An adult child's romantic relationships can be a minefield for parents…

• **Don't confide that you "never liked" an ex-boyfriend or ex-girlfriend** or provide reasons why your adult child is better off without this former mate. Keep in mind that ex-boyfriends and ex-girlfriends sometimes reenter the picture. That could create awkwardness if you've previously expressed a dislike.

• **Don't overlook your adult child's romantic partners at family get-togethers.** If your adult child has been seeing someone for a while, be sure to include the partner in family gatherings, then do your best to make him/her feel welcome and comfortable. The more comfortable your grown child's partner is with you, the more you are likely to see of your child.

More from Jeffrey Jensen Arnett, PhD…

How to Give Advice to an Adult Child

Many young adults spend their 20s acting in ways that seem irresponsible to their parents. They might change jobs or romantic partners frequently or rely on their parents for financial support or housing.

This is all perfectly normal and does not mean that the young adult is destined to act this way forever.

And while adult children might seem to be in desperate need of advice, there's a good chance that they will react poorly if their parents offer it. Such guidance makes them feel as if their parents still see them as children. This puts parents in a difficult position—they want to help their grown-up kids avoid missteps, but any wisdom they offer is likely to be poorly received.

Usually parents' best option is to bite their tongues and not offer their adult children advice when it hasn't been requested. Such advice might harm the relationship, and there is a good chance it won't be heeded anyway. *But speaking up could be wise if…*

• **You believe your adult child's safety is at risk.** It's worth putting the relationship at risk when safety is at stake.

Examples: Don't offer unsolicited advice if you think your adult child is staying out too late—but do if you suspect he's driving home drunk. Don't tell your daughter you don't like her new boyfriend—but do speak your mind if your daughter has a black eye and you suspect that the boyfriend is responsible.

• **The topic is money-related and you're providing financial support.** If your money is on the line, it's perfectly reasonable to voice concerns about the adult child's questionable financial decisions or even set ground rules for spending. But it will help the relationship if after voicing these concerns or setting these rules, you add something such as, "The final decision is yours, and I will continue to support you emotionally whatever you decide. I just can't continue to support you financially if you make this decision."

Example: You're paying your child's rent while he searches for a job, but you notice that he hasn't been looking for work lately.

●**You obtain permission to provide advice.** The odds of a negative reaction decline greatly if you ask the child if he would like your input before you offer it.

Warning: Respect the child's answer. If he says he prefers to work through the problem on his own, keep your advice to yourself.

When you feel you must provide advice, also ask the adult child for his advice on a different topic about which he is knowledgeable. This can keep the relationship balanced.

Simple Questions That Reveal Decline

Two simple questions can reveal an older loved one's decline…

1) For health or physical reasons, do you have difficulty climbing up 10 steps or walking one-quarter of a mile?

2) Because of underlying health or physical reasons, have you modified the way you climb 10 steps or walk one-quarter of a mile?

Any change or increased difficulty climbing steps or walking a short distance can indicate mobility problems and the beginning of functional decline that will make an older person less able to live independently. Physical therapy or the use of mobility-assistance devices may make it possible for seniors to live on their own for a longer time.

Cynthia Brown, MD, associate professor, division of gerontology, geriatrics and palliative care, University of Alabama at Birmingham, and author of an analysis of studies on mobility and aging done from 1985 to 2012, reported at *WebMD.com*

Family History Important

Fewer older individuals are putting priority on leaving money to heirs—86% of baby boomers and 74% of Americans age 72 and older say that keeping family history alive is the most important piece of their legacy…64% of baby boomers and 58% of elders say family mementos and heirlooms are important legacies. If you agree that family history is important when making an estate plan, pay special attention to giving keepsakes to family members who really want and appreciate them. Be sure to share your values—think about making an ethical will, which is not legally binding but can tell heirs a great deal about what you believe and how you have lived your life. The website *PersonalLegacyAdvisors.com* (under "Resources Examples," click on "Ethical Wills") can help in creating this document.

Roundup of experts in estate planning, reported at *MarketWatch.com*.

Creative Funerals Becoming Popular

With creative funerals, you pick a theme, provide for a variety of memorial ideas and even specify how you want mourners to dress.

Examples: A sports enthusiast calls for team memorabilia at the funeral…a gambler asks for a poker party with her name on souvenir poker chips…a medieval ceremony is followed up by a medieval-style banquet, with guests in period costumes…a baker asks each guest to prepare his/her favorite recipe and share it at a memorial potluck.

Specify your wishes as part of your will, and be sure to provide enough funds to carry them out.

Roundup of experts on funeral practices, reported at *MarketWatch.com*.

Best Way to Handle a Troublesome Neighbor

If you have a neighbor who's bringing down your home's value with an unkempt yard, very loud pets or terrible odors, consider doing the following… Schedule a time to talk—don't just drop in or try for a casual conversation. Invite the neighbor to your house as a gesture of goodwill. Research state and local laws and ordinances relating to the issue if a friendly chat is not enough. And, keep a record of the dispute in case you have to go to the authorities or to court.

Example: If a neighbor's dog often barks loudly, make a note of the times at which this happens. Say that you understand why it might be difficult for the neighbor to keep the dog quiet all the time but suggest times when it might be important to do so. If necessary, point out that there's a local ordinance on noise.

If a neighborly discussion does not make headway but you do not want to go to officials, suggest mediation.

Experts on negotiation quoted at *CNNMoney.com*.

Best Devices to Find a Lost Pet

A *microchip*, a tiny electronic chip, can be inserted under a pet's skin. Register the chip's ID number with a tracking service, and the chip can be scanned or tracked by shelters and pounds nationwide. Chips cost about $45, plus about $25 for registration.*

A *GPS collar* is a tracking device that attaches to a pet's collar and reports the location to your computer or smartphone. It sends an alert whenever a pet goes outside a boundary that you set—although it will not prevent the animal from straying. Collar devices cost $100 to $200, plus monthly service fees of $8 to $40.

Roundup of pet-care experts, reported in *Woman's Day. WomansDay.com*

*Prices subject to change.

To Keep Your Pet's Weight Under Control…

Spoil your pet with cuddles, not treats. Use a measuring cup to control the animal's portions. Neutered and spayed dogs should be fed 20% less than what is recommended on the food label—unneutered dogs have faster metabolisms and so can eat more. Switch your cat to wet food, which is higher in meat protein and contains fewer carbohydrates than dry food.

Woman's Day. WomansDay.com

Pets Can Get Depressed, Too

When pets get depressed, they may lose their appetite and become reclusive or lethargic. If you notice these symptoms, go to your veterinarian—depression can indicate arthritis, cancer or other conditions. Comforting your animal can help—so can extra playtime, a set routine and serving food at the same times each day. Try dietary changes—avoid food high in additives and artificial preservatives. You also might consider acupuncture or acupressure—find a vet who knows these techniques through the International Veterinary Acupuncture Society, *IVAS.org*.

Natural Health. NaturalHealthMag.com

EASY-TO-DO…

Don't Sound Angry When Calling Your Dog

When you sound upset or frustrated if your dog is off-leash and gets into trouble…or you yell at the dog for not coming quickly enough…you are teaching your dog that coming to you is unpleasant. Instead, give your dog lots of praise when it comes to you, no matter what it has done.

Your Dog. TuftsYourDog.com

These "Facts" About Dogs Aren't True?

A wagging tail indicates a dog's energy level, not how friendly it is. A dog wagging vigorously is ready to play or to charge. A dog's nose—whether it is dry or wet—tells you nothing about the dog's health. Check its gums, which should be bright pink. Dogs don't eat grass to induce vomiting—many just like the taste and will vomit if they eat too much. Dogs don't necessarily dislike cats—many get along well. Dogs do not need baths—but it's OK to bathe them every month or two if their smell gets strong. Only medium-sized dogs age about seven years for every human year. Dogs less than 20 pounds age about five-and-a-half to six years per human year...dogs more than 90 pounds age about eight years per human year.

Your Dog. TuftsYourDog.com

Swaddling Reduces a Dog's Stress

Placing a snug-fitting jacket around a dog's torso, much like swaddling a baby, reduced the dog's anxiety in as little as 15 minutes in a recent finding. Swaddling can be used to calm dogs that are anxious because of loud noises from fireworks or thunder...travel...or separation. The jacket used in the study, the Thundershirt, is available at pet stores and online at *Thundershirt.com*.

Your Dog. TuftsYourDog.com

Better Leash Training

Why pulling on a dog's leash often brings no response—dogs have little feeling at the base of the neck. To get a better response from your dog, use a head halter. It transmits pressure to the dog's snout and nape.

Avoid: Choke collars or collars with prongs—they can seriously injure a dog.

Your Dog. TuftsYourDog.com

911 for an Injured Cat

What should you do if a cat has been injured by a car or fallen out of a tree? "Scoop and run." Gently pick up the cat...wrap it carefully in a blanket so that it can't scratch or bite you...and rush it to the nearest emergency veterinary clinic.

Armelle de Laforcade, DVM, emergency and critical care team, Foster Hospital for Small Animals, Cummings School of Veterinary Medicine, Tufts University, North Grafton, Massachusetts, writing in *Catnip.*

Cat Droppings Can Make *Anyone* Sick

The parasite *Toxoplasma gondii* in cat feces can cause *toxoplasmosis*, which can be dangerous for anyone—not just pregnant women, who can pass the infection on to their babies, and people with compromised immunity. Toxoplasmosis has been linked to schizophrenia, obsessive-compulsive disorder, rheumatoid arthritis and brain cancer.

Self-defense: Avoid contact with cat litter and cat droppings...keep children's sandboxes covered if you or a neighbor has a cat...and wear gloves when gardening.

Study by researchers at The Stanley Medical Research Institute, Chevy Chase, Maryland, published in *Trends in Parasitology.*

17

House Proud

22 Clever Household Tips: You'll Wonder How You Lived Without Them

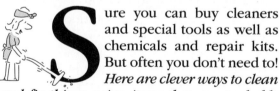

Sure you can buy cleaners and special tools as well as chemicals and repair kits. But often you don't need to! *Here are clever ways to clean and fix things using items that you probably have at home...*

CLEAN & SIMPLE

• **Polish faucets and more with newspaper.** Newspaper ink is a terrific polishing agent that requires no water or liquid, so just crumple a piece of newspaper and rub.

• **Shine shoes and plants with bananas.** Banana peels contain oil and potassium, key ingredients in store-bought shoe polish. Wipe shoes with the inside of the peel (discard the stringy parts of the peel first). Then buff the shoes with a clean cloth. You also can use the peels to clean the dust and debris from leafy houseplants.

• **Clean car tires with mayonnaise.** To rid your tires of tree sap and road tar, dab a bit of mayonnaise onto the marks. Leave on for 10 minutes. Wipe away residue with a clean cloth. The vinegar in the mayo acts as a natural cleaner, and the oil and eggs add shine.

• **Remove mold in a refrigerator drip pan with white vinegar.** Vinegar is a natural sanitizer and bacteria killer. Put some in a spray bottle, and apply directly to the area. Let it sit for 20 minutes before wiping with a clean cloth.

• **Get rid of dishwasher gunk and odors with Kool-Aid.** Fill the dishwasher dispenser

---

Julie Edelman, aka "The Accidental Housewife," is a rich source of everyday tips to maintain your home, family, health and sanity. Based on Florida's Gulf coast, Julie appears regularly on the *Today* show, *Rachael Ray* and *The Doctors*. She is author of *The New York Times* best-seller *The Accidental Housewife: How to Overcome Housekeeping Hysteria One Task at a Time* (Ballantine). *JuliesTips.com*

with a packet of lemonade Kool-Aid or any powdery drink mix that contains citric acid. Run the empty dishwasher for a full normal cycle to remove gunk, lime and rust stains as well as odors.

• **Remove scuff marks on floors and shower curtain scum with tennis balls.**

Scuff marks: Cut an X in a yellow tennis ball (pink could leave color on your floor). Place the ball on the top part of a broomstick. Rub the ball back and forth on the floor to erase scuffs.

Shower curtain scum: Throw one or two tennis balls into your washing machine with your shower curtain along with one cup of white vinegar and your usual amount of laundry detergent. Run on the regular cycle. The ball acts as a scrub to remove scum and mildew...vinegar kills mold.

• **Clean latex paint from your skin with baby oil.** Gently rub baby oil anywhere on your skin that has paint. Then wash with soap and hot water.

• **Remove deodorant marks on clothing with the foam from dry-cleaner hangers.** Remove the foam from a hanger, and rub it back and forth forcefully on deodorant marks. A towel works, too, but foam is gentler on fabric.

CLEVER FIX-ITS

• **Replace lost earring backs with pencil erasers.** Snip the tip of a pencil eraser, and use it to temporarily replace a lost back so that you can wear the earring until you replace the back.

• **Quiet squeaky doors with cucumber.** Take a slice of cucumber, and rub it up and down several times all around the hinge. Have a clean cloth handy to wipe away any excess. I am not sure why it works—it just does!

• **Fix holes in screens with dental floss.** Use dental floss to mend small holes in a window or door screen. Weave in and out by hand or with a sewing needle. Then tie the ends.

• **Mend minor cracks in fine china with milk.** Milk contains casein, a protein that, when heated, turns into a natural plasticlike glue. Place your cracked dish in a pan or pot large enough to cover it completely in milk.

Bring the milk to a boil, and then reduce to a simmer. Let it simmer for 45 to 60 minutes, then let the milk cool. Rinse the plate. The crack should be sealed!

KEEPING BUGS AWAY

• **Deter mealybugs with matchbooks.** You can have mealybugs in your pantry and not know it. To keep the bugs from flourishing, take flour, rice and cereal out of their original packaging right after you bring them home and place them in Tupperware-like containers. As an extra precaution, put a matchbook on top of the food before sealing. The sulfur repels mealybugs.

• **Kill fruit flies with red wine.** Fruit flies love the fermented grape! Fill a glass with one-half inch of leftover red wine. Tightly cover the top of the glass with plastic wrap. Poke small holes in the wrap so that the flies find their one-way ticket in.

• **Repel ants, roaches and fleas with citrus rinds.** Bugs hate *D-limonene*, which is naturally found in the oil in lemon and orange rinds. Place pieces of rind where these pests are likely to enter, such as door and window openings and ledges...cracks between kitchen cabinets...and holes in floors. Replace every few days, as needed.

• **Ward off booklice with silica packets.** Those little packets of silica you find in packaging of electronics, shoes, nutritional supplements, etc., absorb moisture. Booklice live in the damp fungus and mold that thrives in books. Put silica packets behind the books and anywhere you suspect moisture. Packets also are available at *Amazon.com*.

More from Julie Edelman...

Oldies but Goodies

You may have heard some of these tips already, but they work so well that they are worth hearing again...

• **Test egg freshness.** Even though eggs have a "use by" date, they often are perfectly fine beyond that date. You can test their freshness simply by seeing if they sink or swim. Fill a bowl with enough water to cover the eggs, and then gently place them in. If they sink, they're fresh.

- **Dry out a wet cell phone.** If your cell phone winds up in the wash or toilet, immediately remove the battery and memory chip. Place both the battery and phone in a bowl filled with enough uncooked rice to completely cover the items. Leave for two to three days. Remove and use an old toothbrush or pastry brush to gently brush away any remaining rice dust so that it doesn't get trapped in any portals or openings. You might have saved your phone!

- **Fix a wood scratch with walnuts.** For small scratches on your dark wood furniture, gently rub a walnut in a circular motion several times over the scratch. Let the natural oils seep into the scratch for five to 10 minutes. Buff with a clean cloth.

- **Clean a toilet bowl with Alka-Seltzer.** Drop two Alka-Seltzer or Polident effervescent tablets into the bowl. Let them fizz and remain for 15 to 20 minutes. Clean with a toilet brush scrubber and flush.

- **Remove bubble gum from hair with creamy peanut butter.** Before you snip those locks, reach for peanut butter—the oilier, the better! Put a dab on a toothbrush, and brush the gummy area. Use a little at a time. Repeat if necessary, and then shampoo. Plain oil works, too, but kids tend to get a kick out of peanut butter.

Handy Trick to Unscrew a Recessed Bulb

It can be difficult to get your fingers around a recessed bulb. To unscrew a lightbulb from a recessed fixture, fold the ends of a piece of duct tape back over themselves, leaving a sticky section in the middle. After putting the sticky section on the bulb, grab the ends of the duct tape and twist.

Family Handyman. FamilyHandyman.com

EASY-TO-DO...
Fizzy Fix for a Slow Toilet

If a toilet is slow but not completely stopped up, pour one cup of white vinegar and one-half cup of baking soda in the toilet and swish the water around until it fizzes quite dramatically. Give a few more plunges, and flush the toilet. The strong reaction between the vinegar and baking soda should clear the way.

Joan Wilen and Lydia Wilen, health investigators based in New York City, who have spent decades collecting "cures from the cupboard." They are authors of *Bottom Line's Treasury of Home Remedies & Natural Cures* (Bottom Line Books) and the free e-letter *Household Magic Daily Tips*. HouseholdMagicDailyTips.com

Clogged Sink? Skip the Plumber and Try This...

Fill an empty milk jug or a two-liter soda bottle with water. Cover up the overflow drain of the sink with duct tape (to stop air from escaping). In one quick motion, jam the top of the bottle into the drain and squeeze the bottle hard to send a jet of water into the drain. Remove the duct tape, and run the water to see if the clog is gone. If not, you can repeat these steps up to three times. If that doesn't work, it's time to call a plumber.

Men's Health. MensHealth.com

Carpet-Cleaning Tricks from the Queen of Clean

Linda Cobb, "The Queen of Clean," author of *Talking Dirty with the Queen of Clean* (Pocket Books). She previously owned one of the largest cleaning companies in Michigan and hosted a cleaning show on the DIY Network. Based in Phoenix, she currently operates the website *QueenofClean.com*.

There are a lot of carpet-cleaning products on the market that claim to do the same job as professional carpet-cleaning services at a fraction of the price. But choose carefully—many of these products are less effective than they claim to be, and some can do permanent damage to carpets. *The best options…*

SMALL STAINS

Spray-on carpet spot-and-stain removers are an affordable solution for most stains, but effectiveness varies greatly from product to product. I've found Carpet CPR ($9.95 for a 24-ounce bottle,* *LeatherCPR.com*)…Folex Instant Carpet Spot Remover (around $7 for a 32-ounce bottle, *FolexCompany.com*)…and Spot Shot ($6.99 for a 22-ounce bottle, *SpotShot.com*) to be effective. All are available on *Amazon.com*.

Warning: Handheld carpet spot-cleaning machines can do a nice job of cleaning small stains. Trouble is, they create an area of clean rug that's just as obvious as the stain they removed, so I don't recommend them. And never use laundry spot remover, laundry detergent, shampoo or dish soap on carpet stains. These contain detergents and other cleaners that you will never completely get out of your carpet. Dirt and grime are likely to stick to this detergent residue, making the carpet appear even dingier.

STUBBORN STAINS AND
HIGH-TRAFFIC AREAS

A hot-water-extraction machine—which is often called a steam cleaner—is the most effective do-it-yourself alternative for cleaning larger areas and stubborn stains. These apply hot water from your tap and/or cleaning chemicals to the carpet, then use a powerful vacuum to suck the liquid back out. You can rent one for around $25 a day. Renting saves a considerable amount of money. A home with 800 square feet of carpet might cost $200 to clean by a pro, so $25 for a day's rental and a $10 bottle of spot-and-stain remover represents a savings of $165.

The Rug Doctor is a good brand to rent (*RugDoctor.com*).

Or you can buy your own hot-water-extraction machine for less than $200. I like Hoover or Bissell models.

*Prices subject to change.

Example: The Hoover Max Extract Dual V WidePath Carpet Washer (recently available for $209.99 on *Hoover.com*).

If using a hot-water-extraction machine…

• **Put only hot water in the tank, not chemical cleaners.** The chemicals used in these machines often leave a residue behind that can attract grime. If your carpets are stained or have become discolored in high-traffic areas, instead pretreat the affected areas with a carpet spot-and-stain remover, such as those mentioned above. Allow this to remain on the carpet for the amount of time recommended on the bottle, then use the hot-water extractor to apply water only.

• **Limit the amount of water you apply, then remove every drop.** Make only one or two passes when applying hot water, but continue to make passes to extract water until you see no more water coming up the unit's hose. This could take a while—using a hot-water-extraction machine can be a lengthy chore—but if water is allowed to remain in the carpet, it could lead to mold or mildew.

• **If you rent a hot-water-extraction machine,** take it outside and run hot water mixed with vinegar through it to clean it out before using it on your carpet. The people who rented it before you may have used chemicals in it that could damage your carpet.

• **If you own a hot-water-extraction machine,** empty the tank after each use, dry the tank's interior and leave the top of the tank off when you store the machine. This reduces the odds that mold or mildew will develop inside the tank, then be transferred to your carpet.

• **If you use a hot-water-extraction machine to treat a stain within minutes of the stain occurring,** start with cold water before switching to hot. Using hot water initially could set the stain.

Warning: Other types of do-it-yourself devices and products that claim to compete with hot-water extraction for cleaning large areas of carpeting are best avoided. There are dry powders and foams designed to be spread on carpets, then vacuumed up. Trouble is, it's impossible to vacuum up all that's applied. The remainder will work its way down into the carpet and turn into a pasty grime-holding residue the next time the carpet becomes wet, such as when you later use a hot-water-extraction machine. Carpet shampooers are best avoided, too, because they can be abrasive to carpet fibers.

WHOLE-HOME CARPET CLEANING

If you have many large carpeted rooms that require cleaning or want your carpet to be as clean as possible, it's worth hiring a professional carpet cleaner. These pros have cleaning equipment that can heat water to a much higher temperature than the hot water do-it-yourselfers use, and they have vacuums that can extract water more effectively.

The typical pro charges 20 to 30 cents per square foot of carpet. Some carpet-cleaning pros offer coupons in local publications or on their websites that can reduce prices.

Warning: Before hiring a professional carpet cleaner, confirm that he/she has a truck-mounted system. These produce the highest water temperatures and best water extraction. Confirm that the company carries liability insurance. Insurance protects you if your carpet or anything else is damaged, and it suggests that this is a legitimate professional.

CLEANING PET STAINS

Pet urine stains are best treated as soon as possible. First blot up all that you can with paper towels. Once you have done that, spray on a solution of one-third white vinegar and two-thirds cool water. Again blot, blot, blot. Allow to dry, and then treat with carpet spot remover if there is a stain.

For odor, try Odorzout. It is a dry product that eliminates odor by absorbing it instead of covering it up (available on *Amazon.com*). Use according to directions.

If you own a carpet-cleaning machine, now is the time to use it. Blot up all the urine you can, then treat with the vinegar/water mixture and extract it using cool water.

Some pet "messes," including vomit and feces, sit on top of the carpet. These require a special cleaning strategy.

Don't rush to scrape up the mess as most people tend to do. That smears the material deeper into the carpet fibers. Instead, pour a

> **EASY-TO-DO...**
> ## Better Carpet Care
> Your carpet won't require cleaning as often if you vacuum at least twice a week. Most of the dirt will be vacuumed away before it has time to work its way into carpet fibers. Replace your vacuum bag when it's half full—the fuller the bag, the less suction your vacuum has. If your vacuum has a canister rather than a bag, empty it after one or two uses.

significant amount of baking soda onto the mess—cover it completely. Use a whole box if necessary.

The baking soda should draw the moisture out of the mess until the material gets dry enough—you probably want to leave it overnight—to be gently lifted up with a paper towel, plastic bag or a plastic putty knife. Next, vacuum up the remaining baking-soda-and-mess residue using your vacuum's hose with no attachment—a hose alone provides the strongest suction on a vacuum cleaner. If there's discoloration, use one of the carpet spot-and-stain removers listed in the section about small stains.

How to Remove a White Table Ring

A white ring on wood furniture is probably a water stain.

Our favorite fix: Mix plain white toothpaste with an equal amount of baking soda (usually one-half teaspoon of each will work), then massage the mixture into the problem area. Wipe the paste away and buff dry. If the area seems a little dull, rub with furniture polish or even a little olive oil.

Joan Wilen and Lydia Wilen, health investigators based in New York City, who have spent decades collecting "cures from the cupboard." They are authors of *Bottom Line's Treasury of Home Remedies & Natural Cures* (Bottom Line Books) and the free e-letter *Household Magic Daily Tips. HouseholdMagicDailyTips.com*

Be Careful When Cleaning Your TV Screen

Never use window cleaner, alcohol, ammonia or paper towels when cleaning your TV screen. Instead, use a clean, soft, lint-free cloth, similar to the microfiber used to clean eyeglasses. Turn off the TV, and let it cool down. Wipe the screen gently to remove smudges. If the screen is very dirty, add a few drops of mild dish soap or hand soap to lukewarm water and dampen the cloth.

Consumer Reports. ConsumerReports.org

Jewelry Repairs You Can Do Yourself

David Preston, an instructor at the California Institute of Jewelry Training, Carmichael, California. He is a jewelry designer and former bench jeweler. *Jewelry Training.com*

Jewelry repairs can cost anywhere from $20 to hundreds of dollars, but there are certain repairs you can perform safely on your own. *Three jewelry tasks you can try—and three never to try...*

DO: Replace opened jump rings. The jump ring is the circle of metal that often connects a necklace or bracelet to its clasp. But once a jump ring has been pulled open, it is more likely to open again. Silver jump rings are particularly hard to keep shut once opened.

Better to buy a replacement jump ring at a craft-supply store such as Michael's (*Michaels.com*). These often cost less than $1 apiece. You can replace a clasp, too, but those sold at craft stores are gold-plated and won't match the color of real gold.

Be careful how you open this new jump ring to get it onto your jewelry. Rather than pull the circle of metal open into a letter C—which would make it susceptible to pulling open this way again—gently pull the ring open to the side as you would a key ring when you wish to add a key. (Use small pliers that have no teeth if possible—teeth can leave ugly marks on the metal.)

***DO NOT*: Solder breaks in jewelry.** Precious metals require special solders. Conventional solder won't bond properly and could contaminate the precious metal, lowering its quality.

***DO*: Reglue pearls back into their settings.** If a pearl comes loose, you can safely reattach it using a standard five-minute two-part epoxy sold online or at hardware stores. Clean any loose residue out of the setting, add a small amount of epoxy with a toothpick, then put the pearl back in place. If epoxy squishes out around the edges of the pearl, you used too much. Remove the pearl, and wipe off the epoxy with a paper towel dipped in rubbing alcohol. Let dry before you try again.

To string pearls: If the string breaks and pearls are not knotted, the string can be replaced using silk thread intended for restringing—other materials are too weak. If pearls are knotted, restringing is best left to a professional jeweler.

***DO NOT*: Attempt to reglue loose pearls yourself if the small metal post in the setting has broken off.** (There usually is a post that fits a hole drilled into the underside of the pearl.) Have a jeweler replace the post. Also, do not attempt to glue any translucent stones. You will see the glue through the stone. A good rule is that if the stone was glued to begin with, it can be reglued.

***DO*: Inspect gem settings for bent or worn prongs.** Damaged prongs can lead to lost gems. Rub jewelry that has prongs across an inconspicuous spot on a fibrous garment such as a wool sweater. Then examine the settings under a magnifying glass. If fibers have become caught under a prong, it might be on the path to becoming loose enough for the gem to escape.

Similarly, if you have jewelry with "channel set" stones—a row of stones set between two walls of metal—examine these walls under a magnifying glass. If the walls seem to bow outward slightly, the gems could be at risk.

***DO NOT:* Try to fix prongs yourself.** Do-it-yourselfers who attempt this tend to reposition prongs in a way that appears tighter but actually leaves them prone to snagging on clothing and bending back suddenly, such as when a hand bearing a ring is pushed into a pocket. That could allow the gem to fall free. Other risks include chipping a corner off a gem or leaving ugly tool marks on the metal. Prong repair—and channel-setting repair—is best left to a jeweler.

months. Keep potatoes away from onions, but store them with apples to keep them from sprouting. Place asparagus and delicate herbs such as parsley, cilantro and chives stems down in a glass of water kept in the fridge. Store fresh gingerroot in the freezer, and grate it frozen when you need it for cooking. Keep mushrooms in a paper bag in the fridge or in a cool, dry place.

Joseph M. Mercola, MD, an osteopathic physician who provides natural health information and resources, writing at *Mercola.com.*

Ring Stuck on Your Finger? Try This...

To remove a ring stuck on your finger, apply a lubricant such as hand sanitizer so that the ring can slide off. If that doesn't work, hold a bag of ice in your hand above your head until the finger numbs. If this fails, work the end of a piece of waxed dental floss between the ring and your finger, then circle loops of the floss repeatedly around the knuckle, compressing the skin. Position each floss loop close enough to the one before so that the skin doesn't squish out appreciably between loops. The compression and the slickness of the floss might make it possible to twist the ring free. *Do not try to cut a stuck ring off your own finger.* If other ring-removal strategies fail, hospitals and some jewelry stores have special ring cutters that can do this with far less risk for injury.

David Preston, an instructor at the California Institute of Jewelry Training, Carmichael, California. He is a jewelry designer and former bench jeweler. *Jewelry Training.com*

Ways to Make Veggies and Herbs Last Longer

Put onions in old clean pantyhose, and tie a knot between each one to keep them separate. They will stay fresh for up to eight

The Perfect Fried Egg

To cook the perfect fried egg, add four tablespoons of olive oil to a sauté pan and bring it to medium-high heat. Tip the pan so that the oil collects in a small pool, crack the egg and let it slide into the oil. Keep the pan tilted throughout the cooking process. Spoon hot oil over the egg two or three times. After only 30 seconds of cooking, the egg white will form a protective pillow around the yolk. The egg then can be removed from the pan.

José Andrés, dean of Spanish studies at International Culinary Center, New York City, quoted in *The New York Times.*

EASY-TO-DO...

Get Rid of Garlicky Hands in Seconds

If your hands smell like garlic or onion, this helpful hint works like magic. Take a piece of flatware (any metal spoon, dull knife or fork will do), pretend it's a bar of soap and wash your hands with it under cold water. No special kind of metal needed! The garlic or onion smell will disappear in seconds. And you can go back to cooking without a soapy smell on your hands.

Joan Wilen and Lydia Wilen, health investigators based in New York City, who have spent decades collecting "cures from the cupboard." They are authors of *Bottom Line's Treasury of Home Remedies & Natural Cures* (Bottom Line Books) and the free e-letter *Household Magic Daily Tips. HouseholdMagic DailyTips.com*

Better Broiling and Frying

To broil or fry food without triggering a smoke alarm, one option is to use an alarm that has a "hush" button. When pushed, it reduces the alarm's sensitivity for a short period of time and then resets itself unless smoke still is present. Also, be aware that ionization alarms tend to be more sensitive to cooking fumes than photoelectric types. If an alarm is to be positioned within 20 feet of a cooking appliance, use either an ionization alarm equipped with a hush button or the photoelectric kind. Never disable a smoke alarm to keep it from going off—it's too easy to forget to turn it on again.

Lorraine Carli, vice president, outreach and advocacy, National Fire Protection Association, Quincy, Massachusetts.

Make Your Home Smell Divine

Fresh-baked cookies is not the most inviting scent.

Best: Individual natural aromas, such as fresh lemon, green tea, lavender, cedar, pine and basil. Recent research reveals that these scents help sell a home—and thus can make any home more inviting to guests. Try displaying a bouquet of fresh lavender or decorate a table with cut pine branches.

Study of the effects of aromas by researchers at Washington State University, Pullman, reported in *The Wall Street Journal.*

Keep Cut Flowers Looking Fresh

To keep fresh flowers looking their best, mix one tablespoon of sugar, one-half teaspoon of vinegar and one-half teaspoon of bleach into a quart of water. Fill the vase as needed. Also, cut each stem on an angle so that it can absorb more water, and remove any leaves that will be beneath the waterline. Every day or so, trim the end of each stem again and change the water.

Heloise, internationally syndicated lifestyle columnist, San Antonio, and author of *Handy Household Hints from Heloise* (Rodale).

9 Ways to Warm Up a Cold Spot in Your Home

Richard Trethewey, the heating, ventilation and air-conditioning (HVAC) expert for the PBS-TV series *This Old House* since 1979. He is founder and owner of RST Thermal, which provides energy-efficient solutions for home heating and cooling to home owners and businesses in New England. He is based in Westwood, Massachusetts. *ThisOldHouse.com*

Is one room or area in your home much colder than others? There are various ways to solve the problem, some of them simple and inexpensive...others involving greater effort and expense.

We asked heating expert Richard Trethewey how you can figure out what's wrong and what to do about it...

SIMPLE SOLUTIONS

Home owners often think that they have to live with temperature inconsistencies in different parts of their homes because they are reluctant to spend tens of thousands of dollars to upgrade their heating systems and insulation. *But in many cases, the solutions are so simple and inexpensive that people may overlook them...*

• **Check the arrangement of the furniture and drapes** to make sure that heating vents or radiators are not blocked.

• **Shut the damper in the fireplace** firmly when you aren't using it.

• **Feel for drafts along windows** by holding a lit candle along the gap between the window and the trim. Watch if the flame bends or flickers, indicating a leak, and then caulk or weather-strip to close the gap. If a window still feels drafty, pry off the interior wall trim around the window and spray foam sealant between the wall and window frame. Then press the trim back into place.

• **If you need to heat only a specific part of a room** such as the desk area in a home office or a couch near a TV, get an energy-efficient, 1,500-watt portable electric space heater such as the Holmes Eco Smart Energy Saving Portable Heater, which weighs less than five pounds, stands 7.5 inches high and costs about $35* but produces as much heat as larger models.

BIGGER PROBLEMS

Here, cold-spot problems and cost-effective solutions…

Problem: **Major heat loss through exterior walls.** Does one wall or part of a wall feel cold all the time in the winter? Traditional fiberglass insulation in the wall may be inadequate because it has broken down over time or has left gaps around electrical boxes or light fixtures, creating drafts.

Solution: Blow Icynene into the walls. Icynene is a new type of expanding foam insulation that is injected into wall cavities through small holes. It's much denser than fiberglass and reduces air infiltration with double the effectiveness of fiberglass. The Icynene can be sprayed in without removing the fiberglass and directly onto electrical and plumbing work. (If you need to access pipes and wires for repair in the future, the Icynene foam can be cut away). For more information, go to *Icynene.com*.

Cost: About $4 per square foot for the material and installation.

Problem: **Heat from your furnace is not making it to the room that is cold.** If you have a forced-air heating system and the airflow out of a room's vent feels weak, you may be losing heat to tiny cracks and gaps in the ductwork in your walls. In older homes, as much as 20% of the heat never makes it to rooms, especially those farthest from the furnace. Trying to seal ductwork yourself with mastic tape often is ineffective because leaks can be hard to identify and much of the ductwork in a house is not accessible.

*Prices subject to change.

Solution: Use Aeroseal duct sealant, a nontoxic polymer spray that contractors pump into both rigid and flexible ducts, sealing gaps from the inside of the ducts. This product received a Best New Product award from *This Old House* magazine. It has proved so effective at improving heat flow (and saving on heating costs) that it's worth doing in your entire home. Go to *Aeroseal.com* to locate a dealer near you.

Cost: About $1,000 to treat the ductwork of a 2,000-square-foot home.

Problem: **Your thermostat is poorly positioned.** If your thermostat is in a sunny room that cools slowly, there will be a delay before the heat kicks in. If the room warms quickly, it shuts off the furnace too early.

Solution: Install a wireless thermostat in the chilly room. You can easily replace your old wall thermostat with a wireless receiver and place a wireless thermostat, which contains the temperature sensor, anywhere in the house. These units transmit up to 500 feet through walls, ceilings and floors.

Recommended: ZoneFirst Wireless Thermostat and Receiver (*ZoneFirst.com*).

Cost: About $200 plus a one-hour service call from an electrician.

Note: If moving your traditional thermostat wiring to a chilly room is easy to do, consider installing the Nest thermostat (*Nest.com*) instead. It's not wireless, but it can be linked to your computer and/or smartphone so that you can control it remotely, adjusting the temperature up or down on short notice even when you are not at home. The Nest also can learn your daily patterns, so it can turn down the temperature when you leave the house.

Cost: $250 plus a one-hour service call from an electrician.

Problem: **Heat from a room that's warmer is not dispersing into an adjoining colder room.** Rooms that have an additional heating source (for example, a stove or a fireplace), as well as rooms on the south side of a house that get a lot of sun, tend to be warmer than the rest of the house.

Solution: Install a room-to-room ventilator. These ultraquiet fan systems are positioned between rooms right in the wall. One side of the ventilator draws heat from the warm room…the other side disperses it into the cold room. Ventilators run off of a manual wall switch or an automatic thermostat.

Cost: About $100, depending on the size of the ventilator, plus two to three hours for an electrician to open up your wall and install the ventilator.

Problem: **You just want to add extra heat to an entire room without having to turn up the thermostat for the whole house.**

Solutions: Put in a ceiling fan that includes a space heater. The Reiker Room Conditioner with remote control installs and functions just like a regular ceiling fan. But in the winter, with the heater engaged, the fan blades circulate heat quickly through the room.

Cost: $350 plus a two-hour installation service call from an electrician.

Install radiant-floor heating, especially for rooms with cold, ceramic tile floors such as bathrooms, mudrooms and kitchens. Radiant-floor heating is made of ultrathin heating cables in mesh mats—not unlike the wires in an electric blanket—that are installed underneath your flooring.

Drawback: Because the heating system must be installed under the tile, this option is best reserved for when you are planning to redo your floors anyway.

Cost: About $6 per square foot for materials and installation.

If these solutions don't work, your problems may be more complex and you may need a professional energy audit.

How to Use a Space Heater Safely

Space heaters cause 300 deaths and 25,000 residential fires each year.

To use a portable electric heater safely: Keep the heater at least three feet away from furniture and other combustible material…

place it on a hard, level surface where children and pets can't get to it…if an extension cord is needed, make sure that it is of 14-gauge wire or larger…and opt for a heater that has a tip-over safety switch, which automatically shuts off the unit if it falls over.

Consumer Product Safety Commission, Washington, DC. *CPSC.gov*

When Fans Do More Harm Than Good

Electric fans may do more harm than good when temperatures rise above 95°F.

Reason: Fans don't cool the air—they blow air that is warmer than body temperature.

At greatest risk: The very young and very old, and people with compromised immune systems.

Study by The Cochrane Collaboration, an international nonprofit group that analyzes medical research, published in *The Cochrane Library*.

Caution: Your Home's Hot Water May Be *Too Hot*

In a recent finding, 41% of homes had water heaters that produced water above the recommended safe temperature of 120°F. Just three seconds of exposure to 140°F water can cause a serious burn.

Self-defense: Set your water heater's temperature to 120°F or below, and use a thermometer to check the water. When taking a bath or shower, start with cold water and mix it slowly with hot water. Also, do not run water elsewhere in the house, because that can raise the temperature of the tub or shower water.

Study of 708 homes by researchers at The Johns Hopkins Bloomberg School of Public Health, Baltimore, published in *Journal of Burn Care & Research*.

Low-Cost Home-Monitoring Options

Most home-monitoring and control systems let you use a smartphone or tablet to do various tasks remotely, such as adjusting your thermostat, turning lights on and off, and controlling a security system. The Iris system from Lowe's costs $179* for either the "Safe & Secure" kit, which comes with motion and contact sensors (for monitoring windows, doors, more)…or the "Comfort & Control" version, which lets you adjust the thermostat and monitor energy use. You can buy both packages for $299—a savings of $59. Comcast and Verizon offer similar systems. More advanced packages are available from AT&T, Time Warner Cable and ADT Security. Shop around for the best deals, and watch for any short-term promotions.

Kiplinger's Personal Finance. Kiplinger.com
*Prices subject to change.

Fix Your Home's Weak Wi-Fi

Eric Geier, CEO of NoWiresSecurity, a cloud-based Wi-Fi security service, and On Spot Techs, an on-site computer services company. Based in Fairborn, Ohio, he is a certified wireless network administrator and author of numerous books on computer technology, including *Geeks on Call: Wireless Networking: 5-Minute Fixes* (Wiley). His website is *EGeier.com*.

Do Netflix movies keep stopping and starting when you stream them to a laptop or TV over your wireless Internet (Wi-Fi)? Does e-mail take forever to download on your iPad in certain rooms? The problem is likely your wireless router. The radio wave signals that your router emits may be too weak when they reach your devices. *Some smart solutions to get a stronger, steadier signal…*

• **Make sure that the router signals aren't impaired by physical barriers that cause interference and signal degradation.** These may include concrete and brick walls, heavy furniture and metal objects such as tall filing cabinets.

• **Move the router to a more central location** in relation to where you use your wireless devices most.

Resource: Use the free Android smartphone app *Wifi Analyzer* to locate the areas of your home where the router signals are strongest and weakest, and then place the router in the best possible spot that still is close enough to an available Internet cable or phone jack.

Helpful: It's usually best to place the router in a high position, such as on a high shelf or on top of a bookcase, to avoid barriers such as furniture.

• **Pay your Internet service provider for more speed.** No matter what kind of router you have or where it is positioned, it can transmit data only as fast as the connection you have from your cable or telephone company. Internet speed is measured in bits-per-second (bps) and can vary at different times of day based on what else you are doing at that time on your home network.

To stream HD movies, for instance, at least 10 megabits per second (or mbps) is recommended to avoid having the picture freeze up. Keep in mind that having multiple users in your home requires higher speeds. A dial-up modem transmits at up to 56 kilobits per second (1,024 kilobits is a megabit)…DSL service, typically up to 6 mbps…and standard Internet cable service, typically 10 mbps or faster for an extra charge. *More elaborate solutions are possible…*

• **Add a wireless repeater.** Plug one of these small devices into any electrical socket at the outer range of your existing router's coverage, and it acts as a mini router, catching the original router signal and extending it.

Repeater to consider: SharePort Mobile Companion by D-Link (about $40*).

• **Switch your router's channel.** Wi-Fi routers send radio waves on different frequencies or channels. During setup, some routers automatically detect the least crowded channel as

*Prices subject to change.

287

the default setting. But if you live in a neighborhood or apartment building with lots of new wireless connections, those routers may be using the same channel and weakening your signal.

What to do: Start by downloading to your computer the *inSSIDer* diagnostic tool, which will analyze what channel your router is using and which one can offer you the best signal strength ($19.99, *inSSIDer.com*). Then refer to your router owner's manual for instructions on how to change the router channels.

Fix a Computer Problem from Far Away

Robert Siciliano, an online security expert for software company McAfee.

Have you ever asked a friend or relative for computer help over the phone? Or maybe you are the one getting the calls for tech help?

I serve as the unpaid computer guru for my extended family. But when my mother (or any family member) calls with a computer problem, I do not jump in my car and I certainly don't try to talk anyone through a technical fix over the phone.

Instead, I use remote-access software. This software lets me take charge of my mother's computer and see what's appearing on her screen right from my own computer. Both machines must have broadband Internet.

I recommend LogMeIn Free, which is particularly easy to use (Windows or Mac, *LogMeIn. com*). I did have to talk my mother through downloading the LogMeIn software onto her computer, but I made this process easy by e-mailing her the link she needed to click on (*Secure.LogMeIn.com/US/products/free*).

Other free remote-access programs include TeamViewer (Windows or Mac, *TeamViewer. com*) and SkyFex (Windows only, *SkyFex.com*).

I also update the antivirus and anti-phishing security software on my mother's computer every three to six months—you can do this with one of the remote-access programs. Now I chat with my mother about her life, not what's on her computer screen!

Help for Slow iPads and Other Devices

Rod Scher, former editor, *Smart Computing.*

To speed up a sluggish tablet, don't just put the device into "sleep" mode, as you normally would do—instead, shut it off completely, then restart it. For an iPad, hold down the sleep/wake button until the red slider appears allowing you to turn it off. For Android-based tablets, hold the power button down until the shutdown button appears and then select "power off." Restart your device.

To quit unresponsive apps on an iPad, force the app to quit by holding down the sleep/ wake button until the red slider appears. Then hold down the home button for about 10 seconds. Once the app has quit, you should be brought back to the home screen.

For an Android-based tablet operating the 3.2 version or below, tap the menu button, select "Settings," choose "Applications" and tap "Manage Applications." Under the "Running" tab, select the app you wish to close and touch the "force stop" button. For an Android 4.0 or higher, bring up the multitasking pane and swipe the app to the left or right.

To stop getting disconnected from Wi-Fi, make sure that you are not in a "drop out" zone in your home or office. That's where the Wi-Fi signal is weak because of interference from other devices or building materials such as brick, stone or metal.

18

Help Yourself

Feel-Good Strategies for Life's Disappointments

We try to shrug off the little things that make us feel bad. We tell ourselves it does not matter that we were snubbed by a neighbor. We reason that it's no big deal that our plan to get new customers failed. We reassure ourselves that our feelings of loneliness after retirement will pass. But recent research suggests that even minor emotional challenges such as these can lead to major mental-health issues when they are left unaddressed.

Example: A study published recently in *Psychological Science* found that the more minor daily emotional stresses participants reported, the more likely they were to suffer from other serious psychological disorders such as depression 10 years later.

Minor emotional challenges are the psychological equivalent of cuts and scrapes. They don't require surgery, but a little basic first aid will reduce the odds that they will become infected.

Effective first-aid strategies for three common emotional challenges…

REJECTION

Even minor rejections can wound us far deeper than logic suggests they should.

Example: A study published in *Annual Review of Psychology* found that people feel significant emotional pain when two strangers who are throwing a ball back and forth fail to include them in the game, a rejection of seemingly no consequence. Remarkably, this emotional pain persists even after study subjects are told that the rejection is not real—the

Guy Winch, PhD, a clinical psychologist in private practice in New York City. He is author of *Emotional First Aid: Practical Strategies for Treating Failure, Rejection, Guilt, and Other Everday Psychological Injuries* (Plume). *GuyWinch.com*

289

ballplayers were instructed to leave them out of the game as part of the experiment.

The hurt we feel when we're rejected is very real—the brain pathways that react to rejection are the same ones that react to physical pain. In fact, pain and rejection seem so similar to our brains that taking Tylenol temporarily eases the sting of rejection. The reason rejection affects us so deeply is probably evolutionary—early humans could not survive if they were rejected by their social group.

To recover from rejection…

1. Assume it's them. When people end romantic relationships, they sometimes say, "It's not you, it's me." This may be a cliché—but it's also an important distinction. When you feel rejected, go ahead and tell yourself that it really is the person doing the rejecting who has mishandled the situation, not you. That won't eliminate the sting of the rejection, but it should reduce the odds that you will fall into a downward spiral of self-criticism.

2. Focus on aspects of yourself that you deeply value. Take some time to think about this, and pay special attention to talents and attributes related to the aspect of your life where the rejection occurred—your key professional skills if the rejection was career-related, for example. Once you have identified several characteristics, choose one and write a brief essay on why it's important to you. We are more convinced by things we write than by things we think, because writing activates additional parts of the brain.

3. Spend time around people who understand your worth. Being around people who value us can effectively counter the sting of rejection.

Example: If you have a falling-out with a friend, have lunch with another friend who cares about you.

LONELINESS

Surveys suggest that 40% of us will feel lonely at some point in our adult lives. Loneliness is particularly common when we leave our parents' home as young adults and when we retire and no longer have workplace relationships.

Loneliness can become a downward spiral. Lonely people often come off as desperate or defensive, reducing the odds that the people they meet will want to spend time with them. *A three-step plan for coping with loneliness…*

1. Try to figure out what you are doing that's keeping other people away from you (or keeping you away from other people). Lonely people tend to become defensive when it's suggested that they are partially to blame for their loneliness. But if they do accept this as true, they usually can identify and correct some aspect of their behavior that's limiting their ability to form relationships.

Example: Lonely people often feel that they cannot join existing conversations at social functions, even though it's usually perfectly acceptable. Just say, "Excuse me, I don't know anyone here. Is it OK if I join your group?" You will almost always be welcomed in. Outright social rejections do happen among teens, but they're very rare among adults.

2. Replace "it's not worth going" pessimism with "any connection is a good thing" optimism. Lonely people often conclude that it's not worth going out to meet people because previous attempts to make new friends have failed. But while the odds are low that on any particular outing you will meet a lifelong friend or future spouse, there's a good chance that you could make a connection or have a conversation—and a single conversation will make a big difference to your emotional state if you have been feeling lonely.

3. Deepen existing relationships. The best cure for loneliness isn't more relationships, it's deeper relationships. Even very lonely people generally have some social connections—perhaps a distant relative or an old friend they have barely spoken with in years. Search your address book for people such as these, then make an effort to stay in closer contact with them.

Helpful: The best way to deepen your relationships is to make a conscious effort to see things from the other person's perspective and empathize with him/her.

FAILURE

It isn't just the big, life-altering failures that affect us. If we're not careful, small failures can undermine our confidence and optimism, too. *A three-part strategy for overcoming the pain of minor failures...*

1. Blame your goal-setting strategy, not your abilities. People often take on big projects and set themselves tight deadlines—then blame their skills when they fall short. Instead, set a series of smaller, incremental, achievable goals. You're likely to reach at least some of these incremental targets, easing any feelings of failure if others are missed.

Example: Rather than trying to lose 30 pounds in three months, try to lose one pound a week for 30 weeks.

2. Focus on factors within your control. Failing can make you feel helpless, as though you have tried your best and don't know what else you can do. Such feelings can damage your motivation when making future efforts or make you give up entirely. The best thing to do is to focus on factors within your control.

Example: You exhausted your contacts, you're out of leads, and you still haven't found a new job. Focus on the interim goal of expanding your contacts and professional network. Send a quick message to your Facebook friends and other social-media contacts asking if they know people in your field...and/or join relevant LinkedIn groups.

3. Learn the simple trick that could keep you from choking next time. Let's say a bowler makes nine strikes in a row, then rolls a gutter ball on the tenth. What happened? He choked—he became so anxious that he overthought something that didn't require much thought at all. Everyone chokes on occasion. Trouble is, once we've choked, we might start to worry that we'll do so again, undermining our confidence.

There's a simple way to reduce the odds of choking—whistle. This works best when playing sports but can come in handy at other times, too. Whistling requires just enough brainpower to distract the part of our mind that might otherwise overthink things. If you're bowling, start humming or whistling a tune (softly) as you pick up the bowling ball, and continue whistling until the ball is rolling toward the pins.

How to Accept Compliments Graciously

Americans deflect compliments approximately two-thirds of the time, often by suggesting that they don't deserve the praise, a recent study has reported. But deflection contradicts the person who gave the compliment, implying that he/she has poor judgment or taste.

Better: Say, "Thank you"—there is never a time when that is not appropriate. Follow up with, "I appreciate you noticing that" or "I was feeling down, and this is just the encouragement I need to keep going." If what you are being praised for included the work of others, acknowledge their efforts after accepting credit for your own role.

Example: "It could not have happened without Bob's help."

The Art of Manliness, a blog dedicated to uncovering the lost art of being a man. *ArtofManliness.com*

EASY-TO-DO...
To Feel More Confident, Strike These Poses...

When stuck on a problem, cross your arms—people who do this are more persistent at tackling tasks. To make a point effectively, talk with your hands and use relevant hand gestures. To boost your confidence, sit up straight—people who slump are less likely to trust their own words.

WholeLiving.com

Turn on Your Happy Switch

Rick Hanson, PhD, neuropsychologist and author of *Hardwiring Happiness: The New Brain Science of Contentment, Calm and Confidence* (Harmony).

Turns out that we're wired to feel bad. Researchers have determined that the human brain is much better at taking in negative experiences than positive ones. This negativity bias helped our early ancestors remember where dangers lurked. Today it causes unnecessary unhappiness.

We can rewire our brains to better absorb the good. We can start by taking greater notice of the happy moments that happen all the time. We see something beautiful. We experience a moment of comfort or pleasure. A family member says, "I love you." Often we let such things pass by with little notice.

I recommend taking five to 10 seconds to let a positive moment really sink in. We can use this time to reflect upon how it makes our life better.

We also can rewire our brains to not fixate so much on the negative. When something bad happens to us, we should call to mind a related positive thought. If an idea of ours is rejected at a meeting, we can remind ourselves that other ideas have been well-received. If the negativity hijacks your attention, drop it and focus only on the positive. When you feel recentered on the positive, let the negative be present in your awareness again. Linking the positive to the negative like this neutralizes the negative and encourages the brain to call up this positive when we have similar negative feelings in the future.

There's a saying in neurology, "Neurons that fire together wire together."

Facebook Folly

Facebook has been linked to unhappiness. The more a study participant used Facebook over a two-week period, the worse he/she reported feeling—and the more likely he was to report a decline in overall satisfaction with life. In contrast, the more a participant socialized in the real world, the more positive he reported feeling.

Study by researchers from University of Michigan, Ann Arbor, and Leuven University, Belgium, of Facebook users in their late teens or early 20s, published in *PLOS ONE*.

The Best New Thing I Did That You Can Do *Now!*

Jonny Bowden, PhD, CNS, a nutritionist and nationally known expert on weight loss, nutrition and health. Based in Los Angeles, he is board-certified by the American College of Nutrition and coauthor, with Stephen Sinatra, MD, of *The Great Cholesterol Myth* (Fair Winds). *JonnyBowden.com*

Guy Winch, PhD, a clinical psychologist in private practice in New York City. He is author of *Emotional First Aid: Practical Strategies for Treating Failure, Rejection, Guilt and Other Everyday Psychological Injuries* (Plume). *GuyWinch.com*

Bryan Mattimore, president and cofounder of The Growth Engine Company, LLC, an innovation consulting agency based in Norwalk, Connecticut. He is author of *Idea Stormers: How to Lead and Inspire Creative Breakthroughs* (Jossey-Bass). *Growth-Engine.com*

Sandy Weiner, a dating coach, blogger and workshop leader based in Stamford, Connecticut. She specializes in helping people over 40. *LastFirstDate.com*

We asked a diverse group of our experts to identify one thing they tried that went so well for them this past year that they would like to recommend it to our readers…

JONNY BOWDEN, PhD, CNS

I went to couples therapy with my wife—even though our relationship was already strong. Couples typically seek therapy only when their relationships hit hard times. But couples therapy can be particularly productive for couples who already are getting along well. These couples are more likely to listen to each other during counseling sessions and less likely to become defensive and bicker.

With the therapist's assistance, my wife and I learned to talk to each other a lot more effectively and to listen nonjudgmentally. We discovered the joy of taking frequent short vacations together. And we learned that we're sometimes actually reactivating old scripts when we think we're having disagreements about current issues. Our relationship was already great—now it's terrific.

GUY WINCH, PhD

I refused to let myself brood. I dealt with some very stressful events in my life this year, including a family member with cancer. My natural inclination was to worry—what if the chemo treatments don't work? Worry was taking over my life until I resolved not to indulge it any longer. Worry of this sort doesn't serve any purpose. It wasn't going to make my family member any healthier or make either of us feel any better.

I discovered that for a chronic worrier, giving up worrying is a bit like a smoker giving up cigarettes. I experienced cravings periodically throughout the day—times when I felt a desperate need to worry. But I found that I could distract myself from these cravings. When I felt the urge to worry, I would come up with a task that required concentration. Those tasks kept my mind occupied until the cravings passed.

Fortunately, my family member's most recent scan showed a very good response to the chemo.

BRYAN MATTIMORE

I dramatically expanded my range of reading materials to trigger creative ideas. Earlier this year, I challenged myself to come up with a new invention or idea every day for 21 consecutive days. I discovered that the most effective way to generate creative ideas was to break free of my usual reading ruts and explore an extremely broad range of publications and websites.

I read articles aimed at demographics and professions other than my own—everything from fashion magazines to technical journals. I searched the Internet for web pages featuring the phrase "best new products" to find other people's creative ideas, which helped trigger ideas of my own. I also used the free e-mail newsletter *Cassandra Daily* to keep up with the latest trends (*TrendCentral.com*).

SANDY WEINER

I enlisted help to overcome my fear of public speaking. This fear was holding back my career. So in 2014, I stopped trying to hide from it or cope with it on my own and instead got help. I met with a speech coach. I joined Toastmasters International, a nonprofit organization that gives its members an opportunity to practice public speaking in a low-pressure environment (*Toastmasters.org*).

I started saying yes to every public-speaking opportunity that came my way. I even did a TEDx video. (The "x" in "TEDx" stands for an independently organized TED event.)

Within months, I was more confident about speaking in front of crowds. I still feel some fear before a speech, but that fear no longer paralyzes me—it energizes me.

Worry No More! 5 Simple Steps to End Those Troubling Thoughts and Fears

Robert L. Leahy, PhD, director of The American Institute for Cognitive Therapy and a clinical professor in psychiatry at Weill Medical College of Cornell University, both in New York City. He is also an associate editor of the *International Journal of Cognitive Therapy* and past-president of the Association for Behavioral and Cognitive Therapies and author of *The Worry Cure: Seven Steps to Stop Worry from Stopping You* (Harmony). *CognitiveTherapyNYC.com*

People who worry too much have a new problem to worry about. Chronic worriers suffer more from pain than those who are more laid-back. They are also more likely to develop digestive complaints, fatigue and depression. In general, worriers are less likely to be happy and are at higher risk for relationship problems.

The latest development: Researchers now know that traditional psychotherapy and/or medications help only about 20% of chronic worriers. But 77% of patients who receive cognitive behavioral therapy, which helps patients recognize and change distorted thought patterns that fuel chronic worrying, experience significant reductions in their anxiety-related symptoms.

Fortunately, you can try many of these techniques on your own. If the problem persists after two months, you may want to consider getting professional help. To find a therapist near you who is trained in cognitive therapy, consult the Academy of Cognitive Therapy, *AcademyofCT.org*.

How to overcome chronic worry...

STEP 1: WORRY IN IMAGES

Research shows that people who are anxious tend to have worried thoughts rather than form mental images of whatever troubles them.

Reason: Thoughts are less threatening than emotions, which often express themselves visually. People who worry get in the habit of using worry, with all the mental clutter that it causes, to avoid difficult emotions, such as sadness and anger.

Action step: **The next time you're worried, form a visual image of the worst-case scenario.** Someone who is concerned about health, for example, might imagine lying in a hospital bed. At first, you'll probably notice that your worries *increase* when you visualize them. But with repetition, the image—and the worries behind it—will lose their sting. They'll start to seem mundane or even tedious—and you'll find it easier to let them go.

STEP 2: CHALLENGE YOUR WORRIES

Worriers are actually good at solving real-life problems. The problem is that they spend an inordinate amount of time worrying about things that either will never happen, or that they'll handle well if they do come about. One study found that 85% of the things that people worried about eventually had positive—or at least neutral—outcomes.

Chronic worriers suffer from "cognitive distortions"—inaccurate thoughts about themselves or their daily lives. You might worry that you'll lose your job and think, *I'll never get another job if I lose this one.* But the truth is, you don't know that you won't get another job. You have no evidence of that.

Action step: **The next time you have a thought like this, remind yourself that there is nothing you can do to prevent your company from downsizing** and that your odds of not getting laid off will improve if you are performing well in your job. If you also start networking, that will help you land a job if you are laid off.

STEP 3: CLASSIFY YOUR WORRIES

People who worry always have a reason. They tell themselves that they're more responsible than nonworriers. They anticipate what could go wrong. They obsess over details that (they think) will help them organize their lives. But worry that isn't linked to action doesn't solve anything. Productive worry is different because it helps you focus on what you can control.

Action step: **Ask yourself if there's something that you can do *today* that will address your worries.**

Example: I'm giving a workshop in Europe in a few weeks. If I'm worried about a hotel reservation, I can use my time productively by making sure that my room is booked.

Conversely, you can't make an action plan for unproductive worries. I could agonize for weeks about the possibility that my talks won't be well-received or that the participants won't like me, but there's nothing I can do about it beyond being well-prepared.

If you find yourself worrying about something that can't be solved with an action you can put in a to-do list, then turn your attention to something else—ideally, something you enjoy doing, such as visiting a friend or playing a game.

STEP 4: GIVE YOURSELF WORRY TIME

People often avoid this step because they want to worry less—not more. When it's done properly, however, it really is an effective way to prevent negative thoughts from overtaking your life.

Action step: **For at least two weeks, set aside just 30 minutes each day.** During that time, write down *every* worry that comes into your mind. You might be surprised how short the list is. People tend to have the same worries, which they recycle over and over again.

Also spend your "worry time" challenging your thoughts. For example, ask yourself, *What am I predicting, and how likely is this to really happen?…Is there any productive action I can take now?…What advice would I give a friend?*

The rest of the day, do not give any mental energy to your worries. You will recognize that you are worrying if your mind is filled with "what if" thoughts. When these thoughts come into your mind, focus on any productive action you can take. But for those two weeks, try to deal with worries *only* during your official worry time.

People who do this report that they feel a greater sense of control, and their worries gradually become less intrusive.

STEP 5: IDENTIFY DEEPER THREATS

The things that really worry you aren't the harried thoughts that flit in and out of your brain. Worriers focus on minutiae in order to avoid their *core fears*—for example, the fear of abandonment or feeling inferior.

People who are afraid of failure might cope by working too much or being hyper-responsible. They worry excessively about their performance because, deep down, they feel that failure is imminent.

Action step: **Ask yourself what you're really afraid of.** Then judge the truth of your belief. Worriers tend to think in all-or-nothing terms. In their minds, they're either a complete failure or a complete success. This isn't true of anyone. Everyone is a mix of good and bad.

Remind yourself: I'm a human being with positive and negative qualities. I can appreciate myself even if I'm not perfect.

And remember that there will always be matters that are beyond your control. Worrying about those issues won't do any good. Take whatever steps you can to address the problem—then let it go!

Stressed? Call Superman...and Other Tricks to Stay Calm

Marc Schoen, PhD, assistant clinical professor of medicine at David Geffen School of Medicine at UCLA. He has a private practice in Los Angeles focused on how the mind affects the body. He is author of *Your Survival Instinct Is Killing You: Retrain Your Brain to Conquer Fear, Make Better Decisions, and Thrive in the 21st Century* (Plume). *MarcSchoen.com*

Your survival instinct could kill you. It tries to protect you from perceived dangers even when no real physical danger exists. In the process, it often ends up inhibiting your ability to perform well under pressure.

Fortunately, there are steps you can take to keep your survival instinct under control and allow the logical part of your brain to make much better decisions.

DANGER VS. DISCOMFORT

Often when we sense danger, our survival instinct takes charge, mobilizing the automatic "fight or flight" response to steer us from peril. That can be a good thing at the appropriate times—for instance, if we have to run out of a burning building.

But this primitive survival instinct does not understand that in modern America, few of us experience life-threatening danger very often. What we do experience frequently is discomfort and stress. And our threshold for tolerating discomfort and stress has become very low.

We have become accustomed to lives of enhanced technology, safety and comfort, so the *limbic system*—which includes the part of the brain that generates the survival instinct—confuses life's ordinary discomforts, frustrations and pressures with physical danger, triggering our survival instinct when it isn't needed.

As a result, we might react to unpleasant but not unsafe situations as if our lives were on the line.

Examples: We might respond to a mild criticism by flying off the handle. We might become enraged at bad drivers, even if they're only slowing us down, not putting us in jeopardy. Or we might do poorly on exams because our limbic system interprets test-taking stress as danger, diverting blood away from the logical part of the brain just when we need it to excel on the exam. Various studies have estimated that between 35% and 60% of test-takers fall victim to this phenomenon.

The usual advice to people who struggle to cope with uncomfortable or stressful situations is to try meditation or exercise to help them relax...or positive self-talk.

These are tools of the logical part of the brain. Although positive self-talk and meditation can be effective, there are many times when they are not enough to tame the irrational limbic brain. Expecting these methods to be effective at these times is like counting on a well-reasoned argument to sway a young child who is throwing a tantrum—the message simply won't get through. *Instead...*

DILUTE THE FEAR

When the limbic system senses danger, it tries to put us on a nonstop one-way trip to our survival instinct. This trip is extremely difficult to stop once under way—but its impact can be diluted by retraining our brain to make additional stops along the way.

This retraining starts to take place during moments when you are calm—not stressed.

First, you need to select three sensory tools that you can draw upon mentally during times of stress…

1. A song that you consider uplifting—perhaps because it offers upbeat lyrics…was used in an uplifting scene in a memorable movie…or reminds you of a successful moment in your life.

2. Visualize a person you associate with strength. This could be someone fictional, such as Superman, or someone real, such as a strong, steadfast friend.

3. Think of a scent that has a positive association for you—maybe the aftershave worn by your father…or the smell of pine trees at the mountain cottage where you always feel relaxed.

After you have lined up these tools, imagine a stressful situation. Then sing out loud your uplifting song…visualize the person of strength…imagine the pleasurable scent. Practice doing this at least three to six times over the next week.

Once you have mastered this technique, the next time you find yourself in a situation that typically causes you stress or discomfort—or the next time an upcoming stressful event pops into your mind—immediately sing your uplifting song in your head…visualize your strong person…and/or imagine that you are sniffing your uplifting scent.

Drawing on these symbols of strength will make you stronger and better able to dilute the fear.

WHY IT WORKS

By stimulating the auditory, visual and olfactory senses, you are bringing in other parts of the brain that are not part of its fear center. I call this strength in numbers—now there are several parts of the brain involved with the fear situation that have no relationship to fear. This type of conditioning weakens, or dilutes, the impact of the fear center of the brain. That should allow you to maintain some perspective and control.

Example: Where your survival instinct previously left you seeing only red rage when someone cut you off in traffic, this technique might allow you to experience a varied rainbow of feelings, with the survival instinct's rage only part of your mental response. You also might feel a sense of optimism triggered by the uplifting song and a sense of strength from recalling the strong person, keeping any feelings of panic in perspective.

BE GRATEFUL

After you feel a bit calmer, consider naming a few things for which you are grateful. Fear isn't the only feeling processed by the limbic system—it also processes other feelings, including gratitude. Intentionally recalling some things for which you feel gratitude can distract the limbic system's attention away from its survival-instinct–based fears.

Examples: You might be grateful that you're employed…or that your kids are healthy.

When you feel that your panic or agitation is under control, then you can use positive self-talk to give the stress- or discomfort-causing experience a positive spin. Tell yourself something such as, *I love solving problems like these*…or *Working under pressure brings out the best in me.*

IMPROVE YOUR TOLERANCE FOR DISCOMFORT

It's wonderful to live in comfort, but comfort comes at a price. The more accustomed we become to perpetual comfort, the more likely it is that our limbic systems will interpret discomfort as danger, triggering our survival instinct when it isn't needed.

To avoid this, we must become more comfortable with discomfort. This can be done—consider all the discomfort that humans used to endure, and many still do, without complaint! When I was a child, my family lived in a very hot area with no air-conditioning, yet the heat didn't much bother us. It's only now that I'm used to air-conditioning that I feel I can't possibly survive without it.

Here's another example: We used to be out of contact with our colleagues and loved ones for hours every day. Only now that we have cell phones do many people become uncomfortable if they can't check their messages every 15 minutes or even more often.

If we remind ourselves that we're capable of enduring discomfort—and that most discomforts are temporary and trivial—our minds will stop associating discomfort with danger. Eventually our minds even might start associating discomfort with a sense of our own heartiness and resolve. But the only way to accomplish this is to sometimes let discomfort happen rather than rush to alleviate it.

LET IT HAPPEN

Here are some ways to let discomfort "happen" for you…

• **If being hungry causes you discomfort,** let yourself be hungry for a while each day rather than immediately reaching for a snack.

• **If being lost makes you uncomfortable,** occasionally drive somewhere unfamiliar without using your GPS and wander around.

• **If lack of mental stimulation makes you uncomfortable,** force yourself to spend time each week alone with your thoughts without turning on the TV or opening a book.

• **If being out of touch makes you uncomfortable,** spend some time (more than 15 minutes) with your cell phone turned off.

Don't try to distract yourself from these discomforts. Feel uncomfortable. You will grow!

DID YOU KNOW THAT…

Distrust Harms the Brain?

People who habitually distrust others, believing that others act mainly in their own self-interest, are three times more likely to develop dementia than those who do not. That was the finding of a recent eight-year study of older adults (average age 71).

Why: Chronic negative emotions can impair cognitive function.

Anna-Maija Tolppanen, PhD, development director of neurology, University of Eastern Finland, Kuopio.

Tricks to Get Yourself to Meditate Daily

Sharon Salzberg, cofounder of the Insight Meditation Society in Barre, Massachusetts, and author of numerous books, including *Real Happiness: The Power of Meditation* (Workman). *SharonSalzberg.com*

Studies show that daily meditation helps relieve elevated blood pressure, pain, insomnia, depression and more. *Recent research:* When participants did a simple 20-minute meditation for eight weeks, beneficial genes, such as those involved in insulin function, were activated, while genes related to inflammation and cancer were suppressed.

But many of us just can't seem to make meditation part of our everyday routine—it seems so difficult to set aside the time…sit still…or quiet our minds. *Three easy strategies…*

• **5-minute meditation.** *What to do:* Find the place where you feel the breath most clearly—nostrils, chest or abdomen—and bring your attention there. Take a normal breath without trying to change it. Repeat in sets of 10 (counting to yourself) for five minutes. If you take only three breaths before you start thinking about something else, bring your focus back to your breath. You don't need absolute quiet. You can do this in your doctor's waiting room or while walking the dog.

• **Single-task meditation.** Choose a simple activity you do often, like drinking a cup of tea, and pay close attention to the sensations that occur while doing it. Feel the heat of the mug in your hands, the warmth and aroma of the steam, and the taste of the liquid in your mouth. When your mind wanders, draw your attention back to the experience. *Other activities to try this with:* Cooking, mowing the lawn or exercising.

• **"On cue" meditation.** With this type of meditation, you use cues in your environment to prompt you to focus and breathe. Let your phone ring three times before answering it. Use the sound of the phone as a reminder to be in the moment and take a few deep, relaxing breaths. *Other cues:* Stopping at a red light or sitting down at your desk.

How to Defuse a Heated Conversation

Here's what to do if you find yourself in a contentious discussion…don't fight back—retaliation only increases the intensity of the interaction…take a break and ask for a pause so that emotions can become calmer.…apologize for something—such as one part of the conversation or the escalation itself…give a relevant compliment about something the other person has said or suggested, as a reminder that there is an underlying positive relationship—it can be as simple as, "I hadn't thought of things that way"…and acknowledge that the other person has a positive intent, emotion or feeling and say that you appreciate his/her willingness to try to deal with a difficult issue.

Geoffrey Tumlin, CEO, Mouthpeace Consulting LLC, communications consultants, Austin, Texas, and author of *Stop Talking, Start Communicating* (McGraw-Hill).

How to Be More Polite in E-Mails

Daniel Post Senning, social-media etiquette expert and spokesperson for the Emily Post Institute, Inc., Burlington, Vermont, and author of *Manners in a Digital World: Living Well Online* (Open Road Media). He is the great-great-grandson of etiquette pioneer Emily Post.

It seems like people are less polite in e-mails than they are in person. Why is that? The informality of e-mail can come across as rude, but observing some simple courtesies can make all your e-mails more polite—and effective…

• **Make sure that the subject line conveys what the message is about.** If you change the topic after a series of messages, change the subject line.

• **Start the message with a salutation,** such as "Dear" or the more informal "Hi."

• **Indicate whether the message is informational only** ("Just thought you might be interested…") or whether you need a response. If so, give a time frame.

• **Include an official closing.** *Examples:* "Sincerely" (the most formal)…"Regards/Warm regards"…"Best."

• **Read messages back to yourself for substance and tone.** Add "please" and "thank you," and modify the language as appropriate.

• **Always respond within 24 hours.** Check your junk-mail folder regularly to make sure that personal messages have not gone there by mistake.

• **Be understanding if people do not respond to your e-mails.** Something may have gone wrong in the delivery.

• **Don't use e-mail in tense or emotional situations.** Pick up the phone.

DID YOU KNOW THAT…

Scientists Can Now "See" Dreams?

Brain scans can reveal some of what a person is seeing in a dream, such as streets or cars. This is possible because of recent advances in decoding brain signals that correspond with what patients see while they are awake. The process cannot reveal a dream's story line, but its ability to observe detail likely will improve in time.

Study by researchers at ATR Computational Laboratories, Kyoto, Japan, published in *Science*.

Surprising Things That Keep You from Making Good Decisions

Francesca Gino, PhD, associate professor of business administration at Harvard Business School, Boston. She is author of *Sidetracked: Why Our Decisions Get Derailed, and How We Can Stick to the Plan* (Harvard Business Review). *FrancescaGino.com*

Every day, dozens of seemingly inconsequential factors affect the way you behave and the decisions you make—small and big. Many of those factors influence you so much that they derail important plans that you have made and even cause you to abandon or alter goals you set and dreams you held.

Example: A study published in *Psychological Science* found that wearing sunglasses makes people much more likely to make morally questionable decisions. The glasses create the illusion in the wearers' minds that their misdeeds are somehow hidden under a cloak of darkness.

Fortunately, you can learn to identify the ways in which your decisions tend to be influenced by irrelevant factors and you can avoid them or minimize their impact.

Here are the most powerful ways we allow these factors to sidetrack us—and how we can fight back...

• **We allow emotions emanating from one event to spill over and affect unrelated decisions.**

Example: One study found that not only are people less happy on rainy days, they actually conclude on those days that they're significantly less satisfied with their lives overall. Bad weather has been shown to make people less optimistic as investors, too.

What to do: Emotions should not be ignored when making decisions—your emotions could be providing very crucial information about how you truly feel about the options you're considering. But before making any decision, take the time to consider why you're feeling the emotions that you currently feel. Are you really dismayed over the option that you just evaluated...or just feeling down because someone drank the last cup of coffee and didn't make a new pot?

If we're able to track down the root cause of our emotions, we usually can reduce their influence on unrelated decisions. Better yet, postpone important decisions until unrelated strong emotions have passed.

• **We focus too narrowly on one aspect of the decision we are making, neglecting to consider what's the best course of action overall.** The ability to focus can help us get things done—but when it comes to making decisions, we also must zoom out and reflect upon the big picture.

Example: A man decides to take his neighbor to court over a minor matter. He is so focused on the fact that he is likely to win be-cause the law is on his side that he fails to consider that his overall goal—enjoying life on his property—will be hurt, not helped, by pursuing legal action that turns a neighbor into an enemy. You might think that most people would include consideration of good neighborly relations in their decision-making process, but very often, that is not the case.

What to do: Ask yourself, What's my ultimate goal? Is this decision consistent with that?

• **We tend to overestimate our own capabilities and competence and underestimate everyone else's.** Most of us consider ourselves above average in most ways. When psychologists ask people to rate themselves in subjective areas such as honesty, appearance and driving ability, the typical respondent places himself/herself in the top 20% to 30%. This, of course, can't be correct in all cases—half of us must fall into the bottom 50%.

Our tendency to overestimate our own abilities makes us prone to favor the ideas we come up with ourselves over those supplied by others. And it convinces us to rely too heavily on the information we happen to have, downplaying the significance of information we lack. People in positions of power are particularly likely to overestimate their own capabilities.

Exception: People who have paid for advice are very likely to heed that advice—even at the expense of better advice that they received for free. They value more highly what they have chosen to pay for.

What to do: Before making a major decision, review your thinking to see whether you have dismissed viable opinions from others too readily...there might be additional information out there that's worth reviewing...and you're giving excessive weight to advice that you purchased.

• **We allow our decisions to be influenced by those with whom we feel a connection—** and we feel connections very easily. It's no surprise that we're more likely to be influenced by people with whom we feel a connection. What is surprising is how little it takes to create this connection. Researchers have found that even the most tenuous of commonalities can make us substantially more susceptible to influence. Your decision-making abilities could be affected if someone notes that he shops in the same store as you, owns the same breed of dog, drives the same make of car or was born in the same month.

Example: In one study I conducted, a group of college students were led to believe that someone who attended their school had behaved unethically, while another group was led to believe that this unethical student attended a different school. Members of the group that thought the cheater attended their school were significantly more likely to follow his lead and act unethically themselves. *What to do…*

• Consider the decision-making tendencies of people in your social circle—they could be influencing your decisions to a greater degree than you realize.

• Spend less time with people who tend to make decisions you don't like, or at least be conscious of their flawed decisions and monitor your own decisions in this area.

• Consider forming new connections with people who make decisions you wish to emulate. For example, spending time among people who eat well and exercise regularly increases the odds that you will adopt a healthy lifestyle and make similarly healthy choices.

• Be wary when someone you've just met cites a connection he has with you—it could be a salesman or con artist trying to foster the sense of connection to increase the odds that you will part with your money.

• **We make decisions based on how we compare to the people around us.** Rationally, the fact that our neighbor owns a luxury car or that our brother just got a raise should not affect our own car-buying or career decisions—yet such things often do weigh heavily on our thinking, in particular with money-related matters.

Example: A Northwestern University study presented MBA students with a series of hypothetical job offers and asked which they would be most likely to accept. Researchers found that students were more likely to accept a job paying $75,000 than one paying $85,000 if they were told that the company offering $75,000 offered that amount to all new hires…while the one offering $85,000 offered some candidates $95,000.

The grads felt slighted by the second company, which was implying that some job candidates deserved more money than the study participants, even though that second company was offering the participants a better salary than the first was.

What to do: Before making a decision—particularly a major financial decision—reflect on whether you are deciding based on your own needs and priorities or you are being unduly influenced by making comparisons of your own skills and talents with those of others.

Creativity Booster: Take a Hike but Leave This at Home…

Backpackers scored 50% higher in creative problem-solving after taking a four-day hike without any electronic devices. Of the 56 study subjects, 24 took a 10-item creativity test the morning before they began the hike, and 32 took the test on the morning of the trip's fourth day.

Unknown: Whether the greatest creativity booster was the exercise…time in nature…or elimination of electronics.

Study of 56 backpackers, average age 28, by researchers at University of Kansas, Lawrence, and University of Utah, Salt Lake City, published in *PLOS ONE*.

---

12 Things That Make You Look Older

Kim Johnson Gross, cocreator of the Chic Simple book series as well as author of *What to Wear for the Rest of Your Life* (Grand Central Life & Style) and *Chic Simple Dress Smart: Men* (Grand Central). Based in New York City, she is a former Ford model and has been fashion editor at *Town & Country* and *Esquire* magazines and a columnist for *More* and *InStyle*. KimJohnsonGross.com

---

As you get older, wardrobe and style choices that worked when you were younger may no longer be serving you well. This goes for both men and women.

Without knowing it, you may be looking older than you are. This could cause others to treat you as older and potentially hold you back from employment opportunities and advancements. This also can make you feel like you are not up to your game or comfortable in your skin. When you are not style confident, you are less body confident, which makes you feel less life confident.

Helpful: Seek out style mentors—people who look elegant and modern without chasing youth-oriented trends. Observe them carefully, and adapt elements of their style to your own. TV newscasters make good style mentors because they are required to look contemporary while also projecting dignity and authority.

Give yourself a good, hard look, and ask yourself whether you are looking older than your actual age with any of these common signals…

1. Sneakers for everyday wear. Your feet should be comfortable, but sneakers outside the gym just look sloppy and careless. Young people get away with it—but there are more stylish options when you're older. These include loafers or driving moccasins for men and low-heeled pumps with cushioned soles for women. Wedge-soled shoes are a comfortable alternative to high heels.

2. Baggy pants. Although young men may look very trendy in high-waisted, loose-fitting jeans, this style screams old on anyone else. For women, the rear end tends to flatten with age, causing pants to fit loosely in the rear. And front-pleated pants for women generally are unflattering and unstylish.

Better: Spend the time to find pants that fit you well—or figure a tailor into your wardrobe budget. Baggy is dowdy, but overly tight makes you look heavier. Well-fitting clothes make you look slimmer and younger.

3. Boring colors. Skin tone gets duller with age, so the colors you wear should bring light to your face. If you are a woman who has worn black for years, it may be too harsh for you now. Brown makes men fade into the woodwork.

Better: Stand in front of a mirror, and experiment with colors that you never thought you

could wear—you may be surprised at what flatters you. Avoid neon brights, which make older skin look sallow, but be open to the rest of the color spectrum. Try contemporary patterns and prints. For neutrals, gray and navy are softer alternatives to black for women, and any shade of blue is a good bet for men.

4. Boring glasses and jewelry. Men and women should have some fun with glasses. It's a great way to update your look and make it more modern. Tell your optician what you're looking for, or bring a stylish friend with you.

As for jewelry for women, wearing a large piece of fab faux jewelry (earrings, necklace, ring) or multiple bracelets adds great style and youth to your look.

5. Turtlenecks. You may think a turtleneck hides a sagging neck and chin, but it is more likely to draw attention to jowls.

Better: A cowl neckline for women, or a loosely draped scarf. A scarf is the single best item to help a woman look thinner, taller, prettier and more chic. For a video on how to tie a scarf, go to *NYCityWoman.com* and type "Six Ways to Wear a Scarf" in the search box. For a man, an oblong scarf, looped, is a stylish European look that adds a welcome shot of color.

6. Stiff or one-tone hair. An overly styled helmet of hair looks old-fashioned. Hair that's a solid block of color looks unnatural and harsh.

Better: Whether hair is short or shoulder-length, women need layers around the face for softness. As for color, opt for subtle highlights in front and a slightly darker tone toward the back.

Keep in mind that gray hair can be beautiful, modern and sexy. You need a plan to go gray, though, which means a flattering cut and using hair products that enhance the gray. Ask your stylist for recommendations. Also, if your hair is a dull gray, consider getting silver highlights around your face to bring light and "energy" to your hair.

Men who dye their hair should allow a bit of gray at the temples—it looks more natural than monochrome hair. But avoid a combover or a toupee. A man who attempts to hide a receding hairline isn't fooling anyone—he just looks insecure.

Better: Treat your thinning hair as a badge of honor. Either keep it neatly trimmed or shave your head.

7. Missing (or bushy) eyebrows. Women's eyebrows tend to disappear with age. Men's are more likely to grow wild.

Better: Women should use eyebrow pencil, powder or both to fill in fading brows. Visit any high-end cosmetics counter, and ask the stylist to show you how. You may need to try several products to find out what works best. Men, make sure that your barber or hair stylist trims your eyebrows regularly.

Also: Women tend not to notice increased facial hair (especially stray hairs) on the chin and upper lip—a result of hormonal change. Pluck!

8. Deeply tanned skin. Baby boomers grew up actively developing suntans using baby oil and sun reflectors. Now pale is the norm. A dark tan not only dates you, it increases your risk for skin cancer and worsens wrinkling.

Better: Wear a hat and sunscreen to shield your skin from sun damage.

9. Less-than-white teeth. Yellowing teeth add decades to your appearance. Everyone's teeth get yellower with age, but with so many teeth-whitening products available, there is no excuse to live with off-color teeth.

Better: Ask your dentist which whitening technique he/she recommends based on the condition of your teeth—for example, over-the-counter whitening strips, bleaching in the dentist's office or a custom bleaching kit you can use at home.

10. Women: Nude or beige hose. Nude stockings on women look hopelessly out-of-date. Bare legs are the norm now for young women, but they are not a good option for older women who have dark veins.

Better: In winter, wear dark stockings or opaque tights. In summer, use spray-on tanner for a light tan…or wear nude fishnet stockings or slacks or capris.

11. Poor-fitting bra. Get a bra that fits. Most women don't know that bra size changes

as your body does. Giving your breasts a lift will make you look younger and trimmer.

12. Excessive makeup. Thick foundation, heavy eyeliner, bright blusher and red lipstick all add years to your face.

Better: Use a moisturizing (not matte) foundation, and dab it only where needed to even out skin tone. To add color to cheeks, use a small amount of tinted moisturizer, bronzer or cream blush. Use liquid eyeliner in soft shades such as deep blue or brown, and blend it well. For lips, choose soft pinks and mauves, depending on your skin tone.

Bottom line: The idea is to have fun putting yourself together. That inner spark and personal style will show that you are getting better with age.

---

5 Best Brain-Boosting Drinks

David Grotto, RD, LDN, a registered dietitian and founder and president of Nutrition Housecall, LLC, a Chicago-based nutrition consulting firm that provides nutrition communications, lecturing and consulting services, along with personalized, at-home diet and lifestyle counseling. He is also author of *The Best Things You Can Eat* (Da Capo Lifelong). *DavidGrotto.com*

Some of the easiest-to-prepare brain foods—meaning foods that can preserve and even improve your memory and other cognitive functions—are actually very tasty drinks.

You probably already know about green tea, which is high in *epigallocatechin-3-gallate* (EGCG), a potent compound that appears to protect neurons from age-related damage. *But the following five drinks are also scientifically proven to help your brain…*

BEET JUICE

Beets are a nutritional powerhouse—and so is the juice. It increases levels of nitric oxide, a blood gas that improves blood flow. How does that help your brain? Your brain needs good blood flow to function optimally.

A recent study looked at brain scans of participants before and after they drank beet juice. The post-beverage scans showed an increase in circulation to the brain's white matter in the frontal lobes—a part of the brain that's often damaged in people with dementia.

You can buy ready-made beet juice at health-food stores, although it's much less expensive to make your own with fresh beets (include the root and greens, which are nutritious as well).

Beet juice has a naturally sweet taste, but you may want to add a little apple juice or another fruit juice—both for flavor and to make the mixture more pourable.

BERRY SMOOTHIES

Acai, a South American fruit that reduces inflammation, is ranked near the top of brain-healthy foods because it dilates blood vessels and increases blood flow. Its juice has a pleasant taste—something like a cross between raspberry and cocoa—but it's very expensive (typically $30 or more for a quart*).

What I recommend: Blend a variety of everyday frozen berries that have been shown to boost brain health—raspberries, blueberries and strawberries, for example—along with a little acai juice (and a bit of any other fruit juice, if you wish) to make an easy, delicious smoothie.

Why use frozen berries? They retain the nutritional benefit of fresh berries—and they're easy to buy and last a long time in the freezer...they give your smoothie a nice texture, which you can vary by adding more or less juice...and they're less expensive than fresh berries if you buy large bags.

CARROT JUICE

The old adage is that carrots are good for the eyes (indeed they are)—but we now know that carrot juice is absolutely great for the brain. Like other deeply colored vegetables (sweet potatoes, kale, red peppers, etc.), carrots are high in beta-carotene, an antioxidant that reduces inflammation—believed to be a factor in brain deterioration.

If you have tried carrot juice but didn't like the taste (it is surprisingly sweet), that's not a problem. It is a very good "base" for multi-vegetable juices. (Some choices that are good for covering up the carrot flavor include kale, spinach and other dark greens.)

*Prices subject to change.

COCOA

A Harvard/Brigham and Women's Hospital study found that adults who drank two daily cups of cocoa did better on memory tests than those who didn't drink it.

The *flavanols* (a class of antioxidants) in cocoa relax the endothelial linings of blood vessels and help reduce blood pressure. High blood pressure is a leading risk factor for dementia. The antioxidants in cocoa also reduce the cell-damaging effects of free radicals—this may improve long-term brain health.

Important: Do not go overboard with sugar, though—sugar is not good for your brain (and the jury is still out on artificial sweeteners).

Here's my advice: Buy a brand of unsweetened cocoa powder that is processed to remain high in flavanols. You don't have to buy an expensive specialty brand to get the brain-protecting effects. Most major brands of cocoa powder have respectable levels of cocoa flavanols. I advise against using milk chocolate or chocolate syrup—they typically have the least amount of flavanols and the most sugar.

At first, make your hot cocoa with your usual amount of sugar...then slowly cut back. You'll grow to appreciate the deep and pleasantly bitter true taste of the cocoa itself as less and less sugar stops masking it. As for using milk or water for your cocoa, that's your choice.

RED WINE

Everyone knows that red wine promotes cardiovascular health (easy does it). What you might not know is that red wine has been linked to a lower risk for dementia.

One reason is that people who drink moderate amounts of red wine—up to two glasses a day for men or one glass for women—have an increase in HDL "good" cholesterol. Research from Columbia University has found that people with the highest levels of HDL were less likely to develop dementia than those with the lowest levels.

Looking to supercharge the brain-boosting power of your red wine? Make delicious Sangria! You'll get the wine's benefits and extra antioxidants and other nutrients from the fruit.

Sangria is typically made by steeping pieces of fresh fruit—lemon, orange, apple and just about any other fruit you like—in a rich red wine such as Merlot or Cabernet Sauvignon and adding sugar and another liquor, such as brandy or rum.

My advice: Skip the sugar and extra liquor, but go ahead and add some orange juice to dilute the wine a bit and add some sweetness.

More from David Grotto, RD…

Best Juice Machines

Here, a juicer and two blenders that I recommend for quality and affordability…

- **Green Star GS-1000 Juice Extractor** uses a low-speed, low-heat system to preserve nutrients from produce. $449.95, *GreenStar.com*.

- **Ninja Professional Blender** has a powerful 1,100-watt motor and six blades to pulverize produce for drinks with lots of pulp. $100, *NinjaKitchen.com*.

- **Vitamix 5200** is a multipurpose blender that also chops and churns veggies and fruits into smoothies. Easy 30-second self-cleaning. $449, *Vitamix.com*.

Apps That Help You Remember

Here are some apps that can help you remember—*DataVault* stores account and website passwords so that you can use a different password and log-in for each account and website ($9.99,* for iPhone/iPad and Android)… *Cleverbug* (free, iPhone/iPad) sends you an alert about a Facebook contact's birthday. The app also prints and mails a customized card within two to five business days. (Your first card is free, but you pay for the stamp. Thereafter, all cards are $2.99 plus mailing.) Or you can send a free digital card via Facebook, e-mail, Twitter or text message…*RX Pal* sends reminders to take your medication, alerts you when a prescription is low and links to your pharmacy for refills (free, Android).

Reader's Digest. RD.com
*Prices subject to change.

Boost Memory While You Sleep

Volunteers who were exposed at night to sounds that were synchronized to the brain's slow sleep rhythms had better recall than those who were exposed to unsynchronized sounds.

Neuron.

Log on to Facebook to Boost Brain Function

Researchers divided 42 older healthy adults (ages 68 to 91) into three groups—one was taught to use Facebook, another to use a simple online diary and the third got no training.

Outcome: After eight weeks, the Facebook group had a 25% boost in brain function, including working memory (required for learning and reasoning), while the other groups saw no change.

Theory: Learning a new skill that involves complex functions and a strong social component helps to stave off cognitive decline.

Janelle Wohltmann, researcher, department of psychology, The University of Arizona, Tucson.

EASY-TO-DO…

Simple Move Helps You Remember

Clench your right hand while preparing to remember something…and then your left hand when trying to recall it. More research is needed, but scientists speculate that when you clench your right hand, you stimulate the left side of the brain, which is involved in "writing memories." Squeezing the left hand engages the right side of the brain, which is associated with memory retrieval.

Study of 51 right-handed people by researchers at the Cerebral Lateralization Laboratory at Montclair State University, Montclair, New Jersey, published in *PLOS ONE*.

19

At Work

Want to Start Your Own Business? What to Say to Naysayers

Tell people that you plan to start a business, and there's a good chance that they will tell you why you shouldn't. Some of their criticisms might raise a few legitimate concerns about your business plan, but many others will reflect nothing more than the critics' inexperience in business or their personal insecurities. Hearing about business plans brings to the surface people's fears and regrets about their own finances and their careers—feelings they might unknowingly project onto you and your idea, which can undermine your confidence if you let it.

Here's how to respond to the doubts prospective entrepreneurs often face...

• **Why would you give up a secure job to chase a dream?**

Response: "Why would I remain in a job where an employer controls my fate when I could have the security of controlling my own future?"

Would-be entrepreneurs can expect to hear many questions about their decision to give up a steady paycheck for the uncertainty of entrepreneurship. The truth is, the questioner might be unwilling to admit to himself/herself that even his career with an established company is not all that secure. Employees get passed over for raises and promotions. Companies have layoffs.

And the questioner is ignoring the fact that financial security might not be your primary career goal. Consider which scares you more—the possibility that your income might be irregular for a while, or the possibility that

---

Chris Guillebeau, author of *The $100 Startup: Reinvent the Way You Make a Living, Do What You Love, and Create a New Future* (Crown Business). Based in Portland, Oregon, he is founder of *The Art of Non-Conformity*, a blog about changing the world by achieving personal goals. *ChrisGuillebeau.com*

you might spend your life working for others and never know what you could have accomplished if you had taken your own shot. If it's the latter, then the greater risk for you lies in not starting a business.

Alternate response: "Who said I was leaving my job?" Some entrepreneurs launch businesses in their spare time and leave their jobs only when those businesses appear well on their way to success.

● **Why are you trying to launch a business when you should be trying to find a job?**

Response: "Launching a business could actually help me find a job."

If you're unemployed when you decide to start a business, expect people to question your priorities. But submitting résumés isn't the only way to land a job. In fact, it usually isn't the best way—employers often receive hundreds of résumés when they advertise an opening, making it hard for job applicants to even get a foot in the door.

If you start a business (or even investigate the possibility of starting one), you have a better way to get a foot in the door. You can contact business people to discuss the goods or services that your company could provide to them...or projects your companies could explore together. Such meetings can lead to job offers. Many employers are entrepreneurs themselves, making them predisposed to hiring other entrepreneurial types.

Example: While unemployed, Brett Kelly wrote *Evernote Essentials*, an eBook covering the note-taking app *Evernote*. The makers of Evernote were so impressed with the book that they hired him.

Launching a business also avoids having a period of unemployment in your work history. Fair or not, employment gaps are red flags for many potential employers.

● **You're too old to start a business.**

Response: "My decades of experience and business contacts are pluses, not minuses."

One of the underappreciated aspects of entrepreneurship is that your age is more likely to work for you than against you. Older entrepreneurs tend to know their industry sec-

tors and the sectors' key players better than younger people do.

Example: Ray Kroc was in his 50s when he bought a small restaurant chain called McDonald's and started expanding it.

Working for yourself when you're over 50 also is a way around the ageism that might hold back your career if you continued working for others. Also, one of the biggest hurdles facing entrepreneurs above age 50 has become much less of a problem. Starting in 2014 under Obamacare, self-employed people are able to obtain relatively affordable health insurance through the new insurance marketplaces. Previously, individual health insurance could be very expensive or difficult to obtain for self-employed people who were older than 50 and/or who had health problems.

● **Most new businesses fail.**

Response: "According to whom?"

There are some daunting statistics floating around about the failure rate of new businesses. You might hear that more than half fail in the first year. But such statistics are deceptive. Many of those failed new businesses actually were just hobby businesses that were never meant to last long or provide more than a few extra dollars on the side.

What's the true failure rate for new businesses? It's tricky to measure, but figures compiled by the Small Business Administration suggest that about 70% of new firms last at least two years, and about half last five years or more. Even those numbers significantly overstate the rate of failure. Some of the new businesses that didn't last didn't fail. They closed because the entrepreneurs who launched them accepted attractive job offers, identified even better business opportunities or sold out to larger companies.

● **Why do you think you'll succeed this time?** Your previous business ideas failed.

Response: "The fact that I've tried before increases my odds of success."

Previous business failures aren't signs that you shouldn't try again. They're signs that you already have paid your dues learning hard lessons about entrepreneurship. Those lessons should serve you well this time around.

• **This isn't a good time to be starting a business.** The economy still is too unsettled.

Response: "Times of economic uncertainty are great times to launch a business."

Consumers and businesses reevaluate their spending habits during unsettled economic times such as these. That reevaluation makes them more open to working with a new company—particularly one that offers good value.

Examples: Blue-chip companies started during weak economies include FedEx, General Electric, General Motors and Microsoft.

• **No one will want what you are selling.**

Response: "How would you know?"

Is the person making this criticism one of your potential customers? If not, then give much, much more weight to the feedback you have received from people you actually intend to sell to. If potential customers have been enthusiastic, criticism about your service from noncustomers likely can be dismissed.

Example: Genevieve Thiers heard many disparaging comments about her idea for a website that connects babysitters and parents. But the negative comments came mainly from the investment community—the mothers she spoke with liked her idea. The website *Sitter city.com* became a success.

• **What do you know about starting and running a business?**

Response: "I know plenty about the sector I'm entering, and I can learn what I need to know about business. That's the easy part."

It is fair for critics to raise this issue if you haven't started and run a business before—being an entrepreneur does require some basic business skills. But these skills can be acquired relatively quickly. Josh Kaufman's book *The Personal MBA* (Portfolio) and John Jantsch's *Duct Tape Marketing* blog (*DuctTapeMarketing.com/blog*) are great places to start.

• **You can't afford to start a business.**

Response: "So I will start it on the cheap."

It can be very pricey to enter the manufacturing sector or even the retailing sector if your business idea requires an extensive inventory and/or a storefront. But there are plenty of business ideas that can be launched for just a few thousand dollars or less.

Examples: It can cost very little to start an online business or a consulting business.

Crowdfunding for Your Business

Jason Best, cofounder and principal of Crowdfund Capital Advisors, a crowdfunding consulting firm. Located in San Francisco, he coauthored the investing framework used in the JOBS Act that helped change the laws to make crowdfund investing legal in the US. He coauthored *Crowdfund Investing for Dummies* (For Dummies). *CrowdfundCapitalAdvisors.com*

Entrepreneurs, artists and other innovators raised more than $10 billion in 2014 through "crowdfunding" websites such as *Kickstarter* and *Indiegogo*. These websites let people finance projects by soliciting small contributions from large numbers of supporters. The contributors do not receive stock in the company, but they typically receive some other reward for their support. But successful crowdfunding campaigns take time and effort, and more than half eventually fail to reach their monetary goals. *To succeed…*

• **Raise your name recognition before you raise funds.** If you don't already have an extensive network of people who think highly of your ideas, spend two to six months becoming a respected member of relevant online and real-world communities before launching a crowdfunding campaign.

Helpful: Participate in LinkedIn, Twitter and Meetup groups that discuss topics related to your business idea.

•**Market your campaign in waves.** Ask close friends and relatives to contribute as soon as the campaign launches. Solicit contributions from other contacts only when those contributions already are coming in. People who don't know you are more likely to contribute if they see that others are already doing so.

•**Reward your contributors with your product.** That has a lot more appeal than a T-shirt with your company logo.

Example: The Pebble smartwatch company offered backers who contributed $115 a smartwatch when it became available at a discounted price.

•**Set your crowdfunding goal at the amount required to reach a "milestone" for your company.**

Examples of milestones: The cost of your first production run of your product...the amount you need to sign a lease on an office/factory, etc. It is a good idea to start with a small financial goal for your fund-raising, then once you raise that amount, go back to the crowd for follow-up contributions.

While there are a number of $1 million success stories on Kickstarter, the vast majority of successful campaigns on the site raise less than $25,000.

Fast-Growing Franchises

Fast-growing franchises with low start-up costs include Brightway Insurance, which offers coverage for homes, cars and businesses, as well as life insurance, has 115 franchises (*franchise fee:* $45,000 to $60,000*)...ComForcare Senior Services, which provides personal-care services in clients' homes, has more than 165 franchises ($42,000*)...Just Between Friends, which stages consignment sales for children's toys, baby equipment and maternity clothes, has more than 125 franchises ($14,900)...Sport Clips haircuts has 1,250 franchises ($59,000)...and Young Rembrandts art classes and workshops has more than 100

*Prices subject to change.

franchises ($31,500). All have net-worth requirements, which vary.

What to do: Investigate the franchise thoroughly and ask a knowledgeable adviser, such as a lawyer, to review all of the documents.

Kiplinger's Personal Finance. Kiplinger.com

Layoffs Coming? A Shrewd Strategy to Stay Employed

Alan L. Sklover, Esq., an attorney specializing in employment law, executive compensation and severance agreement negotiation. He is founding partner of Sklover & Company, LLC, New York City. *Sklover WorkingWisdom.com*

Requesting a demotion might seem an odd career move, but if layoffs are coming, a step backward on the corporate ladder beats a kick out the door.

An employee might be viewed as a prime layoff candidate in his or her current position but a valued, cost-effective asset in a slightly less well-compensated role. In my experience, employers grant voluntary demotion requests roughly half the time.

Voluntary demotion in the face of layoffs can make particular sense for employees over age 55. Older layoff casualties tend to have a particularly hard time finding new jobs. Volunteering for demotion allows these workers to delay tapping retirement savings and starting Social

DID YOU KNOW THAT...

These Are the Best States for Starting a Business?

The five best states for starting a business are Maryland, Colorado, Virginia, Utah and Massachusetts. The states are ranked by the number of high-tech businesses, programs that support entrepreneurs and concentration of science, technology and engineering jobs.

CNBC.com

Security benefits while providing continued access to the employer's health insurance plan.

But employers almost never think to offer demotions instead of layoffs—employees who wish to pursue this course typically must propose it themselves.

What you need to know...

EVALUATING THE DEMOTION OPTION

Employees facing potential layoffs need to move swiftly if they want to ask for a demotion but should still take time to weigh their priorities. Voluntary demotion is worth considering when the top priority is maintaining health insurance benefits or keeping some money coming in. It usually isn't appropriate when your top priority is continued career growth.

Next, evaluate the current job market in your field. Speak with executive recruiters and contacts to find out whether you would be likely to quickly find another position at close to your current compensation.

Three other factors to consider before requesting a demotion...

• **It could cost you a severance package.** If the severance package is likely to be generous, you might be better off accepting it than volunteering for demotion—particularly if you are nearing your intended retirement age or considering a job change anyway.

• **It could affect your pension.** Some pensions are calculated based in part on the employee's earnings during his/her last five years of service (or some other time period). This is most common with public sector pensions. It probably isn't wise to request a demotion—and corresponding pay cut—if your pension is calculated this way.

On the other hand, volunteering for demotion can make a lot of sense if staying with an employer a little longer will allow valuable stock options to vest.

• **It could be a black mark on your résumé.** Future employers might be wary of applicants who have demotions in their work history—demotions generally signal that the employee failed to perform up to expectations. This isn't an issue if you're nearing retirement age and don't expect to apply for any

more jobs, but it is for anyone who expects to continue working.

Helpful: If you do end up applying for jobs, explain to the interviewers that you were not demoted for performance, but rather because your employer eliminated your prior position when it "flattened its organizational structure" and was anxious to find a way for you to stay. Interviewers often aren't familiar with the concept of voluntary demotion, but they do understand flattening organizational structures.

SEVEN CRUCIAL DEMOTION DETAILS

If you do decide to request a demotion, here's how to get it right...

• **Try to make your demotion request to the person who is making the final layoff decisions.** If you're not certain who this is, your best bet is the individual highest in the hierarchy who has been involved in staffing decisions at your level in the past. The decision maker almost certainly will not be someone in the human resources department unless you work in HR.

Make your proposal during a face-to-face meeting, if possible. People find it more difficult to say no to reasonable offers that are made in person. Explain that you know that layoffs are coming...that you like working for the company...and that you would be willing to accept a demotion to a lesser position and a pay cut in order to stay if your current job is at risk. (You can discuss a specific salary later if the demotion idea is accepted.)

• **Make this proposal too soon rather than too late.** Layoff decisions very rarely change once they've been made, so your demotion proposal must be made before the list of employees to be laid off is finalized, not after you receive word that you've been let go. That means that there is some risk that you might volunteer for demotion when your job actually is safe. If you have a good relationship with your boss or someone else in the company's hierarchy, consider talking with this person about your job security first.

• **Pitch your demotion idea in terms of how it helps the decision maker meet his/her needs.** You might explain that demoting you rather than laying you off allows the company to lower its overhead without losing an experienced employee...it saves the company a severance payout at your level...and it protects the relationships you have with the company's key customers and vendors. Specifically mention any reasons for keeping you on that the decision maker might not know.

Example: "Smith Co. is one of our largest customers—and Mr. Smith and I went to college together. Accepting my demotion proposal means that you don't have to put that client relationship at risk."

Do *not* emphasize the difficulties that a layoff would cause you. Don't try to make your case based on fairness—layoff decisions have little to do with fairness.

• **Consider fine-tuning your proposal to match your priorities.** If your goal is to stay with the company for only a discrete period of time, such as until you vest in the pension plan or qualify for Medicare, you could offer to remain at the lower position for only that length of time, then resign.

• **Follow up your face-to-face meeting with an e-mail to the decision maker.** This e-mail should summarize your offer and reiterate how it would help both the company and the decision maker.

• **Do not share your demotion plan with your colleagues.** There isn't room for everyone to go one rung down the corporate ladder. The odds that your offer will be accepted decrease sharply if you tell your coworkers and then some of them request voluntary demotions, too.

• **Request severance package protection.** If your voluntary demotion offer is accepted, ask for some assurance that if you're laid off from the lower position within a year, you will receive a severance package no lower than you would have received if you had been laid off from your current job. It's best to request this assurance by e-mail so that you have evidence if necessary. The employer might not be willing to make this guarantee, but there's little harm in asking.

Negotiate a Relocation Package

You can get a better relocation package if a company wants you to move. About 27% of firms say that they will increase the number of workers relocating this year. Find out the firm's reimbursement policy—only 60% of companies fully reimburse transferees, and only 50% give reimbursement to new hires. Consider negotiating for extra time or money.

Example: Shipping one vehicle typically is covered—additional vehicles would cost at least $500 each. If your company offers benefits such as help with a down payment or closing costs for buying a new home, find out what happens if you prefer to rent for a while before making a purchase.

Roundup of experts in corporate relocation, published in Money.

Job Market Advice for College Kids

Employers plan to hire 8.3% more new college graduates in 2015 than in 2014.

Reasons: A recovering economy and the need to replace retiring baby boomers.

More employers plan to offer signing bonuses in 2015 than at any time in the past five years.

The most desirable majors: Business, engineering, computer science. For liberal arts majors, hiring is rising in sales-related areas, such as public relations, communications and marketing.

What to do: Consider looking in regions that are particularly favorable for certain kinds of work.

Example: The San Francisco Bay area for science and technology jobs.

Also: Emphasize internships, work experience and participation in co-op work-study programs—they count just as much as grades.

Kiplinger's Personal Finance. Kiplinger.com

Introverted? Consider These 10 Careers...

The best jobs for introverts, with median annual salaries from the Bureau of Labor Statistics—Animal trainer, $25,270*...archivist, $47,340...astronomer, $96,460...court reporter, $48,160...film/video editor, $51,300...financial clerk, $36,850...geoscientist, $90,890...industrial machine repairer, $46,920...medical records technician, $34,160...social-media manager, $54,170.

All these jobs involve limited interaction with other people during the workday. Educational requirements, job availability and job location vary widely.

Analysis by CareerCast, reported at *MoneyWatch.com*

*Figures subject to change.

Looking for a Job? These "Innocent" Facebook Posts Can Ruin Your Chances

Miriam Salpeter, author of *Social Networking for Career Success* (Learning Express). She is owner of Keppie Careers, a social-media-focused career coaching and consulting company based in Atlanta. *KeppieCareers.com*

It is well-documented that improper use of social media can derail careers. However, it's just as likely that social networks such as Twitter, Facebook and LinkedIn could help you land your next job.

A 2013 study by the recruiting technology company Jobvite found that 94% of employers use or plan to use social networks as part of their hiring process. Some employers use social-media tools to locate candidates worth calling in for interviews, and others use them to weed out applicants who seem unprofessional or otherwise problematic. With dozens of qualified job hunters applying for most openings these days, employers often search for any excuse to remove candidates from contention.

Here's how to make the most of your online presence...

REMOVE RED FLAGS ONLINE

It may seem obvious that you should delete posts and photos that you would not want an employer to see such as those showing you partying or in various states of undress. But a surprising number of people don't do this, partly because they think their privacy settings are limiting access to their sites.

Social-networks' privacy settings are supposed to allow us to restrict access to our sensitive posts and photos so that they can be viewed only by the people we choose—but these privacy settings tend to be confusing, and many people's pages aren't as private as they think.

A Columbia University study found that all 65 Facebook users who participated in the study were sharing information in ways they did not intend.

It always is better to err on the side of caution when your career is on the line and simply delete anything that could cause problems or doesn't seem totally professional.

Also, be wary of the following, which can seem innocent but could cost you a job...

•**Complaints.** If you have used your social-media account to vent anger at businesses, bad drivers, former employers, your current boss or anyone else, remove as many of those posts as possible. Excessive complaining may make you appear to be a negative person, and employers don't like to hire people who have poor attitudes.

•**Political commentary.** A potential employer might possess different political opinions—or a company might worry that some of its customers do. At the very least, refrain from political posts that make you seem extreme or inflexible in your views. Such posts could make employers worry that you will have trouble getting along with coworkers.

•**Anything that could be interpreted as insensitive to other people.** This includes jokes that involve race, gender or sexual orientation. You don't want to give employers any reason to even consider the possibility that you might say or do something racist, sexist or otherwise discriminatory.

•**Anything a current or former employer could consider confidential.** If there is something on your social-network page that a past employer might not want shared, other employers might worry that you would not protect their private information either. This includes details about your accomplishments that you include on your LinkedIn profile. If you accomplished something that your company has not made public, don't include details of it online.

When it comes to Facebook or other social networks, avoid mentioning incidents that your employers wouldn't want customers or investors to know. For example, take down any posts poking fun at prior employers' embarrassing strategic missteps or customer relations blunders.

•**Arguments.** Employers might worry that people who become embroiled in heated debates online could become argumentative in the workplace as well. Don't show your temper online.

MANAGE YOUR ONLINE PROFILE

Don't stress out too much if you realize that you won't be able to totally clear your profile of all potentially damaging information. The fact is, you are better off working for a place where the people have similar values to you so that you won't clash down the road.

If you choose not to delete potentially problematic posts—or cannot fully do so because other people have reposted them elsewhere—your best bet is to add numerous posts and updates designed to create the impression that you want people to have of you. For example, if you choose not to remove partisan political commentary, add posts showing that you respect people who hold the opposite viewpoint, even though you don't agree with them.

Bottom line: Look at your social media, and try to put yourself in an employer's shoes. What would he/she think about you if he sees what you post?

MAKE IT WORK FOR YOU

An increasing number of employers are now using social networks—particularly LinkedIn—to locate potential hires. *To make the most of this opportunity...*

•**Paint yourself as an industry insider.** Use LinkedIn and other social networks to comment on important industry news. Join LinkedIn groups, Twitter chats and Google+ communities that include employees and executives at companies where you would like to work. Answer questions posted there, and be generous with your expertise. Don't go overboard and try to answer every question—being too active on social networks may create the impression that your time isn't valuable. Just contribute when you have something especially useful and intelligent to say.

Try to show that you understand the sector's "pain points"—the issues currently causing sleepless nights for executives and key customers.

Example: When a complicated new government regulation affects your sector, write a post or update that helps interpret the regulation or offers a tip for coping with it.

• **Use keywords to make it easier for people to find you online.** What are the keywords an employer might search on the Internet if he were looking to hire someone like you? These might include specific subsectors, in-demand skills or specialized degrees or certifications. Include these keywords in your LinkedIn page headline and prior job titles to help make your page appear higher in the listings when these keywords are searched, improving the odds that employers will find you. Use them in your updates and bios on all of the social networks.

Example: Rather than list a prior job title as "Assistant Manager," list it as "Assistant Manager, Veterinary Pharmaceuticals." This is more targeted.

• **Add a photo.** LinkedIn users who include photos of themselves are seven times more likely to have their profiles viewed, according to LinkedIn's research. This photo should be a head-and-shoulders shot that makes you appear friendly and professional. You should be smiling and well-dressed. Eliminate anything distracting in the photo, either in the background or in your wardrobe.

• **Turn your headlines into your personal elevator pitch.** On LinkedIn, most people simply list their job titles as their headline. For job hunters, that's a wasted opportunity. This headline will appear prominently in LinkedIn's search results, so your goal should be to write something that will quickly pique potential employers' interest. Once you have a great LinkedIn headline, use this for your Twitter bio and adapt it for Google+ and Facebook, too. For example, rather than write, "Project manager," you might write "PMP-certified consumer electronics project manager. Spearheaded successful multimillion-dollar 2014 product launch."

BE AWARE OF PERCEPTIONS

Employers know that when an employee overhauls his LinkedIn page, it's often a sign of an impending career move. To reduce the risk that updating your page will tip off your employer that you are thinking about leaving, select "Turn on/off your activity broadcasts" from LinkedIn's "Privacy & Settings" menu (hover over your picture in the upper right). If the box that appears is checked, uncheck it, then click "Save changes."

An employer or coworkers still could stumble across the fact that you have made LinkedIn changes, however, so have an explanation ready in case someone raises the topic. For example, you could tell a colleague that you want your page to be as impressive as possible because potential clients sometimes use LinkedIn to investigate you.

TO DELETE DAMAGING POSTS

Here's how to delete questionable posts, updates and tweets from social media…

For Facebook: Hover over the post in your Timeline…click the V-shaped icon in the upper-right corner…then select "Delete."

For LinkedIn: Select "Your Updates" from the "All Updates" drop-down list…find the questionable post…then click "Delete."

For Twitter: Go to your profile page…locate the post you want to get rid of…then click "Delete" for that post.

Companies Often Look at the Wrong Things on Facebook When Hiring

Companies routinely eliminate candidates who post content about alcohol or drug use—but a recent study has found that Facebook postings often have nothing to do with an applicant's self-discipline or conscientiousness. In fact, candidates for sales and marketing positions—jobs that require an outgoing personality—are significantly more likely to post about drugs and/or alcohol. So automatically eliminating them reduces the pool of qualified applicants.

One online indicator worth looking for: People who rate high on both conscientiousness and agreeableness are very unlikely to insult other people in Facebook postings.

Study of 175 people by researchers at North Carolina State University, Raleigh, published in *Cyberpsychology, Behavior, and Social Networking.*

Outrageous Résumé Mistakes

One résumé was written in text-speak—using the letter "u" instead of the word "you." One candidate gave his objective as working for someone who was not an alcoholic—like his current employer. One candidate attached her baby pictures. And another mentioned having served a jail term for assaulting a former boss.

What to do: Proofread your résumé, and ask a friend to review it. Omit irrelevant information. For recent college grads, a one-page résumé is ideal...for experienced workers, at least two pages with a focus on jobs relevant to the position.

Roundup of hiring managers surveyed by market-research firm Harris Interactive and employment website *CareerBuilder.com*, reported at *CBSNews.com*.

Overused Career Buzzwords

Overused career buzzwords to delete from your LinkedIn profile and stop using in your job search—*responsible, strategic, creative, effective, patient, expert, organizational, driven, innovative* and *analytical*.

These words have been used so often, in so many contexts, that they have lost meaning and now point to people who have nothing new or interesting to say about themselves.

Instead of using these words, link your skills to specific results that show your competence...use active rather than passive language, showing how you achieved specific results...get endorsements and recommendations from reputable people who can verify your abilities.

Roundup of experts in career advice, reported at *CareerBliss.com* and *FoxBusiness.com*.

EASY-TO-DO...

Better Body Language During a Job Interview

Hunching over makes you seem uninterested and crossing your arms shows a lack of confidence. Keeping your hands in your lap makes you appear timid, so don't be afraid to occasionally gesture with your hands to share your enthusiasm. Avoiding eye contact can make you seem unwilling to connect with the interviewer and therefore with the job—even in a group interview, make eye contact with each person in the room.

Kelly Decker, president, Decker Communications, San Francisco, quoted at *MoneyWatch.com*.

To Get Better Job References...

When asked to give references for a possible job, provide names of anyone in authority over you who is likely to give favorable comments—you need not mention your direct supervisor unless specifically asked. If you know your former boss will give you a poor reference but the recruiter insists on having his/her name, provide it, but explain that you did not see eye-to-eye. Also give the recruiter the name of someone in authority who thought highly of your work. Speak to all your references before listing them to be sure that they are willing to talk to the recruiter on your behalf.

CBSNews.com

How to Handle a Job Interview on Skype

For a job interview on Skype, dress nicely although you can be a bit less formal than for an in-person interview. And choose an appropriate location such as a home office. Avoid wireless connections—use a wired ethernet connection if you can to eliminate the chance of Wi-Fi problems. Have some form of backup, such as a phone number—if your Internet connection does go down, then the interviewer still can reach you. Also, be sure that your Skype user name looks and sounds professional.

MakeUseOf.com

How to Find a Job at a Friend's Company

CareerSonar.com uses your LinkedIn connections and Facebook friends to help you get a job. Sign up for free through Facebook. Then enter a keyword for a position you want. CareerSonar matches up the keyword to jobs available at organizations where your friends and contacts work. Then you can get in touch with a friend or colleague, express interest in the position and ask for help making the right connections.

Suzanne Lucas, a writer who spent 10 years in corporate human resources, writing online at *CBSNews.com*.

Get Credentialed to Get a Job

The federal government helps all 50 states fund CareerOneStop centers where job seekers can obtain credentials certifying that they possess the minimum skills needed for certain jobs.

Example: Even lower-level positions in health care require credentials under federal guidelines.

What to do: Search online for your city, state and "CareerOneStop" to find places providing the training you want—such as community colleges and for-profit centers.

Bankrate.com

Where's Your Wow? 4 Ways to Stand Out from the Pack

Rick Frishman, publisher at Morgan James Publishing and founder of Planned Television Arts, a book publicity company based in New York City. He is coauthor, with Robyn Freedman-Spizman, of *Where's Your Wow: 16 Ways to Make Your Competitors Wish They Were You!* (McGraw-Hill). *RickFrishman.com*

Some people just have a natural ability to "wow"—an effortless charisma and skill in relationships that draw others toward them. But most of us need to learn a few tricks to get the most out of whatever it is that makes us special. This can make a business seem more appealing to customers and an employee less expendable to his/her boss, a crucial consideration in today's slow economy. *Four ways to wow...*

• **Write a book.** The publish-on-demand and self-publishing services that are available today mean that you can have a book in print, either by finding a small publisher interested in your idea or by financing a book yourself, typically for well under $1,000.* (The "Resources" section of my website, *RickFrishman.com*, includes links for information.)

Examples: An insurance salesman could write a book called *How to Buy a Life Insurance Policy.* A real estate agent could write *Choosing the Right Home in a Buyer's Market.*

Give copies of your book to your customers. If you can't write, try to find a ghostwriter willing to work for a modest fee...or simply "talk" the book onto a recording device, then transcribe it. No matter how many copies you sell, having a book in print makes you look like an expert in your field.

• **Feed stories to the local press.** Contact reporters at small newspapers in your region, and offer news related to your area of expertise. It must be truly newsworthy, not just self-interested attempts to obtain free publicity.

Example: An exterminator might direct reporters to recent evidence that a new type of termite is now in the region...or provide

*Price subject to change.

315

advice on how to rid your home of an insect that is unusually prevalent in the area.

Once you have been in the local papers a few times, local radio and television reporters might start calling as well.

• **Always overdeliver.** Meeting expectations and making good on promises is not enough to wow. You must deliver more than people expect every time. Think of something you easily could add that your customer or employer will value. Include this bonus at the end of the transaction, if possible, so that the other party walks away with it on his/her mind.

Examples: A restaurant adds a free small dessert to dinner orders. A jeweler provides free replacement watch batteries to anyone who buys a watch.

• **Give for the sake of giving...and for your own good as well.** Show that you are a charitable, caring individual, and you will be rewarded. People want to do business with—and be friends with—good people.

Examples: Help coworkers with their responsibilities whenever you can. Donate your time to charitable causes. Volunteer to be the employee who represents your company at charity events.

Your Boss Is Watching You and Listening, Too

Lewis Maltby, JD, president of the National Workrights Institute, a not-for-profit organization that researches and advocates on issues related to employee rights. Maltby previously served as general counsel of Drexelbrook Engineering Company and as director of employment rights with the American Civil Liberties Union. He has testified before Congress on employment issues. *Workrights.org*

They can read our e-mails, listen to our phone calls, watch us through hidden cameras, track our movements and monitor our Facebook pages—all legally. They are not federal agents from the National Security Agency—they are our employers.

Few Americans are aware that their bosses have wide-ranging rights to look into their lives. The rapidly dropping cost of high-tech surveillance equipment, including digital cameras and GPS technology, has been making such prying increasingly common.

YOUR E-MAIL AND TEXT MESSAGES

Any e-mail sent through your employer's computer network can be read by your boss—including not only messages in your work e-mail account but also messages in your personal e-mail accounts if you use your employer's network to send or receive them. This includes messages on your own personal laptop, tablet computer or smartphone.

The e-mails most likely to be examined are those containing words that often are used in a sexual context. Many employers use computer programs that call such messages to their attention so that they can stop workplace sexual harassment before it leads to a lawsuit. But the same keywords that appear in sexual harassment e-mails also can turn up in very private messages between sexual partners or in messages about sensitive medical matters.

Employers have a right to read text and e-mail messages sent from company-owned cell phones, smartphones and laptops, too, even if those messages are sent through personal e-mail accounts from outside the workplace. Employers can't easily monitor such messages as they are sent, but they can be uncovered later when the device is returned to the IT department for repairs or upgrade.

What to do: If you must send a private e-mail or text from the workplace, do so through your own mobile computer or cell phone... and if this device is capable of operating over both Wi-Fi and a cellular network, confirm that it currently is accessing the cellular network, not company Wi-Fi. If you must use a company cell phone to send a private message, opt for calling the person rather than texting or e-mailing. That makes it much less likely that the company will learn the content of the message, though the company could determine what person or place you called.

YOUR ONLINE ACTIVITY

Most employees realize that their employers can monitor their Internet use when they're in the office. And most job applicants understand that many potential employers now evaluate applicants' Facebook pages, blogs and other Internet postings. But some employers take it even further, monitoring Internet content by and about their current employees—and occasionally firing those whose personal lives or opinions the employer considers offensive or unprofessional.

Examples: Employees have been fired for posting pictures of themselves holding a beer at a party...or wearing a bikini on a beach while on vacation. One employee was fired for expressing opinions about the Iraq war that ran counter to his employer's views.

In most states, an employer can legally fire an employee for nearly any reason, aside from reasons that are specifically prohibited by federal law (such as race, religion, sex, national origin, age or disability)...by collective bargaining agreements...or by civil service protections for government employees. Apart from laws prohibiting employers from firing employees for smoking, only California, Colorado, Montana, New York and North Dakota have laws restricting the ability of employers to fire employees for legal off-duty activities and statements.

Employers even can require employees to provide their social-media passwords to facilitate their snooping, though some states have begun passing laws to prohibit this.

What to do: Do not post anything online that you would not be comfortable saying or doing in the office. Discourage your friends and relatives from posting pictures of you doing these things as well. Even if your current employer does not monitor your online life, there's a good chance that it will be examined the next time you apply for a job.

TRACKING YOUR MOVEMENTS

If you have a company car or company cell phone, your employer could be tracking your movements—even during your free time.

It's common and reasonable for employers to install GPS in company vehicles to make sure that their salespeople and delivery people are where they're supposed to be during the workday. But nothing legally prevents employers from also tracking company vehicles during nonworking hours to learn where employees go in their spare time.

Modern cell phones have GPS capabilities, too. For as little as $5 per phone per month, an employer can obtain a service that will use this GPS to track employees' movements.

A company might monitor how late an employee stays out on weekends, how often he visits bars or whether he's having an affair with a coworker.

What to do: If you don't want your employer to know about your activities outside the office, leave your company car at home or at least park it several blocks from destinations that you hope to keep private. Leave the company cell phone home.

CAMERAS, LAPTOPS, PHONES

Some of the following types of snooping are not as common, but it may just be a matter of time before they catch on with employers...

• **Digital video camera surveillance.** Although these cameras are present in many workplaces as security devices, employees often don't realize that they're being observed or recorded. These are not the obvious security cameras of old—a modern digital camera can be easily concealed. Courts generally have ruled that employers have the right to record video of their workers and workplaces, though usually not in employee bathrooms or locker rooms.

Example: The Massachusetts Supreme Court ruled that an employer was within his rights to take videos of a female employee who regularly changed into gym clothes in her cubicle after everyone else had left for the day.

• **Laptop surveillance.** If you have a company laptop, your employer—or a rogue employee in your employer's IT department—could activate that laptop's webcam and spy on you, possibly with no obvious sign that the camera is active. We don't yet have evidence of an employer doing this, but it was done with laptops issued to students by a Pennsylvania high school.

• **Audio surveillance.** In most states, employers can place hidden audio recording devices in their workplaces, too, though a state law might require them to disclose to employers that they have done so.

These listening devices generally must be confined to parts of the workplace where

317

conversations are predominantly work-related, so they typically can't be used in cafeterias, break rooms or bathrooms.

Companies can and do monitor and record employee phone conversations, however. By federal law, they must disclose that phone calls are being recorded. Federal laws also require them to stop listening if it becomes clear that a call is not work-related—but don't count on this rule to protect your privacy.

Employees cannot know for sure that their employers are hanging up on personal calls, and employees legally can be disciplined if the call violates employer restrictions limiting personal use of the phone.

Companies legally can monitor calls made on company-owned cell phones as well, but in practice, this is difficult for them to do.

What to do: Do not do anything in your workplace that you would not want your employer to see, even if no one else is around. If you must do something private in the workplace, the bathroom or locker room is the spot least likely to be under observation. Do not say anything on an office phone that you wouldn't want your employer to hear. If you must make a private call, do so from a cell phone—ideally your personal cell phone. If you have a company laptop, turn it off or at least close it when it's not in use. If you never use your company laptop's Webcam, cover it with a piece of tape.

Prepare Now for Major Cyber Outages

Hacker or criminal attacks or natural disasters can take down power and the computers that use it for days or weeks.

What to do: Create a business-continuity plan for an outage lasting more than a few hours...have a backup in case your physical data center goes down...determine what you would do if you could not get to critical data...have fallback vendors in case your usual ones are compromised...test your systems to be sure that they are as secure as possible against possible hacker attack...install antivirus software, and keep it updated...and plan for a banking-system crash, deciding how you would handle payroll and accounts payable and receivable.

Roundup of security experts reported at FoxBusiness. com.

6 Tricks to Sell Absolutely Anything: A Product...Service... and Even Yourself as a Job Candidate

Daniel H. Pink, lecturer and author of books, including *To Sell Is Human: The Surprising Truth About Moving Others...Drive...*and *A Whole New Mind* (all from Riverhead). The books have been published in 34 languages and have sold more than one million copies in the US alone. He lives in Washington, DC. *DanPink.com*

More often than you may realize, you spend a big chunk of your day selling. Beyond selling products and services to customers, selling you do may include pitching your ideas to your bosses and co-workers...convincing your spouse, children and/or other relatives and friends that your advice is sound...persuading a prospective employer to hire you...even coaxing a credit card issuer or phone company—or a grocery store cashier—to correct a mistake. One poll found that 40% of a typical employee's work hours are spent in various forms of "nonsales selling," and the percentage outside of work may not be a lot lower.

And much of what we think we know about all these forms of "selling" is wrong, according to recent research.

In an interview, best-selling author Daniel H. Pink described six surprising ways to increase your chances of succeeding no matter what form of "selling" you engage in...

1. Confess to a (small) negative. Negatives can be positives. A study published in *Journal of Consumer Research* found that buyers were more likely to purchase a product when they were told about a minor problem with it.

Why? The human mind likes to draw comparisons. Whether you are pitching a product or an idea, if you mention a small drawback or flaw along with the many positive attributes, your audience tends to subconsciously weigh the many pluses against this trifling minus and conclude that the idea or product is a good one. It also makes the audience trust you more, since no product or idea is considered perfect. If you fail to list any negatives or doubts, the audience might instead think up more serious ones on their own—or compare your product or idea more carefully to others before making their decision. This strategy tends to work best when your audience is busy or distracted…and when the advantages are discussed before the small negative is mentioned.

Example: If you sell items on eBay, disclose a tiny scratch, missing instruction manual or some other minor flaw in the description.

2. Don't tell yourself you will accomplish a goal—ask yourself whether you can. For decades, we have been told about the power of positive thinking. Proponents claim that thinking I can do this (or other words of confidence) before making a sales pitch boosts your confidence and increases your chances of success. But while positive self-talk is certainly better than negative self-talk, research published in *Psychological Science* pointed to an even more effective strategy. Rather than make positive statements to yourself about your abilities, ask yourself questions that force your mind to consider your abilities—*Can I do this?* instead of *I can do this.*

In one study, participants who were instructed to write "Will I?" 20 times solved nearly twice as many anagram puzzles as those instructed to write "I will."

Asking yourself questions about your abilities encourages your mind to mull things over and think up reasons why you can succeed, which are much more meaningful than simple "I can do it" platitudes. You even might think of strategies that increase your odds of success.

Example: "Will I be able to present my mistake to my wife in a way that doesn't make her angry?"

3. Use a mild profanity. Most of us scrupulously avoid profanity when we present our ideas and products—we don't want to offend the people we're trying to convince. But a study by researchers at Northern Illinois University discovered that inserting a mild curse word into our speech makes us seem to have greater conviction in what we're presenting, which increases our persuasiveness.

Keep the profanity mild, and use this strategy only when your conviction is genuine—listeners tend to be very good at spotting false conviction.

Example: "Excuse my language, but this is a damn good idea."

4. When you think that you have the upper hand in a sales situation, think of reasons why you don't. It's a wonderful feeling to have the best product, idea or skill set—it means that you can make your sales pitch with confidence. But there is an underappreciated downside to being in a strong sales position. A study by researchers at Northwestern University's Kellogg School of Management found that when people see themselves in a position of power in an interpersonal interaction, they become substantially less likely to see things from the other party's point of view, and that reduces their ability to be persuasive.

If you're feeling confident and powerful shortly before making a sales pitch, remind yourself of ways in which you lack power, then think through the situation from the buyer's perspective.

Example: An employer presenting a new compensation system to his/her employees is likely to feel that he's in a position of power because he's the boss. Before the presentation, he should remind himself that the economy is improving—so his employees could find other jobs if they became unhappy—then reconsider how the new compensation system is likely to be received.

5. Stop trying to solve people's problems, and start trying to identify the problems they've missed. In the past, selling was about solving problems—if a customer needed a lightbulb, you sold him a lightbulb…if an employer posted a help-wanted ad, you sold him on your skills and experience.

But in the Internet-age, people can solve problems such as these on their own—a quick web search will turn up great lightbulb prices…and online employment websites can turn up hundreds of qualified job candidates in minutes. Today the most successful salespeople are those who can spot problems that potential customers don't yet even realize they have.

Examples: Rather than sell a lightbulb, evaluate the light fixtures and windows and propose a new illumination strategy that brings in more natural light or saves electricity. Rather than submit a résumé for a job opening, approach a company that hasn't advertised an opening to discuss ways in which you could improve the company's bottom line.

6. Stress potential at least as much as accomplishments. Accomplishments are tangible and verifiable, while potential is subjective and not certain. Logically, accomplishments should carry much greater weight with an audience. But a 2012 study by researchers at Stanford University and Harvard Business School found that the opposite was true—people generally find potential more enticing than actual accomplishments. The researchers speculated that the inherent uncertainty surrounding someone's or something's potential will cause possible buyers to consider it more deeply. And when buyers think deeply about someone or something, they often begin to feel a connection and think of reasons why this relationship will work.

Example: When you are asked about a past accomplishment during a job interview, use it as a springboard to explain your tremendous potential for future accomplishments. "Yes, I led the marketing team on that product rollout. We focused on a social-media–based campaign, which was almost unheard of at the time. That's what I bring to the table—I can come up with new angles for your future product introductions that will get attention."

Assuming the Sale: A Sales Technique You Can Use at Home

Brian Tracy, noted sales trainer and author of *Unlimited Sales Success* (AMACOM).

A technique for closing a sale can be a great way to approach life! The strategy is known as the "directive close" or "assuming the sale."

It works like this. After describing what you have to sell, you ask, "Does this make sense so far?" Typically the customer responds in the affirmative. Then you say, "Well then, the next step is…" and give the details of the purchase process. Then add, "I'll take care of all the details."

When a salesman "assumes the sale," he acts as if the customer already has agreed to make the purchase. It's an effective sales technique in the hands of a confident salesperson that can result in a success rate of around 70%.

"Assuming the sale" could be effective in nonsales situations, too. When we want people to agree with our opinions or ideas, just act as though they already do.

If your family or friends can't decide what to do on a Saturday, where to go for dinner or what color to paint the living room, present the option that you prefer, asking, "Are we all OK with this?" then moving right to, "Well, here's what we need to do to get that done…I'll set it up." Immediately make reservations or do whatever else is necessary to lock in the decision.

Unless others in the group are firmly entrenched in their own preferences—or firmly opposed to ours—they usually will agree and be pleased that someone else is making it happen!

How Would Mom Handle the Situation?

Lee Cockerell, former executive vice president of Walt Disney World Resort and author of *The Customer Rules* (Crown Business)

My mom wasn't a business consultant, and yours probably wasn't either. But asking ourselves, *What would Mom do?* still is a great way to be a better worker and provide superior customer service.

Good moms encourage their kids to believe in themselves. They make them feel secure and valued. They exalt in their kids' triumphs even more than their own. Managers and other professionals who do the same develop loyal, hardworking, productive teams—not to mention professional allies who remain in their corner years after they've moved on to other positions.

Mom's wisdom is particularly valuable in customer service, says Cockerell, who held executive roles at Hilton Hotels and Marriott Corporation. When you're not certain how to treat a customer, ask yourself what a good mother would do if this customer were a guest in her home. She probably would greet him at the door, then do everything in her power to make him feel welcome and comfortable.

Asking, *What would Mom do?* doesn't just remind us what to do—it also reminds us that we owe it to our moms to be the men and women they raised us to be.

What *Not* to Say at Work

Saying the following things at work can diminish your stature...

- **Can I ask a question?** Just ask—don't request permission.
- **I'm sorry to bother you.** Just say, "Excuse me"—don't identify yourself as a bother.
- **I was hoping you could spare a few moments.** Again, just say, "Excuse me."
- **Thank you for listening to me.** A simple "thank you" is enough.
- **I will be honest with you.** This implies that you aren't honest at other times.
- **I was just wondering if perhaps...** This backs into a question—ask what you want to know.

Barbara Pachter, business etiquette and communications speaker and coach, and president, Pachter & Associates, Cherry Hill, New Jersey. She is author of *The Essentials of Business Etiquette: How to Greet, Eat, and Tweet Your Way to Success* (McGraw-Hill).

If Someone Steals Your Ideas...

Don't get angry if someone takes credit for your ideas. Instead, set up a meeting and speak with the person privately. Say that you were disappointed not to get credit, and ask why it was not given. If the oversight was unintentional, the person may correct the mistake voluntarily—which is your goal.

If the person refuses to give you credit, meet with your manager and lay out the facts—again, without accusing or acting angry. Do not come across as a complainer—let the boss know that you are happy with the way the project turned out and will enjoy working on future ones.

Dan Schwabel, managing partner, Millennial Branding, research and consulting firm, Boston, and author of *Promote Yourself: The New Rules for Career Success* (St. Martin's).

How Businesses Can Spur Innovation

Take new ideas from anywhere and anyone in the company, not just a small circle of insiders. In fact, look to mix ideas together—sometimes a great idea comes from combining two good ones. Give employees time to daydream and experiment, but expect mistakes and learn from them—do not punish people for them.

Rosabeth Moss Kanter, PhD, Ernest L. Arbuckle Professor of Business Administration, Harvard Business School, Boston, writing on the *Harvard Business Review* blog network.

How to Disable the "Reply All" Function

The "reply all" e-mail function can clog recipients' in-boxes and lead to embarrassment if clicked on accidentally. Microsoft offers a free *NoReplyAll* add-on to its Outlook program. Other e-mail software provide different ways to disable the function.

There also is *Reply to All Monitor* ($14.95, *SperrySoftware.com*), which sends a user a message every time he/she clicks Reply All, asking whether he really wants to do so.

The Wall Street Journal. WSJ.com

Workers in Small Companies Are Happier

People who work in firms with fewer than 100 employees are 25% more likely to be happy than individuals working at firms with more than 1,000 employees.

Other factors that contribute to happiness at work: Supervising others rather than being supervised…working at a job that in-volves caregiving or direct service rather than one in sales…working in a skilled trade.

Survey of 11,000 employees in more than 90 countries by Delivering Happiness at Work, a consulting company, San Francisco, reported in *The Wall Street Journal.*

Small Business Discounts

Get discounts on car rentals, office supplies and more by using a website that helps small businesses get the same sort of deals that larger firms negotiate directly with suppliers. *ABNSave.com* offers prenegotiated deals and partnerships with firms such as Office Depot. It can lower your costs without requiring you to spend time searching online for deals.

Example: Save up to 20% on a Hertz car rental.*

Forbes.com

*Offer subject to change.

Great Gadgets to Take on Business Trips

• **Martian Watch** can be used to make calls or send voice commands to your phone. It has a 12-character scrolling LED screen that shows e-mail and text-message alerts. *Cost*: $125 to $300, depending on model.*

• **Powerbag** is a backpack-style case with a built-in battery that can charge a smartphone or tablet carried inside. *Cost*: From $120.

• **MyCharge** is an extra smartphone battery that recharges from a laptop. *Cost*: $20 to $130, depending on model.

• **Kensington AbsolutePower** is a small, lightweight unit that can charge three devices at once—including phones, tablets and laptops (excluding Apple laptops). *Cost*: $90.

Forbes.com

*Prices subject to change.

Better Hotel Business Centers

Hotel business centers are becoming more useful. Some are integrating the center with the lobby, offering free Wi-Fi and more comfortable seats. Others provide videoconferencing technology and more configurable seating. Small partitioned workspaces may be available as well as areas where guests can print wirelessly from hotel laptops or their own devices. Ask what the business-center arrangements are when you book a room.

Roundup of experts on business travel, reported in USA Today.

Little-Known Dangers of Desk Jobs

Steven Schoolcraft, vice president of safety, health and environment at Parsons Corporation, an engineering and construction company with more than 11,000 employees.

You know that workplace safety is a very serious concern in construction and manufacturing. But can a desk job always be considered safe? No. Some of the worst injuries my company suffers each year are to office staff, not construction workers. It's not that the office employees aren't aware of the possible dangers...it's that they're lulled into a feeling of safety and get complacent.

Common causes of office injuries...

• **Power cords.** These can become trip wires when strung across places where employees walk. This danger is increasing as employees search for outlets to recharge an ever-increasing arsenal of portable digital devices.

• **File cabinets.** Opening multiple file cabinet drawers at once can cause these heavy cabinets to tip over if they haven't been secured to a wall. Boxes and other objects stored on top of tall file cabinets can be hazards, too.

• **Staircases.** Falls are particularly likely when employees use the stairs while carrying something with both hands, rendering them unable to hold on to handrails.

• **Paper cutters.** When I worked at NASA, the famed space agency, one employee cut off the fleshy end of his thumb with a paper cutter. Even smart people can be injured by seemingly simple office equipment when they don't pay adequate attention.

Working in Poorly Ventilated Spaces Slows Brain Function

Researchers analyzed the decision-making skills of volunteers in nonpolluted work environments that had varying levels of carbon dioxide. The study found that a decline in abilities such as information usage, strategy and task orientation are directly associated with a rise in carbon dioxide.

Study of indoor air quality and performance conducted by Lawrence Berkeley National Laboratory, Berkeley, California, with researchers from State University of New York (SUNY) Upstate Medical University, Syracuse, published in Environmental Health Perspectives.

Exercise May Prevent Job Burnout

In a recent finding, men who did better on a cycling fitness test were less likely to report feeling burned out by work than men with lower fitness scores.

Possible reason: Exercise can help refresh you mentally and—if done with other people—expand your social circle. Both effects may help protect against burnout.

Best: 30 minutes a day of moderate-to-intense activity.

Study by researchers in the department of psychology at University of Basel Institute for Sport and Sport Sciences, Switzerland, published in BMC Research Notes.

You Can Be Fired for Staying Home Sick

If you have to be out of work due to an illness—even for one day or two—you have little protection under the law. Laws protecting those with illnesses apply only to serious medical conditions and legally specified disabilities. The Americans with Disabilities Act does not apply to firms with 14 or fewer employees unless state or local laws cover smaller employers. If your illness makes it unsafe for you to work, you may be protected if you refuse to break the law—for instance, if you are contagious and in the health industry or food service. Protections for a serious medical condition or disability are complex and carefully defined, and allowable absence under the Family and Medical Leave Act is limited by law. Consult a knowledgeable attorney for details.

Roundup of experts on workplace law, reported at Jobs.AOL.com.

You May Be Able to Buy Extra Vacation Time

A few companies—5% of those in a recent survey—let employees buy extra vacation days through payroll deductions. About 9% allow workers to cash out unused vacation time—and 7% permit employees to donate vacation time to other workers.

Boston.com

Where Workers Get the Most Vacation Time...

Workers get the most days off per year in Austria and Portugal. Both countries require 35 vacation days and paid holidays. Germany and Spain give workers 34 days off per year...France, 31.

The US is the only developed country without any legally required paid vacation days or holidays.

Center for Economic and Policy Research. CEPR.net

More Sex = Higher Wages

Employees who have sex more than four times a week have salaries that are 5% higher, on average, than those who are less sexually active. Those who have no sexual activity average 3% less income than those who have sex.

Possible reason: Sexually active workers may have more self-confidence or may be in better physical or emotional shape than other employees. More frequent sex may make people more productive and creative at work. Or the connection may work the other way—people receiving higher wages may have more sexual desire and more money to encourage sexual activity.

Roundup of experts in psychotherapy and economics, reported at MarketWatch.com.

20

Safety Nets

Sneaky New Tricks from Identity Thieves: Protect Yourself from Hotel Wi-Fi, Social Networks, More

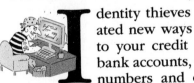I dentity thieves have now created new ways to gain access to your credit card accounts, bank accounts, Social Security numbers and other sensitive data. *Here, the sneakiest threats and ways to protect yourself...*

HOTEL WI-FI

In decades past, criminals who targeted hotel guests typically broke into rooms and stole valuables from luggage. These days, identity thieves can steal from hotel guests without ever setting foot in their rooms. They do this by setting up Wi-Fi networks that appear to be official hotel Wi-Fi networks, then stealing private data from hotel guests who log on. All public Wi-Fi networks should be treated with caution, but hotel Wi-Fi is particularly dangerous because guests tend to feel secure in the privacy of their rooms, making them more likely to access financial accounts, enter credit card details or reveal other supersensitive information. *To protect yourself...*

• **Update your laptop, tablet or smartphone security software immediately before staying at a hotel** (see below under "Smartphones"). This maximizes the odds that the security software will identify threats.

• **Never use hotel Wi-Fi for online banking, credit card account management or investment management.** Don't use a hotel lobby computer for such things, either. "Keyloggers" that track every keystroke and report things such as passwords to identity thieves often are

---

Steve Weisman, an attorney and a member of the National Academy of Elder Law Attorneys. He is a senior lecturer at Bentley College in Waltham, Massachusetts, and host of the syndicated radio program A Touch of Grey. He is author of *50 Ways to Protect Your Identity in a Digital Age: New Financial Threats You Need to Know and How to Avoid Them* (Financial Times). *Scamicide.com*

loaded onto public computers. Consider using your smartphone's network instead for these functions, because it is somewhat safer. Or at least check with the hotel to confirm that you are logging in to the authentic hotel Wi-Fi.

•**If you're prompted to update software or download a program while accessing the Internet through a hotel Wi-Fi system, decline to do so.** Downloading this "update" actually might load malware (malicious software) onto your computer. If you feel that you must update your software as is directed, at least don't click a link in a pop-up window to do so. Instead, visit the software provider's official website, and download the update from there.

•**Don't call the phone number provided on a restaurant menu slipped under your hotel room door.** In one new scam, identity thieves print phony delivery menus, then slip them under hotel room doors. When guests phone to place orders, they're asked for their credit card information, which then is used for fraudulent purchases. If you wish to order from such a menu, look up the restaurant's number on your own.

SMARTPHONES

Smartphones essentially are portable computers, yet many people do not take smartphone security as seriously as they do home computer security. *To protect yourself…*

•**Load antivirus software onto your smartphone, and keep this software updated.** Options for phones that use the Android operating system include Kaspersky Internet Security for Android (*USA.Kaspersky.com*, $14.95*)…ESET Mobile Security (*ESET.com*, $9.95)…BullGuard Mobile Security (*BullGuard.com*, $19.95)…and AVG AntiVirus FREE (*AVGMobilation.com*, free). All of these are available at the websites and at app stores.

For iPhones, iPads and iPods, quality antivirus software is harder to find and less of a necessity because hackers have not gone after them yet, although they probably will before long. Still, Apple smartphone, iPad and iPod users should consider downloading AVG Safe Browser, a free web browser that will

*Prices subject to change.

warn them away from unsafe sites (download it through iTunes or the App Store on your device). While Apple smartphones currently are at low risk for computer viruses, that eventually will change. Apple computers once were very safe from viruses, too, but now are essentially as vulnerable as Windows PCs.

•**Download apps only from usually reliable sources.** If you download an app from the wrong site, you might unknowingly load malicious software onto your phone as well. Trustworthy app sources for iPhones include Apple's App Store.

Trustworthy sources for Android include Google Play (*Play.Google.com*) and Appstore for Android on Amazon.com (*Amazon.com*, select "Appstore for Android" from the "Shop by Department" menu).

•**Set a pass code on your smartphone.** A simple four-digit PIN (or longer pass code) will make it much more difficult for a thief who steals your smartphone to access the data you have stored in it…or for someone who has access to your home or office to load malware onto your phone when you're not watching. The procedure for setting a pass code varies from phone to phone.

CREDIT CARDS

The merchant you buy from might not properly protect your credit card data or the merchant himself could be a thief. Many card issuers now offer two smart ways to reduce this danger. *Contact your card issuers for details and availability…*

•**Ask the issuer to supply a single-use authorization number.** This number is tied to your credit card account but is valid only for a single transaction and would be provided to an Internet merchant in place of the actual credit card number. It's worth considering when buying from Internet merchants that you are not sure you can trust. Even if a crook obtained it, he couldn't use it for additional purchases.

•**Set up a password for online card use through the card issuer.** A box will pop up requesting the password whenever the card is used online. Even online merchants never see this password.

SOCIAL NETWORKS

It isn't news that identity thieves prey upon users of Facebook, pretending to be online friends in order to gather personal data. But many users of Facebook and other social networks don't realize that this is not the only way that identity thieves might target them. *To stay safe...*

•**Don't provide any details about yourself on your Facebook page that could be used to answer the personal security questions you've set up for accounts.** If you forget the password for one of your accounts—anything from an e-mail account to a financial account that can be accessed online—that account provider's website likely will ask you a personal question to confirm your identity before providing access. The personal question might involve your mother's maiden name, the name of your childhood best friend or some other personal detail that strangers are unlikely to know. Trouble is, people often supply these personal details on their Facebook pages or elsewhere.

So much better: Choose personal security questions that cannot be answered using information available on your Facebook page or elsewhere online. Or adjust your answers to personal security questions in a way that you can remember but that no one else is likely to guess. You could tack your favorite number or color onto each response, typing "Larryblue" rather than "Larry" when asked your childhood best friend's name, for example.

•**Don't click links in messages you receive through social networks—even when those messages come from close friends.** When an identity thief breaks into a victim's Facebook account, he/she often will send messages to all of that person's Facebook friends pretending to be this person. These messages typically include a link that, when clicked, secretly loads malware onto the friends' computers, allowing the thief to steal their identities, too.

Damage-Control Plan for Stolen Passwords

Recently, Adobe Systems (maker of Adobe Acrobat software) reported that user names and passwords of 38 million users had been stolen.

If you receive a security-breach warning from any company: Change the password on your main e-mail account first because confirmation of all other password changes will be sent there...change the passwords on your financial accounts...and change the answers to the security questions used to authenticate those passwords.

Adam Levin, chairman and cofounder of Identity Theft 911, which provides identity-theft services for businesses, Scottsdale, Arizona.

Secure Passwords You Won't Forget

Paul Rosenzweig, a professorial lecturer in law at The George Washington University Law School and a former deputy assistant secretary for policy in the Department of Homeland Security.

I don't mind admitting that I have had trouble remembering all of my many online account passwords. I'm not the only one. A recent survey found that in one month, 70% of computer users had forgotten at least one password.

Recently, I learned a clever password trick. Select a favorite quote, then use the first letter of each word of that quote as a password.

For example, you might choose this line from *It's a Wonderful Life*, "Every time a bell rings, an angel gets his wings," then shorten that to the password ETABRAAGHW. Or choose a quote that you love that isn't as famous. That way, even someone who learns about this quote password system won't be able to guess. You can do upper- and lowercase letters in a pattern that you set.

If numbers are required in the password, choose something only you will know. You might select your home phone number when you were a kid and use every third number within the letters of your quotation.

It's still hard to remember multiple passwords for numerous accounts. But with this system, you can jot down a word that will help you recall the quote—"Wonderful" for *It's a Wonderful Life*—rather than write down the passwords themselves. If numbers are needed, jot down another clue.

Example: Phone 3 if three numbers are needed. That is usually enough to help you remember.

For More Secure Online Accounts...

I recently activated a two-step log-in for my online accounts. With "two-step log-in"—also known as "two-step verification" or "two-factor authorization"—a code is sent to me via text message when I attempt to access the account. I then enter this code—in addition to my user name and password—into the website to gain access. It takes me a few extra seconds to log into my e-mail, social-media and online bank accounts, but this means that those accounts are much more secure.

Even if a scammer got his/her hands on my user name and password, he still would not be able to access my account unless he also had hacked my smartphone, which is highly unlikely. Two-step log-in is certainly worth the trouble with ultra-important accounts that are accessed online only rarely, such as investment accounts.

Explore each of your account's security settings menus to find out if two-step log-in is offered.

John Sileo, president of The Sileo Group, a Denver-based identity-theft-prevention consulting and education provider. He is author of *Privacy Means Profit: Prevent Identity Theft and Secure You and Your Bottom Line* (Wiley). *Sileo.com*

EASY-TO-DO...

Reduce Mobile-Banking Risks

For safer mobile banking, follow these helpful tips: Log off before closing banking apps—do not simply exit...download only authorized apps, such as those found in the Apple App Store or Google Play, to reduce the chance of running malware...do not store any log-in information—not even a user ID...and download an antivirus app—several good ones are available in free versions, such as *Avast! Mobile Security* and *Lookout.*

If your phone is stolen or you think you are at risk for a banking security problem, contact your cell phone service provider immediately and ask to freeze service to prevent unauthorized transactions...and watch financial statements closely for at least a few weeks so that you can spot and report any breach.

GoBankingRates.com

Scammers Have a New Partner—Banks

Ken Tumin, cofounder of *DepositAccounts.com*, an independent website that tracks bank and credit union rates and news.

The Justice Department has accused a pair of otherwise reputable banks—Zions Bank of Utah and First Bank of Delaware—of assisting scammers. It is reportedly considering taking action against additional banks as well.

When an unscrupulous telemarketer or Internet scammer gets your bank account information, he/she can't steal money from your account on his own. He needs to find a bank willing to electronically transfer money out of your account and into his own (or into the account of a third-party processor).

According to the Justice Department, Zions Bank and First Bank of Delaware not only made fraudulent transfers on the behalf of scammers, they continued to do so even as the extremely high rate of complaints from those scammers' victims should have made it obvious that the banks were facilitating crimes. Total consumer losses are believed to exceed $100 million. First Bank of Delaware agreed to a $15 million settlement.

Banks have a financial incentive to work with scammers. They earn a fee for each transfer they make on the scammer's behalf.

As a bank customer, your best defense is to not give out your bank account or debit card information over the phone or Internet. Use a credit card to make these payments instead. Credit cards have relatively strong consumer protections, so you are less likely to be on the hook for any unauthorized charges.

If you receive a call requesting your bank account information from someone who has a legitimate reason to have this data—a utility company that you have authorized to automatically debit your account, for example—say that you will call back. Then look up the company's phone number and dial that.

Monitor your bank accounts closely for unauthorized debits. If the bank's online banking system offers automatic notifications, ask to receive an e-mail notification each time there's money withdrawn from your account. If a customer disputes a fraud early enough, the odds are good that he/she will get the money back.

Consumer Protection Now

John Sileo, president of The Sileo Group, a Denver-based identity-theft-prevention consulting and education provider. He is author of *Privacy Means Profit: Prevent Identity Theft and Secure You and Your Bottom Line* (Wiley). *Sileo.com*

We all know that Home Depot got hacked. High-tech scammers stole the credit card and debit card numbers as well as the e-mail addresses of more than 50 million Home Depot customers in 2014.

That's the bad news. Here's the really bad news: We can expect a spate of similar thefts. It's only going to get worse. The massive publicity about the breach is likely to encourage more scammers.

To reduce your risk…

•**Shop with a credit card rather than a debit card.** Some debit card issuers have taken steps to limit customer liability, but credit card consumer protections remain stronger. Monitor all of your accounts closely.

•**Use one of your credit cards only for automatic payments, not retail purchases.** That way, you won't have to update the account information on all your automatic payments (such as phone bills, utilities, etc.) when a retailer data breach forces you to change an account number.

•**Be wary of e-mails or calls from retailers following a data breach, even long afterward.** Scammers posing as the retailer might contact victims, then try to talk them out of other sensitive information, such as their Social Security numbers or other account numbers.

New Scam Seeks Credit Card Security Codes

A thief who has managed to get your credit card number and other information, such as your address, calls claiming to be doing a fraud investigation for the card issuer. The thief provides your card number and other personal information and asks you to confirm it. When you do, you are asked to prove that the card is in your possession by providing the security code (the three- or four-digit code on the back or front of your credit card), which is all the thief needs to make charges on the card.

Never give out the credit card security code to anyone who calls you.

TheDenverChannel.com

CD Caution

Be cautious when buying a certificate of deposit (CD) through an investment specialist called a CD broker. With interest rates on many CDs below 1%, it is tempting to hire one of these brokers to shop around for the best rate. But you must do your due diligence first. Check the broker's reputation—it is best to use a financial planner or a stockbroker you already know and trust. Avoid offers of rates that are well above market—they could be scams or bait-and-switch approaches to put you into riskier investments. Find out where your funds will be deposited if you buy the broker's CD, and check with the FDIC at *Research.FDIC.gov/bankfind* to be sure that the CD is federally insured.

Caution: In case of bank failure, the deposit insurance benefit will be paid to the broker, and you will have to get it from the broker, not from the bank.

DailyFinance.com

Another CD Alert

Scammers claiming to be from brokerages are calling investors with information that purports to be about high-yield CDs. The thieves solicit personal information and use it for identity theft or to steal money from a victim's account. If you are not sure that someone who calls you is legitimate, hang up and call your brokerage directly.

Gerri Walsh, senior vice president for investor education at the Financial Industry Regulatory Authority (FINRA), Washington, DC.

"Pump-and-Dump" Stock Scams Rampant Now

Fraudsters promote stocks of tiny companies via e-mail and social-media sites such as Facebook and Twitter. They try to create a buying frenzy so that the shares they already own will soar, allowing them to cash in, or "dump," the shares. Often they claim to have "inside" information about an impending development or an "infallible" timing system to pick winners.

What to do: Never respond to such e-mails or social-networking come-ons no matter how curious you are.

Lori Schock, JD, director of the US Securities and Exchange Commission Office of Investor Education and Advocacy, Washington, DC. *Investor.gov*

Brokerage-Account Fraud on the Rise

Stephanie Elliott, chief operating officer and chief compliance officer for Chapin Davis Investments, a financial-services and money-management firm that oversees $700 million in client assets, Baltimore. *ChapinDavis.com*

There is a rapidly growing danger that could affect your money if it is managed by a broker or financial adviser. Wire-fraud cases in the securities industry—fraudulent money transfers made over the phone or Internet—are up tenfold over the past decade.

How the scam works: Your broker or financial adviser receives an e-mail that seems to be from a client requesting a wire transfer. For example, the client might want to send money to a daughter's account at a bank near the college she attends. But the bogus e-mail actually is from a scammer who has gathered personal information about you online or hacked into your e-mail account.

When your adviser e-mails you back the required authorization documents to sign, the criminals can intercept it.

Under this scenario, if it is determined that your broker or adviser was negligent or didn't follow the firm's procedures, your account typically will be reimbursed by the firm. If the firm does not reimburse you, you can file a complaint with state regulators, the Financial Industry Regulatory Authority (FINRA) and the Securities and Exchange Commission.

Self-defense: Insist that your broker or financial adviser always phone you before wiring any of your money.

New Dangers for Investors and Small-Business Owners

The North American Securities Administrators Association has released its annual list of dangers posed by scammers, including several relatively new threats.

• **Proxy trading accounts** are set up and/or managed for investors by people who claim to have trading expertise but are unlicensed—often leading to trading losses or theft of assets.

• **Digital currencies,** such as Bitcoins and PPCoins, are not backed by tangible assets, subject to little or no regulation and difficult to understand—creating an environment that is fertile ground for scam artists seeking to take advantage of investors.

• **Raising of capital through such means as crowdfunding** and seeking funds from affluent individuals called "angels" carries risks for both startup businesses and investors. Be very careful to verify the legitimacy of capital-raising services.

North American Securities Administrators Association. *NASAA.org*

Safeguard Your Social Security Payments

John Sileo, president of The Sileo Group, a Denver-based identity-theft-prevention consulting and education provider. He is also author of *Privacy Means Profit: Prevent Identity Theft and Secure You and Your Bottom Line* (Wiley). *Sileo.com*

Block scammers from stealing your Social Security payments electronically. Anyone who uses a bank account with direct deposit is vulnerable.

Thieves first obtain personal information including your Social Security and bank account numbers. Then the scammers use that information electronically to have the Social Security Administration (SSA) reroute your monthly benefits to a different direct-deposit account.

Example: An 86-year-old man received a letter telling him that he won $3.5 million and asking him to submit personal information by phone—after which he became a victim of diverted Social Security payment fraud.

There have been thousands of reports of this type of scheme involving millions of dollars in diverted payments, and several culprits have been arrested and convicted.

Self-defense: Never give out financial information to callers, even if they say that they are from a bank or the government. Always check the real phone number of the institution, and call it before divulging any information.

You can contact Social Security at 800-772-1213 and arrange to block anyone from making changes electronically or by phone to your account or establishing new online access to your account.

You also can use that number to report missing direct-deposit payments and open a fraud investigation. You will be reimbursed by the SSA, but it may take several weeks.

WATCH OUT FOR...

Phony Telemarketing Calls

Dishonest telemarketers illegally call numbers on the Do-Not-Call Registry. They often use robocalls—automated calls that get victims to pick up the line before connecting to an actual telemarketer. And they use spoofing, a technique to hide the originating phone number from caller ID. There were about 3.2 million complaints about do-not-call violations in 2014. The Federal Trade Commission (FTC) goes after only about 50 fraudulent telemarketing firms a year but still advises victims to report the calls at *FTC.gov*.

What else to do: Hang up immediately when you realize a call is unwanted.

Roundup of experts on telemarketing fraud, reported at *LATimes.com*.

Do-Not-Call Registry Scam

Do-not-call-registry scammers call victims and pretend to be registry officials…then ask for personal information, such as Social Security and bank account numbers. They claim that the information is needed to register you for the list or verify that you are on it.

But: These calls are always scams—hang up.

To put yourself on the do-not-call list: Go to *DoNotCall.gov*. There is no charge.

Consumer Reports Money Adviser. *ConsumerReports. org*

2 Utility-Company Tricks

•**Scam 1**—Customers get calls from thieves posing as utility-company workers warning that service will be shut off because of unpaid bills. The thieves demand a credit or debit card to leave service connected.

What to do: If you get a phone or e-mail cancellation notice, call the utility company using the number on your bill.

•**Scam 2**—Alleged energy auditors show up, offering a free inspection. They usually are salespeople pitching unneeded, costly products—or they are burglars.

What to do: Keep your door locked unless you have set up an energy audit yourself.

Sid Kirchheimer, author of *Scam-Proof Your Life* (AARP Books), writing at *AARP.org*.

Emergency-Alarm Scam

Seniors are being targeted by telemarketers selling personal emergency alarm systems costing $30/month or more. Robocalls insist that the alarms are necessary in case of break-ins and medical emergencies. Some of the calls are just pushy…others are scams trying to get credit card information. Watch out for calls that try to create panic or that push for

immediate action. If a call says to press a button to speak to a representative, just hang up.

BBB.org

Cop Con

Scammers posing as police officers often target older people, who are more likely to trust authority figures.

Examples: Someone claiming to be a cop calls and says that you have an unpaid traffic ticket or other violation and must give your credit card number immediately to pay the fine—or you will be arrested. Or a thief claims to be doing a counterfeiting investigation, and asks you to withdraw cash and meet him so that the money can be inspected. Or a crook calls claiming to be a grandchild who has been arrested, then puts another thief on the line to pose as a police officer and demand payment.

Reality: Police never collect debts and do not warn of impending arrests. These and similar calls are always scams—simply hang up.

AARP.org

Signs a Craigslist Rental Is a Scam

Some thieves use Craigslist to steal renters' identities or their first month's rent.

Some warning signs: The listing does not include photos or a city name…the contact's e-mail address looks phony—like "kydixororo-aquep"—because it's an autogenerated e-mail account that's harder to trace…the deal sounds too good to be true—perhaps a security deposit is not required…and/or you are told that prior bad credit won't make a difference—this indicates that the scammer is simply preying on people with substandard credit.

Consumerist.com

Buying Online? Don't Let Them E-Mail You a Photo

David Bakke, consumer advocacy expert with the personal finance website *MoneyCrashers.com*.

Most of the listings on shopping websites such as *Craigslist.com* include a photo of the item for sale, but a few instead say "E-mail me for a photo." Do not make contact with these online sellers—there's a good chance that they're trying to scam you.

If you request a photo of the item, opening that photo might load a virus onto your computer. Or it might open what looks like a web page on a well-known shopping site—perhaps eBay or *Amazon.com*—that asks you to enter your user name and password to view the image. Trouble is, this web page isn't what it seems. If you enter your password—or your credit card or PayPal account information—it will fall into the hands of the scammer.

Also: Someone selling a high-end product online might try to calm your suspicions by suggesting that you send your payment to an escrow service—a company that holds your money until you receive the item. That might sound like a prudent strategy, but escrow is no guarantee that the seller is legitimate. Scammers sometimes set up phony online escrow services. When you send your money to one of these fake escrow services, you're really just sending it to the scammer.

If an online seller insists on using an escrow service, walk away from the purchase or insist on selecting the escrow service yourself, then opt for a well-established company such as *Escrow.com*. Type this escrow company's web address into your browser yourself—don't click a link provided to you by the seller. It could misdirect you to a fake site designed to look like the legitimate escrow company you picked.

Protect Your Online Photos

Photos posted online can easily be reposted in ways you never intended—in ads, in fake dating profiles, even at porn sites.

What to do: Use browser plug-ins and other online tools to track photo use. Firefox has a tool called *Who Stole My Pictures*, and Google's search engine can perform an image search with one of your photos to see if it has appeared anywhere else on the Internet. Check your social-media privacy settings to be sure strangers cannot get easy access to your pictures or personal information. Once a photo is online, it can be virtually impossible to remove it.

MarketWatch.com

Not All ".gov" Links Are from the Government

Scammers have been sending phony links that seem to come from government agencies, but they actually go to sites that download malware.

Before clicking on any link that arrives via e-mail: Hover your cursor over it, and look at the status bar at the bottom of your browser—it will show the actual web address to which the link connects.

Consumer Reports Money Adviser. ConsumerReports. org

"Ransomware" on Your Computer?

Ransomware is a viruslike program that locks a computer, displays the seal of a law-enforcement agency and states that the user has been committing a crime, such as distributing child pornography. The message says that charges will be dropped if the user pays a fine within 72 hours. Some 3% of victims have paid—but the message is phony… the scammers steal users' money and identities…and the computer remains locked. The viruses usually come from a booby-trapped web page or are attached to free downloads from crooked sites.

What to do: If your computer is infected, get instructions on how to remove the ransomware at *US.Norton.com/ransomware.*

NBCNews.com

The FBI Can Read Your E-Mail! What to Do…

FBI officials can read e-mail messages that are more than six months old without a warrant.

To protect your messages: You can encrypt them before sending them if your e-mail provider allows this, but the recipient must have your encryption key to read the message.

Alternative: Delete older e-mails regularly. Or store them on your hard drive, which is protected by the Fourth Amendment (the right to avoid unreasonable search and seizure).

Also: Consider an e-mail service that uses servers based outside of the US. Offshore e-mails are not subject to the same rules as ones within the US. But other countries have their own privacy rules—be sure you know them. And access through offshore servers may be slower than access through domestic e-mail providers.

MarketWatch.com

How to Spot Counterfeit Money

On a real bill, the portrait stands out from the background—on the counterfeit, it tends to blend in…real bills have red and blue embedded fibers—with fake ones, dyed hair sometimes is used and is on the surface, not

embedded…real serial numbers are the same color as the Treasury seal—they may differ on a fake bill…Federal Reserve and Treasury seals should be clear and sharp—they may be uneven or blurred on fakes…borders are sharp on real bills but may be blurred on phony ones…real bills have a raised texture—counterfeits feel flat…and real bills have watermarks matching the portrait—phonies have no watermarks or have mismatched ones.

DailyFinance.com

Little-Known Dangers of Downed Power Lines

Downed power lines can kill you, even if you don't touch them. They can electrify almost anything they touch, including metal fences, poles and mailboxes…standing water… and even supposedly nonconductive materials such as wood when wet after a storm.

If you come across downed power lines: Stay away from them and anything they are near. Don't drive over them.

If your car has made contact with a downed power line: Stay in your car, and call for help through your window or by calling 911 on your cell phone.

About.com

EASY-TO-DO…

Text—Don't Call—During a Disaster

In a disaster, leave phone connections open for first responders. Instead, use your cell phone to text loved ones to say that you are all right and ask them to spread the word. Apps such as *GroupMe* and *Facebook Messenger* can let you reach larger numbers of people. If you have to make one call, make it to your own voice mail—change your outgoing message to say that you are fine but cannot answer the phone. When loved ones call and go directly to voice mail, they will at least know that you are all right.

Wired.com

Index